EAT: LOS ANGELES 2010
The Food Lover's Guide to Los Angeles

For ge –
Happy eating!
thanks for all –
Mellie
12/09

PROSPECT PARK BOOKS

PROSPECT
·PARK·
BOOKS

EAT: **LOS ANGELES** is a trademark of Prospect Park Books.

Published by Prospect Park Books
prospectparkbooks.com
eat-la.com

Distributed to the trade by
SCB Distributors
scbdistributors.com

SPECIAL SALES
Bulk purchase (10+ copies) of EAT: Los Angeles is available to companies, organizations, mail-order catalogs and nonprofits at special discounts, and large orders can be customized to suit individual needs. For more information, contact Prospect Park Books.

Library of Congress Control Number: 2009932185
The following is for reference only:
Bates, Colleen Dunn
        Los Angeles / Colleen Dunn Bates
                p.cm.
        Includes index.
        ISBN: 978-0-9753939-9-4
        1. Los Angeles (Calif.) – Guidebooks. 2. Los Angeles County (Calif.)
– Food / Restaurants.
        I. Bates, Colleen Dunn. II. Title.

Second edition, first printing

Production in the United States of America. Design by Joseph Shuldiner. Printed in China by Four Colour Printing, USA.

This book was printed on FSC-certified, wood-free, environmentally responsible paper.

EAT: LOS ANGELES 2010
The Food Lover's Guide to Los Angeles

EDITOR
Colleen Dunn Bates

CONTRIBUTING EDITORS
Jean T. Barrett
Linda Burum
Miles Clements
Jenn Garbee
Andy O'Neill
Amelia Saltsman
Pat Saperstein
Joseph Shuldiner

PROSPECT PARK BOOKS

[TABLE OF CONTENTS]

[ABOUT THE AUTHORS]

COLLEEN DUNN BATES (editor and publisher) was the American editor of the Gault Millau guides (including *The Best of Los Angeles*) and the restaurant critic for *L.A. Style* for many years. Now she writes about L.A. restaurants for *Westways* and is the co-author of *Hometown Pasadena*, *Storybook Travels* and several other books. She heads up Prospect Park Books, which publishes *EAT: Los Angeles*, the *Hometown* books and other titles. A sixth-generation Southern Californian, Colleen lives in Pasadena.

JEAN T. BARRETT is a food and wine writer whose articles have appeared in the *Los Angeles Times*, *Westways*, *Sky* and *Wine Spectator*, among other publications. The Hollywood Hills resident has also co-authored three books with Colin Cowie, including *Colin Cowie Weddings* (Little Brown).

LINDA BURUM is the author of *A Guide to Ethnic Food in Los Angeles* (Harper Collins) among other books, and she writes regularly about L.A.'s culinary world — with a particular focus on ethnic cuisines — for the *Los Angeles Times* and *Los Angeles* magazine. She lives in Santa Monica.

MILES CLEMENTS writes about food for the *Los Angeles Times*, the *District Weekly* and others. The Long Beach–area resident (and native) also roams the South Bay — and, indeed, all of L.A. — for his blog *Eat Food With Me*.

JENN GARBEE reports on all things ingestible for the *Los Angeles Times*, Squid Ink (the *L.A. Weekly*'s food blog) and Tribune Media's national food and beverage wire. She is the author of *Secret Suppers* (Sasquatch Books) and co-author of *Hometown Santa Monica* (Prospect Park Books), and she is currently writing a book on the history of women and beer. This former pastry chef sidelines as a food stylist and kids' cooking teacher.

ANDY O'NEILL is the masked man known as Bandini — in other words, the hungry guy behind *Daily Taco* (dailytaco.org). He lives in West L.A. and travels far and wide in search of a good taqueria.

AMELIA SALTSMAN is the author of *The Santa Monica Farmers' Market Cookbook* (Blenheim Press). The L.A. native and longtime Santa Monican also writes about cooking, markets and food for such magazines as *Bon Appétit* and is a regular guest on Evan Kleiman's *Good Food* show on KCRW.

PAT SAPERSTEIN is the intrepid eater behind *Eating L.A.* (eatingla.com), one of L.A.'s most respected food blogs. The South Pasadena resident is also a senior editor at *Variety*.

JOSEPH SHULDINER is EAT: Los Angeles's art director and a contributor to eat-la.com. An L.A. native, this artist and former *Los Angeles Times* designer is also a passionate cook. He produced the hit cookbook *Celebrating with Julienne* and is now at work on his own book, *Vaguely Vegan*.

[THE REST OF THE TEAM]

CONTRIBUTORS: Darryl Bates, Troy Corley, Nealey Dozier, Jill Alison Ganon, Sandy Gillis, Lennie LaGuire, Mary Arranaga Landis, Melody Malmberg & Leah Keesun Park

ASSISTANT EDITOR: Skylar Sutton

EDITORIAL ASSISTANT: Darah Gillum

PROOFREADER: Leah Messinger

DATABASE DESIGNER: Anton Anderson

IT DIRECTOR: Darryl Bates

WORDPRESS GURU: John Stephens

[PLEASE CHECK OUT EAT'S WEB SITE AT: eat-la.com]

SPECIAL THANKS to L.A.'s passionate and interconnected food-journalism community, especially the Chowhounds; the Yelpers; the *Los Angeles Times* Food section; Jessica Gelt and the gang at the *Times*'s *Daily Dish*; Jonathan Gold, Amy Scattergood and the other folks at the *L.A. Weekly* and its blog, *Squid Ink*; *Los Angeles* magazine; Evan Kleiman and *Good Food* (KCRW); Lesley Balla at *Tasting Table*; Merrill Shindler; the *Hometown* books and their authors; *Citysearch*; and the city's wonderful blogs, including *Eating L.A.*, *EaterLA*, *FoodGPS*, *la.foodblogging*, *Rameniac*, *Daily Taco*, *Vegetarians in Paradise* (vegparadise.com), *Dig Lounge*, *Tuna Toast* (tokyoastrogirl. com) and *L.A. & O.C. Foodventures*, among many others.

[ABOUT EAT: LOS ANGELES 2010]

IF THERE'S A MORE EXCITING CITY for food lovers in the world than Los Angeles, I don't know it. My hometown may not have the most Michelin stars, but its magic mix of ethnic diversity, prosperity, adventurousness and year-round access to high-quality ingredients has resulted in a metropolis with something really good to eat on almost every corner.

Last year I put together a team of old and new friends to create a guide that would truly reflect the gustatory richness of Los Angeles. We had a wonderful time creating the book we wished we had in our cars, and were gratified to see it welcomed by thousands of hungry Angelenos. But time moves fast in this forward-looking city, and a lot has changed in a year. So we're back with a new book, exhaustively updated and rich with new discoveries, as well as with some improvements to a book that was, of course, a first effort.

This new edition may be 56 pages larger than the first, but it is still by no means a comprehensive guide — that would be so massive you couldn't lift it. **EAT: Los Angeles** is, however, a broad-ranging book, in terms of geography, cuisines and price points. Most of all, it's a discerning one — we don't have every single restaurant in Thai Town, for instance, but we point you toward our favorites. Our goal is to give you interesting, thoughtful, delicious choices in every category across L.A. County, from Long Beach to La Cañada, San Gabriel to Santa Monica. And we explore the food world far beyond restaurants, because if you like to eat, you want to know about worthwhile cheese shops, caterers, taco trucks, farmers' markets and everything that has to do with living a gustatorily rewarding life in Los Angeles.

In these pages you'll find the Why, What and Who for L.A.'s best food businesses, from restaurants and coffeehouses to kitchen-supply stores and food festivals. But we don't know it all, not by a long shot. So if we've missed your favorite Salvadoran market or French bistro or Chinese noodle café, please let us know at eat-la.com.

Colleen Dunn Bates
Editor, EAT: Los Angeles & eat-la.com

P.S. DESPITE OUR BEST EFFORTS . . .
Please forgive us if a business has closed, if prices have been raised or if your experience does not match ours. We labored mightily to verify every scrap of information in this book, but some places will close, change or misbehave, and we can't do a thing about it.

HOW WE DECIDE WHAT TO INCLUDE: **EAT: Los Angeles** has more than 1,200 listings, but of course the L.A. basin has gazillions more places to eat, drink and shop. Our job is to steer you to the best. If we don't like a place, we simply don't include it.

Most importantly, we celebrate the places that are mom 'n pop in spirit — individual businesses and local chains with hands-on ownership and enthusiasm for whatever is being cooked, sold or served. So you'll find loads of smaller cafés, shops and bistros, but you won't find every high-end hotel restaurant, say, or the sort of MBA-managed club-restaurants that run rampant in Hollywood.

A NOTE ABOUT CHAINS: In general, we eschew corporate chains. This isn't because we think they are inherently evil — we'll confess to a weakness for Houston's, and our families would starve without Trader Joe's — but everyone knows about them, and you don't need us to help you find the Cheesecake Factory. Occasionally we'll make an exception, as with Peet's, which has an indie sensibility and is sometimes your only choice for good coffee in certain parts of town.

GOOD FOOD NEIGHBORHOODS: Our first chapter brings you twelve profiles of Good Food Neighborhoods. Some are walkable and some require driving, but each has a strong sense of place and a vibrant food community. Some of the places mentioned in these profiles have separate listings in the book, while others don't — but all are worth visiting. We highly recommend exploring them all... and after you're done, you can call yourself an unofficial L.A. native.

ESSENTIALLY L.A.: In each chapter, we recognize some places as "Essentially L.A." Perhaps it serves exceptional food, or does a better job of selling wine or making coffee than others, or stocks the best selection of cheese or Chinese ingredients in town. Or perhaps its food isn't exactly remarkable, but its atmosphere or history or people are, well, essentially L.A.

DESTINATION DINING: Immigrant groups naturally congregate in certain areas, and therefore immigrant restaurants do the same thing. So accept, for instance, that you will not find great Chinese food on the westside — you need to go to the south San Gabriel Valley to get the real thing. Other cuisines are well represented in many areas but have a particular intensity in one community. You'll find good Armenian food, for instance, in Hollywood and Pasadena, but Glendale has by far the largest Armenian population in the region.

[HERE'S WHERE TO FIND REGIONAL SPECIALTIES]

ARTESIA:
Indian

BRENTWOOD:
Italian trattorias (no one knows why, but tons are here)

CHINATOWN (NORTH DOWNTOWN):
Chinese and Vietnamese, though not as much as
in the San Gabriel Valley

EAST L.A.:
Mexican and Central American

EAST VALLEY:
Thai

GLENDALE:
Armenian & Middle Eastern

HOLLYWOOD (EAST):
Mexican and Central American

HOLLYWOOD (EAST – THAI TOWN):
Thai

KOREATOWN (CENTRAL L.A.):
Korean

LITTLE TOKYO (NORTH DOWNTOWN NEAR CITY HALL):
Japanese and a little Korean

LONG BEACH (NORTH):
Cambodian

SAN GABRIEL VALLEY (SOUTH):
Chinese and Vietnamese

SAWTELLE & CENTINELA, WEST L.A.:

Japanese

STUDIO CITY:
Japanese/sushi bars

TORRANCE:
Japanese

[THE REGIONS]

It's no easy feat to break massive L.A. County into managable chunks, and it requires some semi-arbitrary decisions. Here's how we did it:

CENTRAL CITY: The city of L.A.'s modern core, encompassing Los Feliz, Hollywood, Koreatown, Hancock Park, Beverly/Third, the Mid-City area, Melrose, Miracle Mile, Fairfax and West Hollywood.

EASTSIDE: The city's original core: Downtown, East L.A., Boyle Heights, Westlake (the old name for the area just west of Downtown), Pico/Union, Highland Park, Echo Park, Silver Lake, Eagle Rock and environs. Okay, fussy folks, we know it's sacrilegious to some to say Silver Lake is "eastside," but that's the way things are evolving in L.A., and we're going with the flow.

SAN GABRIEL VALLEY: A huge swath of the east county, ranging from Monterey Park almost to Pomona and encompassing Pasadena, San Gabriel, Sierra Madre and beyond. Yes, we know Glendale and La Cañada aren't technically in the SG Valley, but for simplicity's sake, we're pretending they are.

EAST VALLEY: The San Fernando Valley from Burbank to Sherman Oaks, including Studio City and North Hollywood.

WEST VALLEY: From Encino and the 405 way out northwest and west to the Ventura County line.

WESTSIDE: CENTRAL: The heart of the westside, including Beverly Hills, Culver City, Century City, Rancho Park and Westwood; the 405 is the west border.

WEST OF THE 405: Pretty self-explanatory. Brentwood to the Palisades, Malibu to Venice.

SOUTH BAY TO SOUTH L.A.: Another huge swath of the county, from the South Bay beach towns (Playa del Rey, Manhattan Beach, Redondo Beach), along the coast from Torrance to Long Beach, and across the south basin from Downey to Inglewood.

PRICE SYMBOLS ARE BASED ON AVERAGE ENTREE PRICES:

$	$10-under
$$	$10-$16
$$$	$17-$24
$$$$	$25-$33
$$$$$	$34-up

GOOD FOOD NEIGHBORHOOD
[3rd Street]

IN THE HEART OF LOS ANGELES, 3rd Street has been a food destination since the summer of 1934, when a group of farmers gathered at 3rd and Fairfax to sell their produce. Seventy-five years later, the L.A. Farmers Market hosts millions of tourists annually while remaining a popular gathering spot and food source for locals. The section of 3rd Street extending about a mile west from the market has evolved into one of the city's top shopping rows, with plenty of food shops, restaurants, cafés and wine bars in the mix.

Start your tour at the Farmers Market, of course, with coffee and a bear claw at **BOB'S COFFEE & DOUGHNUTS**. It's a superlative fried-dough experience coupled with unsurpassed people watching: sugar-buzzed screenwriters, tables of elderly regulars on their third cup of decaf and bemused out-of-towners on a bus tour. Nearby, **HUNTINGTON MEATS** sells Harris Ranch beef as well as an impressive array of house-made sausages and a hamburger blend ground to chef Nancy Silverton's specifications. Huntington is next to **MONSIEUR MARCEL GOURMET MARKET**, which aims to satisfy all cravings, from anchovies to Zinfandel; the adjacent café serves authentically French salade de chèvre chaud and poulet rôti.

Just steps away is **LITTLEJOHN'S CANDIES**, an old-fashioned candy shop where visitors can watch the confectioners make their justly famous English toffee. At the other end of the market is **MARCONDA'S MEATS**, a butcher shop that custom-cuts meats to the most demanding standards and offers its own meatloaf blend in ready-to-bake pans. If it's time for lunch, head to **LOTERIA GRILL**, a Mexican counter spot that serves superb tacos (try the cochinita pibil, carne asada or a vegetarian option).

There are many other worthy options here, but with 3rd Street beckoning, head west to **AOC**, a wine bar and dinner-only restaurant owned by Suzanne Goin and Caroline Styne, where you can pair tastes from one of L.A.'s most interesting wine lists with delicious appetizers and roasted items from the wood-burning oven. The wine theme continues with **TASCA**, another very good wine bar about a block west (also only open for dinner), specializing in Spanish and Italian-style tapas.

Farther along the same side of the street, the ultra-charming,

pricey, open-air restaurant
THE LITTLE DOOR now has
a companion café/market,
LITTLE NEXT DOOR, which
sells house-made preserves
from kumquat jelly to duck
confit, along with pastries,
prepared foods, cheeses
and charcuterie. Another
great spot for browsing is
JOAN'S ON THIRD, a café,
bakery, gourmet-to-go and
caterer with one of L.A.'s
best selections of gourmet
items. We're heartbroken to
report that neighborhood
landmark the Cook's Library
closed recently, but you'll
find many good food-related
travel books next door at
TRAVELER'S BOOKCASE.

Since reading about food
and travel stimulates the
appetite, it's fortunate that
the bookstore isn't far from
MINESTRAIO TRATTORIA,
chef Gino Angelini's newish
spot in the Orlando Hotel.
Sit down and relax over a
glass of prosecco and some
salumi. You can stay for dinner (delicious and surprisingly
inexpensive handmade pasta
dishes), or backtrack a few
blocks east to Tasca or AOC.
As long as you stay on 3rd,
you can't lose.

— *Jean T. Barrett*

**IN THE FARMERS MARKET
AT 3RD AND FAIRFAX:**

Bob's Coffee & Doughnuts
323.933.8929

Huntington Meats
323.938.5383

Littlejohn's Candies
323.936.5379

Loteria Grill
323.930.2211

Marconda's Meats
323.938.5131

Monsieur Marcel Gourmet
Market
323.939.7792

ALONG 3RD:

AOC
8022 W. 3rd St., 323.653.6359

Joan's on Third
8350 W. 3rd St., 323.655.2285

Minestraio Trattoria
8384 W. 3rd St., 323.782.8384

The Little Door
8134 W. 3rd St., 323.951.1210

Little Next Door
8142 W. 3rd St., 323.951.1010

Tasca
8108 W. 3rd St., 323.951.9890

Traveler's Bookcase
8375 W. 3rd St., 323.655.0575

GOOD FOOD NEIGHBORHOOD
[Abbot Kinney, Venice]

JUST BLOCKS FROM THE OCEAN, the six-block strip of Abbot Kinney Boulevard epitomizes the sun-drenched, lazy-afternoon surfboard vibe of Venice Beach. Though parking can be tight, you can usually find a spot; if not, try the valet at Joe's. Either way, you won't need a car to explore the cafés, upscale restaurants and funky shops.

Start on the northwest end of Abbot Kinney near Westminster and enjoy a leisurely weekend patio brunch or lovely lunch at **JOE'S**, the neighborhood pioneer known for its stellar Cal-French food, reasonable prices and hospitable chef-owner Joe Miller. Next door at **PRIMITIVO WINE BISTRO**, fans of less formal dining can have a glass of Riesling and a petite salad for lunch, a glass of Bordeaux and steak frites for dinner or a glass of Vin Santo and the warm bread pudding with Calvados, caramel and vanilla bean ice cream at any time. A few doors down at **LILLY'S FRENCH CAFÉ**, the ethereal *île flottante* (caramel-drizzled floating meringue islands atop crème anglaise) is reason enough to linger in the lush outdoor garden, but the reasonably priced croque monsieurs and heaping bowls of moules frites don't hurt, either.

Those with heartier appetites can head across the street to **GLEN-CREST BAR-B-QUE**, where the smoky pork ribs are best taken to go for a picnic, unless you can nab one of the rickety stools. Don't bother with the sides; instead save room for dessert. **N'ICE CREAM** provides you with excellent gelati and sorbets, made fresh daily by a lovely Danish couple. Made with organic milk and fresh fruits, all the flavors are creative and delicious.

One block further on you'll find **HAL'S BAR AND GRILL**, an artists' hangout where the menu is packed with solid California salads, pastas and grilled meats. But it's the massive 40-foot bar that's the real draw. Order a round of cocktails made from freshly squeezed juices and a platter of fries to share, and take in the scene — on Sunday and Monday nights there's even live jazz.

If you're more in the mood for caffeine, cross the street again and head down one block to **ABBOT'S HABIT** for a strong cup of java (skip the food). Next door is **ABBOT'S PIZZA**, the beloved home of the self-named "bagel crust" pizza. The classic pies are good, but don't knock the California-inspired pizzas laden with such ingredients as spinach and sun-dried tomatoes. Toss back a slice like a real New Yorker at the tiny stand-up counter, or order a whole pie to go.

You could end your stroll here, but if you've got a hungry four-legged friend in tow, it's worth the two-block trek to **MODERN DOG**, where the friendly owners will pop treats into your pooch's mouth. And if it's happy hour at **WABI SABI** a few doors down, where the sundown specials are too good to pass up, order a round of spicy tuna rolls and a slice of yuzu cheesecake and call it a day.

But wait... on your way home, stop at **MARKET GOURMET**, which not only has its own parking but is a treasure trove of goodies to take home: cheeses, chocolates, sauces, grains and lots more, including a refrigerator case stocked with fresh pasta, pumpkin-seed pesto and puff pastry.

Food lovers also take note that Abbot Kinney is also a destination for the city's wave of hyper-trendy food trucks, so keep an eye out for Barbie'sQ, FishLips Sushi, Kogi and more.

— Jenn Garbee

Abbot's Habit
1401 Abbot Kinney Blvd.
310.399.1171

Abbot's Pizza
1407 Abbot Kinney Blvd.
310.396.7334

Glencrest Bar-B-Que
1146 Abbot Kinney Blvd.
310.399.9641

Hal's Bar and Grill
1349 Abbot Kinney Blvd.
310.396.3105

Joe's Restaurant
1023 Abbot Kinney Blvd.
310.399.5811

Lilly's French Café
1031 Abbot Kinney Blvd.
310.314.0004

Market Gourmet
1800 Abbot Kinney Blvd.
310.305.9800

Modern Dog
1611 Abbot Kinney Blvd.
310.450.2275

N'Ice Cream
1410 Abbot Kinney Blvd.
310.396.7161

Primitivo Wine Bistro
1025 Abbot Kinney Blvd.
310.396.5353

Wabi Sabi
1637 Abbot Kinney Blvd.
310.314.2229

GOOD FOOD NEIGHBORHOOD
[Boyle Heights]

JUST OVER THE BRIDGE FROM DOWNTOWN L.A., Boyle Heights combines traditional Mexican flavors with East L.A.–style Chicano traditions. Bounded by the 101, 10 and 60 freeways, it's close enough for Downtown workers to head over for lunch, but the bustling carnicerias and crowded shops are a world away. This neighborhood, which now boasts light-rail service from Downtown and Pasadena via the Gold Line extension, is clearly L.A.'s next in line for gentrification. Though the area's a bit rough around the edges, it's perfectly safe for shoppers and diners, and the rewards are many.

Start on East Cesar Chavez Avenue by stopping for breakfast, lunch or dinner at **LA PARRILLA**, which specializes in parrillada grills with meats and seafood and guacamole prepared tableside.

Adventurous eaters won't want to miss the **FOOD STANDS** in front of the Big Buy Foods market on Breed Street, open Thursday to Sunday from 7 to 10 p.m. Specialties from various areas of Mexico and Central America include *pambazo* (filled bread with chile sauce), red pozole soup and Mexico City–style fried quesadillas.

A stop at longtime L.A. hangout **EL TEPEYAC** is a must, for gargantuan Hollenbeck or even larger Manuel burritos.

Where Cesar Chavez Avenue meets Indiana Street is called Five Points, or Cinco Puntos. At **LOS CINCOS PUNTOS** meat market, all the makings for an authentic feast are ready to be assembled, starting with corn tortillas made while you watch, prepared carnitas and other meats, and cactus salad, guacamole and salsa in bulk.

Cross over to East 1st Street and head east to **TERESITAS**, where homestyle dishes like albondigas soup, *costillas* (ribs) and enchiladas are served with homemade tortillas. Heading back toward Downtown on 1st Street, stop in at **TAMALES LILIANA**. Take home a bag of freshly made tamales or try chilequiles or *huevos divorciados* (eggs "divorced" by a row of beans down the middle) for breakfast at this homey diner, which also makes menudo on weekends. Just down the street is **EL MERCADO**, a marketplace that's similar to Downtown's Grand Central Market, but with the addition of mariachis and margaritas at the upstairs restaurants. Stalls sell everything from chiles and seafood to toys and cowboy hats. Further west on 1st Street, the large, colorful **EL RINCONCITO DEL MAR RESTAURANT** is the place for seafood cocktails of shrimp or octopus and hearty seafood stews called *caldos.*

Heading south toward Whittier Boulevard, pick up a snack at **LA MASCOTA**, one of L.A.'s best Mexican bakeries. Choose heavenly smelling bolillo rolls fresh from the oven, pan dulce pastries or tamales.

Finish your walk or drive at **MARIACHI PLAZA**, the closest thing to a Boyle Heights meeting point, on East 1st Street near Boyle Avenue. Mariachi musicians hoping to be hired for parties gather in the small park, which includes a charming old-world bandstand. Near the plaza is the area's most upscale restaurant, **LA SERENATA DE GARIBALDI**, where diners often spot the mayor and other politicos. The handsome place (which now has two westside offshoots) emphasizes creative preparations of Mexican seafood and offers valet parking. Finish off the evening at **EASTSIDE LUV**, a sure sign — along with the Metrolink that just opened right outside — that the neighborhood is on the rise. The wine bar/music venue is livening up the neighborhood with everything from burlesque shows to Chicano art exhibits.

— *Pat Saperstein*

Breed Street food stands
Cesar Chavez Ave. & Breed St.

Los Cinco Puntos
3300 E. Cesar E. Chavez Ave.
323.261.4084

Eastside Luv Wine Bar
1835 E. 1st St., 323.262.7442

El Mercado De Los Angeles
3425 E. 1st St., 323.268.3451

El Rinconcito Del Mar Restaurant
2908 E. 1st St., 323.269.8723

El Tepeyac Café
812 N. Evergreen Ave.
323.267.8668

La Mascota Bakery
2715 Whittier Blvd., 323.263.5513

La Parrilla Restaurant
2126 E. Cesar E. Chavez Ave.
323.262.3434

La Serenata de Garibaldi
1842 E. 1st St., 323.265.2887

Tamales Liliana
3448 E. 1st St., 323.780.0839

Teresitas Restaurant
3826 E. 1st St., 323.266.6045

GOOD FOOD NEIGHBORHOOD
[Culver City]

THIS ENTERTAINMENT STUDIO HUB turned foodie mecca
is home to an ever-increasing collection of gourmet hot dog stands,
stellar cocktails and rogue new chefs. It's divided into two areas,
with the hot new restaurants on Culver Boulevard, where Park and
Lock should be renamed Park and Nosh, and the Helms Bakery
home-furnishings complex, where you can grab a hot dog or toss
back a pint while shopping for that perfect loveseat. Plan ahead
(translation: Bring an ice-filled cooler) and you can cart home everything from takeout fried chicken to roasted vegetables.

Start off with a lunchtime quest for inner peace — or at least
darn good star anise–ginger short ribs with parsnip purée — at
AKASHA, part of the new wave of sustainable restaurant/bakery/
bars. If after achieving clarity you'd like to celebrate with a nice
drink, stop into **BOTTLEROCK** wine bar for a glass of your favorite
grape and an order of bacon-wrapped dates. Grab a bottle to take
home while you're there, then head around the corner to **FRAÎCHE**
for an herb-infused homemade absinthe cocktail. Stay to enjoy the
lamb *spezzatino* (stew) with ricotta gnocchi, then round the corner
to **UGO - AN ITALIAN BAR** to grab an authentic Italian espresso
con panna (skip its restaurant next door). Next to that is **TENDER
GREENS**, a vegetable-lover's cafeteria with organic fare galore,
plus wine, beer and desserts. A few doors down you can get your
carnivore fix with the cured meat platters at **FORD'S FILLING STA-
TION**, where Harrison's son Ben turns out stellar appetizers and
flatbreads; the mains take second stage. Or revel in the charms of a
pitch-perfect French bistro at the new **LE SAINT AMOUR**, where the
soup is onion and the moules have frites. Before you leave Culver,
consider stopping into **HONEY'S KETTLE** to pick up some fried
chicken for later.

Next, hop in the car and head down Washington to the Helms
complex — or walk to work up an appetite, because it's only three-
quarters of a mile. La Dijonaise, Beacon, Father's Office … let your
preference decide where to stop. At **BEACON**, Cal-Asian fusion food
is served up in the former Beacon Laundromat building, and the
happy-hour dishes will set you back about the same as a load of
laundry. At **FATHER'S OFFICE**, you'll find the same famous grilled
onion-blue cheese bacon burger as at the Santa Monica original,

with a bonus: This one has a larger menu and a heck of a lot more space, though that doesn't mean the line to nab a seat is any shorter. If you're lucky, the **LET'S BE FRANK** cart will be parked across the street, serving its grass-fed beef dogs with caramelized onions on freshly baked buns to tide you over. Or get a four-pack to take home for later.

Stroll back toward Washington Boulevard and check out the exhibition at the Museum of Design Art and Architecture on the corner of Sherbourn Drive. **WILSON**, the museum's self-proclaimed global-cuisine restaurant, is worth a stop for the rabbit sloppy joe. Wrap up the gloriously gluttonous day with a shopping spree at **SURFAS** on the bustling corner of Washington and National. It's a cook's Disneyland, filled with hard-to-find kitchen items you didn't know you needed and ingredients you've only read about. Make sure to pick up some of the delicate little canelés from the café for tomorrow's breakfast.

— *Jenn Garbee*

Akasha
9543 Culver Blvd., 310.845.1700

Beacon
3280 Helms Ave., 310.838.7500

BottleRock
3847 Main St., 310.836.9463

Father's Office
3229 Helms Ave., 310.736.2224

Ford's Filling Station
9531 Culver Blvd., 310.202.1470

Fraîche
9411 Culver Blvd., 310.839.6800

**Honey's Kettle
Fried Chicken**
9537 Culver Blvd., 310.202.5453

La Dijonaise
8703 Washington Blvd.
310.287.2770

Le Saint Amour
9725 Culver Blvd., 310.842.8155

Let's Be Frank Dogs
Helms Ave. parking lot across from
Father's Office, 415.515.8084

Surfas
8777 W. Washington Blvd.
310.558.1458

Tender Greens
9523 Culver Blvd., 310.842.8300

Ugo - An Italian Bar
9501 Culver Blvd., 310.204.1222

Wilson
8631 Washington Blvd.
310.287.2093

[Koreatown]

CHAPMAN PLAZA, THE LATE 1920S MARKETPLACE
on 6th Street with Churrigueresque flourishes and romantic drive-
through archways, is a striking icon of old Los Angeles. The plaza is
also a symbol of the new L.A. — a bustling, high-style warren that's
the perfect starting point for exploring Koreatown, which boasts a
staggeringly diverse concentration of eateries, from upscale barbecue palaces and soulful country-style roadhouses to glam night
clubs and delicious dives. In this part of town, where the cool factor
runs high but the restaurant signage can verge on the overwhelm-
ing, Chapman Plaza is a manageable touchstone.

Start your tour at Chapman Plaza's **TOE BANG**. With its open patio and rustic paneling, Toe Bang attracts a hip and casual crowd,
serving good bar food and drinks in a traditional Korean country-
side setting (close your eyes and you might think you're in a South
Bay surfers' hangout). The glamour quotient rises on the upper level
of the plaza, where you'll find **GAAM**, a slick yakitori and sake bar.
Back at street level, **KYOTO**, a stylish sushi bar, offers huge portions
of glistening sashimi.

Next, head south on Vermont to check out **SAN SOO DANG**, a
tiny storefront in a Latino-skewing strip mall. It specializes in *duk*,
traditional, mochi-like rice cakes. Try a *juhl pyun* — made from
plain white rice with just a hint of sesame oil — before moving on
to Olympic Boulevard, where **WIEN KONDITOREI UND CAFE**, a
Euro-Korean patisserie/tea room, is a quiet oasis behind bougain-
villea-draped lattices. Order a green-tea chiffon cake or sweet rice
doughnut to enjoy at a little marble table on the shaded patio,
where a sign reminds, "Do Not Feed the Bird."

Head west on Olympic until you spot the blocky, greenery-cov-
ered building that houses **CHOSUN GALBEE**. With its airy, attractive bar, seductively tented patio and waitresses in pink-and-blue
hamboks, this is the choice of upscale diners — just check out all
the fancy cars at the valet station. The specialty is grill-at-the-table
Korean barbecue, along with a notable selection of *panchan*,
the small side dishes that come with a traditional Korean meal.
Nang myun, the cold buckwheat noodle soup that's popular in hot
weather, is on the menu, too, along with hot pots and casseroles.

If you want to go strictly old school, head to **DONG IL JANG** on
West 8th for roast *gui*, a grilled meat-and-scallion feast. Like most

Koreatown restaurants, Dong Il Jang also offers *bibim bap* (white rice with steamed veggies, egg, and meat layered on top, mixed at the table with a spicy paste called *kochu-jang*) and has a sushi bar. (Theirs has a koi pond and a prominent display of costly liquor bottles, complete with, yes, a John Wayne decanter.)

Around the corner on Western, **BCD TOFU HOUSE**'s pleasant dining room displays slender silver chopsticks and large spoons at each place — the perfect utensils for tucking into kickass spicy tofu soup (*soon tubu*), offered in the original formulation or with such add-ons as the deliciously doughy dumplings called *man-doo*.

Finally, if you've been out sampling Koreatown's soju-and-karaoke boîtes (Palm Tree or Viking Café, anyone?) you just might end up, in the wee hours, needing some fast food to tide you over till daybreak. Head to the bright strip-mall outpost **HODORI** on Vermont. Open 24 hours a day, 365 days a year, Hodori posts oversize photos of its dishes, so you can just point. The night's still young, and that boiled chicken in broth with ginseng is calling your name.

— *Lennie LaGuire & Leah Keesun Park*

BCD Tofu House
869 S. Western Ave.
213.380.3807

Chosun Galbee
3330 W. Olympic Blvd.
323.734.3330

Dong Il Jang
3455 W. 8th St., 213.383.5757

Gaam
3465 W. 6th St., #300
213.388.8850

Hodori
1001 S. Vermont Ave.
213.383.3554

Kyoto Sushi
3465 W. 6th St., 213.389.4000

San Soo Dang
761 S. Vermont Ave.
213.487.1717

Toe Bang Restaurant
3465 W. 6th St., 213.387.4905

Wien Konditorei und Café
3035 W. Olympic Blvd.
213.427.0404

GOOD FOOD NEIGHBORHOOD
[Little India]

ALIVE WITH THE COLOR of brilliant silk saris, the aroma of a hundred curries and the rhythms of Bhangra-inspired folk hits pouring out of music shops: This is Pioneer Boulevard, the heart of Little India on a typical weekend. It sits in the middle of Artesia, a suburb north of Long Beach just off the 91 Freeway — which, conveniently for the widely dispersed Indian community (and the rest of us), connects to the 405, the 110, the 710 and the 605 freeways. Most restaurants here, unlike those catering to the American palate, serve regional specialties and street foods. More than half are vegetarian, reflecting the way most Indians eat. A short stroll gives food lovers total immersion into the varied cuisines of the Subcontinent.

Start at **WOODLANDS** on the northeast corner of Artesia and Pioneer. The Karnataka-style southern vegetarian cuisine is so diverse and complex it renders meat irrelevant. From humble grains and legumes come crisp crêpes, crunchy fritters, thick pancakes and breads, all eaten with dozens of curries and dipped into fresh coconut chutney. Across the street the northern-style **AMBALA DHABA** gets it name from the funky roadside spots in the Punjab region. But this is a comfortable restaurant, offering beer and wine along with a lengthy menu of chicken, lamb, goat and vegetarian specialties. Still further south, **LITTLE INDIA GRILL**, an ultra-casual order-at-the-counter spot, turns out bargain northern-style combo meals and a wonderful array of breads, like keema naan stuffed with spiced, minced lamb.

Casual snack sellers known as *chat* shops are everywhere, and each has its own specialties. **PIONEER SWEETS & SNACKS** carries all the famous southern vegetarian items such as dosas, prathas and a wide range of sweets. But its five different *thalis* — essentially combo meals — make ordering easy. A few shops further south, the separately owned **AMBALA SWEETS** sells an array of *namkeen* — crunchy, savory tidbits made from flours, lentils and nuts. You eat them plain or in salad-style dishes topped with tamarind and cilantro chutneys. Among the many sweets here are *rasmalai* and *cham cham*, spongy milk-based balls in sweetened cream or syrup.

At the center of Little India, on 186th Street just east of Pioneer, is **SURATI FARSAN MART**, an elegant Gujarat-style snack shop. Worth a stop for the beautiful gift boxes alone, the café serves stellar chat and sweets. The *pani puri,* crunchy fried ping-pong ball-size orbs you fill with beans and minty water, are a must-try.

Close to 186th is **FARM FRESH**, where you can stock up on lentils, beans and spices, as well as masala dosa mix. Nearby is **SHAN**, serving the meat-intensive cuisine of Hyderabad. The central Indian city, long a crossroads, takes a smattering of flavors from many regions. There are 17 lamb curries in addition to five tandoor-cooked lamb items — yet the ruggedly spicy vegetable dishes are among the best on the street. A few steps south, the neat-as-a-pin **UDUPI PALACE**, named for the southern temple city in Karnataka state, makes dosas as long as baseball bats. Its *kadis* (little fritters) come submerged in sumptuous coconut curry.

You come to the end of Little India at the Little India Village mall. Upstairs sits the neo-moderne **TIRUPATHI BHIMAS**, serving the classic vegetarian fare of Andhra Pradesh state. The thalis and *tiffins* — multi-dish meals served on a tray — are the way to go. Follow these delights at **SAFFRON SPOT**, where Indian-style ice creams come in spectacular flavors, and the ice cream–topped rose or saffron milk drinks are studded with cooling basil seeds.

— *Linda Burum*

Ambala Dhaba
17631 Pioneer Blvd.
562.402.7990

Ambala Sweets
18433 Pioneer Blvd.
562.402.0006

Farm Fresh
18551 Pioneer Blvd.
562.865.3191

Little India Grill
18383 Pioneer Blvd.
562.924.7569

Pioneer Sweets & Snacks
18413 Pioneer Blvd.
562.402.1155

Saffron Spot
18744 Pioneer Blvd.
562.809.4554

Shan
18621 Pioneer Blvd.
562.865.3838

Surati Farsan Mart
11814 E. 186th St.
562.860.2310

Tirupathi Bhimas
18792 Pioneer Blvd., 2nd floor
562.809.3806

Udupi Palace
18635 Pioneer Blvd.
562.860.1950

Woodlands
11833 Artesia Blvd.
562.860.6500

GOOD FOOD NEIGHBORHOOD
[Little Tokyo]

LITTLE TOKYO STARTED OUT as the hub of L.A.'s early 1900s Japanese immigrant community, complete with temples, movie theaters and traditional restaurants. Japanese-Americans have mostly moved to the Torrance area, but the Downtown neighborhood has retained its Asian roots while adding a burst of energy from residents of recently built lofts. Downtown streets are often sparsely populated at night, but Little Tokyo — also called J-Town by some Angelenos — has more foot traffic than some other areas.

Starting at the Japanese American Museum, walk west on 1st Street, the area's most historic block. The Chinatown-era neon Chop Suey Café sign is a landmark for generations who celebrated family occasions there. Have a drink at the adjacent **FAR BAR** lounge, but eat somewhere else. **SUEHIRO CAFÉ** serves Japanese diner food until 3 a.m. on weekends, including sturdy bowls of nabeyaki udon and bargain combination dinners. Nearby, **DAI-KOKUYA** draws raves and crowds for deeply flavored pork-broth ramen.

Japanese Village Plaza is a short car-free block full of unique flavors. **MITSURU CAFE**'s well-worn imagawayaki molds have been turning out crispy, lightly sweetened red bean cakes for several generations. Also in the plaza, **MIKAWAYA** invented the ice cream–filled mochi that are found all over now, but there are more flavors here at the home base. Try the red bean, coffee and peanut butter flavors, or the Italian gelato with a light Japanese touch. Next door, the compact **NIJIYA MARKET** is jam-packed with Japanese items and even a Hawaiian products department.

Near San Pedro and 1st streets, Weller Court is a modern office plaza full of restaurants. Spice lovers will appreciate **OROCHON RAMEN**, where steamy bowls of noodles come in seven levels of heat, with the bravest diners opting for the "hyper" and "extreme" levels. Around the corner, the Kyoto Grand Hotel is designed with Japanese touches, including a lovely Zen garden and Little Tokyo's only tempura bar at the **THOUSAND CRANES** restaurant.

Japanese restaurants are usually categorized by their specialties, and 2nd Street is home to top-quality sushi, shabu-shabu and *izakaya* — small plates of cooked food that go well with beer. **HARU ULALA** is a fun izakaya where diners watch the chef grill fish and vegetables. Had enough sushi? **SPITZ** features Turkish doner kebabs and a carefully selected beer and wine list.

A bit farther east on 2nd Street, Honda Plaza is home to **SUSHI GEN**, one of the area's most beloved, and crowded, sushi bars. If you continue east on 2nd to Alameda, you'll find the Little Tokyo Shopping Center, housing the Korean-owned **LITTLE TOKYO GALLERIA** supermarket, which stocks a wide selection of Asian ingredients; the bento boxes make a quick and tasty lunch. Other worthy spots in the indoor mall include **SUSHI GO 55**, **HONDA-YA** izakaya and an outlet of the **BEARD PAPA'S** cream-puff empire.

Across Alameda Street on 3rd Street is **WURSTKÜCHE**, which is packed with young customers sampling Belgian brews in a dimly lit, high-style beer hall that serves a wacky array of sausages, including rabbit, alligator and rattle-snake. To recover from your sausage and beer, you can caffeinate a couple of doors down at the **NOVEL CAFÉ**, the coffeehouse that's become the hub for this increasingly inhabited loft neighborhood.

— *Pat Saperstein*

Beard Papa's
333 S. Alameda St., 213.620.0710

Daikokuya
327 E. 1st St., 213.626.1680

Far Bar
347 E. 1st. St., 213.617.9990

Haru Ulala
368 E. 2nd St., 213.620.0977

Honda-Ya
333 S. Alameda St., 213.625.1184

Little Tokyo Galleria
333 S. Alameda St., 213.617.0030

Mikawaya
333 S. Alameda St., 213.613.0611

Mitsuru Café
117 Japanese Village Plaza, 1st St. and Central Ave., 213.613.1028

Nijiya Market
124 Japanese Village Plaza, 1st St. and Central Ave., 213.680.3280

Novel Café
811 E. Traction Ave., 213.621.2240

Orochon Ramen
123 S. Onizuka St., 213.617.1766

Spitz
371 E. 2nd St., 213.613.0101

Suehiro Café
337 E. 1st St., 213.626.9132

Sushi Gen
422 E. 2nd St., 213.617.0552

Sushi Go 55
333 S. Alameda St., 213.687.0777

Thousand Cranes
Kyoto Grand Hotel, 120 S. Los Angeles St., 213.253.9255

Wurstküche
800 E. 3rd St., 213.687.4444

GOOD FOOD NEIGHBORHOOD

[San Gabriel Valley]

DRIVE A FEW MILES EAST of Downtown on the 10 Freeway and you'll hit the south San Gabriel Valley, which Taiwanese and Hong Kong venture capital has turned into the largest, splashiest suburban Chinatown in North America. Monterey Park was the first enclave, but as the Chinese population has escalated, this new-era Chinatown has spread like peanut butter into Alhambra, San Gabriel, Arcadia and Rowland Heights.

How to find your way around? Simply imagine a grid. The two main drags run east and west, parallel to the 10 Freeway: Valley Boulevard on the north end and Garvey Avenue on the south. Several north-south commercial streets intersect these thoroughfares: Atlantic Boulevard Garfield Avenue and San Gabriel and Rosemead boulevards.

The multi-level Focus Plaza at Valley and Del Mar Avenue in San Gabriel, nicknamed the Great Mall of China, is crammed with restaurants, noodle shops, boutiques and a huge 99 Ranch supermarket. **NEW CAPITAL SEAFOOD**, on the 4th floor, is a favorite for its reasonably priced traditional dim sum. Its neighbor, **DONG TING SPRING**, a Hunanese spot, serves dishes incorporating grand quantities of chiles and funky condiments. Must haves: stir-fried smoked pig's ear and dried tofu steamed with fresh garlic tops.

Further west on Valley Boulevard in Alhambra is **SAVOY KITCHEN**, a tiny corner cafe with a sidewalk patio and a constant crowd of people waiting for a chance to order the Malaysian-style Hainan chicken. It doesn't look like much — plain-looking poached chicken with stock-infused rice and a trio of sauces — but it's richly flavorful and rewarding; cough up the extra two bucks for the dark meat. A little further west, at **101 NOODLE EXPRESS**, it's the Shandong-style scallion beef roll, miraculously seasoned beef wrapped in lightly crisped Chinese pancakes, that people drive across town to eat.

Returning east on Valley to Atlantic Boulevard going south you'll find a row of restaurant-laden malls. In the Mar Center is **OCEAN STAR**, one of the best traditional live seafood and dim sum halls. The cavernous room with ladies steering burnished dumpling carts is preferable after noon, when they roll out the more exotic items. For fancier, more au courant dim sum ordered from a menu, **ELITE RESTAURANT** serves Thai-style papaya salad garnished with goose tendons, and luscious steamed live shrimp with their roe.

A meal at the northern-style **LITTLE SHEEP,** on Atlantic at Garvey Avenue, reveals just how diverse Chinese cuisine can be. Shabu-shabu–style dining is taken to new and extraordinarily spicy heights. Lamb comes in many styles: dumplings, pancakes, meatballs and slices for the pot.

Traveling east on Garvey you come to **SEAFOOD VILLAGE**, a Chiu Chow spot serving ethereally flavored dishes like duck soup with pickled lemon. Meals can be made of the appetizer plates: crisp-fried shrimp balls, oyster omelet, whole cold crab. Keep heading east to **MAMA LU'S DUMPLING HOUSE**, where the *xiao long bao* — dumplings with soup inside — and the won tons are as good as anything you will find in Hong Kong. Still further east is the not-to-be-missed **CHINA ISLAMIC** restaurant, with its multi-layered sesame breads, spectacular lamb hot pots and hand-shaved noodle dishes of the north.

Continue east to San Gabriel Boulevard and go north to **CHUNG KING**, our favorite down-home Sichuan restaurant famous for its dry-chile-covered diced chicken with peanuts.

— Linda Burum

101 Noodle Express
1408 E. Valley Blvd., Alhambra
626.300.8654

China Islamic Restaurant
7727 E. Garvey Ave., Rosemead
626.288.4246

Chung King
1000 S. San Gabriel Blvd.
San Gabriel, 626.286.0298

Dong Ting Spring Hunan Restaurant
Focus Plaza, 140 W. Valley Blvd.
2nd floor, San Gabriel
626.288.5918

Elite Restaurant
700 S. Atlantic Blvd., Monterey Park
626.282.9998

Little Sheep
120 S. Atlantic Blvd., Monterey Park
626.282.1089

Mama Lu's Dumpling House
153 E. Garvey Ave., Monterey Park
626.307.5700

New Capital Seafood
Focus Plaza, 140 W. Valley Blvd.
4th floor, San Gabriel
626.288.1899

Ocean Star
145 N. Atlantic Blvd., Monterey Park
626.308.2128

Savoy Kitchen
138 E. Valley Blvd., Alhambra
626.308.9535

Seafood Village
684 W. Garvey Ave., Monterey Park
626.289.0088

GOOD FOOD NEIGHBORHOOD
[Sawtelle]

THE WESTSIDE'S "LITTLE OSAKA," along a three-block stretch of Sawtelle west of the 405, throbs with nightlife and the sort of restaurants you're likely to see in modern Tokyo. This enclave between Olympic and Santa Monica boulevards was once farmland for immigrants and later drew Japanese-Americans returning from internment camps. Today, apart from a few extant bonsai nurseries, Sawtelle is all about anime shops, izakaya and noodle bars.

At the southern end in the Olympic Collection complex sits ultra-casual **YAKITORI-YA**, serving nothing but skewered chicken parts grilled over imported hardwood charcoal. Its neighbor is **KIRIKO SUSHI**, where the house-smoked salmon salad with mango lures a devoted clientele, who also rave about the house-made ice creams.

Across the street, the Sawtelle Place Mall holds many delights. **NIJIYA**, a small supermarket, carries goods that seem plucked from the Tokyo suburbs: fresh cut sashimi, bento meals to go, Japanese cookware and pocky sticks. A few doors down, two delightful bakeries are shoehorned into a single shop: international chain **BEARD PAPA'S**, where cream puffs get filled only after you order, and **MOUSSE FANTASY**, which turns out elegant cakes and light takes on French pastries. The more virtuous like **TOFU VILLA**, a Korean-style soon dubu restaurant serving spicy tofu stews.

The Sawtelle Centre strip mall across the street holds **MANPUKU**, a *yakiniku* house (the Japanese version of a cook-at-your-table Korean barbecue). Walk a few shops north to **BLUE MARLIN**, where the walls shimmer with an underwater seascape and the menus offer *youshoku*, popular "foreign" dishes tailored to Japanese palates. The pastas are al dente, the chicken free-range and the curries sing with flavor. A few steps more gets you to **2117 RESTAURANT** a small, pleasant space where Japan's love affair with French food is aptly demonstrated with light modern fare emphasizing organic ingredients: elegant pastas, duck confit and soft-shell crab — and a pretty good wine list, too.

Back across the street is the casual izakaya **FURAIBO**, whose jocular style attracts young families and college kids for pub-style small dishes and tebasaki chicken fried to a crackling crispiness and washed down with shochu. Further north is the venerable **HIDE SUSHI,** the bar that introduced many boomers to sushi with an appeal to the American idea that more is more; its bargain prices and pristinely fresh fish ensure a wait.

Further north, chef Hideo Yamashiro (of Shiro in South Pasadena) offers sophisticated renditions of izakaya at the sleekly minimalist

ORRIS, where you can order a platter of charcuterie along with tempura with house-made curry powder and choose from a beautifully edited wine selection. In the same complex, Mako Tanaka, former Chinois chef and proprietor of Mako in Beverly Hills, brings his modern take on Japan's traditional grill houses at **ROBATA YA**. The small, casual space emphasizes pristine ingredients; grilled skewers go beyond chicken to several cuts of Wagyu (Kobe-style) beef, along with a menu of hot and cold small plates. In the next space is **MIZU 212**, a modern shabu-shabu bar (the name references water's boiling point), where you poach your meal of thinly sliced beef, pork or chicken to dip in the kitchen's outstanding sauce of freshly ground sesame seeds.

Cross the street and walk toward Santa Monica Boulevard to find **BAR HAYAMA** in a converted cottage with a bamboo shaded patio, fire pit and two sake bars. Here graduates of the California Sushi Academy turn out lovely *kozara* (equivalent of tapas) that go beyond standard sushi and sashimi to the likes of beef tartar with quail egg and yellowtail sashimi with myoga.

— *Linda Burum*

2117 Restaurant
2117 Sawtelle Blvd., 310.477.1617

Bar Hayama
1803 Sawtelle Blvd., 310.235.2000

Beard Papa's
2130 Sawtelle Blvd., 310.479.6665

Blue Marlin
2121 Sawtelle Blvd., 310.445.2522

Furaibo
2068 Sawtelle Blvd., 310.444.1432

Hide Sushi
2040 Sawtelle Blvd., 310.477.7242

Kiriko Sushi
11301 Olympic Blvd., 310.478.7769

Manpuku
2125 Sawtelle Blvd., 310.473.0580

Mizu 212
2000 Sawtelle Blvd., 310.478.8979

Mousse Fantasy
2130 Sawtelle Blvd., 310.479.6665

Nijiya Market
2130 Sawtelle Blvd., 310.575.3300

Orris
2006 Sawtelle Blvd., 310.268.2212

Robata Ya
2004 Sawtelle Blvd., 310.481.1418

Tofu Villa
2130 Sawtelle Blvd., 310.477.8987

Yakitori-Ya
11301 Olympic Blvd., 310.479.5400

GOOD FOOD NEIGHBORHOOD
[Silver Lake]

ONE OF L.A.'S MOST QUICKLY changing neighborhoods, Silver Lake is a mix of young musicians, writers and creative types, film-business workers and professionals who enjoy the hilly streets lined with architecturally significant homes and the proximity to Downtown Los Angeles. In the past few years, the neighborhood has gained still more gourmet food shops, under-the-radar restaurants and funky boutiques.

Start a walking tour of Silver Lake at Sunset Junction, the area starting around Sunset Boulevard and Sanborn Avenue, where several tasty shops are close together. **INTELLIGENTSIA COFFEE & TEA**, which originated in Chicago, kicked up the local coffee competition by several notches; its shady terrace is a great place for lingering over carefully drawn lattes. After fueling up on coffee, stop by the **CHEESE STORE OF SILVERLAKE**, one of the city's top cheesemongers, and stock up on cheeses, condiments, charcuterie, olives and wine for your pantry.

For a leisurely dinner, dine next door to the Cheese Shop at **CAFE STELLA** for French bistro food in a bohemian sidewalk-café atmosphere. You'll find the perfect dessert right across the street at **PAZZO GELATO**, which carries unusual flavors of hand-crafted gelati. Or head east on Sunset to pick up some salted caramels or red velvet cupcakes at the dainty **LARK SILVER LAKE CAKE SHOP**.

Make sure to allow time for a stop at Joe Keeper's new shop, **BAR KEEPER**, in the Sunset Junction area. It's a wonderland of goods for cocktail lovers and mixologists, and it's just the place to pick up a gift of an absinthe spoon for that friend who has everything — or thought he did.

While the area is more ethnically diverse than it once was, it's still rich in Latino culture and food, and you'll see lots of Mexican restaurants. Try the fish tacos at the popular **EL SIETE MARES** taco stand; for lighter, updated Mexican dishes, a tasty mole and good vegetarian choices, head to **ALEGRIA ON SUNSET**. And if it's a drink you're after, you'll find margaritas and a killer tequila selection at **MALO**, a hip hangout whose drinks are better than its food.

Breakfast is the favorite meal for a certain sort of Silver Lake resident. Late sleepers favor grungy old-school diner **MILLIE'S**, while those who value sustainability and local ingredients head to **LOCAL** for brioche french toast or tofu chilequiles; Local also has a terrific new-age salad bar. People who want room to spread out in a booth with the newspaper settle in at **DUSTY'S BISTRO**, which has a full bar and French-Canadian specialties.

Vestiges of the area's scruffier past can be found at **CAFÉ TROPICAL**, a Cuban café serving up café con leche, fresh-squeezed juices and baked goods, like the iconic guava cheese pastry. Or dig into a bowl of steaming pho noodle soup into the wee hours at **PHO CAFÉ**, a Vietnamese mini-mall spot with a modern décor but no sign out front.

As you leave the area, head north onto Silver Lake Boulevard to check out **LA MILL**, a high-style coffee emporium with baroque brewing methods and top-notch food conceived by Michael Cimarusti, chef of Providence. Continue along the Silver Lake reservoir to Glendale Boulevard to find **SILVERLAKE WINE**, where regular tastings (as well as the every-Thursday appearance of the Let's Be Frank truck) draw enthusiastic crowds of oenophiles.

— *Pat Saperstein*

Alegria on Sunset
3510 W. Sunset Blvd., 323.913.1422

Bar Keeper
3910 W. Sunset Blvd., 323.669.1675

Café Stella
3932 W. Sunset Blvd., 323.666.0265

Café Tropical
2900 W. Sunset Blvd., 323.661.8391

Cheese Store of Silverlake
3926 W. Sunset Blvd., 323.644.7511

Dusty's Bistro
3200 W. Sunset Blvd., 323.906.1018

El Siete Mares
3131 W. Sunset Blvd., 323.665.0865

**Intelligentsia
Coffee & Tea**
3922 W. Sunset Blvd., 323.663.6173

LA Mill
1636 Silver Lake Blvd., 323.663.4441

**Lark Silver Lake
Cake Shop**
3337 W. Sunset Blvd., 323.667.2968

Local
2943 W. Sunset Blvd., 323.662.4740

Malo
4326 W. Sunset Blvd., 323.664.1011

Millie's
3524 W. Sunset Blvd., 323.664.0404

Pazzo Gelateria
3827 W. Sunset Blvd., 323.662.1410

Pho Café
2841 W. Sunset Blvd., 213.413.0888

Silverlake Wine
2395 Glendale Blvd., 323.662.9024

GOOD FOOD NEIGHBORHOOD
[South Pasadena]

QUAINT SOUTH PASADENA has done its utmost to preserve its leafy, small-town flavor, and the arrival of the Metro Gold Line service cemented its pedestrian-friendly status. Just a few blocks long, the charming Mission Street area is rich with food-centric places, as well as boutiques and antiques shops; shady El Centro Street, one block south, is also part of this district.

Starting at the Gold Line's Mission station, walk north across Mission to find **HEIRLOOM BAKERY**, the neighborhood's best breakfast place, with sturdy coffee, homey baked goods, generous egg dishes and a large outdoor eating area. If you just want coffee, stop at quirky **BUSTER'S**, which also has Fosselman's ice cream.

Next, walk south a block to find El Centro, a pretty little street that parallels Mission. It seems almost European here — the first place you'll see, right next to the tracks, is **NICOLE'S GOURMET FOODS**, run by the *charmant* Nicole Grandjean. A wholesaler of French cheeses and goodies for restaurants, she also has a retail store and café complete with a flower-lined patio. The store opens early for *cafés et croissants* and offers cheese and charcuterie to take home or to be made into sandwiches (try the prosciutto, pecorino and arugula) at lunchtime. Nicole's also stocks hard-to-find baking items, kitchenware and frozen croissant dough and tart shells. **BISTRO DE LA GARE** completes the block's French theme, with indoor and outdoor dining on such traditional French fare as steak frites, onion soup and roast chicken.

A few steps east on El Centro is **KALDI**, the antithesis of chain coffeehouses, with funky couches and chairs, free WiFi, good cappuccino and snacks. Also on El Centro is **FIREFLY BISTRO**, a quintessentially Californian spot whose dining "room" is a large, tented, twinkle-lit patio. The eclectic menu draws from the South (shrimp and grits), the Mediterranean (grilled calamari with olives, pine nuts and arugula) and the modern American playbook (a great BLT for lunch, crab hash for brunch).

Note that if you plan your visit for a Thursday afternoon, you'll find El Centro taken over by the small but very good weekly **FARMERS' MARKET**, a fine fate for a food lover!

Head north a block back to Mission and stop in at friendly **MISSION WINE**, which pours tasting flights every day and also has beer on tap. Owner Chris Meeske's selection of small-production wines includes some good values. If it's time for dinner, choose from **MIKE & ANNE'S**, which has a lively new bar, delicious upscale comfort food (get the burger and the sweet potato fries) and yet another lovely patio, or **BRIGANTI**, a convivial Tuscan trattoria with an excellent burrata caprese salad, light pastas and grilled fresh fish. The old-timer of the neighborhood is **SHIRO**, a modern space with imaginative French-Japanese cooking that emphasizes seafood; its sizzling whole catfish with ponzu is legendary, but by no means should you limit yourself to that one dish.

Just make sure somewhere in your day to fit in an old-fashioned sundae or milkshake at the historic corner **FAIR OAKS PHARMACY**, complete with an antique soda fountain and counter.

— *Pat Saperstein*

Bistro de la Gare
921 Meridian Ave., 626.799.8828

Briganti
1423 Mission St., 626.441.4663

Buster's Ice Cream & Coffee Shop
1006 Mission St., 626.441.0744

Fair Oaks Pharmacy
1526 Mission St., 626.799.1414

Firefly Bistro
1009 El Centro St., 626.441.2443

Heirloom Bakery & Café
807 Meridian Ave., 626.441.0042

Kaldi
1019 El Centro St., 626.403.5951

Mike & Anne's
1040 Mission St., 626.799.7199

Mission Wine
1114 Mission St., 626.403.9463

Nicole's Gourmet Foods
921 Meridian Ave., 626.403.5751

Shiro
1505 Mission St., 626.799.4774

South Pasadena Farmers' Market
El Centro St. & Diamond Ave.
Thurs. 4-8 p.m.

GOOD FOOD NEIGHBORHOOD
[Ventura Boulevard, Studio City]

WE'LL ADMIT IT: Ventura Boulevard lacks the cachet of such other important streets "over the hill" as Wilshire and Sunset. The main surface artery through the San Fernando Valley has long, utterly forgettable stretches lined with strip malls, auto dealerships and low-end motels. However, as Ventura heads into Studio City, it's studded with some of the Valley's best food finds — ones that are even worth a drive over the hill.

Start around the corner from Universal City at the celebrated **SU-SHI NOZAWA**, located on the eastern end of Sushi Row, the section of Ventura named for its cluster of sushi restaurants. At his original Studio City place chef Kazunori Nozawa, known to some as the Sushi Nazi, offers a distinctive style of chef's-choice omakase ("trust me" is his motto) to cowed but doting customers (he also operates Sugarfish in Marina del Rey). In the same Ventura Boulevard strip mall is the humbler but more hospitable **DAICHAN**, a family-run hole-in-the-wall that serves excellent homestyle Japanese dishes, such as udon noodles, poki bowls, curries and tempuras.

A short hop west on the same side of Ventura is chef Katsuya Uechi's original **KATSU-YA**, which has now grown into a sushi empire with a branch in Encino and high-style Katsuya by Starck offshoots in Hollywood, Brentwood and Glendale. Katsu-Ya in Studio City specializes in elaborate rolls and intricate presentations, and if you can swing a reservation it's a fun spot for a small group. A few blocks west on the same side of Ventura is Uechi's latest creation, **KIWAMI**, an elegant, contemporary spot for sushi connoisseurs to savor omakase or nosh less formally on soba noodles, tempura and miso-marinated black cod. If you're on an expense account, try **ASANEBO**, which despite its unprepossessing location (in a strip mall across the boulevard from Kiwami) was awarded one star from the Michelin guide in 2007. Asanebo serves a limited selection of nigiri sushi but is better known for superb sashimi and a range of imaginative cooked dishes; omakase starts at $75 per person and ascends from there.

Since man does not live by yellowtail alone, you might want to stop at **LAUREL TAVERN** for a draft California brew or glass of wine with some irresistible skewers of pork belly. Or if it's cheese you're craving, head to **ARTISAN CHEESE GALLERY**, just east of Laurel Canyon Boulevard. It purveys handmade cheeses from all over the world, as well as Fra Mani salumi, a variety of gourmet food products and an amazing duck confit sandwich. On Sundays, Ventura Place behind the Cheese Gallery is home to the **STUDIO CITY FARMERS' MARKET**, a small market that is hugely popular with the locals (parking can be a challenge). And every morning, the venerable **DU-PAR'S** is a magnet for hungry folk chowing down on buttermilk pancakes and french toast; it's also a great place to spot rumpled, not-yet-caffeinated celebrities.

A block west of Laurel Canyon you'll find a chic little bakery called **BIG SUGAR BAKESHOP**. Every day the bakers create a different lineup of temptations, from red velvet cake and tender scones to luscious brownies, but Big Sugar is perhaps best known for creating the doughnut muffin, which combines the best of both baked goods into one toothsome breakfast treat.

Last, for a relaxing capper to this culinary crawl, stop in at **THE FLASK**, which has been satisfying local needs for premium bottlings for more than four decades. After all, pounding the pavement in search of good eats is thirsty work.

— *Jean T. Barrett*

Artisan Cheese Gallery
12023 Ventura Blvd.
818.505.0207

Asanebo
11941 Ventura Blvd.
818.760.3348

Big Sugar Bakeshop
12182 Ventura Blvd.
818.508.5855

Daichan
11288 Ventura Blvd.
818.980.8450

Du-par's
12036 Ventura Blvd
818.766.4437

The Flask
12194 Ventura Blvd.
818.761.5373

Katsu-Ya
11680 Ventura Blvd.
818.985.6976

Kiwami
11920 Ventura Blvd.
818.763.3910

Laurel Tavern
11938 Ventura Blvd.
818.506.0777

Studio City Farmers' Market
Ventura Pl. at Ventura Blvd.
Sun. 8 a.m.-1 p.m.

Sushi Nozawa
11288 Ventura Blvd.
818.508.7017

Restaurants

In these pages you'll find nearly 500 of L.A.'s most interesting restaurants, from the humblest to the *haute*-est. Look for more good eating in Food That's Fast, Breakfast + Lunch, Drink + Eat, Gourmet-to-Go and Bakeries + Sweets.

[ESSENTIALLY L.A.]

CENTRAL CITY

Angeli Caffé, Melrose (PAGE 40)
Animal, Fairfax District (PAGE 41)
AOC, Beverly/Third (PAGE 41)
Bistro LQ, Beverly/Third (PAGE 43)
Campanile, Miracle Mile (PAGE 44)
Chosun Galbee, Koreatown (PAGE 45)
Fred 62, Los Feliz (PAGE 48)
Grace, Beverly/Third (PAGE 49)
Hungry Cat, Hollywood (PAGE 50)
Jar, Melrose (PAGE 50)
Jaragua, East Hollywood (PAGE 50)
Jitlada, Hollywood (PAGE 51)
Loteria Grill, Hollywood (PAGE 52)
Lucques, Melrose (PAGE 53)
M Café de Chaya, Melrose (PAGE 53)
Madeo, West Hollywood (PAGE 54)
Osteria Mozza & Pizzeria Mozza, Beverly/Third (PAGES 56 & 57)
Providence, Melrose (PAGE 57)
Soot Bull Jeep, Koreatown (PAGE 60)
Taylor's Steakhouse, Koreatown (PAGE 61)
Umami Burger, Miracle Mile (PAGE 63)

🏛 ESSENTIALLY L.A. ☺ LATE ♥ ROMANTIC 💲 VALUE 🔉 QUIET ♻ SUSTAINABLE

EASTSIDE

Blair's, Silver Lake (PAGE 65)
Bottega Louie, Downtown (PAGE 66)
Café Pinot, Downtown (PAGE 67)
Casa Bianca Pizza Pie, Eagle Rock (PAGE 67)
Chaya Downtown (PAGE 67)
Church & State, Downtown (PAGE 68)
El Taurino, Pico-Union (PAGE 70)
Fatty's, Eagle Rock (PAGE 71)
Gingergrass, Silver Lake (PAGE 72)
Kagaya, Little Tokyo/Arts District (PAGE 73)
La Serenata de Garibaldi, Boyle Heights (PAGE 74)
Mo-Chica Peruvian, USC (PAGE 75)
Moles la Tia, East L.A. (PAGE 75)
Pacific Dining Car, Westlake (PAGE 76)
R-23, Downtown (PAGE 77)
Teresitas, East L.A. (PAGE 79)
Tiara Café, South Park/Fashion District (PAGE 79)
Water Grill, Downtown (PAGE 80)
Yang Chow, Chinatown (PAGE 81)

SAN GABRIEL VALLEY

Babita Mexicuisine, San Gabriel (PAGE 82)
Celestino, Pasadena (PAGE 85)
Chang's Garden, Arcadia (PAGE 85)
Cook's Tortas, Monterey Park (PAGE 86)
Din Tai Fung, Arcadia (PAGE 86)
Duck House, Monterey Park (PAGE 87)
Elite, Monterey Park (PAGE 88)
Green Village Shanghai, Rowland Heights (PAGE 89)
La Cabanita, Montrose (PAGE 91)
Luscious Dumplings, San Gabriel (PAGE 92)
Palate Food & Wine, Glendale (PAGE 96)
Sea Harbour, Rosemead (PAGE 98)
Shiro, South Pasadena (PAGE 99)
Southern Mini Town, San Gabriel (PAGE 100)
Vietnam Restaurant, San Gabriel (PAGE 102)
Zeke's Smokehouse, Montrose (PAGE 104)

VEGETARIAN ⊙ KID FRIENDLY ✿ PATIO DINING 🚗 DELIVERY 🏛 PRIVATE PARTY

[ESSENTIALLY L.A.]
EAST VALLEY
Asanebo, Studio City (PAGE 104)
Caioti Pizza Café, Studio City (PAGE 105)
Kiwami, Studio City (PAGE 107)
Krua Thai, North Hollywood (PAGE 107)
Pinot Bistro, Studio City (PAGE 108)
Smoke House, Burbank (PAGE 109)
Sushi Nozawa, Studio City (PAGE 110)

WEST VALLEY
Brent's Delicatessen, Northridge (PAGE 111)
Puro Sabor Peruvian Food, Van Nuys (PAGE 113)
Saddle Peak Lodge, Calabasas (PAGE 114)
Woodlands, Chatsworth (PAGE 116)

WESTSIDE: CENTRAL
Craft, Century City (PAGE 117)
Cut, Beverly Hills (PAGE 117)
Grill on the Alley, Beverly Hills (PAGE 119)
Guelaguetza, Palms (PAGE 119)
Koutoubia, Westwood (PAGE 120)
Lawry's the Prime Rib, Beverly Hills (PAGE 120)
Le Saint Amour, Culver City (PAGE 121)
M Café de Chaya, Culver City (PAGE 121)
Matsuhisa, Beverly Hills (PAGE 122)
Spago, Beverly Hills (PAGE 123)
Urasawa, Beverly Hills (PAGE 124)
Versailles, Culver City (PAGE 124)
Wolfgang's Steakhouse, Beverly Hills (PAGE 125)

[ESSENTIALLY L.A.]
WEST OF THE 405

Antica Pizzeria, Marina del Rey (PAGE 126)

Border Grill, Santa Monica (PAGE 127)

Catch, Santa Monica (PAGE 129)

Drago Ristorante, Santa Monica (PAGE 130)

Gjelina, Venice (PAGE 132)

Inn of the Seventh Ray, Topanga (PAGE 133)

Joe's, Venice (PAGE 134)

Josie, Santa Monica (PAGE 134)

Mélisse, Santa Monica (PAGE 137)

Michael's, Santa Monica (PAGE 137)

Musha, Santa Monica (PAGE 137)

Orris, West L.A. (PAGE 139)

Piccolo, Venice (PAGE 140)

Pizzicotto, Brentwood (PAGE 140)

Riva, Santa Monica (PAGE 141)

Rustic Canyon, Santa Monica (PAGE 141)

Tlapazola Grill, West L.A. & Venice (PAGE 143)

Typhoon, Santa Monica (PAGE 143)

Vincenti, Brentwood (PAGE 144)

SOUTH BAY TO SOUTH L.A.

Benley, Long Beach (PAGE 146)

Chaba Thai Bay Grill, Redondo Beach (PAGE 148)

Dal Rae, Pico Rivera (PAGE 148)

Enrique's, Long Beach (PAGE 150)

George's Greek Café, Long Beach (PAGE 151)

Izakaya Yuzen Kan, Torrance (PAGE 152)

Komatsu Tempura Bar, Torrance (PAGE 153)

La Casita Mexicana, Bell (PAGE 154)

Musha, Torrance (PAGE 155)

Otafuku, Gardena (PAGE 156)

Pann's Restaurant, Inglewood (PAGE 156)

Renu Nakorn, Norwalk (PAGE 157)

Restaurant Christine, Torrance (PAGE 157)

Tirupathi Bhimas, Artesia (PAGE 158)

🍃 VEGETARIAN ☺ KID FRIENDLY ☼ PATIO DINING 🚐 DELIVERY 🎩 PRIVATE PARTY

CENTRAL CITY

[8 oz. Burger Bar] 7661 Melrose Ave., Melrose, 323.852.0008, 8oz-burgerbar.com. L & D daily. American. Full bar. AE, MC, V. $$ **WHY** The short-rib grilled cheese, which is every bit as heavenly as it sounds; the high-quality build-your-own burgers, made with grass-fed beef or a blend of Angus steak, tri-tip, chuck and short rib; and the light, wonderful onion rings. **WHAT** This upscale burger bar occupies the former Table 8 space and shares the same owners. The feel is more casual than when it was Table 8, but it's still chic, with wainscoting and a handsome bar. The surprise is why it's not more crowded, given the surprisingly moderate prices and very good burgers. 📷 🍸

[Ackee Bamboo] 4305 Degnan Blvd., Leimert Park, 323.295.7275, ackeebamboo.com. B, L & D daily. Jamaican. BYOB. MC, V. $ **WHY** Zingy Jamaican food in a casually hip Leimert Park café. **WHAT** Close your eyes and the sea of L.A. concrete outside might just morph into the blue Caribbean, thanks to the vividly flavorful, bargain-priced Jamaican cooking at this friendly neighborhood spot. If you like spicy, have the classic jerk chicken; if you like it mellower, try the beef stew, meat patties, barbecued ribs or the namesake *ackee* (the meat of a Jamaican flower) with salt cod, the traditional Jamaican breakfast dish. 📷 ☼

[Ago] 8478 Melrose Ave., Melrose, 323.655.6333, agorestaurant.com. L Mon.-Fri., D nightly. Italian. Full bar. AE, MC, V. $$$ - $$$$$ **WHY** For celebrity cachet and hearty, South Beach–friendly Tuscan meals of salads followed by delicious bistecca fiorentina, flattened chicken or veal chops with rustic beans. **WHAT** The star power burns bright at this manly (and pricey) Tuscan trattoria, where the ingredients are good and the plastic surgery is better. **WHO** With co-owners like Robert De Niro and the Weinstein brothers, it's no surprise that the place is packed with famous faces and wannabes day and night.

[Amarone Kitchen & Wine] 8868 W. Sunset Blvd., West Hollywood, 310.652.2233, amarone-la.com. D Mon.-Sat. Italian. Beer & wine. AE, MC, V. $$$ - $$$$ **WHY** It's like escaping to Florence right there on Sunset Boulevard. **WHAT** While the rest of the Sunset Strip screams for attention, this dollhouse of a ristorante is happy to be invisible — its clientele cares more about food, service and charm than being noticed. Couples and friends reminisce about their last trip to Italy while the young Bolognese chef sends out grilled octopus with white beans, squid-ink spaghetti with seafood, risotto with porcini and parmigiano and flawlessly cooked *spigola* (a cousin of branzino). **WHO** Handsome people old enough to be the parents (grandparents?) of the crowd hanging out in front of the Viper Room down the block. ♥ 🍸

[Angeli Caffé] 🏛 7274 Melrose Ave., Melrose, 323.936.9086, angelicaffe.com. L Tues.-Fri., D Tues.-Sun. Italian. Beer & wine. AE, MC, V. $ - $$$ **WHY** Wonderful pizzas, panzanella, perfectly dressed salads and toothsome pasta dishes. Delivery, too! **WHAT** Back in the early days of Melrose, Evan Kleiman set the L.A. standard for casual, affordable trattorie serving robust and delicious food. Today Angeli continues to be a standard-bearer. An L.A. treasure, and a great place to have a private party. **WHO** Old-time Melrosers sporting L.A. Eyeworks glasses and only the subtlest of tattoos. 👓🔖☺�,🏛

[Angelini Osteria] **7313 Beverly Blvd., Beverly/Third, 323.297.0070, angeliniosteria.com. L Tues.-Fri., D Tues.-Sun. Italian. Beer & wine. AE, MC, V. $$$ - $$$$ WHY** Rich oxtails, braised artichokes, green lasagne and other delicious pastas, and wonderful branzino. **WHAT** There are fancier Italian restaurants in town, but few with better food than this one (and chef Gino Angelini's other restaurant, La Minestraio). The minimalist storefront is packed a little too tightly, and the room's a little too loud, but that only seems to make the food taste better. If only it wasn't so expensive, we'd eat this Italian soul food every week. **WHO** A sophisticated crowd that cares more about the cooking than the scene, although there is a bit of a scene anyway.

[Animal] 🏛 **435 N. Fairfax Ave., Fairfax District, 323.782.9225, animal-restaurant.com. D nightly (to 2 a.m. Fri.-Sat.). Modern American. Beer & wine. AE, MC, V. $$$ - $$$$ WHY** Bacon in your salad, bacon for your main course, bacon in your dessert. **WHAT** L.A.'s current foodie sensation is a bare-bones room roiling with noise and filled with people who aren't even mad that they had to wait 45 minutes… with a reservation. It helps that the staff is remarkably kind, but really it's because who can stay mad when the food is so damn good? The smart way to go is to share plates, so you don't OD on the meltingly rich squares of pork belly with kim chee. Owners/chefs Jon Shook and Vinny Dotolo, the "Two Food Dudes" of brief TV fame, are indeed dudes, but they are not slackers — they work hard to make sure you will be happy with your kale salad with pecorino, polenta with slow-cooked bolognese, crisp-tender pork ribs with a balsamic glaze, and bacon-chocolate crunch bar. And you will be. Unless you're a vegetarian. **WHO** A thundering herd of handsomely tousled carnivores. ☺

[AOC] 🏛 **8022 W. 3rd St., Beverly/Third, 323.653.6359, aocwinebar.com. D nightly. Mediterranean/wine bar. Full bar. AE, MC, V. $$ - $$$ WHY** AOC has an NYC bistro feel with excellent wines by the glass and perfectly ripe cheeses — and staff members who know more than just their name. The Cal-Med food is always reliable, if a smidge less so than at sister restaurant Lucques. **WHAT** Anything vegetable (or animal, for that matter) is coddled by the cooks at this oh-so-hot wine bar and small-plates restaurant — even cod haters will be converted by the fritters with citrus salad and aioli. Don't skip dessert — all the better to linger with a glass of Muscat and take in the scene, complete with the requisite high-decibel chatter. **WHO** D girls, agents and food-and-wine lovers traveling from the Palisades and Pasadena. 🔖

🔖 VEGETARIAN ☺ KID FRIENDLY ✿ PATIO DINING 🚍 DELIVERY 🏛 PRIVATE PARTY

[Atlacatl] 301 N. Berendo St., East Hollywood, 323.663.1404. L & D daily. Salvadoran. Beer & wine. Cash only. $ **WHY** Wonderful and wonderfully inexpensive Salvadoran home cooking: pupusas, empanadas with cream, *sopa de res* (a stew-like beef soup) and thick Salvadoran-style horchata. **WHAT** In a faded cottage on a worn stretch of Beverly lies a wonderful Salvadoran café staffed with incredibly nice women who deliver hefty pupusas filled with cheese and *loroco* (flower buds reminiscent of asparagus) or beans, cheese and *chicharron* (pork); tender-crisp-sweet fried plantains; and complimentary sides of *curtido*, the tangy and delicious Salvadoran cole slaw. **WHO** Neighborhood families, including many Salvadorans, who don't mind waiting 20 minutes for a table, and who keep an eye on soccer on the TV while they wait. 🐷☺

[The Bazaar at SLS Hotel] 465 S. La Cienega Blvd., West Hollywood, 310.246.5555, thebazaar.com. Tea & D daily, brunch Sat.-Sun. Spanish/modern American. Full bar. AE, MC, V. $$$$ - $$$$$ **WHY** That only-in-Vegas memorable experience complete with over-the-top, pause-worthy food by celebrity chef José Andrés, a jaw-dropping modern décor by Philippe Starck, and a host/manager who has a wire in his ear and looks like a celebrity bodyguard. **WHAT** In two adjoining über-chic tapas bars, famed Spanish chef Andrés serves small dishes unlike anyone else's: cotton candy–foie gras lollipops (amazing, trust us), Philly cheese steaks with "air bread" (really mini bread-like shells topped with Kobe beef that pops open to reveal melted cheese) and an ever-changing menu of don't-try-this-at-home creations — most of which are quite wee, so you'll need to order lots of them to make a meal. Brunch, afternoon tea or nibbling at the separate (and fantastic) patisserie are good lower-priced options if you haven't hit the jackpot yet. The sexy Bar Centro makes outrageously expensive cocktails that are wildly creative yet balanced (think a Manhattan with a "liquid" cherry that explodes in your mouth). Gorgeous waiters might take good care of you or might forget about you — and the kitchen races dishes out, seemingly in hopes of turning tables fast to make room for more Platinum cards. **WHO** A see-and-be-seen crowd that mixes *The Hills* with *Real Housewives*. 🏠

[Beverly Soon Tofu House] 2712 W. Olympic Blvd., Koreatown, 213.380.1113. L & D daily. Korean. Beer & wine. AE, MC, V. $ **WHY** For the *soon dubu jigae*, a spicy, garlicky stew of soft, fresh tofu that roils and bubbles like volcanic lava in its individual iron pot. The superheated dish cooks a raw egg that the server cracks in at your table. Your choice of seafood or bits of meat add extra flavor to the extravaganza. **WHAT** Rivals of this 23-year-old café — including a well-known chain — may seek to encroach on its long-held supremacy, but we're drawn back for the cloud-like texture of its tofu, the spot-on balance of its broth and the charming rural ambience, with rustic tables fashioned from sliced trees. 🐷🥄

🏛 **ESSENTIALLY L.A.** ☺**LATE** ♥**ROMANTIC** 🐷**VALUE** 🌙**QUIET** ♻**SUSTAINABLE**

[Bistro LQ] 🔒 8009 Beverly Blvd., Beverly/Third, 323.951.1088, bistrolq.com. D Tues.-Sun. French/modern American. Beer & wine. AE, MC, V. $$$ - $$$$ **WHY** Because the cooking of one of L.A.'s most talented and inventive chefs finally has the setting and service it deserves. **WHAT** The late Mimosa is now a small, chic dining room with artful lighting, abstract paintings and a fleet of handsome French and Latino waiters. It really feels like Paris — 21st-century Paris, that is. Chef/owner Laurent Quenioux (formerly of many places, including Bistro K) doesn't care that Angelenos aren't big eaters of such offal as duck hearts, goat tripe and lamb tongue; he cooks with them anyway, and they're so wonderful that they sell. He's all about pushing the culinary envelope, complementing and contrasting textures, spices and flavors of sweet and savory. Not every dish succeeds — braised baby goat with guajillo peppers, for instance, was dense and heavy — but many are marvels, and they're all available in half-portions, so you can try more. Consider the uni tapioca pudding with yuzu kocho, which tastes like essence of the sea; the incredible oatmeal topped with cinnamon-scented roasted lobster; the smoked herring with warm potatoes and a sautéed quail egg; the very French cheese cart; and the "composition around dark chocolate." **WHO** Fans who've followed Quenioux all over town and culinary adventurers tired of the same old beet salads and grilled salmon. ♥ 🍽

[BLT Steak] 8720 Sunset Blvd., West Hollywood, 310.360.1950, bltsteak.com. D nightly. American/steakhouse. Full bar. AE, MC, V. $$$$$ **WHY** NYC chef Laurent Tourondel understands the true meaning of the Holy Trinity: meat, potatoes and pastry. **WHAT** There are a lot of things to like about BLT: sauces that are actually worthy of the top-quality steaks (three-mustard, chimichurri); non-beef mains that are often even better than the excellent steaks; potatoes nine ways (the gratin is so worth the calories); and too many tempting caramelized/souffléd/creamed desserts to choose from. Save big bucks (you are not going to skip dessert here) with the daily blackboard menu, a $60 three-course dinner. **WHO** At these prices, and with the Sunset Boulevard location, a celebrity or two is inevitable, and Bentleys are parked three deep at the valet stand. 🏛

[BoHo] 6372 W. Sunset Blvd., Hollywood, 323.465.8500, bohorestaurant.com. L & D nightly, brunch Sat.-Sun. Modern American. Full bar. AE, MC, V. $$ - $$$ **WHY** It's the perfect fit for the neighborhood: a relaxed, reasonably priced place for before or after outings at the Pantages, the Arclight and Amoeba. **WHAT** Chef André Guerrero hits the nail on the head with his new place next to the Arclight theaters. Decorated with deliberately ugly flea-market art and lamps, the vast, brick-walled space manages to be both cozy and quiet, and the menu is exactly as good as it needs to be, with something for everyone: crisp pizzas (try the Korean barbecue), excellent burgers, a perfect Caesar, all-American desserts. The tap beer list is astonishing. **WHO** Attractive young film buffs at the bar, and an appealing diverse mix in the booths and around the flea-market tables. ☉ 🎥 🎵 🥡

[Bulan Thai Vegetarian Kitchen] 7168 Melrose Ave., Melrose, 323.857.1882, bulanthai.com. L & D daily. Thai/vegan. No booze. AE, MC, V. **$ WHY** Truly delicious vegan Thai cooking, served by nice people in a homey setting — and free delivery, too! **WHAT** Bulan serves good Thai food first — the vegan part seems almost secondary. Faux chicken and shrimp dishes are specialties; try the satay, the green curry and the pad kee mao noodles. **WHO** Vegans bringing their carnivorous mates, who always leave happy. 🎥 ♻ 🥡 🚗

[Café des Artistes] 1534 N. McCadden Pl., Hollywood, 323.469.7300, cafedesartistes.info. D nightly (to 2 a.m. Thurs.-Sat.). French. Full bar. AE, MC, V. $$ - $$$$ **WHY** Well-prepared French bistro classics in a hidden, romantic spot. Try the perfectly dressed salads, steak sandwich with thin, crisp fries, cassoulet, and one of the tarts for dessert. **WHAT** Although large, with a front patio, a fireplace-warmed dining room and a huge tented back patio, this French bistro seems intimate. For a while it was a player on the see-and-be-seen circuit; thankfully, those days are gone. The back patio is a great place for a private party. **WHO** Low-key dealmakers (think software developers more than A-list movie producers) and romancing couples. ☉♥🎵☼

[Campanile] 🏛 624 S. La Brea Ave., Miracle Mile, 323.938.1447, campanilerestaurant.com. L Mon.-Fri., D Mon.-Sat., brunch Sat.-Sun. Californian/Mediterranean. Full bar. AE, MC, V. $$$ - $$$$$ **WHY** For Mark Peel's mastery of simple grilled meats, for the desserts, for Thursday grilled-cheese night and for the handsome, old-L.A. setting that makes everyone happy. **WHAT** Lucques may be the Campanile of the 2000s, but that doesn't mean Campanile peaked in the '90s. It remains the perfect L.A. restaurant, the sort of place that doesn't make us want to up and move to San Francisco or Portland, like so many of our scene restaurants do. Owner/chef Mark Peel loves bold, rustic flavors that are carefully built but not complicated — a California-Mediterranean cuisine that focuses on exceptional ingredients. If you haven't been here in ages, come back — you won't be sorry. **WHO** Business folks at lunch, stylish families on Thursdays for grilled-cheese night and, for dinner, longtime regulars. ♥♻🥡☼

[Carlitos Gardel] 7963 Melrose Ave., Melrose, 323.655.0891, carlitosgardel.com. L Mon.-Fri., D nightly. Argentinean. Beer & wine. AE, MC, V. $$$ - $$$$ **WHY** First-rate Argentinean wine and food: beef empanadas, matambre, sausages, remarkable french fries and, of course, the baked garlic to squish over your bread. **WHAT** Less showy than the Brazilian churrascarias that are currently the rage but every bit as devoted to delicious grilled meat, Gardel's has been L.A.'s go-to Argentinean restaurant for years. Good service, a reasonably priced wine list, a romantic setting and, in case your loved one is a vegetarian, tasty meat-free pastas. **WHO** Carnivores. ♥

[Chameau] 339 N. Fairfax Ave., Fairfax District, 323.951.0039, chameaurestaurant.com. D Tues.-Sat. Moroccan/French. Beer & wine. AE, MC, V. $$$ **WHY** Sublime Moroccan-French dishes without all the belly-dancing folderol: house-made breads, sweet-savory duck b'stilla, long-cooked lamb of astonishing tenderness and flavor and delicate couscous served with tagines. Good wines, too. **WHAT** This chic Moroccan bistro is more Parisian in look than kitschy Moroccan, and the menu shows the influence of three cultures: Moroccan, French and Californian. Chef Adel Chagar does a superb job of executing the rich North African staples, from his couscous to his steaming b'stillas, but he also serves California-friendly salads (cucumber, tomato, olives and goat cheese) and French-influenced entrees (roasted scallops with fish fumet). **WHO** Romance seekers. ♥ 🦞

[Chaya Brasserie] 8741 Alden Dr., West Hollywood, 310.859.8833, thechaya.com. L Fri., D nightly, brunch Sun. Asian/French. Full bar. AE, MC, V. $$$ - $$$$ **WHY** Because it's an L.A. pioneer that set the standard for French-Japanese-American cooking that's inventive but not silly. And it has a great and affordable bar menu. **WHAT** It's too easy to forget about this chic bistro near Cedars-Sinai, and indeed we did forget it in our last edition. But we were sorry: It's a quintessential L.A. restaurnt with consisently good food and a cool vibe. Excellent lunchtime salads and dinnertime burgers and miso-marinated sea bass. **WHO** Agents, writers and such stars as Zac Efron and David Byrne.

[Cheebo] 7533 W. Sunset Blvd., Hollywood, 323.850.7070, cheebo.com. B, L & D daily. Italian/Californian. Beer & wine. MC, V. $$ - $$$ **WHY** For a robust, modestly priced meal after an Arclight movie. And if you live or work around here, they deliver! **WHAT** This noisy, cheerful café has something for everyone — breakfast burritos, panini, chopped salads, vegan lentil soup, a kids' menu — but we're most partial to the rectangular pizzas. A fun spot for a casual Hollywood meal with friends. **WHO** A boisterous crew of young'uns. 🖼️ ☼ 🦞 ☺ �: 🚚

[Chosun Galbee] 🏠 3330 W. Olympic Blvd., Koreatown, 323.734.3330, chosungalbee.com. L & D daily. Korean. Full bar. AE, MC, V. $$$ - $$$$ **WHY** Groups can mix orders of short ribs, sliced beef, chicken, shrimp and pork and then help servers tend to the meats on the grill in the center of the table, creating a fun and interactive meal. **WHAT** This stylish, modern setting is more upscale than the typical Korean barbecue restaurant, with a sleek, chic décor, a lovely outdoor patio and private rooms that are often packed with business groups or parties. A Koreatown must. **WHO** Upscale Korean couples on dates, large celebratory groups. ☺ ☼ 🏮

🦞 **VEGETARIAN** ☺ **KID FRIENDLY** ☼ **PATIO DINING** 🚚 **DELIVERY** 🏮 **PRIVATE PARTY**

[Cobras & Matadors] **7615 Beverly Blvd., Beverly/Third, 323.932.6178. D nightly. Spanish. Beer & wine from the neighboring shop. AE, MC, V. $$ - $$$ WHY** One of the best sangrias in town, and some tasty (if inconsistently prepared) little dishes to have with it, including the addictive socca cakes with a cilantro dipping sauce. Save room for the churros with chocolate sauce. **WHAT** One of the first ventures by Steven Arroyo, this original Cobras & Matadors (the East Hollywood one recently closed to become an Umami Burger) is as cramped as ever, but at least now it takes reservations. Pick up a bottle of wine from Arroyo's shop next door and dabble in the mostly good small-plate dishes: grilled octopus, prawns with garlic, asparagus with Machego cheese, and pa amb tomaquet, tomato-rubbed toast with jamon serrano. **WHO** Neighborhood locals who seem to come here weekly.

[Comme Ça] **8479 Melrose Ave., West Hollywood, 323.782.1104, commecarestaurant.com. L & D daily, brunch Sat.-Sun. French. Full bar. AE, MC, V. $$$ - $$$$ WHY** Good classic French bistro fare: bouillabaisse, steak frites (great), sole meunière. The cheese bar is a dairy addict's heaven. **WHAT** Dubbed a slice of Paris in L.A., David Myers's place is really a Paris brasserie gone Hollywood, with slick Marilyn Monroe–white booths and old-school bartenders making excellent drinks. Some regulars come just for the duck confit; others come for the gorgeous cheese counter, the charcuterie plate or the desserts, although we've had some dessert disappointments. And some service issues, too. Nonetheless, this is a fun place with generally terrific food and lots of atmosphere. **WHO** David Myers fans who can't afford Sona, and lots of neighborhood foodies. ♥

[Cube Café] **615 N. La Brea Ave., Melrose, 323.939.1148, cubemarketplace.com. L & D Mon.-Sat. Italian/modern American. Beer & wine. AE, MC, V. $$ - $$$ WHY** For the complimentary prosecco and cheese to "toast" your arrival, as well as the in-the-know staff, eager to pair the perfect Barbera with your tagliatelle with Fatted Calf sausage ragú. Oh, and for the spiffy upscale market. **WHAT** This intimate neighborhood café, cheese bar and marketplace serves a pricey Italian-driven menu rich with farmers' market produce, house-made pastas, an evolving selection of more than 85 varieties of cheese, and salumi from Salumi Salame, the Fatted Calf and Pio Tosini, to name but a few. **WHO** Attractive, youthful Hollywood people, including a pop starlet or two. Don't be afraid to sit at the bar and mingle with the knowledgeable bartender and cheese guru. 🏠

[Dominick's] **8715 Beverly Blvd., West Hollywood, 310.652.2335, dominicksrestaurant.com. D nightly. Italian. Full bar. AE, MC, V. $$ - $$$ WHY** The steal is the $15 three-course Sunday supper with $10 bottles (yes, whole bottles) of house wine. Brilliant? No. Fun and economical? You bet. Dominick's is a great place to take out-of-towners. **WHAT** An old-school Rat Pack hangout restored to its original red-sauce Italian splendor with black-and-white photos lining the walls and plenty of filling red-sauce Italian dishes to share. Ask for a seat on the back patio near the fireplace and cozy up with some meatballs. 🖼

[El Cholo] 1121 S. Western Ave., Mid-City, 323.734.2773, elcholo. com. L & D daily, brunch Sun. Mexican. Full bar. AE, MC, V. $$ **WHY** To experience an L.A. landmark, drink a large, sweetish margarita and, in season, have green corn tamales. **WHAT** If you're a native Angeleno, you've been to El Cholo at least once. It's a formula but a fun one: Waitresses in hokey Mexican get-ups swoop through the many stuccoed, frescoed, old-style Mexican rooms taking orders for margaritas, substantial plates of enchiladas ("Careful! The plate is hot!"), smoke-spewing fajitas and the famed sweet green-corn tamales. It's not the best Mexican food you'll ever have, but it's a classic L.A. Cal-Mex experience. **WHO** Big groups of friends celebrating birthdays, tourists, families that have been coming here for generations. 👁🏛

[El Nido] 2112 S. La Brea Ave., Mid-City, 323.939.6506, restaurantel-nido.com. L & D Mon.-Tues. & Thurs.-Sun. Nicaraguan. Beer & wine. AE, MC, V. $ - $$ **WHY** The *empanadas de maduro*. These fried turnovers, stuffed with mashed ripe bananas and melted cheese and served in a pool of cultured cream, are candidates for our Best Dish Ever list. **WHAT** The stuffed parrots and Nicaraguan knickknacks add an air of festivity, but the food alone is enough to get the party started. Plantains are more than bit players here, often showing up in sides with the grilled or braised meat and fish dishes. Another nice surprise: Nicaraguan enchiladas aren't like their Mexican counterparts — El Nido's are soufflé-like packets stuffed with shredded beef and rice. And the freshly squeezed fruit and vegetable juices are a refreshing treat. 🖼

[Fabiolus Café] 6270 Sunset Blvd., Hollywood, 323.467.2882, fabio-lus.org. L Mon.-Fri., D nightly. Italian. Beer & wine. AE, MC, V. $$ - $$$ **WHY** A charming patio and simple, affordable Italian food that goes down well after a movie or a play. **WHAT** We love this place, not for the food (which is just fine) but because of ebullient owner Fabio and the convenience to the Arclight and the Pantages. Prices are modest, the Chianti is palatable, and the gnocchi al pesto and traditional lasagne are good accompaniments to a post-film discussion. 🖼👁☼

[Fat Fish] 3300 W. 6th St., Koreatown, 213.384.1304, fatfishla. com. L Mon.-Sat., D nightly. Japanese/sushi. BYOB. MC, V. $$ **WHY** For surprisingly good *kaiten* (conveyor-belt) sushi at exceptionally low prices, and a fun, Jetsons-in-2010 setting. **WHAT** Sleek, chic and more modern than an Austin Powers movie set, Fat Fish quickly became a Koreatown hot spot even though it lacks that critical liquor license (in the works). Sushi floats past you on a conveyor belt, a gimmick to be sure, but with prices so low (lunch is a total bargain) and the sushi so good, who cares? **WHO** Young folks stuffing themselves. 🖼

🍃 VEGETARIAN 👁 KID FRIENDLY ☼ PATIO DINING �: DELIVERY 🏛 PRIVATE PARTY

[Figaro] 1802 N. Vermont Ave., Los Feliz, 323.662.1587, figarobis-trot.com. B, L & D daily. French. Beer & wine. AE, MC, V. \$\$ - \$\$\$ **WHY** Honest French-bistro charm, a civilized breakfast, a dreamy chocolate soufflé and a good happy hour, with \$5 Kirs and wine and tasty small plates. **WHAT** The service is often problematic, the kitchen can be slow, and the prices could be lower. But we still love Figaro, which bursts with Parisian charm, from the sidewalk tables to the zinc bar to the terribly romantic chandelier room. The excellent onion soup and a glass of Côtes du Rhône make for a perfect supper. ☺ ♥ ☼

[The Foundry] 7465 Melrose Ave., Melrose, 323.651.0915, thefoundryonmelrose.com. D Tues.-Sun. Modern American. Full bar. AE, MC, V. \$\$\$\$ **WHY** Because the food is much better than at most Hollywood scene restaurants. Extras are the good bar menu (tater-tot fondue!) and the live jazz. **WHAT** Owner/chef Eric Greenspan, ex of Patina, may be rumpled, exuberant and sometimes annoyingly loud, but his cooking is elegant and sophisticated. He set out to create a destination restaurant that combines serious food and professional service with an informal conviviality and good live jazz. And he has succeeded. The details snap: a terrific, fairly priced wine list, one of the best cheese plates in town, and smart service. **WHO** A remarkably normal crowd for such a hot spot — sure, they're attractive, but they're all ages and don't look overly Botoxed and lip-plumped. ☼

[Fred 62] 🏠 1850 N. Vermont Ave., Los Feliz, 323.667.0062, fred62.com. B, L & D 24 hours daily. Californian. Beer & wine. AE, MC, V. \$ - \$\$ **WHY** Postmodern yet homey diner food (e.g. White-Trash Tuna Sandwich), served 24 hours a day in comfy booths at modest prices. **WHAT** Not only is Fred 62 one of the few 24-hour eateries in L.A., but it also achieves that rare state of being all things to all people. High school kids looking to share after-school chili-cheese fries? Check. Eddie Bauer–clad boomers looking for a movie-night Chardonnay 'n BLT? Check. Pierced-tongued twentysomethings looking for an after-midnight hangout to slurp udon noodles? Check. Hip grandmas taking the grandkids out for Sunday-morning waffles? Check. The prices are low, and the setting is bright and retro-diner, with booths, counter stools and a too-cool-for-you staff. **WHO** Everyone who's anyone in Los Feliz. ☺ 🕶 🥄 ☺ ☼

[Girasole] 225 1/2 N. Larchmont Blvd., Hancock Park, 323.464.6978, girasolecucina.com. L Wed.-Fri., D. Tues.-Sat., brunch Sun. Italian. BYOB (no corkage). AE, MC, V. \$\$ **WHY** Pillowy spinach or pumpkin gnocchi, various pastas with a rich homemade ragú, and a sublime linguine with shrimp, fresh tomato and olive oil. **WHAT** This tiny, family-run storefront trattoria is one of the best-kept secrets on Larchmont. Sweet people, low prices and delicate yet flavorful pastas. Our only regret is the limited hours. **WHO** Hancock Park couples who like the modestly romantic vibe and the fact that they can bring their own wine. ♥ 🕶 🥄

🏠 ESSENTIALLY L.A. ☺ LATE ♥ ROMANTIC 🕶 VALUE 🥄 QUIET ☼ SUSTAINABLE

[Grace] 🔒 7360 Beverly Blvd., Beverly/Third, 323.934.4400, gracerestaurant.com. D nightly. Modern American. Full bar. AE, MC, V. **$$$$ - $$$$$ WHY** Creative cooking that stays on the fun side of intelligent. **WHAT** Neil Fraser has matured into one of L.A.'s most exciting yet reliable — no, those two things aren't necessarily oxymoronic — chefs, and he gets all the support he needs from the flawlessly run front room, a modern, handsome space. He seeks out great products from the markets and local sources, and creates artful dishes. Desserts, especially the doughnuts, are divine. **WHO** A mix of Angelenos who look more bookish (in a moneyed way) than pierced-navelish. ♥ 🍴 🍸

[Guelaguetza] 3337 1/2 W. 8th St., Koreatown, 213.427.0601, guelaguetzarestaurante.com. B, L & D daily. Mexican/Oaxacan. Full bar. AE, MC, V. **$$ WHY** Intensely flavorful, stick-to-your-ribs Oaxacan food served in a sunny yellow room by nice people. The branch on Olympic has live marimba music most nights. **WHAT** Only loosely affiliated with the better Guelaguetza in Palms (they're owned by siblings, but the restaurants themselves aren't related), this one and its nearby actual sibling (3014 W. Olympic Blvd., 213.427.0608) are still good, authentic Oaxacan places serving moles of every color, enchiladas, camarones and other tasty things, all in hefty portions. 🍴 ☺

[Hatfield's] 6703 Melrose Ave., Melrose, 323.935.2977, hatfieldsrestaurant.com. D Mon.-Sat. Modern American/Californian. Full bar. AE, MC, V. **$$$$ - $$$$$ WHY** Carefully prepared combinations (like roasted branzino with red onion soubise, dried apricots and almonds) by a talented husband-and-wife team, with a new setting and service that match the food's quality. **WHAT** Quinn and Karen Hatfield are serious about their cooking, and now they have a larger setting for it, in the spot that held Red Pearl Kitchen. You'll be so comfortable and well fed that you might not even mind the high New York/San Francisco prices. (That's where they most recently cooked — he does the "real" food and she does pastry.) The $49 market menu, however, is a superb value. **WHO** People you feel like you should know — is that a neighbor? — but don't. ♥

[Hodori] 1001 S. Vermont Ave., Koreatown, 213.383.3554. Daily 24 hours. Korean. No booze. MC, V. **$ WHY** Decent and cheap Korean standards served 24/7. **WHAT** The short list of L.A. restaurants open 24 hours a day includes this Koreatown diner, and you could do far worse at 3 a.m. than Hodori's bibim bap or bulgogi. Parking's a pain, and the service and setting are basic, but the hours and price are right. ☺ 🍴

[Holy Cow Indian Express] 8474 W. 3rd St., Beverly/Third, 323.852.8900. L & D daily. Indian. Beer & wine. MC, V. **$ WHY** One of L.A.'s better chicken tikka masalas. **WHAT** An offshoot of the more elegant Suriya on Third Street, Holy Cow serves lightened up Indian dishes that are still full of flavor. There are a few tables in the minimall storefront, and they also deliver in the area. 🍴 🍸 ☺ �foodtruck

---

🍸 VEGETARIAN ☺ KID FRIENDLY ✿ PATIO DINING 🚚 DELIVERY 🎩 PRIVATE PARTY

[Hungry Cat] 🔒 1535 N. Vine St., Hollywood, 323.462.2155, thehungrycat.com. L & D daily. Seafood/modern American. Full bar. AE, MC, V. $$$ - $$$$ **WHY** A pristine raw bar, impeccable New England seafood dishes and a smart wine list — and it's all served until midnight, with the raw bar open until 1 a.m. **WHAT** Always full of hungry hepcats sharing oversized seafood platters, this glass-and-metal bistro may not be L.A.'s most elegant or sophisticated seafood restaurant, but it's certainly its most exciting. It keeps the formula simple: You come here for New England-style seafood, a good glass of wine and one killer dessert, the chocolate bread pudding. If you're with someone who doesn't like seafood, comfort them with the pug burger. **WHO** Arclight filmgoers. ☉ ☼

[Ita-Cho] 7311 Beverly Blvd., Beverly/Third, 323.938.9009, itachores-taurant.com. L Mon.-Fri., D Mon.-Sat. Japanese. Beer & wine. AE, MC, V. $$$ **WHY** Lovely small dishes — Japanese fried chicken, crab claws with cucumber, black cod with miso, braised eggplant — at reasonable prices given the quality. **WHAT** Years ago, in its original low-rent Hollywood location, this restaurant introduced *izakaya* (small plates) to Angelenos, who followed the place when it moved to this more stylish industrial space on Beverly. What's on the menu? Classical Japanese preparations of whatever the chefs decide is right for the moment — along with some very good sushi, too. **WHO** Japanese and non-Japanese business people and date-nighters. 🌇 ☼

[Jar] 🔒 8225 Beverly Blvd., Beverly/Third, 323.655.6566, thejar.com. D nightly, brunch Sun. Modern American/steakhouse. Full bar. AE, MC, V. $$$ - $$$$$ **WHY** Superb steaks and chops, succulent side dishes (duck fried rice, Japanese purple yams with crème fraîche) and comfort foods (pot roast, coq au vin). Oh, and a Sunday brunch that *Los Angeles* has twice declared the city's best. **WHAT** Suzanne Tracht's retro-contemporary (think *Mad Men*) chophouse delivers a superior dining experience in a civilized yet comfortable setting. Entrees can be pricey, but the meltingly tender coq au vin is a bargain at $21, and Mozzarella Monday brings a dozen cheesy dishes for $12 or less. Side dishes are exceptionally good. **WHO** Well-dressed residents of the nearby hills, who consider Jar their country club, along with younger hipsters who like the cocktails and the cool vibe.

[Jaragua] 🔒 4493 Beverly Blvd., East Hollywood, 323.661.1985. L & D daily. Salvadoran. Beer & wine. MC, V. $ **WHY** Perhaps the most beautifully executed Salvadoran food in the city. **WHAT** The rich golden paint on this corner restaurant on a shabby stretch of Beverly lets you know that the place has ambitions, and boy, does it achieve its ambitions. Inside the large, even-more-colorful dining room, happy regulars attack plates of expertly made pupusas (try the rice-flour one with squash and cheese, or the *chicharron* (pork) with a corn crust); gorgeous shrimp cocktails; medium-rare grilled rib-eye; plantains in every sort of preparation; and a massive sandwich made of fresh-roasted turkey rubbed with herbs and spices. **WHO** East Hollywood immigrants and eaters from Hancock Park and Los Feliz. 🖼️☺

[Jitlada] 🏠 **5233 1/2 Sunset Blvd., East Hollywood, 323.663.3104. L Tues.-Sun., D nightly. Thai. Beer & wine. AE, MC, V. $$ WHY** Such amazing specialties as the *yam priaw dawng* (pickled crab salad), soft-shell crab curry and crispy morning glory stems with shrimp and fried shallot slices. **WHAT** Over the last couple of years Jazz Singsanong and her chef brother Suthipom have turned one of Thai Town's better restaurants into a destination dining spot, thanks to her devotion to making her customers happy, and his devotion to the dishes of Pak Panang, their home region in southern Thailand. The menu is huge, so ask for Jazz's advice if possible — or know that you won't be sorry with the mango salad with fresh coconut, shrimp, nuts and chile, the jungle curry, the whole fried sea bass and the famous rice salad (*khao yam*). Warm service and a nicer dining room than the Thai Town norm. **WHO** Chefs and food lovers from across the country. 🖼️ 🔊 🥡

[Katana] **8439 W. Sunset Blvd., West Hollywood, 323.650.8585, katanarobata.com. D nightly. Japanese/sushi. Full bar. AE, MC, V. $$ - $$$ WHY** The Sushi Roku of robata, this place serves reasonably authentic skewers of tasty meats and veggies at prices that reflect the neighbor-hood and the scene. **WHAT** "Our food comes from three kitchens," the waiter will explain to first-timers dining at this trendsetting West Hol-lywood spot ensconced in a stunning '20s-era Mediterranean structure. Nibble on grilled robata foods from the display speared on slender skewers, long-simmered homestyle dishes in miniature, or sushi — or a little of each. **WHO** Little-black-dress women and the men who chase them.

[KyoChon Chicken] **3833 W. 6th St., Koreatown, 213.739.9292, kyochon.com. L & D daily. Korean. No booze. MC, V. $$ WHY** They really mean it when they say "super-spicy" fried chicken. Or take a safer route and order the soy-marinated crispy-style chicken. **WHAT** It's fried chicken, but it's not fast. In fact, they don't start cooking it at this stylish Korean café until you order it, which can mean a wait of 25 minutes or so. But the payoff is a deeply flavorful bird accompa-nied by a refreshing side dish of pickled white radishes.

[La Morenita Oaxaqueña] **3550 W. 3rd St., Koreatown, 213.365.9201. L & D daily. Oaxacan/Mexican. No booze. MC, V. $ - $$ WHY** For the enormous, flopppy-crusted *tlayuda con todo*, Oaxaca's answer to pizza, the red mole and the delicate, delicious Oaxacan-style empanadas filled with things like *huitlacoche* (a mushroom-like fungus) or *flor de calabaza* (zucchini flower) — or even *chapulines* (grasshoppers). **WHAT** The vibrant colors inside this strip-mall café on the edge of Koreatown hold the promise of equally vibrant cooking,

🌿 **VEGETARIAN** ☺ **KID FRIENDLY** ☼ **PATIO DINING** 🚗 **DELIVERY** 🎩 **PRIVATE PARTY** and La Morenita delivers on that promise. A few dishes disappoint, notably the expensive mixed grill and the bland mole amarillo, but most everything else here is redolent with the spices and sophistication of good Oaxacan cooking. Don't miss the coloradito, a red mole that shines with the open-faced enchiladas al gusto. **WHO** Mexican-American families and young singles from the neighborhood. 👓☺

[La Paella] 476 S. San Vicente Blvd., West Hollywood, 323.951.0745, usalapaella.com. L Mon.-Fri., D Mon.-Sat. Spanish/Mediterranean. Beer & wine. AE, MC, V. $$$ **WHY** Catalan warmth and hospitality and outstanding paellas. Try the squid ink one or the paella marinara, with saffron and seafood. *Los Angeles* magazine proclaimed this the best flan in town. **WHAT** An intimate (read: make reservations) and fetching cottage with a devout following for its delicious paellas. The tapas aren't anything to shout about, but the paellas — and the romantic charm of the place — are worth a trip. **WHO** Spaniards, Argentineans and couples or groups of friends reliving that trip to Spain they took two years ago. ♥ 🍸

[Little Dom's] 2128 Hillhurst Ave., Los Feliz, 323.661.0055, little-doms.com. B, L & D daily. Italian. Beer & wine. AE, MC, V. $$ - $$$ **WHY** Red-sauce Italian, served with modern flair and a wink of the eye. The three-course Monday Night Supper is a steal at $15, with house wine for just $10 a bottle. **WHAT** A lot of people consider this handsome, booth-lined, retro trattoria to be a great bargain, which we don't quite get — starters are $10 to $15, a burger's $15, and sides are $8, which ain't cheap in our book. On the other hand, the food shares well, so a group can have a tasty and affordable meal if they order carefully, particularly if they add one of the good pizzas into the mix. Make sure to share one of the sweet focaccias. **WHO** Mod Los Feliz families. ☺ ☼

[The Little Door] 8164 W. 3rd St., Beverly/Third, 323.951.1210, thelittledoor.com. D nightly. Mediterranean. Beer & wine. AE, MC, V. $$$$$ **WHY** For the deeply romantic atmosphere, lovely patio and we're-so-cool L.A. scene. **WHAT** The food's not the point at this sign-less restaurant, although it's just fine. It's all about the décor, the atmosphere, the patio and the scene, all of which are memorable. Service meanders, but there's good wine to drink, so what's your rush? Nonsmokers note that the candlelit patio is full of smokers, and wallet-watchers note that the vegetable couscous is the least expensive entree — and it's $30. **WHO** Young men with artfully sculpted bed head and three-day stubble and the willowy women who accompany them. ♥👝☼

[Loteria Grill Hollywood] 🏛 6627 Hollywood Blvd., Hollywood, 323.465.2500, loteriagrill.com. B, L & D daily. Mexican. Full bar. AE, MC, V. $$ - $$$ **WHY** Our favorite Farmers Market stall got a liquor license and nicer digs. **WHAT** Plenty of high-style Mexican food is flooding into Downtown right now, but what's the rest of L.A. to do? Assuming you're ready to brave Hollywood Boulevard (don't try this on Oscar weekend), the answer is to eat at Loteria Grill. No, not the little stand that's been one of Farmers Market's best bets for several years, but the big new one with great margaritas and a swell sidewalk patio. The menu is similar to the one at the stand — tacos, tostadas, sopes and burritos with richly flavorful fillings like cochinita pibil, nopalitos and shrimp with spicy morita salsa. If you can't make up your mind, get the fantastic twelve-mini-taco sampler platter and try 'em all. **WHO** Aficionados of real Mexico City cooking. ☼

[Lucques] 🏛 **8474 Melrose Ave., Melrose, 323.655.6277, lucques.com. L Tues.-Sat., D nightly. Mediterranean/modern American. Full bar. AE, MC, V. $$$ - $$$$ WHY** For the farm-fresh ingredients that shine with just the right amount of chef behind them — fried squash blossoms with manchego, Jidori chicken with hand-cut noodles, pancetta, shell beans and chanterelles, grilled Niman Ranch steak with potatoes parisienne — which show up here before being copied at other L.A. restaurants. Don't pass up the pastry chef's remarkable desserts: chocolate bread pudding with bourbon, pecans and vanilla ice cream, acacia honey panna cotta. **WHAT** Relaxed and beautiful, homey yet elegant, with attentive service that's never pretentious, Lucques is the reigning Chez Panisse of Los Angeles. It's one of the best patio dining spots in town, but being inside by the fireplace is pretty nice, too. The beloved Sunday Supper brings gorgeous home-style cooking, served generously and family-style, for $45 per person. **WHO** Attractive but not plastic people who really care about what goes into their mouths. ♥🍸☼

[Luna Park] **672 S. La Brea Ave., Miracle Mile, 323.934.2110, lunaparkla.com. L Mon.-Fri., D nightly. Modern American. Full bar. AE, MC, V. $$ - $$$ WHY** Modern comfort food (goat cheese fondue, grilled chicken with cornbread pudding, make-your-own s'mores) at modest prices in a funky-chic setting. Miracle Mile locals can get it delivered, too. **WHAT** Vintage mismatched chandeliers, curtained booths and deep colors lend an air of shabby-chic romance to this lively San Francisco transplant, whose cocktails and chow make everyone happy. Dinnertime is generally packed and noisy, but lunch is quieter — and weekend brunch is a well-kept secret. **WHO** Girlfriends meeting for lunch, lively groups of friends at night. ♥📷🍸🚗

[M Café de Chaya] 🏛 **7119 Melrose Ave., Melrose, 323.525.0588, mcafedechaya.com. B, L & D daily. Modern American/vegetarian. No booze. AE, MC, V. $ - $$ WHY** Macrobiotic, organic, vegetarian and/or vegan cooking that's better than you might think is possible. **WHAT** Shigefumi Tachibe, founding chef of the late, lamented La Petite Chaya and executive chef of Chaya Venice and Chaya Brasserie, became an avid student of macrobiotic cooking years ago, and his studies finally paid off with this chic little restaurant and deli, which has spawned a larger offshoot in Culver City. His menu eschews red meat, poultry, dairy, eggs and refined sugar — and yet it's full of delicious things to eat. A fine place for a lovely, light meal. ☼❧♡🚗

[Madeo] 🏛 8897 Beverly Blvd., West Hollywood, 310.859.4903. L Mon.-Fri., D nightly. Italian. Full bar. AE, MC, V. $$$ - $$$$ **WHY** Carpaccio, simple roast veal carved tableside, light gnocchi with pesto and Tuscan fish soup, served with deference at a quietly A-list Hollywood canteen. **WHAT** Well-dressed, middle-aged folks with business to discuss feel very much at home in this traditional ristorante, where the service is smooth and the food is consistently satisfying. It's the kind of place that people come to every week for years and always order the same thing. **WHO** Agents, producers, movie stars, studio execs and doctors from Cedars-Sinai. ♥ 🍸

[Magnolia] 6266 1/2 Sunset Blvd., Hollywood, 323.467.0660, magnoliahollywood.com. B Sun., L & D daily to 1 a.m. (2 a.m. on weekends). Modern American. Full bar. AE, MC, V. $$$ **WHY** Something for everyone, served into the wee hours, and convenient to the Arclight and the Hollywood club scene. **WHAT** A handy place to know about, whether you want a Cobb salad for lunch, crab cakes and cosmopolitans before an Arclight movie, or a burger after making the club scene. The food isn't remarkable, but it's satisfying. Magnolia fancies itself a rock 'n roll restaurant, so the noise can overwhelm at night; ask for a patio table if you want quiet. **WHO** Hollywood business folk by day, moviegoers in the early evening, and a glam club crowd late at night. ☾ ❧♡

[Mario's Peruvian & Seafood] 5786 Melrose Ave., Hollywood, 323.466.4181. L & early D daily. Peruvian/seafood. No booze. MC, V. $ - $$ **WHY** Ceviche, the seafood platter and the chicken or shrimp *saltado*, a stir-fry with red onions and tomato served with a heap of very good fries (potatoes come from Peru, after all). **WHAT** There's usually a wait at Mario's, and for good reason — its food is drop-dead delicious, and inexpensive to boot. The strip-mall setting is basic, and the parking lot is always full, but you won't be sorry for your trouble. Great for takeout, too. **WHO** A studio lunch crowd and, on weekends, fans who drive here from all over. 📷 ☺

[Minestraio Trattoria] Orlando Hotel, 8384 W. 3rd St., Beverly/Third, 323.782.8384, minestraio.com. B, L & D daily. Italian. Full bar. AE, MC, V. $$ **WHY** Carb counts be damned; sometimes you just want a plate of delicious homemade pasta at a good price. **WHAT** Gino Angelini's answer to the recession, Minestraio has replaced his fancier La Terza, and the less expensive menu features a good Caesar salad, superb eggplant parmigiana and the usual array of trattoria-style secondi (grilled sausages with potatoes, a rib-eye tagliata). But the real stars are the house-made pastas, such as tortelli filled with butternut squash and lasagne with beef ragú and béchamel, ably prepared by chef/partner Gianluca Sarti, who hails from Bologna. Unfortunately, scant attention has been paid to the dull, limited wine list; consider BYO for a $15 corkage fee. **WHO** Out-of-towners blissfully surprised to find Italian comfort food of this level in a hotel restaurant. 🝔 🝕

[Monsieur Marcel] **Farmers Market, 6333 W. 3rd St., Fairfax District, 323.939.7792, mrmarcel.com. B, L & D daily. French. Beer & wine. AE, MC, V. $ - $$ WHY** L.A.'s best-kept-secret French bistro. **WHAT** Almost hidden in a corner of the Farmers Market is a café as authentically French as any in Lyon. It's part of the adjacent Mr. Marcel market, home of French cheeses, olives, wines, table linens and an array of gourmet foods. Unlike most Farmers Market eateries, which are order-at-the-counter stands, this is a proper table-service bistro, serving delicious quiche, salade de chèvre chaud, roast chicken, great garlic fries and wine by the glass. ☼

[Natalie Peruvian Seafood] **5759 Hollywood Blvd., Hollywood, 323.463.8340. L & D Mon.-Sat. Peruvian/seafood. No booze. MC, V. $ - $$ WHY** Peru's Chinese influence is evident in the wonderful fried-rice dishes; also try the fried calamari and classic pescado saltado with french fries, and wash it down with an Inca Cola. **WHAT** This rival to Mario's goes a little easier on the chiles but turns out Peruvian food that's still powerfully flavorful. It's a pleasant little café that doesn't get as crowded as Mario's, although the parking's no better. Delicious food, low prices. 🝔 ☺

[Nishimura] **8684 Melrose Ave., West Hollywood, 310.659.4770. L Mon.-Fri., D Mon.-Sat. Japanese/sushi. Beer & wine. AE, MC, V. $$$$$ WHY** Sushi, sashimi and cooked dishes of tremendous beauty and flavor. **WHAT** The classicist's sushi served in this serene and minimal-ist space is not for the faint of wallet, and neither is it for the person looking for a scene. Hiro Nishimura is very serious about his food, and that's exactly how his fans like it. You can easily drop $200 for a meal here. **WHO** Fans who would follow chef Nishimura to Panorama City if necessary — but they're much more at home in the shadow of the Pacific Design Center. ♥ 🝕

[Ortolan] **8338 W. 3rd St., Beverly/Third, 323.653.3300, ortolanrestau-rant.com. D Tues.-Sat. French. Full bar. AE, MC, V. $$$$$ WHY** Pause-worthy haute French dishes from Christopher Emé that tend to elicit comments like "wow" and "what was that exactly?" — like the escar-got with lettuce emulsion and parmesan crust. If you can handle the investment, it's worth tasting Emé's culinary explorations. **WHAT** The elegant, special-occasion setting is, refreshingly, one of the few places you'll see more ties than not — no doubt in part due to the special-oc-casion prices. Beautiful people sit at cream-colored banquettes under equally beautiful crystal chandeliers, and the service makes everyone feel rich and important. **WHO** A well-dressed, high-dollar crowd whose handbags cost more than our cars. ♥ 🝕 ☼ 🝙

🝔 **VEGETARIAN** ⊙ **KID FRIENDLY** ☼ **PATIO DINING** 🚐 **DELIVERY** 🝙 **PRIVATE PARTY**

[Osteria Mozza] 🏛 **6602 Melrose Ave., Melrose, 323.297.0100, mozza-la.com. D nightly. Italian/modern American. Full bar. AE, MC, V. $$ - $$$$ WHY** The mozzarella tasting plate, grilled octopus with potatoes, celery and lemon, orecchiette pasta with sausage and swiss chard, pan-roasted sea trout with Umbrian lentils — in fact, pretty much everything. **WHAT** The frenzy that built around the opening of this joint venture between Mario Batali, Joe Bastianich and Nancy Silverton may have subsided, but getting a table in this simply handsome dining room is still not easy. Happily, it's well worth the effort, thanks to the terrific pastas, hearty Batali-style main courses and a lavish array of cheese-based nibbles made in front of the dozen people who managed to score seats at the mozzarella bar. The (pricey) wine list is a whirlwind tour of Italy, from Alto Adige to Sicilia. **WHO** Batali and/ or Silverton groupies, celebrities, and pretty much everyone else who can snag a reservation. 🔖 🏛

[Papa Cristo's] **2771 W. Pico Blvd., Mid-City, 323.737.2970, papacristo.com. L Tues.-Sun., early D Tues.-Sat. Greek. Beer & wine. AE, MC, V. $ - $$ WHY** Savory, straightforward Greek classics at low prices: spanakopita, baba ganouj, kebabs, gyros and lots more. **WHAT** Founded as a market in 1948 by Sam Chrys, this funky, rambling place is now run by Sam's son, Chrys Chrys, who grew it into a full-fledged restaurant in the early '90s, in time to cash in on the *My Big Fat Greek Wedding* phenomenon. You order at the chaotic counter, look for a table (in the big dining room, the market or out on the covered patio), and soon you'll be served plates heaped with lamb souvlaki or roast chicken. Thursday is the Big Fat Greek dinner, complete with Greek dancing. **WHO** Students and teachers from Loyola High, businesspeople from the neighborhood's many little warehouses. 🔖 🔖 ☺ ✿

[Park's BBQ] **955 S. Vermont Ave., Koreatown, 213.380.1717, parksbbq.com. L & D daily. Korean/barbecue. Beer & wine. MC, V. $$$ - $$$$ WHY** A particularly lavish and beautiful array of *panchan*, the small appetizers that accompany traditional Korean barbecue, and meat of very high quality. **WHAT** As far in atmosphere from smoky, funky barbecue joints like Soot Bull Jeep as you can get, Park is spare and industrial-chic, with a gorgeous and fairly formal serving staff and powerful ventilation whisking away smoke from the tabletop grills. It's an investment to cook your own meat here, but it's a worthwhile one: the prime short ribs, bulgogi, pork belly and Kobe-style beef are all superb. **WHO** Businesspeople and well-heeled couples.

[Paru's] **5140 W. Sunset Blvd., Hollywood, 323.661.7600, parusrestaurant.com. L Sat-.Sun., D nightly. Indian/vegetarian. Beer & wine. AE, MC, V. $ - $$ WHY** Richly flavorful southern Indian cooking that is all vegetarian with many vegan choices, too, served on an atmospheric secret patio. **WHAT** Paru's has a speakeasy feel to it — you have to be buzzed in, and there's a hidden tree-filled garden in back — which lends it an aura of romance that is continued with the cooking. The tasty (and vegetarian) dosas, samosas, sambar (potato-squash soup) and lassi drinks are fun to share, and the prices are more than fair. **WHO** Family groups and vegetarian date-nighters getting cozy in the twinkle-lit garden patio. ♥🗺🗨☺☼

[Petrossian] **321 N. Robertson Blvd., West Hollywood, 310.271.0576, petrossian.com. L & D daily, brunch Sun. Russian/French. Beer & wine. AE, MC, V. $ - $$$ WHY** The happy hour (3 to 8 p.m.) is a hell of a deal — $5 specials include luscious country pâté with freshly made toast points, eggplant caviar à la russe and those charming almond sweetmeats from Provence. The $35 brunch (including a glass of good Champagne) is also a good value. **WHAT** This newly expanded Euro-moderne outpost of the Parisian fancy food emporium has a caviar-and-crème fraîche décor and a surprisingly affordable restaurant — assuming, of course, you avoid the Caspian caviar. Try the sweet-tart borscht puréed to a brilliant magenta velvet; the unfortunately named Petrossian Jello, which turns out to be a refreshing scallop ceviche in a yuzu gélée with green apple foam; orecchiette with truffle cheese, pancetta and parmesan; and the wonderful thick-sliced, cold-smoked salmon belly (think Russian toro). It's a shame the blini are tough and uninteresting. **WHO** Well-dressed people having a civilized lunch. ♥

[Pizzeria Mozza] 🏛 **641 N. Highland Ave., Melrose, 323.297.0101, mozza-la.com. L & D daily. Italian/pizzeria. Beer & wine. AE, MC, V. $$ - $$$ WHY** Pizza dough of perfect flavor and bite, paired with damned fine toppings; the margherita is simple the way E=MC2 is simple. **WHAT** Is Mozza's pizza the second coming of Christ? You'd think so with all the hullabaloo around this pizzeria and its celebrity-chef parents, Nancy Silverton and Mario Batali. But the result is something more earthy than celestial — heaven on earth, we'll call it. The food, and not just the pizzas (try the bruschetta, roasted brussels sprouts and salads), really is worth all the fuss. We draw the line at the $8.50 valet parking, though — it's not that hard to find a space on the street. **WHO** Food groupies so happy to have scored a tiny table or a counter seat. ☼🗨🏛

[Providence] 🏛 **5955 Melrose Ave., Hollywood, 323.460.4170, providencela.com. L Fri., D nightly. Seafood/modern American. Full bar. AE, MC, V. $$$$$ WHY** Because it's one of best fine-dining seafood restaurants in the United States. Okay, maybe it is the best. **WHAT** Michael Cimarusti's seafood dishes are constructed as carefully as paintings, and they're as delicious to eat as they are to gaze upon. The former chef at Water Grill has hit his creative stride at his own place, the serene and appropriately elegant former home of Patina. All the details — service, wine, tableware — are seamlessly tended to so diners can feel as important as they think they are, or actually are. Every dish is worthwhile, even if it's not seafood — the foie gras a la plancha, for

instance, is divine, and the cheese selection is among L.A.'s finest.
WHO Expensively dressed captains of L.A. industry and food lovers
(chefs, journalists, aficionados) from around the country, checking it
out while they're in town. ♥ ⏺

[Pure Luck] 707 Heliotrope Dr., East Hollywood, 323.660.5993,
pureluckrestaurant.com. L & D Mon.-Sat. Vegan/American. Beer & wine.
MC, V. $ - $$ **WHY** Sweet potato fries and fried dill pickle chips that
will make you feel virtuous, even if they're fried. **WHAT** This fetching
cottage-style restaurant may be vegan, but about half of the diners are
carnivores who aren't the least bit annoyed that their friends made
them come here. Attractive dishes are made with quality ingredients,
and there's local beer (including Craftsman) and French-press coffee
to drink. Try the grilled beet salad, "carnitas" burrito and sloppy joe,
and to be safe you should order both the regular and sweet potato
fries. For dessert, walk across the street to Scoops. **WHO** Preschoolers,
their tattooed parents and East Hollywood locals. ⏺ ⏺ ⏺ ⏺

[Rahel Ethiopian Veggie Cuisine] 1047 S. Fairfax Ave., Miracle
Mile, 323.937.8401, rahelveggiecuisine.com. L & D daily. Ethiopian/
vegetarian. BYOB. AE, MC, V. $ - $$ **WHY** Hearty stews made from
chickpeas and lentils accompany plenty of vegetable side dishes, like
greens with garlic or tomatoes with green pepper, while the fluffy injera bread adds healthy touches like flax, sunflower seeds and sesame.
Flaxseed and barley also make appearances in smoothie-like drinks.
WHAT Most of the Ethiopian restaurants on Fairfax serve meat dishes,
but this one is all vegan, with dishes cooked in olive oil instead of butter. The simple, colorful room is decorated with messob tables, and a
traditional Ethiopian coffee ceremony finishes the meal. ⏺ ⏺ ⏺

[Red Corner Asia] 5267 Hollywood Blvd., East Hollywood,
323.466.6722, redcornerasia.com. L & D daily. Thai/Asian. Beer & wine.
AE, MC, V. $$ **WHY** RCA's signature dishes, including flaming whole
volcano chicken, crispy catfish with apple salad, fish cakes on lemon-
grass skewers and spicy shrimp with cashews and fried basil leaves.
WHAT This clean, modern addition to the Thai Town dining scene has
a user-friendly menu and a devoted clientele, thanks in part to its late
hours (until 2 a.m. most nights). Prices are a little higher than the Thai
Town norm, but the food and setting are worth it. ⏺ ⏺ ⏺

[Roscoe's House of Chicken & Waffles] 1514 N. Gower St.,
Hollywood, 323.466.7453, roscoeschickenandwaffles.com. B, L & D daily.
Southern/soul food. Beer & wine. MC, V. $ - $$ **WHY** Fried chicken and
big waffles, of course. **WHAT** The name pretty much says it all. The
original location of this small chain of gut-busting L.A. soul-food cafés,
Roscoe's is a Hollywood institution, and it's a haven for people who
can't stand the idea of one more vegan scramble or nonfat chai latte. The
fried chicken, waffles and other Southern standards are high-fat, high-

sugar and all-around bad for you — in a very good way. **WHO** Music-industry folks, African-American families and the young 'n hungry. 🖼️😊

[Ruen Pair] **5257 Hollywood Blvd., East Hollywood, 323.466.0153. L & D daily to 4 a.m. Thai. No booze. Cash only. $ WHY** Don't miss the papaya salad and authentic dishes like shredded fish salad, fried rice with Chinese sausage and stir-fried morning glories. **WHAT** The homey, reasonably priced restaurant is cash only with no liquor, but it's worth it for excellent and inexpensive renditions of Thai specialties, which are served until 4 a.m. **WHO** Hollywood denizens and, in the midnight hours, the post-club crowd. 😊 🖼️🔖

[Sake House Miro] **809 S. La Brea Blvd., Miracle Mile, 323.939.7075, sakehousemiro.com. L Mon.-Fri., D Mon.-Sat. Japanese. Beer & wine. AE, MC, V. $ - $$ WHY** Beer and sake happy-hour specials, serviceable sushi and a fun selection of izakaya small plates. Korean bibim bap is surprisingly good here. **WHAT** Koreatown hipsters and Miracle Mile office workers populate the heavy wooden tables at this spot that reveals the Japanese fascination with '50s-era Tokyo memorabilia. A faux alley at the rear of the bar is lined with replicas of old storefronts, signage and posters, while Asian movie one-sheets grace the dining room walls. Multiple menus offer satay-like skewers of grilled kushiyaki, sushi rolls, fruit juice–laced shochu "martinis" and the kind of quick-bite snack food found everywhere in urban Japan. **WHO** Young women with streaked hair in denim microskirts and bobby socks and their Blackberry-toting dates. 😊

[Sanamluang Café] **5170 Hollywood Blvd., East Hollywood, 323.660.8006. L & D daily to 4 a.m. Thai. No booze. Cash only. $ WHY** Noodle dishes are the stars — standouts include *pad see euw* (drunken noodles) and boat soup noodles, and they're served every night until 4 a.m. **WHAT** This venerable spot offers a late-night Thai fix that's hard to beat, despite the bare-bones atmosphere and crowded parking lot. Good food at a great price, and it tastes even better after midnight. **WHO** The after-hours club crowd, along with hospital workers from nearby Kaiser and Children's. 😊 🖼️

[Sapp Coffee Shop] **5183 Hollywood Blvd., East Hollywood, 323.665.1035. B, L & D Mon.-Tues. & Thurs.-Sun. Thai. No booze. Cash only. $ WHY** Thai food cooked for the Thai palate. **WHAT** This 20-year-old Thai Town luncheonette (open through dinner as well) has been spiffed up in modish citrus shades. But the full-throttle onslaught of capsicum heat in its po-tak soup, stir-fried pork or chicken reminds Thais and the rest of us how food tastes in the homeland. 🖼️

[Simon/L.A.] **Sofitel, 8555 Beverly Blvd., West Hollywood, 310.278.5444, simonlarestaurant.com. B, L & D daily. Modern American. Full bar. AE, MC, V. $$$$ WHY** The fantastic, funky outdoor patio, the

---

🔖 **VEGETARIAN** ☉ **KID FRIENDLY** ❁ **PATIO DINING** 🚗 **DELIVERY** 🏛 **PRIVATE PARTY**

great Bloody Mary and the junk food platter (the pastry chef's version of Ding Dongs and Ho Hos) are an odd combo, but secretly you've got to love it for brunch. **WHAT** The restaurant for the trendy Sofitel hotel, Simon/L.A. is a bit over the top, but there's no doubting the appeal of Kerry Simon's modern comfort food. If you've got the bucks, go early for the food — like truffle mac 'n cheese or tuna with crab and red chile aioli — and leave before the young Hollywood crowd takes over. **WHO** Uber-trendy hotel guests and Nicole Ritchie wannabes. ☼

[Sona] 401 N. La Cienega Blvd., West Hollywood, 310.659.7708, sonarestaurant.com. D Tues.-Sat. Modern American. Full bar. AE, MC, V. $$$$$ **WHY** Small, beautiful plates filled with ingredients you can't pronounce and may never have in quite the same combination ever again. Go for the culinary thrill of it, and if you can't afford the six- or nine-course tasting menus, stay home. **WHAT** The Riedel stemware is washed in a special chemical-free dishwasher that is guaranteed to leave no residual taste on the glass — Sona is that kind of place It's also the kind of place where tipping more than one person is always required. It's a serene and beautiful dining space to showcase the artful dishes and boundary-pushing but delicious desserts (fried lemon meringue pie with English peas and popcorn ice cream) of chef David Myers. The experience is worth it, if you can afford it. **WHO** Bentley-driving retirees and couples on "important" dates. ♥🛎

[Soot Bull Jeep] 🔒 3136 W. 8th St., Koreatown, 213.387.3865. L & D daily. Korean/barbecue. Beer & wine. MC, V. $$ - $$$ **WHY** For the quint-essential, grill-your-own, Koreatown experience — it's a great place to bring out-of-towners. **WHAT** You'll smell like meaty smoke all night after dinner here, and you won't mind a bit. It's one of Koreatown's best-known places, a dive with brusque service and a constant wait for a table. The *panchan* (side dishes) aren't as complex and interesting as at some of its competitors, but the mesquite-fueled tabletop grills are the real thing, and the meat you cook over that mesquite is satisfying in a deeply primal way. **WHO** Korean businesspeople, hungry young folks and Koreatown explorers. 🗐 ☺

[Spicy BBQ Restaurant] 5101 Santa Monica Blvd., East Hollywood, 323.663.4211. L & D Mon.-Tues. & Thurs.-Sun. Thai. BYOB. Cash only. $ **WHY** To taste rarely found northern-style Thai cooking at its best. **WHAT** A super talent plies the stoves at this minuscule northern-style restaurant hidden in a strip mall next to a falafel place. The special-ties listed toward the back of the menu include *gaeng hung lae*, pork curry spiked with whole garlic cloves and ground peanuts, *nam prik num*, an explosively hot roasted chile and eggplant dip, *nam prik oom*, the milder tomato pork dip, and *khao sawy*, the north's impossibly delicious curry noodle dish. **WHO** Homesick northern Thais and in-the-know Thai food lovers. 🗐

🔒 ESSENTIALLY L.A. ☺LATE ♥ROMANTIC 🗐 VALUE 🍸QUIET ☘SUSTAINABLE

[Street] **742 N. Highland Ave., Melrose, 323.203.0500, eatatstreet. com. L & D daily, brunch Sun. International. Beer & wine. AE, MC, V. $$ - $$$$ WHY** For its celebration of street foods from around the world, and the skill and enthusiasm of owner/chef Susan Feniger. **WHAT** Celebrity chef Susan Feniger (Border Grill, Ciudad, Too Hot Tamales) is a warm-hearted Midwestern gal whose culinary passions are truly global, and at her new place she shares all those passions, from Cuban stuffed potato cake to Egyptian basbousa lime cake (two of the best dishes on the menu). Not everything works, and the prices are high for street food (though not high for a hip restaurant with this location and quality of service), but Street adds something new to L.A.'s restaurant mix. **WHO** Feniger's chef pals, tattooed hard-body moms with adorable babies, and aging L.A. foodies who sport L.A. Eyeworks glasses and drive Priuses. 🌱 ☺ ☼

[Talésai] **9043 Sunset Blvd., West Hollywood, 310.275.9724, talesai. com. L Mon.-Fri., D nightly. Thai. Full bar. AE, MC, V. $$ - $$$ WHY** A sane and serene retreat in the heart of the Sunset Strip, with beautifully presented and delicious Thai food. **WHAT** This Thai pioneer has a new lease on life, thanks to a major renovation and the energy and good cooking of young Kris Yenbamroong, grandson of the 26-year-old restaurant's original chef. In a stylish black-and-white room, regulars share pretty, artfully spiced Thai classics, with a few modern twists: beef larb, salmon steamed in banana leaf, and fried chicken with sticky rice and *noom* (a Thai salsa); make sure to start with the Hidden Treasures, heavenly little bites of crab, shrimp and calamari. **WHO** Musicians, actors and other longtime residents of the Hollywood Hills who've been coming here for years. ☺ 🚐

[Taylor's Steakhouse] 🏛 **3361 W. 8th St., Koreatown, 213.382.8449, taylorssteakhouse.com. L Mon.-Fri., D nightly. American/ steakhouse. Full bar. AE, MC, V. $$ - $$$$ WHY** Effortlessly retro steakhouse classics, old-L.A. atmosphere and good cocktails. **WHAT** This 1953 matriarch is a genuine outpost of all we know and love about steakhouse ambience and cuisine: red Naugahyde booths, the dimmest possible lighting, iceberg wedges smothered with blue cheese, icy martinis, generous steaks for less than $30. **WHO** Old-school Angelenos who remember when Sam Yorty was mayor. 🗐 ☺ 🏠

[Tere's Mexican Grill] **5870 Melrose Ave., Hollywood, 323.468.9345. B, L & D Mon.-Sat. Mexican. No booze. MC, V. $ WHY** Homemade Mexican food that's anything but generic in a generic strip-mall setting. There's no beer to drink, but you can have a Mexican Coke, made with cane sugar instead of corn syrup. (That Coke alone draws a loyal clientele.) **WHAT** Although the bare-bones, order-at-the-counter setting isn't much, Tere's cooking provides all the atmosphere you need. Robert and Maria Teresa Melgar make everything from scratch: the soft tortillas, the chunky, fantastic guacamole,

---

🌱 VEGETARIAN ☺ KID FRIENDLY ☼ PATIO DINING 🚐 DELIVERY 🏠 PRIVATE PARTY

the light, almost pungent verde sauce on the enchiladas, the hearty fideo soup, the savory chorizo-filled empanadas, and much more. **WHO** Paramount folks, post-production house workers and Hancock Park families picking up takeout. 🎞️ ☺ ✿

[Terroni] 7605 Beverly Blvd., Beverly/Third, 323.954.0300, terroni.ca. L & D daily. Italian. Full bar. AE, MC, V. $$ - $$$ **WHY** Pastas and pizza are the focus: Thin-crust pizzas in the Naples style are topped with gorgonzola, pears and walnuts or spicy sausage; a wide selection of Sicilian-style pastas include an excellent penne alla Norma. **WHAT** The stylish import from Toronto brought a lively café to a neighborhood hungry for mid-priced, casual Italian. From the Eames chairs, to the open shelving and sidewalk tables, to the extensive menu (salads, panini, pastas, mains), Terroni has perfectly captured the L.A. vibe, despite its Canadian birthplace. 🎞️ ✿

[Tower Bar] Sunset Tower, 8358 W. Sunset Blvd., West Hollywood, 323.848.6677, sunsettowerhotel.com. L & D daily. French/modern American. Full bar. AE, MC, V. $$$$ - $$$$$ **WHY** The elegance, the view, the impeccable service run by famed maître d' Dimitri Dimitrov ... and the food's good, too. **WHAT** Is it a movie set or a restaurant? This restaurant atop the Sunset Tower Hotel is a little of both, a dazzlingly glamorous set with equally dazzling city views; outside is a separate operation, the Terrace, a poolside boîte that's filled with *Entourage* types. Inside, you'll be served special-occasion cooking (shrimp cocktail, caviar, poulet rôti) that's better than it needs to be, given that Olive Garden food could sell in this setting. **WHO** Anniversary and birthday celebrants, rich tourists and some famous faces. ♥ 🍷 ✿ 🏨

[Trattoria Farfalla] 1978 Hillhurst Ave., Los Feliz, 323.661.7365, trattoriafarfalla.com. L & D daily. Italian. Beer & wine. AE, MC, V. $$ - $$$ **WHY** Penne alla Norma, insalata Farfalla (a salad on a pizza crust), thin-crust pizza with pesto and goat cheese, and good (if pricey) wine by the glass. **WHAT** A pioneer in the new-generation makeover of Los Feliz, Farfalla has been slinging pasta and Chianti to a constant crowd of regulars for many years, and it's every bit as good as it was in the early days — and every bit as packed. The kitchen knows how to get a ton of flavor into a very simple dish: say, tagliolini with shrimp or gnocchi with pesto. **WHO** Actors, writers, Los Feliz families. 🚐

[Tropicalia] 1966 Hillhurst Ave., Los Feliz, 323.644.1798, tropicaliabraziliangrill.com. L & D daily to midnight. Brazilian. Beer & wine. AE, MC, V. $ - $$ **WHY** To sample Brazilian food in a cheerful room warmed with Brazilian music, or out on the terrace overlooking the Los Feliz parade. **WHAT** Owned by the neighboring Trattoria Farfalla, Tropicalia serves its own take on the vibrant, flavorful cooking of Brazil. There's *moqueca de peixe*, a wonderful coconut-milk-based sauce served with shrimp or white fish, and classic grilled marinated steak and chicken, but also California-influenced salads, like the delicious *salada brasileira*, with quality greens, hearts of palm, avocado and a heap of sautéed shrimp. Fun food at modest prices. **WHO** Los Feliz locals who need a break from Farfalla and Mexico City. ☺ ☼

[Umami Burger] 🔒 850 S. La Brea Ave., Miracle Mile, 323.931.3000, umamiburger.com. L & D daily. American. No booze. MC, V. $ **WHY** For what is quite possibly the best burger in town. Sorry, Father's Office. **WHAT** Adam Fleischman, owner of this new sit-down burger bistro and co-owner of BottleRock, tried every burger of note in L.A. while planning his place, and he figured out how to do it right. He grinds the beef from flap steak and short ribs, gets soft, shiny yet sturdy buns from a Portuguese bakery, and offers such toppings as grilled onions, parmesan cheese crisps and shiitake mushrooms. The signature Umami burger has a rich savoriness; other choices include the Triple Pork, the Turkey Confit and the Truffle Cheese, and soon there'll be a homemade veggie burger. Our only complaint is that the fries, while triple-fried and crisp, are too thick. **WHO** Young and hungry foodie men. 📷☺☼

[Umami Burger] 4655 Hollywood Blvd., East Hollywood, 323.669.3922, umamiburger.com. L & D Mon.-Sat. American. Beer & wine. MC, V. $ **WHY** Los Feliz and East Hollywood were surprisingly weak on the burger front. Not anymore. And Umami's eastern outpost adds a Japanese beer-and-oyster bar to the mix. **WHAT** First Adam Fleischman found success with BottleRock, then Umami, and now he's taken over the former Cobras & Matadors and Sgt. Recruiter space to expand his Umami empire (there should be a third branch in Fred Segal Santa Monica by the time you read this). His burgers are a sensation (see listing above). This new spot is sure to be a big hit. 📷

[Vegan Glory] 8393 Beverly Blvd., Beverly/Third, 323.653.4900, veganglory.com. L & D daily. Vegan/Thai. Beer & wine. MC, V. $ - $$ **WHY** A consistently good vegan Thai-American café with very good fake chicken, fish and meat dishes; pass on the vegan burger in favor of the vegan tacos, three-flavor fish, pad Thai, curries and coconut ice cream. **WHAT** At this bright and cheerful strip-mall spot near the Beverly Center, the only shortcoming is the lack of parking, although there is a valet option. Other than that, it's a godsend for vegans and the people who love them, because they can eat well, too. **WHO** Devout regulars, including some famous vegans. 📷🥬🚚

[Vermont] 1714 N. Vermont Ave., Los Feliz, 323.661.6163, vermontrestaurantonline.com. L Mon.-Fri., D nightly. Modern American. Full bar. AE, MC, V. $$$ - $$$$ **WHY** Chic elegance in a neighborhood more known for casual bistros. Check out the lobster bake on Wednesdays. **WHAT** Now that the cocktail-lounge action has moved out back to the adjacent Rockwell, Vermont is more about the dining

🥬 VEGETARIAN ☺ KID FRIENDLY ☼ PATIO DINING 🚚 DELIVERY 🎩 PRIVATE PARTY experience. Stephane Beaucamp's food is as elegant as the space: warm Medjool date salad, prime flat-iron steak with black peppercorn sauce, crispy whitefish with a watercress-basil sauce. A lovely date-night destination that's not cheap but not as expensive as it could get away with being — especially on Sundays and Mondays, when a three-course dinner is just $28. **WHO** A tastefully beautiful gay and straight crowd — if they've had work done, you'd never be able to tell. ♥

[Xiomara] 6101 Melrose Ave., Melrose, 323.461.0601, xiomararestaurant.com. L Mon.-Fri., D Mon.-Sat. Cuban. Full bar. AE, MC, V. $$$ - $$$$$ **WHY** The lunch-only cubano sandwiches are delightful, especially the *pan con lechón* (shredded pork with Spanish peppers). And the Cuban club is a tasty fusion of marinated turkey breast with applewood-smoked bacon on sourdough. **WHAT** This is no ordinary cubano sandwich joint — although they do serve them, elegantly, and garnished with microgreens, no less. Xiomara Ardolina's Nuevo Latino eatery is high-style all the way, from the house-pressed sugarcane juice in the mojitos to the Christofle silverware. The cream of L.A.'s Cuban crop.

[Yai Restaurant] 5757 Hollywood Blvd., Hollywood, 323.462.0292. L & D daily. Thai. Beer & wine. Cash only. $ **WHY** Jungle curry, a subtly spicy, coconut-milk-based seafood stew; grilled beef salad with Chinese broccoli; pad Thai with a fiery spiciness instead of an American sweetness; and the succulent BBQ beef appetizer. **WHAT** Thai Town has lots of fine cafés, but this one stands out. You don't come here for the setting: Formica tables jammed into a brightly lit room in a grimy mini-mall. You come for the fabulous, and fabulously cheap, food. Surprisingly, you also come for the service, provided by friendly young women who are happy to introduce this cooking to newcomers. **WHO** Local Thais and adventurous non-Thai food explorers. 📷🍷

[Yai's on Vermont] 1627 N. Vermont Ave., Los Feliz, 323.644.1076. L & D daily. Thai. No booze. Cash only. $ **WHY** Spicy papaya salad, minced chicken with red curry and fried trout are recommended; make sure to specify your desired spice level. **WHAT** On the easternmost end of Thai Town with ample free parking, this offshoot of the original offers a chance to try authentic Thai dishes without the grunge factor of the Yai on Hollywood Boulevard. **WHO** A mix of Thai families and bargain-seeking Los Feliz hipsters. 📷🍷☺☼

EASTSIDE

[Birriería Jalisco] 1845 E. 1st St., East L.A., 323.262.4552, birrieriajalisco.com. B, L & D daily. Mexican. No booze. MC, V. $ **WHY** This 35-year-old institution turns out Southern California's most refined birria. **WHAT** Unlike most birrierías specializing in Guadalajara's famous roasted kid specialty, *birria*, this place doesn't hedge its bets by serving combination plates or other entrees. The drill is simple: You pile soft shreds of the sweet roasted meat onto a fresh tortilla and moisten the crispy-edged flesh with an accompanying broth that's the color of sun-drenched terra cotta and as complexly seasoned as Oaxacan mole. Six meat cuts are listed in Spanish on a card at every table: No. 1, the *surtida*, includes leg, rib and back meat. No. 2, leg and back alone, is the leanest, while No. 3, the rib and leg, offers lots of wonderful gelatinous cartilage to gnaw. The homemade desserts and iced drinks are also wonderful. **WHO** Connoisseurs of kid and Mexican ex-pats for whom the dish is pure comfort food. 🗺

[Blair's] 🏛 2903 Rowena Ave., Silver Lake, 323.660.1882, blairsrestaurant.com. L & D daily. Modern American. Beer & wine. AE, MC, V. $$$
WHY Owner/chef Marshall Blair, ex of Downtown's Water Grill, is not only adept at preparing seafood (don't miss the tuna tartare with spiced ginger vinaigrette), but he's also got a way with meat and pastas, like the dreamy strozzapretti with short ribs, roasted shiitakes and wilted spinach. **WHAT** Blair's has all the hot-spot requirements: a Silver Lake location, a dimly lit, romantic atmosphere, an artistically attractive clientele, a clever list of boutique wines and au courant modern American comfort food. What it doesn't have, fortunately, is the attitude, noise and scene that you might expect of such a stylish bistro. **WHO** The same eastside intelligentsia you see at Palate. ♥ 🍷 🔍

[Blue Hen] 1743 Colorado Blvd., Eagle Rock, 323.982.9900, eatatbluehen.com. L Mon.-Fri, D nightly. Vietnamese. No booze. MC, V. $ **WHY** Organic chicken and vegetarian-friendly cuisine in a casual space that makes you feel like part of Eagle Rock's ascent into hipdom. **WHAT** At this mini-mall organic Vietnamese place, the music on the stereo is a cool as the art on the walls. Try the baguette-based Vietnamese sandwiches, the crisp spring rolls, the steaming bowls of *pho* (noodle soup) and the iced coffee with sweet condensed milk. 🔍 ☕

[Blue Velvet] 750 S. Garland Ave., Downtown, 213.239.0061, bluevelvetrestaurant.com. L Mon.-Fri., D nightly. Modern American. Full bar. AE, MC, V. $$$ - $$$$ **WHY** For the *Sex in the City* vibe with rooftop views of Downtown and creative West Hollywood-worthy fare. **WHAT** Blue Velvet manages to be funky and elegant at the same time – and that applies to both the décor and the food. Lunch and dinner appetizers are the way to go here, with most under $12. Don't miss the seared foie gras starter with apple purée, pickled mushrooms and foie gras bread pudding. **WHO** An expense-account business crowd and local loft owners hanging by the pool, sipping fig-thyme martinis. ♥ 🍷 🎉

🔍 VEGETARIAN ☉ KID FRIENDLY ✿ PATIO DINING 🚚 DELIVERY 🎉 PRIVATE PARTY

[Bottega Louie] 700 S. Grand Ave., Downtown, 213.802.1470, bottegalouie.com. B Sat.-Sun., L & D daily. Italian. Full bar. AE, MC, V. $$ - $$$ **WHY** Crisp, puffy-edged pizzas, delicious salads and seemingly hundreds of fun small plates. **WHAT** In a vast, open space with white marble floors, white walls and a white ceiling way up high, an army of well-trained staff serve solidly satisfying trattoria fare to a constant crowd. At this writing this is Downtown's hottest hot spot, roiling with noise and conviviality. Weekend breakfast is both quieter and very good, and Downtown dwellers frequent the long, gleaming deli for prepared dishes, sandwiches and cookies to take home or back to the office. **WHO** After-work professionals and Hancock Parkers meeting their Pasadena friends before a show at the Music Center or Club Nokia, even though none of them can hear each other talk.

[Bulan Thai Vegetarian Kitchen] 4114 Santa Monica Blvd., Silver Lake, 323.913.1488, bulanthai.com. L & D daily. Thai/vegan. No booze. MC, V. $ **WHY** Truly delicious vegan Thai cooking, served by nice people in a homey setting — and delivery, too! **WHAT** This Silver Lake outpost of the Melrose vegan destination has found the success of its sibling; even though vegan restaurants are as plentiful as tattoos in Silver Lake and Los Feliz, few are as good as this place. **WHO** Vegans bringing their carnivorous mates, who leave happy.

[CaCao Mexicatessen] 1576 Colorado Blvd., Eagle Rock, 323.478.2791, cacaodeli.com. L & D Tues.-Sun. Mexican. BYOB. MC, V. $ - $$ **WHY** Warmth, a strong sense of neighborhood and a serious approach to food — and, more importantly, to Mexican chocolate in all its forms. **WHAT** The name was a poor choice — everyone stumbles over it — but everything else about this richly colorful new café/deli/market succeeds. Lovely people offer table service in the café or out on the patio, as well as takeout food and a fine coffee bar that adds Mexican chocolate drinks to the usual mix. Try the cochinita pibil tacos, Tijuana-style Caesar salad, tortilla soup, cubano torta and the cheese plate. Some balk at the $2.75 tacos, but this is not a truck, this is a nice café with table service and flowers on the table, and you can bring your own wine. **WHO** Eagle Rock people flocked from day one, including vegetarians grateful for the good choices.

[Café Beaujolais] 1712 Colorado Blvd., Eagle Rock, 323.255.5111. D Tues.-Sun. French. Beer & wine. AE, MC, V. $$ - $$$ **WHY** Because the onion soup, steak frites and dark-chocolate mousse are intensely comforting for Francophiles; the flippant, funny black-T-shirted French waiters are the lagniappes. **WHAT** Just like an ordinary corner bistro in one of Paris's lesser arrondissements, Café Beaujolais is nothing to go out of your way for but is a blessing for locals. Straightforward, old-fashioned French bistro food at fair prices, served with élan or attitude, depending on your tolerance for French bistros.

ESSENTIALLY L.A. ☺ LATE ♥ ROMANTIC VALUE QUIET ☼ SUSTAINABLE

[Café Pinot] 🏛 700 W. 5th St., Downtown, 213.239.6500, patinagroup.com/cafePinot. L Mon.-Fri., D nightly. Modern American/French. Full bar. AE, MC, V. $$$ - $$$$$ **WHY** Sitting under the olive trees in front of the L.A. Central Library, sipping a Viognier and eating the famed mustard-crusted rotisserie chicken with fries, is one of Downtown's greatest pleasures. **WHAT** When the weather's good, book a table on the terrace at this chic bistro owned by celebrity chef Joachim Splichal. If the weather's not good, you'll still have a very fine French-Californian bistro meal in the concrete-and-glass dining room staffed by skilled waiters. **WHO** Well-dressed attorneys, bankers and real estate brokers, often entertaining clients. 🍷 🥢 ☼ 🏛

[Canelé] 3219 Glendale Blvd., Atwater, 323.666.7133, canele-la.com. D Tues.-Sun., brunch Sat.-Sun. Modern American/French. Beer & wine. AE, MC, V. $$ - $$$ **WHY** The most extraordinary plain omelet in town, served in a casual, open-kitchen room alongside a short list of really good French-American-Mediterranean dishes. **WHAT** Owner/chef Corina Weibel cooked at Campanile and Lucques, but her ambitions for Canelé are more modest: a convivial neighborhood bistro serving quality Cal-French-Mediterranean food at affordable prices. Her cooking is simple and robustly flavorful, particularly notable for the meats (lamb chops, beef bourguignonne), fish (whole roasted branzino) and desserts. Be prepared for cheek-by-jowl seating, and enjoy the we're-in-on-the-secret eastside vibe. No reservations, so come early or late. **WHO** Everyone here looks like an artist, writer, software developer or actor on an HBO series, and they probably are. 🥢

[Casa Bianca Pizza Pie] 🏛 1650 Colorado Blvd., Eagle Rock, 323.256.9617, casabiancapizza.com. D Tues.-Sat. Italian/pizzeria. Beer & wine. Cash only. $ - $$$ **WHY** The crust is thin, the cheese and sauce are in fine balance, and the vintage sign out front still calls it a "Pizza Pie." **WHAT** Their pizza is an L.A. legend, but this funky Eagle Rock landmark is no place for a quick bite; waits are fearsome, and even ordering a to-go pie can take an hour. The payoff is a thin crust, New York-style pizza with a flavor that usually makes you forget how long it took to get seated (try it topped with eggplant). Smart regulars place their order when they put in their name for a table, so the pizza's ready by they time they sit down. The rest of the basic Italian food is fine but forgettable. **WHO** Old-school Eagle Rock and the entire pizza-loving populations of Pasadena and Glendale. 🥢 🥢 ☺

[Chaya Downtown] 🏛 525 S. Flower St., Downtown, 213.236.9577, thechaya.com. L Mon.-Fri., D Mon.-Sat. French/Asian. Full bar. AE, MC, V. $$$$ **WHY** Terrific L.A.-style Euro-Asian fusion food and a swinging happy hour make this a good spot for a business lunch, an after-work cocktail or a chic date night. **WHAT** The latest member of L.A.'s great Chaya family is a hit. The serene, Asian-accented space has an impressive art-glass chandelier in the bar and comfy outdoor booths that, on

🥢 VEGETARIAN ⊙ KID FRIENDLY ☼ PATIO DINING �- DELIVERY 🏛 PRIVATE PARTY a warm summer evening, make you forget you're in a sterile office-tower neighborhood. The kitchen is particularly adept at seafood dishes (sushi, seafood crudo, squid ink fettuccine with prawns and calamari, miso-marinated white sea bass), and the happy-hour menu boasts $5 cocktails and great-value sushi and small plates. **WHO** Downtown suits who think McCormick & Schmick's is too stodgy and the Standard is too annoying. ♥ 🍷 ☼ 🏚

[Chichen Itza] 2501 W. 6th St., Westlake, 213.380.0051, chichenitza-restaurant.com. L & D Tues.-Sun. Mexican/Yucatan. Beer & wine. AE, MC, V. $$ **WHY** Seductive dishes from the Yucatan: panuchos with shredded turkey, tomato, pickled red onion and avocado; shrimp ceviche with a splash of Yucatecan green oil; cochinita pibil; and a remarkable queso relleno made with edam cheese and ground pork seasoned with almonds, raisins and capers. **WHAT** Near MacArthur Park, on the western edge of Downtown, sits this terrific Yucatecan restaurant, a cheerful space with polished wooden tables, beams and kind, professional service. The flavors are rich, with such ingredients as black beans, fried plantains, pickled red onions, achiote and citrus. Excellent seafood and pork dishes, and tasty vegetarian fare, too. **WHO** Workers from the nearby nonprofits and St. Vincent's Hospital. 🍴🍸☺

[Church & State] 🏚 1850 Industrial St., Downtown, 213.405.1434, churchandstatebistro.com. L Mon.-Fri. D Mon.-Sat. French. Full bar. AE, MC, V. $$ - $$$ **WHY** Walter Manzke's first-rate execution of French bistro classics, at near-bargain prices. **WHAT** This too-loud, brick-walled restaurant got off to a weak start, but when owner Steven Arroyo snagged chef Manzke, things took a marked turn for the better. He makes his own charcuterie, procures pristine oysters, makes a mean bouillabaisse and knows enough not to tinker with such classics as moules marinière, steak frites and an elegant omelet (all terrific). Be warned that the ultra-flaky Alsatian-style tarts are huge and best shared with a group as an appetizer, and note that the onions on the tarte flamiche are caramelized to the point of ultra-sweetness (heaven for some, too sweet for others). Also a big hit with the regulars are the tasty, reasonably priced French wines and that milk of modern yuppiedom, absinthe. **WHO** The chic folks who live upstairs in the Biscuit Company lofts or across the street in the Toy Company lofts. 🍴☼

[Ciudad] Union Bank Plaza, 445 S. Figueroa St., Downtown, 213.486.5171, ciudad-la.com. L Mon.-Fri., D nightly. Latino. Full bar. AE, MC, V. $$ - $$$$ **WHY** Great margaritas and mojitos (which taste better during the $4 happy hour Monday to Friday and Sunday in the early evening) and winning small plates, from goat-cheese fritters to delicious Peruvian ceviche. **WHAT** Ciudad distinguishes itself from Santa Monica sister restaurant Border Grill by trying to be all things Latin for all people, and it doesn't always work as well as Border Grill's Mexican food does. But the enclosed patio is inviting, the cocktails are swell, and the bar food is fun. **WHO** Suits from the Downtown towers, and a lively happy-hour crowd. ☺🍷☼

[Cliff's Edge] 3626 W. Sunset Blvd., Silver Lake, 323.666.6116, cliff-sedgecafe.com. D Mon.-Sat., brunch Sat.-Sun. Italian/modern American. Full bar. AE, MC, V. $$ - $$$ **WHY** For the most beautiful outdoor dining on the eastside, with food that suits the setting; try the leek and onion tart with an arugula salad, the rigatoni with wild-boar ragú, and the warm seafood salad. Brunch is lovely, too. **WHAT** We'd eat Arby's fare in this setting — a hidden walled garden built around a massive ficus tree, with levels and nooks and, at night, flickering candles — so we're all the more grateful that the food is good, if pricier than we'd like. The shocker is that the staff is actually nice — a place like this about ten miles west would be dripping with attitude. **WHO** TV directors keeping a low profile and production assistants splurging on a big night out. ♥☼

[Cole's] 118 E. 6th St., Downtown, 213.622.4090, colesfrenchdip.com. L & D daily. American. Full bar. AE, MC, V. $ - $$ **WHY** Whether the French dip sandwich was invented here or not, lots of thought has gone into the redo of this historic spot. **WHAT** Chef Neal Fraser consulted on the menu when the oldest public house in L.A. re-opened after a restrained remodel, featuring red leatherette booths and historic black-and-white photos. The compact menu offers hand-sliced French dip sandwiches of beef, pork, turkey and lamb with au jus and "atomic" pickle spears, paired with sides including bacon-potato salad and mac 'n cheese.

[Colori Kitchen] 429 W. 8th St., Downtown, 213.622.5950, colorikitchen.wordpress.com. L Mon.-Fri., D Wed.-Sat. Italian. Beer & wine. MC, V. $ - $$ **WHY** Because it's the best-value sit-down restaurant in Downtown L.A. **WHAT** Past a fairly grim-looking doorway in a transitional block (over here, $750,000 lofts, over there, a shabby residence hotel) is a charming room with brick walls and an open kitchen, where the owner/chef (formerly of Ca'Brea) turns out delicious Italian classics at bare-bones prices: rigatoni melanzane or spaghetti and meatballs for $6.50, and a tasty chicken pesto sandwich for $6.50. Specials are pricier but worth the investment. **WHO** An interesting Downtown mix: fire captains and lawyers sitting next to loft-dwelling screenwriters and Fashion District hipsters. 🍴🍷

[Domenico] 1637 Silver Lake Blvd., Silver Lake, 323.661.6166, domenicoristorantesilverlake.com. L & D daily. Italian. BYOB (wine license pending). AE, MC, V. $$ - $$$$ **WHY** Elegant Italian dishes in a relaxed Silver Lake sidewalk café with excellent service. **WHAT** Tiny and white inside, with a spacious front patio, this neighborhood restaurant is culinarily ambitious for the neighborhood. Handmade pastas — think lasagne with oxtails, beet tortelli or Peruvian blue-potato ravioli — and hearty, creative mains like braised rabbit make it a sophisti-

🍷 VEGETARIAN ☺ KID FRIENDLY ☼ PATIO DINING �. DELIVERY 🎉 PRIVATE PARTY

cated alternative to the area's profusion of pizzerias. It's pricier than we'd like, but it's delivering the goods. **WHO** Date-night couples; a smattering of local actors. ☼

[El Caserio] **401 Silver Lake Blvd., Silver Lake, 213.273.8945, elcaseri-ola.com. L & D Tues.-Sun. Mexican/Latino. Beer & wine. AE, MC, V. $$ - $$$$ WHY** A pretty place to explore the cuisine of South America. **WHAT** This dramatically enhanced sibling to William Velasco's revered 25-year-old restaurant has the mood of a gracious old hacienda, and the food is less Ecuatoriano and more contemporary pan–South American. The libations match luscious tropical fruits with appropriately flavored alcohol: bright, citrusy *naranjilla* (fruitier cousin of the tomato) with gin, or tart-sweet *lulo* (mountain blackberry) with cachaça, for example. Slightly retooled favorites from the older menu include *llapingachos*, crisp-edged potato patties filled with melting cheese, the Andean answer to the quesadilla. ☼

[El Puerto Escondido] **3345 N. Eastern Ave., El Sereno, 323.909.1008, elpuertoesc.com. L & D daily. Mexican/seafood. Beer & wine. MC, V. $ WHY** Ultra-fresh Mexican-style seafood, including Happy Oysters, freshly shucked and topped with a vibrant chopped shrimp cocktail, and *caldo de siete mares*, a light, fresh soup stocked with Alaskan crab legs, mussels and shrimp. **WHAT** This eastside branch of the Inglewood original serves the seafood dishes of Mexico's Pacific beach towns, and while it's not open 24/7 like the mothership, it has the same terrific shrimp cocktails, camarones al mojo de ajo, ceviches and whole fried fish, all at very low prices. **WHO** El Sereno locals and South Pas surfers pining for Mexico's beaches. 🗒️☺

[El Taurino] 🏠 **1104 S. Hoover St., Pico-Union, 213.738.9197. L & D daily to 4 a.m. Mexican. Beer & wine. Cash only. $ WHY** Juicy carne asada burritos, tacos al pastor, famously fiery salsa roja, a divey bull-fighting décor, and a 4 a.m. closing time. **WHAT** Some complain about the long lines and the fact that they charge 40 cents for the salsas, but this is just petulant whining. El Taurino is a gift to Angelenos, and not just because of its late-night hours and parking. The meats (carne asada, barbacoa, al pastor, carnitas, lengua) are all excellent and the salsas addictive (get the verde instead of the roja if your mouth isn't coated in flame retardant). **WHO** USC students, Koreatown residents and, late at night, the post-party crowd. ☺ 🗒️

[El Tepeyac] **812 N. Evergreen Ave., Boyle Heights, 323.267.8668. B, L & D Mon. & Wed.-Sun. Mexican. BYOB. MC, V. $ WHY** Machaca burrito, guacamole and taquitos, all in massive portions. **WHAT** This venerable L.A. dive is famed for its monstrous burritos, especially the Hollenbeck, which we find dull. Try the machaca instead, and plan to share it with another hungry soul. You can bring your own beer or sip a good horchata. **WHO** Almost always a line of college students, working men and families from the Valley having an adventure. 🍸☼

[Elf] 2135 Sunset Blvd., Echo Park, 213.484.6829, myspace.com/elfcafe. D Wed.-Sun. Vegetarian/Mediterranean. BYOB ($5 corkage). Cash only. $$ - $$$ **WHY** Homey vegetarian fare (mac 'n cheese, vegetable tarts, tagines) served out of a tiny, charming Sunset Boulevard storefront. **WHAT** The owners of this candlelit chocolate box of a café are folk musicians who turn out organic fare with a retro feel from a minuscule kitchen. Mediterranean-inspired vegan and vegetarian dishes (roasted tomato-feta tarts, kale salad, delicious chickpea crêpe with chevre butter) taste like earnest home cooking. With friendly service, Elf captures the groovy vibe of the new Echo Park. **WHO** Bearded musicians, hot yoga babes, pierced parents pushing designer strollers. 🍸🌀🔖☺

[Empress Pavilion] 988 N. Hill St., Chinatown, 213.617.9898, empresspavilion.com. L & D daily. Chinese/dim sum. Full bar. AE, MC, V. $$ **WHY** The best dim sum in Chinatown, and good Hong Kong–style seafood for dinner, too. **WHAT** Chinatown's most elegant restaurant, Empress Pavilion is packed for weekend dim sum; we prefer coming during the week. It's lesser known for dinner, but the more than respectable cooking (steamed Dungeness crab with flat noodles in garlic sauce) and professional service make it a good place to know about, especially for groups. **WHO** Chinese and Occidental businesspeople, large family groups and friends meeting for dim sum. ☺🏮

[Fatty's] 🔒 1627 Colorado Blvd., Eagle Rock, 323.254.8804, fattyscafe. com. D Wed.-Sun. Vegetarian/modern American. Beer & wine. AE, MC, V. $$ - $$$ **WHY** This is the place to bring your friends who distrust vegetarian cooking; they'll be blown away by the rich and elegant fare. Standouts from the kitchen, which delights in witty juxtapositions, include vegetarian dumplings, huge homemade potato chips with two kinds of dip, and the sticky and decadent maple sugar cotton candy, which everyone orders. **WHAT** If you never trust a skinny cook, you'll be drawn to this gem for the name alone. It's a post-ironic title for a sensual vegetarian/vegan restaurant that cooks some seriously delicious food and has fun doing it. The staff is attentive and knowledgeable, the wine is well selected and well priced, available in flights or "glass-and-a-halfs," and the food is outstanding — a tightly composed menu that includes tapas, salads, pizza, entrees and fondues. 🍸🌀🔖☺

[Folliero Pizza] 5566 N. Figueroa St., Highland Park, 323.254.0505. L & D daily. Pizzeria/Italian. Beer & wine. MC, V. $ **WHY** A little bit of Queens in Highland Park (which is, now that we think of it, the Queens of L.A.). **WHAT** It's not the lightest pizza in town — the crust is on the substantial side, and the cheese overpowers the sauce — but there's no denying the appeal and comfort of this old-school New York Italian pizza, especially when you eat it inside this old-world, brick-walled Italian restaurant. Skip the rest of the menu, as well as the

---

🍸 VEGETARIAN ☺ KID FRIENDLY ☼ PATIO DINING �: DELIVERY 🏮 PRIVATE PARTY

more complicated pies, and stay faithful to a plain cheese or a sausage and mushroom. **WHO** Highland Park gentrifiers and local Latino families — this hasn't been an Italian neighborhood for decades. 🎢 😊 🚗

[Gingergrass] 🏛 2396 Glendale Blvd., Silver Lake, 323.644.1600, gingergrass.com. L & D daily. Vietnamese. Beer & wine. AE, MC, V. $ - $$ **WHY** Vast bowls of delicate noodles crowned with flowering basil tops and mint; char-grilled meats arranged over hillocks of raw greens; shrimp rolled around sugarcane sticks; sweet-tart jackfruit salad with pickled lotus roots; and more such crowd-pleasing dishes. **WHAT** Vietnamese cafés are hip and happening — the light, intensely colorful, vividly flavorful food perfectly suits the L.A. aesthetic, and with nearly a half million Vietnamese-Americans living in California, there's no shortage of skilled chefs. Gingergrass is a great example of the trend, an always-jammed spot fragrant with the aromas of mint, basil, grilled meat and pickled vegetables. It's great fun with a group, though you'll have to shout to be heard at the other end of the table. **WHO** A Silver Lake–eclectic mix of families and friends packed tightly into the high-ceilinged, glass-walled, noisy space. 🎢 🥢 😊

[Good Girl Dinette] 110 N. Ave. 56, Highland Park, 323.257.8980, goodgirlfoods.com. L Sat.-Sun., D Tues.-Sun. Vietnamese/American. BYOB. MC, V. $ **WHY** Viet-American comfort food in a stylishly barren new Highland Park café. **WHAT** Why a place calls itself a dinette and chooses not to serve lunch during the week is beyond us, especially because the Grandma's Pho, pork baguette sandwich, spicy fries and curry chicken pot pie are great lunch dishes. Oh well, we're happy to come for dinner, especially because we can bring our own wine. **WHO** New-era Highland Parkers in straw porkpie hats. 🎢 🥢 😊

[Hawaiian Chicken] 686 N. Spring St., Chinatown, 866.319.3867, hawaiianchicken.com. L & D Mon.-Wed. & Fri.-Sat. Hawaiian. Beer & wine. MC, V. $ **WHY** Sensational grilled chicken now available to those who can't wait for farmers' market day to roll around. **WHAT** This family-run restaurant expands on the Hawaiian *huli huli* (literally, "turn turn") concept that's made its rotisserie chicken such a hit on the farmers' market circuit around town. The birds roast over mesquite-like kiawe charcoal, and in this Chinatown location, you can get such fusion dishes as grilled chicken in guava-chile sauce. Call ahead for takeout if you don't want to wait. 🎢 😊

[Izakaya Haru Ulala] 368 E. 2nd St., Little Tokyo/Arts District, 213.620.0977. D Mon.-Sun. (to 2 a.m. Fri.-Sat.). Japanese. Beer, wine & sake. AE, MC, V. $$ **WHY** Tasty dishes to accompany sake or beer: noodles, yellowtail with daikon, slow-cooked Kurobuta pork belly, shiitake tempura and robata-yaki, served until midnight during the week and 2 a.m. on weekends. **WHAT** Whimsical menus written in crayon set the tone at this casual space dominated by a U-shaped

🏛 **ESSENTIALLY L.A.** 😊 **LATE** ♥ **ROMANTIC** 🎢 **VALUE** 🍜 **QUIET** ♻ **SUSTAINABLE** counter around the open robata-style kitchen, where chefs work grilling yakitori, steaming vegetables, stuffing eggplant and bell peppers and charring bananas for dessert. **WHO** A business and jury-duty crowd at lunch, and in the wee hours, clubgoers looking to refuel. ☉

[Izayoi] 132 S. Central Ave., Little Tokyo/Arts District, 213.613.9554. L Mon.-Fri., D Mon.-Sat. Japanese. Beer & wine. AE, MC, V. $$ - $$$ **WHY** For good unfiltered sakes and the best *izakaya* (Japanese pub fare) in Little Tokyo: grilled yellowtail collar, black cod, braised pork belly, scallop sashimi, seafood cream croquette and fried chicken. **WHAT** A sparkly clean, almost sterile ambience prevails at this Little Tokyo spot, where the chefs in the open kitchen and behind the sushi counter take advantage of the nearby wholesale fish market. Organized by technique, the menu proffers such dishes as succulent grilled baby barracuda, vinegary mozuku seaweed and richly flavored braised pork belly. **WHO** Date-nighters and Downtown lofties.

[Kagaya] 🏠 418 E. 2nd St., Little Tokyo/Arts District, 213.617.1016. D nightly. Japanese. Beer & wine. MC, V. $$$$ - $$$$$ **WHY** Real shabu-shabu made with exceptional ingredients, notably the Wagyu beef. Best of all: When you finish cooking and eating your meat, seafood and veggies, they take the pot back to the kitchen and turn the now-rich broth into a heavenly thick soup with rice or udon. **WHAT** It's a modest-looking place, and *shabu-shabu* (meat, seafood and vegetables cooked at the table in bubbling broth) is typically pretty ordinary stuff here in the U.S. But Kagaya has brought it up a few notches, thanks to exceptional meats (including Kobe and Wagyu beef) and such elegant touches as chrysanthemum leaves in the mounds of seasonal greens to cook in the pot. You pay dearly for this — $41 to $128 per person for a fixed-price meal — but it's worth a splurge, especially if you get the good beef. **WHO** Expense-account adventurers. 🍷

[La Caridad] 2137 W. Temple St., Westlake, 213.484.0099. B, L & D Mon.-Sat. Cuban. No booze. Cash only. $ **WHY** The *media noches* (Cuban sandwiches made on eggy bread that's just a little sweet) just might be the best in the city. **WHAT** This Filipinotown hole-in-the-wall features a Formica countertop and an ancient iron stove where sandwich magic is regularly performed: The classic cubano sandwich is composed of fresh-roasted pork piled on enormous slices of bread with the requisite ham, cheese and pickles. You'll also find fresh squeezed carrot and orange juices, and good Cuban coffee. 🍴

[LA Mill] 1636 Silver Lake Blvd., Silver Lake, 323.663.4441, lamillcoffee.com. B, L & D daily. Modern American. No booze. AE, MC, V. $$ - $$$ **WHY** The food is conceived by Providence chef Michael Cimarusti, with imaginative desserts by Providence pastry chef Adrian Vasquez. Eggs with crab, an Asian BLT made with pork belly, and a deconstructed sweet potato pie are standouts. **WHAT** This elegant, high-design coffeehouse and restaurant features deluxe coffee preparations as well as breakfast, lunch and dinner. This is surely the most ambitious coffeehouse food in town, annoyingly pretentious to some and long overdue to others — but everyone's talking about it. **WHO** Eastside ladies who lunch and hardcore coffee connoisseurs. ☼

[La Parrilla] 1300 Wilshire Blvd., Westlake, 213.353.4930; 3129 W. Sunset Blvd., Silver Lake, 323.661.8055, laparrillarestaurant.com. B, L & D daily. Mexican. Full bar. AE, MC, V. $ - $$ **WHY** Smoky, aromatic parrilladas, where you grill meat (marinated Cornish hens, steak, pork chops) on tabletop grills. **WHAT** Going back 30 years and now boasting four locations, La Parrilla is known for its parrilladas and brochetas, but the rest of the food is good, too. Try the *pollito en pipian* (young chicken with pumpkin seeds). Good happy hour, and the Wilshire location has a patio right out of Ensenada. 📷 ☺ ☼ 🏠

[La Serenata de Garibaldi] 🏛 1842 E. 1st St., Boyle Heights, 323.265.2887, laserenataonline.com. L & D daily, brunch Sat.-Sun. Mexican/seafood. Beer, wine & agave margaritas. AE, MC, V. $$ - $$$ **WHY** Beautiful Mexican seafood in a landmark Boyle Heights setting, with kind service. Try the shrimp gorditas for lunch and a fresh-fish special for dinner. **WHAT** An L.A. treasure, La Serenata continues to serve carefully prepared, sometimes elegant Mexican seafood dishes to a loving and longtime clientele. It now has two branches on the westside, and they're fine, but this is the holy ground. Seafood is the focus, but vegetarians are tended to, as are people who insist on having beef tacos. **WHO** Politicians, *L.A. Times* people, leaders in the Latino community and really smart tourists. 📷 🎵 🍷 ☺

[La Taquiza] 3009 S. Figueroa St., USC, 213.741.9795. B, L & D daily. Mexican. No booze. AE, MC, V. $ **WHY** The *mulita*, a sort of taco-quesadilla hybrid made with two fresh corn tortillas encasing meat, cheese, guacamole and salsa — the L.A. sandwich of your dreams. **WHAT** Tortillas are made fresh here all day, and the al pastor is slow-roasted on a vertical spit... clearly this is more than your typical strip-mall Mexican dive. Everyone gets the mulita, but the tacos, burritos and combination plates are also terrific, as are the horchatas. **WHO** A wonderful multiethnic and cross-class mix of Angelenos, including lots of USC students and staff. 📷 ☺

[Larkin's] 1496 Colorado Blvd., Eagle Rock, 323.254.0934, larkinsjoint. com. D Wed.-Sun., brunch Sat.-Sun. Soul food/Southern. Beer & wine. MC, V. $$ **WHY** Skillet-fried chicken and other Southern comfort dishes served in an atmospheric old home. **WHAT** Everyone loves the charm of the restored Craftsman house, but opinion is divided on Larkin Mackey's Southern cooking. Portions are small by soul-food standards, waits for tables can be painful (no reservations), and service is typically lax. But the chicken is skillet-fried the right way, and the banana pudding is comfort in a crock. Worth checking out for eastsiders. New this year: a beer and wine license. **WHO** Tastefully tattooed parents with gorgeous multiethnic toddlers, and other modern-era Eagle Rockers. 😊 ☼

[Mae Ploy] 2606 W. Sunset Blvd., Echo Park, 213.353.9635. L & D daily. Thai. Beer & wine. AE, MC, V. $ **WHY** All the Thai stalwarts (try the chicken with mint leaves) are well prepared, as are the special dishes, like crab noodles and eggplant salad. **WHAT** Straddling the Silver Lake/Echo Park dividing line, this long-established eatery delivers tasty home-style Thai food throughout the area. You can also eat this delicious food in-house and accompany your meal with Thai beer served in a frosty mug. 📋🥡😊�

[Mandarin Chateau] 970 N. Broadway, Chinatown, 213.625.1195. L & D daily. Chinese/Shanghai. Beer & wine. AE, MC, V. $ - $$ **WHY** When you're in the mood for red-cooked pork ribs or lion's head meatballs but don't want to head out to the San Gabriel Valley, this venerable spot (formerly known as Mandarin Shanghai) is the ticket. **WHAT** Hidden in a strip mall, this little place is a good find off the Chinatown tourist path for war won ton soup, respectable seafood dishes, better-than-the-norm kung pao chicken and hot pots. 📋

[Mo-Chica Peruvian] 🏠 Mercado la Paloma, 3655 S. Grand Ave., USC, 213.747.2141, mo-chica.com. L & D Mon.-Sat. Peruvian. No booze. MC, V. $ **WHY** What may be the best ceviches in L.A. **WHAT** Mercado la Paloma may technically be a food court, but this is no Westfield mall. For one thing, the place is a nonprofit, designed to help small neighborhood entrepreneurs. For another, it's home to this new Peruvian café, where former sushi chef Ricardo Zarate is turning out such dishes as scallop ceviche with sweet potato, toasted corn and seaweed; lamb shank with white canary beans and cilantro sauce; and a refined *lomo saltado* (a stir-fry of beef and vegetables with fried potatoes) that's almost French in execution and flavor. **WHO** Pilgrims eager to explore Peruvian food in greater depth. 📋😊�

[Moles la Tia] 🏠 4619 E. Cesar Chavez Ave., East L.A., 323.263.7842, moleslatia.com. B, L & D daily. Mexican. No booze. AE, MC, V. $ - $$$ **WHY** There's more than the usual Mexican bill of fare here — this spot elevates sauces to the main attraction. **WHAT** Red, green and black moles are just the beginning of the rainbow of dishes here. Neither divey nor fancy, it's the perfect informal place for a party or group dinner, the better to experience dozens of flavors of moles, including coffee, hibiscus and tequila. Mole sauces are paired with chicken, quail, pork and fish, while the non-mole fare (including a good cochinita pibil) is just as carefully prepared. Homemade tortillas and several flavors of flans round out the menu. **WHO** Culinary explorers ready to explore Boyle Heights. 📋😊

🥬 VEGETARIAN ☺ KID FRIENDLY ☼ PATIO DINING � DELIVERY 🏠 PRIVATE PARTY

[New Moon] 102 W. 9th St., South Park/Fashion District, 213.624.0186, newmoonrestaurants.com. L Mon.-Sat. Chinese/Cantonese. Beer & wine. AE, MC, V. $$ **WHY** Chinese chicken salad. **WHAT** It's not the most authentic Chinese food, not by a long shot, but New Moon makes a damn fine Chinese chicken salad and perfectly acceptable won ton soup, fried rice and stir fries — and the won ton strips with a plum dipping sauce are a tasty variation on chips and salsa. A convenient lunch spot for a group that's hitting the fashion or jewelry marts. **WHO** Garment District workers and shoppers. ☺

[Noé Restaurant & Bar] Omni Los Angeles Hotel, 251 S. Olive St., Downtown, 213.356.4100, noerestaurant.com. D nightly. Modern American. Full bar. AE, MC, V. $$$$ - $$$$$ **WHY** Civilized surroundings, excellent cocktails, foie gras three ways — and they know how to get you out in time for the curtain. **WHAT** Noé's sophisticated menu has won the hearts and loyalty of many Downtowners. The food is delicious and elegantly served, and the prix-fixe menu is a good value, given the prices, quality and setting. The restaurant and its adjoining lounge have become favorite meeting spots before performances at Disney Hall and the Music Center. **WHO** Hotel guests, California Plaza professionals and Music Center patrons. 🍸🏛

[Otomisan] 2506 E. 1st St., Boyle Heights, 323.526.1150. L & D Mon.-Sat. Japanese. Beer & wine. MC, V. $ **WHY** When you're in Boyle Heights but don't want Mexican food. **WHAT** You'll feel like you're walking into the film *L.A. Confidential* when you pull open the screen door to this diner, which has just five stools and three leatherette booths. It's a vestige of when Boyle Heights was a hub of Japanese immigrants, before World War II, but it's not just a relic — the sweet couple that owns it does a fine job. She handles service, and he handles both the cooking (made-from-scratch miso, good old-school sukiyaki, cold udon, classic teriyaki) and the dishwashing. **WHO** A few elderly Japanese-Americans who've lived in the neighborhood for 50 years, and their Mexican-American neighbors. 🗒

[Pacific Dining Car] 🏛 1310 W. 6th St., Westlake, 213.483.6000, pacificdiningcar.com. B, L & D 24 hours daily. American/steakhouse. Full bar. AE, MC, V. $$$$ - $$$$$ **WHY** For delicious, expensive steaks; satisfying, expensive breakfasts; 1920s elegance and food served 24 hours a day. Great for serious business meetings and gleeful middle-of-the-night splurges. **WHAT** Dating to 1921, this former railroad dining car on the fringes of Downtown is as beloved as Musso & Frank — but the food's a lot better. Steaks are the specialty, and they're terrific if someone else is buying; stick with breakfast if you're buying. Note that the room temp is akin to a meat locker, so dress warmly. The Santa Monica branch is less noteworthy. **WHO** L.A.'s power brokers, writers channeling the ghost of Raymond Chandler (who ate here), the rich and elderly and, at 3 a.m., the young, drunk and bleary. ☺ ♥ 🍸

🏛 **ESSENTIALLY L.A.** ☺ **LATE** ♥ **ROMANTIC** 🗒 **VALUE** 🍸 **QUIET** ♻ **SUSTAINABLE**

[The Park] 1400 Sunset Blvd., Echo Park, 213.482.9209, thepark-1400sunset.com. L Tues.-Fri., D Wed.-Sun., brunch Sat.-Sun. Modern American. No booze (license pending). AE, MC, V. $ - $$ **WHY** Jidori chicken, cornmeal pancakes with grilled shrimp and chipotle cream and Mexican Coke; hopefully there'll be wine by the time you read this. **WHAT** One of the leaders of the Echo Park boom (it's not evil gentrification, it's a renaissance!), the Park is stylish in a barren, homespun way, with empty frames on the stark walls and a simple patio that's the place to be for weekend brunch. Young chef/owner Joshua Siegel serves eminently affordable modern home cooking — composed salads, artful burgers, pot pies, roast chicken — that is just the thing for this era of modest consumption. **WHO** Carefully scruffy young families and silver-haired Silver Lake adventurers. 🚚 ☺

[Patina] Walt Disney Concert Hall, 141 S. Grand Ave., Downtown, 213.972.3331, patinagroup.com. D Tues.-Sun. Modern American/seafood. Full bar. AE, MC, V. $$$$ - $$$$$ **WHY** For fine dining in the French Laundry style, but in the dazzling Walt Disney Concert Hall instead of the Napa Valley. **WHAT** Seafood is a focus at this elegant Joachim Splichal flagship restaurant, with dishes like diver scallops carpaccio with kumquat liquid sphere and black truffle, or a Mediterranean loup de mer with spring minestrone and pesto crouton. Those headed for a concert typically have a two-course meal; destination diners celebrating an occasion are wise to choose the often-extraordinary seven- or eleven-course tasting menus — assuming, of course, that their net worth is sufficient to allow for the investment. **WHO** Concert-goers, high-end business-lunchers and anniversary celebrants. ♥ 🍷 🏛

[Pete's Café & Bar] 400 S. Main St., Downtown, 213.617.1000, pet-escafe.com. L & D daily (to 2 a.m.). American. Full bar. AE, MC, V. $$ - $$$ **WHY** Well-prepared modern-American comfort food — mac 'n cheese, Caesar salad, flat-iron steak with blue-cheese fries — at fair prices in a swell old building. **WHAT** High ceilings, old tile floors and burnished wooden tables give Pete's a look usually more associated with San Francisco or New York. This is a fine place for a weekend lunch after a MOCA visit or gallery crawl; it's also a comforting haven for a drink and a Hellman burger after a long day of lawyering. Check out jazz night on Tuesdays. **WHO** Businesspeople, artists, families — a rumpled-stylish Downtown mix. ☺ ☺

[R-23] 🔒 923 E. 2nd St., Downtown, 213.687.7178, r23.com. L Mon.-Fri., D Mon.-Sat. Japanese/sushi. Beer & wine. AE, MC, V. $$ - $$$$ **WHY** Dungeness crab salad, grilled yellowtail collar, simple and ultra-fresh sushi and rolls. **WHAT** Find your way to this all-but-hidden space off a gritty loading dock in the warehouse district east of Downtown, and you'll be transported into an almost cinematically perfect loft/gallery scene (huge paintings, exposed brick walls, Frank Gehry–designed cardboard chairs) with impressively fresh sushi

🌿 VEGETARIAN ☺ KID FRIENDLY ✿ PATIO DINING 🚐 DELIVERY 🏛 PRIVATE PARTY

and well-prepared grilled dishes. Service can be slow but is always thoughtful and friendly. **WHO** Media and business types mingle with loft-dwellers, artists and musicians. (That *was* Leonard Cohen at the next table, right?)

[Rambutan Thai] **2835 W. Sunset Blvd., Silver Lake, 213.273.8424, rambutanthai.com. L & D daily. Thai. Beer & wine. AE, MC, V. $$** **WHY** Delicious Thai tapas — such small plates as Thai rolls, crab rolls, larb and fried shrimp cakes — along with good sakes and Asian beers. **WHAT** A grim mini-mall is home to this sleek and stylish Thai boîte, which now has an adjacent nightclub that's a weekend scene. Avoid the too-sweet mee krob, but try all the rest of the small plates; the happiest people come with a group, so they can try more delectable little dishes. Come for lunch or early dinner if you want to talk to your companions. **WHO** Silver Lake sophisticates — quiet by day, convivial by night. ☉🌙🚗

[Reservoir] **1700 Silver Lake Blvd., Silver Lake, 323.662.8655, silverlakereservoir.com. D Tues.-Sun., brunch Sun. Modern American. Beer & wine. AE, MC, V. $$$ WHY** Open-faced lasagne with pork, roasted tomatoes and braised artichoke. **WHAT** The site of the former Netty's is now a clean-lined, almost Craftsmanish bistro with elbow-to-elbow tables but not too much noise. Owner/chef Gloria Felix's menu is a little odd — the core is simple grilled or pan-seared salmon, steak or tofu that you pair with your choice of "setups," a structure more suited to a country-club restaurant than a Silver Lake spot. Pass on those in favor of the good salads, pastas and burger. Reservoir hasn't yet lived up to its potential, but we're hopeful that it's moving in the right direction. **WHO** Silver Lakers who might still be pining for Netty's. ♥☼

[Rivera] **1050 S. Flower St., South Park/Fashion District, 213.749.1460, riverarestaurant.com. L Mon.-Sat., D nightly (to midnight Thurs.-Sat.). Latino/modern American. Full bar. AE, MC, V. $$$ - $$$$ WHY** For the inventive (if pricey) cocktails, the suave Staples-convenient setting and some pretty wonderful flavors. **WHAT** We're mixed about this swank new South Park spot, where '80s wünderchef John Sedlar has resurfaced — on the one hand, it's a sophisticated space with a good bar and some very good cooking. On the other hand, the portions are wee, and there's a pretentiousness to Sedlar's style, most visually evident in his spice stencils. If you come, try the ahi ceviche, the Basque lamb chops, the Kurobuta pork chop in mole, and the Donjai (basically a pomegranate margarita), but feel free to skip dessert. **WHO** Expense-account studs on a tequila-tasting adventure. ☉

[Suehiro Café] **337 E. 1st St., Little Tokyo/Arts District, 213.626.9132. L & D daily to 1 a.m. (to 3 a.m. Fri.-Sun.). Japanese. Beer & wine. MC, V. $ - $$ WHY** For good, inexpensive Japanese comfort food, especially udon, served late into the night. **WHAT** A Little Tokyo icon, Suehiro is a simple, affordable café that serves satisfying udon noodle soups, cold soba noodle dishes, bento-box meals and katsudon bowls. Extras include friendly service and a library of Japanese fashion magazines and manga. **WHO** City Hall and *L.A. Times* people at lunch, MOCA visitors on weekends and, late at night, people refueling after making the Downtown bar scene. ☺ ▦ ☺

[Sushi Go 55] **333 S. Alameda St., 3rd Fl., Little Tokyo/Arts District, 213.687.0777, sushigo55.com. L & D daily. Japanese/sushi. Beer, wine & sake. AE, MC, V. $$$ WHY** High-quality, old-school sushi that's a bargain at lunch — the $10 special gets you miso soup, five pieces of sushi and a blue-crab hand roll; many regulars opt for the chirashi sushi box for $15. **WHAT** Owned by a pioneering family who started the second sushi bar in America and has been running restaurants in Little Tokyo for six decades, Sushi Go 55 is profoundly traditional — this is not a rock 'n roll sushi joint. Chefs are focused and quiet, the shopping-center setting is conventional, and the emphasis is on very fresh food. Reasonable prices, by sushi standards. **WHO** A primarily Asian crowd at lunchtime and a more diverse mix at night. ▦

[Teresitas] ▦ **3826 E. 1st St., East L.A., 323.266.6045, teresitasrestaurant.com. B Sat.-Sun., L Tues.-Sun., D Tues.-Sat. Mexican. Beer & wine. MC, V. $ - $$ WHY** Wonderful, traditional Mexican cooking: goat stew on weekends and always-good daily specials, like albondigas on Monday, pork ribs in chile negro sauce on Wednesdays and pozole on Fridays. **WHAT** This East L.A. landmark family restaurant serves simple, very good home cooking. Weekend breakfasts are worth rolling out of bed for. **WHO** Politicians and police officers. ▦ ☺

[Tiara Café] ▦ **127 E. 9th St., South Park/Fashion District, 213.623.3663, tiara-cafe-la.com. B & L daily, D Wed.-Sun., brunch Sat.-Sun. Modern American. Beer & wine. AE, MC, V. $ - $$$ WHY** Panache, casual glamour and great food at modest prices — notable are the vegan/vegetarian dishes and Downtown's best pizza. There's also a small gourmet-to-go/market section. **WHAT** Owner/chef Fred Eric (Fred 62) has always known what a certain sort of stylish Angeleno wants to eat, and he's hit the nail on the head here: fab pizzas, lovely salads, great vegan dishes and worthwhile desserts, all as organic, healthful and sustainably produced as possible. The setting suits the Fashion District: massive columns, pink walls studded with huge fake jewels, and a gregarious and campy (think: men who evoke pirates) staff. **WHO** A mob of fashion industry folks by day, and quiet tables of artists and loft people by night. ▦ ☺ ▨

[Traxx] **Union Station, 800 N. Alameda St., Downtown, 213.625.1999, traxxrestaurant.com. L Mon.-Fri., D Mon.-Sat. Modern American. Full bar. AE, MC, V. $$$ WHY** To eat a good meal in the splendor of L.A.'s Union Station. **WHAT** Chef/owner Tara Thomas serves a concise,

---

▨ **VEGETARIAN** ☺ **KID FRIENDLY** ☼ **PATIO DINING** ☷ **DELIVERY** ▦ **PRIVATE PARTY**

appealing menu of modern American dishes (with Asian and Latino influences) in a great-looking streamline moderne dining room or out on the "patio" under the painted beams of Union Station. The separate bar is one of L.A.'s best-kept bar secrets — atmospheric and generally uncrowded. **WHO** Business lunchers, upscale train travelers and couples enjoying the romance of Union Station. ♥ ⏾ ☼

[Viet Noodle Bar] 3133 1/2 Glendale Blvd., Atwater, 323.906.1575. L & D daily. Vietnamese. BYOB. Cash only. $ **WHY** A hip scene with respectable noodles and a fun communal table for solo diners. **WHAT** This minimalist modern setting offers communal tables (for groups and singles) and a shelf of intellectual tomes to peruse while eating. The menu's also minimalist, with vegetarian and fish noodle dishes hailing from southern Vietnam, Vietnamese coffee and restorative pennywort juice. **WHO** The coolest of the cool kids. ▧

[Warung Café] 118 W. 4th St., Downtown, 213.626.0662, warung-cafela.com. L Mon.-Fri., D Mon.-Sat. Asian. Beer, wine & sake. AE, MC, V. $$ - $$$ **WHY** Pretty, carefully composed Asian-fusion dishes served in a serene space. **WHAT** This chic little spot looks like it belongs on Abbot Kinney in Venice, but instead it's in a Downtown neighborhood that needs more such moderately priced bistros. Nothing is remarkable, but the small plates — Asian pork ribs, grilled chicken tandoori, asparagus-crab salad, cold ramen in a tangy peanut sauce — are just the thing for informal business lunches and happy-hour snacking, and they take out well for office lunch meetings. **WHO** Women in power suits and the men who lunch with them. ☉ ♻ ▧ 🚗

[Water Grill] 🏛 544 S. Grand Ave., Downtown, 213.891.0900, water-grill.com. L Mon.-Fri., D nightly. Seafood/modern American. Full bar. AE, MC, V. $$$$ - $$$$$ **WHY** For A-list service, a beautiful setting and elegant, thoughtfully prepared seafood. Splurge on the chilled seafood platter if you can afford it. **WHAT** Original star chef Michael Cimarusti has moved on to his own place, Providence, and although the Water Grill's cooking no longer has foodies in New York buzzing, it's still very, very good. David LeFevre makes things like striped-bass ceviche with mint, pineapple, candied black beans, butternut squash and achiote oil, or the slightly less complicated seared wild big-eye tuna with beluga lentils and pear-celery root purée. His talent with flavors, along with the high-quality ingredients, swank interior and excellent service, make the prices less painful than they otherwise might be. **WHO** Downtown's movers and shakers wearing good suits and carrying well-fed Platinum cards. ♥ ⏾ 🏛

[Wood Spoon] 107 W. 9th St., South Park/Fashion District, 213.629.1765. L Mon.-Sat., D Tues.-Sat. Brazilian. BYOB. MC, V. $ - $$ **WHY** For a short, delicious menu of Brazilian dishes, including a fabulous (and massive) chicken pot pie made with hearts of palm, corn, roasted potatoes and olives. **WHAT** The bright, minimalist space in the heart of the fashion district is warmed with yellow flowers, the rich flavors of Brazil and the presence of the owner/chef, an engaging woman who makes a mean pot pie, an addictive pork burger and great sweet potato fries. New bonus: delivery Downtown. **WHO** Fashion-industry workers at lunch, loft-dwellers at dinner. 🖭 🚐

[Yang Chow] 🏠 819 N. Broadway, Chinatown, 213.625.0811, yangchow.com. L & D daily. Chinese. Beer & wine. AE, MC, V. $ - $$ **WHY** It may be Chinese food designed for white people, but it's still seriously tasty, and for many people, addictive. **WHAT** Two simple rooms are permanently packed with regulars who have been coming here for 20 years and always order the same things: sweet-spicy slippery shrimp, hefty pan-fried dumplings, dried-fried string beans with pork, and cashew-rich cashew chicken. This is not diet food — it's the sort of place you take Grandpa for his birthday, and he has to loosen his belt buckle afterwards. **WHO** Always jammed with noisy tables of Downtown businesspeople, Dodgers-bound friends and big family groups celebrating birthdays. Don't come without a reservation. 🕲

[Yxta Cocina Mexicana] 601 S. Central Ave., Downtown, 213.596.5579, yxta.net. L Mon.-Fri., D Mon.-Sat. Mexican. Full bar. AE, MC, V. $$ - $$$ **WHY** For 40 years, Jesse Gomez's family has been turning out "careful-the-plate-is-hot" Mexican food at El Arco Iris, an old-school hub of Highland Park life. Now Gomez has created a new-school, loft-like place serving regional Mexican dishes, as well as 20-some tequilas and what may well be the best margarita Downtown. **WHAT** This is not Jesse's father's Cal-Mex cooking — the reasonably priced menu is filled with things like squash blossoms with Oaxacan cheese, an artfully composed and delicious tostada with sashimi-grade ahi, and camarones with garlic and cilantro-lime rice. But it also has the comfort-food standards we Angelenos sometimes require to make it through another day: enchiladas suizas, carnitas (juicy and tender) and, of course, tacos and sopes of various stripes. **WHO** Youngish after-work folks drinking margaritas and sharing tastes of the food.

[Zucca] 801 S. Figueroa St., Downtown, 213.614.7800, patinagroup. com. L Mon.-Fri., D nightly. Italian. Full bar. AE, MC, V. $$$ - $$$$ **WHY** A terrific happy hour and a fantastic room aglow with wood-work, Murano chandeliers, mirrors and frescoes. The free shuttle to the Music Center is a plus, too. **WHAT** Generally reliable Italian classics are served in what may be the most beautiful restaurant Downtown, part of Joachim Splichal's Patina-based family. Locals skip the dinner and come for the excellent happy hour, with free pizza and affordable mini-dishes. Great for pre-theater. **WHO** Downtown executives, theater-goers and, increasingly, residents. ♥🖭🏠

🥬 VEGETARIAN 🕲 KID FRIENDLY 🌣 PATIO DINING 🚐 DELIVERY 🏠 PRIVATE PARTY

SAN GABRIEL VALLEY

[888 Seafood] 8450 E. Valley Blvd., Rowland Heights, 626.573.1888. L & D daily. Chinese/dim sum/seafood. Full bar. AE, MC, V. $ - $$$ WHY High-quality Chiu Chow dim sum, and lots of it. Don't miss the taro and the exceptionally juicy sui mai. **WHAT** This vast and grand restaurant is famed for the incredible range of its dim sum — 60 choices most weekdays and 80 on weekends — and its Chiu Chow expertise also extends to dishes like the whole perch poached in broth and a succulent braised goose. ☺ 👜

[Arroyo Chop House] 536 S. Arroyo Pkwy., Pasadena, 626.577.7463, arroyochophouse.com. D nightly. American/steakhouse. Full bar. AE, MC, V. $$$$ - $$$$$ WHY New York strip, spinach with caramelized sweet onions, well-mixed drinks, and, for those who are splurging, chocolate soufflé. **WHAT** The setting is retro-modern — rich mahogany, white linens, etched glass, Craftsman-influenced light fixtures — and the fare is reliable comfort food for the captains-of-industry set. Prime steak and chops are a specialty, along with simple and carefully prepared sides (asparagus, garlic mashed potatoes). **WHO** Well-dressed, Jaguar-driving professionals. ♥ 🍸 👜

[Azeen's Afghani Restaurant] 110 E. Union St., Old Pasadena, 626.683.3310, azeensafghanirestaurant.com. L Mon.-Fri., D nightly. Afghani. Beer & wine. MC, V. $ - $$$ WHY A fascinating cuisine; squint at the menu and you'll recognize derivatives (or ancestors) of such Indian, Pakistani, Persian and Chinese dishes as pakoras, curries, dumplings and pilafs. **WHAT** Azeen's is an elegant, white-tablecloth restaurant tucked away on a fairly quiet block of bustling Old Pasadena. Share a sampler plate of appetizers followed by tender beef kebabs or *quabili pallaw* (lamb with carrots and raisins.) Sweet, translucent butternut squash (*kadu*) is a delicious side. 🍸

[Babita Mexicuisine] 🏠 **1823 S. San Gabriel Blvd., San Gabriel, 626.288.7265. L Tues.-Fri., D Tues.-Sun. Mexican. Beer & wine. AE, MC, V. $$ - $$$ WHY** Great Oaxacan food from a serious and attentive chef. **WHAT** It looks like a dive from the outside, but inside it's inviting and charming — the perfect setting for owner/chef Roberto Berrelleza's outstanding regional Mexican cooking with an Oaxacan focus. The standouts include seriously good Yucatecan cochinita pibil, filet mignon with pimiento-mint sauce, and habañero-blazed camarones topolobampo. The food can be slow to appear, but that's because of Berrelleza's personal attention to each dish. The flan just might be the best anywhere. **WHO** Some people drive across town just for the chiles en nogada — a fall-only pork specialty. 🍸

[Bamboodles] 535 W. Valley Blvd., San Gabriel, 626.281.1226, bamboodlesrestaurant.com. L & D daily. Chinese/noodles. No booze. MC, V. $ WHY The pleasure of the food coupled with the fun of watching the noodle master hopping on a wooden platform while holding a huge dough-draped bamboo pole in a fairly suggestive manner, using gravity to work the dough. **WHAT** This strip-mall café revolves around bamboo, both in the handsome décor and the cannon-thick hunk of bamboo used by the noodle maker. The resulting noodles are delicate and light, but not so remarkable that they seem worth all that effort. What makes this outpost of a small China-based chain worth the trip are the flavors surrounding the doughy products, from the juicy perfection of the celery and pork steamed dumplings to the robustness of the long-cooked beef soup noodle, marred only by a high fat-to-meat ratio (but then again, that's why it tastes so good).

[Bashan] **3459 N. Verdugo Rd., Montrose, 818.541.1532, bashanrestaurant.com. D Tues.-Sun. French/modern American. Beer & wine. AE, MC, V. $$$$ WHY** Burrata and bresaola salad, braised pork belly with cranberry beans, and the tasting menus. **WHAT** Chef Nadav Bashan (Providence, Michael's, the Lobster) and his wife, Romy, have created a welcoming, modern eatery serving exceptionally refined cuisine that is at the level of the best restaurants in Los Angeles — yet it's far from the *Entourage* crowd, on a leafy street in a north Glendale suburb. It's not cheap, but you'd pay more for food this good in Santa Monica. **WHO** Food lovers who can't believe a place of this quality exists on Verdugo in Montrose.

[Basil Thai] **411 E. Huntington Dr., Monrovia, 626.447.8845. L Mon.-Fri, D Mon.-Sat. Thai. Beer & wine. MC, V. $ - $$ WHY** A rare family-owned café in the heart of chainland, serving tasty and healthy Thai food. **WHAT** Not only is this stylish little strip-mall café a friendly family operation (husband Poki cooks, wife Nina serves, and their teenage son helps out), but it's a great value — both the regular menu and the $6.95 lunch buffet. Poki's cooking is several notches above the suburban strip-mall standard — vegetables are crisp and fresh, flavors are skillfully balanced, and chiles are used for flavor, not just to make your face sweat. Try the *tom yum* (spicy-sour) soup with shrimp, the stir-fried chicken with cashews and onion, the *yum pla muek* (a vibrant salad of fresh greens, grilled squid, lime and chile) and any of the rice noodle dishes. 🍽🦐☺

[Bistro 45] **45 S. Mentor Ave., Pasadena, 626.795.2478, bistro45. com. L Tues.-Thurs., D Tues.-Sun. French/modern American. Full bar. AE, MC, V. $$$ - $$$$$ WHY** Exemplary wine list; creative and confident cooking. **WHAT** This is certainly a contender for the title of Best Upscale Restaurant in the San Gabriel Valley, with a livelier buzz and (just slightly) lower prices than some others. The patio's the place for lunch; for dinner, the suavely modern dining rooms beckon. Stand-outs include the superb bouillabaisse and the grilled beef tenderloin. There's usually a bread pudding on the dessert menu, and you should order it. **WHO** Pasadena's beautiful people. ♥ 🕐 ☼🏛

🍃VEGETARIAN ☺KID FRIENDLY ☼PATIO DINING 🚐DELIVERY 🏛PRIVATE PARTY

[Bistro de la Gare] 921 Meridian Ave., South Pasadena, 626.799.8828, bistrodelagare.com. L & D Wed.-Sun., Brunch Sat.-Sun. French. Beer & wine. AE, MC, V. $$ - $$$ **WHY** Great setting in a lively neighborhood, steps from the Gold Line station that inspired its name. **WHAT** This lovely red-walled space features a traditional French bistro menu and charm galore. Service can be slapdash and the kitchen uneven but the crowds of spirited locals packing the small bar and dining rooms don't seem to mind. **WHO** Well-dressed locals, farmers' market foodies and Francophiles. ☼

[Briganti] 1423 Mission St., South Pasadena, 626.441.4663, brigantisouthpas.com. L Mon.-Fri., D nightly. Italian. Beer & wine. AE, MC, V. $$ - $$$ **WHY** Seafood salad, burrata with pesto and roasted tomatoes, ethereal thin-crust pizzas, classic pastas, excellent fresh-fish specials. **WHAT** Briganti is the sort of lively Tuscan trattoria that's common on the westside but rare on the eastside, and South Pasadenans can't get enough of it. The joint is always jumping, with noise bouncing off the brick walls of the enclosed patio (ask for a table in the main room if you want a quieter conversation). Be warned that the service can be slow and distracted. **WHO** An over-40 crowd from Pasadena, South Pas and San Marino, many of whom know each other from Junior League or Little League. ☼

[Café Bizou] 91 N. Raymond Ave., Old Pasadena, 626.792.9923, cafebizou.com. L Wed.-Fri., D nightly, brunch Sat.-Sun. Modern American/ French. Full bar. AE, MC, V. $$ - $$$ **WHY** Monkfish on saffron-shrimp risotto with a lobster sauce. Need we say more? **WHAT** Upscale style + moderate prices = busy restaurant. This Old Pasadena bistro draws a crowd with all entrees priced at less than $20. And $1 more buys salad or soup (try the carrot-rosemary) with any main course. It's nothing exciting, but the roast chicken with fries, seafood with black tagliolini, and pepper steak are satisfying. ♥ ▧

[Café Spot] 500 W. Valley Blvd., Alhambra, 626.308.3233. L & D daily. Chinese/coffee shop. Beer & wine. MC, V. $ **WHY** A spirited scene, plus lots to choose from on the long menu. **WHAT** One of the San Gabriel Valley's many Hong Kong–style coffee shops, Café Spot stands out for the quality of its food. This is the place to go for dishes like Grand Mom's braised pork belly and the Hong Kong–style waffle. ▧

[Carousel] 304 N. Brand Blvd., Glendale, 818.246.7775, carouselrestaurant.com. L & D Tues.-Sun. Lebanese/Middle Eastern. Full Bar. AE, MC, V. $$ - $$$ **WHY** Lebanese *mezzas* (small plates) galore, including creamy hummus, spicy muhammara, fattoush salad and frogs' legs with lemon and garlic. Plus, it's just steps from the Alex Theatre. **WHAT** Delicious food, speedy service and an attractive décor make Carousel one of Brand Boulevard's most reliable and rewarding dining options. Don't miss the *fatteh oberjhin* (toasted pita and eggplant appetizer) and the many versions of *kebbeh*, Lebanese steak tartare. For main courses, there are succulent grilled kebabs (*lula* is excellent) and schwarma. Late on Friday and Saturday evenings, the place jumps to live music and belly dancing with a prix-fixe dinner menu. **WHO** Local Lebanese families and a pre-theater crowd. ☺

[Celestino] 🏛 141 S. Lake Ave., Pasadena, 626.795.4006, calogerodra-go.com. L Mon.-Fri., D Mon.-Sat. Italian. Full bar. AE, MC, V. $$ - $$$$ **WHY** Terrific pastas in a convivial but not chaotic setting. **WHAT** The San Gabriel Valley's most consistently excellent Italian restaurant, combining warm service, a serious wine list and downright delicious food. Don't miss the baby lettuces with roasted peppers, eggplant and goat cheese; the black and white tagliolini with scallops and saffron sauce; and the whole grilled branzino. **WHO** Madison Heights neighbors running into each other. ☼ 🎵 🏛

[Central Park] 219 S. Fair Oaks Ave., Pasadena, 626.449.4499, centralparkrestaurant.net. B, L & D daily. American. Beer & wine. AE, MC, V. $$ - $$$ **WHY** A convenient, moderately priced café just south of the Old Town madness — with free parking! **WHAT** Part of a small local chain that also owns Wild Thyme, Central Park feels generic, and yet it fits the bill in many ways. The short-rib hash, Thai beef salad, pizzas and brick-flattened chicken are of the moment and actually quite satisfying — think a better-value Smitty's. **WHO** Writers and the self-employed for breakfast, business people for lunch, seniors for the early-bird bargain dinner menu, and families for a nice after-soccer meal. 🎵 🚚 🛋 ☺

[Chang's Garden] 🏛 627 W. Duarte Rd., Arcadia, 626.445.0606. L & D daily. Chinese/Shanghai. Beer & wine. MC, V. $$ **WHY** Eat like a Shanghai connoisseur, starting with wonderful lotus-leaf-wrapped pork ribs. **WHAT** Chef Henry Chang's cooking represents both the ethereal and earthy sides of Shanghainese food. The shrimp sautéed with Dragon Well tea has the fresh tastes of spring, and his delicate Westlake soup of shredded yellowfish in a pale broth captures the essence of fresh fish. Opposite in style and flavor are the savory caramel-sauced clay pot chicken smothered in roasted chestnuts and a dish called Famous Poet Su Tung Po's Pork, a book-size rectangle of ultra-slow, red-cooked pork belly. A fold-out Chinese-only portion of the menu lists regional dishes made famous at Louwailou, a renowned Hangzhou restaurant that dates back to the 1840s. ☼

[Chung King] 1000 S. San Gabriel Blvd., San Gabriel, 626.286.0298. L & D daily. Chinese/Sichuan. Beer. Cash only. $ **WHY** Hot, hot, hot — just like back in Sichuan province. **WHAT** This plain little café sizzles with exceptionally fiery dishes. Go for the Sichuan standards: beef hot pots, Chinese bacon with leeks, spareribs with Sichuan peppercorns, fried chicken with hot peppers. A little less spicy but still delicious are

🌿 VEGETARIAN ☺ KID FRIENDLY ☼ PATIO DINING 🚚 DELIVERY 🛋 PRIVATE PARTY the dry-fried soybeans and the fried potato shreds. Cool down like a Sichuan native with a few of the cold dishes from the buffet. 🗟

[Cook's Tortas] 🔒 1944 S. Atlantic Blvd., Monterey Park, 323.278.3536, cookstortas.com. B, L & D Mon.-Sat., brunch/lunch Sun. Mexican. No booze. AE, MC, V. $ **WHY** For a totally different take on the ubiquitous Mexican sandwich, served in a minimalist, casually stylish café. **WHAT** Cook's — which takes its name from the discoverer of the Sandwich Islands — takes sandwiches to a new plane with soft, house-baked rolls and a rotating menu selected from hundreds of filling choices. Traditional tortas like the fiery ahogada are executed with more flair than the corner torta shops, while original varieties like *bacalao* (Spanish cod and garlic), chicken mole verde and pork mojito create a fiesta of flavors. Refreshing aguas frescas in a rainbow of fruit flavors and imaginative sides and baked goods are also standouts. **WHO** Students from nearby East L.A. City College and culinary explorers from all over L.A. 🗟 ☺

[Daisy Mint] 1218 E. Colorado Blvd., Pasadena, 626.792.2999, daisymint.com. L & D daily. Asian. BYOB (no corkage). AE, MC, V. $$ **WHY** Brightly flavored and affordable Korean-Thai-Chinese dishes, from addictive Shanghai-style soup dumplings and Thai noodle dishes to savory Korean rib-eye. **WHAT** This modern mom-and-pop — he's Korean and she's Thai — is decorated with empty flea-market frames and vintage chandeliers, and it's filled to the brim with the kind of people you'd see shopping for those exact same items at the Rose Bowl swap meet. Wine lovers adore the no-corkage policy (a license has been pending for ages), and everyone likes the family-style Asian-fusion dishes to share. **WHO** A hip Pasadena crowd from Art Center, the Playhouse, PCC and Caltech. 🗟 🥢 ☺ ✿

[Derek's Bistro] 181 E. Glenarm Ave., Pasadena, 626.799.5252, dickensonwest.com. D Tues.-Sat. Modern American. Full bar. AE, MC, V. $$$ - $$$$$ **WHY** Luxe food in a romantic setting, plus a swell private room for a dinner party. Excellent wine list. **WHAT** Hidden in a strip mall, this is Pasadena's swank secret. Irish-born Derek Dickenson knows what his upscale clientele craves, and he delivers the goods: seared foie gras with a kumquat marmalade; beef Wellington; wild salmon with lentils, bacon and a mustard beurre blanc. Intimate nooks and lovely flowers and table settings make this one of the most romantic restaurants in town. **WHO** Well-heeled oenophiles. ♥ 🍷 🏛

[Din Tai Fung] 🔒 1108 S. Baldwin Ave., Arcadia, 626.574.7068, dintaifungusa.com. L & D daily. Chinese/dumplings. No booze. AE, MC, V. $ **WHY** Drop-dead amazing dumplings. **WHAT** Be prepared to wait in line, but don't expect to mind the minute you bite into your first dumpling. (That said, nothing is worth a 90-minute wait, so try to come outside of prime hours, when the wait might be just 20 minutes.)

This American branch of a Taipei dumpling house is famed for its Shanghai-style soup dumplings, whose mix of broth, pork and crab explodes in your mouth. But all the dumplings, from the vegetarian to the shrimp-and-pork sui mai, are dreamy. **WHO** A never-ending stream of Angelenos from every walk of life. 📷🗽☺

[The Dining Room] 1401 S. Oak Knoll Ave., Pasadena, 626.585.6218, pasadena.langhamhotels.com. D. Tues.-Sat. Modern American. Full bar. AE, MC, V. $$$$$ **WHY** Luxury — from the amuse-bouches to the chilled glasses of Champagne and the light from the crystal chandeliers. **WHAT** Chef Craig Strong put this luxe hotel dining room on L.A.'s culinary map, and when he departed for Laguna Beach in 2009 it caused Pasadena's deep-pocket gourmands to worry that the food might slip back to hotel-boring. Their fears were allayed when *Top Chef* candidate Michael Voltaggio, ex of José Andrés's Bazaar, took over — his food is anything but boring, full of boundary-pushing partnerships, foam-style sauces and touches of molecular gastronomy. We found it more intellectual than good in its early days, and service has been sub-par; we're holding out hope that Voltaggio and team hit their stride soon. **WHO** Upstanding upper-middle-class folks with something to celebrate. ♥ 🍷 🎩

[Duck House] 🏛 501 S. Atlantic Blvd., Monterey Park, 626.284.3227, pearlcatering.com. L & D daily. Chinese/Beijing. Beer & wine. MC, V. $$ **WHY** One word: Duck. **WHAT** Recently relocated to somewhat grander digs in Monterey Park, the former Lu Din Gee appears to be the only truly authentic Beijing duck restaurant in L.A. There are lots of good things to order (scallion pancakes, beef with garlic, the mountain yam jelly called *konnyaku*) but it's really all about the three-course duck dinner, a great feast to share with friends. It starts with a platter of crisp, salty-sweet skin and moist meat to wrap in pancakes with a bit of scallion and a smear of hoisin, then proceeds to stir-fried duck with bean sprouts and concludes with an aromatic and wonderful duck soup. Note that you must call at least an hour ahead to order your duck. **WHO** Lots of birthday-party and other celebratory groups. 📷☺

[Elena's Greek-Armenian Cuisine] 1000 S. Glendale Blvd., Glendale, 818.241.5730, elenasgreek.com. L & D Mon.-Sat. Armenian/Greek. No booze. AE, MC, V. $ - $$ **WHY** Terrific homemade stuffed grape leaves, gyros and kebabs for cheap. **WHAT** How can a tiny restaurant in an out-of-the-way Glendale location with no parking thrive for more than three decades? By offering satisfying, tasty food at unbelievably low prices. We are addicted to Elena's version of stuffed grape leaves, but occasionally fall off the wagon to indulge in the generous gyros or shish kebab platters. You really have to work hard to spend more than $15 per person. At these prices, don't expect a fancy décor — the dining room is basically a patio enclosed with canvas and clear plastic. **WHO** Budget-conscious folks who love to eat. 📷☺

🌿VEGETARIAN ☺KID FRIENDLY ☼PATIO DINING 🚗DELIVERY 🎩PRIVATE PARTY

[Elite] 🏛 700 S. Atlantic Blvd., Monterey Park, 626.282.9998, elitechinerestaurant.com. B, L & D daily. Chinese/Cantonese/dim sum. Beer & wine. MC, V. $ - $$ **WHY** The best dim sum in town, and a superb Cantonese dinner menu, too. **WHAT** L.A.'s reigning dim sum house eschews the rolling carts in favor of a large menu of beautiful dumplings and small dishes: deep-fried peanut and sesame cake, flawless sui mai, Macau roasted pork, Macau egg custard pies and many more. The shame is that so many of its dim sum fans never think to return for dinner, when attentive waiters deliver such wonderful things as roast squab, seafood soup with bitter melon and ham, steamed live prawns, and Maine lobster with butter, black pepper, garlic and ginger. **WHO** A crowd of devoted fans, especially for dim sum on weekends. 🏛

[Firefly Bistro] 1009 El Centro St., South Pasadena, 626.441.2443, eatatfirefly.com. L Tues.-Fri., D Tues.-Sun., brunch Sat.-Sun. Modern American. Beer & wine. AE, MC, V. $$ - $$$$ **WHY** Hip and friendly, with a sangria and tapas menu on Thursdays, when the bustling local farmers' market comes to life outside its door. **WHAT** This tented bistro is bright by day and romantic at night, with an interesting and usually wonderful menu of multi-ethnic offerings, from red chile vegetable egg rolls to warm spinach salad, grilled pork chop with bacon-wrapped asparagus to famed shrimp and grits. The lunchtime salads are excellent, and the wine list is creative and affordable. ♥ ☼ 🏛

[Gale's Restaurant] 452 S. Fair Oaks Ave., Pasadena, 626.432.6705, galesrestaurant.com. L Tues.-Sat., D Tues.-Sun. Italian. Full bar. AE, MC, V. $$ - $$$$ **WHY** You get to drink your wine out of silver-encrusted goblets from Brighton Collectibles (which belongs to Gale's fabulously successful brother). **WHAT** Run by hometown girl Gale Kohl and her husband, Rene Chila, Gale's features a talented Italian chef, warm atmosphere and professional staff. Favorite dishes include mussels with white wine and garlic, caprese salad, Caesar salad and rosemary lamb chops. But for the best eating, check out the specials menu; the lunchtime salads are particularly excellent. **WHO** Pasadena's connected people: politicians, volunteers, community leaders.

[Giang Nan] 306 N. Garfield Ave., Monterey Park, 626.573.3421. L & D daily. Chinese/Shanghai. BYOB. MC, V. $$ **WHY** Skinny fried eel with shrimp are crunchy and addictive, and the braised pork knuckle is among the best in town. **WHAT** China may have had its Cultural Revolution, but dignitaries always seemed to eat beautifully at the Jin Nan Guest House in Shanghai, where, before the mid-'90s wave of high-end restaurants, chef Hongwei Kong worked the stoves. Now Kong is at this modest restaurant, nearly invisible at the back of a large mini-mall. And while most dishes are casually served, the occasional stylish presentation hints at the chef's past and reveals his skill, as with the fingers of yellowfish in their airy tempura-like coating seasoned with salty crumbled seaweed, a dish that melts like cotton candy on the tongue. **WHO** Homesick Shanghainese flock to the restaurant for the marinated crab appetizer and the comforting, soupy fish-head casserole afloat with slippery, wide rice noodles. ⬛

[Golden Deli] 815 W. Las Tunas Dr., San Gabriel, 626.308.0803, goldendelirestaurant.com. L & D Mon.-Tues. & Thurs.-Sun. Vietnamese. No booze. Cash only. $ - $$ **WHY** The fresh, light banh mi sandwiches and those fabulously crisp spring rolls. **WHAT** This no-frills diner packs 'em in with appealing and cheap Vietnamese food: oniony pho, shrimp paste on sugar cane, myriad noodle dishes and justly popular spring rolls accompanied by a fragrant heap of fresh green herbs. Also consider the related and new Vietnam Restaurant down the street. ⬛ ☺

[Green Street Tavern] 69 W. Green St., Old Pasadena, 626.229.9961, greenstreettavern.net. L Mon.-Fri., D nightly, brunch Sat.-Sun. Modern American. Beer & wine. AE, MC, V. $$$ - $$$$ **WHY** A pretty little restaurant off the Old Town chain highway, with personality and good Cal-Med-fusion cooking. **WHAT** Not to be confused with Green Street Restaurant, this cozy, upscale little boîte is sculpted with art nouveau curves and holds just a couple of booths, a few tables and a small backlit bar, which pours a good selection of wines and beers. Service is attentive, ingredients are quality (often organic and/or local), and the cooking is accomplished. It can get noisy at peak hours, so sit on the sidewalk terrace if the weather's nice. **WHO** Pasadena date-nighters in on the secret. ♥ ☼

[Green Village Shanghai] ⬛ 1390 Fullerton Rd., Rowland Heights, 626.810.5698. L & D daily. Chinese/Shanghai. Beer & wine. MC, V. $$ **WHY** The lightness of the dishes and the many fish offerings are what set the place apart, but sybarites will be happy to learn it serves (under the name "braised pork knuckle") what was once famously known as Pork Pump, the foie gras-like, long-stewed pork joint made popular at the now-declining Lake Spring. **WHAT** Shanghai's reputation for exquisite food gave the city its nickname "Heaven on Earth," and this disciplined cooking shows us why. Try the cold appetizers: Zhen Jiang jellied cured pork, with a dipping sauce of dark vinegar (the Chinese answer to head cheese or jambon persillé) or super-fragrant, wine-marinated "special flavored" crab. This kitchen demonstrates the underacknowledged virtues of eel with more than half a dozen preparations, including Wuxi crispy eels and eel-paste-flavored sautéed leeks. There are such rarities as hairy crab, and sea cucumber with shrimp eggs, alongside such homey dishes as ten-ingredient pan-fried noodles. **WHO** Devout fans who have followed this place as it moved to a seemingly endless series of locations.

[Gus's BBQ] 808 Fair Oaks Ave., South Pasadena, 626.799.3251, gussbbq.com. L & D daily. Barbecue/Southern. Full bar. AE, MC, V. $$ - $$$ **WHY** The sons of the guy who owns the original Tops learned well at their daddy's knee: Focus on good, unfussy food that makes people, if not their cardiologists, happy. So you get tasty dry-rub ribs, sweet baked beans, salty and rich pulled pork and fresh Southern greens. **WHAT** For years people came here just for the 1940s neon sign outside, and now that it's under new management, Gus's is actually worth visiting. It's great looking, with dark-wood floors, an old-school diner kitchen, padded booths and a proper bar (rare in South Pas). Nothing is mind-blowing, and it's on the pricey side (especially for lunch), but the Southern classics are consistently good, homey and satisfying. **WHO** Local business folks, grandparents taking the grandkids out for dinner and old-time South Pasadenans. ☺ 👜

[Happy Sheep] 227 W. Valley Blvd., San Gabriel, 626.457.5599. L & D daily. Chinese/dumplings/noodles. Beer & wine. MC, V. $ - $$ **WHY** Tasty, make-it-your-way hot-pot soups, low prices and a convivial, family-friendly vibe. **WHAT** A chain of hot-pot emporiums popular throughout Asia, this place specializes in a bubbling broth perfect for a foggy winter day. Order chile-red spicy broth or clear mild for the burner in the middle of the table, then check off a variety of soup additions such as meats, vegetables, tofu or noodles. Lamb dumplings and scallion pancakes make good side dishes to the main-attraction hot pots. **WHO** Large Chinese groups with soup-slurping toddlers. 📷 ☺

[Ho Ho Kitchen] 10053 Valley Blvd., El Monte, 626.442.6689. L & D Mon.-Tues. & Thurs.-Sun. Chinese/dumplings/noodles. No booze. Cash only. $ **WHY** Go for the tofu lovers' pièce de résistance: fine-cut tofu "noodles" dotted with ham shreds and shrimp in a rich-tasting translucent sauce. **WHAT** Ho Ho Kitchen is a charming hole-in-the-wall where you're greeted with Styrofoam plates, big smiles and little English but wonderful home-style cooking. *Xiao long bao*, or soup dumplings, although not on the menu, are usually available for the asking; they come with slivers of ginger and black vinegar for dipping. Tender "lion's-head" pork meatballs are also great. 📷 🔖 ☺

[Indo Kitchen] 5 N. 4th St., Alhambra, 626.282.1676, indokitchen-alhambra.com. L & D daily. Indonesian. No booze. MC, V. $ **WHY** Pretend you're voyaging through Indonesia and order the *nasi pecel leme*, deep-fried catfish with a dried shrimp-chile sambal. **WHAT** Indo Kitchen's *nasi campur* combination plates, which might include barbecued pork, chicken strips and a variety of garnishes, are some of the best bargains this side of Jakarta. They're also delicious, as are the *longtong cap goh me* (a creamy chicken curry over rice and green jackfruit) and the *nasi rames* plate featuring Sumatran beef curry. 📷

[J & J Restaurant] 301 Valley Blvd., San Gabriel, 626.308.9238. L & D daily. Chinese/Shanghai/noodles. No booze. Cash only. $ **WHY** Soup noodle dumplings, scallion pancakes, Shanghai fried noodles and other such comfort food. **WHAT** The mini-mall storefront offers a selection of traditional eastern Chinese breakfast items on the weekends and good and inexpensive noodle soups, dumplings and traditional northern and Shanghai dishes all the time. **WHO** Noodle and dumpling lovers on a budget who don't want to wait in Din Tai Fung's line.

[Japon Bistro] 927 E. Colorado Blvd., Pasadena, 626.744.1751, japonbistro-pasadena.com. L Mon.-Fri., D Tues.-Sun. Japanese. Beer & wine. MC, V. $$ - $$$ **WHY** A lively sushi bar, an engaged staff and very good Japanese food, including appealing vegetarian choices. **WHAT** Don't let the home-lettered signs and uninviting, tunnel-like space dissuade you from discovering this fine and eclectic Japanese spot. The knowledgeable young staff can't wait to introduce you to the live sea urchin, the sake collection and the terrific izakaya (salmon carpaccio, Hawaiian-style poke, beef kushiyaki). **WHO** Caltech foodies discussing nanotechnology and black holes.

[Java Spice] 1743 Fullerton Rd., Rowland Heights, 626.810.1366. L & D Tues.-Sun. Indonesian. No booze. MC, V. $ **WHY** The *nasi bungkus* is a magnificent meal, a picnic banquet swathed in fresh-cut banana leaf that looks something like a pregnant shoe box. Inside are chunks of coconut-infused chicken, smoldering chile-laced beef rendang, brightly spiced jackfruit curry, chunky fish cake, tofu nuggets and a blazing scarlet sambal-topped egg, all atop a rice plateau that soaks up the flavors. **WHAT** If you can't make it to this generic-looking strip-mall place on weekends for nasi bungkus, not to worry — the regular menu during the week is rich with aromatic, spicy-sweet Javanese classics, including the amazing fried chicken; shrimp and egg fried rice; elegant butter-sautéed frogs' legs with caramelized shallots; and beef rendang and rice disks floating on an amazing broth of coconut and chile. **WHO** Lively multi-generational Indonesian families fill the place on weekends for the nasi bungkus feasts.

[La Cabanita] 🏠 3447 N. Verdugo Rd., Montrose, 818.957.2711. B Sat.-Sun., L & D daily. Mexican. Full bar. AE, MC, V. $$ **WHY** Very good food, plus tasty (and strong) margaritas. **WHAT** La Cabanita is a cheerful neighborhood café offering superb food. After 20 years, we think it's as wonderful as ever, especially the beans, the green mole, the sopes compuestos, the new pork in chile verde, the mole enchiladas and the chicken soup. **WHO** Locals, plus salsa-to-go customers from Echo Park and beyond.

[La Caravana] 1306 N. Lake Ave., Pasadena, 626.791.7378. L & D daily. Salvadoran. No booze. MC, V. $ **WHY** This is the place to get your fill of pupusas and empanada-like meat-filled *pepitos*. **WHAT** Plush booths and Central American art and woodwork create a handsome setting for sampling hearty, tasty Salvadoran specialties like savory chicken sautéed with onions and potatoes.

🍃 VEGETARIAN ☺ KID FRIENDLY ☼ PATIO DINING 🚚 DELIVERY 🎩 PRIVATE PARTY

[La Grande Orange] 260 S. Raymond Ave., Pasadena, 626.356.4444, lgostationcafe.com. D nightly. Modern American. Full bar. AE, MC, V. $$ - $$$ **WHY** Although it's the kind of restaurant that MBAs create, Grande Orange is an undeniably winning place, especially the bar, the taco platters, the burgers and the excellent pizzas emerging from the brand-new wood-burning ovens. **WHAT** The owners of this newish spot in the handsomely restored 1925 Santa Fe Depot at Del Mar Station have thought of everything. Good-value happy hour? Check. Retro-hip mac 'n cheese? Check. Grilled ahi tacos? Check. It's got it all, from name-dropping martinis to a thoughtful kids' menu, so all of Pasadena is showing up. **WHO** Early-bird seniors on the patio, young families and middle-aged friends in the dining room and a lively, youngish, after-work crowd in the bar. 🗫 ☺ ☼

[La Vie] 2547 San Gabriel Blvd., Rosemead, 626.571.1180. D nightly. French. Beer & wine. AE, MC, V. $$ - $$$ **WHY** Carefully prepared classic French food at low prices. Make sure to order a soufflé for dessert. **WHAT** The chef may be Vietnamese, but he's not putting any lemongrass in his sauces — this is French cooking through and through, from duck à l'orange (much better than you might expect) to coq au vin. The place is hidden in a strip mall in a neighborhood best known for Chinese noodles, but that makes an outing here all the more fun. It's romantic in a somewhat hokey way, and it's a bargain in the best possible way — entrees are around $20 and come with very good soup, a butter lettuce salad, bread and good coffee. **WHO** Francophiles on a budget, some of whom drive a distance to eat here. ♥🗫 ᕫ

[Lunasia] 500 W. Main St., San Gabriel, 626.308.3222, lunasiachinesecuisine.com. L & D daily. Chinese/dim sum. Beer & wine. AE, MC, V. $$ **WHY** Well-crafted dim sum by day and well-executed Cantonese cooking by night, served in an attractive dining room for surprisingly modest prices. **WHAT** The dim sum gets more attention at this swank place on Alhambra's auto row, but we think the dinner is equally worthy. As is the trend now in your classier joints, dim sum is made to order, not served from wheeled carts, so it's fresher than the norm. But consider the dinner menu: whole, crisp-skinned Beijing duck served with fat pancakes, stir-fried prawns in tea sauce, fresh lobster with black pepper and butter (a bargain at $28), a first-rate kung pao chicken, delicious and vibrantly green pea shoot tips with garlic and, for groups of about ten, a celebratory whole roast suckling pig ($188). **WHO** Large, prosperous Chinese-American family groups. 🗫 ☺ 🛗

[Luscious Dumplings] 🏠 704 W. Las Tunas Dr., San Gabriel, 626.282.8695. L & D Tues.-Sat., brunch Sun. Chinese/dumplings. No booze. Cash only. $ **WHY** Pan-fried pork dumplings that will have you eating far more than propriety or good health demand. **WHAT** Given the amount of competition, particularly in this neighborhood, it takes a lot of chutzpah to call yourself "Luscious Dumplings," but this simple café's wares deserve the appellation. Each dumpling's covering sports a different decorative pleating that indicates its filling type. Steamed pork dumplings hold the requisite pool of interior broth to suck out before polishing off the rest. Empanada-shaped, golden fried dumplings balance chive, pork, egg and crunchy bits of dried shrimp; a bit of savory pork brings fish and napa cabbage together for an ethereal filling. Be warned: The early bird gets the dumpling — a line often forms when it opens, and the kitchen sometimes runs out of the popular ones. **WHO** Devotees who eat here as often as possible. 🗺️ 🕐

[Maison Akira] 713 E. Green St., Pasadena, 626.796.9501, maison-akira.com. L Fri., D Tues.-Sun., brunch Sun. French/Japanese. Beer & wine. AE, MC, V. $$$$ - $$$$$ **WHY** Chef Akira Hirose, who trained with Joel Robuchon and has cooked at Citrus and L'Orangerie, brings his particular brand of culinary artistry to the French-Japanese restaurant that bears his name. **WHAT** Picture a townhouse on the Upper East side of Manhattan and you'll have an idea of Maison Akira's décor. Its quiet opulence — in the dining room and on the menu — may lack flash but you'll eat as well here as you will anywhere. Simple yet dazzling main dishes include a grilled Chilean sea bass with a miso marinade and a rack of lamb with rosemary sauce and potato mousseline. The Sunday brunch is spectacular. **WHO** Pasadena Playhouse season-ticket holders. ♥ 🕐 🗺️ 🏠

[Malbec] 1001 E. Green St., Pasadena, 626.683.0550, malbeccuisine. com. L & D daily. Argentinean. Beer & wine. AE, MC, V. $$ - $$$ **WHY** Good, honest Argentinean cooking and wines at modest prices. **WHAT** The space that once held a deli now boasts good lighting and comfortable booths, as well as a collection of tasty and affordable Argentinean wines and a menu of well-prepared classics at more-than-reasonable prices: empanadas, *matambre* (rolled meat stuffed with vegetables and herbs), garlic fries, handmade pastas and such hearty entrees as grilled short ribs (great flavor but too chewy), skirt steak chimichurri (delicious) and grilled salmon. Hardly anyone has room for dessert. **WHO** Everyone who's anyone in Pasadena, often coming with friends, who then run into their friends… 🗺️

[Mandarin Noodle Deli] 9537 Las Tunas Dr., Temple City, 626.309.4318. L & D daily. Chinese/dumplings/noodles. No booze. Cash only. $ **WHY** Dumplings and noodles are the star attractions, while scallion pancakes and hot and sour soup are also winners. **WHAT** When a craving hits for Chinese comfort food, this busy coffee shop–like spot full of hungry families hits the mark. **WHO** Happy families slurping noodles. 🗺️ 🕐

[Mandarin Noodle House] 701 W. Garvey Ave., Monterey Park, 626.570.9795. L & D daily. Chinese/dumplings/noodles. No booze. Cash only. $ **WHY** Those "thin onion pancakes" — scallion-laced, layered

🌿 VEGETARIAN ⊙ KID FRIENDLY ✿ PATIO DINING � DELIVERY 🏠 PRIVATE PARTY

and crunchy, and the cha-jiang mien noodles. **WHAT** Come here for the food, not the ambience. You'll soon forget the harsh light and less-than-nurturing service when you start slurping a steaming bowl of Family Handmade Noodle Soup with hand-cut noodles and lots of other tasty stuff. The pan-fried dumplings and the pork or shrimp soup noodle are good, too. 📷☺

[Max's of Manila] 313 W. Broadway, Glendale, 818.637.7751, maxschicken.com. B Sat.-Sun., L & D daily. Filipino. Beer & wine. AE, MC, V. $ - $$ **WHY** The *chicharrón de pollo* (deep-fried chicken skin) sets the gold standard. **WHAT** Mildly seasoned chicken, fried whole to keep it juicy, is the house specialty at this branch of the Filipino chain. You can order it spicy, too, and the palm vinegar dip that accompanies both versions is garlic studded and terrific. 📷☺

[Mayumba] 3514 Rosemead Blvd., Rosemead, 626.572.9558. L & D Tues.-Sun. Cuban. Full bar. AE, MC, V. $$ - $$$ **WHY** The sandwich de cerdo with caramelized onions is mind-blowingly good. And there's dancing to a Cuban orchestra on weekends! **WHAT** It's got a lively weekend bar scene, a fine, buttoned-down dining room and all-around good Cuban cooking, but Mayumba's sandwiches — cubanos and media noches fueled by a terrific *lechón asado* steeped in a garlic/sour orange marinade — are a huge draw in their own right.

[Mei Long Village] 301 W. Valley Blvd., San Gabriel, 626.284.4769. L & D daily. Chinese/Shanghai/dumplings. Beer & wine. MC, V. $ - $$ **WHY** Go for the Shanghai-style dumplings filled with crab and pork and the light, pastry-style dumplings filled with sautéed leeks — but also try the Shanghai spareribs and the jade shrimp with a spinach purée. **WHAT** Originally known as Dragon Villages, this was one of the first formal restaurants to introduce Shanghai-style cooking to Los Angeles. The main draw for regulars these days: the beloved dumplings — crab, pork and steamed vegetable — and pot stickers. 📷🍴☺

[Mezbaan Indian] 80 N. Fair Oaks Ave., Old Pasadena, 626.405.9060, mezbaan.net. L Mon.-Fri., D nightly, brunch Sun. Indian. Beer & wine. AE, MC, V. $ - $$$ **WHY** Great lunch buffet. **WHAT** One of the original Old Town eateries, Mezbaan offers tandoori, benghan bharta, palak paneer and distinctive curries that diners can spice on a sliding scale of one to ten. Hyderabad specialties (like the delicious lamb pasinda) also are served. Live Indian music on weekends, too. ☺

[Mike & Anne's] 1040 Mission St., South Pasadena, 626.799.7199, mikeandannes.com. B, L & D Tues.-Sun. Modern American. Full bar. AE, MC, V. $$ - $$$ **WHY** The lovely rosemary-lined patio and the refreshingly uncomplicated modern American food — grilled sandwiches, crisp-skinned chicken, a terrific burger, and its decadent deep-fried trio of delight: sweet potato fries, french fries and the best onion rings in Pasadena. **WHAT** In the space of a few short years, South Pasadena has become a really good town to be hungry in, and this place is one of the foodie focal points. The sunny-by-day, twinkle-lit-by-night patio is still the place to be in good weather, but now that the restaurant has expanded to a second dining room and a spiffy new bar, there's room for everyone. The kitchen stocks its larders from the local farmers' markets, including the Thursday one across the street. **WHO** A typical South Pas mix — Republican Junior Leaguers next to Koi-clad artists. ♥☺☜☺☼

[Newport Seafood] **518 W. Las Tunas Dr., San Gabriel, 626.289.5998, newportseafood.com. L & D daily. Chinese/seafood. Beer & wine. AE, MC, V. $ - $$$ WHY** A glistening mountain of lobster, sautéed with lots of garlic, scallions and ginger. **WHAT** Recently relocated from a small, grungier spot into a bright former coffee shop, Newport is handsome enough to attract business lunchers by day and upscale celebrators by night. And because the specialties are four- to six-pound lobsters, as well as crab and aptly named elephant clams, this is a place for celebrating. (The lobsters are a far sight cheaper than at, say, the Palm, but they're still an investment.) Don't bother with the glutinous hot and sour soup, and don't feel compelled to try the Vietnamese dishes; just stick with the lobster, clams and excellent vegetables (especially the pea sprouts). **WHO** A well-dressed mix of Asian and Occidental diners out for a seafood splurge. ☺

[Noodle Island] **800 W. Las Tunas Dr., San Gabriel, 626.293.8839. B, L & D daily. Chinese/noodles. No booze. MC, V. $ WHY** Ancient ginger chicken soup with your choice of noodles (rice noodles are best). **WHAT** This strip-mall noodle café is more elegant than most, with dark colors, bamboo details and poultry objets d'art that let you know that this is a place for consuming chicken. At most of the tables you'll see the two house specialties: the fragrant, delicious "ancient ginger" chicken soup with noodles, tender meat and cilantro, and the steamed Hainan chicken served with three dipping sauces and a mountain of addictive chicken-broth-infused rice. **WHO** Chinese-American businesspeople at lunch, families with noodle-happy kids at dinner. ☜☺

[Oba Sushi Izakaya] **181 E. Glenarm St., Pasadena, 626.799.8543, obasushi.com. L Mon.-Sat., D nightly. Japanese/sushi. Beer, wine & sake. MC, V. $$ - $$$ WHY** Excellent izakaya: fish cake tempura, an incredible poke salad, the Oba roll with cucumber, avocado, jalapeño and paper-thin beef, and carefully prepared sashimi, notably the organic, farm-raised hamachi. **WHAT** Pasadena's newest Japanese spot is also its best – and with a Mexican sushi chef, no less. You can sit at the sake/wine bar, the small sushi bar or in one of two dining areas, and you'll be well served by very nice people. Lunchtime bento boxes are a good value. ☜☺

☙VEGETARIAN ☺KID FRIENDLY ☼PATIO DINING ⛟DELIVERY ☗PRIVATE PARTY

[Ocean Star Seafood] 145 N. Atlantic Blvd., Monterey Park, 626.308.2128. L & D daily. Chinese/seafood. Full bar. AE, MC, V. $$ - $$$$ **WHY** Don't-miss dishes like salt-and-pepper shrimp, whole steamed fish and crab in black bean sauce. **WHAT** Vast and glossy, this reliable Cantonese restaurant is chaotic for dim sum and a bit more refined at dinner. The fresh and varied dim sum is served from rolling carts, and the seafood is consistently excellent. A seafood feast in a private room makes for a great party. ☺🏠

[Palate Food & Wine] 🏠 933 S. Brand Blvd., Glendale, 818.662.9463, palatefoodwine.com. D nightly. Modern American/French. Full bar. AE, MC, V. $$ - $$$ **WHY** Little crocks of "porkfolio" (a charcuterie plate including a suave pork pâté), gorgeous cheeses, pickled vegetables (and fruits!), sous vide–cooked steak of astonishing flavor, Valrhona chocolate pudding and terrific wines poured by the halfglass, glass or bottle. The three-course Sunday Supper is $35, a relatively good buy. **WHAT** Chez Panisse in Glendale? Before you laugh, get over to Octavio Becerra's place and prepare to get caught up in his joy in robust, simple, reasonably priced (very) small plates served with exuberant wines. Everything either comes from a local farmers' market (or someone's garden), a small-scale craftsman (as with the cheeses) or is made in-house: house-churned butter, handmade pasta, house-cured prosciutto. In back is a retail wine store with a tasting area, an oversize table for parties and a culinary library that Becerra encourages guests to browse. We've had some failures here, notably risotti and pastas, but those were the exception, not the rule. **WHO** A devoutly loyal crowd of hybrid-driving foodies (and wine geeks) from north Glendale, Atwater, Silver Lake and Pasadena. ♻🏠

[Parkway Grill] 510 S. Arroyo Pkwy., Pasadena, 626.795.1001, theparkwaygrill.com. L Mon.-Fri., D nightly. Californian. Full bar. AE, MC, V. $$$$ **WHY** It's the Spago of Pasadena. **WHAT** Its California pizzas, organic vegetables, open kitchen and inventive cookery made a big splash in once-stodgy Pasadena when it opened in 1985, and the Parkway Grill is still an appealing destination today. Classic dishes — lobster-filled cocoa crêpes, ahi niçoise salad, seasonal fruit crisps — are the way to go. There's a good wine list and the bar is great, particularly on the weekends, when live jazz is on the menu. **WHO** Well-dressed local power people. ♥🏠

[Pearl's Restaurant] 644 W. Garvey Ave., Monterey Park, 626.284.2761. L & D daily. Chinese/Shanghai. No booze. Cash only. $ **WHY** Shredded-pancake beef soup, delicate shrimp dumplings, and low prices. **WHAT** A tiny café with a big following, Pearl's offers Shanghai-style rice plates and lots more: cold noodles and shredded chicken in peanut sauce, stewed pork leg with greens, and beef simmered in a spicy sa-ta sauce with preserved vegetables. **WHO** Dedicated enthusiasts from as far away as Irvine and Ventura. 📷☺

🏠 ESSENTIALLY L.A. ☺ LATE ♥ ROMANTIC 📷 VALUE 🔇 QUIET ♻ SUSTAINABLE

[Penang Malaysian Cuisine] **971 S. Glendora Ave., West Covina, 626.338.6138. L & D daily. Malaysian. No booze. MC, V. $ WHY** For hard-to-find Malaysian classics, from satays and curries to coconut rice and ice *kacang*, a red-bean shaved-ice dessert that's more delicious than you might think. **WHAT** This plaza café turns out Indian griddle breads (*roti canal*) and scalding Indo-Malay *rendangs*, long-simmered chicken, lamb or beef cooked in a thick coconut cream infused with massive quantities of curry spices. Noodle dishes and rice plates are best for single diners, while specials such as spicy Thai sauce shrimp and stir-fried eggplant with belacan are more suitable for groups to share. **WHO** Malaysian food buffs who drive a long way, and West Covina locals brave enough to try something different from their usual Thai joint. ☺

[Phoenix Inn] **208 E. Valley Blvd., Alhambra, 626.299.1238, phoenixfoodboutique.com. L & D daily (to 1 a.m.). Chinese/Cantonese. Beer & wine. MC, V. $ - $$ WHY** Top-notch ingredients and consistently high quality cooking. Try the boneless chicken, a deceptively simple but fabulous chicken-soy stir-fry. **WHAT** Cantonese cooking is the house specialty, and hearty dishes like lo mein and spareribs with salt and pepper are particularly good. Bonus fun fact: Local legend says this place is haunted by a woman ghost who sits at various tables and admires what you're eating. ☺ 📠☺🏠

[Porto Alegre] **Paseo Colorado, 260 E. Colorado Blvd., Pasadena, 626.744.0555, portoalegre-churrascaria.com. L & D daily. Brazilian. Full bar. AE, MC, V. $$$ - $$$$ WHY** One of the best churrascarias around, with a generous and beautiful buffet (salads, roasted vegetables, prosciutti, cheeses, garlic rice, bananas fritas) and quality meats. **WHAT** Hidden on the second floor of the Paseo, where P. F. Chang's and Yard House get all the attention, this Brazilian barbecue place is more subdued than the wacky Gaucho's Village, has better food than Picanha in Burbank and is less expensive than Fogo de Chao in Beverly Hills — making it a fine choice for a carnivorous feast. Handsome men carve glistening meats tableside until you cry uncle; just make sure to get one of the lamb chops before you quit. **WHO** Special-occasion celebrants. ♥ 🍴☺

[The Raymond] **1250 S. Fair Oaks Ave., Pasadena, 626.441.3136, theraymond.com. L Tues.-Fri., D Tues.-Sat., brunch Sat.-Sun. Modern American. Full bar. AE, MC, V. $$$$ WHY** An elegantly conceived menu and a setting oozing historic charm. **WHAT** Newish owners and an ambitious young chef have breathed life into this 1901 Craftsman bungalow. It's the epitome of Pasadena charm, with gleaming wood floors, leaded glass, flower-filled patios and an air of tranquility. The upscale California cooking isn't always flawless — the roasted bruschetta was bitter on one visit — but it's generally very good. Try the crab cakes; the endive and baby frisée salad; the roast salmon with asparagus, potato risotto and wild thyme; and the hot-fudge sundae. **WHO** Pasadena movers and shakers, anniversary-celebrating couples, Craftsman-loving visitors. ♥ 🍷 ☼

[Red White + Bluezz] **70 S. Raymond Ave., Old Pasadena, 626.792.4441, redwhitebluezz.com. L & D daily. Modern American/wine bar. Full bar. AE, MC, V. $$ - $$$ WHY** The menu focuses mainly on updated American classics, and includes a wide selection of artisanal cheeses and charcuterie for sampling with the wines. **WHAT** Quality live jazz is at the heart of this candlelit bistro, but the surprise is how good the food is, too. Try the Snake River Farms Kobe beef burger with sweet potato fries — it's sensational. The crab cakes are also very good, as is the "duo of beef sliders" appetizer of succulent grilled skirt steak and tender, savory short ribs on potato gaufrettes. There are plenty of wines by the glass for less than $10, which we appreciate. **WHO** Diners enjoying the jazz in a dark and intimate setting. ♥🏨

[Robin's Wood-Fire BBQ] **395 N. Rosemead Blvd., East Pasadena, 626.351.8885, robinsbbq.com. L & D Tues.-Sun. American/barbecue. Full bar. AE, MC, V. $$ - $$$ WHY** When the 'cue zealots start debating who does it best, Robin's usually ranks among the finest. **WHAT** There's Pabst Blue Ribbon on tap, a kitschy Americana décor and a swell lineup of side dishes (blueberry cornbread, pecan cole slaw) but those are just supporting players to the deservedly popular meats, smoked over mesquite and hickory. There are some good deals, too, including Sunday "family feasts" and half-price kids' dishes on Tuesday and Sunday. **WHO** Convivial families. 💵☺

[Saladang] **363 S. Fair Oaks Ave., Pasadena, 626.793.8123. L & D daily. Thai. Beer & wine. AE, MC, V. $$ WHY** Some of the best Thai food in the San Gabriel Valley. **WHAT** Saladang's dining room is chic and modern — with exposed ducts, colorful table settings and handsome rattan chairs — and its food deliciously fresh and well-presented. The yellow curries, satays, light fried calamari and spinach-and-duck salad are all excellent. The menu is thoughtfully laid out with vegetarian-friendly options and the service is quick and professional. 🍷🥢

[Savoy Kitchen] **138 E. Valley Blvd., Alhambra, 626.308.9535. L & D Mon.-Sat. Chinese/coffee shop. No booze. Cash only. $ WHY** Twenty-six years of creating first-rate comfort food. **WHAT** Come early to eat at this popular but tiny Hong Kong–style coffee shop. Tables are hard to come by, but when you get one, order the generous and tasty Hainan-style chicken, which almost every table orders. Other standouts include the shrimp rolls, curries and the smoked duck salad. 💵☺

[Sea Harbour] 🏛 **3939 N. Rosemead Blvd., Rosemead, 626.288.3939. L & D daily. Chinese/seafood. Full bar. AE, MC, V. $$ WHY** Seafood selections such as shrimp-stuffed eggplant, tofu rounds topped with scallops and shrimp and shark fin dumplings are standouts. **WHAT** Dim sum doesn't roll on carts at this temple to tea snacks; instead the jewel-like dumplings, noodles and other refined small plates are pictured on the extensive, often-changing menu. Hard-core foodies choose the crunchy fried chicken knees and gelatinous chicken feet. Finish the meal with dessert-like dim sum, such as fried durian puffs, flaky egg tarts and the unusual lowfat milk bun. Waits can be long, but reservations and private rooms are available. ◎🍴

[Shamshiri] **122 W. Stocker St., Glendale, 818.246.9541. L & D daily. Persian. Beer & wine. AE, MC, V. $ - $$ WHY** Abundant, interesting and delicious Persian food at low prices. Try the *fesenjon*, a sort of Persian mole, rich and complex, with pomegranate and walnuts. **WHAT** The kindly service can be erratic at this Glendale Persian restaurant, but it's easy to forgive when you taste the food — and even easier to forgive when you pay the bill. Very good kebabs and stews, with dill, mint and saffron-scented garnishes keeping the plates beautiful and the palate refreshed. 📷◎

[Shanghai Restaurant] **140 W. Valley Blvd., San Gabriel, 626.288.0991. L & D daily. Chinese/Shanghai. No booze. MC, V. $$ WHY** Ambitious cuisine for discriminating eaters. **WHAT** In its coveted spot — the second floor of the huge Chinese Focus Plaza — Shanghai could get by serving the usual cold wine chicken, spicy cold beef tendon and pedestrian hot pots. Those are on its menu, but the kitchen turns out more sophisticated fare, such as poached dumpling-like rolled tofu sheets stuffed with meat and the Chinese green chi-tsai. Tender savory custard with clams is another wonder. And those fond of assertive flavors might try a thin fish fillet coated in deep red wine lees (an inspiration from Fujian to the south). But avoid the braised pork knuckle with soy sauce, a sad mound of congealed fat. 📷◎

[Shiro] 🔒 **1505 Mission St., South Pasadena, 626.799.4774, restaurant-shiro.com. D Wed.-Sun. French/Japanese. Full bar. AE, MC, V. $$$$ WHY** The signature whole sizzling catfish with ponzu sauce, but don't stop there — it's all delicious. For a memorable experience, ask chef Shiro to surprise you. **WHAT** Chef Hideo Yamashiro knows his seafood and the menu reflects it, with lots of fresh, interestingly sauced fish offerings. As competition has intensified in increasingly food-obsessed South Pasadena, Shiro's, once the only game in town, is fighting back by offering an excellent $35 four-course menu on Wednesdays. We wish the modern white setting was more charming, but the food and kind service more than compensate. ♥ 🍸

[Song] **383 S. Fair Oaks Ave., Pasadena, 626.793.5200. L & D daily. Thai. Beer & wine. AE, MC, V. $$ WHY** Romantic patio setting and an evocative, just-challenging-enough Thai menu. **WHAT** The glass-walled dining room is attractive, but the open-air patio — set off

🥬 VEGETARIAN ◎ KID FRIENDLY ◌ PATIO DINING 🚗 DELIVERY 🍴 PRIVATE PARTY

by 15-foot-tall steel panels laser-cut to suggest the patterns of Thai fabrics — is the ideal setting for consuming the street food-inspired dishes served at this sister restaurant to neighboring Saladang. Standouts include the crispy, addictive corn cakes, a salad of asparagus and chicken, and the fish balls with curry. **WHO** Date-night couples and post–mee krob Thai food enthusiasts looking for the kind of dishes you won't find everywhere else in town. ♥❦☼

[Southern Mini Town] ⌂ **833 W. Las Tunas Dr., San Gabriel, 626.289.6578. L & D daily. Chinese/Shanghai. No booze. MC, V. $ - $$ WHY** Because the spot-on cooking at this supremely nondescript place is something no food lover will want to miss. **WHAT** With small appetizer plates of Shaoxing-marinated blue crab, red-cooked Jia Xing duck and cool jade celery seasoned with sesame oil, plus a few orders of its satisfying pastries and dumplings (steamed or fried, with meat or with vegetable filling) you might be tempted to forgo entrees. Don't. The kitchen has honed the flavors of almost every dish: the supremely rich deep-fried and red-cooked spareribs; the delicate gluten puffs in a soup lively with the contrasting textures of bow-tied fresh tofu sheet, glass noodles and torn napa cabbage; even the simple al dente noodles dressed only with a modicum of scallion-infused oil. ▧❦☺

[Supreme Dragon] **18406 Colima Rd., Rowland Heights, 626.810.0396. L & D daily. Chinese/dim sum. No booze. Cash only. $ WHY** Crusty-bottomed pan-fried pork bao with slightly fluffy coverings, the fresh scallion dumplings, the salted vegetables stir-fried with torn bean curd sheet, and more such little treasures. **WHAT** At Supreme Dragon, diners are given a long sushi bar-style list of about 80 northern and Shanghai-style pastries and small dishes. The restaurant's attempts at elegance — waterfall curtains, the golden and red placards in its two dining rooms — are beside the point. You're here to eat. The delicate bottle gourd squash makes an excellent balance for richer dishes such as braised duck with meaty black mushrooms and leeks, or pork belly chunks braised with lightly pickled vegetables whose tang plays against the richness of the meat. ▧❦☺

[Tasty Garden] **228 W. Valley Blvd., Alhambra, 626.300.8262, tastygarden.us. L & D daily to 1 a.m. (to 3 a.m. Fri.-Sat.). Chinese/coffee shop. No booze. AE, MC, V. $ WHY** Exceptional menu, cross-generational clientele. **WHAT** The fare at this lively, Hong Kong–style coffee shop is well made, fantastically tasty and definitely eclectic. Crowds come for the filet mignon with pepper and basil and (no kidding) the peanut butter pizza. **WHO** Seniors at tea time, clubbers in the wee hours. ☺ ▧

[Taylor's Steakhouse] **901 Foothill Blvd., La Cañada, 818.790.7668, taylorssteakhouse.com. L Mon.-Fri., D nightly. American/ steakhouse. Full bar. AE, MC, V. $$ - $$$$ WHY** Effortlessly retro steakhouse classics and a bar that's jumping enough to give sleepy

---

⌂ ESSENTIALLY L.A. ☼LATE ♥ROMANTIC ▧ VALUE ♪QUIET ❀ SUSTAINABLE

La Cañada an actual hot spot. **WHAT** This is no poseur steakhouse. Taylor's, the only branch of the beloved 1953 L.A. mothership, is a genuine outpost of all we know and love about steakhouse ambience and cuisine: red Naugahyde booths, iceberg wedges smothered with blue cheese, icy martinis, generous and prime steaks for less than $30. It's packed every night, so reservations are essential. **WHO** The blue-blazer crowd. 🍽 🍷

[Three Drunken Goats] **2256 Honolulu Ave., Montrose, 818.249.9950, 3drunkengoats.com. L & D daily. Spanish/wine bar. Beer & wine. AE, MC, V. $$ - $$$ WHY** You'll be tempted to continue ordering tapas until you're full, but save room for the churros with chocolate dipping sauce, one of the best desserts ever invented. **WHAT** This Montrose hot spot (no, that's not an oxymoron) has a huge menu of delicious, light small bites (bacon-wrapped dates, croquettes, mushrooms of many kinds, grilled octopus, steamed clams, excellent stuffed peppers, small and complex salads) and larger grilled dishes (New York steak with blue-cheese butter), plus a fun selection of wines and live gypsy music some nights. The point is to order a bottle of wine or a carafe of sangria, then linger over a parade of interesting dishes in the warm, high-ceilinged, barn-like space. 🍷

[Tibet Nepal House] **36 E. Holly St., Old Pasadena, 626.585.0955, tibetnepalhouse.com. L & D Tues.-Sun. Nepalese. Beer & wine. AE, MC, V. $ - $$ WHY** The award-winning buffet lunch is inexpensive and wonderful. **WHAT** The mountaineer/photographer/chef trained in Austria and brings a gourmet sensibility to Tibetan and Nepalese cuisine, which is reminiscent of both Chinese and Indian food but more subtly flavored. Karma Tenzing Bhotia's menu spans the Himalayas, from lowland curries and dals to highland yak, noodles and momos (dumplings). Try the savory, soup-like Tibetan butter tea. 🍷🍴☺

[Tonny's] **843 E. Orange Grove Blvd., Pasadena, 626.797.0866. B, L & D daily. Mexican. No booze. MC, V. $ WHY** Some of the most delicious guacamole ever, chunky and fragrant with cilantro and limes. Homemade tortillas wrap *delicioso* burritos and seafood tacos, and the chile verde is heavenly. **WHAT** Warm and welcoming, this little family restaurant has an open kitchen, a tiny patio out back, about eight tables and very good home cooking. A small but sparkling gem in the heart of working-class Pasadena. 🍽☺✿

[Tre Venezie] **119 W. Green St., Pasadena, 626.795.4455. L Fri., D Wed.-Sun. Italian. Full bar. AE, MC, V. $$$$ - $$$$$ WHY** It's a gem among the Italian restaurants that litter Old Pasadena. **WHAT** This romantic little cottage on Green Street features a dining room decorated like someone's (tasteful) home, a kind Italian staff and often-extraordinary dishes from Venice, Friuli and the rest of northeastern Italy. Bring your Gold Card, and savor a superb caprese made with

🍷 VEGETARIAN ☺ KID FRIENDLY ✿ PATIO DINING � DELIVERY 🏠 PRIVATE PARTY

homemade smoked buffalo mozzarella, exquisite handmade pastas and fresh fish cooked simply and perfectly with olive oil, garlic and a splash of vinegar. There's an acclaimed grappa collection and a fine list of wines at gasp-inducing prices. **WHO** Elegant grown-ups willing to make the investment. ♥ 〽

[Vietnam House] **710 W. Las Tunas Dr., San Gabriel, 626.282.3630. L & D Mon. & Wed.-Sun. Vietnamese. Beer & wine. MC, V. $ - $$ WHY** A multi-course beef extravaganza at bargain prices. **WHAT** An all-purpose menu is served at this large sibling to Golden Deli, which serves beer and takes credit cards, which is not often the case. Try the seven courses of beef for a meaty experience, or concentrate on the terrific spring rolls. Barbecued meats, pho soup and bahn mi sandwiches round out the extensive menu. 〽⦿

[Vietnam Restaurant] ▣ **340 W. Las Tunas Dr., San Gabriel, 626.281.5577, vietnamrestaurantsg.com. L & D. Mon.-Wed. & Fri.-Sun. Vietnamese. No booze. MC, V. $ WHY** The it spot of the moment for pho, crisp spring rolls and a hugely portioned and delicious seven-course beef dinner. **WHAT** The result of a squabble in the family that owns the famed Golden Deli and Vietnam House led to two members of the family — including the former Vietnam House cook — splitting off to open this tidy little place. The result is yet another, even better Vietnamese café with all the standard dishes and a superb $13 seven-course beef dinner that can easily feed two. **WHO** Former Vietnam House groupies who followed the cook here. 〽⦿

[Wahib's Middle Eastern] **910 E. Main St., Alhambra, 626.281.1006, wahibsmiddleeast.com. B, L & D daily. Middle Eastern. Beer & wine. AE, MC, V. $ - $$ WHY** Great specials, fantastic hummus, fresh baklava and slightly lower prices for takeout. **WHAT** This workaday warehouse of Lebanese and Armenian food has a large dining room with banquet-style tables. It's open for breakfast, has a bakery and offers great specials off the beaten kebab-and-falafel path, including crunchy fried frogs' leg with lemon and garlic, served over french fries. Cucumber salad, the tender lamb dishes, a Greek-style moussaka and the roast chicken specials also are tasty. 〽⦿

[Wang Jia] **156 S. San Gabriel Blvd., San Gabriel, 626.291.2233. L & D Mon. & Wed.-Sun. Chinese/Shanghai. No booze. Cash only. $ - $$ WHY** Fine home-style cooking for a bargain tariff. **WHAT** This spot's spartan white room is as brightly lit as any hospital operating room; it's the varied crowds that give the room its color. Following Shanghai custom, meals begin with small eats: roasted peanuts flecked with herb-like dry seaweed, seasoned jelly fish strips with scallions or deeply flavored wine-marinated chicken. Inevitably, a huge clay hot pot graces almost every table. The ingredients in the herbal duck hot pot — bits of Virginia ham, toothsome dry bamboo shoots and tofu knots — have a delectable synergy. Sweets include the eastern rice balls with wine sauce. 🍸😊

[Xiang Wei Lou] 227 W. Valley Blvd., San Gabriel, 626.289.2276. L & D daily. Chinese/Hunan. Beer & wine. Cash only. $ **WHY** Perhaps the best Hunanese food in the San Gabriel Valley. **WHAT** There's considerable talent behind the stoves at this plain but spiffy café next to the San Gabriel Hilton. The dishes showcase a multiplicity of chile types and styles: dried to an almost black-red or sun-bleached; whole or crushed into flakes; soft and almost sweet, yet blazing; and so forth. Try the cumin beef laced with dry and fresh red peppers; lamb riblets with a musky herbal heat; the broth with several varieties of fresh mushrooms; and, to cool your palate, fresh cucumber cubes.
WHO Spicy-food lovers who also appreciate the late (by Chinese-restaurant standards) closing time of 11:30 p.m. 😊 🍸

[Yang Chow] 3777 E. Colorado Blvd., East Pasadena, 626.432.6868, yangchow.com. L & D daily. Chinese. Beer & wine. AE, MC, V. $$
WHY The slippery shrimp is twice-cooked, bathed in a subtly sweet, mildly hot sauce, and just about impossible to stop eating, unfortunately for your heart (it's a notoriously fatty and caloric dish). **WHAT** This branch of the Chinatown classic draws a huge and devoted clientele. The slippery shrimp is famous, and also good are the cashew chicken, fiery Sichuan won ton soup, pan-fried dumplings and dry-sautéed asparagus and green beans. Good service, too. **WHO** Families who come here once a week. 🍸😊🌀

[Yujean Kang's] 67 N. Raymond Ave., Old Pasadena, 626.585.0855, yujeankangs.com. L & D daily. Chinese/French. Full bar. AE, MC, V. $$$
WHY Dishes like duck salad with black-bean sauce and Chinese "polenta" with shrimp, mushrooms and scallions, along with a wine list created by the oenophile chef to harmonize with his elegant menu. **WHAT** The setting is sophisticated and so is the menu, reflecting a French chef's panache and a Chinese gourmand's sense of robust flavor. Don't miss the tea-smoked duck, won ton soup, crispy beef with sautéed vegetables and the stir-fried Blue Lake green beans. A good place for a business lunch in Old Pasadena. **WHO** A mature crowd, including lots of oenophiles. ♥ 🍸🥢

[Yunnan Garden] 545 W. Las Tunas Dr., San Gabriel, 626.308.1896. L & D daily. Chinese. Beer. MC, V. $ **WHY** To discover the flavors of China's Yunnan province. **WHAT** A brightly lit Chinese café like a thousand others in the area, with the brusque service that's the norm. But the culinary style is less common: the robust, chile-laden food of the mountainous Yunnan province, which fills China's southwest corner. Try the crossing-the-bridge noodles, cumin lamb, and won tons in an addictive chile broth. 🍸

🥬 VEGETARIAN ⊙ KID FRIENDLY ⊙ PATIO DINING � DELIVERY 🏠 PRIVATE PARTY

[Z Sushi] 1132 N. Garfield Ave., Alhambra, 626.282.5636. L Mon.-Sat., D nightly. Japanese/sushi. Full bar. AE, MC, V. $$ - $$$ **WHY** It's one of the better places for sushi east of the 5 Freeway. **WHAT** Knotty-pine walls and two bars — one for drinking, one for sushi — give Z an interesting look, and the good food is matched by the friendly, quick and solicitous service. The sashimi's fresh, the sushi rolls are imaginative, and the cooked dishes, like salmon and baby lobster with a subtle wasabi cream sauce, are appealing. Try the plum martini. ☺

[Zeke's Smokehouse] 🏛 2209 Honolulu Ave., Montrose, 818.957.7045, zekessmokehouse.com. L & D daily. American/barbecue. Beer & wine. AE, MC, V. $$ - $$$ **WHY** Sweet potato fries, pulled-pork sandwiches and Memphis-style baby-back ribs. **WHAT** A partnership between chefs Leonard Cohen (Maple Drive, 72 Market St.) and Michael Rosen (Reign) along with the Gelsinger family (Gelsinger's Meats) opened Zeke's in 2002. It's become a Montrose mainstay for its top-quality regional American barbecue and smokehouse cooking, as well as its charming retro-style interior. There's another branch in West Hollywood with the same good cooking. ☺ ♻

EAST VALLEY

[Asanebo] 🏛 11941 Ventura Blvd., Studio City, 818.760.3348. L Tues.-Fri., D Tues.-Sun. Japanese. Beer & wine. AE, MC, V. $$$$ - $$$$$ **WHY** The omakase. **WHAT** Despite its unprepossessing location, Asanebo is a destination restaurant (and a favorite of night-off chefs) that serves top-quality sashimi, sushi and cooked specialties. It's expensive, so be sure to ask prices of specials if they are not posted. Omakase starts at about $75 per person. **WHO** Loyal regulars, including some of L.A.'s top chefs, and visitors who want to eat at a Michelin one-star in a Valley strip mall.

[Bistro Provence] 345 N. Pass Ave., Burbank, 818.840.9050, bistroprovence.net. L Mon.-Fri., D Mon.-Sat. Californian/French. Beer & wine. AE, MC, V. $$ **WHY** For a great-deal prix-fixe dinner that includes such things as the delicious roast chicken with garlic fries, beef bourguignonne and homemade French desserts. **WHAT** Patina alum Miki Zivkovic has created a welcoming neighborhood restaurant in an unattractive Burbank strip mall next to a Starbucks. After the success of a weekly prix-fixe night, Zivkovic made the entire dinner menu prix-fixe, and it's a bargain — $29 for a generous and delicious three-course meal with plenty of choices to please everyone. **WHO** Local studio workers and Toluca Lake residents in on the secret. ♥ 🗐

[Boneyard Bistro] 13539 Ventura Blvd., Sherman Oaks, 818.906.7427, boneyardbistro.com. D nightly, brunch Sun. Barbecue/American. Beer & wine. AE, MC, V. $$ - $$$ **WHY** Pulled pork potstickers, barbecued tri-tip, grilled bone-in rib-eye steak and more than a hundred beers. **WHAT** Chef/owner Aaron Robins has successfully merged an upscale bistro with a barbecue joint, and the locals love it. Between the 'cue and the bistro sides of the menu, there's something to satisfy any palate; plus, the daily specials are usually excellent. Portions are extremely generous. **WHO** Big eaters.

[Bua Siam] 12924 Sherman Way, North Hollywood, 818.765.8395. L & D daily. Thai. No booze. MC, V. $ **WHY** Consistently excellent cooking that doesn't pander to the sweet-craving American palate. Free delivery, too. **WHAT** It's not just the array of tapas-size plates that draws us to this stylish, boxcar-size spot. Although who can argue with $2.99 appetizers that include skewered meatballs, crunchy rice cakes with Thai chile, the Thai spaghetti called *knom jean* and southern fish curry? Regulars know to share entree-size orders of mussel omelets or shatteringly crisp ground catfish on an incendiary green-papaya salad. Note that the blazingly spicy stir-fries are geared to Thai palates unless otherwise requested. **WHO** Lots of Thais, and non-Thais who like their cooking authentic. 🖼️🥡☼🚐

[Ca' Del Sole] 4100 Cahuenga Blvd., Toluca Lake, 818.985.4669, cadelsole.com. L Mon.-Fri., D nightly, brunch Sun. Italian. Full bar. AE, MC, V. $$ - $$$ **WHY** Charm, consistently good rustic Italian cooking, and the chance that you might run into that producer who hasn't been returning your calls. **WHAT** Although it's full of showbiz people, Ca' Del Sole is not a scene — most people come here because they want to eat well and have a good conversation with their companions, whether on the walled Venetian patio or in the handsome, rambling interior. Try the octopus, the salumi, the baby artichokes with wild arugula and parmesan, and any of the house-made pastas. **WHO** At lunch it's a virtual commissary for folks from Warner, Universal, Disney and CBS Radford; at dinner, it's more filled with over-50 Toluca Lake locals having a date night. ♥☼🏛️

[Caioti Pizza Café] 🏛️ 4346 Tujunga Ave., Studio City, 818.761.3588, caiotipizzacafe.com. L & D daily, brunch Sat.-Sun. Pizzeria. BYOB. MC, V. $ - $$ **WHY** Superb salads (try the Humble Salad, a romaine wedge with bacon, goat cheese and roma tomatoes, or the "The" salad, said to induce labor in pregnant women) and Caioti's rightly famed individual pizza; don't forget to order some garlic rolls, too. **WHAT** Ed LaDou may have shuffled off this mortal coil, but the California pizza he invented (that's right, it was LaDou, not Puck) lives on in this casual, noisy café. Fun, affordable and delicious. **WHO** Valley families sharing salads and pizzas. 🥡☼☼

[Carnival] 4356 Woodman Ave., Sherman Oaks, 818.784.3469, carnivalrest.com. L & D daily. Lebanese/Middle Eastern. Beer & wine. AE, MC, V. $$ **WHY** Creamy hummus, fattoush salad with crispy pita chips, kebabs, and grilled quail are all well prepared. Nightly specials run

---

🥬 VEGETARIAN ☺ KID FRIENDLY ☼ PATIO DINING 🚐 DELIVERY 🏛️ PRIVATE PARTY

to such things as an unusual okra stew with lamb. **WHAT** With a huge menu of Lebanese specialties as well as takeout and catering, this comfy restaurant serving the Valley's large Middle Eastern community will please both vegetarians and carnivores. Try the combination appetizer plate, which lets everyone taste a few salads. 📷🍸☺

[Cedar House Café] **4805 Whitsett Ave., Valley Village, 818.769.9994. L & D daily. Middle Eastern/Lebanese. Beer & wine. MC, V. $ - $$ WHY** Wonderful lentil soup, robustly garlicky hummus and kebabs of exceptional tenderness and flavor. **WHAT** Consistently delicious Lebanese food is the draw at this friendly neighborhood spot, known for its chicken and lamb kebabs, hummus, falafel and schwarma. Weekdays are relaxed, but weekend nights bring live music, so it gets loud. 🍸☺☼

[Chadaka Thai] **310 San Fernando Blvd., Burbank, 818.848.8520, chadaka.com. L & D daily. Thai. Full bar. AE, MC, V. $ - $$$ WHY** Full bar service (yes!) and tasty Thai cooking make a great happy hour combo. **WHAT** Amid all the mega-chain restaurants of the Burbank Media Center is a branch of Silver Lake's popular Rambutan Thai serving fresh, authentic Thai food in a gorgeous modern room overlooked by a large Buddha above the bar. A great spot before or after a movie at the nearby cinemas. **WHO** Movie-goers and studio workers. ♥🍸

[D'Cache] **10717 Riverside Dr., Toluca Lake, 818.506.9600, dcacheres-taurant.com. L Tues.-Fri., D Tues.-Sat. Spanish/Californian. Full bar. AE, MC, V. $$ - $$$ WHY** Charm and intelligent food in an old Spanish-style house — in a neighborhood that needed a good restaurant. **WHAT** At first, this newish place looked like it was angling to become the romantic spot in Toluca Lake, and it sort of is, but in a noisy way, with live flamenco music and even dancing on weekends. (Lunch is much quieter.) The Chilean, Spanish and Italian wines suit both the setting — a carefully restored 1930s Spanish house — and the mostly Spanish food: paella, Catalan-style chicken picada, giant prawns with pasta, serrano ham and spinach, and good lamb chops. ♥☼🍶

[El Katracho] **14838 Burbank Blvd., Sherman Oaks, 818.780.7044. L & D Mon. & Wed.-Sat. Honduran. Beer & wine. MC, V. $ - $$ WHY** Well-prepared Honduran *baleadas* (fat quesadillas), marinated chicken and conch soup served by non-English speakers in a spotless storefront restaurant. **WHAT** Overmortgaged on your Van Nuys house? Then come to El Katracho for one of the $6 lunch specials, and you'll be fed for the day — and then some. Honduran cooking is rich and hearty (but not spicy), and here it's served in abundance: mountains of plantains, hillocks of very good rice, heaping bowls of not-so-great beans, big scoops of shredded-cabbage salad and big hunks o' chicken, pork or beef. Choose the subtly sweet marinated chicken over the dry fried chicken or, better yet, order the conch soup like the regulars do. 📷☺

🏛 ESSENTIALLY L.A. ☺ LATE ♥ ROMANTIC 📷 VALUE 🍶 QUIET ♻ SUSTAINABLE

[Katsu-Ya] 11680 Ventura Blvd., Studio City, 818.985.6976, katsu-yagroup.com. L & D daily. Japanese. Beer & wine. AE, MC, V. $$$ - $$$$ **WHY** Spicy tuna on crispy rice, seared spicy albacore sashimi, daily specials. **WHAT** The original Studio City location of the mini Katsu-Ya empire has gotten way too popular for many, but that doesn't deter hordes of sushi lovers from waiting in line for a table or a coveted seat at the sushi bar. Elaborate rolls and intricate presentations are a hallmark, but the fish is fresh and the vibe is hip and fun. **WHO** Stylish Valleyites, including plenty of show people, who don't mind the crowds or the noise level.

[Kiwami] 11920 Ventura Blvd., Studio City, 818.763.3910, katsu-yagroup.com. L & D daily. Japanese/sushi. Beer & wine. AE, MC, V. $$$ - $$$$ **WHY** At the time of this writing, über-sushi-chef Katsuya Uechi is not only in the house; he's preparing omakase in the small sushi bar at the back. **WHAT** After Katsu Michite closed Tama to open Katsu Sushi in Beverly Hills, Uechi took over the old space, notwithstanding the fact that he has the perennially popular Katsu-Ya just up the block. At Kiwami (which means "the ultimate" in Japanese), Uechi has created an elegant, sleek dining room where you can go high-end and savor superb omakase, or order à la carte and enjoy daily nigiri sushi and sashimi specials or classics such as miso-marinated black cod. To experience sushi prepared by Uechi himself, call well ahead of time to reserve seats in the back sushi bar. **WHO** Universal and CBS staffers on lunch break or after work, sushi hounds from all over, and Studio City families with sophisticated, chopsticks-wielding kids in tow.

[Krua Thai] 13130 Sherman Way, North Hollywood, 818.759.7998. L & D daily. Thai. No booze. MC, V. $ - $$ **WHY** Pad Thai, pan-fried noodle dishes, papaya salad with blue crab. **WHAT** A standout among the many excellent establishments in NoHo's "Thai Gulch," Krua Thai serves robustly flavored dishes that can be dialed up or down in heat level to suit your taste. Don't miss its excellent version of pad Thai as well as *pad kee mao*, flat noodles stir-fried with green chiles, mint leaves and pork. **WHO** Foodies, young people on a budget, Thai families.

[Malbec] 10150 Riverside Dr., Toluca Lake, 818.762.4860, malbeccuisine.com. L & D daily. Argentinean. Beer & wine. AE, MC, V. $$ - $$$ **WHY** Good, honest Argentinean cooking and wines at modest prices. **WHAT** This offshoot of the successful Pasadena original has the same affordable Argentinean wines, an equally nice staff, and the same menu of well-prepared classics: empanadas, *matambre* (rolled meat stuffed with vegetables and herbs), garlic fries, handmade pastas and such hearty entrees as grilled short ribs (great flavor but too chewy), skirt steak chimichurri (delicious) and grilled salmon. **WHO** Toluca Lake neighbors running into each other.

[Marche] 13355 Ventura Blvd., Sherman Oaks, 818.784.2915, maxrestaurant.com. D nightly. Modern American/Californian. Full bar. AE, MC, V. $$$ - $$$$ **WHY** Sherman Oaks was ready for something new and wonderful, and we're hopeful that this will be it. **WHAT** Just as we went to press, the longtime Max was becoming Marche. Owner/ chef André Guerrero, who's busy with his new BoHo in Hollywood, brought in as a partner Gary Menes from Palate. The setting and service should remain pretty much the same, but with Menes at the helm, the cooking will change significantly. Look for a market-driven, modern-American, small-plates menu with ingredients procured from local growers — including Guerrero's own home garden. 🦪

[Mistral] 13422 Ventura Blvd., Sherman Oaks, 818.981.6650, mistral-restaurant.com. L Mon.-Fri., D Mon.-Sat. French. Full bar. AE, MC, V. $$$ - $$$$ **WHY** A reliably good and well-run French bistro with an elegant décor, a proper bowl of onion soup, excellent steak frites and a perfect chocolate soufflé. The steak tartare has a loyal following. **WHAT** Stick to the brasserie classics served in this wood-paneled, chandelier-lit spot and you'll be as happy as everyone else who packs the place day and night: frisée lardon, steak tartare, steak frites covered in golden shallots and simple whitefish. Crackerjack service. **WHO** French ex-pats and south-of-Ventura folks planning their next trip to France.

[Pinot Bistro] 🗝 12969 Ventura Blvd., Studio City, 818.990.0500, patinagroup.com. L Mon.-Fri., D nightly. Californian/French. Full bar. AE, MC, V. $$$ - $$$$ **WHY** Belgian endive salad with Roquefort, whitefish fillet with brandade and a great roast chicken with frites, all served in a place right out of the 8th arrondissement. **WHAT** Pinot Bistro is the oldest and most reliable of Joachim Splichal's Patina spinoffs. Avant-garde when it opened, this handsome, artfully lit bistro has evolved into a neighborhood favorite that fits its upscale Sherman Oaks location to a T. A no-corkage-fee policy brings in the wine buffs. **WHO** An older, well-dressed crowd that appreciates good French food and professional service. ♥ 🍸 🏛

[Shiraz] 15472 Ventura Blvd., Sherman Oaks, 818.789.7788, shirazrestaurant.net. L & D daily. Persian/Middle Eastern. Beer & wine. AE, MC, V. $ - $$ **WHY** The kebabs and Middle Eastern classics are good, but live a little and try some of the seasonal Persian specialties, like chicken stewed with cherries. **WHAT** This fine old-timer is good for Persian classics; a specialty is fish pilaf, a traditional dish for the Iranian New Year. But most regulars return for the chicken kebabs, hummus and robust stews served over basmati rice. Service can be grumpy, and the setting is nothing special, so the local delivery is popular. 🕙�.

[Skaf's Grill] 6008 Laurel Canyon Blvd., North Hollywood, 818.985.5701. L & D Mon.-Sat. Lebanese/Middle Eastern. No booze. AE, MC, V. $ **WHY** Scrumptious, cheap Lebanese specialties, including a

---

🗝 ESSENTIALLY L.A. 🕙 LATE ♥ ROMANTIC 💲 VALUE 🍸 QUIET ♻ SUSTAINABLE

great cabbage salad, richly flavored hummus and excellent kebabs. **WHAT** Overlook the funky strip mall and cramped parking lot; Skaf's is a find if you enjoy Middle Eastern food but don't feel like spending a lot of dough. It has a slick new branch in Glendale, but the NoHo location is somehow more real. In addition to the kebabs, the daily specials can be good choices. **WHO** An eclectic crowd of budget-conscious diners. 📷🔪☺

[Smoke House] 🏠 4420 W. Lakeside Dr., Burbank, 818.845.3731, smokehouse1946.com. L Mon.-Sat., D nightly, brunch Sun. American. Full bar. AE, MC, V. $$$ - $$$$ **WHY** Famous for the garlic bread, the Smoke House is best at old-school dinner-house fare like steak Sinatra, prime rib and shrimp Louie. A popular brunch buffet on weekends, early-bird specials and live entertainment in the lounge also draw fans. **WHAT** Judy Garland is no longer dining at the Smoke House, but the faux-Tudor restaurant looks nearly the same as it did in her day. Studio workers from Warner and Disney, couples on dates and old-timers who have been eating here since opening day in 1946 love the vintage atmosphere, generous cocktails and retro menu. We usually stick to the cocktails. **WHO** Your dad — and maybe your grandpa, too. 🍷🍸

[Sompun] 12051 Ventura Pl., Studio City, 818.762.7861. L Mon.-Sat., D nightly. Thai. Beer & wine. MC, V. $ **WHY** A long list of traditional noodle dishes infrequently seen outside Thai Town. **WHAT** In its hidden location, this simple spot has been surprising folks for more than 25 years with the quality of its food. Besides the excellent noodle dishes, you must try the swoon-worthy yet rarely seen "Indian"-style coconut curry and its northern cousin, *kao soi*. Also setting this place apart from the usual mom 'n pop Thai café are such dsihes as the eastern-style sausage salad with chopped ginger and the flaky roti griddle bread that you dunk into rich curries. 📷🔪�GROUP

[Spark Woodfire Grill] 11801 Ventura Blvd., Studio City, 818.623.8883, sparkwoodfiregrill.com. L Mon.-Fri., D nightly. Italian/Californian. Full bar. AE, MC, V. $$ - $$$$ **WHY** Fashionable cocktails, pretty salads and delicious pizzas and meat dishes cooked in the wood-burning oven. **WHAT** You name the trendy dish, this friendly Cal-Italian bistro serves it: burrata with tomatoes, grilled artichokes, individual pizzas, flat-iron steaks, retro-hip meatloaf, "smashed" potatoes, white chocolate bread pudding — what's not to like? Good bar and grill fare in a convenient Studio City location, at prices that are neither high nor low. 🍸

[Sushi House of Taka] 4627 Van Nuys Blvd., Sherman Oaks, 818.784.8777. L & D daily. Japanese/sushi. Beer & wine. AE, MC, V. $$$ - $$$$ **WHY** Generously sized, tasty pieces of sushi in a low-key setting. **WHAT** Don't be put off by the dated-looking interior of this restaurant around the corner from Ventura Boulevard. The sushi spots

🔪 VEGETARIAN ☺ KID FRIENDLY ✿ PATIO DINING 🚐 DELIVERY 🍸 PRIVATE PARTY

on Ventura may get more attention, but chef "Taka" Tanaka serves up impeccably fresh sushi and sashimi as well as tempura and teriyaki. Ordering off the specials board is the best approach. **WHO** Sushi fans from Sherman Oaks and Encino who would rather that their local find doesn't get discovered.

[Sushi Nozawa] 11288 Ventura Blvd., Studio City, 818.508.7017, sushinozawa.com. L & D Mon.-Fri. Japanese/sushi. Beer & wine. MC, V. $$$$ - $$$$$ **WHY** A limited selection of impeccably fresh sushi prepared with warm rice. **WHAT** Kazunori Nozawa is one of the chefs who put Studio City's Sushi Row on L.A.'s culinary map, thanks to his rigid standards for seafood — not to mention for customer behavior You either tolerate his "my way or the highway" approach or you're offended by it, but many who understand the subtleties of traditional sushi service are big fans of Nozawa's omakase. **WHO** Sushi purists and out-of-towners curious about "the Sushi Nazi."

[Swan Restaurant] 12728 Sherman Way, North Hollywood, 818.764.1892, swanthaifood.com. L & D daily. Thai. No booze. MC, V. $ **WHY** Unusual dishes like acacia omelet curry and a standout Crying Tiger beef with a complex dipping sauce. **WHAT** Despite the modest interior, there's some serious Thai cooking going on here. Ask one of the very kind servers for the special small-plates menu.

WEST VALLEY

[Adagio] 22841 Ventura Blvd., Woodland Hills, 818.225.0533. L Thurs., D Tues.-Sun. Italian. Full bar. AE, MC, V. $$$ **WHY** Upscale Italian food and service of a higher caliber than you'd expect from such a modest-looking place, at prices that are more than fair. **WHAT** A real find in the West Valley, Adagio is all about comfort: a cozy but not too fancy setting, solicitous but not too formal service, and well-prepared Italian food that makes everyone happy: tableside Caesars, excellent soups, rich osso buco and a large roster of daily specials. **WHO** West Valley boomers taking their parents out for a nice dinner.

[Alcazar] 17239 Ventura Blvd., Encino, 818.789.0991, al-cazar.com. L & D Tues.-Sun. Lebanese/Middle Eastern. Full bar. AE, MC, V. $ - $$$ **WHY** Chef's hummus, spicy muhammara, chicken livers with pomegranate juice, grilled kebabs. **WHAT** This spacious restaurant with a covered outdoor dining area for hookah smoking serves terrific Lebanese specialties, ranging from the familiar (hummus, kebabs) to the exotic (quail, frogs' legs, lamb tongue, beef brains). The vegetarian plate is a great option for sharing, and a side dish of toasted bulgur (*firik*) is a delicious complement to the kebabs. Come on a Friday or Saturday evening for live music. **WHO** The Lebanese diaspora, and a lot of non-Lebanese folks who think this is the best Middle Eastern restaurant around.

ESSENTIALLY L.A. LATE ♥ROMANTIC VALUE QUIET SUSTAINABLE

[Brandywine] **22757 Ventura Blvd., Woodland Hills, 818.225.9114. L Tues.-Fri., D Mon.-Sat. French/modern American. Beer & wine. AE, MC, V. $$$$ - $$$$$ WHY** Personal service and cooking in an intimate, romantic, special-occasion setting. **WHAT** In a good twist on the old French standard, at Brandywine the wife does the cooking and the husband runs the front room, and it's clearly a harmonious relationship. This tiny place is romantic as all get-out, and chef Peggy McWilliams makes the kind of food you want when you're celebrating or seducing: caviar, tableside Caesars, rack of lamb, Muscovy duck, even chateaubriand for two. **WHO** Couples who want to cozy up in one of the booths. ♥ 🍴

[Brent's Delicatessen] 🏛 **19565 Parthenia St., Northridge, 818.886.5679, brentsdeli.com. B, L & D daily. Deli. No booze. AE, MC, V. $ - $$ WHY** Whitefish salad, tender corned beef on rye, silken cheesecake. **WHAT** Smoked-fish and corned-beef addicts from such deli-starved places as Pasadena and Burbank think nothing of driving 40 minutes to eat at Brent's. This is the real thing, with the full range of deli essentials, from hand-sliced lox and kreplach soup to brisket dips and a famed Cobb salad, all served in a basic coffee-shop setting. **WHO** A constant crush of West Valleyites, from young families to seniors who've been eating pastrami here for 40 years. 🍴 ☺

[Chopan Kebab House] **8910 Reseda Blvd., Northridge, 818.885.1616. L & D Tues.-Sun. Afghani. No booze. V. $ - $$ WHY** A chance to sample an L.A. rarity: Afghan cuisine. **WHAT** The Afghan cooking is terrific at this modest café (which also sells pizza!). The silky-skinned chive dumplings, *aushak*, and their meat-filled cousins, *manti*, with their creamy, tangy sauce topped with swirls of saffron-infused butter, give reason enough to seek out this charmer. The *bulani*, a spice-infused potato leek turnover the size of a yoga mat, reflects the influence of the Indian Subcontinent on food that also borrows from central Asia and Iran. **WHO** Local Afghanis and curious gourmands. 🍴 🥡 ☺

[Copper Chimney] **19737 Ventura Blvd., Woodland Hills, 818.932.9572, copperchimneywoodlandhills.com. L Mon.-Fri., D nightly, brunch Sat.-Sun. Indian. Beer & wine. AE, MC, V. $$ - $$$ WHY** Tandoori dishes, homemade Indian pickles, mint chicken and naan stuffed with cheese, minced lamb, or nuts and cherries. **WHAT** The buffet counter wraps around an open kitchen, leaving scant space for tables, but this is compensated for with crisp white linens and chic tableware. Oh, and the food! Chef Dewan Bisht started his training at five-star hotels in New Delhi and went on to work at many high-end Indian kitchens; this is his first solo venture. His lunch and dinner buffets are gorgeous; there's a substantial list of vegetarian and vegan dishes; and he is happy to make any dish mild, medium or spicy. **WHO** Business lunchers by day, date-nighters by evening. 🥡 ☺ ☼

🥡 **VEGETARIAN** ☺ **KID FRIENDLY** ☼ **PATIO DINING** 🚚 **DELIVERY** 🏛 **PRIVATE PARTY**

[Hummus Bar & Grill] 18743 Ventura Blvd., Tarzana, 818.344.6606, hummusbargrill.com. L & D daily. Israeli/Middle Eastern. No booze. AE, MC, V. $$ - $$$ **WHY** The velvety hummus, of course, as well as a toothsome array of all-you-can-eat salads and side dishes for just $6 per person with a main-course order. **WHAT** Conversations, many in Hebrew, fill the air in this popular casual-dining restaurant, along with the slapping sound of fresh dough being formed into *laffa*, a puffed Iraqi bread that is brought hot to every table. Skewered beef, chicken and lamb are popular entrees, but vegetarians can have a field day with the piquant salads, the hummus combos (it's served with chickpeas, pine nuts, or marinated mushrooms) and the falafel with tahini. **WHO** The Israeli diaspora and West Valleyites who simply like terrific, freshly prepared Middle Eastern food. ☉ 🥄

[Itzik Hagadol Grill] 17201 Ventura Blvd., Encino, 818.784.4080, itzikhagadol.com. L & D daily. Israeli/Middle Eastern. Beer & wine. AE, MC, V. $$ - $$$ **WHY** For the dazzingly colorful appetizer of 20 Israeli salads, the homemade flatbread and the array of grilled things on skewers. **WHAT** Come hungry to this upscale *shipudia* (Israeli skewer house), because regardless of your intentions, you'll eat too much. Pretty much every table orders the signature appetizer of 20 salads (carrots, eggplant, tabbouleh, mushrooms, etc.), and whichever ones you finish, the nice waiters will refill, no charge. Warm flatbread will magically appear on the table as fast as you eat it. And then there are the mesquite-grilled skewers: sizzling baby chicken thighs, chicken livers, filet of beef, foie gras and, yes, turkey testicles. It's not cheap, but it's good and it's great fun, especially for special occasions. **WHO** People who've been to the parent restaurant in Tel Aviv. 🥄 ☉

[Koko's Middle Eastern Restaurant] 16935 Vanowen St., Van Nuys, 818.708.1877. L & D Tues.-Sun. Armenian/Middle Eastern. No booze. AE, MC, V. $ - $$$ **WHY** Mezze good enough — and generous enough — to make an entire meal. **WHAT** The ginormous bowl of pickled vegetables and tower of pita that show up as soon as you sit down set the tone for the staggeringly generous portion sizes that are to come. Arrive hungry, or go with a group and share. *Muhammara* (crushed walnut dip with pomegranate juice), smoky eggplant dip, hummus and sliced lamb tongue in a lemon marinade are good choices from the appetizer list; a fine share-worthy entree is *arayes-maria*, a garlicky round of ground lamb and beef laced with pine nuts. ☺

[La Porteña] 16150 Nordhoff St., North Hills, 818.920.3894. L & D Tues.-Sun. Argentinean. Beer & wine. MC, V. $ - $$$ **WHY** Well-prepared Argentinean food in a West Valley area that needs interesting places to eat. **WHAT** Now run by the Mercado Buenos Aires folks, this no-frills restaurant serves tasty milanese, empanadas, *parrillada* (mixed grill) and pastas, notably gnocchi specials. Plan on taking food home. **WHO** Argentinean ex-pats and carnivores. 🗺️ ☺

🍴 ESSENTIALLY L.A. ☉ LATE ♥ ROMANTIC 🗺️ VALUE 🍃 QUIET 🌿 SUSTAINABLE

[Lum-Ka-Naad] **8920 Reseda Blvd., Northridge, 818.882.3028, lumkanaad.com. L & D daily. Thai. No booze. MC, V. $ - $$ WHY** Rewarding Thai dishes not often seen outside of Thai Town, served in a warm little Northridge storefront. **WHAT** The brash tart heat of the south and the warm mellow flavors of the north come together in this rustically styled dining room, where the restaurant's forward-thinking owners aim to spread the word about "true" Thai flavors. The food is meticulously prepared — *laap plaa duk* (crispy catfish salad) and *laap kua* (ground pork salad), for example — and often comes with the restaurant's signature platters of palate-cooling fresh vegetables. 🥗

[Madeleine Bistro] **18621 Ventura Blvd., Tarzana, 818.758.6971, madeleinebistro.com. L Wed.-Fri., D Wed.-Sun., brunch Sat.-Sun. Modern American/vegan. Beer & wine. AE, MC, V. $$ - $$$ WHY** Tasty, seasonally changing risotto and pasta entrees, shiitake mushroom sushi, chicken-fried seitan with mashed potatoes and delicious, homey desserts; to drink are organic wines, beers and inventive juice drinks. **WHAT** David Anderson, former chef at Real Food Daily, and his wife, Molly, have brought the same sort of inventive vegan fare to a West Valley neighborhood that's grateful for it. The storefront bistro has a handsome modern-Craftsman look, a nice little wine bar and a menu that focuses as much on satisfaction as it does on health. **WHO** Goodlooking, yoga-practicing vegetarians. 🔵🖐

[Mercado Buenos Aires] **7540 Sepulveda Blvd., Van Nuys, 818.786.0522. L & D daily. Argentinean. Beer & wine. AE, MC, V. $ - $$ WHY** Excellent and authentic Argentine classics: empanadas, milanesa, white fish, huge platters of sizzling meat, mashed potatoes and bread pudding, all at more than reasonable prices. **WHAT** At this quirky café in the middle of a deli and meat market, patrons cheer their soccer team on TV or simply kibitz while munching on sandwiches slathered with herby chimichurri or on a grilled steak from the meat department, where every cut for a good parillada is sold. After your lunch or dinner, you can pick up pastries, tortas, cold cuts and upscale Latin American groceries from the market. **WHO** Who knew there were so many Argentineans in the Valley? 🥗☺

[Puro Sabor Peruvian Food] 🛡 **6366 Van Nuys Blvd., Van Nuys, 818.908.0818. B, L & D daily. Peruvian. BYOB. MC, V. $ - $$ WHY** Pure, unadulterated Peruvian flavors (*puro sabor* means "pure flavor") in a sweet Valley spot with modest prices. **WHAT** This isn't the most scenic neighborhood in Van Nuys, but inside is a cheerful, spotless café that showcases the accomplished cooking of chef Juana Paz, a bank teller from Peru who succeeded in achieving her twin dreams of moving to the United States and having her own restaurant. Everything she makes is wonderful: sparkling, well-balanced ceviches; a superb *parihuela*, the South American answer to bouillabaisse; *seco de chivo*, a rich, long-simmered kid stew; lumberjack-size Peruvian breakfasts on weekends; and, for dessert, heavenly *picarones*, tempura-light pumpkin doughnuts. 🕸

[Rincon Taurino] 8708 Van Nuys Blvd., Panorama City, 818.892.7444. B, L & D daily (to 3 a.m. Sat.-Sun.). Mexican. No booze. Cash only. $ **WHY** Tender al pastor with a crunchy glaze, pit-barbecued lamb and chicken on weekends, and rich-tasting but lean *pierna de cerdo* (pork leg), served in burritos or tortas. **WHAT** First-timers come for the excellent tacos and burritos, then return for the Saturday and Sunday *barbacoa*, whole pit-roasted lamb, served in two courses: lamb soup, followed by the roasted lamb with rice, beans and guacamole. **WHO** North Valley carnivores — and even a few vegetarians, who come for the fine vegetarian burrito. ☺ 🕸🔖☺

[Saddle Peak Lodge] 🏛 419 Cold Canyon Rd., Calabasas, 818.222.3888, saddlepeaklodge.com. D Wed.-Sun., brunch Sun. Modern American. Full bar. AE, MC, V. $$$$ - $$$$$ **WHY** The country-rustic, ultra-atmospheric setting, not to mention the seared foie gras, elk tenderloin and a wine list bulging with trophy cabs. **WHAT** Decorated like a rustic hunting lodge and set in the spectacular mountains that divide Malibu from the Valley, Saddle Peak is that rarest of birds: a special-occasion restaurant that has remained special for years, despite several changes of chef. Expect a menu heavy on exotic meats and poultry (quail, venison, elk), excellent and attentive service and, at the end of the evening, a whacking big bill. **WHO** Well-heeled, well-dressed Angelenos who may have driven quite a distance to get here, and they're typically celebrating something. ♥ 🌙 ☺ ✿ 🏛

[Sako's Mediterranean Cuisine] 6736 Corbin Ave., Reseda, 818.342.8710, sakosmediterraneancuisine.com. L Sat.-Sun., D Wed.-Sun. Turkish/Armenian. No booze. MC, V. $ - $$ **WHY** *Iskender kebab*, an astonishingly tasty dish of seasoned ground beef cooked on a rotisserie then sliced very thin and served in a heap with a splash of light, fresh tomato sauce, grilled pita and yogurt swirled with brown butter. **WHAT** You have to really look to find this place, which is hidden behind a Del Taco and the Venetian Palace Gourmet Hall. In the cheerful, simple dining room you'll sample the delicious food of Istanbul: kebabs, surprisingly delicious fried eggplant, tripe soup and a beautiful *borek*, thin, flaky tubes of phyllo filled with seasoned feta. Try the candied apple for dessert. **WHO** Homesick Turks and West Valleyites grateful for the good, inexpensive food. 🕸☺

[Sol y Luna] 19601 Ventura Blvd., Tarzana, 818.343.8448, solyluna-restaurant.com. L Tues.-Fri., D Tues.-Sun. Mexican. Full bar. AE, MC, V. $$ **WHY** Cal-Mexican food that's a notch above most; try the fresh tableside guac, house-made sopes and tamales, and luscious (if mild) chile verde. **WHAT** The family that owns the funkier Las Fuentes has done a fine job providing the West Valley with a good all-around full-bar Mexican restaurant. It's colorful and just kitschy enough, the food is better than it needs to be (places like this that serve margaritas seem to be packed no matter what refried gloop they serve), and the cadillac margaritas are excellent (but avoid the fruity ones). Cons: No reservations, so there's often a wait for dinner, and lots of noise when it's full. **WHO** Local working folks at lunch, and cheerful groups of families and friends at night. 📷😊

[Springbok Bar & Grill] **16153 Victory Blvd., Van Nuys, 818.988.9786, thespringbok.com. L & D daily. South African. Full bar. AE, MC, V. $ - $$$ WHY** Well-executed versions of South Africa's culinary hits: curries, chile sauces, meaty barbecues, a subtly spice Naidoo's Durban curry, tasty kebabs called *sosaties* and much more. **WHAT** Because this is L.A.'s only South African restaurant, you might envision a modest, family-owned spot where you could sample a few of those wonderful South African wines and explore a delicious multicultural cuisine with European, Malaysian, East Indian and African elements. A cuisine, it would seem, perfectly suited to L.A. tastes. At first, the fantasy is completely crushed by the sports bar setting — it looks like a burger-and-beer place. But chef Trevor Netmann is turning out the real thing in a sea of flat-screen TVs and rugby matches. **WHO** South African ex-pats, rugby fans and curious diners. 😊 📷

[Sushi Ichiban Kan] **19723 Ventura Blvd., Woodland Hills, 818.883.8288, sushiichiban-kan.com. L Mon.-Fri., D nightly. Sushi/Japanese. Full bar. AE, MC, V. $$ - $$$ WHY** Yes, Virginia, there is good sushi in the West Valley. **WHAT** The family that owned the popular Hirosuke in Encino sold it in 2007, then opened Sushi Ichiban-Kan in affluent, restaurant-hungry Woodland Hills. The menu is extensive, with cooked Japanese specialties such as tempura, teriyaki and grilled seafood, as well as sushi, sashimi and a variety of creative cut rolls. Regulars rave about the lunch combo specials, but at lunch or dinner the kitchen's real talent is behind the sushi counter. Service is warm and deferential; after a meal, you'll be ushered out with a flurry of bows from every staffer you pass. **WHO** A cross-section of sushi-loving West Valleyites. ♥ 🍴

[Sushi Iki] **18663 Ventura Blvd., Tarzana, 818.343.3470, sushiiki.com. L Tues.-Fri., D Tues.-Sun. Japanese/sushi. Beer & wine. AE, MC, V. $$$$ - $$$$$ WHY** Spectacular, if pricey, sushi. **WHAT** In addition to the familiar sushi and sashimi offerings, chef "Crazy Eddie" Okamoto offers exotic and unusual seafood items imported from around the world. If you're not on a budget, this is a great West Valley sushi option. ♥ 🍴

[Top Thai Cuisine] **7333 Reseda Blvd., Reseda, 818.705.8902. L Mon.-Tues. & Thurs.-Sat., D Mon.-Tues. & Thurs.-Sun. Thai. Beer & wine. AE, MC, V. $ - $$ WHY** Superb northern Thai food in an unlikely Reseda location — it's a blessing for Northridge and Reseda locals and is worth a trip for Thai aficionados. **WHAT** It may be on a less-than-hip stretch of Reseda Boulevard, but the dining room is handsome and the china elegant. Proceed directly to the back page of the menu for the northern specialties — proprietress Noi Sriyana will be happy to make recommendations. Don't miss the *muu ping*, garlic-infused strips of pork; *khao sawy* noodle curry; or *sai ua* pork sausage. 🍸

[Uerukamu] 19596 Ventura Blvd., Tarzana, 818.609.0993. D Mon.-Sat. Japanese. Beer & wine. AE, MC, V. $$ - $$$ **WHY** An excellent range of sakes and a lot of very good food to accompany your sake. **WHAT** The menu at this izakaya and sake bar in a mini-mall offers carefully made classical dishes such as *chawan mushi* (steamed egg soup), fried eggplant with a miso glaze, and pork chunks braised in sukiyaki sauce, as well as some good sushi standards. The extensive sake selection includes several flights and monthly sake deals. 🍸

[Woodlands] 🏛 9840 Topanga Canyon Blvd., Chatsworth, 818.998.3031, woodlandschatsworth.com. L Tues.-Fri., D Tues.-Sun., brunch Sat.-Sun. Indian/vegetarian. Beer & wine. AE, MC, V. $ - $$ **WHY** For "Dosa Nights" (Wednesdays and Fridays), when you can pick a dosa and gorge yourself at the sumptuous buffet — all for $10. **WHAT** Who needs meat when you can feast on south Indian vegetarian fare that's this scrumptious? Go-to dishes include tamarind and lemon rice, coconut chutney and the amazing *chana batura* — fried bread that's as crisp as an eggshell and as big as a volleyball. **WHO** South Indians and vegetarians making a pilgrimage. 🗺🥄☺

WESTSIDE: CENTRAL

[Annapurna Cuisine] 10200 Venice Blvd., Culver City, 310.204.5500, annapurnacuisine.com. L & D daily. Indian/vegetarian. Beer & wine. AE, MC, V. $ - $$ **WHY** Dosas and southern-style curries in a tech-savvy setting complete with Bollywood offerings on plasma screens. **WHAT** Annapurna showcases classic southern Indian cooking in an urbane setting (complete with WiFi). Try the ultra-thin paper dosa or a curry accompanied by pickles, chutneys and sambars. 🗺🥄

[Beacon] 3280 Helms Ave., Culver City, 310.838.7500, beacon-la.com. L Mon.-Sat., D Tues.-Sun. Modern American/Asian. Beer & wine. AE, MC, V. $ - $$$ **WHY** Elegant but unpretentious Cal-Asian food made by the founding chef of Chinois-on-Main — without the scene or the high prices of his former culinary home. The midweek prix-fixe meals are a great value. **WHAT** Now that Culver City has another dozen or so hot spots for the hordes to hit, Beacon has mellowed into becoming exactly the sort of everyday bistro that husband-and-wife owners Kazuto Matsusaka and Vicki Fan hoped it would be. In a concrete-modern space in the old Beacon Laundry building (with lots of outdoor seating), regulars sustain themselves on udon with braised pork belly, addictive chicken wings with a soy-ginger glaze, a tasty chopped salad and, for those who want a proper dinner, salmon trout over grits or grilled organic chicken with a Thai marinade. **WHO** Culver City families having a quiet weeknight dinner and studio folks and friends meeting for lunch on the large, sunny patio. 🖼 🍴 🥢 ☺ ✪

[Blue on Blue] Avalon Hotel, 9400 Olympic Blvd., Beverly Hills, 310.407.7791, avalonbeverlyhills.com. B, L & D daily. Californian/French. Full bar. AE, MC, V. $$$ - $$$$ **WHY** For fabulous happy-hour people-watching and happy-hour prices that are hard to beat: $6 scallop BLTs and black trumpet mushroom risotto. **WHAT** The Avalon has surprisingly good hotel food — this is 90210, so they can afford a real chef — and even regular folk can score a Jetsons-modern poolside table, although you might want to pull out the Juicy jeans or you might get a once-over. Monday night is the good-value "bistro burger night." **WHO** Chihuahuas in Birkin bags nibbling treats while their owners discreetly down bacon burgers in private poolside cabanas. ♥ 🍴 ✪ 🏛

[Café Bella Roma S.P.Q.R.] 1513 S. Robertson Blvd., Pico-Robertson, 310.277.7662, bellaromaspqr.com. B, L & D Tues.-Sun. Italian. BYOB. AE, MC, V. $$ **WHY** The sort of friendly, affordable, garlic-scented trattoria that every neighborhood deserves and this one finally got. **WHAT** A mamma-and-pappa spot with more tables on the sidewalk than inside, Bella Roma is a modest Italian café with a better kitchen than you might expect. Don't be in a big hurry, because the food's made from scratch: seasonal soups, house-made gnocchi, tagliatelle frutti di mare, tasty small pizzas and late-breakfast (it doesn't open until 10 a.m.) frittatas. Pass on dessert, but do have a good espresso. **WHO** Pico-Robertson neighbors who can walk here. 🖼 🥢 ☺ ✪

[Craft] 🏛 10100 Constellation Blvd., Century City, 310.279.4180, craftrestaurant.com. L Mon.-Fri., D nightly. Steakhouse/American. Full bar. AE, MC, V. $$$$ - $$$$$ **WHY** Servers who make you feel like Trump, special-occasion food (veal sweetbreads with kumquats, rabbit saddle with wild cherries) and a Wall Street atmosphere for those times when laid back L.A. just won't do. **WHAT** Part of Tom Colicchio's New York–based mini-empire, this elegant new place has a design-your-own menu where everything is à la carte — at upscale steakhouse prices (think $15 for a side of forest mushrooms, although to be fair, dishes are larger to share). But if you have deep pockets, it's worth it. If your stocks just flopped, hit the adjacent Craftbar for superb cured meats and cheeses at half the price of the dining-room dishes. **WHO** Power suits and handsome families with adult kids celebrating birthdays, big-boy style.

[Cut] 🏛 Beverly Wilshire Hotel, 9500 Wilshire Blvd., Beverly Hills, 310.276.8500, fourseasons.com/beverlywilshire. D Mon.-Sat. Steakhouse. Full bar. AE, MC, V. $$$$$ **WHY** Bone-marrow flan with parsley salad,

🥢 VEGETARIAN ☺ KID FRIENDLY ✪ PATIO DINING � DELIVERY 🏛 PRIVATE PARTY

dry-aged prime rib-eye steak and possibly the best people-watching in Beverly Hills. **WHAT** With its sleek Richard Meier–designed interior and menu showcasing the finest beefsteaks and seafood from all over the world, Wolfgang Puck's Cut has been a runaway success since its 2006 opening. If you're on an expense account or have money to burn, get a reservation and settle in for exceptional service, expertly selected wines and a superb meal. **WHO** Celebrities galore, young turks from the studios, Maybach drivers. ♥ 〃

[Fogo de Chao] 133 N. La Cienega Blvd., Beverly Hills, 310.289.7755, fogodechao.com. L Mon.-Fri., D nightly. Brazilian. Full bar. AE, MC, V. $$$$ - $$$$$ **WHY** When you're starving, celebrating and have $55 to blow on a single dinner, not counting drinks, tax and tip (or dessert, but you won't have room for it anyway). **WHAT** Of Southern California's several churrascarias, none has been more successful than this grand temple of meat, where spits of lamb, beef, pork and chicken turn day and night on a massive, mesquite-fed rotisserie grill. It costs a bundle but is worth it for a splurge, thanks to the most spectacular salad bar in L.A. and the quality of the meat, carved tableside by swashbuckling gauchos. **WHO** Lots of upscale family groups celebrating birthdays and graduations with vast quantities of gorgeous meats. 〃 ☺

[Ford's Filling Station] 9531 Culver Blvd., Culver City, 310.202.1470, fordsfillingstation.net. L & D daily. Modern American. Full bar. AE, MC, V. $$ - $$$$ **WHY** For a robust scene and modern comfort food: platters of cured meats, fried Ipswich clams, pizza-like flatbreads, oxtail soup and a hearty pub burger, all accompanied by boutique beers (it considers itself a gastropub) and chic wines. **WHAT** Emblematic of the new Culver City, this is one of the hottest of a dozen hot restaurants that are drawing Angelenos to the town that was once L.A.'s sleepiest secret. Owner/chef Ben Ford has capitalized on both his celebrity name (he's Harrison's son) and his talent for making food that people want to eat now. It's jam-packed, screamingly loud, a little overpriced and undeniably fun. **WHO** People who wouldn't have been caught dead in Culver City a decade ago. ☼

[Fraiche] 9411 Culver Blvd., Culver City, 310.839.6800, fraicheres-taurantla.com. L & D Mon.-Sun., brunch Sun. French/Italian. Full bar. AE, MC, V. $$ - $$$ **WHY** Because neighborhood food at these prices is rarely this good: beef tartare with bacon sabayon, striped bass with haricots verts, baby artichokes, fingerling potatoes and a carrot nage, pappardelle with oxtail, mustard greens and crucolo cheese. **WHAT** Yet another Culver City hot spot, this time with a husband-and-wife top chef-pastry chef team and an atmosphere that's like your favorite pair of jeans – it just seems right for everything. If not for the snooty sommelier – and the feeling that the investors are always around sniffing for more – it'd be perfect. If you can't score a reservation, hit the bar for moules frites and a good cocktail. ☞

[Gardens] Four Seasons Hotel, 300 S. Doheny Dr., Beverly Hills, 310.273.2222, fourseasons.com. B, L & D daily. Californian/Mediterranean. Full bar. AE, MC, V. $$$$$ **WHY** Hey, isn't that Amy Adams over there? **WHAT** The Four Seasons has always made sure to have a seriously talented chef in the kitchen of its dining room, and Ashley James holds the torch high. The weekend buffet brunch is what Gardens is famed for, but if you can afford it (not many can), come for dinner and discover how talented he is. **WHO** Rich grandmas taking the family out for Sunday brunch and journalists interviewing celebrities. ♥ 🍷 🏛

[The Grill on the Alley] 🏠 9560 Dayton Way, Beverly Hills, 310.276.0615, thegrill.com. L Mon.-Sat., D nightly. American. Full bar. AE, MC, V. $$$ - $$$$ **WHY** The Cobb and Caesar salads, and the chance to sit in the same room with the people who greenlit the movie your kids saw last weekend. **WHAT** This clubby institution offers an old-school menu (shrimp cocktail, chicken pot pie, meatloaf) to its power-lunching Hollywood faithful. Even though some of the lunch-hour heat has migrated elsewhere, the Grill is still a draw, and its table assignments are a time-honored barometer of mogul status. **WHO** Everybody who's anybody in Hollywood and (way) beyond, including a certain moon-walking astronaut. 🍷

[Guelaguetza Palms] 🏠 11127 Palms Blvd., Palms, 310.837.1153. B, L & D daily. Mexican/Oaxacan. Beer & wine. MC, V. $ - $$ **WHY** Heavenly huevos rancheros with rice and black beans, green-mole soup, empanadas with various fillings and carefully made moles of complex and rewarding flavors. **WHAT** Soledad Lopez's offshoot of her brother's larger chain is the winner in the group — a warm, tidy, modest neighborhood restaurant serving outstanding Oaxacan food. If you come for a Saturday-night dinner of chicken with green mole, chayote and potatoes, you'll want to return on Sunday morning for a breakfast of café con leche and huevos rancheros. **WHO** Oaxacan families from the neighborhood and fans who travel to eat here. 🪑 🍷 ☺

[Haifa] 8717 W. Pico Blvd., Pico-Robertson, 310.888.7700, haifala. com. L Sun.-Fri., D Sun.-Thurs. Israeli/Middle Eastern. No booze. AE, MC, V. $ - $$ **WHY** For kosher, Israeli-style Middle Eastern cooking that's fresher and lighter than most. **WHAT** This storefront looks cheesy, but inside is a cheerful café with vintage French posters and granite café tables. Haifa calls its cooking Middle Eastern, but it's a bit different from the Lebanese norm: easier on the oil and garlic, with an abundance of colorful vegetables and less of an emphasis on sour/tart flavors. The salads are standouts, from the cumin-infused carrots to the tangy dice of cucumber, tomato and onion. Kebabs are tender, the chicken dishes have lots of flavor, the falafel is crisp, and the rich hummus is as addictive as the fresh pita. Service is brusque but good. **WHO** Middle-aged businessmen talking on cell phones, locals who keep kosher, and falafel-and-hummus junkies from all over. 🪑🥬

🥬 VEGETARIAN ◌ KID FRIENDLY ☼ PATIO DINING � DELIVERY 🏛 PRIVATE PARTY

[Hokusai] 8400 Wilshire Blvd., Beverly Hills, 323.782.9717, hokusaires-taurant.com. L Mon.-Fri., D Mon.-Sat. Japanese/French. Full bar. AE, MC, V. $$$$ **WHY** Traditional Japanese combinations at lunch and French-inflected dinner entrees, as well as a sushi bar. Appetizers include rock-shrimp tempura, lavish foie gras with eggplant and yuzu sauce, and lobster with truffles, while entrees include salmon with lobster bisque sauce, Kobe beef and Jidori chicken. **WHAT** Beverly Hills has several upscale sushi options, and Hokusai is one of the more recent and elegant entries, with attentive service and a dramatic interior and accomplished cooking. With a full bar and happy-hour selections, it's a good choice before a movie or play, or for a business lunch. ♥ �

[Industry Cafe & Jazz] 6039 Washington Blvd., Culver City, 310.202.6633, industrycafeandjazz.com. L & D daily. Ethiopian. Beer & wine. AE, MC, V. $ - $$ **WHY** Friendly Ethiopian food and even friend-lier live jazz — with no cover charge. **WHAT** This simple little spot is fun for a change-of-pace dinner: tasty Ethiopian food, with some American soul food for good measure, paired with jazz on weekends and Wednesdays and comedy on Thursdays. ☺ 🎦

[The Ivy] 113 N. Robertson Blvd., Beverly Hills, 310.274.8303. L & D daily. Modern American. Full bar. AE, MC, V. $$$$$ **WHY** To channel Danny DeVito in *Get Shorty*. **WHAT** There's a white picket fence to keep the looky-loos out and the celebrities in, and the remarkable thing is how well it works. Movie and music stars really do come here, as do the agents, managers and publicists who feed off of them, and they're all delighted to pay $30 for a burger or a bowl of spaghetti. The surprise is that the hearty regional American food (especially the corn chowder, crab cakes and desserts) is actually good. It's nowhere near worth the money, of course, but can you put a price on sitting next to Mandy Moore or Conan O'Brien? **WHO** The famous, semi-famous and wanna-be-near-the-famous. ☼

[Koutoubia] 🏛 2116 Westwood Blvd., Westwood, 310.475.0729, koutoubiarestaurant.com. D Tues.-Sun. Moroccan. Full bar. AE, MC, V. $$$ **WHY** For L.A.'s best full-experience (ritual hand washing, sitting on pillows, belly dancing on weekends) Moroccan restaurant. **WHAT** Longtime Koutoubia owner Michel Ohayon is one of L.A.'s most legendary hosts. More often than not, it will be he who washes your hands with rosewater and he who checks on you a half-dozen times during your dinner. His careful attention has kept this place at the top of the heap, with delicious traditional Moroccan food (tagines, couscous, b'stilla) and an enveloping and romantic atmosphere and experience. **WHO** Celebrators, romantics and b'stilla junkies. ♥ ☺ 🏛

[Lawry's the Prime Rib] 🏛 100 N. La Cienega Blvd., Beverly Hills, 310.652.2827, lawrysonline.com. D nightly. American. Full bar. AE, MC, V. $$$$ - $$$$$ **WHY** Luscious prime rib and a theatrical sense of "going out." **WHAT** It's kinda like the Disneyland of restaurants. Lawry's has characters (waitresses in uniforms and perky caps and imposing carving men in stiff toques), adventures (salad tossed tableside in a huge spinning bowl, prime rib carved from a silver cart) and tons of Japanese tourists. But don't let the kitschy show have you thinking this place isn't good — it's great. **WHO** Three-generation families celebrating occasions, couples on special dates and lots of happy Japanese business people and travelers. ☺

[Le Saint Amour] 🔒 9725 Culver Blvd., Culver City, 310.842.8155, lesaintamour.com. L Mon.-Fri., D nightly, brunch Sun. French. Beer & wine. AE, MC, V. $$ - $$$ **WHY** A meal at this reasonably priced, entirely charming bistro is way cheaper than a ticket to France — with a wait staff that's as professional as in Paris, but so much nicer. **WHAT** This fantastic and blessedly affordable (and quiet) new French bistro is the creation of charcuterie maker and former Angelique Café owner Bruno Commereuc (whose pâté and head cheese are also available a few doors down at Fraîche). It's got it all: a tree-shaded sidewalk patio, romantic bistro interior, easy-drinking French wines, and textbook onion soup, frisée aux lardons, moules frites and duck confit — simple comfort food of the highest order. **WHO** Francophiles and well-dressed, grown-up couples and groups of friends. ♥ 📷 ☼

[M Café de Chaya] 🔒 9343 Culver Blvd., Culver City, 310.838.4300, mcafedechaya.com. B, L & D daily. Modern American/vegetarian. No booze. AE, MC, V. $$ **WHY** Everything — from barbecue seitan sandwiches to soy-based desserts — tastes good. **WHAT** This more spacious cousin to the Melrose original has a pleasant patio and an easygoing atmosphere. Both locations offer a communal table and surprisingly good macrobiotic, organic, vegetarian and/or vegan cooking that's the most interesting of its kind in L.A. right now. **WHO** Girlfriends brunching, families with adorably organic children. ☺ 🔍 ☺ ☼

[Mako] 225 S. Beverly Dr., Beverly Hills, 310.288.8338, makorestaurant. com. L Tues.-Fri., D Tues.-Sat. Asian. Full bar. AE, MC, V. $$ - $$$ **WHY** Everything on the menu is tempting, from sizzling soft shell crab with ginger dressing and grilled sweet Japanese prawns to Beijing duck and Kobe meatballs. **WHAT** The former chef at Chinois runs this tranquil, softly lit Asian small-plates spot with an open kitchen (sit at the counter and watch the cooks) and carefully nuanced dishes with an accent on seafood. A good date-night spot. ♥ 📷 🍴

[Mastro's Steakhouse] 246 N. Cañon Dr., Beverly Hills, 310.888.8782, mastrossteakhouse.com. D nightly. Steakhouse. Full bar. AE, MC, V. $$$$$ **WHY** The Beverly Hills comedy writ large, with really good steaks to boot. **WHAT** It's loud, it's showy, the bar's a scene, the prices are high, and everyone is having a blast at Mastro's, which has held firm as one of Beverly Hills's "it" spots for several years now. What's kept it so popular is not just the scene, which is considerable, but the fact that the prime steaks, as well as the cocktails, onion rings, potatoes and spinach, are skillfully cooked and massively portioned. **WHO** Movie stars, plastic-surgery victims, anniversary celebrants from Van Nuys. 🍸

[Matsuhisa] 🏛 129 N. La Cienega Blvd., Beverly Hills, 310.659.9639, nobumatsuhisa.com. L Mon.-Fri., D nightly. Japanese. Beer & wine. AE, MC, V. $$$ - $$$$ **WHY** For Nobu Matsuhisa's Peruvian-influenced Japanese cuisine, which came to fame here and later swept the food world. **WHAT** The Nobu craze started here, in a restaurant far simpler than its overwrought Beverly Hills neighbors, and while the Nobus in Malibu, New York, Aspen and beyond may be a bigger deal these days, we still prefer the parent. The famed dishes — black cod with miso, mussels in spicy garlic sauce, shrimp with caviar, the range of rolls and sushi — are pretty much the same, but somehow they seem better served and, well, more real here. **WHO** The scene people have long since moved on, but the loyal fans remain. ♥ 🍸

[Napa Valley Grille] 1100 Glendon Ave., Westwood, 310.824.3322, napavalleygrille.com. L & D daily. Californian. Full bar. AE, MC, V. $$$$ - $$$$$ **WHY** The creative sandwiches and burgers, including the "Coastal Oregon sushi-quality smoked albacore tuna melt" and the Niman Ranch cheeseburger. **WHAT** A burnished take on wine-country rusticity, the Napa Valley Grille is a good option for a business lunch or dinner before the curtain goes up at the Geffen. It serves good salads, grilled fish, pastas and a nice selection of cheeses accompanied by raisin-pecan bread, along with a wine list that draws prominently — but not exclusively — on bottles from its namesake county. **WHO** Well-dressed folks headed to or from the Geffen. 🍸 📷 ۞ 🍸

[Pampas Grill] 3857 Overland Ave., Culver City, 310.836.0080, pampas-grill.com. L & D daily. Brazilian. Beer & wine. AE, MC, V. $$ **WHY** For affordable and casual Brazilian barbecue. **WHAT** This larger offshoot of the Farmers Market original is built around a large buffet laden with all the Brazilian churrascaria standards: barbecued meats, garlic rice, black beans, plantains, salads, roasted vegetables, fried yucca and that dreamy cheese bread. It's sold by weight, so go easy on the meats for the best value — and your cardiologist will thank you. 📷 ☺ ۞

[Polo Lounge] Beverly Hills Hotel, 9641 Sunset Blvd., Beverly Hills, 310.276.2251, beverlyhillshotel.com. B, L & D daily. American. Full bar. AE, MC, V. $$$$ - $$$$$ **WHY** For a slice of old Hollywood, with a gentlemen's club-style lounge, a pretty garden dining room and lovely tables under the overhanging oak trees on the patio. **WHAT** Food isn't the main attraction at this fabled spot, although the eggs Benedict at brunch are one of the city's best versions, and the ladies who lunch enjoy the Molly salad. Mostly you come for the atmosphere and history — and perhaps one of the sturdy drinks served in the lounge. **WHO** Beverly Hills dowagers, industry players of all ages. ♥ 🍸 ☼

[Shaherzad Restaurant] 1422 Westwood Blvd., Westwood, 310.470.3242. L & D daily. Persian/Middle Eastern. Beer & wine. AE, MC, V. $$ - $$$ **WHY** A fun and affordable choice for Westwood Village dining. Just don't fill up on that amazing bread. **WHAT** The only restaurant around that serves you hot flatbread straight from the tandoor-style oven, Shaherzad is a good place for kebabs, fluffy Persian rice, beef barg and traditional stews. **WHO** Middle Eastern UCLA students and Iranian ladies who lunch. ☺

[Spago] 🔒 176 N. Cañon Dr., Beverly Hills, 310.385.0880, wolfgang-puck.com. L Mon.-Sat., D nightly. Modern American/Californian. Full bar. AE, MC, V. $$$$$ **WHY** To worship at the shrine of California cuisine. **WHAT** Wolfgang Puck still works the room from time to time, when he's not off overseeing his global empire, but this is really Lee Hefter's kingdom, and it's a magical kingdom indeed. (Although now that Hefter's spending time at Cut it may be in the process of becoming chef de cuisine Thomas Boyce's kingdom.) Hefter-Boyce-Puck have kept the creativity and standards at peak level for years, and the tasting menu today is every bit as exciting, beautiful and delicious as it was a decade ago. And Sherry Yard's desserts are fantastic, too. The setting and service do the kitchen justice. **WHO** International hot shots, movie stars and serious eaters. ♥🥡☼🏛

[Sushi Zo] 9824 National Blvd., Palms, 310.842.3977. L Mon.-Fri., D Mon.-Sat. Japanese/sushi. Beer & wine. AE, MC, V. $$$$ - $$$$$ **WHY** Rich ankimo liver, blow-torched butterfish, blue crab hand roll, luscious toro — it's best to just sit back and let it roll out. **WHAT** This austere spot is many people's favorite L.A. sushi bar; there's no scene, fancy rolls or cellphone use allowed, just the freshest fish, simply presented. Reserve ahead, sit at the granite-topped bar and order *omakase*, or chef's choice, for the full experience. **WHO** Serious sushi lovers. 🍸

[Tender Greens] 9523 Culver Blvd., Culver City, 310.842.8300, tendergreensfood.com. L & D daily. Modern American/vegetarian. Beer & wine. AE, MC, V. $ - $$ **WHY** Have-it-your-way salads and healthy entrees at low prices, given the mostly organic and local produce.
WHAT Long lines snake out the door of this pioneering invent-your-own salad spot with a buzzing patio. Diners wait at the counter while their salads are tossed from fresh vegetables and meats, then choose beer, wine, lemonade and cupcakes to go with the salads or main courses. **WHO** Families with active children, retirees and everyone else for miles around. 🍴♻🥡☺ ☼

🥬 **VEGETARIAN** ☺ **KID FRIENDLY** ☼ **PATIO DINING** � **DELIVERY** 🏛 **PRIVATE PARTY**

[Torafuku] 10914 W. Pico Blvd., Century City, 310.470.0014, torafuku-usa.com. L Mon.-Sat., D nightly. Japanese. Beer & wine. AE, MC, V. $$ - $$$ **WHY** Very good, close-to-the-earth country-style meals you might expect at a *ryokan*, or Japanese country inn. **WHAT** Locavores will love the ingredients — organic vegetables; local free-range chicken and eggs; Santa Barbara prawns; grass-fed beef — that chef Tetsuya Harikawa sources for his simply cooked meals. For rice connoisseurs, the star of the show is the early-crop rice cooked in 500-pound ceramic kamado pots that give it a toasty flavor.

[Totoraku Teriyaki House] 10610 W. Pico Blvd., Century City, 310.838.9881. By reservation only. Japanese. BYOB (no corkage). AE, MC, V. $$$$$ **WHY** To pole-vault into the league of the coolest foodies in town. **WHAT** One might assume from the "Pico Teriyaki House" sign outside that this might be a divey neighborhood spot for a cheap plate of chicken teriyaki and shrimp tempura. And one would be very, very wrong. This is L.A.'s great "secret" restaurant, where you can only get a reservation through a personal connection to chef Oyama, and you'd better bring him a serious bottle of wine if you hope to return. In return for your considerable trouble, and upwards of $200 of your money, you'll get a many-course beef-based meal that you may never forget. **WHO** Chefs and people who know people. 🖋

[Tuk Tuk] 8875 W. Pico Blvd., Pico-Robertson, 310.860.1872, tuktukla.com. L & D daily. Thai. Beer & wine. AE, MC, V. $ - $$ **WHY** Beef salad makes a light supper, and curries are also satisfying. **WHAT** One of the best Thai options on the westside, with clean, updated versions of favorite dishes, served in a pleasant Asian-style décor. 🖋🥢☺

[Urasawa] 🏠 218 N. Rodeo Dr., Beverly Hills, 310.247.8939. D nightly. Japanese/Sushi. Full bar. AE, MC, V. $$$$$ **WHY** For an omakase meal of astonishing complexity, diversity and luxury. **WHAT** If you have to ask how much it costs, you can't afford it — so we can't afford it. L.A.'s most expensive sushi restaurant (and that's really saying something) requires an outlay of what would be a month's rent in some parts of the country. But if you're serious about sushi and are ready put yourself in the hands of a master, Hiroyuki Urasawa will present you with 30-plus tiny dishes that will amaze you. **WHO** Not everyone who dines here is rich — some save for months and consider the effort worth it. 🖋

[Versailles] 🏠 10319 Venice Blvd., Culver City, 310.558.3168, versaillescuban.com. L & D daily. Cuban. Beer & wine. AE, MC, V. $ - $$ **WHY** Succulent, irresistible roast pork and Cuban-style roast chicken, and (when it's available) amazing oxtail, too. **WHAT** A no-frills, cheap L.A. landmark beloved for its garlicky marinated roast chicken, juicy, salty Cuban roast pork, plantains, black beans and rice. Branches on South La Cienega and in Encino and Manhattan Beach. 🍽

🏠 ESSENTIALLY L.A. ☺ LATE ♥ ROMANTIC 🍽 VALUE 🖋 QUIET ✿ SUSTAINABLE

[WakaSan] 1929 Westwood Blvd., Westwood, 310.446.5241. D Mon. & Wed.-Sun. Japanese. Beer & wine. MC, V. $$$ **WHY** A great-value $35 omakase meal, usually 11 or 12 carefully made courses. A real find. **WHAT** At this rustic charmer in a Westwood strip mall, a delicious multi-course *omakase* (chef's choice) menu of home-style dishes is the only option — but no one is complaining. It's a great deal for a complex and interesting meal. **WHO** UCLA professors and Japanese-food lovers seeking an affordable splurge. ☉ ⬚

[Wolfgang's Steakhouse] ⬚ 445 N. Cañon Dr., Beverly Hills, 310.385.0640, wolfgangssteakhouse.com. L & D daily. Steakhouse. Full bar. AE, MC, V. $$$$ - $$$$$ **WHY** You can't underestimate the amusement factor of seeing emaciated middle-aged Beverly Hills social x-rays being presented with massive, glistening porterhouses. **WHAT** Wolfgang Zwiener learned a lot of things in his decades as headwaiter at Peter Luger in New York, especially the importance of good service in an expensive steakhouse. So he has this handsome outpost of his growing chain running like a Swiss train station. Everyone gets the massive porterhouse for two (or an even more massive one for four), and it's a gorgeous piece of meat, tasting of its age (in a good way) and unadorned with sauces or fripperies. It's worth going easy on the steak (which takes home well) and the excellent onion rings and spinach to save room for the purist's cheesecake. **WHO** A parade of beautiful-but-not-young people who are old enough to appreciate the impeccable service, not to mention to be able to afford the tab. ☼ ⬚

WEST OF THE 405

[26 Beach Café] 3100 Washington Blvd., Venice, 310.823.7526, 26beach.com. B Mon.-Fri., L & D daily, brunch Sat.-Sun. Californian/ American. Full bar. AE, MC, V. $$ - $$$$ **WHY** House-made buns with the burgers and a nice, casual vibe. **WHAT** So what if it's not really at the beach? The food is good, the prices are reasonable and the setting is flea-market cute, complete with a covered garden. Splurge on the strip steak or wild salmon, or follow the regulars' lead and go with the burgers, which come in variations including salmon, turkey and veggie, or one of the entree salads, such as the ginger-infused salmon with asparagus, mushrooms, greens and soy dressing. Breakfast is also a winner; try the famed french toast. ⬚ ⬚ ☼

[Anisette Brasserie] 225 Santa Monica Blvd., Santa Monica, 310.395.3200, anisettebrasserie.com. B & L Mon.-Fri., D nightly, brunch Sat.-Sun. French. Full bar. AE, MC, V. $$$ **WHY** All the classic French dishes are present, from onion soup to duck à l'orange, raw seafood platters, bourride and potatoes lyonnaise, and they're generally very good. Open all day, Anisette also serves breakfast, from a decadent pastry basket to a full English spread. **WHAT** Longtime L.A. French chef Alain Giraud spent several years conceptualizing his own restau-

---

⬚ VEGETARIAN ☉ KID FRIENDLY ☼ PATIO DINING ⬚ DELIVERY ⬚ PRIVATE PARTY

rant, and when Anisette opened in 2008, it turned out to be a stunning room perfectly replicating a Parisian brasserie, despite its beach-adjacent location. Dark woods, red leather booths, tile floors that look like they've been there forever and gleaming copper cookware complete the Gallic look. As well as a serious wine list, there's a selection of modern, creative cocktails. **WHO** Francophiles with money. ☉ ☺

[Antica Pizzeria] 🏛 Villa Marina Marketplace, 13455 Maxella Ave., 2nd Fl., Marina del Rey, 310.577.8182, anticapizzeria.net. L & D daily. Pizzeria/Italian. Beer & wine. AE, MC, V. $$ **WHY** The perfect and characteristic char on the bottom crust of each exquisitely baked pizza. The margherita is simple, sauceless and spectacular. **WHAT** Even the Neapolitan pizza police (aka the Associazione Verace Pizza Napoletana) recognize the deliciously authentic fare being turned out by Peppe Miele at this Marina del Rey trattoria and pizzeria. The Naples native was the first U.S. resident accepted into the pizza society and his restaurant follows its strict rules on baking methods (wood-burning ovens) and dough (just flour, natural yeast and water.) The result: smallish pizzas that taste utterly *fantastico*. Good salads and pastas, too. **WHO** True believers who know how it's done back in the old country (and we don't mean New York). 🍴☺🚗

[Axe] 1009 Abbot Kinney Blvd., Venice, 310.664.9787, axerestaurant. com. L Wed.-Fri., D Wed.-Sun., brunch Sat.-Sun. Modern American. Beer & wine. AE, MC, V. $$$ **WHY** That Abbot Kinney esprit, plus a chance to feel virtuous and catered-to at the very same meal. **WHAT** From the sidewalk, Axe (pronounced "ah-shay") looks so understated as to be practically unmarked, but that hasn't stopped the hordes from discovering its green-friendly menu and tastefully minimalist vibe. The entrees, like the porterhouse pork chop with a cider reduction, tend to be overpriced, heavy on the organic hype and light on flavor. Stick with the small plates. such as shaved baby artichokes in lemon dressing or soy-braised short ribs with chestnuts. **WHO** Venice habitués too cool to make a scene over spotting celebs like Orlando Bloom. ☺🍴☼

[Bar Hayama] 1803 Sawtelle Blvd., West L.A., 310.235.2000, bar-hayama.com. L Mon.-Fri., D nightly. Japanese. Beer & wine. AE, MC, V. $$$ - $$$$ **WHY** To sip sake and nibble on gorgeous small plates and sushi on the patio, next to the romantic fire pit. **WHAT** The current star of the Sawtelle Japanese scene, Hayama is a winner for its bamboo-lined patio, its two sake bars and the excellent small-plates-and-sushi food of Toshi Sugiura: scallop sashimi, grilled yellowtail collar, soft-shell crab salad, age dashi tofu and more. ♥🍴☼

[Beachcomber Café] Malibu Pier, 23000 Pacific Coast Hwy., Malibu, 310.456.9800, thebeachcombercafe.com. B, L & D daily. American. Full bar. AE, MC, V. $$ - $$$$ **WHY** Because it's on the Malibu Pier and the food doesn't suck. **WHAT** The folks behind the fetchingly restored

1940s Beachcomber at Crystal Cove won the restaurant concession on the recently rehabbed Malibu Pier. The look is identical to the one in Crystal Cove: green leather booths, warm wood paneling and plenty of windows to bring in the Pacific. There's large bar, a row of outdoor tables with dreamy views of the Santa Monica Bay, and a dining room with views north toward Surfrider Beach. The cooking is a little bit better than it needs to be, given the location: breakfast scrambles; albacore tuna melts and burgers for lunch; and for dinner, festive cocktails, grilled seafood and meat (choose those over the heavy seafood pot pie) and big, sugary desserts. **WHO** Rich surfers, date-nighters, tourists and Malibu families celebrating birthdays. ♥ 🍸 ☺ ☼ 🏛

[Beechwood] **822 W. Washington Blvd., Venice, 310.448.8884, beechwoodrestaurant.com. D Tues.-Sat., bar menu nightly. Modern American. Full bar. AE, MC, V. $$ - $$$ WHY** Killer french fries and sweet potato fries, a suave croque madame and desserts as comfy as grandma's lap. **WHAT** Located where way-cool Abbot Kinney meets the more prosaic Washington, Beechwood is rich in Venice style but free of hipster attitude — and its bar menu is one of the best values around. The midcentury-modern building houses a booth-lined dining room, a spacious lounge, and a terrific bar patio warmed by a big fire pit. No matter where you eat, it's all good, it's all stylish, and it's all reasonably priced. **WHO** Handsome twenty- and thirtysomethings in the bar, with date-night boomers in the quieter dining room. ☺ 🍸 🍽 ☼

[Border Grill] 🏛 **1445 4th St., Santa Monica, 310.451.1655, bordergrill.com. L & D daily, brunch Sat.-Sun. Mexican. Full Bar. AE, MC, V. $$ - $$$$ WHY** Designer margaritas and superb appetizers from two California-cuisine pioneers. **WHAT** Chef/owners Susan Feniger and Mary Sue Milliken are foodie rock stars whose first, shoebox-size restaurant City morphed into the original Border Grill. Today, TV's "Two Hot Tamales" have an empire that includes this Border Grill, another in Vegas, Downtown's Cuidad and Feniger's new Street. This is where Santa Monica meets for happy hour: margaritas, mojitos, aged tequilas and wonderful appetizers, such as shrimp ceviche, wild-mushroom quesadillas, chicken panuchos and great guacamole. The main courses are less rewarding (and a lot more expensive) so the savvy stick to appetizers and drinks. The setting matches the food: vibrantly colorful, cheerfully festive and powerfully noisy. **WHO** Santa Monica's happy (hour) people; out-of-town admirers of the Two Hot Tamales. 🍽

[Caché] **3110 Main St., Santa Monica, 310.399.4800, cacherestaurant. com. D nightly. Modern American/French. Full bar. AE, MC, V. $$$ - $$$$ WHY** The plump, crunchy fries alone are worth a visit to Josiah Citrin's new spot. **WHAT** The Mélisse chef's new place in the old Schatzi and Hidden space is an indoor-outdoor late-night bar with the requisite firepit, plus indoor, patio and cabana dining. The kitchen's focus is on the decadent: mason jars of duck confit and foie gras parfait;

🍽 **VEGETARIAN** ☺ **KID FRIENDLY** ☼ **PATIO DINING** 🚚 **DELIVERY** 🏛 **PRIVATE PARTY**

fire-roasted bone marrow with wild mushroom toast; and those fries — half-inch-thick batons, creamy inside and translucently crisped out — seasoned with Basque red pepper or truffle and parmesan. Those same fries are scattered over the steamed mussels, the better to soak up the broth. Citrine's longstanding devotion to the farmers' market is evident, and there are enough apps, mains, flatbreads and seasonal sides (carrots with passionfruit and thyme) to keep a vegetarian happy. **WHO** South Santa Monicans who want something less formal (and expensive) than haute cuisine Mélisse. ♥▨☼

[Café Brasil] 11736 Washington Blvd., Mar Vista, 310.391.1216, cafe-brasil.com. B, L & D daily. Brazilian. Beer & wine. AE, MC, V. $ - $$ **WHY** Tasty, inexpensive Brazilian sandwiches, grilled meats, collard greens, black beans and *feijoada*, the famed pork stew. **WHAT** It's a simple order-at-the-counter café but an exceptionally charming and colorful one, with a greenery-lined sidewalk terrace and an intensely colorful dining room. There's beer and wine, but don't neglect the fresh mango juice or excellent coffee. ▨☺☼

[Café del Rey] 4451 Admiralty Way, Marina del Rey, 310.823.6395, cafedelreymarina.com. L & D daily. Californian/modern American. Full bar. AE, MC, V. $$$ - $$$$$ **WHY** The view and the excellent weekend prix-fixe brunch. **WHAT** In a modern space overlooking bobbing boats, the dinner crowd sips cocktails and dines on oysters, sushi and Alaskan halibut with braised fennel and baby artichokes. The cooking's appealing and consistent, though not quite worth the steep dinnertime tab. Lunch or brunch is a better option, and the bar is a good spot for a nightcap. Welcoming service. **WHO** Boat owners, business folk, Marina residents, all sporting judicious tans. ♥☼

[Caffe Pinguini] 6935 Pacific Ave., Playa del Rey, 310.306.0117, caffepinguini.com. L Tues.-Fri., D Tues.-Sun. Italian. Beer & wine. AE, MC, V. $$$ - $$$$ **WHY** Meticulously prepared Italian classics in a charming spot near the ocean. **WHAT** This funky pocket beach neighborhood in Playa del Rey is a well-kept secret, as is its surprisingly upscale Italian restaurant with a silly name. There's a romantic patio, a cozy dining room, attentive service and some very good dishes, notably the seafood salad, smoked mozzarella with sauteed shiitakes, fresh pastas and traditional piccatas. If only the prices weren't so high. **WHO** Playa date-nighters and visiting LMU parents. ♥☽☼

[Capo] 1810 Ocean Ave., Santa Monica, 310.394.5550, caporestaurant.com. D Tues.-Sat. Italian. Full bar. AE, MC, V. $$$$ - $$$$$ **WHY** A Bruce Marder gem worth finding amid the posh Ocean Avenue hotels. **WHAT** The luxuriously simple, farm-fresh fare served in this tiny, romantic Italian restaurant is worth a special-occasion splurge. Meats are a specialty, so resist the handmade pastas and dive into the steaks and chops, grilled in the wood-burning fireplace in the corner of the dining room. The service and wine list are both excellent, as well they should be at these prices. ♥ 🕸

[Catch] 🏛 **Hotel Casa del Mar, 1910 Ocean Way, Santa Monica, 310.581.7714, catchsantamonica.com. B, L & D daily. Seafood/sushi. Full bar. AE, MC, V. $$$ - $$$$$ WHY** Chef Michael Reardon's perfectly realized Cal-French-Asian seafood is well worth the splurge. **WHAT** High ceilings, crisp white walls and floor-to-ceiling windows frame the dazzling view at this privileged outpost of exceptional, yet un-showoffy, cuisine. Why complicate that piece of snapper from Thailand when it tastes so fabulous just sautéed till crisp and placed next to a salad of calamari, cannelli beans and herbs? For another take on the gorgeous seafood offered here, there's a serene sushi bar in the middle of the dining room. Try the Meyer lemon tart for dessert. **WHO** Beautiful people with big bank accounts, sipping $15 pre-dinner cocktails in the adjacent lounge. ♥ 🕸

[Chalet Edelweiss] **8740 Sepulveda Blvd., Westchester, 310.645.8740, chaletedelweiss.us. Swiss/German. Beer & wine. AE, MC, V. $$ WHY** Because L.A. is very short on Swiss restaurants — this is about it. **WHAT** This is not destination dining, but it's good to know about if you're in the Westchester/LAX area and have a hankering for a whole lotta cheese and some accordian music. Try the raclette, the fondue, the schnitzels with good späetzle, and the gut-busting Swiss mac 'n cheese, but skip dessert. That way you might be able to manage another Bitburger Pils, which they have on tap. **WHO** Westchester families and birthday celebrants. 🖼️ ☺

[Chaya Venice] **110 Navy St., Venice, 310.396.1179, thechaya.com. L Mon.-Fri., D nightly. Asian/Californian. Full bar. AE, MC, V. $$$ - $$$$ WHY** Lobster enchiladas, and one of the best happy hours in town. **WHAT** Chaya Venice's once-pioneering East-meets-West cuisine is now found all over L.A., but it's good to revisit the source for good sushi, seaweed salads, pastas and such French-Japanese hybrids as miso-marinated sea bass with a wasabi-tamarind beurre blanc. **WHO** Venice artists and musicians, when they can afford it, and Hollywood moguls, who can always afford it. 🍸

[Chez Jay] **1657 Ocean Ave., Santa Monica, 310.395.1741, chezjays. com. B Sat.-Sun., L Mon.-Fri., D nightly. American. Full bar. AE, MC, V. $ - $$$ WHY** Jay Fiondella has passed on, but his place remains an oasis in a sea of gentrification. **WHAT** This tiny shack festooned with Christmas lights lives on amid the upscale hotels and overpriced restaurants that now dominate Ocean Avenue. Chez Jay still packs 'em in nightly with old-school food that fills you up just fine. It's also fun for a drink after dinner, when the red leatherette booths start to empty out. **WHO** Those who can't resist the old-school appeal and celebrity-dive cachet (Warren Beatty and Sean Penn were regulars for years). 🏛

🍸 **VEGETARIAN** ☺ **KID FRIENDLY** ☼ **PATIO DINING** 🚗 **DELIVERY** 🏛 **PRIVATE PARTY**

[Chinois on Main] **2709 Main St., Santa Monica, 310.392.9025, wolfgangpuck.com. L Wed.-Fri., D nightly. Asian. Full bar. AE, MC, V. \$\$\$\$ - \$\$\$\$\$ WHY** It's a delicious '80s-era time warp — noisy, pricey and crowded — with desserts worth sticking around for, like the dim sum dessert box and the crème brûlée trio. **WHAT** It's been a quarter-century since Wolfgang Puck opened Chinois on Main, and not much has changed — which, oddly enough, turns out to be a good thing. It all works: that hot-pink-and-turquoise décor, those Cal-Asian dishes that started the craze, and such deserving menu staples as Shanghai lobster in ginger-curry sauce with the paper-thin, crispy fried spinach that so mysteriously dissolves on your tongue. 🏛

[Divino] **11714 Barrington Ct., Brentwood, 310.472.0886. L & D daily. Italian. Beer & wine. AE, MC, V. \$\$ - \$\$\$ WHY** Personal service, carefully cooked pastas and charm galore in a hidden Brentwood location. **WHAT** Italian trattorias are as plentiful in Brentwood as Guatemalan nannies, and most of them are good. This is one of the least known — and one of the best. The high-ceilinged space is decorated with old black-and-white family photos of brothers/owners Davor and Goran Milic, who hail from the Yugoslav side of the Adriatic, where the cooking is comparable to the Italian side. Seafood is a specialty (wonderful basil-bathed orecchiette with branzino), as are crisp pizzas, lemony salads, light gnocchi porcini and good gelati. **WHO** Down-to-earth Brentwood locals who are in on the secret. ♥ 🖼

[Drago Ristorante] 🏛 **2628 Wilshire Blvd., Santa Monica, 310.828.1585, celestinodrago.com. L Mon.-Fri., D nightly. Italian. Full bar. AE, MC, V. \$\$\$ - \$\$\$\$\$ WHY** Simple, handmade and delicious trattoria fare, and fellow diners who remember what it means to dress for dinner. **WHAT** This showpiece of Celestino Drago's mini-empire offers hearty regional cooking in an elegant setting. But all pretense vanishes when Celestino strolls from table to table, grinning and chatting as customers dine on dishes such as handmade pumpkin tortelloni in sage cream and fettuccine with pheasant-morel sauce. Things like veal chops and fresh fish can get pricey, but we're happy to pay \$16 for the venison ragú with fresh cavatelli. The wine-by-the-glass route makes more sense than the inflated wine list **WHO** Dolled-up habituées and special-occasion diners, with no shortage of baubles on display. ♥🏛

[Echigo] **12217 Santa Monica Blvd., West L.A., 310.820.9787. L Mon.-Fri., D Mon.-Sat. Sushi/Japanese. Beer & wine. AE, MC, V. \$\$ - \$\$\$ WHY** Because sushi masters are judged by their rice. **WHAT** "No cooked stuff," warns a hand-scribbled notice at this no-frills Tokyo-style sushi restaurant in a generic West L.A. strip mall. They're not kidding — there's no miso soup, no California rolls, no attitude. Just Hitoshi Kataoka's glistening sushi rice topped with supremely fresh fish. "Trust me," proclaims the daily chalkboard — it's *omakase* (chef's choice) only at the sushi counter, although tables can be à la carte or omakase. Echigo offers one of the best lunch specials around: a $14 "sushi lunch set," with five pieces and a blue crab hand roll. **WHO** Westside sushi buffs who want everything from ankimo to uni at a more reasonable price than at the better-known competition. 🥢

[El Texate] **316 Pico Blvd., Santa Monica, 310.399.1115, eltexate.com. B, L & D daily. Mexican/Oaxacan. Full bar. MC, V. $ WHY** Cheap and tasty moles, goat tacos and chicken soup with rice and avocado. **WHAT** Just a few blocks from the Pacific, you can have a Oaxacan meal for less than $12, and it tastes equally good whether you live in a $5 million north-of-Montana chateau or a rent-controlled south-of-Pico shack. The soccer-watching bar makes a decent margarita on the rocks. **WHO** Ocean Park locals, and not enough of them — the colorful dining room and shabby patio are often empty. 🥢 ⊙ ☼

[Fig] **Fairmont Miramar, 101 Wilshire Blvd., Santa Monica, 310.319.3111, figsantamonica.com. B daily, L Mon.-Sat., D Tues.-Sat., brunch Sun. Modern American/French. Full bar. AE, MC, V. $$$ - $$$$ WHY** Because if beef tongue is the must-have dish, when tarte flambé and amazing sweetbreads with mushroom fricassée are also on the menu, chef Ray Garcia must be on to something. **WHAT** If you didn't have to walk past the spa, you'd never guess this is the Fairmont Miramar's new bistro. The food is top-notch, the atmosphere laid-back, and the wine and beer selection actually interesting and fairly priced — hardly your typical hotel restaurant. Only the desserts are uninteresting. Try to find time for the bacon-centric Sunday brunch — yes, there's even a bacon Bloody Mary. **WHO** Well-heeled locals spreading arugula butter on warm baguettes at the bar and chatty hotel guests tossing back fig mojitos on the patio. ♥ 🍸 🥢 ☼ 🏛

[Furaibo] **2068 Sawtelle Blvd., West L.A., 310.444.1432. L Mon.-Fri., D nightly. Japanese. Beer & wine. MC, V. $$ - $$$ WHY** Small, tapas-like plates of fried chicken wings, calamari, grilled tofu, various yakitoris and other things that go down very well indeed with pitchers of cold beer. **WHAT** Situated in the former traditional-style pub space of Yoro No Take, this izakaya place specializes in tebasaki, Japanese-style fried chicken wings. They head an enormous à la carte menu that includes about 30 varieties of grilled fish, dozens of vegetable dishes and kushiyaki. **WHO** This noisy, lively place is a favorite haunt of Japanese university students and young professionals. ⊙ 🥢

[Gaby's Mediterranean] **20 Washington Blvd., Marina del Rey, 310.821.9721; 10445 Venice Blvd., Venice, 310.559.1808, gabysexpress. com. L & D daily. Mediterranean. No booze. AE, MC, V. $ - $$ WHY** Savory stuff, served outdoors by the beach at low prices. **WHAT** The inside room is rather grim, with too-loud music, but on the sidewalk, with a constant parade of people headed for the sand and nearby Venice Pier, this is a perfect beach café. Fat, soft pita bread, smooth

🥬 **VEGETARIAN** ⊙ **KID FRIENDLY** ☼ **PATIO DINING** 🚚 **DELIVERY** 🏛 **PRIVATE PARTY**

hummus, fresh tabbouleh and roasted chicken make a fine lunch on a sunny day, and the wraps are tasty, so it's easy to forgive any kitchen haphazardness — or that too-tart dressing on the salads. There's a branch in a parking-lot tent in Palms. **WHO** Flip-flop people. 🕞 ☺ ✿

[The Galley] 2442 Main St., Santa Monica, 310.452.1934, thegalley-restaurant.net. L Sun, D nightly. American/steakhouse. Full bar. AE, MC, V. **$$ - $$$$$** **WHY** A crooner's jukebox, a nostalgia-inducing menu and lighting dim enough to make you fall in love with the person across from you — and with this old-school steakhouse — all over again. **WHAT** Santa Monica's oldest restaurant/bar has been a local treasure since it opened in 1934. Regulars love the martinis with mermaid toothpicks, along with the steaks, littleneck clams and signature salads with the "secret-recipe" dressing (tastes like a tangy Green Goddess to us). The nautical décor is one of its many old-fashioned charms. ♥ 🍸

[Gjelina] 🏛 1429 Abbot Kinney Blvd., Venice, 310.450.1429, gjelina. com. L Mon.Fri., D nightly, brunch Sat.-Sun. Modern American. Beer & wine. AE, MC, V. **$$ - $$$** **WHY** The kitchen knows when to take a fish off the grill and how to bring out the best in each dish — without overcomplicating it. The It spot of the moment in Venice. **WHAT** This newcomer has a '70s Big Sur vibe but a decidedly more modern menu and a seriously skilled kitchen. Try the plump steamed mussels in a pungent fat-free broth, served with a hunk of grilled sourdough; the delicious thin-crust pizzas; the fresh fish; and any of the vegetable dishes: excellent fries, roasted cauliflower with garlic, parsley and chiles, brussels sprouts with caramelized figs. The noise can be crush-ing inside, so try to score a table on the back patio. **WHO** A constant crowd of Venice cool people — make reservations well in advance for weekends, especially if you want to sit on the quieter back patio. 🍶 ✿

[Hakata Sushi & Sports Bar] 2830 Wilshire Blvd., Santa Monica, 310.828.8404. L & D daily. Japanese/sushi. Full bar. AE, MC, V. $$ - $$$ **WHY** Riki's lobster roll — stuffed with rich tempura-fried lobster and drizzled with a sweet, creamy sauce — just might be the best non-des-sert dessert in town. **WHAT** Don't run when you spot the plasma TVs and beer ads hanging overhead at this quirky hybrid sushi restaurant and sports bar. Stay clear of the drab teriyaki and combo plates in the main dining room and grab a seat at the sushi bar, where the goods are always fresh, simply prepared and reasonably priced. 🕞

[Hal's Bar & Grill] 1349 Abbot Kinney Blvd., Venice, 310.396.3105, halsbarandgrill.com. L & D daily. Californian. Full bar. AE, MC, V. $$ - $$$$ **WHY** No cover, no drink minimum, no kidding. **WHAT** Listening to jazz and sipping martinis at this stylish neighborhood restaurant on a Sunday night — when the rest of the world is nodding off during 60 Minutes — is deliciously fun and indulgent. Grab a seat at the bar to hear such accomplished musicians as blues guitarist Phil Upchurch

🏛 **ESSENTIALLY L.A.** ☺ **LATE** ♥ **ROMANTIC** 🕞 **VALUE** 🍶 **QUIET** ✿ **SUSTAINABLE**

and sax player Cal Bennett, and enjoy one of the very good salads, burgers or modern-American main courses. **WHO** Venice artists, musicians and the occasional celebrity.

[Hama Sushi] 213 Windward Ave., Venice, 310.396.8783, hamasushi. com. D nightly. Japanese/sushi. Full bar. AE, MC, V. $$ - $$$$
WHY Inventive sushi rolls and exuberant chefs. (If you stay until closing, you'll get to hear them belt out "Hotel California," accompanied by a few well-served patrons.) **WHAT** One of the nation's first sushi restaurants, Hama has been hot since 1979, combining a flip-flops-friendly atmosphere with fresh, carefully prepared sushi, sashimi and cooked Japanese classics such as spicy tuna shiso, seaweed salad, and grilled yellowtail collar with ponzu. With its surf videos and free-flowing Asahi and sake, this is a must-visit in Venice. ☼

[The Hump] Santa Monica Airport, 3221 Donald Douglas Loop South, Santa Monica, 310.313.0977, typhoon.biz. L Tues.-Fri., D nightly. Japanese/sushi. Full bar. AE, MC, V. $$$$ **WHY** Artful sushi in an artful space at Santa Monica Airport, with dreamy views and romance to spare. It's an intimate spot that's a date-night winner. **WHAT** Sister restaurant Typhoon, one floor down, gets more attention because of its bar scene and the insects on the menu, but Hump is every bit as deserving. Get one of the window-side tables for an early dinner and you'll be treated to a panoramic view and, most likely, a gorgeous sunset sky. The sushi and sashimi taste as good as the view looks. ♥ ☼

[Il Grano] 11359 Santa Monica Blvd., West L.A., 310.477.7886, il-grano.com. L Mon.-Fri., D Mon.-Sat. Italian. Full bar. AE, MC, V. $$$ - $$$$
WHY High-quality fresh fish, Italian style; try the crudos, the squid ink pasta with sea urchin and the salt-baked sea bass. The three-course business lunch is a good value. **WHAT** Sal Marino grew up in the restaurant business (at Marino's), and now, in his own modern, elegant place, he's exploring his own culinary passions: ultra-fresh seafood and handmade pastas. Il Grano has matured into a fine and sophisticated ristorante with delicious, celebratory cooking. The tasting menus (including a vegetarian one) are worth trying. Serious wine list, too. **WHO** Chic, modern westsiders in a chic, modern space. ♥ ☼ 🍴🏠

[Inn of the Seventh Ray] 🏠 128 Old Topanga Canyon Rd., Topanga, 310.455.1311, innoftheseventhray.com. L Mon.-Sat., D nightly, brunch Sun. Vegetarian/Modern American. Beer & wine. AE, MC, V. $$ - $$$$
WHY As they say, "partake of the angelic vibrations of the violet ray," baby. The food's great. **WHAT** Although it's tempting to make fun of this 1970s-era hippie landmark, the food is no joke. The menu ranges from raw food dishes (summer-squash lasagne) to vegetarian choices (agave-glazed vegan duck) and even carnivore pleasers (naturally raised filet mignon with a mirepoix of asparagus). The Sunday brunch, while not cheap, is serene and lovely. **WHO** Wedding parties drawn to

its gardens, gazebos and fountains, plus raw-food enthusiasts, vegetarians and even the occasional carnivore. ♥ 🌙 🐚 ◔ ✿ 🏛

[Javan] 11500 Santa Monica Blvd., Brentwood, 310.207.5555, javan-restaurant.com. L & D daily (to midnight Fri.-Sat.). Persian/Middle Eastern. Full bar. AE, MC, V. $$ - $$$ **WHY** Tasty kebabs, delectable little grilled lamb chops, saffron rice and other Persian dishes. Local delivery, too. **WHAT** The leading Iranian restaurant on Santa Monica Boulevard, with excellent kebabs and a particularly suave-looking bar. Pass on the salads in favor of the kebabs, lamb chops and delicious lentil-based ashjoe soup. 🌙 🚗

[JiRaffe] 502 Santa Monica Blvd., Santa Monica, 310.917.6671, jiraf-ferestaurant.com. D nightly. Californian/French. Full bar. AE, MC, V. $$$$ - $$$$$ **WHY** The seafood's usually outstanding, including pancetta-wrapped tiger shrimp with lemon-harissa nage or crispy salmon with braised fennel and parsnip purée. **WHAT** JiRaffe epitomizes the California bistro, with its elegant chandeliers hung above cozy tables, first-rate service and the creative, market-based California-French cuisine of surfer chef Raphael Lunetta. Bargain hunters, take note of Lunetta's fantastic three-course Wednesday-night dinner inspired by the morning farmers' market: an appetizer, a ravioli entree, a dessert and two three-ounce pours of wine, all for $29. Mondays bring a swell $38 three-course bistro-night menu. **WHO** Santa Monica creative types, businesspeople and politicians. ♥✿🏛

[Joe's] 🏛 1023 Abbot Kinney Blvd., Venice, 310.399.5811, joesrestau-rant.com. L Tues.-Fri., D Tues.-Sun., brunch Sat.-Sun. Modern American. Full bar. AE, MC, V. $$ - $$$$ **WHY** The best deal in town is lunch at Joe's, where for $13 to $16 you get either "soup of today" or a salad with greens, roasted squash, caramelized walnuts and pomegranate vinaigrette, followed by such main courses as grilled shrimp on saffron risotto. Great brunch, too. **WHAT** Before Abbot Kinney was the coolest place in L.A., Joe Miller gambled and opened a tiny restaurant there. His first-rate cooking and the warmth of the handsome little place paid off; he expanded into a neighboring space and watched the neighborhood gentrify. This still-young chef now ranks as a Venice old-timer, respected for the excellence of his food, which is served with skill in this clean-lined, California-elegant bistro. **WHO** Attractive middle-aged surfers, clothing designers and software developers. ♥

[Josie] 🏛 2424 Pico Blvd., Santa Monica, 310.581.9888, josierestau-rant.com. D nightly. Modern American/Californian. Full bar. AE, MC, V. $$$$ **WHY** Thoughtful, creative dishes made from seasonal ingredients — perhaps a peach and wild arugula salad followed by a whole boneless trout cooked "campfire" style (fabulous) or a buffalo burger with truffle fries, and concluding with a Meyer lemon cheesecake with roasted blueberries. **WHAT** Josie Le Balch grew up in an L.A. restaurant, and now she has become one of the city's best chefs. Her restaurant is grown-up and serious about its food, yet it's unpretentious in an east Santa Monica kind of way. When you need to eat really well but don't want an overblown scene, come here. **WHO** Intelligent food lovers, often celebrating an occasion. ♥ 🍸

[Katsuya Brentwood] 11777 San Vicente Blvd., Brentwood, 310.207.8744, sbeent.com. L & D daily. Japanese. Full bar. AE, MC, V. $$$ - $$$$$ **WHY** Who knew Brentwood could be this happening? **WHAT** This upscale, always-packed, almost manic place is very *Lost in Translation* — lots of neon, purple and white leather, all of it created by famed French designer Philippe Starck. The menu, from sushi chef Katsuya Uechi, includes a variety of hot and cold items, including scallops with kiwi in yuzu vinaigrette, baked black cod and very good sushi rolls. The robata bar turns out delectable skewers of grilled shrimp, chicken meatballs, vegetables and steak. **WHO** Brentwood's beautiful people.

[La Cachette Bistro] 1733 Ocean Ave., Santa Monica, 310.470.4992, lacachettebistro.com. L Mon.-Fri., D nightly, brunch Sat.-Sun. French/Californian. Full bar. AE, MC, V. $$$ **WHY** A prime location on Ocean near the hotels, serving a market-based menu of sophisticated Cal-French bistro dishes and stylish mixologist-designed cocktails. **WHAT** In his many years at La Cachette, Jean Françcois Meteigner earned a reputation as one of L.A.'s best French chefs. As befits the times, he decided to shut down the fancy-schmancy place and devote himself to cooking rather more affordable modern bistro fare, in a beach-adjacent spot with a large patio, comfortable bar and handsome bistro décor. it was just opening at press time, so we haven't tried the food, but it looks most promising. 🛍 ☼ 🏠

[La Grande Orange] 2000 N. Main St., Santa Monica, 310.396.9145, lagrandeorangesm.com. B, L & D daily. American. Full bar. AE, MC, V. $$ - $$$ **WHY** A crisp margarita on the sidewalk patio is a beautiful thing. **WHAT** The right place at the right spot and at the right price, this new La Grande Orange, a branch of the Phoenix original and Pasadena sibling, suits its relaxed Ocean Park neighborhood perfectly. The menu tries with mixed success to satisfy every perceived GenX craving; skip the dull main courses in favor of the generous and well-prepared sushi rolls, tasty ahi or steak taco platters, and perfect cheeseburger. Breakfast (great egg sandwich and already-legendary English muffins) and lunch are order-at-the-counter; dinner brings good table service. **WHO** A diverse crowd of twentysomething cocktail kids, tousled young families and date-night boomers. 🚬 ☺ ☼

[Lares] 2909 Pico Blvd., Santa Monica, 310.829.4559, laresrestaurant.com. B, L & D daily. Mexican. Full bar. AE, MC, V. $ - $$ **WHY** Chiles rellenos, lengua en mole and good margaritas, all at low prices.

🥬 VEGETARIAN ◎ KID FRIENDLY ☼ PATIO DINING 🚗 DELIVERY 🏠 PRIVATE PARTY

WHAT Manny Lares seems to be the main man at this family restaurant, but then there's his brother, his two sisters, his niece.... "We all cook, we all wash dishes, we all go to the bank," he says. Downstairs is a quiet room for eating enchiladas in peace, but the place to be is upstairs, where the flamenco guitarist entertains the diners, many of whom return weekly for the hearty southern Mexican classics. **WHO** Rent-controlled south Santa Monicans. 📷 ☺

[Le Petit Café] 2842 Colorado Ave., Santa Monica, 310.829.6792, lepetitcafebonjour.com. L Mon.-Fri., D Mon.-Sat. French. Beer & wine. AE, MC, V. $$ - $$$$ **WHY** Honest fare at great prices: *pourquoi pas*? **WHAT** So many restaurants claim to be a neighborhood bistro these days, but it's a shock to actually find one. Le Petit Café is the real deal, with chalkboard-toting waiters, tiny bistro tables topped with Provençal linens and fine, straightforward bistro food at surprisingly good prices. **WHO** By day, a business crowd from nearby studios; in the evening, locals take over, with couples sharing escargots and friends lingering long after their steak au poivre has been cleared. 📷

[Lilly's French Café] 1031 Abbot Kinney Blvd., Venice, 310.314.0004, lillysfrenchcafe.com. L Mon.-Sat., D nightly, brunch Sun. French. Beer & wine. AE, MC, V. $$ - $$$$ **WHY** French bistro food at reasonable prices — especially the $12 brunch specials — in a convivial setting. **WHAT** In a charming old house in the heart of Abbot Kinney lies a French café that combines Venice style with traditional bistro cooking. Terrine de canard, salade frisée aux lardons, moules frites, entrecôte grillée, soufflé au chocolat chaud — it's all here, just like at your favorite Parisian bistro. ♥📷 ☼

[The Lobster] 1602 Ocean Ave., Santa Monica, 310.458.9294, thelobster.com. L & D daily. Seafood/modern American. Full bar. AE, MC, V. $$$ - $$$$$ **WHY** Cosmopolitan cooking without pretension, with a beach-friendly location that can't be beat. **WHAT** It has every right to be a tourist trap, but Allyson Thurber's pierside seafood restaurant is anything but. Always packed and always noisy, the modern concrete-and-glass space gives diners stellar views of the sea, sky and Ferris wheel — along with a daily-changing menu of fine seafood. You might find fat scallops seared and served with a simple trio of sides (grilled tomatoes, spinach and grilled asparagus) or black bass with sesame seeds, grilled shiitake mushrooms and a ginger-wasabi sauce. Don't even think of coming without a reservation.

[Locanda Portofino] 1110 Montana Ave., Santa Monica, 310.394.2070, locandaportofino.com. L Mon.-Sat., D nightly. Italian. Beer & wine. AE, MC, V. $$$ - $$$$ **WHY** It's the kind of intimate, authentic trattoria you dream of finding in your own backyard. **WHAT** You arrive to seductive, garlicky odors wafting through the door and the attentions of cute, heavily accented Italian waiters — and food that lives up to the anticipatory promise, from the hearty pasta arrabbiata to a hand-cut grilled swordfish of a quality that's hard to find these days. The risotti and pasta are appealing and the filet mignon is superb. It's a little place, so make reservations. **WHO** North of Montana locals, including famous folks who just want a nice, quiet dinner. ♥ ☼

[Mélisse] 🔒 1104 Wilshire Blvd., Santa Monica, 310.395.0881, melisse. com. D Tues.-Sat. French/modern American. Full bar. AE, MC, V. $$$$$
WHY The seasonally inspired and hard-to-resist four-course tasting menu; at $105 without wine, it's a serious indulgence, but one you're not likely to forget. Beautiful vegetarian tasting menu, too.
WHAT Mélisse is luxuriously French, with just a bit of California flair and a farmers' market sensibility. Josiah Citrin has created a romantic, dimly lit space, with formal tables set with French cutlery, an occasionally haughty wait staff and, yes, an actual cheese cart brimming with oozing, stinking delicacies. The dry-aged côte de boeuf (for two) with potato-leek torte, wild mushrooms and braised lettuce deserves its status as a menu classic. **WHO** Food- and romance-lovers willing to invest in a memorable meal. ♥ 🍴 ♻ 🔒 🏠

[Michael's] 🔒 1147 3rd St., Santa Monica, 310.451.0843, michael-ssantamonica.com. L Mon.-Fri., D Mon.-Sat. Californian. Full bar. AE, MC, V. $$$ - $$$$$ **WHY** Its patio, its still-amazing art collection and its wine list. **WHAT** Michael McCarty opened his namesake restaurant back in 1979 and was hugely influential in defining what was dubbed California cuisine and went on to become modern American cooking. His kitchen helped make goat cheese, arugula and caramelized onions a wildly popular culinary trinity, and he took California wines seriously long before many others did. It still seems caught in that era, dishing up pricey food that's lacking in modern flair. Perhaps it's time for a little nip and tuck? Still, lunching on this patio on a sunny day remains one of those things you've gotta do. **WHO** Artists, writers, actors and tourists who can afford it. ♥ 🔒 ☼

[Monte Alban] 11927 Santa Monica Blvd., West L.A., 310.444.7736. B, L & D daily. Mexican/Oaxacan. Beer & wine. AE, MC, V. $ **WHY** For the many mole sauces — black, yellow, green, red, colorado — served inside tamales, with chicken, and in all sorts of dishes. Good huevos for breakfast, too. **WHAT** At press time, fire had shuttered this fine and most affordable Oaxacan café known for its moles and its breakfast (lovely cinnamon-infused coffee), but it should be back by the time you read this. Try the mole negro tamale and the huitlacoche and *frijoladas*, a wonderful mix of beans, chicken and mole. 🍴 ☼

[Musha] 🔒 424 Wilshire Blvd., Santa Monica, 310.576.6330. D nightly. Japanese/Californian. Beer & wine. AE, MC, V. $$ - $$$ **WHY** Fatty pork belly (you know you want it), kim chee udon, tuna poke, seafood-filled baguette au gratin ... amazing and delicious dishes that typify the

🔒 VEGETARIAN ☼ KID FRIENDLY ☼ PATIO DINING 🚗 DELIVERY 🏠 PRIVATE PARTY

best of modern Japanese-L.A. fusion cooking. **WHAT** It's crowded and the waitresses are harried — yet Musha's diners always seem relaxed and happy. Perhaps it's the slow-cooked pork belly. Or the moderate prices. Or the sake. Or the communal table that inspires new friendships. Whatever the reason, this modern small-plates Cal-Japanese bistro is lots of fun, and the food is terrific. ☺ 🗒️

[Nanbankan] 11330 Santa Monica Blvd., West L.A., 310.478.1591. D nightly. Japanese. Beer & wine. MC, V. $$ - $$$ **WHY** Trust your waiter and order the specials he recommends, perhaps corn, Australian lamb, mushrooms, burdock rolled in pork, *yaki onigiri* (rice ball) and *ninniku no me* (garlic sprouts sautéed with mushrooms and scallops). And an order of the amazing chicken wings. **WHAT** For three decades Nanbankan has been L.A.'s yakitori destination, long before everyone was rushing to the latest *izakaya* (small plates) hot spot. The aroma of grilling meat, chicken and vegetables fills the modest room, where small groups of friends (seating is tight) share orders of things on skewers. If you haven't been in years, go back — you won't be sorry.

[Nobu] Malibu Country Mart, 3835 Cross Creek Rd., Malibu, 310.317.9140, nobumatsuhisa.com. D nightly. Japanese/sushi. Full bar. AE, MC, V. $$$ - $$$$ **WHY** Celeb spotting, perfectly fine food and a chance to make like one of the Malibu locals who've adopted Nobu as their neighborhood canteen (baseball cap, flip flops and iPhone optional). **WHAT** It's Disneyland Malibu here: a perfectly orchestrated miniature version of clichéed Malibu life, complete with omnipresent celebrities (think: Cindy Crawford, David Duchovny, Courtney Cox, Kelsey Grammer...), hilarious cosmetic-surgery chatter in the restrooms and good though largely unexciting food: delectable black cod in miso, basic sushi, tasty but soggy rock-shrimp tempura, yellowtail sashimi with jalapeño. **WHO** The famous, the fabulous, the families with kids — sometimes all at the same table.

[Noma Sushi] 2031 Wilshire Blvd., Santa Monica, 310.453.4848. L & D daily. Japanese/sushi. Beer & wine. AE, MC, V. $$ **WHY** High-quality sushi and regional specialties served in an intimate setting. **WHAT** Step inside this curbside sushi joint on a Friday night and you'll be transported to a bustling Manhattan hot spot with its shotgun interior, cozy booths and frantically busy staff delivering quality sushi with a few unexpected surprises (think: black pig sausage from your waiter's hometown, with a side of ballpark mustard). **WHO** Anyone who loves a booth: couples, families with neighborhood kids in tow, and friends meeting after work. 🗒️☺

[Nook Bistro] 11628 Santa Monica Blvd., West L.A., 310.207.5160, nookbistro.com. L Mon.-Fri., D Mon.-Sat. Modern American. Beer & wine. AE, MC, V. $$ - $$$ **WHY** Farmers' market–fresh comfort food like shrimp and grits (the house special), shiitake-and-Gruyère bread

🏠 ESSENTIALLY L.A. ☺ LATE ♥ ROMANTIC 🗒️ VALUE 🔊 QUIET ♻ SUSTAINABLE

pudding, and pear crumble. Extras include a big communal table, a modest $10 corkage and no corkage on Mondays. **WHAT** Nook Bistro is indeed a nook, a tiny spot hidden in the back corner of a little strip mall with not enough parking. It's hard to spot, but that hasn't stopped it from becoming very popular, thanks to its excellent prices and simple, well-prepared dishes. It's the kind of place a chef would open for other chefs, and the loyal locals are the beneficiaries. **WHO** Regulars who know to make a reservation and come before 8 p.m. — after that the wait can be brutal. 🖅🌀🌂☺

[Orris] 🏠 2006 Sawtelle Blvd., West L.A., 310.268.2212, orrisrestaurant. com. D Tues.-Sun. French/Asian. Beer & wine. AE, MC, V. $$ - $$$
WHY Such exquisite French-influenced small plates as shrimp-mousse-filled ravioli with shiitake sauce, grilled hearts of romaine salad, filet mignon with roquefort butter and foie gras with Japanese eggplant. **WHAT** After running Franco-Japanese restaurant Shiro in South Pasadena for many years, chef Hideo Yamashiro flipped the name (sort of) and opened the smaller and more casual Orris on Sawtelle's Japanese restaurant row. Reservations aren't accepted for the spare, modern eatery, but there is seating at the chic granite bar and on the patio. Premium sakes and good wines. 🖅🌣

[Osteria Latini] 11712 San Vicente Blvd., Brentwood, 310.826.9222, osterialatini.com. L Mon.-Fri., D nightly. Italian. Beer & wine. AE, MC, V. $$ - $$$$ **WHY** There are lots of Italian eateries in Brentwood; this one stands out because it's friendly, homey and has reasonable prices. **WHAT** Trieste native Paolo Pasio has the warmth required of a good trattoria owner, and his dining room is inviting and often crowded. His kitchen turns out very fine Italian comfort food: beet salad, burrata with red and yellow tomatoes, buttery whole roasted branzino, delicious lobster risotto, excellent pastas. Our only complaints: weak desserts and the recitation of far too many daily specials to remember.

[Paco's Tacos] 4141 Centinela Ave., West L.A., 310.391.9616, pacoscantina.com. L & D daily. Mexican. Full bar. AE, MC, V. $ - $$
WHY Cal-Mex cuisine at its gut-busting best, plus an excellent cadillac margarita and low prices. **WHAT** If you grew up in Southern California, this is the kind of restaurant you dreamt of when you went away to college. It boasts every Mexican-restaurant cliché: paintings of hokey Mexican scenes, a logo with a sombrero-sporting hombre and a costumed señora making tortillas on a griddle. (Plus walls crammed with antlers, armor and St. Patrick's Day decorations.) There's often a wait, but the food's worth it: juicy carne asada, fresh tortillas, a huge tostada and gooey, cheesy enchiladas with rice and beans. 🖅☺

[Pecorino] 11604 San Vicente Blvd., Brentwood, 310.571.3800, pecorinorestaurant.com. L Mon.-Sat., D nightly. Italian. Beer & wine. AE, MC, V. $$$ **WHY** Basic pastas like *cacao e pepe* (spaghetti with

🍃 VEGETARIAN ☺ KID FRIENDLY 🌣 PATIO DINING 🚐 DELIVERY 🏮 PRIVATE PARTY pecorino, parmesan and pepper) that are so satisfying you'll wonder what else they're sneaking into the bowl. **WHAT** Step inside Pecorino, and you'll be greeted by a gush of warmth — brick walls, cozy bistro tables, rustic chandeliers — and exuberant host Mario Sabatini. As he hops around the dining room, his twin brother Raffaele is in the kitchen cooking up dishes from their hometown of Abruzzo and beyond. The food's good — even the amaretto-soaked tiramisu (really). No reservations, so come early or you'll have to wait.

[Piccolo] 5 Dudley Ave., Venice, 310.314.3222, piccolovenice.com. D nightly. Italian. Beer & wine. AE, MC, V. $$$ - $$$$$ **WHY** It's not fancy, but Piccolo's charm and superb Italian food make it ideal for a memorable date or celebration. Just be prepared to pay. **WHAT** For now this beachside trattoria has but 12 tables (more are coming with a planned expansion), so you'll feel like you've been invited to a friend's house for dinner — a friend who is passionate about Italian food and wine and can cook like nobody's business: homemade tagliolini with venison ragú, stuffed rabbit with polenta, scallops with black truffles, flourless chocolate cake. The monthly *centro al contrario* (reversal) dinner is great fun — you choose your wines, and the chef makes your meal accordingly. **WHO** Moneyed Venice artists and entrepreneurs. ♥ ☼

[Pizzicotto] 11758 San Vicente Blvd., Brentwood, 310.442.7188. L Mon.-Sat., D nightly. Italian. Beer & wine. AE, MC, V. $ - $$$ **WHY** The irresistible *pesce cuocopazzo*, fresh whitefish with a horseradish-pistachio crust and sauce of white wine, garlic, lemon and fresh tomatoes. **WHAT** There's always a crowd at this Brentwood trattoria, perhaps the best of the large Italian bunch in the neighborhood — so don't even think of coming without a reservation. The ceilings are high (and so are the noise levels) and everybody looks happy tucking into bruschetta, panini, crisp-crusted pizzas and risotto with wild mushrooms.

[Raku] 11678 W. Olympic Blvd., West L.A., 310.478.3090. D Mon. & Wed.-Sun. (to 1:30 a.m. Fri.-Sun.). Japanese/Korean. BYOB (no corkage). AE, MC, V. $$ - $$$ **WHY** With a long, elegant dining counter, a lengthy menu of homey dishes and late hours, this simple strip-mall spot is a boon for night-owl industry types working in West L.A.'s studios and creative offices. **WHAT** A motherly woman behind the stoves of the open kitchen turns out tamago with free-range eggs, braised black pork chunks, simmered fiddlehead fern tops and for the brave, home-style pickled squid guts to perk up your rice. ☺

[Real Food Daily] 514 Santa Monica Blvd., Santa Monica, 310.451.7544, realfood.com. L & D daily, brunch Sun. Vegan/American. No booze. AE, MC, V. $$ **WHY** The Ciao Bella — roasted veggies with pesto on hemp bread. **WHAT** Chef/owner Ann Gentry serves enticing meat-free and dairy-free fare in her casual café. The faux Reuben and mock club try too hard to mimic their meat counterparts, so try instead the seasonal vegetables in a wasabi vinaigrette, the Yin Yang veggie salad with peanut-sesame dressing and the chunky miso soup. **WHO** Westside vegans, vegetarians and plain old vegetable lovers. ♻🗒◔🚐

[Riva] 🏛 312 Wilshire Blvd., Santa Monica, 310.451.7482, rivarestaurantla.com. L Mon.-Fri., D & late supper nightly. Italian. Full bar. AE, MC, V. $$ - $$$$ **WHY** Because there really are some late-night Promenade shoppers searching for a reasonably priced bistro with good, not gimmicky, food. Honest. **WHAT** When chef Jason Travi and sommelier Thierry Perez of Fraîche launched Riva, it served upscale Italian food with darn good pizza. When Perez left eight months later, Travi revamped the menu. The thin-crust, wood-fired pies are still available Sundays and Mondays, but now small plates, such as a braised veal cheek tart and spicy octopus crostini, have replaced the once-over-priced entrees. Travi tests new dishes (a recent example was marinated lentils topped with a fried egg) during his bargain early- and late-hour menu, which also offers wines and beer for less than $5 a glass — so if you come early or late, you can have food and drink for less than $15. **WHO** Bentley-driving locals lingering with friends over dinner and trendy young things pulling out their last pennies at the bar. ◔ 🗒

[Robata Bar] 1401 Ocean Ave., Santa Monica, 310.458.4771, robatabar.com. D nightly to midnight. Japanese. Full bar. AE, MC, V. $ - $$$ **WHY** A funky, fun, after-work hangout for ginger-lychee mojitos, sake and very share-able robata skewers. **WHAT** This easy-to-miss space next to parent restaurant Sushi Roku features authentic *robata* (Japanese grilled meats and veggies), chicken cartilage (for the brave) and a good-enough raw bar with interesting combos — try the wasabi Bloody Mary oyster shooter. ◔

[Rustic Canyon] 🏛 1119 Wilshire Blvd., Santa Monica, 310.393.7050, rusticcanyonwinebar.com. D nightly. Modern American/wine bar. Beer & wine. AE, MC, V. $$$ - $$$$ **WHY** The burger — Meyer beef, Niman Ranch bacon, wild greens, a brioche bun and sharp Tillamook cheddar — rivals the one at Father's Office. Mondays bring more creative burgers that chef Evan Funke pairs with craft beers. **WHAT** We wish all neighborhood restaurants were this fine. The market-inspired menu served in this high-ceilinged, candlelit dining room changes monthly; there are always gossamer-light pastas and an Italian feel, reflecting Funke's time in Emilia-Romagna. Not to worry, though — the pan-roasted half chicken with caramelized baby onions is always offered. Don't miss the desserts from Huckleberry: salted chocolate caramel tart, plum and grape crostata, and perhaps the best chocolate chip cookie in town. Expect pricey, small-producer varieties on the wine list, great beers (there's a beer sommelier) and a serious commitment to organic farmers'-market and sustainable products. **WHO** An after-work wine-sipping crowd at the bar and a food-focused crowd (including some off-duty chefs) at the tables. ♻

🗒 VEGETARIAN ◔ KID FRIENDLY ✿ PATIO DINING 🚐 DELIVERY 🏛 PRIVATE PARTY

[SaSaYa] 11613 Santa Monica Blvd., West L.A., 310.477.4404, izakaya-sasaya.com. D nightly. Japanese. Beer & wine. MC, V. $$ - $$$ **WHY** Excellent izakaya is paired with a vast collection of sakes and shochus. Good weeknight happy hour, too. **WHAT** In a rustic, wood-paneled space that looks like a Japanese country inn, customers share tips at the massive communal table. Signs in calligraphy describe special sakes and seasonal dishes that are simple yet perfectly cooked. ⓢ

[Tasting Kitchen] 1633 Abbot Kinney Blvd., Venice, 310.392.6644, thetastingkitchen.com. D nightly, brunch Sun. Modern American. Full bar. AE, MC, V. $$$ - $$$$ **WHY** An elegant Lucques-meets-Portland gem with an ever-changing selection of two dozen inspired, intensely flavored but not at all fussy creations, ranging from delicate market greens tossed with walnut anchoïade to pork cheek ravioli nestled among balsamic-laced radicchio. The $50 four-course tasting menu has got to be one of the best fine-dining deals in town. **WHAT** The AK space (same owner, new chef) has been reinvented by former Clark-Lewis folks whose who've brought not only great food but an infectious enthusiasm that fills the buzzing dining room. Casey Lane works the stoves, while 26-year-old manager and Italian wine buff Maxwell Leer chats up guests about the unfiltered Prosecco and Sagrantino (an indigenous grape from Umbria). The beer, wine and cocktail list may contain only two dozen options, but somehow here it feels complete. Don't skip the fantastic desserts, such as a summery lemon semifreddo with pistachios, by pastry chef Joey Messina. **WHO** Married couples out for a special night and young singles gathered around the bar. ⓢ

[Tavern Brentwood] 11648 San Vicente Blvd., Brentwood, 310.806.6464, tavernla.com. B Mon.-Fri., L & D daily, brunch Sat.-Sun. Modern American. Full bar. AE, MC, V. $$$$ **WHY** Except for low prices, this place has everything that's missing from Suzanne Goin and Caroline Styne's other restaurants with similar farmers'-market-friendly Cal-French cuisine: breakfast, brunch, kids' menus, cocktail bar, even a takeout counter. **WHAT** This latest glammed-up addition to the Lucques/AOC family is light-filled by day and romantic by night, with a takeout-friendly café as a bonus. (You'd never guess this used to be a Hamburger Hamlet.) The food's excellent, if affordable only to 90049 residents. We also love the clever kids' menu ("no parsley" pasta with butter and parmesan), the great but overpriced bar ($14 vodka gimlets?) and, finally, bread worthy of Goin's food, made by in-house baker Nathan Dakdouk, who is sure to be christened L.A.'s next sourdough king. **WHO** Goin worshippers with deep pockets in the dining room; locals picking up prepared salads, multigrain cherry-cashew bread and cookies from the takeout "larder." ☺

[Terried Sake House] 11617 Santa Monica Blvd., West L.A., 310.477.9423. D nightly. Japanese. Beer & wine. Cash only. $$ **WHY** Katsuhiko Terada grills succulent yakitori, fries asparagus, sautés tofu steak, broils cod and short ribs and, on the spot, expertly cooks up anything on his lengthy small-plates menu. **WHAT** Cherished by a cadre of locals, Terada has been working behind his open kitchen counter at this very utilitarian space for more than 20 years. The food, sake and prices make up for the lack of atmosphere. 🖼️

[Tlapazola Grill] 🏠 **636 Venice Blvd., Venice, 866.377.7930, tlapa-zolagrill.com. L & D daily. Mexican/Oaxacan. BYOB; license pending. AE, MC, V. $$ - $$$ WHY** Lobster chile relleno with tamarind-hoisin sauce, grilled salmon with mole pipian and a spinach-garlic quesadilla, and grilled half-chicken with two moles. **WHAT** This nouvelle Oaxacan café recently moved from Marina del Rey to the former Pam's Place in Venice, and it was a wise move. Now you can enjoy these very good southern Mexican dishes on a quiet and comfortable walled patio, at the same modest prices. Note that while it shares a name with the (also good) Tlapazola in West L.A., they are run by different family members. **WHO** A loyal crowd who's sick of the typical beach-town melted-cheese Mexican food. 🖼️ 🍷 ☼

[Tlapazola Grill] 🏠 **11676 Gateway Blvd., West L.A., 310.477.1577. L & D Tues.-Sun. Mexican/Oaxacan. Full bar. AE, MC, V. $$ WHY** Inventive and rewarding modern Oaxacan food and superb margaritas. **WHAT** The two Cruz brothers started this sweet place, but their business partnership split, and each brother has his own Tlapazola. This one is more gracious than its strip-mall setting would suggest, serving a delicious hybrid cuisine that combines Oaxacan staples (awesome mole negro) with Mexican classics (carnitas with rice and black beans) with a California approach to fresh vegetables, seafood, sauces and presentation. Kind people, moderate prices and great margaritas make it a westside winner. 🖼️

[Typhoon] 🏠 **3221 Donald Douglas Loop South, Santa Monica, 310.390.6565, typhoon.biz. L Mon.-Fri., D nightly, brunch Sun. Asian. Full bar. AE, MC, V. $$ - $$$ WHY** Pan-Asian delicacies, with an unforgettable side serving of small planes taking off over the Pacific at sunset. **WHAT** This place is just plain fun. With a window-lined dining room overlooking retro Santa Monica airport, a chic Asian décor with aeronautical touches, a good bar and a fairly priced menu of dishes from Singapore, Korea, China, Thailand, Vietnam, the Philippines and Burma, Typhoon can't go wrong. Thrill seekers will try the deep-fried white sea worms or Singapore-style scorpions; everyone else shares small plates of such good stuff as sui mai, Vietnamese egg rolls, Korean-style short ribs and Thai river prawns with a cilantro-garlic-peanut paste. Upstairs is Hump, an affiliated sushi bar with even better views. **WHO** Adventurers, aviation enthusiasts, Asian-food lovers and savvy hosts with hard-to-wow out-of-town guests. ♥ ☺

🍃VEGETARIAN ◎ KID FRIENDLY ☼PATIO DINING 🚌 DELIVERY 🎪 PRIVATE PARTY

[Valentino] 3115 Pico Blvd., Santa Monica, 310.829.4313, valentinorestaurant.com. L Fri., D Mon.-Sat. Italian. Full bar. AE, MC, V. $$$$$
WHY To search for a good buy on owner Piero Selvaggio's huge and lovingly maintained wine list — and to pay homage to the restaurateur who set the West Coast Italian standard for many years and influenced countless Italian chefs in town. **WHAT** This groundbreaking Italian restaurant has impeccable silver and service, the atmosphere exudes self-satisfied wealth, and the kitchen is accomplished, turning out such delicacies as truffle-topped risotto, agnolotti filled with braised Sonoma lamb, and a garlic-rubbed veal chop served over wilted wild greens. But at well over $100 a head for dinner with wine (and a lot more if you go nuts with the wine), we're looking for something a little more interesting for our investment. **WHO** Serious wine lovers and mature romantics with cash to burn. ♥ ⑨ ⑪

[Vincenti] 🏛 11930 San Vicente Blvd., Brentwood, 310.207.0127, vincentiristorante.com. L Fri., D Mon.-Sat. Italian. Full bar. AE, MC, V. $$$$ - $$$$$ **WHY** Owner Maureen Vincenti's contagious laugh and doting attention to each guest, plus the house-made porchetta, spit-roasted until it's a perfectly charred, juicy hunk of pure pork bliss.
WHAT Step inside the elegant dining room, with its marble counters and slick leather banquettes, and it's clear this isn't your average homespun trattoria. Chef Nicola Mastronardi turns out gutsy cuisine, such as osso buco tortelloni with wild mushroom sauce and sliced steak with herb ravioli, endive and green peppercorn sauce. For dessert, try one of pastry chef Willy Sifuentes's creations: a delicious twist on tiramisu, served in a martini glass, or the light, heavenly lemon ricotta cake. This kind of dining experience doesn't come cheap, but Vincenti is one Italian that's worth the price. **WHO** Well-heeled, well-dressed westsiders. ♥ ⑨ ⑪

[Wabi-Sabi] 1637 Abbot Kinney Blvd., Venice, 310.314.2229, wabisabisushi.com. D nightly. Japanese/Asian. Beer & wine. AE, MC, V. $$$
WHY Crunchy shrimp rolls, Thai snapper over summer beans, lovely sushi and sashimi. **WHAT** One of the better restaurants on a restaurant-choked street, Wabi-Sabi is stylish yet relaxed, with consistently good sushi and Asian-fusion dishes. **WHO** Neighborhood locals — which means very attractive creative types who can afford a $1 million Venice cottage and chic sushi cafés like this one. ☼

[Warszawa] 1414 Lincoln Blvd., Santa Monica, 310.393.8831. D Tues.-Sun. Polish. Full bar. AE, MC, V. $$ - $$$ **WHY** In winter, sustaining pierogis, stroganoff and heavenly hot dried plums wrapped in bacon; in summer, a table on the pretty patio and a bowl of the best cold borscht you've ever had, at least around here. **WHAT** L.A.'s longstanding center of Polish culinary life continues to thrive in this charming cottage on not-so-charming Lincoln. The rich food — pierogis, roast duckling with apples, hunter's stew, potato pancakes — is consistently good. **WHO** Eastern European ex-pats and romance seekers who want a break from Italian food. ♥ 🍷 ☼ 🏠

[Whist] **Viceroy, 1819 Ocean Ave., Santa Monica, 310.260.7511, viceroysantamonica.com. B, L & D daily, brunch Sun. Modern American. Full bar. AE, MC, V. $$$$ - $$$$$ WHY** An only-in-L.A. combo: top-notch creative French-American dishes meet Justin Timberlake–worthy poolside dining. **WHAT** Former chef Warren Schwartz opened the door for a new style of inspired hotel dining; now new cook in town Taite Pearson is going for the slam dunk. He's turning out rabbit rillette with quince gelée, chicken liver mousse with onion jam, marrow flan with parsley salad — and those are just the potted meat starters. It was no surprise to learn that Pearson had been executive sous chef at Joel Robuchon's renowned Vegas restaurant. He's a whiz with unusual flavor combos like diver scallops with zucchini blossoms and bacon jus. **WHO** International hotel guests with fat wallets, fashionistas lounging in the bar, and locals who know if they order carefully, they can walk out with enough greenbacks to come back for Sunday brunch. ♥ ☼

[Wilshire] **2454 Wilshire Blvd., Santa Monica, 310.586.1707, wilshirerestaurant.com. L Mon.-Fri., D Mon.-Sat. Modern American/steakhouse. Full bar. AE, MC, V. $$$$ - $$$$$ WHY** With its California-dream patio and organic market food, Wilshire is bucking to be the Michael's for the new millennium. **WHAT** Wilshire has a too-cool country-club vibe, complete with leather club chairs and a martini-sipping crowd at the packed bar, but it's not just the latest hot spot to jump on the organic, sustainable bandwagon. Chef Andrew Kirschner is on his game, turning out farmers'-market inspired dishes like ricotta gnocchi with fava beans, hedgehog mushrooms and toasted breadcrumbs, or whole fried Thai snapper with citrus-soy dipping sauce. Save room for the updated comfort-food desserts, like the espresso float with cinnamon-sugar doughnuts. **WHO** A moneyed crowd that's as beautiful as the enclosed patio, with its fireplace and burbling fountains. ♥☼☼🏠

SOUTH BAY TO SOUTH L.A.

[Aimee's] **800 S. Pacific Coast Hwy., Redondo Beach, 310.316.1081, aimeesbistro.com. D Tues.-Sun. French. Beer & wine. AE, MC, V. $$ - $$$ WHY** The warmth of owner Aimee Mizrahi, the heartwarming French bistro cooking and the modest prices. **WHAT** Homey beyond its strip-mall setting, Aimee's is beloved by locals for its great service and fine food: bouillabaisse, scallops with foie gras, coq au vin and crème brûlée. Tables are tightly packed, so don't plan on gossiping much. 🗐

[Aki Sushi] **665 Redondo Ave., Long Beach, 562.439.4025. D Tues.-Sun. Japanese/sushi. Beer & wine. AE, MC, V. $$$ WHY** To sit at the sushi bar and let Aki make you some very good things. **WHAT** Chef Aki developed a following years ago at Sushi of Naples, and his fans

🥬VEGETARIAN ⊙KID FRIENDLY ☼PATIO DINING 🚗DELIVERY 🏠PRIVATE PARTY followed him to a couple more locations. Now he's well settled here (don't confuse this with the other Aki on 7th). His fish is carefully selected, and his prices are fair. **WHO** Loyal regulars.

[At Last Café] 204 Orange Ave., Long Beach, 562.437.4837. L & D Tues.-Sat. American. BYOB. AE, MC, V. $ - $$ **WHY** Simple Americana with refined flair. **WHAT** At Last Café may be a tiny place, but size doesn't matter, as it has quickly become one of the most popular neighborhood spots in a city full of them. Behind its success is approachable American cooking that capably twists the classics. At lunch, expect good sandwiches headlined by a charred burger and a vegetarian option stuffed with grilled zucchini, eggplant, peppers, lettuce and olives. Dinner brings on the acclaimed brick chicken, which is flattened (yes, with a brick) and cooked to a crisp, as well as pot roast, lamb shoulder and a supremely creamy mac 'n cheese. **WHO** A diverse chunk of Long Beach folks looking for gourmet on the cheap and happy to bring their own wine. 🗺🍷☺

[Azuma Izakaya] 16123 S. Western Ave., Gardena, 310.532.8623. L Mon.-Fri., D nightly. Japanese. Beer & wine. MC, V. $$ **WHY** Bargain izakaya dishes served in a casual, fun setting: udon, fresh mussels, fried chicken, miso black cod and more. **WHAT** Grill chefs send out excellent food until midnight from a menu with at least 100 items. Sake drums and beer kegs stacked in a corner decorate the tiny room, which has the feel of a '40s-era coffee shop and is usually packed. ☺ 🗺

[Bamboo Island] 816 E. Anaheim St., Long Beach, 562.435.3877. L & D daily (to midnight). Cambodian. Full bar. AE, MC, V. $ **WHY** A taste of L.A.'s Little Cambodia with an easy-to-navigate colored picture menu and helpful servers to introduce this often unfamiliar cuisine. **WHAT** If you've never tried Cambodian curry noodles, anchovy cake or coconut curry fish, this friendly, open-late café will get you started sampling food from the home of Angkor Wat. **WHO** Mostly Cambodians craving prahok ktee and other specialties of their homeland. ☺ 🗺

[Belacan Grill] 2701 190th St., Redondo Beach, 310.370.1831, belacangrill.com. L & D Tues.-Sun. Malaysian. Beer & wine. AE, MC, V. $$ - $$$ **WHY** A chance to try some of L.A.'s best-prepared Malaysian food, served in a hip and handsome setting. **WHAT** Chef Kean Tan, who's apprenticed in five-star hotels, offers live crab plucked from tanks and cooked in curry spices or deep fried with garlic. Tofu is served Hakka style stuffed with poached shrimp or as a satay filled with peanut-sauced vegetables. **WHO** Well-traveled Beach Cities dwellers and discriminating Malay ex-pats. ♥

[Benley] 🏠 8191 E. Wardlow Rd., Long Beach, 562.596.8130. L & D Tues.-Sat. Vietnamese. Beer & wine. AE, MC, V. $ - $$ **WHY** Upscaled Vietnamese cuisine prepared with an eye toward authenticity.

WHAT Stashed away in a strip mall that butts up against the Orange County border, Benley is one of Long Beach's most consistent restaurants. That's because it has a very clear handle on the kitchen, which turns out refined and thoughtful Vietnamese cuisine: great bowls of pho and expert renditions of bun cha that are highlighted by fantastically crisp sheets of pork. The pan-seared salmon and chicken curry are worthy, too, though you'll want to save room for the warm cassava cake drizzled with vanilla crème anglaise. **WHO** Middle-aged east Long Beachers and young couples bonding over spring rolls. 🍷

[Bento Asian Kitchen] 1000 Torrance Blvd., Redondo Beach, 310.792.5185, bentoasiankitchen.com. L & D Mon.-Sat. Japanese. No booze. AE, MC, V. $ - $$ **WHY** A lengthy menu of carefully prepared boxed lunches from a sparkling kitchen. **WHAT** When you don't want to pony up big bucks for the omakase at your favorite sushi bar, this place is a bargain alternative. They offer great variety: 20 options of made-to-order bento, including many sushi roll combinations. **WHO** Harried parents and sushi lovers on a budget. 🚙☺

[Bistro Beaux] 21605 S. Western Ave., Torrance, 310.320.5820. D Mon.-Sat. (to 1 a.m.). Japanese/Mediterranean. Full bar. AE, MC, V. $$ **WHY** Beef carpaccio salad, soft scrambled egg with *mentaiko* (spicy cod roe), salmon fried rice ... and a 1 a.m. closing time that draws the late-night crowd. **WHAT** Corrugated aluminum siding decorates the walls of this South Bay, design-forward restaurant serving such Japanized Mediterranean cuisine as flash-fried calamari, spicy cod roe spaghetti, scallop gratin and seafood salad tossed with garlic vinaigrette. **WHO** The young and the stylish, Blackberries optional. ☺

[Bouchees Bistro] 515 Long Beach Blvd., Long Beach, 562.951.8222, bouchees.com. B, L & D daily. American. Beer & wine. AE, MC, V. $ - $$ **WHY** A Blue Line-adjacent eatery that makes the best burgers in Long Beach — and it's now open for good breakfasts, too. **WHAT** Defined by its customizable cast of burgers (including mini sliders), Bouchees has a simple concept that it executes perfectly. Choose your patty (Angus sirloin, turkey, ahi, organic homemade veggie), your toppings (caramelized onions, shiitakes and jalapeño salsa, to name but a few) and your sauces (peppercorn dijonnaise and lemon caper aioli, among others). There are house burgers if you don't feel like designing your own, as well as such non-burger options as an enormous jumbo lump crab cake and a trio of salads. Burgers of the month are made of things like elk or wild boar. **WHO** Downtown office dwellers, Metro riders, theatergoers and dedicated burger lovers. 🍷☺

[Brix@1601] 1601 Pacific Coast Hwy., Hermosa Beach, 310.698.0740, brix1601.com. D nightly. Modern American/wine bar. Full bar. AE, MC, V. $$ - $$$$ **WHY** An excellent wine list, fried calamari, duck confit spring rolls, diver scallops. fresh fish and wonderful desserts. **WHAT** Affili-

🍷VEGETARIAN ☺KID FRIENDLY ☼PATIO DINING 🚙DELIVERY 🏠PRIVATE PARTY

ated with the neighboring wine shop, this Hermosa spot is as much about wine as food — but the food is certainly no afterthought. Chef Michael McDonald turns out consistently good modern American food that's exactly what everyone wants to eat right now. Brix manages to be both lively and romantic, and the service is enthusiastic. A boon for South Bay food lovers. **WHO** South Bay wine and food folks, some of whom travel a ways to be here. ☺ ♥🍸

[Can Coon] **9887 Alondro Blvd., Bellflower, 562.925.0993. L & D Tues.-Sun. Thai. No booze. Cash only. $ WHY** Any one of the blistering salads, seasoned with *pak pai*, a Thai herb that tastes like cilantro raised to the tenth power. **WHAT** Although its setting is beyond nondescript, the flavors at this six-table Isaan-style place leap from the plate. The fermented sour rice sausage and shrimp laap (*larp kroong* on the menu) are some of the best in town. 🗺 🍸

[Chaba Thai Bay Grill] 🏛 **525 S. Pacific Coast Hwy., Redondo Beach, 310.540.8441, chabarestaurant.com. L & D daily. Thai. Full bar. AE, MC, V. $ - $$$ WHY** Sumptuous New Thai cookery and a full bar. **WHAT** For the best of new-generation Thai cooking, this handsome bistro is the place. The dishes blend pure Thai ingredients and techniques with a presentation style that's almost French in its elegance. The fusion is particularly true of the daily specials, which can run from braised lamb in panang curry on a bed of cabbage to filet mignon with shiitake-green peppercorn sauce and galangal rice. ☼🚗

[Cucina Picarelli] **5096 E. Pacific Coast Hwy., Long Beach, 562.494.5118, cucinapicarelli.com. L Tues.-Fri., D Tues.-Sun. Italian. Full bar. AE, MC, V. $$ - $$$ WHY** For the best fried calamari in town, and a few very good pasta dishes, some of which are made by the owner's mom, who comes in once a week to make pasta. Try a special if she made it, or have the penne with a tri-tip meat sauce from an old family recipe. **WHAT** Not everything's good at this small trattoria, but the atmosphere's great (owner Joe Picarelli seems to know everyone in town), and the dishes that are good — calamari, homemade salad dressings, pasta specials — are thoroughly satisfying. **WHO** Devoted regulars have made this the Cheers of Long Beach; some frequent diners even keep their private stash of vodka at the bar. ☼

[Dal Rae] 🏛 **9023 E. Washington Blvd., Pico Rivera, 562.949.2444, dalrae.com. L Mon.-Fri., D nightly. Continental/American. Full bar. AE, MC, V. $$$ - $$$$$ WHY** When nothing will do but oysters Rockefeller, prime rib and a one-man band in a tux singing Springsteen's *Pink Cadillac*. **WHAT** This landmark was founded in 1958, and inside it remains 1958. The lobster is still being Thermidored, the bananas still flambéed, and the spinach salad still wilted. "Ah," you might be thinking, "that sounds like a depressing, off-the-Vegas-strip hangout for fourth-rate goombas and washed-up Peggy Lee wannabes." But you

🏛 ESSENTIALLY L.A. ☺ LATE ♥ ROMANTIC 🗺 VALUE 🍸 QUIET ☼ SUSTAINABLE

would be wrong. The sons of the founder have kept the Dal Rae fresh and first-rate. The booths are high-backed, the cocktails are stiff, and the Caesar is prepared tableside. A little bit of high-fat, high-calorie heaven. **WHO** A cross-section of folks from Pico Rivera, Downey and Whittier, from families out to celebrate Grandma's 85th birthday to young couples splurging on a special date. ♥ 🌙 ☺ 🏠

[Darren's Restaurant & Bar] 1141 Manhattan Ave., Manhattan Beach, 310.802.1973, darrensrestaurant.com. D nightly. Modern American. Full bar. AE, MC, V. $$$ - $$$$ **WHY** Inventive, flavorful, beach-friendly Cal-Asian fusion cooking is served in a ten-table boîte closely overseen by the friendly owner/chef, who doubles as sommelier. Great happy-hour menu at the tiny bar. **WHAT** Lately this nachos-friendly beach neighborhood is drawing a more food-serious crowd with wine bars and upscale restaurants, most notably this intimate place. Local boy Darren Weiss, perhaps L.A.'s only deaf owner/chef, spent his formative years cooking in swank Hawaiian restaurants, so it makes sense that he loves to blend sweet and spicy, as with the lobster chowder, which marries a coconut-milk broth with a spicy undercurrent. Most of the time his mélanges work beautifully. Desserts are a weak spot. Excellent service, expensive wines, well-made cocktails. **WHO** Middle-aged moms/triathletes celebrating a birthday, Tommy Bahama couples, small groups of twentysomething friends who can afford good food and wine. ♥🦞☼

[The Depot] 1250 Cabrillo Ave., Torrance, 310.787.7501, depotrestaurant.com. L Mon.-Fri., D Mon.-Sat. Californian/modern American. Beer & wine. AE, MC, V. $$$ - $$$$ **WHY** For a good business lunch or a lively dinner with friends. **WHAT** Owner/chef Michael Shafer is one of the culinary leaders in the South Bay, and his Depot is one of the best destinations in the area for martinis, steaks and Asian-influenced California cuisine. **WHO** The Torrance A-list of business leaders, politicians and social sorts. 🏠

[El Pollo Inka] 15400 Hawthorne Blvd., Lawndale, 310.676.6665, elpolloinka.com. L & D daily. Peruvian. Beer & wine. AE, MC, V. $ **WHY** Fantastic roast chicken or traditional saltado de pollo. Add some of the famed cilantro sauce and an order of plantains and you'll be in heaven. **WHAT** The name may imply a competitor to El Pollo Loco, but this is actually a sweet little sit-down restaurant with seductive and inexpensive Peruvian food, most notably the juicy, wood-smoked pollo a la brasa and the *saltado de pollo*, a stir-fry of chicken with onions and tomatoes, served with a double-carb whammy of potatoes and rice. **WHO** Families attacking orders of roast chicken. 🍴☺

[El Puerto Escondido] 915 Arbor Vitae St., Inglewood, 310.670.1014, elpuertoesc.com. B, L & D 24 hours daily. Mexican/seafood. Beer & wine. MC, V. $ - $$ **WHY** Ultra-fresh Mexican-style seafood,

🥬 VEGETARIAN ☺ KID FRIENDLY ☼ PATIO DINING 🚗 DELIVERY 🏠 PRIVATE PARTY

including Happy Oysters, topped with a vibrant chopped shrimp cocktail, and *caldo de siete mares*, a light, fresh soup generously stocked with Alaskan crab legs, mussels and shrimp — served 24 hours a day, a stone's throw from LAX! **WHAT** There are now three branches of this beloved restaurant, which serves the seafood dishes of Mexico's Pacific Coast beach towns, but this is the original and the only one open 24 hours a day. Stick with the same dishes you'd order in Los Cabos — camarones al mojo de ajo, ceviches, shrimp cocktails, whole fried fish, even cold Coronas in a bucket — and you'll be as happy as the regulars. **WHO** LAX workers and construction workers. ☺ 📝

[El Puerto Escondido] 4182 W. El Segundo Blvd., Hawthorne, 310.978.9609, elpuertoesc.com. L & D daily. Mexican/seafood. Beer & wine. MC, V. $ **WHY** Ultra-fresh, ultra-cheap Mexican-style seafood. **WHAT** This newest branch of the Inglewood original doesn't have the 24-hour appeal of the mothership, but it does have the same terrific shrimp cocktails and platters of seafood appetizers big enough to make into meals. And this new branch makes freshly squeezed orange, carrot and celery juices, too. **WHO** Blue-collar workers and surfers pining for Mexico's beaches. 📝

[Enrique's] 🏠 6210 E. Pacific Coast Hwy., Long Beach, 562.498.3622. L & D daily. Mexican. Beer & wine. MC, V. $ - $$ **WHY** Absolutely superb Mexican food: a huge, tender pork shank with tomatillo sauce, addictive potato taquitos, grilled shrimp and achiote-infused chicken, rice so good it makes Mexican-Americans weep in memory of their grandmothers, and heavenly chocolate bread pudding. **WHAT** Enrique Perez can make a burrito if that's what you really want, but you're better off letting this Guadalajara native show you his real stuff, perhaps the roasted peppers filled with cheese and potatoes and served with guac and a tomato-onion pico de gallo. Between the ranchera music, the low prices and the outstanding food, this place give its regulars lots of reasons to be happy. **WHO** A great Long Beach cross-section, minus the party-hearty margarita crowd (beer and wine only): upscale couples, working-class families, golfers from the neighboring course, college students, other restaurateurs. 📝☺

[Fora Restaurant] 5730 E. 2nd St., Long Beach, 562.856.9494, fora-naples.com. D Tues.-Sun. Modern American. Full bar. AE, MC, V. $$$ - $$$$ **WHY** A charming little place whose modern bistro cooking is best showcased in the four- or five-course tasting menus paired with a wine flight ($57 and $66, respectively). **WHAT** An intimate spot on intimate Naples Island, Fora has an appealing, not-too-overpriced menu of modern classics: lobster martini, roasted tomato soup, seared sushi-grade tuna and, most surprisingly and deliciously of all, beef stroganoff. Good cheeses and even better soufflés. **WHO** Beach-dwelling locals looking for a little romance, a good glass of wine and the delicious ahi tower. ♥ 🍷 🦞

[Frenchy's Bistro] **4137 E. Anaheim St., Long Beach, 562.494.8787, frenchysbistro.com. L Fri., D Tues.-Sun. French. Beer & wine. AE, MC, V. $$$$ WHY** A fetching proper French bistro in an unlikely neighborhood, serving delicious truffled foie gras terrine, sand dabs, rack of lamb with a mustard and herb crust and flawless soufflés. **WHAT** A French husband-and-wife team run this romantic bistro, where the cooking is classic and carefully prepared, the wine list is good (if pricey), and the service is serious, sometimes a little too much so. A fine place for a celebratory dinner. **WHO** A generally well-dressed crowd that can afford $30 entrees. ♥ 🍸

[Gardena Bowl Coffee Shop] **15707 S. Vermont Ave., Gardena, 310.532.0820. B, L & D daily. Hawaiian/Japanese. No booze. MC, V. $ WHY** Teriyaki chicken and bacon fried rice ... need we say more? **WHAT** A down-and-dirty bowling-alley coffee shop with authentically good and cheap Hawaiian food. 📷☺

[George's Greek Café] 🏛 **135 Pine Ave., Long Beach, 562.437.1184, georgesgreekcafe.com. L & D daily. Greek. Beer & wine. AE, MC, V. $ - $$$ WHY** Dolmathes, saganaki, taramosalata, gyros, grilled lamb chops — and bonhomie. **WHAT** George Loizides greets customers like family at this Pine Avenue institution serving hearty Greek specialties at reasonable prices. (Long Beach once had a vibrant Greek community, and this place carries on the tradition.) It's a great place to go with a group and share the array of dips and appetizer combinations as well as the fun of *saganaki*, cheese flamed with brandy. Opa! **WHO** Birthday partiers and families. 📷☺

[The Green Temple] **1700 S. Catalina Ave., Redondo Beach, 310.944.4525, greentemple.net. B Sun., L & D Tues.-Sun. Vegetarian/ Californian. No booze. MC, V. $$ WHY** Vegetarian and vegan meals in a bucolic garden setting. **WHAT** The board of changing daily specials at this serene, Buddha-filled indoor-outdoor eatery may offer sweet white corn chowder or a nut-strewn salad. House dressings include balsamic-virgin olive oil vinaigrette and sesame-tamari-lemon. And the delicious house favorites, enchiladas and the kamut spaghetti with a rich tofu cream sauce, keep the clientele loyal. 🍃🚚☺☼

[Iccho] **25310 Crenshaw Blvd., Torrance, 310.325.7273. D nightly (to 2 a.m.). Japanese. Beer & wine. MC, V. $$ WHY** Pitchers of Japanese beer, bottles of sake and fun small dishes, from the udon-and-yakitori standards to such novelties as fried kim chee with pork and caterpillar sushi rolls. **WHAT** In the shopping-intensive locale of Rolling Hills Plaza, this family-style izakaya comforts everyone with an enormously long menu that ranges from the basic to the inventive, and it's all served until 2 a.m. ☼ 📷

[Izakaya Yuzen Kan] 2755 Pacific Coast Hwy., Torrance, 310.530.7888, izakayakan.com. L Mon.-Sat., D nightly. Japanese. Beer & wine. AE, MC, V. $$ - $$$ **WHY** Intelligent and sometimes almost whimsical dishes like ground chicken with a light miso glaze in lettuce wraps, as well as exquisitely fresh, flown-in-from-Japan sashimi. **WHAT** This modern izakaya hidden in a shopping center has an airy open kitchen and sleek lines that give it a quiet dignity. Ultra-fine as well as more modest sakes have been smartly selected to pair with the modern Japanese fare. **WHO** Izakaya diners more interested in the quality of the food than a noisy scene.

[Japonica] 1304 1/2 S. Pacific Coast Hwy., Redondo Beach, 310.316.9477, japonicadining.com. D nightly. Japanese. Beer & wine. AE, MC, V. $ - $$ **WHY** Sake, romance, careful service and excellent izakaya. **WHAT** Curtained booths allude to the tatami rooms of the past at this sleek South Bay looker serving great food and an extensive sake list that includes several flights. Every dish, including crunchy fried baby Spanish mackerel, fresh salmon roe omelet and seared albacore with spicy sauce, confirms the kitchen's skill. ♥ 🦢

[Johnny Reb's] 4663 Long Beach Blvd., Long Beach, 562.423.7327, johnnyrebs.com. B, L & D daily. Southern/American. Beer & wine. AE, MC, V. $$ **WHY** Fried pickles, fried green tomatoes, fried chicken and, if you're trying to go easy on the fried foods, mac 'n cheese. It's a theme restaurant, but a good one. **WHAT** Southern-food buffs (and really, does anyone not love fried chicken and cornbread?) wept when Johnny Reb's burned down a couple of years ago, but it's back and thriving. Choose the chicken, catfish or pulled pork over the baby-back ribs and explore the interesting sides, which include black-eyed peas and Brunswick stew. **WHO** Big eaters. 🗗 ☺

[Katsu] 302 Rosecrans Ave., Manhattan Beach, 310.546.3761, katsu-sushi.com. L Mon.-Fri., D nightly. Japanese. Beer & wine. AE, MC, V. $ - $$ **WHY** Superb lunchtime sushi bento boxes ($12.95) and excellent happy-hour deals. **WHAT** A pleasant and modest sushi bar, Katsu bears no relation to the über-trendy Katsu-ya chain. Very good, reasonably priced sashimi, sushi, spicy tuna and tempura are served in a modest lime-green dining room just a roll's throw from the ocean. **WHO** Locals who come here weekly. 🗗 ☺

[Kelly's] 5716 E. 2nd St., Long Beach, 562.433.4983, kellysrestaurantinc.com. D Tues.-Sun. American/steakhouse. Full bar. AE, MC, V. $$$$ - $$$$$ **WHY** For the complimentary pâté and lavosh (why doesn't every restaurant offer this?), the strong drinks (watch out!) and the clubby atmosphere. **WHAT** At this Naples institution, politicians and business leaders kibitz over huge martinis while hungry folks with well-stocked wallets sit in cushy booths and eat prime rib and Caesar salad. Good old-school service. **WHO** Everyone who's anyone. 🦢

🏛 ESSENTIALLY L.A. ☺ LATE ♥ ROMANTIC 🗗 VALUE 🦢 QUIET 🌿 SUSTAINABLE

[The Kettle] 1138 Highland Ave., Manhattan Beach, 310.545.8511, thekettle.net. B, L & D 24 hours daily. American. Beer & wine. AE, MC, V. $ - $$$ **WHY** A 24/7 godsend for insomniacs, students and night-shifters. **WHAT** The food's fine, but the real value of this woodsy-in-a-'70s-way coffee shop is that it's open 24/7, a rarity for a large, full-service restaurant anywhere in L.A., let alone a beach town. Regulars get the muffins, crab cake Benedict, burgers and egg dishes. **WHO** It all depends on the hour: seniors for early breakfast and dinner, families and beach-goers during the day and a sometimes rowdy post-party crowd late at night (which is when the bouncer shows up). ☺ 🍽 ☺ ☼

[Khun Lek Kitchen] 9208 Alondra Blvd., Bellflower, 562.804.6602. L & D Mon.-Tues. & Thurs.-Sun. Thai. BYOB. MC, V. $ - $$ **WHY** For the specials menu, listed on a handwritten daily menu. **WHAT** Crisp white tablecloths, contemporary art and a mirrored karaoke room mark this as a restaurant with aspirations, and the light, clean food lives up to the look. Check the menu and daily specials board for such Isaan favorites as raw shrimp laap or catfish salad.

[Komatsu Tempura Bar] 🔒 1644 W. Carson St., Torrance, 310.787.0787. L Mon.-Fri., D Mon.-Sat. Japanese. Beer & wine. MC, V. $$ - $$$ **WHY** For exquisitely made tempura and high-caliber izakaya-style little dishes. **WHAT** If there were a Tempura Olympics, chef Hiroshi Komatsu would surely get the gold. He plucks your tempura from his proprietary blend of scalding oil and serves the lacy, crackle-crusted fish and vegetables one piece at a time so they never cool and wilt. He also comes up with such novelties as tempura chestnuts stuffed with umeboshi plums. **WHO** Discriminating, tradition-loving Japanese and anyone wanting to graduate from mundane fried chicken.

[Kotosh] 2408 Lomita Blvd., Lomita, 310.257.1363, kotoshrestaurant.com. L & D Mon.-Sat. Japanese/Peruvian. Beer & wine. AE, MC, V. $ - $$ **WHY** Intercontinental fusion food informed by 100 years of immigration. **WHAT** Born out of history, this quaint place is the result of a century of Japanese immigration to Peru. Its success stems from its ability to take two disparate cuisines and forge a strong, seafood-based middle ground. On the Peruvian side of things, try the *pulpo al olivo* (tender slabs of octopus streaked with botija olive sauce) and solid ceviche. The Japanese menu is sushi intensive, dominated by California-style rolls that, despite some predictability, owe their excellence to generally inventive combinations and quality fish. **WHO** Indecisive South Bay residents who want the best of two continents.

[KyoChon Chicken] 2515 Torrance Blvd., Torrance, 310.320.9299. L & D daily. Korean. No booze. MC, V. $$ **WHY** They really mean it when they say "super-spicy" fried chicken. Or take a safer route and order the soy-marinated crispy style. **WHAT** It's fried chicken, but it's not fast. In fact, they don't start cooking it at this stylish Korean café

🥬 VEGETARIAN ⊙ KID FRIENDLY ✿ PATIO DINING � DELIVERY 🎩 PRIVATE PARTY

until you order it, which can mean a wait of 25 minutes or so. But the payoff is a deeply flavorful bird accompanied by a refreshing side dish of pickled white radishes. 🗟 ☺

[La Casita Mexicana] 🔒 4030 E. Gage Ave., Bell, 323.773.1898, casitamex.com. B, L & D daily. Mexican. No booze. AE, MC, V. $$ **WHY** Food just like Grandma's — if Grandma happened to be a meticulous Mexican village cook committed to using locally grown ingredients. Try to come on a Wednesday — it's pozole day. **WHAT** Spanish-language media cooking stars Jaime Martin del Campo and Ramiro Arvizu have created a place that draws fans from all over the L.A. basin. Absolutely everything — from table salsas to *refrescos* (juice drinks) and *raspados* (snow cones) — is made from scratch. Unfamiliar veggies like *huauzontle* and *romerito* may adorn the Lenten menu, although most dishes will be familiar. But even the enchiladas and moles have a particular flair. Remarkable Mexican home cooking that's worth a trip. **WHO** Devotees who drive long distances for a special meal here. 🗟 ☺ ۞

[La Concha] 2612 E. Anaheim St., Long Beach, 562.438.9499. L & D daily. Mexican. Beer. MC, V. $ **WHY** Hunger-killing *tortas ahogadas*. **WHAT** An unassuming place crammed into a corner strip mall that often goes unnoticed on this busy block, this place covers all the expected Mexican bases— but the real reason to visit is the Guadalajaran specialties. La Concha's torta ahogada is the best around: slabs of crusty bread stuffed with crisp pork and drowned in a manageably spicy chile de árbol sauce. If you're not up for the torta, try a plate of diced pork tossed with strips of cactus or a stout bowl of carne en su jugo instead. **WHO** Local heat seekers and Chivas fans cheering on every goal. 🗟

[La Huasteca] Plaza Mexico, 3150 E. Imperial Hwy, Lynwood, 310.537.8800, lahuasteca.com. B, L & D daily. Mexican. Full bar. AE, MC, V. $$ - $$$ **WHY** Chicken with mole negro, chile en nogada, panuchos, steak in huitlacoche, snapper with a chipotle-ginger sauce and many other complex, richly flavorful dishes. Consistency is sometimes an issue, but it's all worth trying. **WHAT** In a vast and grand space reminiscent of an outdoor Mexico City plaza, this is a destination restaurant with mariachis (warning: it gets loud), tequila-tasting events, private parties and ambitious southern Mexican cooking. ☺ 🍶

[La Parolaccia] 2945 E. Broadway, Long Beach, 562.438.1235, laparolacciausa.com. L Sat.-Sun, D nightly. Italian. Beer & wine. AE, MC, V. $$ **WHY** Charming plates of Italian classics. **WHAT** Though it's not completely unique to Long Beach (there's a Claremont branch), La Parolaccia is as entrenched in local stomachs as any of the city's famous greasy spoons. The reason is clear: Its osteria-style cooking stands well above the nearby red-sauce joints. Consider trying the fluffy gnocchi, rich risotto, penne cinque terre (with goat cheese, pesto and sun-dried tomatoes) and great, simple pizzas from the wood-burning oven. **WHO** Bluff Heights residents. 🦐

[Michael's Ristorante] 5620 E. 2nd St., Long Beach, 562.439.7080, michaelsonnaples.com. D nightly. Italian. Full bar. AE, MC, V. $$$ - $$$$ **WHY** Sophisticated Italian cooking, including light yet flavorful lasagne, various homemade pastas and gorgeous branzino with olives and capers, best enjoyed on the rooftop terrace on a warm summer evening. **WHAT** Naples's most sophisticated restaurant is this handsome, modern Italian with comfortable booths downstairs and a fab upstairs terrace with a heated dining area and fireplace-warmed hanging-out area. The service is young and inexperienced, but the cooking is assured and delicious, and the wine list is worthy. Good-value happy hour, too. **WHO** Well-heeled couples and effervescent gaggles of friends sharing bottles of wine. ♥ 🍸 🦐 ✿

[Musha] 🏠 1725 Carson St., Torrance, 310.787.7344. D nightly. Japanese/Californian. Beer & wine. AE, MC, V. $$ **WHY** Fatty pork belly (you know you want it), kim chee udon topped with butter and caviar, tuna poke, seafood-filled baguette au gratin ... amazing and delicious dishes that typify the best of modern Japanese-L.A. fusion cooking. **WHAT** The loud, chaotic (and fun) Torrance branch is a contrast to the more sedate (and fun) Santa Monica location of this anything-goes pub, where European ingredients and concepts (roasted garlic, dips and crackers) are incorporated into Japanese pub fare. ☺ 🗺

[New Orleans Cajun Café] 140 Pier Ave., Hermosa Beach, 310.372.8970, neworleanshermosa.com. L & D Mon. & Thurs.-Sun. Cajun/Southern. Beer & wine. MC, V. $$ - $$$ **WHY** A New Orleans native, the owner/chef knows how to cook Cajun-Creole food. Sit at the counter to enjoy some easygoing repartee while the cooks make mounds of red beans and rice, jumping jambalaya and hush puppies. **WHAT** This busy, narrow, corner café reminiscent of Louisiana's shotgun houses serves catfish, seafood and sausages flown in from New Orleans. Just-right spices sizzle but don't scorch. Note that parking is a pain in the Big Easy; head for the structure by the pier. **WHO** Anyone aching for a real Creole meal, surfside residents and singles out for a date. 🍸 🦐

[Open Sesame] 5215 E. 2nd St., Long Beach, 562.621.1698, opensesamegrill.com. L & D daily. Lebanese/Middle Eastern. Beer & wine. AE, MC, V. $ - $$ **WHY** For one of the most convivial, food-celebrating places in Belmont Shore, with happy groups sharing *fattoush* (a chopped salad), schwarma, crisp-soft fried potatoes, vegetarian platters, Belmont Brewing beers on tap and, of course, baklava. But whatever you order, just make sure you include some of those potatoes. **WHAT** Ali Kobeissi's Lebanese bistro is so popular that he took over the lease for a failed restaurant a few doors down, and now that Open

🦐 VEGETARIAN ⊚ KID FRIENDLY ✿ PATIO DINING 🚗 DELIVERY 🏠 PRIVATE PARTY

Sesame is every bit as crowded as its parent; expect to wait at least a half-hour at either place. The original is well designed, with comfortable booths and a noise level that's manageable even at peak times, and the service is prompt and cordial. 📠🐾☺☼

[Otafuku] 🏛 16525 S. Western Ave., Gardena, 310.532.9348. L & D Mon.-Sat. Japanese. Beer & wine. AE, MC, V. $ - $$ **WHY** The best soba noodles in the South Bay. Great izakaya, too. **WHAT** Noodles made by hand in small batches are the draw at this dinky, hard-to-find noodle and izakaya spot (hint: enter from the back parking lot). While it makes fine eel tempura, grilled steak and and wild mushrooms over rice, the reason to drive out of your way for a meal here is the absolutely superb soba noodles, either cold with a dipping sauce with green onions and wasabi or hot in a delicious soup. Since you're there, make sure to try the Otafuku fried chicken, too. 📠☺

[Pann's Restaurant] 🏛 6710 La Tijera Blvd., Inglewood, 323.776.3770, panns.com. B, L & D daily. Coffee shop/American. Beer & wine. AE, MC, V. $ - $$$ **WHY** An L.A. classic for its 1950s roots and Googie architecture alone — but when you add the waffles, patty melt, fried chicken and incredible biscuits... well, it's a downright treasure. **WHAT** George and Rena Panagopoulos opened this Jetsons-style restaurant in 1958, and the family still runs it They've kept the place in tip-top shape, and the food is exactly what you would hope for in such a place: good egg dishes, country-fried steak, patty melts, shakes, and perhaps the best fried chicken and biscuits in town. The burgers, however, are surprisingly blah, and everyone knows that the vegetables are best left uneaten. **WHO** Seniors, college students, travelers coming and going from LAX, and pretty much every sort of Angeleno. 📠☺

[Petros] 451 Manhattan Beach Blvd., Manhattan Beach, 310.545.4100, petrosrestaurant.com. L & D daily. Greek. Full bar. AE, MC, V. $$$ - $$$$ **WHY** The exuberant Greek flavors go down well so close to the ocean. **WHAT** Don't expect plate-smashing hokum at this modern Greek bistro, just very good food: feta bruschetta; grilled octopus; shrimp saganaki with tomato, basil and feta; grilled pita with a dip of olives and sun-dried tomatoes; lovely fresh-fish entrees; a hearty lamb pasta and terrific cheeses. The setting is cool and whitewashed, with an awning-shaded patio that's great for lunch, and the Greek music in the background doesn't interfere with conversation. ☺☼

[Pho Pioneer] 17701 Pioneer Blvd., Artesia, 562.809.9250. L & D daily. Vietnamese. No booze. MC, V. $ **WHY** The Pioneer rice special, a combination of crispy minced shrimp cake, slabs of grilled marinated pork, delicate steamed egg loaf and a salad garnish, has customers returning again and again. **WHAT** Artesia may be famed for Little India, in which this Vietnamese place sits, but in fact it's as multinational as Coca-Cola — so Pho Pioneer has thrived here. Its phos include a seafood version, a shrimp version, a vegetarian version and one with chicken breast — one for every taste. And to keep pace with trends, it offers traditional Vietnamese smoothies with boba tapioca pearls. **WHO** Indian-American families checking out the pho scene. 🖼🦐☺

[Ramen California] **24231 Crenshaw Blvd., Torrance, 310.530.2749. L & D Tues.-Sun. Japanese/modern American. Beer & wine. AE, MC, V. $ - $$ WHY** A new, radical wave of ramen that fuses Japanese tradition with Californian innovation. **WHAT** Ramen California sprang from the mind of Shigetoshi Nakamura, a Japanese ramen prodigy who has taken on the task of reinventing the noodle soup. Indeed, diners should be advised to abandon all previous ramen knowledge — Nakamura's noodle soups are all about fresh, market-driven produce. In the signature California ramen, more than 30 vegetables bob through the powerful and clean chicken broth. The heirloom tomato ramen is a study in fresh flavor, while the wildly inventive Reggiano-tofu ramen is all about experimentation. There's a rotating selection of small plates, too, including excellent bao-like bread crusted with rosemary and sea salt and consistently good carpaccios. **WHO** Ramen lovers who are willing to set their purist tendencies aside. ☺🦐

[Renu Nakorn] 🏠 **13019 E. Rosecrans Ave., Norwalk, 562.921.2124. L & D daily. Thai. Beer & wine. MC, V. $$ WHY** Robustly seasoned and beautiful food: jackfruit curry with pork, khao soi curry with noodles and chicken, an incendiary papaya salad, lemongrass-infused Isaan sausages and much, much more. **WHAT** Anxious fans can breathe easy — the destination Isaan-style Thai restaurant is back after a major remodel, and it's still worth the drive to Norwalk. The basics — pad Thai, panang curry, satay — are excellent, but it's the northern Isaan dishes that are worth the trip. The dining room is pleasant now, and the service is good. **WHO** Serious Thai food fans. 🖼

[Restaurant Christine] 🏠 **24530 Hawthorne Blvd., Torrance, 310.373.1952, restaurantchristine.com. L Mon.-Fri., D nightly. Mediterranean/Asian. Beer & wine. AE, MC, V. $$$ - $$$$ WHY** The avocado tower, lobster salad and the tasting menu. **WHAT** Christine Brown combines flavors of the Mediterranean and the Pacific Rim in her color-washed bistro, and the results are generally quite successful. The "greens and grazing plates" are big enough to share as a starter; half the room seems to get the avocado tower, with napa cabbage, mango and sesame. For an entree, depending on your global mood, you can go Italian (cioppino) or Asian (sesame-glazed Atlantic salmon). ☼🏠

[Riviera Mexican Grill] **1615 S. Pacific Coast Hwy., Redondo Beach, 310.540.2501. L & D daily. Mexican. Full bar. AE, MC, V. $ - $$ WHY** Great margaritas, grilled fish tacos and a chill surf-town atmosphere. **WHAT** An active member of the local ocean community, Riviera sponsors an annual paddle contest and keeps the prices low

🦐 **VEGETARIAN** ☺ **KID FRIENDLY** ☼ **PATIO DINING** 🚗 **DELIVERY** 🏠 **PRIVATE PARTY**

to keep hard-surfing regulars properly stoked with Mexican food. The Cal-Mex food is simple and satisfying, and the cadillac margaritas really are the best in Redondo. **WHO** Old and young surfers, blond families and Rainbow-shod friends sharing pitchers. 🗺️ ☺ ☼

[Siem Reap] 1810 E. Anaheim St., Long Beach, 562.591.7414. L & D daily. Cambodian. Full bar. MC, V. $ - $$ **WHY** A decades-old centerpiece of Cambodia Town. **WHAT** A lot of heat courses through Siem Reap — sometimes a subtle, slow burn, other times a fully loaded assault. Beef *loc lac* (on a mound of rice with tomato, cucumber, green eggplant, a fried egg and lemon sauce) is an easy entry point, but also consider *amok*, a powerfully spicy fish curry steamed and formed into patties. The menu can be daunting, but don't hesitate to ask for help. And make sure to grab a taro shake to cool off. **WHO** Cambodian locals. 🗺️

[Starling Diner] 4114 E. 3rd. St., Long Beach, 562.433.2041, star-lingdiner.com. B & L Tues.-Sun., D Thurs.-Sat. American. Beer & wine. AE, MC, V. $$ **WHY** For neighborhood charm with gourmet soul. **WHAT** Surrounded by a quaint neighborhood of historic homes and breezy apartments, this bright, quirky café has become a hub of local life. (Come in alone and you can sit at a long communal table with soon-to-be friends.) For breakfast, try the mascarpone-stuffed french toast or the sweet and creamy polenta with seasonal berries and cream. At lunch and dinner, the menu is all about sandwiches and pizzettes, well-conceived cheesy flatbreads that keep the neighbors coming back. **WHO** Early risers, hungry friends and dog-walking diners. 🗺️☺

[Tin Roof Bistro] 3500 Sepulveda Blvd., Manhattan Beach, 310.546.6180, tinroofbistro.com. L & D daily. Modern American. Full bar. AE, MC, V. $$ - $$$ **WHY** Excellent and affordable cocktails and wine by the glass, a killer burger and farmers' market produce. **WHAT** Mike Simms has a winner in his new indoor-outdoor bistro that rises above its shopping-mall setting. Skip the blah, undercooked pizzas in favor of the terrific curry spinach dip, thick burgers, salads, roast chicken, fresh fish and shoestring fries. At this writing the desserts were weak, but we expect they will improve. **WHO** Shaggy old surf hippies, golf-shirt-wearing business folk and blond families. 🗺️🍴☺☼

[Tirupathi Bhimas] 🏠 18792 Pioneer Blvd., Artesia, 562.809.3806, tirupathibhimas.com. L & D daily. Indian/vegetarian. No booze. AE, MC, V. $ **WHY** Lunchtime *thali* — an assortment of beautiful small dishes with big flavor. **WHAT** Spicy vegetarian fare in the Andhra style is the focus of this spacious Little India restaurant that's one of the best of the neighborhood. Carrot cubes with grated coconut and a lentil stew called *kootu* are accompanied by roti, rice and dessert. 🗺️🍴☺

[Toko Rame] 17155 Bellflower Blvd., Bellflower, 562.920.8002. L & D Tues.-Sun. Indonesian. No booze. MC, V. $ **WHY** A long-standing source of Indonesian excellence. **WHAT** The decades-old, family-run Toko Rame touches on what seems like every possible Indonesian entree, from lightly charred satay and dishes constructed around the glutinous rice cake known as *lontong* to carefully executed curries and combination plates like *nasi bungkus*. There are more than 100 options, giving you many reasons for a return trip. **WHO** Indonesian families and hungry drivers pulling in off the 91. 🖼️🍷

[Torihei] **1757 W. Carson St., Torrance, 310.781.9407. D nightly. Japanese. Beer & wine. AE, MC, V. $ - $$** **WHY** A relatively rare but harmonious pairing of yakitori and oden. **WHAT** Torihei's yakitori is made from tender, flavorful Jidori chicken. Its *oden* is the more unusual of the specialties, a homey dish that's typically prepared as a one-pot stew — but here items are presented à la carte. The fresh fish cake is essential, a pillowy triangle that's airier than a marshmallow. But the ultimate oden item is the soft-boiled egg set afloat in a pool of dashi and topped with little piles of brilliant orange cod roe. Like so many of Torihei's dishes, it's an ode to simple, precise flavor. **WHO** Torrance businessmen fresh off work and young couples sharing skewers. ☺

[Udupi Palace] **18635 Pioneer Blvd., Artesia, 562.860.1950, udupipalace.net. L & D Tues.-Sun. Indian. No booze. MC, V. $** **WHY** The dosa are among the biggest — and lightest — in Little India. **WHAT** Maybe you can't spell it, but you should definitely order the *kancheepurum idli*. The ginger-and-cashew dumplings are a specialty at this restaurant, which is named for a temple city in India's Karnataka state. Also check out the *kadi* fritters in coconut curry and the "tomato omelet," actually a pizza-like uttappam made with chickpea flour. 🖼️🍷☺

[Woodlands] **11833 Artesia Blvd., Artesia, 562.860.6500, woodlandsartesia.com. L & D Tues.-Sun. Indian/vegetarian. Full bar. MC, V. $ - $$** **WHY** Go on Dosa Nights (Wednesday and Friday), when you can gorge yourself at the sumptuous buffet — all for $10. **WHAT** Who needs meat when you can feast on south Indian vegetarian fare that's this scrumptious? Go-to dishes include tamarind and lemon rice, coconut chutney and the amazing *chana batura* — fried bread that's as crisp as an eggshell and as big as a volleyball. 🖼️🍷☺

[Yuzu Torrance] **1231 Cabrillo Ave., Torrance, 310.533.9898. L Mon.-Fri., D Mon.-Sat. Japanese. Beer & wine. AE, MC, V. $$$ - $$$$** **WHY** It brings the spirit of *washoku* — traditional Japanese flavors and methods updated with today's artisanal ingredients — from Japan to California. **WHAT** Two bars, wine bar, open robata-style kitchen, tatami rooms and outdoor seating add up to a luxe, sexy environment for elegant Japanese fare: sashimi from the Tsukiji market, honey-marinated Kurobuta pork, skewered Kobe beef balls, tempura-fried sweet potato and more. **WHO** Always full with an upscale crowd, including many Japanese; make reservations a few days in advance. ♥☼🏠

🍃 VEGETARIAN ⊙ KID FRIENDLY ☼ PATIO DINING 🚗 DELIVERY 🏠 PRIVATE PARTY

Drink + Eat

Sometimes the sustenance you seek is as much about the liquids as the solids. But that's not to say you want to drink your dinner. Los Angeles is enjoying a boom in places that celebrate the art of the cocktail, the brew and/or the grape, and many of them serve good food, too. Here are our favorite wine bars, pubs and cocktail lounges.

$$[\text{ESSENTIALLY L.A.}]$$

Bar Marmont, West Hollywood (PAGE 162)

Cat & Fiddle, Hollywood (PAGE 162)

Cole's, Downtown (PAGE 165)

Craftbar, Century City (PAGE 171)

The Edison, Downtown (PAGE 161)

Father's Office, Culver City & Santa Monica (PAGES 171 & 173)

Lou, Hollywood (PAGE 162)

Musso & Frank Grill, Hollywood (PAGE 163)

Varnish Bar, Downtown (PAGE 167)

Vertical Wine Bistro, Pasadena (PAGE 169)

Ye Olde King's Head, Santa Monica (PAGE 176)

The York, Highland Park (PAGE 168)

ESSENTIALLY L.A. ☺ LATE ♥ ROMANTIC VALUE QUIET SUSTAINABLE

CONVIVIAL WINE-SHOP TASTINGS

55 Degrees, Atwater (PAGE 324)
Brixwine, Hermosa Beach (PAGE 324)
Colorado Wine Co., Eagle Rock (PAGE 325)
Mission Wines, South Pasadena (PAGE 327)
Off the Vines, San Pedro (PAGE 327)
Red Carpet, Glendale (PAGE 327)
Silverlake Wine, Silver Lake (PAGE 328)

RESTAURANT BARS OF NOTE

The Bazaar at SLS, West Hollywood (PAGE 42)
Beechwood, Venice (PAGE 127)
Blue on Blue, Beverly Hills (PAGE 117)
Blue Velvet, Downtown (PAGE 65)
Chaya Downtown (PAGE 67)
Chaya Venice, Venice (PAGE 129)
Chez Jay, Santa Monica (PAGE 129)
The Depot, Torrance (PAGE 149)
The Grill on the Alley, Beverly Hills (PAGE 119)
Kelly's, Long Beach (PAGE 152)
Hal's Bar & Grill, Venice (PAGE 132)
Hungry Cat, Hollywood (PAGE 50)
La Grande Orange, Pasadena (PAGE 92)
Lucques, Melrose (PAGE 53)
Luna Park, Miracle Mile (PAGE 53)
Mastro's Steakhouse, Beverly Hills (PAGE 121)
Mike & Anne's, South Pasadena (PAGE 94)
Noe Restaurant & Bar, Downtown (PAGE 76)
Pete's Café & Bar, Downtown (PAGE 77)
Rustic Canyon, Santa Monica (PAGE 141)
Smoke House, Burbank (PAGE 109)
Tin Roof Bistro, Manhattan Beach (PAGE 158)
Tower Bar, West Hollywood (PAGE 62)
Typhoon, Santa Monica (PAGE 143)
Vermont, Los Feliz (PAGE 63)
Wilshire, Santa Monica (PAGE 145)

VEGETARIAN ⊙KID FRIENDLY ✿PATIO DINING 🚐DELIVERY 🎩PRIVATE PARTY

CENTRAL CITY

[Bar Marmont] Chateau Marmont, 8221 W. Sunset Blvd., West
Hollywood, 323.656.1010, chateaumarmont.com. D nightly. Modern American. Full bar. AE, MC, V. $$$ - $$$$ **WHY** For the eternal Hollywood
scene. **WHAT** You're probably not cool enough to come here — we're
certainly not — but you might want to come anyway, just to check out
the never-ending scene, have an overpriced cocktail and taste some of
Carolynn Spence's rustic food (oxtail bruschetta, burger with bacon,
avocado and onion rings, roasted halibut with garlic sauce), which is
much better than it needs to be, given that nobody comes here just to
eat. **WHO** People who are younger, richer, better looking and more
gregarious than you — or at least appear to be in the moment. ☺ 🎩

[Cat & Fiddle] 6530 W. Sunset Blvd., Hollywood, 323.468.3800,
thecatandfiddle.com. L & D daily (to midnight Fri.-Sat.). Pub/English.
Full bar. AE, MC, V. $ - $$ **WHY** English-pub warmth mixed with California style, with excellent house-made bangers, crisp pasties, hilariously decadent Scotch eggs and a sherry trifle with fresh sweet cream.
WHAT Founded in 1982 by the late British rocker Kim Gardner and
his wife, Paula, a fashion retailer, this landmark Sunset pub has been
a music- and movie-industry hangout since the beginning. Outside is a
courtyard with a friendly vibe and a real California feeling; inside the
1920s Mission Revival building is a cozy fireside seat and a dart room.
WHO An after-work crowd of creative types from studios and music-
biz offices nearby. ☺ ☼

[The Golden State] 426 N. Fairfax Ave., Fairfax District,
323.782.8331, thegoldenstatecafe.com. L & D Tues.-Sun. American. Beer
& wine. AE, MC, V. $ **WHY** Locally sourced foods meet excellent beers
at this tiny, order-at-the-counter café. **WHAT** A minimalist ode to the
joy of pairing craft brews — mostly from the Golden State, California
— with food from the state's purveyors, including Scoops' unexpected
ice cream flavors (including beer- and wine-inspired tastes), Let's Be
Frank dogs and sausages, and naturally raised beef. Don't miss the
crunchy fish 'n chips and zingy jalapeño cole slaw. Ask knowledgeable owner Jason Bernstein to help select the perfect beer for the food.
WHO Daytime families, nighttime club-goers and sports fans (there's a
TV for the big games). 📺

[Lou] 724 Vine St., Hollywood, 323.962.6369, louonvine.com.
D Mon.-Sat. Wine bar/Mediterranean. Beer & wine. MC, V. $$ - $$$
WHY Terrific, reasonably priced wines by the glass, a dreamy cheese
and charcuterie platter, and the famed pig candy (basically, thick bacon caramelized with brown sugar). **WHAT** The perfect neighborhood
bistro, Lou is a dark and fetching spot hidden next to a laundromat in a
crummy strip mall. Stop in for a quick glass of biodynamic Coteaux du
Languedoc and a bit of cheese, or settle in with friends for a relaxed
dinner. Trust their advice on wine, make sure to try some cheese, and

---

🏛 ESSENTIALLY L.A. ☺ LATE ♥ ROMANTIC 📺 VALUE 🍴 QUIET ♻ SUSTAINABLE

come on Mondays for the fantastic three-course, five-wine French-bistro supper. **WHO** Savvy baby boomers from Hancock Park and not-insufferably-hip GenXers from Hollywood. ♥ 🗐

[Melrose Bar & Grill] **8826 Melrose Ave., West Hollywood, 310.278.3684, melrosebarandgrill.com. L Mon.-Fri., D Mon.-Sat. Modern American. Full bar. AE, MC, V. $$ - $$$ WHY** A great collection of wines and tap beers, good martinis, the Mediterranean platter and the duck burger. **WHAT** What's not to like about such a convivial and comfort-able spot? It's clubby, it's fairly priced, it has a fabulous wine list, and it serves excellent, unfussy bar-and-grill fare: crisp calamari, juicy pork chops, Irish salmon and homey desserts. If you come alone, there's a friendly counter or a spot for you and your laptop (free WiFi). **WHO** People talking shop at lunch (it's quiet enough for seri-ous business lunches); at dinner, grown-up wine lovers and regulars stopping in for a drink or a meal. 🗐 🍸

[Musso & Frank Grill] 🏛 **6667 Hollywood Blvd., Hollywood, 323.467.7788. B, L & D Tues.-Sat. American. Full bar. AE, MC, V. $$$ WHY** Martinis, atmosphere, flannel cakes, atmosphere, chicken pot pie and atmosphere. **WHAT** God knows it isn't the cooking that makes this place an essential L.A. restaurant — it's the rich blend of traditional architecture and Hollywood history, faded smoke and legendary lies, all aged to an irresistible patina. (Okay, the cocktails are part of the draw, too.) Don't eat the vegetables or try to chat up the old-school waiters, but do linger at the bar as long as possible. **WHO** Crusty old showbiz men, young bucks. 🍸

[The Village Idiot] **7383 Melrose Ave., Melrose, 323.655.3331, villageidiotla.com. L & D daily to 2 a.m. Pub/American. Full bar. AE, MC, V. $ - $$ WHY** A fairly deep and thoughtful tap-beer selection, excellent fish 'n chips and spinach pie, and a pretty normal crowd for Melrose, especially midweek. **WHAT** The crush is too much for us on weekend nights, but otherwise we're always happy to stop into this brick-walled pub and restaurant (the longtime home of Chianti) for a Guinness and a steak sandwich or something fried. The wine selection isn't nearly as good as the beer, but sometimes there's a good buy by the bottle. **WHO** Beer boys and girls seeking Boddingtons or Craftsman beers, something good to eat, and a jovial time. ☺

EASTSIDE

[Allston Yacht Club] **1320 Echo Park Ave., Echo Park, 213.481.0454, allstonyachtclub.com. D Tues.-Sun. Wine bar/modern American. Full bar. AE, MC, V. $$ - $$$ WHY** A smart, international wine list, tasty small plates and good-value specials. **WHAT** A sign if there ever was one of Echo Park's gentrification, Allston is a small, dark, clubby place with very good wines, a full bar, tasty small-plate dishes

---

🍃 VEGETARIAN ☺ KID FRIENDLY ☼ PATIO DINING �"DELIVERY 🏛 PRIVATE PARTY

and a couple of very nice owners who are longtime Silver Lake/Echo Park residents — but who originally hailed from Boston, hence the eccentric name. Check the web site for frequent happy-hour and special-night bargains. **WHO** Echo Park Town Council folks, locals from the hills above and adventurers from Silver Lake and Downtown. 🏷️ 𝕺

[Bacaro] 2308 S. Union Ave., USC, 213.748.7205, bacarolosangeles. com. Nightly from 5 p.m. Wine bar/Italian. Beer & wine. AE, MC, V. $ **WHY** Because you're bored with most wine-bar offerings and tired of paying through the nose for a glass of wine. **WHAT** On a funky block between Pico-Union and USC is a tiny haven for wine lovers, where the wines of the day are artfully written in chalk on the blackboard walls. In back is a kitchen that turns out Venetian-style *cicchetti* (small bites), including bruschetta, crostini and such heartier dishes as grilled asparagus topped with a fried egg, and a deconstructed BLT made with Niman Ranch bacon; almost all the dishes are a mere $7. Bacaro is one of those spots you wish would open within walking distance of your house, a place where enthusiasm for esoteric Italian bottlings is matched by a menu of unfussy, simply delicious snacks. We're nuts about the joint and juiced about the owners' plan to open another outpost in the heart of Downtown. **WHO** Oenophiles with more taste than dough from USC and West Adams. 🏷️ 𝕺

[Barbrix] 2442 Hyperion Ave., Silver Lake, 323.662.2442, barbrix.com. Nightly from 6 p.m. Wine bar/Mediterranean. Beer & wine. AE, MC, V. $ - $$ **WHY** Silver Lake's relaxed new indoor/outdoor wine bar has spot-on Mediterranean-inspired small plates. **WHAT** Interesting, well-priced wine selections from California to Croatia are the centerpiece of this former house. The food's just as good, from cheese and charcuterie samplers to flavorful farmers' market vegetable salads and meaty plates of pork belly, lamb chops and wild boar sausage. If you hope to hold a conversation, reserve a table on the quieter patio in what used to be the house's front yard — inside, at the small tables, charcuterie counter or wine bar, it's downright deafening. **WHO** Casually stylish wine lovers. ☺ ☼

[BottleRock] 1050 Flower St., South Park/Fashion District, 213.747.1100, bottlerock.net. L & D daily. Wine bar/modern American. Beer & wine. AE, MC, V. $$ **WHY** To taste oddball whites, rare reds and exotic microbrews and banter about the same with BottleRock's urbane, wine-savvy GM George Skorka, former sommelier at an impressive list of high-end Los Angeles eateries. **WHAT** On the ground floor of the Metropolitan Lofts building, in a series of starkly modern rooms lined with shelves displaying hundreds of intriguing bottles, BottleRock (a branch of the Culver City original) is Downtown's most intelligent and adventuresome wine-and-food destination. The open kitchen, helmed by Jared Levy, turns out tempting, wine-friendly treats during rush hour (4 to 6:30 p.m.) and an extensive menu of artisan cheeses, charcuterie and small plates (green curry mussels, pork-belly risotto and agnolotti with bacon and dates are just a sampling). The more than 900 wine and beer selections are all available for retail sale, a boon for nearby loft-dwelling oenophiles. **WHO** A crowd as sophisticated and eclectic as the wine list. ☺ 🍸

[Casey's Irish Bar & Grill] **613 S. Grand Ave., Downtown, 213.629.2353, bigcaseys.com. L & D daily. Pub/Irish. Full bar. AE, MC, V. $ - $$ WHY** A classic pub setting and food that's a big cut above most pubs — fish 'n chips are almost delicate, and the shepherd's pie is rich with lamb and parsnips. **WHAT** This below-street-level Downtown pub, with its dark wood paneling, pressed-tin ceiling, brass rails and mahogany bar, is a popular filming location (*Good Night, and Good Luck, The X-Files*). Six British beers on tap, as well as Belgian ales and microbrews, with good pub fare to match. **WHO** Downtown professionals and businesspeople knocking back a pint after a day of deal making. ☺

[City Sip] **2150 W. Sunset Blvd., Echo Park, 213.483.9463, citysipla. com. D Tues.-Sun. Wine bar/Mediterranean. Wine. MC, V. $ - $$ WHY** "Wine for the people" (or so says its slogan), in working-people's Echo Park, with affordable tastings, charcuterie and small plates, as well as fun wine classes. **WHAT** A groovy wine bar for an increasingly groovy neighborhood, City Sip is part wine bar and part wine school. Six nights a week, owner Nicole Daddio pours wine (for as little as $3 during the midweek happy hour) and serves charcuterie (Spanish chorizo, prosciutto with figs, speck with sauerkraut), cheeses, panini (including the Nutella-esque chocolate and hazelnut), and a salad or two. The two-hour, $50 wine classes are unpretentious and very worthwhile. 📝

[Cole's] 🍸 **118 E. 6th St., Downtown, 213.622.4090, colesfrenchdip. com. L & D daily. American. Full bar. AE, MC, V. $$ WHY** Classic cocktails and sandwiches in an old-timey setting in the heart of Downtown. **WHAT** Cole's French Dip has been cleaned up and relaunched, and the casual, woodsy bar area got a makeover, too, so it's warmer and more inviting, while still evoking old Los Angeles. It's appropriate that for a tavern that claims to be the city's oldest public house, the featured (and very well-made) cocktails are longtime favorites like Manhattans and Sazeracs. And the dips — beef, turkey, lamb or pastrami — and their accompaniments (cole slaw, fries, mac 'n cheese) hit the spot.

[Corkbar] **403 W. 12th St., South Park/Fashion District, 213.746.0050, corkbar.com. L & D daily. Wine bar/modern American. Beer & wine. AE, MC, V. $$ WHY** Wholly addictive *gougères* (cheddar pastry puffs), excellent if somewhat pricey California wines by the glass, easy street parking and a location within walking distance of Staples Center and L.A. Live. **WHAT** Corkbar distinguishes itself from the 7,000 other

🌱 VEGETARIAN ◎ KID FRIENDLY ☼ PATIO DINING 🚐 DELIVERY 🏠 PRIVATE PARTY new places to get a drink downtown by its smart roster of California wines, its smart, wine-loving staff and its menu of tasty food that goes well with wine: salads, shrimp risotto, a burger, veggie sandwich, and the usual cheese and charcuterie. Food prices are pretty reasonable, but wine's on the higher end. The clean, modern space is relaxed and easy to hang out in — and blessedly quiet. **WHO** South Park residents and a quietly hip pre- and post-Club Nokia crowd.

[The Doheny] **714 W. Olympic Blvd., Downtown, No phone, thedoheny. com. Varies. Modern American. Full bar. AE, MC, V. $$$$ WHY** You have country clubs in your genes and money to burn. **WHAT** This members-only high-end cocktail lounge has annual fees of more than $2,000 and an initiation fee to match — but for that you get gigantic ice cubes that supposedly won't melt in your drink as quickly. **WHO** If we could afford to get in the door, we'd expect to find the eternally cool, if not always young, sipping whiskey beneath the dim glow of bar lamps made from absinthe fountains.

[The Edison] **108 W. 2nd St., Downtown, 213.613.0000, edisondowntown.com. Wed.-Fri. from 5 p.m., Sat. from 8 p.m. American. Full bar. AE, MC, V. $ - $$ WHY** To take a glamorous step back in time — and for the double-take you'll experience the first time you spot the Absinthe Fairy. **WHAT** This nostalgic bar reignites 1920s elegance in an unbelievable multi-level space that was L.A.'s first private power plant. Each night brings new revelries, from live music to burlesque, but it's enough of a show just to wander through the endless nooks and crannies, decorated with leather wing chairs, tufted velvet and old power-plant equipment. Mixologists from all over the country visit, so the cocktail list changes, but absinthe is always a favorite, sold by an ethereal winged woman pushing a glowing green cart. To soak up the liquor, try the sweet potato Tesla fries, the grilled cheese with tomato soup, or a couple of Auntie Em's cupcakes. The foolish few who show up in T-shirts or flip flops are turned away by a beautiful blond wearing seemingly nothing but beads. **WHO** The hippest of the hip (often dressed to the nines) and rockabilly types on Friday and Saturday, and a surprisingly diverse after-work crowd midweek.

[Golden Gopher] **417 W. 8th St., Downtown, 213.614.8001, golden-gopher.la. Nightly to 2 a.m. American. Full bar. AE, MC, V. WHY** One of the first spruced-up bars of Downtown's renaissance. Kogi fans take note that the taco truck sometimes parks outside. **WHAT** The funky name and neon sign date from the bar's original incarnation, but the new version is a sleek stop on the Downtown bar-hopping itinerary, with an outdoor smoking area complete with couches. Also left over from the previous century: It's one of the city's few bars where it's legal to buy a bottle to take home. **WHO** The after-work cocktails crowd gives way to seriously partying young folks later in the evening.

[Redwood Bar & Grill] **316 W. 2nd St., Downtown, 213.680.2600, theredwoodbar.com. L Mon.-Fri. & Sun., D nightly. Pub/American. Full bar. AE, MC, V. $ - $$ WHY** Solid pub grub, stiff drinks and good tunes. **WHAT** Ink-stained *L.A. Times* staffers used to hang out here when it was a true dive bar, but the pirate-theme update retains a certain divey feel. Fish 'nchips, crunchy cole slaw and hefty burgers go down well with ale or cocktails, which in turn are well suited to the often-worth-while live music that happens most nights. **WHO** Downtown office workers during the day; music-loving younger folk at night. ☺

[Varnish Bar] 🏠 **Inside Cole's, 118 E. 6th St., Downtown, 213.622.9999, thevarnishbar.com. Nightly until 2 a.m. American. Full bar. AE, MC, V. $$ WHY** The closest L.A. has to a speakeasy, with a discreetly marked door at the back of Cole's and exquisitely crafted cocktails. **WHAT** 1920s-style barmen, a jazz soundtrack and fresh fruit juices make the Varnish old-school — yet it's up to date on the latest in mixology. **WHO** The Downtown bar-crawling crowd is youngish, but high-end cocktails keep out drinkers looking for cheap well drinks and a loud party scene.

[Verdugo] **3408 Verdugo Rd., Glassell Park, 323.257.3408, verdugobar. com. Mon.-Sat. from 6 p.m., Sun. from 1 p.m. Pub/American. Full bar. AE, MC, V. $$ WHY** Well-selected beers from small breweries in a location that's a bit hard to find, but worth the search. **WHAT** Choose from two rooms and a beer garden with picnic tables for sampling rare Belgian and California craft brews at this hidden-away hot spot. There's a full bar, wine and special cask-beer nights, but no food — ah, but you can find plenty of taco trucks and street vendors nearby. **WHO** Craft-brew geeks from Eagle Rock, Highland Park, Silver Lake and environs.

[Wurstküche] **800 E. 3rd St., Little Tokyo/Arts District, 213.687.4444, wurstkucherestaurant.com. L & D daily; open late Thurs.-Sat. German. Beer & wine. AE, MC, V. $ WHY** The perfect blend of juicy sausage, substantial-but-not-huge bun and sweet-savory onions and peppers — just the thing to eat alongside a pint or two of Belgian beer. **WHAT** The two young turks behind this industrial-hip beer garden at 3rd and Traction keep it simple: You got your beer, your sausage and your fries. What more could you possibly need? Ranging from the classic (brats, kielbasa) to the Californian (several vegetarians) to the adventurous (rattlesnake-rabbit-jalapeño), the sausages are grilled to order, tucked in a compact bun and topped with grilled onions, sweet peppers and/or sauerkraut. There are mustards galore, and even more dipping sauces to try with the thick but crisp Belgian fries. To drink are appealing Belgian and German draft beers and cool bottled sodas. **WHO** By day, a youngish crowd of creative types; by night, an even younger crowd of Downtown bar-hoppers. ☺ 🍽

🍃VEGETARIAN ⊙KID FRIENDLY ✿PATIO DINING 🚐DELIVERY 🛎PRIVATE PARTY

[The York] 5018 York Blvd., Highland Park, 323.255.9675, they-orkonyork.com. D nightly, brunch Sat.-Sun. Pub/American. Full bar. AE, MC, V. $ - $$ **WHY** Local microbrews, good wine by the glass and tasty, affordable gastropub chow. Try the quick-fried garbanzo beans, the soups, the shrimp bruschetta and the fish 'n chips. **WHAT** A high-ceilinged old brick building in gentrifying Highland Park is home to this simple but stylish pub, our favorite of L.A.'s new wave of pubs. Order your homemade soup, Caesar salad, Cuban pulled-pork sandwich, very good burger or cheese platter from the bartender, and someone will deliver the food (and drink) to your table. A godsend for hungry and thirsty eastsiders. **WHO** The hip and savvy of Highland Park and Eagle Rock, along with slummers from Pasadena and Los Feliz. ☺ ▧

SAN GABRIEL VALLEY

[The Bar] Langham Huntington Hotel, 1401 S. Oak Knoll Ave., Pasadena, 626.568.3900, pasadena.langhamhotels.com. Sun.-Thurs. until midnight, Fri.-Sat. until 2 a.m. American. Full bar. AE, MC, V. $$$ - $$$$ **WHY** Suave elegance, live music on weekends, and a good-value happy hour Monday through Friday. **WHAT** The crystal is real and the setting is old-money luxurious, so it should come as no surprise that the cocktails are $15 to $18 and the bar dishes are $8 to $19. But the quality is high, and it's the most elegant place for miles around to celebrate or to spoil someone. A pianist plays Tuesday through Thursday; Friday night is live jazz; and Saturday night brings solid blues bands. Prices plunge to normal on happy-hour specials. **WHO** Well-dressed Pasadenans, business travelers and, during college breaks, moneyed Pasadena private-school kids reuniting with old friends. ☺ ♥ ○

[Lucky Baldwins] 17 S. Raymond Ave., Old Pasadena, 626.795.0652, luckybaldwins.com. B, L & D daily. Pub/English. Beer & wine. AE, MC, V. $ - $$ **WHY** Sixty-three beers on tap, including wonderful Belgians, along with such reliable pub standards as meat pies and a tasty chicken curry. **WHAT** Co-owner David Farnsworth is originally from the north of England, and with partner Peggy Simonian he's created an authentically English pub in a brick-walled Old Town space, with nooks, crannies and a lovely patio on the pedestrian alley in back. Aficionados come from far away for such annual events as the Belgian beer festival in February and Oktoberfest, when German beers are front and center. **WHO** Caltech students, professors and others who prefer earnest conversation over a pint to a raucous bar scene. 🍺 ○

[Lucky Baldwins Delirium Pub & Café] 21 Kersting Court, Sierra Madre, 626.355.1140, luckybaldwins.com. B, L & D daily. Pub/English. Beer & wine. AE, MC, V. $ - $$ **WHY** Forty-six beers on tap, with great choices from Ireland, England and Belgium, and solid English fare, including a good chicken curry and lovely pasties.

WHAT A pleasantly old-school pub (pressed tin ceilings, polished wooden floors, walled patio) that perfectly suits its old-fashioned setting in Sierra Madre's village center. In the back is a tiny but richly rewarding package shop with a few British foodstuffs and hard-to-get beers. **WHO** Patagonia-clad locals taking a break from restoring their Craftsman cottages and hiking the Mt. Wilson Trail. 🖻 🌙 ☼

[Madeleines] **1031 E. Green St., Pasadena, 626.440.7087, madeleinesrestaurant.com. L Tues.-Fri., D Tues.-Sun., brunch Sun. Wine bar/modern American. Full bar. AE, MC, V. $$ - $$$ WHY** A romantic, hidden spot where the wine and food are taken seriously, but not in a pretentious way. **WHAT** One of the more romantic spots in the San Gabriel Valley, Madeleines meanders through an historic building. There's a dining room, a bar, a courtyard, a couple of private rooms and a very handsome wine bar, stocked with a large and appealing collection from around the world. To go with them is excellent wine-bar fare: tempura shrimp and zucchini, charcuterie, grilled lollipop lamb chops. Every Tuesday night you'll find the fun folks from the Pasadena branch of Drinking Liberally, a progressive group that likes to have a good glass of wine while they talk politics. **WHO** Pasadena wine lovers who alternate between this place and Vertical. ♥ 🌙 🏛

[Vertical Wine Bistro] 🔒 **70 N. Raymond Avd., Old Pasadena, 626.795.3999, verticalwinebistro.com. D nightly. Wine bar/modern American. Full bar. AE, MC, V. $$$ - $$$$ WHY** About 100 wines by the glass, with all sorts of flight options, and delicious small dishes to accompany those wines. **WHAT** A-list movie producer and Pasadena resident Gale Anne Hurd brought a little Hollywood zing to non-showy Pasadena with her wine-focused restaurant — although the look is actually more New York sleek than Hollywood glitz, and it suits Pasadena well. So does the menu of mini grilled-cheese sandwiches, composed salads and small-plate mains like wild salmon with lentils and bacon. The vast wine-by-the-glass selection has elite choices, of course, but also a few tasty $8 glasses for the cheapskates among us, and the happy hour is a relative bargain. **WHO** A handsome crowd of professionals, eastside entertainment-industry folks and oenophiles. ♥

EAST VALLEY

[Laurel Tavern] **11938 Ventura Blvd., Studio City, 818.506.0777, laureltavern.net. L Sat.-Sun., D nightly until 11 p.m. (bar until 2 a.m.) Pub/American. Beer & wine. AE, MC, V. $ - $$ WHY** A well-edited lineup of scrumptious bar food, including skewered chunks of pork belly so succulent they'll make you weak in the knees. **WHAT** The Valley's coolest gastropub is a long, streamlined room with exposed brick walls and French doors opening onto the busy boulevard. Some of the nicest barkeeps in town make sure patrons are well-lubricated with an ambitious all-California draft beer list and an unpretentious selection

🥬 **VEGETARIAN** ◎ **KID FRIENDLY** ☼ **PATIO DINING** �Delivery **DELIVERY** 🏛 **PRIVATE PARTY**

of wines by the glass (almost all under $10) or bottle. The limited menu is heavy on terrific burgers; the arugula salad is topnotch and you can make a meal out of the steamed Penn Cove mussels. **WHO** Industry folk unwinding after a long day behind the cameras and neighbors who have adopted the place as their local pub. ☺ 🗺

WEST VALLEY

[Ireland's 32] 13721 Burbank Blvd., Van Nuys, 818.785.4031, irelands32pub.com. L & D daily. Pub/Irish. Full bar. AE, MC, V. $ - $$ **WHY** A friendly Irish pub in the heart of the Valley, with fresh beer (Guinness, Harp, Bass, Smithwick's), well-made burgers and good, crisp fish 'n chips. **WHAT** It's a bit gloomy at first, but once your eyes adjust you'll find a handsome room, friendly locals and fresh beer. If the bar's too crowded, grab a table by the dance floor. Hungry? Check out the board list, then mosey over to the kitchen door and tell the cook what you'd like, and a good meal will be in front of you a few minutes later. **WHO** Couples watching football or meeting friends for a pint and some grub. 🗺

[Pickwick's Pub] 21010 Ventura Blvd., Woodland Hills, 818.340.9673, pickwickspub.org. L & D daily. Pub/English. Full bar. AE, MC, V. $ - $$ **WHY** Fourteen draft beers (stouts, lagers, ales and ciders) at modest prices, live music and, to eat, Cal-Val standards (salads, barbecued chicken breast) and pub classics (juicy, salty onion rings and comforting mashed potatoes and peas). **WHAT** Rebuilt after being destroyed by fire, the fresh room of this 34-year-old pub is still comfortable and homey. The food's been updated, too — lightened with fresh fish and salads. The extensive menu is inviting, and the pretty, open-layout room is equally comfortable for dining or just getting together for drinks. **WHO** Friendly and loyal West Valley regulars, mostly young, including some very good darts players. 🗺 🍸

WESTSIDE: CENTRAL

[Alibi Room] 12236 Washington Blvd., Culver City, 310.390.9300, alibiroomla.com. D Mon.-Sat. to midnight (bar to 2 a.m.). American/Korean. Beer & wine. AE, MC, V. $ **WHY** To eat Kogi's tacos without having to stand in a 90-minute line at the truck — plus you can have a Duvel Golden Ale or Los Carlos Malbec with your kim chee sesame quesadilla. **WHAT** We loved this chill pub before Kogi took over the kitchen, and now we love it more, although now too many other people do, too. Come early (it opens at 5:30) if you want to snag some of the comfy, low-slung seating, and go wild sampling the Korean tacos, Korean spiced fries, tofu and citrus salad. To drink are good-value wines by the glass, bottled beers and a handful of draft craftsman brews. **WHO** Twentysomething studio toilers meeting after work, with some middle-aged Culver City locals for good measure. ☉ 🖼️🥂

[BottleRock] **3847 Main St., Culver City, 310.836.WINE, bottlerock. net. L Tues.-Sat., D nightly. Wine bar/Modern American. Beer & wine. AE, MC, V. $ - $$ WHY** Plenty of wine by the glass and good bar snacks (fried Marcona almonds, charcuterie and cheese plates), plus (surprisingly, for a wine bar) one of the most interesting beer menus in town. **WHAT** This hybrid wine bar/wine shop sits on the cusp of trendy, but fortunately it stays just this side of cozy. A good stop for a pick-me-up and a snack. **WHO** Folks waiting for their reservation at Fraîche and post-movie sippers.

[Craftbar] 🏛️ **10100 Constellation Blvd., Century City, 310.279.4180, craftrestaurant.com. L Mon.-Fri., D nightly. Modern American. Full bar. AE, MC, V. $$ WHY** An affordable version of Tom Colicchio's terrific (and adjacent) Craft restaurant, a sleek brother to the New York original. **WHAT** Everything on the menu in the front lounge and patio at Craft is $10 or less and just as interesting: hush puppies with bacon jam, sausage ravioli with clams, rhubarb-honey shortcakes with candied pistachios. **WHO** Junior ICM agents reveling in their potential while their bosses seal the deal on $50 steaks inside. ♥🖼️☼

[Father's Office] 🏛️ **3229 Helms Ave., Culver City, 310.736.2224, fathersoffice.com. L Fri.-Sun., D nightly. Pub/American. Full bar. AE, MC, V. $$ WHY** The justly famed medium-rare burger topped with caramelized onions, smoked applewood bacon and blue cheese is worth the wait, the price and the fat grams. Only you can decide if it's worth the hype. **WHAT** The square footage is greatly improved from the Santa Monica original, with lots of patio seating, but don't think you still won't have to stand in line to enjoy one of Sang Yoon's famous burgers, some sweet potato fries and a small-producer tap beer or two — and now you can even have a cocktail, thanks to the full bar. No substitutions on the famous burger, no kids (21 and over only). Take heart that the line moves quickly. **WHO** Youngish men who take their beer and burgers very seriously. ☉ ☼

[The Lounge at Bond St.] **Thompson Beverly Hills Hotel, 9360 Wilshire Blvd., Beverly Hills, 310.601.2255, bondstrestaurant.com. L & D Mon.-Sat. Japanese/Asian. Full bar. AE, MC, V. $$ - $$$ WHY** This New York import is known for its fusion sushi, like hamachi with jalapeño, and you can get it at slightly lower prices than in the main dining room below. **WHAT** This elegant mezzanine cocktail lounge with a handful of small tables becomes a standing-room only hot spot on the weekends. **WHO** Agents and scene hoppers grasping sake-sangria glasses with expertly manicured hands while hotel guests soak up the free sightseeing tour of the Beverly Hills spectacle.

🥬 **VEGETARIAN** ☉ **KID FRIENDLY** ☼ **PATIO DINING** 🚚 **DELIVERY** 🎩 **PRIVATE PARTY**

[Nic's Martini Lounge] **453 N. Cañon Dr., Beverly Hills, 310.550.5707, nicsbeverlyhills.com. D Mon.-Sat. American. Full bar. AE, MC, V. $$ - $$$$ WHY** Dress-up fun in the heart of Beverly Hills, with a piano bar, often-good jazz and a walk-in vodka freezer that brings out the Russian in everyone. **WHAT** Larry Nicola was well ahead of the cocktail craze that's swept L.A. — he decamped from Silver Lake several years ago to open this swank (and only slightly tongue-in-cheek) Beverly Hills boîte. Come for a martini, come for a meal, come for some jazz — but note that the scene gets louder and more intense after 9 p.m. on weekends. **WHO** Suave youngsters and hip middle-agesters who value a well-made cocktail, a proper platter of oysters and a good piano player. Some are famous, but Larry keeps 'em on the down low. ☺ ♥ ☼

[Rush Street] **9546 Washington Blvd., Culver City, 310.837.9546, rushstreetculvercity.com. L & D daily, brunch Sat.-Sun. Pub/modern American. Full bar. AE, MC, V. $$ - $$$ WHY** Food that's much, much better than it has to be, given the owners' concept of an eatery styled after Chicago's Rush Street, a strip known for its bar scene, not fine dining. Order the truffle asiago fries while you peruse the menu. Good happy hour, too. **WHAT** In an enormous, barn-like room in the heart of Culver City, Rush Street serves snazzy cocktails and an eclectic array of dishes, from terrific sandwiches and salads at lunch to an even more varied and extensive assortment at dinner — lobster and shrimp egg rolls, Mongolian pork lettuce cups and a spinach, shiitake and gorgonzola pizza are among the offerings. At a recent lunch we had the best tortilla soup we'd ever eaten, followed by a tangy Asian salad topped with a half-dozen enormous, impeccably fresh shrimp impaled on lemongrass skewers. There's some real talent in Rush Street's kitchen, but the word is out — the crowds can be considerable. **WHO** Sony Studios foodies and lots of young, goateed guys in plaid fedoras. ♥ ☼

[X-Bar] **Hyatt Regency Century Plaza, 2025 Avenue of the Stars, Century City, 310.551.3332, xbarla.com. D Mon.-Sat. until 2 a.m. Modern American. Full bar. AE, MC, V. $$ - $$$ WHY** Because mall shopping requires constant refueling with both mocha-espresso martinis and chile-lime crab cakes. **WHAT** Cocktails with cheesy names like the astrology-inspired Leo and Scorpio (which arrive tableside in the appropriate birthstone color) are actually pretty good, if overpriced and on the sweet side. Garlic fries with chipotle aioli will come to the rescue to temper the sweetness. A good spot for a Century City drinks-and-hors d'oeuvres rendezvous. **WHO** Shoppers and CAA agents who have discovered this gorgeous open-air outdoor patio, as well as out-of-towners convinced that all L.A. bars are required to have the same slick designer with a penchant for white-on-white. ♥ ☼

🏛 ESSENTIALLY L.A. ☺ LATE ♥ ROMANTIC 📷 VALUE 🔈 QUIET ♻ SUSTAINABLE

WEST OF THE 405

[Bar Pintxo] 109 Santa Monica Blvd., Santa Monica, 310.458.2012, barpintxo.com. L & D daily. Wine bar/Spanish. Beer & wine. AE, MC, V. $ - $$ **WHY** Quick, authentic and California-inspired tapas, including jamón serrano, served until midnight. **WHAT** This New York shotgun-style bar has tapas lined up behind a counter up front, a sidewalk "counter" and a half-dozen bar tables in back for a delicious — though pricey — snack and glass of vino. **WHO** Fans of chef/owner Joe Miller who don't want the commitment of a full meal at Joe's; couples out for a glass of wine and a light bite after a movie in an area dominated by louder pubs and bars. ☺ ☼

[Copa D'Oro] 217 Broadway, Santa Monica, 310.576.3030, copadoro. com. Mon.-Sat. from 6 p.m. American. Full bar. AE, MC, V. $$ **WHY** For cocktails you won't find at the corner bar — really good ones. **WHAT** Cocktail guru Vincenzo Marianella's Promenade-adjacent lounge feels like a cozy Manhattan bar, thanks to its weathered brick walls, French-mod leather wingbacks, well-coiffed bartenders and big-city prices. If you want to spend $11 for a gin and tonic here, that's your business, but the smart money's on such concoctions as the Smoke of Scotland (two scotches, dry vermouth and elderflower liqueur) and the Emerald (gin, elderflower liqueur, lemon juice, black grapes and sage). Add a very good Black Forest ham sandwich, and you've got a well-balanced meal, at least in some circles. **WHO** The newsboy-cap and belly-button-length gold-necklace crowd.

[Daily Pint] 2310 Pico Blvd., Santa Monica, 310.450.7631, thedailypint.net. Daily from 2 p.m. to 2 a.m. Pub/American. Full bar. AE, MC, V. $$ **WHY** At least two cask-conditioned "real" ale firkins on tap and what has to be the largest Scotch collection in California. **WHAT** This dark, tattered bar hardly looks like much — until you open the menu and discover hundreds of interesting beers and whiskeys. The cask ales, typically from San Diego breweries, vary weekly, and the fantastic house-made potato chips go down just as easy. **WHO** Regulars who look as tired as the barstools, home brewers after a club meeting, and college students pretending that they always spring for good beer.

[Father's Office] 🍺 1018 Montana Ave., Santa Monica, 310.393. BEER, fathersoffice.com. L Sat.-Sun., D nightly. Pub/American. Beer & wine. AE, MC, V. $$ **WHY** A chance to decide for yourself whether this is the best burger in America. **WHAT** When Sang Yoon, formerly chef at Michael's, said goodbye to haute cuisine to open a pub, he set about creating a world-class hamburger. It's a rare, dry-aged beef patty topped with Maytag blue cheese, smoked applewood bacon and caramelized onions — and don't even think about asking for substitutions. The dark, shotgun-style bar has only a few bistro tables, and even

🥬 VEGETARIAN ☺ KID FRIENDLY ☼ PATIO DINING 🚚 DELIVERY 🎩 PRIVATE PARTY

with the new branch in Culver City, the line's often out the door. The ever-changing selection of seasonal boutique beers is worth waiting for, but the over-21 rule is strictly enforced, so leave the kids at home. **WHO** Beer and burger aficionados.

[Finn McCool's] 2702 Main St., Santa Monica, 310.452.1734, gerrigilliland.com/finn. L & D daily. Pub/Irish. Full bar. AE, MC, V. $$ **WHY** For a fantastic carved wooden bar from Ireland, Guinness, good Irish appetizers (try the mini Yorkshire puddings) and, on Sunday afternoon, musicians playing Irish tunes around an old wooden table, just like in Galway. **WHAT** The bar gets boisterous late on weekend nights, but at other times this handsome, high-ceilinged pub from L.A.'s best-known Irish chef, Gerri Gilliland, is a surprisingly sweet spot. The extensive menu is tempting, but we'd advise passing on the dinner entrees in favor of the much better appetizers, snacks and desserts. They move a lot of Guinness here, and the deft bartenders are fun to watch. **WHO** Families for weekend lunches; mates meeting for a few pints and a meal in the evening. ☺

[Library Alehouse] 2911 Main St., Santa Monica, 310.314.4855, libraryalehouse.com. L & D daily until 11 p.m. Pub/American. Beer & wine. AE, MC, V. $$ **WHY** For dozens of beers on tap, mainly Californian, Belgian and German brews, which you can try in four-ounce, five-shot sample flights. **WHAT** This aptly named bar has a polished professor vibe with better-than-average bar food: chipotle shrimp quesadillas, a solid build-your-own beef, turkey, veggie or salmon burger, and salmon fish 'n chips that tastes healthier than its cod cousin. The outdoor patio is quite appealing, but you'll get better service if you can snag a seat at the bar. **WHO** Beer-loving regulars at the bar and Santa Monica families on the outdoor patio. 🗺 🍸 ☼

[O'Brien's Irish Pub and Restaurant] 2941 Main St., Santa Monica, 310.396.4725, obriensonmain.com. L & D daily. Pub/Irish. Full bar. AE, MC, V. $$ - $$$ **WHY** Food that's a notch above the pub norm, including the generous slices of Scottish smoked salmon on wheat toast with capers, green onions and horseradish, or the banger sandwich, a crusty baguette filled with sausage and grilled onions. **WHAT** This comfortable Irish pub, with its plank floors, brick walls and flat-screen TVs, is popular for its better-than-average food, lunch specials and sports, sports, sports. Skylights and windows keep football afternoons from having that Lost Weekend feeling. Sunday afternoons bring live music on the front patio. **WHO** Lively, sometimes rowdy Ocean Park locals, sports fans and young singles. ☺ ☼

[On the Waterfront Café] 205 Ocean Front Walk, Venice, 310.392.0322, waterfrontcafe.com. L & D daily, brunch Sat.-Sun. German/American. Beer & wine. AE, MC, V. $ - $$ **WHY** Good German brats, fat pretzels and German beer on tap, including a Hefeweizen that goes down very well on a sunny beach afternoon while the Boardwalk parade flows by. **WHAT** A refreshing break from the generic sidewalk cafés that line the Venice Boardwalk, this place is a German beer garden with decent food and convivial picnic-table seating. Fun for a weekend lunch or weekday sunset happy-hour beer-and-brat. **WHO** An amusing mix of scruffy local regulars and tourists, all of whom seem happy all the time; sometimes after a few Erdingers on tap they can get really happy. 🍽 ☼

[Primitivo Wine Bistro] 1025 Abbot Kinney Blvd., Venice, 310.396.5353, primitivowinebistro.com. L Mon.-Fri., D nightly. Wine bar/ Mediterranean. Beer & wine. AE, MC, V. $$ - $$$ **WHY** Wine-friendly and delicious small dishes such as paella, asparagus risotto with lemon and parmesan, and roasted salmon with couscous, plus some satisfying true tapas like marinated olives, cheeses and cured meats. **WHAT** Is it a set design or tapas bar? You be the judge. First, though, you'll have to land one of the small wooden tables in the high-ceilinged space that's filled with columns, old stained-glass church windows and acres of linen drapes. The by-the-glass collection of wines is extensive and interesting, if on the costly side, and the food runs to appealing small dishes, designed to share and to go well with wine. **WHO** Lots of beautiful Venice folk. ♥

[Venice Beach Wines] 529 Rose Ave., Venice, 310.606.2529, venicebeachwines.com. L & D daily. Italian/Mediterranean. Beer & wine. AE, MC, V. $ **WHY** A lovely covered sidewalk patio, worthy wines to drink here or take home, and mighty fine panini. **WHAT** Part retail wine shop and part outdoor café, this new place was cleverly designed to keep the indoors temperature controlled for the wine while having that indoor-outdoor flow so essential to Venice living. The wine-by-the-glass list is relatively short but deeply appealing: an international collection of lesser-known choices at fair prices, including some for under $10. To accompany your Portuguese Vale de Torre or Argentin-ean Zolo Viognier is a reasonably priced menu of cheese, charcuterie, salads and panini, all of which are good enough to attract lunchtime folks who are drinking Pellegrino instead of Pinot. **WHO** Mostly locals who can walk here for a drink and a panini. 🚗 ☼

[The Yard] 119 Broadway, Santa Monica, 310.395.6037, theyardsm. com. D Tues.-Sun. Pub/American. Full bar. AE, MC, V. $$ - $$$ **WHY** Funky wine bar meets art gallery space, with a laid-back neigh-borhood pub vibe and a terrific happy hour menu. **WHAT** The vibe is great, with its rotating art on the walls, lounge-type atmosphere and friendly staff. Stick to the classic cocktails (margaritas, cosmos) unless you're a Heineken fan (with original art on the walls you'd think they'd have more craft beers). This is more of a watering hole than a gastropub, although the food is better than the average bar fare: pulled-pork sandwiches, Spanish meatballs, parmesan fries. Savvy snackers know to come between 5:30 and 7:30 for the happy-hour menu — everything tastes better at $5 to $6 a pop. **WHO** Young and artsy. 🗒️

[Ye Olde King's Head] 🏠 116 Santa Monica Blvd., Santa Monica, 310.451.1402, yeoldekingshead.com. B, L & D daily. Pub/English. Full bar. AE, MC, V. $$ - $$$ **WHY** Fresh beer, tasty English pub fare and a gregarious and interesting crowd. **WHAT** L.A.'s best-known pub has grown over the decades, now boasting two pub rooms and a dining room stretching between the Promenade and the shore. It's touristy as hell, but it's saved by the quality of food and the twentysome beers on tap. Try the sausage rolls, vegetable samosa, fish 'n chips or shepherd's pie. **WHO** College students and tourists (including visitors from England) in the busier pub side, quieter conversationalists in the "snug" and fish-'n-chip-eating families in the dining room. ☺ ☺

SOUTH BAY TO SOUTH L.A.

[4th Street Vine] 2142 E. 4th St., Long Beach, 562.343.5463, 4thstreetvine.com. Mon.-Fri. from 4 p.m., Sat.-Sun. from 2 p.m. Wine bar. Beer & wine. AE, MC, V. $ - $$ **WHY** Generous pours of good, modestly priced wines in a very cool Retro Row shop — with $3 glasses on Thursdays. **WHAT** Almost every afternoon and evening, bartender Evan mans the small, living-room-like wine bar in back of the store, and regulars stop in to ask him what he's pouring and to hear what he's playing on the stereo. For just $10, he'll pour you a taste of four wines and give you a smart, succinct explanation of each. **WHO** Pre-dinner wine sippers and people coming out of the Art Theater across the street, looking for a place to sip and talk. 🗒️ 🏛️

[Auld Dubliner] 71 S. Pine Ave., Long Beach, 562.437.8300, aulddubliner.com. L & D daily. Full bar. Pub/Irish. AE, MC, V. $$ - $$$ **WHY** The classic Irish dish boxty is often an awkward potato pancake folded over messy fillings, but here it's a graceful, crêpe-like dish with simple, tasty fillings. Chips (fries) are dusted with curry powder. Try the Irish whiskey brulée for dessert. **WHAT** It is a small chain, and it's situated in an impossibly corporate-looking site near a bunch of chain stores and the Convention Center, but the Auld Dubliner feels lived in and comfortable, it has a fine lineup of draft beers (Guinness, Harp, Newcastle, Smithwick's), and the Irish food is terrific. **WHO** Downtown Long Beach suits relaxing after work.

[Friends of the Vine] 221 Avenida Del Norte, Redondo Beach, 310.792.5940, friendsofthevine.net. D Tues.-Sat. Wine bar. Beer & wine. AE, MC, V. $ - $$ **WHY** A very friendly and neighborly spot to sample from a large list of wines. **WHAT** In the late afternoon, this rambling, somewhat cluttered wine shop turns into a lively wine bar, and it almost feels like a party in a friend's house. Owners Fred and Tracy play their favorite CDs and pour wine by the glass or the flight, or you can buy a bottle, pay a modest corkage, and drink it here. Accompaniments include a generous cheese plate, charcuterie and a few other snacks. **WHO** PV and south Redondo locals meeting friends for a drink and a cheese plate before moving elsewhere for dinner.

[Manhattan Beach Brewing Company] 124 Manhattan Beach Blvd., Manhattan Beach, 310.798.2744, manhattanbeachbrewingcompany. com. L & D daily. Pub/American. Full bar. AE, MC, V. $ - $$
WHY House-brewed beers, cozy booths and food that's better than the pub norm, all an easy walk from the pier and the beach. **WHAT** The beer brewed onsite in large copper vats isn't as good as Craftsman's, but their Hefeweizen and Manhattan Beach Blonde go down great after a walk on the beach. Regulars crowd into the small four-top booths, share pizzas, sesame-ahi tuna, fish tacos and pesto-shrimp salad, and sometimes watch a game on the big TV. **WHO** Sun-washed folks in their 20s and 30s who've had a good day at the beach. 🖼️ ☼

[The Pike Bar & Fish Grill] 1836 E. 4th St., Long Beach, 562.437.4453, pikelongbeach.com. L & D daily, B Sat.-Sun. American. Full bar. AE, MC, V. $ - $$ **WHY** A plate of retro charm and a side of rock and roll. **WHAT** A key in the rise of Retro Row — the vintage-loving stretch of 4th Street famous for its pin-up poses and deadstock designs — the Pike is owned by former Social Distortion drummer Chris Reece. The bar is themed around the (mostly) nautical icons of lost Long Beach — namely the long-gone Pike amusement park. When DJs aren't spinning everything from Lee Hazlewood to Os Mutantes, the bar becomes more of a restaurant, cooking up high-quality sandwiches and burgers, pastas and a number of seafood staples. The Pike's fish 'n chips is the essential dish, a basket of golden, beer-battered sole that's perfectly paired with a draft ale. **WHO** A well-inked crowd hungry for simple cocktails — lobster and otherwise. ☺ 📝

[Simmzy's] 229 Manhattan Beach Blvd., Manhattan Beach, 310.546.1201, simmzys.com. L & D daily. Pub/American. Beer & wine. AE, MC, V. $ - $$ **WHY** Finally, an open-air beach bar in Manhattan Beach with good food and drink. **WHAT** Not much more than a single room opening onto a street patio, this tiny gastropub has two dozen really good rotating tap beers, gobs of wine by the glass and an Angus burger with sweet smoked onions, cheddar, and garlic aioli that rocks. Don't skip the fries. **WHO** Bikini-clad locals who've never heard of "No shoes, no shirt, no service," yet somehow don't look out of place. ☼

🍃 VEGETARIAN ☺ KID FRIENDLY ☼ PATIO DINING 🚙 DELIVERY 🎩 PRIVATE PARTY

Breakfast + Lunch

Fancy restaurants are all well and good, but nothing makes most of us happier than a simple café that specializes in breakfast. Except perhaps a place that makes a really great lunchtime salad, panini or pastrami on rye.

[ESSENTIALLY L.A.]

Auntie Em's Kitchen, Eagle Rock (PAGE 183)

BLD, Beverly/Third (PAGE 180)

Ed's Coffee Shop, West Hollywood (PAGE 181)

Euro Pane, Pasadena (PAGE 187)

Figtree's Café, Venice (PAGE 197)

Fisherman's Outlet, Downtown (PAGE 184)

Fountain Coffee Room, Beverly Hills (PAGE 194)

John O'Groats, Rancho Park (PAGE 194)

Jongewaard's Bake N Broil, Long Beach (PAGE 200)

Julienne, San Marino (PAGE 188)

Langer's Deli, Downtown (PAGE 185)

Homegirl Café, Chinatown (PAGE 184)

Huckleberry, Santa Monica (PAGE 197)

Hugo's, West Hollywood (PAGE 182)

Marmalade Café, Malibu (PAGE 198)

Mi India Bonita, East L.A. (PAGE 186)

Nickel Diner, Downtown (PAGE 186)

North End Café, Manhattan Beach (PAGE 201)

Pie 'n' Burger, Pasadena (PAGE 189)

Studio Café Magazzino, Toluca Lake (PAGE 191)

ESSENTIALLY L.A. ☺LATE ♥ROMANTIC VALUE QUIET SUSTAINABLE

THE FOLLOWING RESTAURANTS ARE PARTICULARLY
KNOWN FOR BREAKFAST OR BRUNCH:

Beachcomber Café, Malibu (PAGE 126)

Bottega Louie, Downtown (PAGE 66)

Brent's Deli, Northridge (PAGE 11)

Campanile (brunch), Miracle Mile (PAGE 44)

Café del Rey (brunch), Marina del Rey (PAGE 128)

Cliff's Edge (brunch), Silver Lake (PAGE 68)

Guelaguetza, Palms (PAGE 119)

Jar (brunch), Beverly/Third (PAGE 50)

Joe's (brunch), Venice (PAGE 134)

Johnny Rebs', Long Beach (PAGE 152)

La Grande Orange, Santa Monica (PAGE 135)

LA Mill, Silver Lake (PAGE 73)

La Parrilla, Westlake & Silver Lake (PAGE 74)

Little Dom's, Los Feliz (PAGE 52)

Luna Park (brunch), Miracle Mile (PAGE 53)

Pacific Dining Car, Downtown (PAGE 76)

Pann's Restaurant, Inglewood (PAGE 156)

Roscoe's House of Chicken & Waffles, Hollywood (PAGE 58)

Rush Street (brunch), Culver City (PAGE 172)

THESE DIM SUM/DUMPLING/NOODLE PLACES ARE
ALSO GREAT FOR LUNCH OR BRUNCH:

888 Seafood, Rowland Heights (PAGE 82)

Bamboodles, San Gabriel (PAGE 82)

Din Tai Fung, Arcadia (PAGE 86)

Dumpling House, Arcadia (PAGE 237)

Elite, Monterey Park (PAGE 87)

Empress Pavilion, Chinatown (PAGE 70)

J & J Restaurant, San Gabriel (PAGE 90)

Lunasia, Alhambra (PAGE 92)

Mandarin Noodle Deli, Temple City (PAGE 93)

Mandarin Noodle House, Monterey Park (PAGE 93)

Noodle Island, San Gabriel (PAGE 95)

Ocean Star Seafood, Monterey Park (PAGE 96)

Sea Harbour, Rosemead (PAGE 98)

Supreme Dragon, Rowland Heights (PAGE 100)

VEGETARIAN ◎ KID FRIENDLY ☼ PATIO DINING ⛟ DELIVERY ⌂ PRIVATE PARTY

CENTRAL CITY

[Alcove Café & Bakery] **1929 Hillhurst Ave., Los Feliz, 323.644.0100, alcovecafe.com. B, L & D daily. Modern American. Beer & wine. AE, $$ WHY** Excellent, custardy omelets, prepared with a delicate hand, as well as very good baked goods and a terribly charming patio. **WHAT** Lunch and dinner dishes can be uneven, but you can't go wrong with breakfast and desserts at this order-at-the-counter café with a rambling, greenery-lined front patio and a famed desk inside in which people leave little notes — a neighborhood literary happening in progress. **WHO** Writers, musicians, costume designers, blind-daters and Los Feliz women sporting subtle tattoos and Kingsley-clad preschoolers. ☺ ♥☞♻☙☺☼

[BLD] 🏛 **7450 Beverly Blvd., Beverly/Third, 323.930.9744, bldrestaurant.com. B, L & D daily. Modern American. Beer & wine. AE, MC, V. $$ - $$$ WHY** Fried-egg sandwich (made with Gruyère, sourdough and thick-cut Nueske's bacon), frittata with bacon-wrapped asparagus, big salads, good burgers, great cheese platter, gingerbread pudding with vanilla ice cream, and more modern classics. **WHAT** A coffee shop for the goat-cheese-and-mizzuna crowd, BLD is a casual offshoot of nearby Grace, a superb restaurant run by Neal and Amy Fraser. Short for "Breakfast, Lunch and Dinner," BLD turns out everything from ricotta-blueberry pancakes to house-cured salmon salads. It's hip but not too trendy, busy but not too noisy, upscale but not overpriced. Expect a long wait for brunch. Note that at press time, Pasadena's food lovers were anxiously awaiting their own BLD, headed for a prime spot on Raymond in Old Town. **WHO** Miracle Mile office workers, low-key industry types, Hancock Park moms out for lunch. ☙☺

[Bloom Café] **5544 W. Pico Blvd., Mid-City, 323.934.6900, go2bloom. com. B, L & D daily. Modern American. BYOB (no corkage). AE, MC, V. $ - $$$ WHY** Organic eggs are used in breakfast dishes like poached eggs with goat cheese and smoked bacon. There are plenty of vegetarian choices, and lunches include grass-fed beef burgers and free-range chicken and apple salad. **WHAT** This zippy, modern café on an up-and-coming stretch of Pico draws neighborhood faithfuls for breakfasts with a healthy touch. An adjacent pizzeria turns out creative pies at lunch and dinner. Delivery in the area. ☞♻☙☺🚗

[Du-par's] **Farmers Market, 6333 W. 3rd St., Fairfax District, 323.933.8446, du-pars.com. B, L & D 24 hours daily. American. No booze. AE, MC, V. $ - $$ WHY** Nostalgic charm for natives, and decent coffee-shop fare at 3 a.m. **WHAT** Thoroughly renovated L.A.'s original Du-par's in the Farmers Market is back, red Naugahyde booths and all. Seen-it-all waitresses in gingham-trimmed uniforms and tiny white caps deliver huge (if overcooked) omelets, good (if not as good as in our childhoods) french toast, classic pancakes and steaming pot pies. Outside is a spiffy patio that looks like a French sidewalk café; would

🏛 ESSENTIALLY L.A.　☺ LATE　♥ ROMANTIC　☞ VALUE　♻ QUIET　☙ SUSTAINABLE

that the lukewarm coffee was as good as in France. Oh well, the cooking is satisfyingly homey — and Du-par's is open 24/7. **WHO** Seniors, high-school kids and screenwriters on a budget. ☺ 📷 ☺ ☼

[Ed's Coffee Shop] 🏠 460 N. Robertson Blvd., West Hollywood, 310.659.8625. B & L Mon.-Sat. American. No booze. MC, V. $ **WHY** First-rate short-order cooking served in a classic lunch-counter diner that's been here for 50 years. **WHAT** With its lunch counter, black-and-white linoleum floor and retro feel, this small coffee shop would seem more suited to the Midwest than West Hollywood. But it's beloved by locals for just that old-time atmosphere (and service), as well as the blessedly updated diner fare: great huevos rancheros, omelets, blueberry pancakes, fresh-spinach quesadillas and tuna melts. **WHO** Some of L.A.'s best chefs, who just want a good plate of eggs and turkey sausage. 📷🥄☼

[The Farm of Beverly Hills] 189 The Grove Dr., Fairfax District, 323.525.1699, thefarmofbeverlyhills.com. B, L & D daily. American. Beer & wine. AE, MC, V. $$ - $$$ **WHY** The brownies and lattes at the coffee bar. **WHAT** It serves three meals a day, plus weekend brunch, but we like it best for breakfast: good brewed coffee, chocolate croissants, frittatas built to order, brioche french toast and homemade granola. Lunch is fine, but on crowded days service can be slow. The Farm's real claim to fame is its dense, fudgy brownies, which they sell at all three branches and online. Pick one up to smuggle into the movie theater, and you'll never order Milk Duds again. Other locations at 439 N. Beverly Dr. in Beverly Hills (the original) and at L.A. Live Downtown. **WHO** Grove shoppers and movie-goers. 🥄☺ ☼

[Food + Lab] 7253 Santa Monica Blvd., West Hollywood, 323.851.7120, foodlabcatering.com. B, L & D daily. American/Austrian. No booze. AE, MC, V. $ - $$ **WHY** Fantastic sandwiches, excellent espresso, lovely patios both front and back, and all sorts of good food to take home and pretend you made. **WHAT** Nino Linsmayer and his chef mom Esther built a successful business as caterers before opening this café and gourmet-to-go market, so they came into the business already knowing how to make crowd-pleasing food. They haven't been here long but already have a devout following for their sandwiches (Austrian meatloaf, prosciutto with ricotta and honey, vegetarian pesto), salads, soups and breakfast dishes, made with organic ingredients. They're Austrian, which explains the Viennese coffee and good Austrian strudels. **WHO** Mostly neighborhood locals, including people who actually walk here. 🚗🥄☼

[Grub] 911 N. Seward St., Hollywood, 323.461.3663, grub-la.com. B Sat.-Sun., L & D daily. American. No booze. MC, V. $ - $$ **WHY** If you work in the heart of production Hollywood, this is a fine spot for lunch. **WHAT** Lunch — or weekend breakfast — at a table in the

🥄 VEGETARIAN ☺ KID FRIENDLY ☼ PATIO DINING 🚗 DELIVERY 🎩 PRIVATE PARTY walled patio behind this long, narrow bungalow is a fine thing indeed, and it's almost as nice sitting inside. Chef Betty Fraser had her Hollywood moment on Top Chef, and now she's back to making tasty Peruvian saltado, rosemary-steak salad, a hearty beet salad and her beloved "After School Special," a suave grilled-cheese sandwich served with a cup of tomato soup. **WHO** Below-the-line production people from places like Glen Glenn Sound and Laser-Pacific. 🕸🍸☼

[Hugo's] 🏛 **8401 Santa Monica Blvd., West Hollywood, 323.654.3993, hugosrestaurant.com. B, L & D daily, brunch Sat.-Sun. Modern American. Full bar. AE, MC, V. $$ WHY** Pasta Mama and Pasta Papa, two of the most addictive pasta-egg scrambles imaginable. **WHAT** Hugo's serves dinner, and it's a good dinner, but what brings the crowds back again and again are the breakfasts and brunches. Organic, generally lowfat ingredients are turned into terrific scrambles, pancakes, vegan breads and, for true brunch sybarites, a tasty but potent cocktail called the Mangorita. Lunchtime brings things like hummus wraps, mac 'n cheese and turkey burgers. A modern L.A. classic with consistently delicious food. **WHO** An exceptionally handsome crowd, both gay and straight, including lots of once-a-week regulars and some famous faces. ✿🍸☺

[Milk] **7290 Beverly Blvd., Beverly/Third, 323.939.6455, themilkshop. com. B, L & D daily. American. No booze. MC, V. $ WHY** The media noche Cuban sandwich is great, and there's also an unusual soba shrimp salad, burgers and a kids' menu, so the critters can get something solid before they start in on the cupcakes. **WHAT** It's not all about desserts at this stylish bakery and café — eat a proper sandwich and then try an ice cream creation, or pick up lunch to take back to the office. **WHO** Hip Hancock Park families and Miracle Mile office workers. ☺

[Nite Moon Café] **Golden Bridge Yoga Center, 6322 De Longpre Ave., Hollywood, 323.988.4052, goldenbridgeyoga.com. B & L daily, D Mon.-Thurs. Vegetarian. No booze. AE, MC, V. $ WHY** The terrific vegan BLT could make a person forsake meat, while the salad bar offers out-of-the-ordinary choices such as roasted cauliflower. The truly virtuous can order mung beans and rice. Hot tip: Magical chocolates sold in the herb shop are said to improve skin tone and overall health. **WHAT** It's actually possible to find inner peace while chowing down on a tasty vegan brownie at this café inside the cavernous Golden Bridge Yoga Center. Order cafeteria-style and then sit at long communal tables to enjoy your tasty vegetarian fare. **WHO** Pregnant ladies ravenous after prenatal yoga class, turbaned Sikhs, hungry yogis glowing from within. 🕸✿🍸☺

[Square One] **4854 Fountain Ave., East Hollywood, 323.661.1109, squareonedining.com. B & L daily. American. No booze. AE, MC, V. $ - $$ WHY** It's hard to decide between farm-fresh egg dishes with chorizo, eggs Benedict with smoked salmon, banana-caramel french toast and creative lunchtime sandwiches and salads, so you'll have to return often — as we do — to try them all. **WHAT** This sunny diner with a large walled patio cooks up some of the best breakfasts on the eastside, using top-quality ingredients and farmers' market produce. A great spot that is blessedly quiet during the week. **WHO** Los Feliz locals, including families with really cute babies. 🌱🥄☺☼

[The Trails] 2333 Fern Dell Dr., Los Feliz, 323.871.2102, thetrailslosfeliz.com. B & L Tues.-Sun. American/Vegetarian. No booze. Cash only. $
WHY Fresh, simple café fare is served at picnic tables under the pine trees in Fern Dell, making it paradise for people (and their dogs) returning from a long hike. Good vegetarian choices. **WHAT** Had a long hike or a hard day cutting your student film at neighboring AFI? Then head to Trails to refuel with a tasty avocado sandwich and a fresh lemonade or, even better, a piece of apple pie with Fosselman's ice cream. A little bit of country in the heart of the city. **WHO** Hikers, dogs, kids, American Film Institute folks and dessert lovers. 🌱🥄☺☼

EASTSIDE

[Auntie Em's Kitchen] 🏠 4616 Eagle Rock Blvd., Eagle Rock, 323.255.0800, auntieemskitchen.com. B & L daily, early D Mon.-Fri. Modern American. No booze. AE, MC, V. $ - $$ **WHY** Open-faced breakfast sandwiches, the grilled steak salad and spectacular cupcakes, scones and brownies. **WHAT** This funky and fetching retro-American roadhouse features delicious modern-diner cooking. For breakfast, try an open-faced egg sandwich topped with bacon, Cajun turkey sausage or portobello mushroom and roasted red peppers. For lunch, the turkey meatloaf sandwich and the grilled-steak salad are standouts. The homemade baked goods are all fab, especially the huge chocolate cupcakes. **WHO** Eagle Rock hipsters, from Oxy professors to tattooed Highland Park performance artists. 🥄☺☼

[Bar-B-Kosher] 113 E. 9th St., South Park/Fashion District, 213.623.4955. B & L Sun.-Fri. Middle Eastern/Kosher. No booze. MC, V.
$ - $$ **WHY** Pita sandwiches, omelet baguette sandwich, Moroccan carrots and hummus. **WHAT** Convenient for regulars of Downtown's Fashion District, this kosher café has developed a loyal following for its delicious baguette and pita sandwiches, as well as its Middle Eastern classics (baba ganouj, falafel, hummus). Take note that the "side salads" are actually served on your sandwich, so choose them wisely. **WHO** Fashionable Fashion District workers and shoppers. 🍴🥄

[Blue Star Restaurant] 2200 15th St., Downtown, 213.627.2022, bluestarrocks.com. B & L Mon.-Sat. Modern American. Beer & wine. AE, MC, V. $ - $$ **WHY** A great tuna sandwich, fresh salads, a huge enclosed patio, a swell jukebox and a relaxed, hang-out-as-long-as-you-

🥄 **VEGETARIAN** ☺ **KID FRIENDLY** ☼ **PATIO DINING** 🚗 **DELIVERY** 🎉 **PRIVATE PARTY**

like vibe. **WHAT** Surely the coolest secret spot Downtown, Blue Star sits on the edge of the scrap-metal yards off Alvarado in Vernon — in other words, the last neighborhood you'd expect to find a modern diner serving caprese sandwiches and ahi niçoise salads. It's not open for dinner, which makes it a great place for evening private parties. **WHO** A diverse mix of rag traders (from Guess and other local fashion companies), produce-warehousers, art-lofters and adventurers from further north in Downtown. 🖼️🔌☼🎁

[Café Tropical] **2900 W. Sunset Blvd., Silver Lake, 323.661.8391. B, L & D daily. Cuban/Mexican. No booze. MC, V. $ WHY** Café con leche, fresh-squeezed fruit juices, guava cheese pastry and a hearty Cuban sandwich. **WHAT** Catch a vestige of Silver Lake before it was completely gentrified at this funky Cuban café, which was once filled with actual cigar-smoking refugees. **WHO** A regular and longstanding crowd of bohemians. ☺ ☼

[Coffee Table Bistro] **1958 Colorado Blvd., Eagle Rock, 323.255.2200, coffeetablebistro.com. B, L & D daily. American. Beer & wine. AE, MC, V. $ - $$ WHY** Breakfast burritos are a favorite, and the wide selection of cakes makes a good accompaniment to coffee drinks. **WHAT** Chat or work in this Eagle Rock offshoot of the original Silver Lake screenwriter's paradise. Thanks to the liquor license and adjacent bar and lounge, it's easy to move from coffee to evening entertainment. **WHO** Eagle Rock writers, entrepreneurs and families. 🖼️☺

[Fisherman's Outlet] 🏛️ **529 S. Central Ave., Downtown, 213.627.7231, fishermansoutlet.net. B & L Mon.-Sat. Seafood/American. Beer & wine. Cash only. $ - $$ WHY** Very fresh char-broiled fish (yellowfin tuna, mahi mahi, catfish, swordfish) that is not overcooked like it usually is at these kinds of places, served with rice or perfect fries. **WHAT** Don't be put off by the paper plates, concrete picnic tables or lunchtime crowds — this seafood-market and café has fish better than at many a white-tablecloth restaurant. We prefer the char-broiled choices over the fried, which are a little more generic; the lobster is worth the splurge. Some, though, swear by the fried scallops and sand dabs. **WHO** Working men and families who have been coming here for three generations. 🖼️☺☼

[Homegirl Café] 🏛️ **130 W. Bruno St., Chinatown, 323.526.1254, ext. 301, homeboy-industries.org. B & L daily, D Thurs.-Sat. Mexican/ Californian. No booze. MC, V. $ WHY** Fresh, modern Mexican fare with lots of vegetarian choices (tofu chorizo, anyone?) — and eating here supports a fantastic nonprofit. It's now open for dinner a few nights a week, too. **WHAT** What started as a bakery in East L.A. intended to give young people an alternative to gangs has grown into a multi-faceted enterprise (tattoo removal, silkscreening, bakery) on the edge of Chinatown. The showpiece is the Homegirl, where young women learn the restaurant business. It's a bright space with art for sale and an open kitchen, which turns out tasty, healthful salads, tacos and breakfast dishes, all at low prices. Tip well! **WHO** City Hall workers, suited business folks and pierced punks. 🗊🎔🕑

[Kim Chuy] **727 N. Broadway, Chinatown, 213.687.7215, kimchuy. com. B, L & D daily. Chinese. No booze. AE, MC, V. $ - $$ WHY** For Chiu Chow noodles and nothing but: egg noodles with sliced pork; beef noodle soup; chow mein with beef, Chinese broccoli and oyster sauce; or, for special occasions, Pork Variety (aka intestines) noodle soup. **WHAT** Richly flavored, sustaining noodle soups and fried noodle and rice dishes from the Chaoshan region of southeastern China are the focus at this plain little Chinatown café. Start your morning with a bowl of egg-noodle soup, and move on at lunchtime to the heartier beef chow mein. 🗊🕑

[Langer's Deli] 🏠 **704 S. Alvarado St., Westlake, 213.483.8050, langersdeli.com. B & L Mon.-Sat. Deli. Beer & wine. MC, V. $ - $$ WHY** The best pastrami on rye in Southern California; very good corned beef, too. **WHAT** Langer's is so beloved that the city named the intersection of 7th and Alvarado "Langer's Square" — and Metrolink put a subway stop right across the street. The subway furthers the happy feeling of a proper New York deli, from the vinyl booths to the chewy rye bread to the dames who serve the chow. But this is no New York pretender — it's an L.A. classic. **WHO** Downtown's Brooks Brothers crowd meets Mid-City seniors and working folks ... a great mix. 🗊

[Local] **2943 W. Sunset Blvd., Silver Lake, 323.662.4740, silverlakelocal. com. B & L daily, D Tues.-Sat. American. No booze. AE, MC, V. $ - $$ WHY** Delicious and indulgent breakfast served until the afternoon (but as befits Silver Lake, not until after 9 a.m.). **WHAT** Local does justice to its name — the ingredients are local, the diners all know each other and the staff is incredibly friendly. For breakfast, try the brioche french toast lathered in butter and powdered sugar; for lunch, consider the curried chicken salad sandwich — reminiscent of that British darling, Coronation Chicken — which shares the plate with fantastic spicy fries. Or opt for a trip to the full-wall salad bar, complete with every vegetable imaginable and many organic and/or vegan dressings. Everything seems overpriced at first glance, but the portions are huge, so if you share dishes, it's pretty reasonable. **WHO** Every breed of Silver Lake indie kid and an extraordinary number of pregnant women trying to eat healthfully when they also need to eat a lot. 🎔🕑

[Los Feliz Café] **3207 Los Feliz Blvd., Atwater, 323.660.8144. B & L daily. American. No booze. MC, V. $ WHY** Keep it basic: bacon and eggs, corned beef hash, BLTs and burgers. Finish with a root beer float. **WHAT** Come here for old-fashioned diner food at rock-bottom

---

🍃 VEGETARIAN ⊙ KID FRIENDLY ☼ PATIO DINING 🚗 DELIVERY 🏛 PRIVATE PARTY prices, served on a tranquil patio with outdoor tables overlooking the public golf course in Atwater. **WHO** Hungover hipsters and their dogs, families with kids, golfers. 🕼 ⑨ ☺ ☼

[Mi India Bonita] 🏠 4731 E. Olympic Blvd., East L.A., 323.267.8505. B & L Mon.-Sat. Mexican. No booze. MC, V. $ **WHY** Huevos rancheros, huevos Oaxaqueños, tender barbacoa, weekend pozole and everyday albondigas soup just like you wish your grandmother made. **WHAT** Substantial breakfasts and meaty, nourishing soups are the specialty at this hole-in-the-wall café, where fans get weepy over the quality of the fluffy albondigas, pozole, *cocido de res* (beef and vegetable soup) and menudo. Worth a trip. 🕼 ☺

[Millie's] 3524 W. Sunset Blvd., Silver Lake, 323.664.0404, milliescafe. net. B & L daily. American. No booze. MC, V. $ - $$ **WHY** Famous for the Devil's Mess egg dish, but also good for biscuits, gravy and healthier alternatives like spinach, pine nuts and eggs. Try the chipotle grilled cheese at lunch. **WHAT** The tiny Silver Lake diner has been sort of a punk rock commissary for more than 20 years and was a real diner for 40 years before that. The history that griddle has seen.... Sit at the counter to kibitz with the colorful fry cooks, or try the small adjacent dining room or sidewalk seating with a bit more breathing room. Note that the management has a strict no-cell-phone policy. **WHO** The half of Silver Lake that gets up at noon on weekend mornings and the half that seems to never go to work on weekdays. 🕼 ❧ ☼

[My Taco] 6300 York Blvd., Highland Park, 323.256.2698. B, L & D daily. Mexican. No booze. MC, V. $ **WHY** Gut-pleasing Mexican breakfast dishes served all day. Good carne asada, too. **WHAT** Come here for a $5.50 breakfast of huevos rancheros or chorizo and eggs and you won't need lunch. The chilequiles are like nachos that have gone to heaven and, as their reward, got covered in eggs and cheese. If you come for lunch or dinner, try the goat tacos, the barbacoa plate or, if you are a 17-year-old boy who burns calories like a jet burns fuel, the carne asada fries with guacamole. 🕼

[Nickel Diner] 🏠 524 S. Main St., Downtown, 213.623.8301, 5cdiner.com. B & L Tues.-Sun., D Tues.-Sat. American. No booze. AE, MC, V. $ **WHY** Bacon maple doughnuts. **WHAT** This retro diner at Main and 5th (5th being called "the Nickel" by the tougher locals in this hardscrabble neighborhood) has won local fame for bringing L.A. the bacon doughnut, which is already a staple in such foodie towns as Portland. But that's just the beginning. Come for any of the very good breakfast dishes, like the egg scramble with bacon, goat cheese, garlic and spinach, or a lunchtime sandwich or salad, or skip all that and go straight for the chocolate peanut-butter potato-chip layer cake. **WHO** Not nearly as many annoying hipsters as you might think — instead, it's a good mix of Downtown residents, workers and explorers. 🕼

🏠 ESSENTIALLY L.A. ☺ LATE ♥ ROMANTIC 🕼 VALUE ⑨ QUIET ☼ SUSTAINABLE

[Shekarchi Downtown] **914 S. Hill St., South Park/Fashion District, 213.892.8535. L Mon.-Fri. Persian. No booze. AE, MC, V. $ WHY** Excellent kebabs (try the *koubideh*, a ground-beef blend), particularly good rice and refreshing yogurt drinks. And they deliver throughout Downtown. **WHAT** This very good Iranian businessman's lunch place in an historic part of Downtown has a far more fashionable décor than you'd suspect from the outside. It's open on weekdays only and is packed at prime lunch time, so don't be in a big rush. 🖼️�

SAN GABRIEL VALLEY

[Billy's Deli] **216 N. Orange St., Glendale, 818.246.1689, billysdeli. com. B, L & D daily. American/deli. Beer & wine. AE, MC, V. $ - $$ WHY** Classic deli fare, plus customer-pampering waitresses straight out of Central Casting. **WHAT** Established in 1948, Billy's is an institution that runs on homemade pickles, towers of lox and pastrami and lots of rye bread. A deli case and bakery case complement a dining room hung with sepia photos of a Glendale with Red Cars (and without high-rises or smog). The bill will be on the expensive side, but everything is high in quality. Don't miss the food wall that adorns the outside of the restaurant, with tiles cast from real deli meats and breads. Who knew? 🙂

[Dish] **734 Foothill Blvd., La Cañada, 818.790.5355, dishbreakfast-lunchanddinner.com. B, L & D daily. American. Full bar. AE, MC, V. $ - $$ WHY** Good, no-frills home cooking, only you don't have to do the dishes. **WHAT** This is the best spot in the area for an all-American breakfast: cornmeal johnnycakes, applewood-smoked bacon and the usual egg dishes. Lunch brings simple sandwiches, soups and salads. The Americana theme extends to the décor and the Awesome Dish Root Beer Float on the kids' menu. **WHO** Families with kids and empty-nester couples. 🖼️🍴🙂

[Euro Pane] 🗝️ **950 E. Colorado Blvd., Pasadena, 626.577.1828. B & L daily. American/French. No booze. MC, V. $ WHY** Breakfast croissants that are the best for many miles, and fab lunchtime sandwiches: egg salad, chicken salad and an amazing BLAT (bacon, lettuce, avocado and tomato). Excellent coffee, too. **WHAT** Sumi Chang's extraordinary bakery is also a swell place for lunch. Her staff doesn't always display her kindness and people skills, and the seating is basic, but the devout fans don't mind when they get their breakfast goodies or pressed sandwiches. **WHO** Pasadena's intelligentsia read their *New Yorkers* at small café tables over pains aux chocolats or lunchtime sandwiches. 🌿🍽️🙂

[Green Street Restaurant] **146 S. Shoppers Ln., Pasadena, 626.577.7170, greenstreetrestaurant.com. B, L & D daily. American. Full bar. AE, MC, V. $$ - $$$ WHY** Ordering the Dianne salad marks

---

🌿 **VEGETARIAN** ◎ **KID FRIENDLY** ✷ **PATIO DINING** � **DELIVERY** 🏛️ **PRIVATE PARTY**

you as a true Pasadenan. **WHAT** This institution does a brisk business in Cal-American cuisine. There's a popular outdoor patio and a modern-coffee-shop interior, but wherever you choose to sit, the go-to dish is the Dianne salad, its ginormous take on Chinese chicken salad (for a more reasonable serving, get the "dinner" size, not the full). It's impossible to stop eating, as thousands of Pasadenans before you have discovered. **WHO** Pasadena moms and their moms. 📠 🌱 ⊙ ☼ 🚗

[Julienne] ⌂ 2649 Mission St., San Marino, 626.441.2299, julienneto-go.com. B & L Mon.-Sat. Modern American. Beer & wine. AE, MC, V. $ - $$$ **WHY** Signature rosemary bread for toast and sandwiches, not one but two great bacon offerings (applewood smoked and candied) on the breakfast menu and killer chocolate-mint brownies in the dessert case. Plus fantastic takeout baskets for the plane or the Hollywood Bowl. **WHAT** Breakfast or lunch on the shaded sidewalk terrace fronting this impossibly charming café and gourmet-to-go store is a fine treat, and well worth the wait if you come at peak hours. Lunch standouts include the lamb sandwich with caramelized onions and the chopped salad with grilled chicken, roasted vegetables and pesto. At breakfast, try the wonderful salmon hash or a perfectly cooked omelet. **WHO** San Marino ladies who lunch, families with out-of-town guests and folks on the bridal/baby-shower circuit. ♥ 🌱 ☼

[Le Pain Quotidien] 88 W. Colorado Blvd., Old Pasadena, 626.396.0956, painquotidien.com. B, L & early D daily. Modern American/French. Beer & wine. AE, MC, V. $ - $$ **WHY** Our favorite breakfast in Pasadena: flawless omelets (try the pesto-parmesan), fresh fruit with yogurt, fresh juices and pains aux chocolats. **WHAT** Yes, we're doing our best to eschew chains, but these Belgian-based cafés offer a level of quality that's almost never seen on a large scale. Fresh, flavorful, often organic ingredients go into the delicious open-face sandwiches, quiches, salads, soups and sweets. The bread, *naturellement*, is substantial and flavorful. And even with the prime Old Town location, we can always snag a good table. **WHO** The Patagonia-and-Prius crowd, some toting the cutest babies in town. ♻ 🌱 ⊙ ☼

[Lovebirds] 921 E. Colorado Blvd., Pasadena, 626.583.8888; 10 S. 1st St., Alhambra, 626.281.9999, lovebirdscafe.com. B & L Mon.-Sat. American. No booze. AE, MC, V. $ **WHY** Simple, satisfying sandwiches on homemade bread. **WHAT** Part bakery, part coffeehouse, part lunch purveyor, these spacious, friendly, order-at-the-counter cafés are fine places for lunchtime sandwiches. Generous and made on an array of homemade breads, they are thoughtfully offered in three sizes: regular, large and half. **WHO** Office workers flock to both locations. 📠 ⊙

[Marston's] 151 E. Walnut St., Pasadena, 626.796.2459, marstons-restaurant.com. B & L daily, D Wed.-Sat. American. Beer & wine. AE, MC, V. $ - $$$ **WHY** Legendary cornflake-coated french toast. **WHAT** The breakfasts are excellent, as are the lunch salads, but insanely long weekend waits for a table are an unfortunate fact of life at this charming old Pasadena bungalow. Come on a Tuesday to more easily snag a lovely front-porch table to eat your generous omelet in peace. ♥ ☺ ☼

[Nicole's Gourmet Foods] **921 Meridian Ave., South Pasadena, 626.403.5751, nicolesgourmetfoods.com. B & L Mon.-Sat. French. Beer & wine. AE, MC, V. $ WHY** Excellent, well-edited selection of cheese and wine in a friendly, low-key setting. **WHAT** Nicole Grandjean has created a little corner of Paris by the Mission Gold Line station. Order at the counter, grab a table on the flower-lined sidewalk patio and enjoy a delicious baguette sandwich, salad or quiche. Don't leave without stocking up on cheese (from France, California and many points in between), pâté, fine chocolate, wine and one of the frozen delicacies: puff pastry, raviolis, mini tart shells. **WHO** Eclectic mix of locals, serious Francophiles and foodie chefs. ☼

[Pie 'n' Burger] ⬛ **913 E. California Blvd., Pasadena, 626.795.1123, pienburger.com. B, L & D daily. American. No booze. Cash only. $ WHY** Cheeseburgers and banana cream pie. **WHAT** This no-frills diner with a long counter and even longer lines serves fantastic burgers, very good short-order breakfasts and house-made pies that are famous enough to draw folks from around Southern California. In fact, just about every food group on the wall-mounted menu has its passionate devotees, including the toast and the bacon. **WHO** Caltech students and profs, older couples, paperback-toting singles. ⬛ ☺

[The Terrace] **Langham Huntington Hotel, 1401 S. Oak Knoll Ave., Pasadena, 626.568.3900, pasadena.langhamhotels.com. B, L & D daily. Modern American. Full bar. AE, MC, V. $$ - $$$$ WHY** A chance to live the California dream without actually checking in. **WHAT** Ah, the good life: lunch at an umbrella-shaded table overlooking the pool of this grande dame hotel, iced tea or Chardonnay in hand. Order a flawless chicken Caesar, a gorgeous Cobb or a rich turkey pesto panini and watch the world's troubles drift away. **WHO** Lunching ladies, business folk and lucky hotel guests with time to linger poolside. ♥ ♪ ⬛ ☼

[Ugo's Italian Deli] **74 W. Sierra Madre Blvd., Sierra Madre, 626.836.5700, ugoscafe.com. B, L & D Tues.-Sun. Italian. Beer & wine. MC, V. $ WHY** Excellent panini, a green salad with semi-dried pear tomatoes, sublime cheese-filled risotto cakes and crunchy cold broccollini peppered with garlic slices. Oh, and the most incredible baked goods east of Euro Pane — by all means have a cupcake. **WHAT** The Hamptons have arrived in Sierra Madre, thanks to this spiffy new Italian bakery, deli and café with a few inside tables and some nice sidewalk seating. The food is terrific, the people are nice, and the prices are fair. ☼

⬛ VEGETARIAN ☺ KID FRIENDLY ☼ PATIO DINING ⬛ DELIVERY ⬛ PRIVATE PARTY

EAST VALLEY

[Aroma Café] 4360 Tujunga Ave., Studio City, 818.508.0677, aromacoffeeandtea.com. B, L & D daily. American. No booze. MC, V. $ - $$
WHY Good breakfasts served until 2:30 p.m., with huge salads and chic sandwiches for those who don't want breakfast. **WHAT** Owned by the same folks behind Alcove in Los Feliz, this café/coffeehouse/bookstore is in a fetching old cottage with an enclosed brick patio. The menu is extensive; try a breakfast burrito, the scrambled eggs atop spinach puff pastry, or a vegetarian scramble. Partial table service (order at the counter) can be spotty and a little full of attitude, and you'll have to wait at peak times, but the food and setting are usually worth it. **WHO** Studio City beautiful people, including lots of TV writers, actors and young PAs. ♥◐☼

[Art's Delicatessen] 12224 Ventura Blvd., Studio City, 818.762.1221, artsdeli.com. B, L & D daily. Deli. Beer & wine. AE, MC, V. $ - $$
WHY When you don't have time to drive to Brent's and you've gotta have deli. **WHAT** We're not as fond of Art's as its diehard fans, but neither will we turn down a corned beef on rye here. An all-around traditional deli: vinyl booths, Formica tables, smoked fish, deli sandwiches and always-amusing people-watching. **WHO** Seniors, TV writers and studio folks, many of whom have been coming here for 30 years. ☺🚗

[Du-par's] 12036 Ventura Blvd., Studio City, 818.766.4437, du-pars. com. B, L & D 24 hours daily. American. No booze. AE, MC, V. $ - $$
WHY For classic American breakfasts, including custardy french toast, corned beef hash with poached eggs and a short stack of pancakes, served 24 hours a day. **WHAT** The Studio City branch of the L.A. Farmers Market icon is a Valley favorite for hearty breakfasts served by staffers who know regulars by name. Du-par's bacon is crisp and flavorful and the eggs are cooked to order, even if the place doesn't serve those new-fangled coffee drinks such as espresso and cappuccino. If you like thinner pancakes, ask for them; sometimes if the batter has been sitting overnight they come out too thick. **WHO** Folks from the 'hood, including a smattering of celebs trying to avoid attention before they've had their coffee. ☺☺

[Good Neighbor] 3701 Cahuenga Blvd., Studio City, 818.761.4627. B & L daily. American. Beer & wine. MC, V. $ **WHY** Breakfast, and a good one at that, served all day, along with good American coffee and personal service. **WHAT** The parking stinks, but that keeps the crowds at bay, so the wait's not too bad for a table in this fine mom 'n pop diner in the Cahuenga Pass. Generous omelets, a delish pancake sandwich and surprisingly good vegetarian options. Lunchtime sandwiches are perfectly fine. **WHO** Below-the-line working folk from the local studios, some of whom have been coming here for decades. 🗺◐☺

[Hugo's] 12851 Riverside Dr., Studio City, 818.761.8985, hugosrestaurant.com. B, L & D daily. Modern American. Full bar. AE, MC, V. $$
WHY Pasta Mama and Pasta Papa, two of the most addictive pasta-egg scrambles imaginable. **WHAT** Hugo's serves dinner, and it's a good dinner, but what brings the crowds back again and again are the breakfasts and brunches. Organic, hormone-free, processed-sugar-free, generally lowfat ingredients are turned into scrambles, pancakes, vegan breads and, for true brunch sybarites, a tasty and potent cocktail called the Mangorita. Lunchtime brings things like hummus wraps, focaccia sandwiches (so-so) and turkey burgers (better). **WHO** Hip and healthy Valley families, studio people and some famous faces. ○◑☺

[Jinky's Cafe] 14120 Ventura Blvd., Sherman Oaks, 818.981.2250, jinkys.com. B, L & D daily. American. No booze. AE, MC, V. $ - $$
WHY Santa Fe egg scramble, pumpkin pancakes, french toast coated in honey nut cornflakes and, at lunch, good quesadillas and a Chinese chicken salad. **WHAT** Not everything is good at this health-conscious, fairly pricey café, but many of the breakfast dishes are, which is why it's so hard to find parking on weekend mornings, and the wait for a table can be interminable. Come instead on a weekday for the famous french toast or some very good pancakes. **WHO** A huge throng on weekend mornings — come early or on a weekday. ◑☺☼

[Paty's] 10001 Riverside Dr., Toluca Lake, 818.761.0041, patysrestaurant.com. B, L & D daily. American. Beer & wine. AE, MC, V. $ - $$
WHY Because breakfast is served all day, either out on the patio or in among the photos of celebrities, some of whom actually come here. **WHAT** An all-around good vintage coffee shop, no more and no less. You can hang out on the patio or in a booth with a screenplay and some scrambled eggs, or treat your kids to a shake. Service can be slow, but what's your rush? **WHO** Toluca Lake grandmas, TV actors, teens and office workers. ▦♪☺☼

[Studio Café Magazzino] ▣ 109 N. Pass Ave., Toluca Lake, 818.953.7220. B & L Mon.-Fri. American. No booze. AE, MC, V. $
WHY Excellent soups, a killer tuna sandwich, good vegetarian options, peach iced tea and very nice people — in short, the perfect little lunch café. **WHAT** A charming neighborhood spot with spitting distance of Warner Bros., this treasure is packed at lunch but quieter for breakfast. Let Rose take your order at the counter and hope you can snag one of the half-dozen tables inside or two outside. Rose's kitchen makes delicious daily soups (including a fabulous split pea) and generous and fresh sandwiches and salads. After the lunch rush, you can linger over an espresso and one of the good-looking desserts. **WHO** A steady stream of studio people. ▦◑☼

◑ VEGETARIAN ☺ KID FRIENDLY ☼ PATIO DINING ▦ DELIVERY ▣ PRIVATE PARTY

[TallyRand] 1700 W. Olive St., Burbank, 818.846.9904, thetallyrand. com. B, L & D daily. American. Full bar. AE, MC, V. $ **WHY** Honest diner food at honest diner prices. **WHAT** A neighborhood staple since 1959, the TallyRand is a good spot for a well-prepared American breakfast (eggs 'n bacon, homemade muffins, superb buttermilk pancakes) and a delicious chicken club sandwich for lunch. Solid chow served to solid folks settled into padded vinyl booths. **WHO** Large family groups, early-bird seniors, hipster coffee-shop aficionados. 🗺️😊☘️

[Watercress] 13565 Ventura Blvd., Sherman Oaks, 818.385.1448, watercresscafe.com. B & L daily. American. No booze. MC, V. $
WHY Lovely breakfasts and lunches made from quality organic ingredients. **WHAT** Next door to the affiliated Coffee Roaster, this bright, modern café has a short menu of very good food: organic steel-cut oatmeal, chorizo scrambles, a rich salami and brie sandwich and great blueberry pie. **WHO** A quiet crowd of local regulars. 🔕☘️🗺️

WEST VALLEY

[More Than Waffles] 17200 Ventura Blvd., Encino, 818.789.5937, morethanwaffles.com. B & L daily. American. No booze. MC, V. $ - $$
WHY Waffles. Okay, maybe pancakes, too. **WHAT** This strip-mall café is quite the place to be on weekend mornings, when a musician plays on the patio and dogs and kids are everywhere. Even though the name implies otherwise, waffles are the thing to get. 😊☘️

[Nat's Early Bite] 14115 Burbank Blvd., Van Nuys, 818.781.3040. B & L daily, D Tues.-Fri. American. No booze. MC, V. $ **WHY** For a satisfying American breakfast (delicious scrambles and omelets, carrot muffins, truly crisp hash browns) and a well-made cup of coffee. **WHAT** Pass on lunch and dinner, but don't miss the chance for breakfast at this honest, old-school diner. There's a wait on weekends, but it's worth it. **WHO** Regular Van Nuys diner folks — it's not a hipster scene. 🗺️🔕😊

[Vinh Loi Tofu] 18625 Sherman Way, Reseda, 818.996.9779, vinhloitofu.com. B, L & early D daily. Vietnamese. No booze. MC, V. $
WHY Fresh and tasty Vietnamese fare, all vegetarian and most of it vegan, with many dishes featuring fresh tofu made in the adjacent factory. **WHAT** In a dining room barely bigger than a lunch truck, Kevin Tran mans the counter and chats with regulars at his café next to his tofu factory. Try any of the vegan soups, the spring rolls, the soy shrimp, the fake meat dishes, the carrot cake ... it's all delicious. **WHO** A steady stream of regulars, as diverse as they come: Asian chefs, vegan moms with toddlers in tow, bikers, women in hijabs. 🗺️☘️🔕😊

🏛️ ESSENTIALLY L.A.   😊 LATE   💜 ROMANTIC   🗺️ VALUE   🔕 QUIET   ☘️ SUSTAINABLE

WESTSIDE: CENTRAL

[Al Gelato] 806 S. Robertson Blvd., Beverly Hills, 310.659.8069.
L & D daily. Italian. No booze. Cash only. $ - $$ **WHY** For red-sauce
dishes like rigatoni, as well as pizza, prosciutto or meatball sandwiches and salads. The tuna sandwich and the chili have many admirers.
WHAT Gelato is the ending, but the meal starts with hearty pastas and
soups and sandwiches. Behind the tempting, extensive gelato counter
is a casual, no-frills dining room with table service. Good for a low-key Beverly Hills lunch. ☺

[Bluebird Café] 8572 National Blvd., Culver City, 310.841.0939,
bluebirdcafela.com. B & L Mon.-Sat. American. Beer & wine. AE, MC, V. $
WHY Excellent cupcakes and reliable lunch fare: pressed chicken-and-cheddar or prosciutto-and-mozzarella sandwiches, a delish turkey
Reuben and parsley-flecked fries. **WHAT** A cheerful, simple neighborhood café with a pleasant enclosed patio and justly famed cupcakes.
Breakfast is usually pretty quiet during the week. It's not cheap, but
this isn't a cheap neighborhood anymore. **WHO** Culver City studio and
creative types, who try to score tables on the patio for lunch. 🍽☺☼

[Cabbage Patch] 214 S. Beverly Dr., Beverly Hills, 310.550.8655,
cabbagepatchbh.com. L & D Mon.-Sat. Modern American. No booze.
AE, MC, V. $ - $$ **WHY** Beautiful salads, bowls and sandwiches made
from ingredients as fresh, locally sourced and organic as possible,
served in a bright, cheerful café. **WHAT** Handsome young owner Samir
Mohajer was chef at Rustic Canyon for two years, and he's brought
the same devotion to high-quality ingredients seen at his old home to
this casual, order-at-the-counter café. Salads are generous and perfectly balanced; try the one made with baby greens, free-range Jidori
chicken (raised locally), applewood-smoked bacon, brioche croutons
and a Champagne vinaigrette. Bowls are generous and gorgeous, and
sandwiches hold things like Niman Ranch ground beef, wild arugula,
shaved parmesan and eggplant caponata. **WHO** Beverly Hills locals
who value quality food over a scene. ☼

[Café Flore] 214 S. Robertson Blvd., Beverly Hills, 310.659.6877,
cafeflore.us. B Mon.-Sat., L daily, D Wed.-Sun., brunch Sun. French/
Californian. Beer & wine. AE, MC, V. $ - $$ **WHY** French-style sandwiches, omelets, salads and tartines, to eat in the friendly café or take
out — and free delivery in the area! **WHAT** A find in high-rent Beverly
Hills for a tasty, peaceful, reasonably priced meal. Try the Valrhona
chocolate pancakes or eggs Benedict for breakfast, the saffron-scented
grilled chicken sandwich for lunch and the *flammekueche* (Alsatian
pizza) for supper. 🍽☺🚚

🥬 VEGETARIAN ◌ KID FRIENDLY ☼ PATIO DINING 🚚 DELIVERY 🏠 PRIVATE PARTY

[The Farm of Beverly Hills] 439 N. Beverly Dr., Beverly Hills, 310.273.5578, thefarmofbeverlyhills.com. B, L & D daily. American. Beer & wine. AE, MC, V. $$ - $$$ **WHY** The breakfasts, weekend brunch and brownies. **WHAT** This original of the three-branch mini-chain serves three meals a day, plus weekend brunch, but we like it best for breakfast: good brewed coffee, chocolate croissants, frittatas built to order, brisket omelets and homemade granola. Lunch brings excellent club sandwiches and good salads and cheeseburgers, but the Farm's real claim to fame is its dense, fudgy brownies, which they sell at all three branches and online. Be prepared to wait, and have patience with the service. Other locations at the Grove and at L.A. Live Downtown. **WHO** Beverly Hills tourists and locals alike, including lots of pretty people. 🛍️☺☺

[Fountain Coffee Room] 🏛 Beverly Hills Hotel, 9641 Sunset Blvd., Beverly Hills, 310.276.2251, thebeverlyhillshotel.com. B & L daily. American. No booze. AE, MC, V. $$ - $$$ **WHY** To treat a special kid or grandkid to waffles or a big ol' ice cream sundae, but only if your wallet isn't easily offended. **WHAT** Dripping with old Beverly Hills panache, this 20-seat 1949 diner counter is overpriced, of course, but you're paying for the setting, and it's a great one. Splurge on the caviar and sour cream omelet if you must, but you'll be just as happy with pancakes and good coffee. A real milkshake makes a heavenly afternoon indulgence. **WHO** Big spenders having a treat. ☺

[John O'Groats] 🏛 10516 Pico Blvd., Rancho Park, 310.204.0692, ogroatsrestaurant.com. B, L & D daily. American. No booze. AE, MC, V. $ - $$ **WHY** Corned beef hash, biscuits, thick-cut bacon and pumpkin or fresh-fruit-topped pancakes. **WHAT** Fans line up every weekend morning (and sometimes on weekdays) for a spot at a table or the counter in this rustic-charming diner named for a village in Scotland. The food isn't authentically Scotch (a good thing, perhaps), but the breakfasts are hearty and totally delicious. **WHO** Stroller-pushing families and couples with their newspapers to read over breakfast. ☺

[Leaf Organics] 11938 W. Washington Blvd., Culver City, 310.390.6005, leaforganics.com. B, L & D daily. Vegan. No booze. AE, MC, V. $ **WHY** A chance to worship the holy trinity of gastronomic virtues — vegan, raw and organic — in a pleasant, light-filled space. **WHAT** Served inside an engagingly bright chartreuse building, this organic, raw, vegan fare has an international tilt, gallivanting from the Flying Falafel salad on baby greens with tahini sauce to the curried-lentil Bombay burrito. The tasty and equally well-traveled appetizers include miso-carrot-ginger soup and good guacamole. There's another branch at 14318 Ventura Blvd., Sherman Oaks. ☺🛍️

[S & W Country Diner] 9748 Washington Blvd., Culver City, 310.204.5136. B & L daily. American/Southern. No booze. Cash only. $ **WHY** Substantial, inexpensive Southern breakfasts: grits, eggs,

---

🏛 ESSENTIALLY L.A. ☺ LATE ♥ ROMANTIC 💵 VALUE 🔈 QUIET ☺ SUSTAINABLE biscuits and gravy, sausage and similar such non-diet food. **WHAT** A greasy spoon of a breakfast nook, with a too-long wait and often-over-whelmed service on weekends but a nice vibe during the week. **WHO** Sony workers and local residents walking from home for breakfast. The regulars expect a wait and don't mind.

WEST OF THE 405

[3 Square Cafe & Bakery] 1121 Abbot Kinney Blvd., Venice, 310.399.6504, rockenwagner.com. B, L & D daily. American/German. Beer & wine. AE, MC, V. $$ **WHY** Pretzel bread, the pretzel burger, avocado fries and outdoor seating on Abbot Kinney. **WHAT** Accomplished chef Hans Röckenwagner has had everything from a swank restaurant to a bakery, and now he's created this elegant modern café and bakery. His German heritage is evident in the brats and famed pretzel bread, and all the food is excellent, if on the pricey side. Still, this is Abbot Kinney, and you pay for such prime real estate. **WHO** Venice beautiful people enjoying a quiet breakfast or lunch.

[Back on the Beach Café] Annenberg Community Beach House, 415 Pacific Coast Hwy., Santa Monica, 310.393.8282, backonthebeach-cafe.com. B & L daily, D Tues.-Sun. American. Beer & wine. AE, MC, V. $ - $$$ **WHY** Tables on the sand, smack in the middle of Santa Monica Beach. **WHAT** After closing for a remodel, Back on the Beach is back, now part of the new public beach club at the neighboring Marion Davies estate. The straightforward fare is pretty much the same — nothing amazing, but that omelet, breakfast quesadilla or burger tastes so much better when the sun is sparkling on the Pacific and you've just had a ride on the bike path. A fun and affordable place to bring out-of-town guests on a sunny day. **WHO** Local volleyball players, families with little kids, bike-path cruisers.

[Blue Plate] 1415 Montana Ave., Santa Monica, 310.260.8877, blue-platesantamonica.com. B, L & D daily. American. Beer & wine. AE, MC, V. $ - $$$ **WHY** The turkey-avocado wrap and chopped salad. **WHAT** This cute-as-a-button coffee shop isn't as good as we wish it would be — the service can be spotty, the prices are on the high side for such simple fare, and the kitchen is inconsistent. That said, it's got a good vibe and is a pleasant place to meet a friend. **WHO** Chic women starting or ending a Montana shopping spree.

[The Bookmark Café] Santa Monica Main Library, 601 Santa Monica Blvd., Santa Monica, 310.587.2665. B Mon.-Sat., L daily, D Mon.-Thurs. American. No booze. AE, MC, V. $ **WHY** It's the best secret café in Santa Monica. **WHAT** You don't have to keep this quiet: The café in the fabulous Main Library offers good, made-to-order food including turkey burgers, panini, wraps and an amazing range of salads (chef's, Cobb, Greek, apple walnut). You can eat in a large, sunny courtyard, and savor the fact that almost everything on the menu costs less than $7. It serves breakfast, too, including omelets, pancakes and good coffee. **WHO** Quiet, studious types. 🖼 🎵 🍽 ☺ ✿

[Bread & Porridge] 2315 Wilshire Blvd., Santa Monica, 310.453.4941, breadandporridge.com. B, L & D daily. American. Beer & wine. AE, MC, V. $ - $$ **WHY** Omelets made with a variety of interesting sausages, goat cheese salad, tender brisket. **WHAT** High-backed wooden booths, chalkboard menus and retro tile make for a setting of Rockwellian charm, just the place to wallow in the comfort of eggs, sausages, pancakes, fashionable salads and hearty entrees. Now that it has a license, locals come for an early supper with a glass of good wine. Quality ingredients at fair prices. **WHO** Folks who shop the Santa Monica Farmers' Market and hip nursing moms coming from the Pump Station a couple of doors over. 🖼 ♻ 🍽 ☺

[Broadway Deli] 1457 3rd St. Promenade, Santa Monica, 310.451.0616, broadwaydeli.com. B, L & D daily. American. Full bar. AE, MC, V. $ - $$ **WHY** Good location, quality wine and a diverse menu that runs the gamut from matzo ball soup to pizza puttanesca. **WHAT** Despite a great, all-things-to-all-people concept, this part deli/part brasserie doesn't live up to its considerable promise. The service is often chaotic and the kitchen is wildly inconsistent. It does a good business, though, thanks to the steady tourist trade and its relatively reasonable prices, roomy booths and ideal location on the south end of the Third Street Promenade. ☺ 🍽 ☺

[Café Vida] 15317 Antioch St., Pacific Palisades, 310.573.1335. B, L & D daily. American/Mexican. BYOB (no corkage). AE, MC, V. $$ **WHY** A chance to lunch with the Palisades set, plus no corkage fee. **WHAT** This is the place that triggered a local epiphany: "Healthy" food can actually taste good! Winning dishes include a delicious egg-white frittata with sausage and roasted vegetables. Get there before 11:30 for brunch or lunch and before 6 p.m. for dinner, or you'll wait, wait, wait. **WHO** Prosperous, huevos rancheros-lovin' locals. 🖼 🍽 ☺ ✿

[Cora's Coffee Shoppe] 1802 Ocean Ave., Santa Monica, 310.451.9562, corascoffee.com. B & L daily. Modern American. Beer & wine. MC, V. $ - $$ **WHY** Surprise: Aging starlet gets a good facelift and emerges lovelier than ever. **WHAT** High-end restaurateur Bruce Marder bought this miniature and adorable old diner and restored it, adding a funky but fetching bougainvillea-shaded patio furnished with marble tables and bistro chairs. It's a lovely place to linger over a burrata caprese omelet or the organic rotisserie chicken. You may linger longer than you intended (the service can be spotty) and pay more than you'd like, but nothing out of line for an outdoor café with really good food a block from the beach. **WHO** Everyone looks like a movie star trying not to be noticed, wearing jeans and no makeup. ♥ 🎵 🍽 ✿

[Cynthia's on the Corner] 1518 Montana Ave., Santa Monica, 310.394.7178, cynthiasonthecorner.com. B, L & D daily. American. BYOB. AE, MC, V. $ - $$ **WHY** The blackberry cobbler of your dreams, not to mention the bread pudding, mud pie and pecan pie. The food that comes first is great, too, especially the chopped salad, the fried chicken and the breakfast dishes. **WHAT** Cynthia Hirsh developed some notoriety some years ago at Cynthia's on 3rd Street, where her homey American food developed a huge following, but she herself was known for erratic, diva-like behavior. Eventually she shut the place down and went on a three-year sabbatical in Spain. Now she's back with this bright café and gourmet-to-go spot; her food's pretty much the same — which means terrific — and the sabbatical seems to have done her good. Excellent American comfort food at surprisingly low prices, sometimes served on the slow side. **WHO** Montana Avenue ladies who lunch — and who aren't afraid of real food. ⬚ ☺

[Figtree's Café] ⬚ 429 Oceanfront Walk, Venice, 310.392.4937, figtreescafe.com. B & L daily. American. Beer & wine. AE, MC, V. $ - $$ **WHY** Sunny-side-up tables overlooking the Venice Boardwalk and the beach beyond. **WHAT** Of the parade of tourist-bait sidewalk cafés on the Boardwalk, this has been our favorite since the '70s, when sandwiches with avocado and sprouts were considered exotic. Today we like the egg scrambles, turkey burgers and big salads. **WHO** Aged hippies and a new generation of tastefully tattooed young parents and their progeny. ⬚⬚☺ ⬚

[Huckleberry Bakery & Café] ⬚ 1014 Wilshire Blvd., Santa Monica, 310.451.2311, huckleberrycafe.com. B, L & early D daily. American/Bakery. No booze. AE, MC, V. $ - $$ **WHY** Really fantastic café food: sandwiches on fresh-made bread, homemade soups, a perfect chopped salad, wonderful desserts. **WHAT** The new bakery and café from the husband-and-wife chefs at Rustic Canyon, Josh Loeb and Zoe Nathan, is a place of deafening noise and recession-resistant crowds, who line up at breakfast and lunch to order not-inexpensive ciabatta sandwiches filled with burrata, marinated peppers and prosciutto; irresistibly aromatic rotisserie Jidori chicken; salads of flawless ingredients; and the best cookies we've had in ages. **WHO** Impeccably manicured westside women who don't bat an eye at $8 tarts. ⬚☺

[Izzy's Deli] 1433 Wilshire Blvd., Santa Monica, 310.394.1131, izzysdeli.com. B, L & D 24 hours daily. Deli. Beer & wine. AE, MC, V. $$ **WHY** Good, honest food served 24 hours a day — and valet parking is free during the day! **WHAT** An essential place to know about for anyone who's likely to find himself hungry on the westside at 3 a.m. Even at the more conventional hours, Izzy's serves reliable matzo ball soup, pastrami sandwiches, lox and bagels, brisket and all the deli classics. **WHO** A wonderful cross-section of old and young Santa Monica, including lots of families. ☺ ⬚☺

⬚ VEGETARIAN ☺ KID FRIENDLY ☼ PATIO DINING ⬚ DELIVERY ⬚ PRIVATE PARTY

[The Lazy Daisy] 2300 Pico Blvd., Santa Monica, 310.450.9011.
B & L daily. American. No booze. AE, MC, V. $ **WHY** A chance to hang
out with the local hipsters in a laid-back neighborhood café. **WHAT**
This funky-cute cottage across the street from Virginia Park is
emblematic of the gentrification of Santa Monica's Pico neighborhood. Pull up a chair at one of the adorable little tiled tables on the
ivy-shaded patio and enjoy one of the good-to-okay egg scrambles
or rosemary turkey burgers. Lackadaisical (maybe even lazy) service
lives up to the café's name, but hey, it's cool. 🍴🦞☺☼

[Le Pain Quotidien] 316 Santa Monica Blvd., Santa Monica,
310.393.6800; 11702 Barrington Ave., Brentwood, 310.476.0969,
painquotidien.com. B, L & D daily. Modern American/French. Beer & wine.
AE, MC, V. $ - $$ **WHY** Great chicken curry and egg salad open-face
sandwiches; good lemon tarts; inviting communal table with loaves
of bread serving as idiosyncratic napkin holders; excellent vegan and
vegetarian options. **WHAT** These Belgium-based cafés offer a level of
quality that's almost never seen in chains. Fresh, flavorful, often organic ingredients go into the delicious open-face sandwiches, quiches,
salads, soups and sweets. The bread, *naturellement*, is substantial and
flavorful. **WHO** Transplanted New Yorkers and others happy to see
their favorite Belgian import arrive in California. 🔄🦞☺☼

[Marmalade Café] 📖 3894 Cross Creek Rd., Malibu, 310.317.4242,
marmaladecafe.com. B, L & D daily. Modern American. Beer & wine. AE,
MC, V. $$ **WHY** Though not on the water, this is one of the best coastal
cafés around — and a perfect lunch stop if you're driving up the coast.
WHAT This branch of the Marmalade restaurant/caterer mini-chain
serves wine and has a fancier dining room than the Santa Monica
flagship. The draw is very good food in a casual, indoor/outdoor set-
ting and a chance to rub shoulders with Malibu types in their native
habitat. **WHO** Beautiful people — really beautiful people. ☼

[Panini Garden] 2715 Main St., Santa Monica, 310.399.9939,
paninigarden.com. B, L & D daily. Italian. No booze. AE, MC, V. $ - $$
WHY A hidden bit of heaven right on bustling Main Street. **WHAT** This
modest café is a sleeper find on Main Street — a welcome alternative
to the many overpriced or overly touristy eateries. Take your crisp,
absolutely delicious panini to the hidden rear garden, where umbrellas
shade the tables, lavender lines the walk and a fountain burbles. There
are also lots of good salads with organic fixings. 💵🍴🦞☺☼

[Patrick's Roadhouse] 106 Entrada Dr., Santa Monica,
310.459.4544, patricksroadhouse.info. B & L daily. American. No booze.
MC, V. $ **WHY** Tried and true classics served in vintage beach-bum
splendor. **WHAT** What looks like an oceanside Irish pub thanks to
the jolly green paint job is actually a booze-free greasy spoon that's
been greeting PCH passersby since 1974. The one-time hot dog joint

is now a hearty breakfast dive, complete with flea-market antiques, worn wood tables and a hodgepodge of photos (including of Arnold Schwarzenegger, who's been known to polish off a few rounds of scrambled eggs here). Go for the pancakes, omelets and scrambles. **WHO** Surfers, body builders, newspaper-toting locals.

[Sauce on Hampton] 259 Hampton Dr., Venice, 310.399.5400, sauceonhampton.com. B, L & D daily. American. BYOB. MC, V. $ **WHY** Shiraz frittata, a scramble with grilled onions, roma tomatoes and turmeric; luscious breakfast sandwiches; the chopped baby spinach salad; and a turkey burger that is juicier and more flavorful than most, topped with baby spinach, sliced tomato, red onion, applewood-smoked bacon and cheddar. **WHAT** A teeny café with teeny tables, this new spot is the product of gregarious chef/owner Sassan (Sass) Rostamian, formerly the lunch chef at Rustic Canyon. It perfectly suits the neighborhood: It's a breakfast place that doesn't open until 10 (Venice can make Silver Lake seem uptight and suburban), and everything is organic and carefully prepared but costs less than $11. **WHO** The sort of Venice folks who have breakfast at 10 a.m. — on weekdays.

SOUTH BAY TO SOUTH L.A.

[Claire's at the Museum] Long Beach Museum of Art, 2300 E. Ocean Blvd., Long Beach, 562.439.2119, ext. 270, lbma.org. B Sat.-Sun., L Tues.-Sun. Californian. Beer & wine. AE, MC, V. $$ **WHY** One of the most civilized spots in Long Beach for lunch and weekend breakfast, with a dazzling view of the harbor and good ladies-who-lunch food: crème brûlée french toast, salmon BLTs, chicken Caesars. **WHAT** Occupying the Arts & Crafts Elizabeth Milbank Anderson House on the museum grounds, with a lovely patio next to Claire Falkenstein's huge and dynamic water sculpture and a killer view of the harbor, this is a great place to take out-of-towners for a California dreamin' lunch or weekend breakfast. **WHO** Museum-goers, ladies who lunch, date-lunchers, Long Beach State professors.

[Coffee Cup Café] 3734 E. 4th St., Long Beach, 562.433.3292. B & L daily. American. No booze. Cash only. $ **WHY** The perfect coffee shop, with properly cooked omelets, amazingly good vegetarian chorizo and great coffee. **WHAT** No one seems to mind waiting 45 minutes for a table in this cheery yellow diner on weekends, and not just because of the free while-you-wait coffee — the food is that good. From the vegetarian breakfast burrito to the banana pancakes, everything is fresh and delicious. **WHO** Young couples with babies and strollers, over-70 couples, neighbors running into neighbors.

[Eat at Joe's] 400 N. Pacific Coast Hwy., Redondo Beach, 310.376.9570, i-eat-at-joes.com. B & L daily, D Mon.-Fri. American. Beer & wine. AE, MC, V. $ - $$ **WHY** Hearty diner breakfasts that are just what

VEGETARIAN **KID FRIENDLY** **PATIO DINING** **DELIVERY** **PRIVATE PARTY**

the hung-over Sunday morning crowd needs to cure what ails them. The really hungry get the John Wayne omelet. **WHAT** Huge portions of straightforward American breakfast chow (omelets, home fries, biscuits and gravy) are served to gregarious groups seated at big communal tables lined with picnic benches. Good burgers at lunchtime. **WHO** Families and shaggy twentysomethings recovering from a few too many the night before. 📷🍴☺

[Jitters Café] **190 Hermosa Ave., Hermosa Beach, 310.372.4712. B & L daily, D Thurs.-Sun. American. Beer & wine. MC, V. $ WHY** Very good breakfast fare, including locally famous muffins, served in a cheerful corner cottage a block from the beach. **WHAT** Jitters knows exactly what beach people want to eat, and it delivers the goods: excellent smoothies, great muffins, generous omelets and satisfying pancakes. Lunch is fine, but breakfast is the meal to get, and the wait isn't usually a problem — although service is often slow. **WHO** Volleyball players, surfers, dudes and retired beach people. 📷☺☼

[Jongewaard's Bake n Broil] 🏠 **3697 Atlantic Ave., Long Beach, 562.595.0396. B, L & D daily to 9 p.m. American. No booze. AE, MC, V. $ WHY** To sit at the counter and revel in a perfect pot pie and, to keep the theme going for dessert, a piece of brownie pie with vanilla ice cream. If you can't stay, pick up some frozen pot pies to take home, and for your next summer party, make sure to order the French peach pie. **WHAT** The Bake & Broil (which is what everyone calls it) has been Long Beach's comfort-food destination for ages, and it remains as good as its ever been. Hand-made burgers, fresh strawberry pancakes, Mexican breakfast scrambles, hot turkey sandwiches, red velvet cupcakes better than at all those trendy cupcakeries... it's the diner food you remember from the happy childhood you probably didn't have. **WHO** Bixby Knolls locals and families who've been driving a distance to eat here for many years. 📷☺

[Martha's 22nd Street Grill] **25 22nd St., Hermosa Beach, 310.376.7786. B & L daily. American. No booze. AE, MC, V. $ WHY** Very good breakfasts served outdoors overlooking the Hermosa Strand and the ocean. **WHAT** The parking's a nightmare, and you'll have to wait on weekends, but these are minor annoyances when faced with the reward of enjoying a glass of house-squeezed orange juice, a proper cup of coffee, very good fresh fruit and near-perfect eggs Benedict and omelets. A little bit of California heaven. **WHO** Bike-path cyclists, surfers and their dogs, who must wait patiently on the other side of the fence enclosing the patio. 📷🍴☺☼

[Mishi's Strudel] **309 W. 7th St., San Pedro, 310.832.6474, mishis-strudel.com. B & L Tues.-Sat. Hungarian. No booze. AE, MC, V. $ WHY** Fresh-baked strudel with Old World charm. **WHAT** This family-owned spot brings a taste of Hungary to the historic waterfront. Styled like a country café, Mishi's specializes in both sweet and savory strudels and crêpes. There are plenty of fruit-centric fillings, including apricot-almond and apple walnut, as well as such savory options as spinach, mushroom and cabbage. Slow down and stay awhile with a cup of coffee or tea. ☺ ◕

[North End Café] 🏠 **3421 Highland Ave., Manhattan Beach, 310.546.4782. B, L & D daily. American. No booze. MC, V. $ WHY** For the best breakfast in Manhattan Beach, and a terrific lunch, too — with a view of the ocean! The fries are worth the fat grams. **WHAT** Great coffee (try the coffee with a hint of orange peel) and excellent ingredients make this cheerful little café the breakfast and lunch spot of choice in Manhattan Beach. It's located well north from the mobs near the pier, but that doesn't mean you won't have to wait for a table. Panini are a specialty, for breakfast and lunch, and they all feature quality produce on fresh baguettes. Try the egg-bacon-cheese, the pesto-brie or the Cuban. **WHO** Locals who can walk here and El Porto surfers. ◕ ☺ ○

[Nosh Café] **617 S. Centre St., San Pedro, 310.514.1121. B & L daily. American/Australian. No booze. AE, MC, V. $ WHY** Thoughtful café cooking with a taste of Australia. **WHAT** Owner Susan McKenna is Australian, so her downtown San Pedro spot has a few Down Under offerings, including organic Weetabix for breakfast and flaky meat pies for lunch. Other fine dishes include the banana, Nutella and ricotta wrap; the rice pudding with poached pears and fresh fruit; the roast beef sandwich with caramelized onions, horseradish, grain mustard and greens; the delicious cookies and sweets (try the sticky date pudding) and a deli case full of great takeout. **WHO** Brunching neighbors and moms picking up takeout. ◕ ☺

[Pacific Diner] **3821 S. Pacific Ave., San Pedro, 310.831.5334. B & L Mon. & Wed.-Sun. American. No booze. MC, V. $ WHY** Hearty omelets, calamari and eggs, chicken-fried steak. **WHAT** Of San Pedro's several old-school breakfast diners, this is probably the most revered, more for its longevity and funky charm than its food — although the egg dishes go down just fine. **WHO** Cops, old longshoremen and assorted crusty San Pedro folks. ▧ ○

[Uncle Bill's Pancake House] **1305 Highland Ave., Manhattan Beach, 310.545.5177, unclebills.net. B & L daily. American. No booze. AE, MC, V. $ WHY** The coffee's so-so, but the pancakes, omelets and potato dishes are all very good. You're at the beach, you're eating banana pancakes ... what's not to be happy about? **WHAT** As you can guess from the name, breakfast is the name of the game at this not-far-from-the-beach café, where the weekend crowds are considerable (unless you arrive before 8:30 or 9 a.m.) and the buttermilk pancakes are as good as you'd hoped. **WHO** Families, businesspeople meeting over omelets, surfers refueling after a dawn session. ▧ ☺ ○

◕ **VEGETARIAN** ☺ **KID FRIENDLY** ○ **PATIO DINING** ▧ **DELIVERY** 🏠 **PRIVATE PARTY**

Coffee, Tea + Juices

Finding a decent coffee, tea or juice drink is easy in L.A. — in some areas you can't go more than a block without seeing a Starbucks, Coffee Bean or Jamba Juice. But instead, please explore the independent places found in almost every neighborhood. Here you'll find our favorites.

[ESSENTIALLY L.A.]

Aroma Café, Studio City (PAGE 212)
Café Corsa, USC (PAGE 206)
The Conservatory, Culver City (PAGE 214)
Funnel Mill, Santa Monica (PAGE 216)
Graffeo Coffee, Beverly Hills (PAGE 214)
Intelligentsia, Silver Lake (PAGE 206)
Intelligentsia Venice Coffeebar (PAGE 217)
Jin Patisserie, Venice (PAGE 210)
Jones Coffee, Pasadena (PAGE 210)
LA Mill, Silver Lake (PAGE 207)
Langham Huntington Hotel, Pasadena (PAGE 211)
Oaxacalifornia Juice Bar, USC (PAGE 208)
Royal/T Café, Culver City (PAGE 215)
Sanjang Coffee Garden, Silver Lake (PAGE 205)
Ten Ren Tea, Chinatown (PAGE 208)
Tierra Mia Coffee, South Gate (PAGE 221)
Tudor House, Santa Monica (PAGE 219)
Urth Caffé, Santa Monica (PAGE 219)

🏛 ESSENTIALLY L.A. �》LATE ♥ROMANTIC 🗟 VALUE ⑨ QUIET ❀ SUSTAINABLE

THESE CAFÉS AND BAKERIES
ALSO SERVE QUALITY COFFEE AND TEA DRINKS
AND WILL OFTEN MAKE THEM TO TAKE OUT:

3 Square Café & Bakery, Venice (PAGE 195)
Alcove Café & Bakery, Los Feliz (PAGE 180)
Amandine Patisserie, West L.A. (PAGE 290)
Belwood Bakery, Brentwood (PAGE 291)
BLD, Beverly/Third (PAGE 180)
Bloom Café, Mid-City (PAGE 180)
Bookmark Café, Santa Monica (PAGE 195)
Bread & Porridge, Santa Monica (PAGE 196)
Breadworks, West L.A. (PAGE 275)
Butter Tart, Glassell Park (PAGE 278)
CaCao Mexicatessen, Eagle Rock (PAGE 66)
Café Tropical, Silver Lake (PAGE 184)
Clementine, Century City (PAGE 287)
Coffee Cup Café, Long Beach (PAGE 199)
Euro Pane, Pasadena (PAGE 187)
The Farm of Beverly Hills, Fairfax District &
Beverly Hills (PAGES 181 & 194)
Food + Lab, West Hollywood (PAGE 181)
Heirloom Bakery, South Pasadena (PAGE 282)
La Maison du Pain, Mid-City (PAGE 276)
Le Pain Quotidien, Pasadena, Brentwood &
Santa Monica (PAGES 188 & 198)
Little Flower Candy Co., Pasadena (PAGE 283)
Marmalade Café, Malibu (PAGE 198)
Milk, Beverly/Third (PAGE 182)
Ugo's Italian Deli, Sierra Madre (PAGE 189)

CENTRAL CITY

[Beverly Hills Juice Club] **8382 Beverly Blvd., Beverly/Third, 323.655.8300, beverlyhillsjuice.com. Mon.-Fri. from 7 a.m., Sat. from 10 a.m. MC, V. WHY** Cold-pressed apple juice blends that are totally delish — try the apple strawberry or apple ginger. **WHAT** It's not really in Beverly Hills, but a harmless bit of false advertising is no reason to shun this teeny place, which specializes in cold-pressed fruit juices, wheatgrass, carrot juices and smoothie-like, banana-based creations. **WHO** Healthful sorts on their way to Spinning or Pilates. ☺�]

[Chado Tea Room] **8422 W. 3rd St., Beverly/Third, 323.655.2056, chadotea.com. Daily from 11:30 a.m. MC, V. WHY** More than 200 varieties of tea, a tranquil setting and a yellow-coconut cake that you'll want to lie down in, because it's so hypnotically sweet and moist. **WHAT** It's really all about the tea — hundreds of teas, actually, from Darjeeling biodynamic green tea to intensely smoky Tarry Souchong, all properly brewed in a pot. A good selection of delicate sandwiches and pastries and a decadent afternoon tea menu make Chado a perfect stop for lunch or an afternoon pick-me-up. **WHO** Lots o' women celebrating birthdays, taking their teens out for a treat and pausing for a shopping break. But men aren't afraid of the place. 🕝 🍴🌿

[Groundwork] **1501 N. Cahuenga Blvd., Hollywood, 323.871.0107, lacoffee.com. Mon.-Fri. from 7 a.m., Sat.-Sun. from 8 a.m. AE, MC, V. WHY** Organic drip coffee (Ethiopian Nile) good enough to convert a latte lover; friendly baristas who know their foam drawings. **WHAT** A small, hip, L.A. coffee roaster with a social conscience and locations in areas that need them most — like this heart-of-Hollywood spot. Good coffee and perfectly decent pastries. **WHO** Hollywood night owls straggling in late in the morning for a hangover-killing jolt of java. 🕝☺☼

[Insomnia Café] **7286 Beverly Blvd., Beverly/Third, 323.931.4943. Daily from 10 a.m. Cash only. WHY** A convenient location, comfy furniture and no-cell-phone policy make this a good spot for working or meeting someone, although parking can be tricky, and the WiFi's not free. **WHAT** This longtime caffeination station is a relaxed, friendly and very quiet place, with respectable coffee drinks and good snacks — and it's open until 1:30 a.m. **WHO** Screenwriters, freelance writers, students and a post-theater crowd. ☺ 🕝 🍴

[Psychobabble] **1866 N. Vermont Ave., Los Feliz, 323.664.7500. Mon.-Sat. from 7 a.m., Sun. from 8 a.m. AE, MC, V. WHY** Quality looseleaf teas, respectable lattes, WiFi and an artsy-fartsy Los Feliz vibe. **WHAT** A neighborhood coffeehouse in one of L.A.'s coolest neighborhoods, this place shows work from local artists, hosts stand-up comics on Friday nights and offers an open-mic night on Sundays. It also makes a good panini and provides two hours of WiFi with any purchase. **WHO** Screenwriters, songwriters, letter writers ... lots of people scribbling in notebooks or tapping on keyboards. ☺ ☼

[Sabor y Cultura] 5625 Hollywood Blvd., Hollywood, 323.466.0481, saborycultura.com. Mon.-Fri. from 6:30 a.m., Sat.-Sun. from 7:30 a.m. AE, MC, V. **WHY** A friendly vibe, fairly easy street parking, free WiFi and skilled baristas. **WHAT** A double-wide storefront in Little Armenia, this spacious, inviting coffeehouse doesn't display the sort of Latin influences you might expect from its name. It's just an all-around good place to hang out over a latte, a hot breakfast sandwich, a frozen yogurt or a snack. Check for events: art openings, music perfor-mances, perhaps even flamenco dance. **WHO** A typical coffeehouse crowd, East Hollywood style. ☺ ☽ ☼

[Sanjang Coffee Garden] 🏛 101 S. Virgil Ave., East Hollywood, 213.387.9190. Daily from 11 a.m. Korean. AE, MC, V. **WHY** Coffee and tea drinks such as boba, Korean snacks, desserts and sandwiches. Drink prices are on the high side because many patrons stay for hours just ordering one drink. **WHAT** The lavish space catering to the Korean community features several heated outdoor areas, including one with a firepit. All the amenities are provided including free WiFi and blan-kets for snuggling by the fire, and it's open until 2 a.m. **WHO** Young Korean night owls — mostly smokers — and the occasional curious non-Korean. ☺ ☼

[Stir Crazy] 6903 Melrose Ave., Melrose, 323.934.4656. Mon.-Fri. from 7 a.m., Sat.-Sun. from 8 a.m. MC, V. **WHY** A mellow (despite the name) hangout with good coffee and smoothies. **WHAT** A friendly neighborhood coffeehouse with free WiFi, lots of Laptop People (but note that laptops are banished after 7 p.m.) and good coffee made until midnight, sometimes even later. **WHO** Writers and locals who want to look like writers, tapping away on their MacBooks while sipping nonfat lattes. ▦ ☼

[T] Farmers Market, 6333 W. 3rd St., Fairfax District, 323.930.0076, farmersmarketla.com. Daily from 9 a.m. MC, V. **WHY** Bypass the chains for this charming stall with hundreds of bulk teas, and tea drinks to en-joy in the Farmers Market bustle. **WHAT** Have a cuppa and a sandwich or take home exotic varieties of herbal and traditional teas. ☺ ☼

[Urth Caffé] 8565 Melrose Ave., West Hollywood, 310.659.0628, urthcaffe.com. Daily from 9 a.m. MC, V. **WHY** Spanish lattes, tea lattes and all-around good drinks, most of which are organic and/or sustain-ably produced. Don't mind the poseurs and enjoy the coffee and excel-lent oatmeal or pumpkin pie. **WHAT** Sure, it's a Hollywood scene, and the parking is terrible, but you could do far worse in this 'hood for coffee, tea and/or a light meal. The baristas are skilled, the products are good, and the patio is a fine place to catch up with an old friend.

🌿VEGETARIAN ⊙ KID FRIENDLY ☼ PATIO DINING 🚗 DELIVERY 🏠 PRIVATE PARTY

WHO Actors, screenwriters and assorted pretty people — a stereotypical L.A. crowd. 🌀🍸☽

EASTSIDE

[Café Corsa] 🏛 2238 S. Figueroa St., USC, 213.746.2604. Daily from 7 a.m. MC, V. **WHY** It's the least pretentious — and least expensive — place in town to enjoy coffee brewed by individual cup in a Clover machine. **WHAT** Hidden in a strip mall on South Figueroa between Staples Center and USC, this place is a total find for serious coffee lovers. It has a good and often-varying selection of fair-trade beans from around the world, a skilled barista and a cherished Clover machine, which allows aficionados to sample all sorts of coffees for as low as $2 a brewed cup (take that, LA Mill!). **WHO** The coffee-savvy from Downtown, USC and West Adams. 📝🌀

[Café de Leche] 5000 York Blvd., Highland Park, 323.551.6828, cafedeleche.net. Daily from 7 a.m. Cash only. **WHY** This young café is everything that this gentrifying neighborhood promises to be: accessible, affordable and full of adorably attired babies. **WHAT** At the corner of York and Avenue 50, this is a perfect little coffeehouse in a neighborhood that needed it. The menu is small, but the staff takes care with what is there, and everything is delicious (try the hot jalapeño bagels). There's a fantastic selection of organic teas, as well as the expected lattes and mochas — and an amazingly creamy hot chocolate that's full of spices. A row of little tables is perfect for laptops, and there are enough outlets for them all — plus free wireless. **WHO** Twentysomethings working at their laptops and indie parents with cute indie children. 📝🌀🍸☺

[Coffee Table] 2930 Rowena Ave., Silver Lake, 323.644.8111. Daily from 7 a.m. AE, MC, V. **WHY** Because the front patio and back porch are spacious and the menu is broad enough for any time of day. **WHAT** This Silver Lake stalwart offers not only a full range of coffee drinks but also hearty breakfast burritos, a decent burger, salads and desserts. **WHO** Silver Lake moms, screenwriters jousting over power outlets, and dog owners. 🍸☺☽

[Intelligentsia Coffee] 🏛 3922 W. Sunset Blvd., Silver Lake, 323.663.6173, intelligentsiacoffee.com. Daily from 6 a.m. AE, MC, V. **WHY** A very serious approach to coffee, but without the snobbiness seen at some other Clover-stocked joints. **WHAT** Silver Lake's intelligentsia — those who can afford your higher-end coffees, that is — belly up to the bar or snag a Sunset Junction patio table to linger over aromatic, beautifully prepared Clover coffee or espresso drinks. **WHO** Silver Lake cool people — and isn't everyone who lives in Silver Lake cool? 🌀☽

🏛 **ESSENTIALLY L.A.** ☽ **LATE** ♥ **ROMANTIC** 📝 **VALUE** 🔔 **QUIET** 🌀 **SUSTAINABLE**

[Kaldi] **3147 Glendale Blvd., Atwater, 323.660.6005. Mon.-Fri. from 6:30 a.m, Sat.-Sun. from 7 a.m. MC, V. WHY** Smaller than the South Pasadena location, this funky coffeehouse offers free WiFi and sidewalk tables that are prime for people-watching. **WHAT** This is the place to come for sturdy cappuccinos and plenty of other coffee and tea permutations, but don't come hungry — food selections are minimal. **WHO** Trendy young couples and families from Atwater's quickly gentrifying population. 📷 ☼

[LA Mill] 📖 **1636 Silver Lake Blvd., Silver Lake, 323.663.4441, lamillcoffee.com. Daily from 7 a.m. AE, MC, V. WHY** For an obsessive approach to perfect coffee, made in a Clover or tableside via Chemex, served in the swankiest coffee shop in town. Excellent cold-brewed iced coffee, too. **WHAT** Is it a coffeehouse or a restaurant? Lately the answer seems the latter, with consulting chef Michael Cimarusti (Providence) having created what is surely the poshest coffeehouse menu in town. But you can still come here just for a cup of hand-brewed coffee or a meticulously crafted latte, though you'll have to order it from a waiter instead of at a counter, and you'd better not be in a rush. If you're a serious coffee person, you've probably already been here. If you're not, it's probably not worth it just for a cup of coffee — but it might be worth it for a foodie lunch. **WHO** People who can order a $7 cup of coffee and live with themselves. ☼

[Lot 44 Coffee] **257 S. Spring St., Downtown, 213.626.4646, lot44coffee.com. Mon.-Fri. from 7 a.m. MC, V. WHY** Organic, fair-trade drip coffee that's ground and brewed to order, as well as free WiFi and plenty of seating to make use of it. **WHAT** In the heart of Downtown's gallery row, this new coffee bar is full of ambition. It's showing art in its 2,500-square-foot industrial-chic space, it hires seriously schooled baristas, and it clearly has ambitions to be a chain. Baked goods come from Blue Cupcake next door, and you'll also find light breakfast and lunch dishes. All in all, Downtown residents (of whom there are more every day) should be thrilled with this new neighbor. At this writing it wasn't open on weekends, but that may well change by the time you read this. **WHO** A lot more tattooed, skinny-jeans kids than you'd expect in such a modern Downtown setting. 🏠📷 ☼

[The Novel Café] **811 E. Traction Ave., Little Tokyo/Arts District, 213.621.2240, novelcafe.com. Mon.-Fri. from 7 a.m., Sat.-Sun. from 8 a.m. AE, MC, V. WHY** Good-enough Groundworks coffee, a hang-as-long-as-you-like vibe and a location in the hip Arts District. **WHAT** This ahead-of-the-curve Arts District coffeehouse changed from a Groundworks into an offshoot of Venice's fast-expanding Novel Café, but hardly anything changed. It's still scruffily pleasant, staffed by heavily tattooed young folks, and it has a big menu of wraps, pastries, salads and such — although we stick to the coffee and do our eating on the next block at Wurstküche, home of terrific sau-

---

🍃 **VEGETARIAN** ☼ **KID FRIENDLY** ☼ **PATIO DINING** 🚐 **DELIVERY** 🏠 **PRIVATE PARTY**

sage sandwiches. **WHO** Rocker-artist loft kids and a few casual-Friday types getting their dogs out of the loft for a walk. 🗊 ⟳ ☼

[Oaxacalifornia Juice Bar] 🏠 Mercado la Paloma, 3655 S. Grand Ave., USC, 213.747.8622, mercadolapaloma.com. Daily from 8 a.m. Mexican/Oaxacan. MC, V. **WHY** Delicious, fresh licuados, smoothies and juices. **WHAT** In Mercado la Paloma, a nonprofit community center with restaurants, shops and meeting spaces, this Oaxacan spot makes very good juice drinks that go beautifully with the tacos from neighboring Taqueria Vista Hermosa. Homemade ice creams, too. **WHO** Latino families and USC students. 🗊 ⬛ ☼

[Primera Taza] 1850 1/2 1st St., Boyle Heights, 323.780.3923, primerataza.com. Mon.-Fri. from 7 a.m., Sat.-Sun. from 8 a.m. MC, V. **WHY** A place to hang in bitchin' Boyle Heights. **WHAT** On the verge of opening at press time, this coffeehouse is emblematic of the gentrification of Boyle Heights (in case you didn't know, it's the new Echo Park, which in turn was the new Silver Lake only yesterday), thanks in part to the new Metro station out front, not to mention the residential settling of nearby Downtown. It has all the essentials: free WiFi, art for sale on the walls, occasional live music and the expected roster of coffee drinks and pastries. **WHO** Boyle Heights cool people and east Downtowners making the trek over the 1st Street bridge. 🗊 ☼

[Swörk] 2160 Colorado Blvd., Eagle Rock, 323.258.5600, sworkcoffee. com. Daily from 6 a.m. AE, MC, V. **WHY** Dark-roast Truck Driver blend coffee; free WiFi; and kids' drinks like the Princess Potion. **WHAT** This hip corner storefront with Ikea-style décor opened in 2000 and brought good coffee, free WiFi and a stylish yet family-friendly vibe to no-longer-sleepy Eagle Rock. **WHO** Moms and dads drawn by the irresistible combo of strong caffeine and a kids' play area; loyal locals with laptops or screenplays to read. ⬛ ☼ ⟳

[Ten Ren Tea] 🏠 727 N. Broadway, Chinatown, 213.626.8844, tenren.com. Daily from 9:30 a.m. Chinese. AE, MC, V. **WHY** Bulk teas, ginseng and hot teas, iced teas and iced milk teas to sip in the shop. **WHAT** This Chinatown branch of the international tea company has a loyal following for its bulk teas from around the world: green, jasmine, black, Pouchong, Ti Kuan, organic teas, flavored teas and more. Take a break and sit down with an iced bubble (*boba*) tea or a pot of King's Tea. 🗊

[Tropical Zone Ice Cream & Juice Bar] Grand Central Market, 317 S. Broadway, Downtown, 213.617.2233. Daily from 9 a.m. Cash only. **WHY** This vintage juice bar is a throwback to the days when fruit juices were considered exotic health foods. **WHAT** This venerable stand offers a large selection of juices, including tropical fruits, and

smoothie combinations at reasonable prices. There's ice cream, too.
WHO Grand Central Market's endless parade of Downtown office
workers, Latino shoppers and dutiful citizens on jury duty. ⊞ ☺

[Urth Caffé] 451 S. Hewitt St., Little Tokyo/Arts District, 213.797.4534,
urthcaffe.com. Daily from 6 a.m. MC, V. **WHY** Spanish lattes, tea lattes
and all-around good drinks, most of which are organic and/or sustain-
ably produced. And did we mention free, guarded parking? In the
heart of Downtown's Arts District, no less?? **WHAT** It's pricey, and
sometimes too crowded, but when you factor in the free parking, free
WiFi and high-quality food (try the turkey burger and pumpkin pie),
you could do far worse Downtown. The baristas are skilled, the bakery
is good, and the patio is a pleasant place to talk shop. **WHO** Young
Downtowners who look like they'd live in Santa Monica. ☺ ☙ ☼

SAN GABRIEL VALLEY

[Au 79 Tea Spirit] 1635 S. San Gabriel Blvd., San Gabriel,
626.569.9768. Daily from 11 a.m. Asian. MC, V. **WHY** A huge selection of tea drinks and bobas; we love the lavender infusion. **WHAT** A
happening Taiwanese tea and boba hangout, with a TV blaring by day,
music playing by night and very good tea drinks all the time.
WHO Young Taiwanese hipsters in animated conversation. ☺ ☺

[Bean Town Coffee Bar] 45 N. Baldwin Ave., Sierra Madre,
626.355.1596, beantowncoffeebar.com. Daily from 5:30 a.m. MC, V.
WHY Because it makes you want to move to Sierra Madre just so you
can hang out here. **WHAT** This just might be the perfect coffeehouse —
robust java, funky-but-comfortable furniture and a terrifically diverse
crowd. All that plus bluegrass and folk music on the weekends, WiFi,
board games, sidewalk tables and homemade baked goods. **WHO** Book
clubbers, retirees, moms with strollers, teens, dogs. ⊞ ☺ ☼

[Buster's] 1006 Mission St., South Pasadena, 626.441.0744. Daily
from 7 a.m. Cash only. **WHY** Lime rickeys, Fosselman's ice cream and
gentle baristas. **WHAT** A few steps from the Gold Line, this colorful neighborhood hub offers prime people-watching from a handful
of sidewalk tables. Or grab an inside table (upstairs or down) to sip
a latte or savor a scoop of mint chip. **WHO** School kids, commuters,
nearby loft-dwellers and music fans (local performers are showcased
on weekend nights). ☺ ☼

[Chado Tea Room] 79 N. Raymond Ave., Pasadena, 626.431.2832,
chadotea.com. Daily from 11:30 a.m. MC, V. **WHY** More than 200 varieties of tea, and a yellow-coconut cake that you'll want to lie down in,
because it's so hypnotically sweet and moist. **WHAT** An afternoon tea
room with an English look, knowledgeable servers, full high-tea

⬙ VEGETARIAN ◉ KID FRIENDLY ✿ PATIO DINING ⇛ DELIVERY ☗ PRIVATE PARTY service and many good teas. **WHO** Lots o' women celebrating birthdays, taking their teens out for a treat and pausing for an Old Town shopping break. 📷 📍 🔖

[The Coffee Gallery] 2029 N. Lake Ave., Altadena, 626.398.7917, coffeegallery.com. Mon.-Fri. from 6 a.m., Sat.-Sun. from 7 a.m. MC, V. **WHY** You can hang out as long as you like, and the private room is great for a committee meeting. **WHAT** Maybe it's not the best coffee in town — and the service is often bizarrely slow — but there's something endearing about this appealingly scruffy place anyway. For one thing, the live music in the separate concert room is often amazing. **WHO** A cast of Altadena characters, from local politicians to aging hippies to moms 'n kids. 📷 📍 ☺ ☼ 🏠

[Fresh Roast] 308 S. San Gabriel Blvd., San Gabriel, 626.451.5918. Daily from 7 a.m. MC, V. **WHY** Roasted-on-site coffee, in bulk or to drink here, prepared by the Chinese-American owner, Jimmy, who's brought his passion for coffee to a neighborhood that needed it. Great prices, too. **WHAT** This coffee roaster, coffeehouse and juice bar is a real find in the neighborhood, run by a friendly guy who wants everyone to love coffee as much as he does. Fresh-roasted beans are just $8 a pound; espressos and lattes are carefully made; and the juice selection (coconut, orange, sugar-cane) is seductive. Best of all, each cup of of brewed coffee is made to order — Jimmy doesn't believe in having coffee sit around. 📷 ☼

[Jones Coffee] 🏛 537 S. Raymond Ave., Pasadena, 626.564.9291, thebestcoffee.com. Mon.-Fri. from 7:30 a.m., Sat.-Sun. from 9 a.m. AE, MC, V. **WHY** The best latte on the eastside, great house-roasted beans and free WiFi. **WHAT** This small warehouse is filled with giant roasters, burlap bags of coffee beans and a few nooks for sipping and reading. The globe-hopping selection of coffee (including organic choices) includes green beans for home-roasting and offerings from the proprietors' Guatemalan coffee plantation. The prices can't be beat, with a weekly special for just $6.95 a pound. And the espresso drinks are exquisitely crafted. **WHO** Writers, moms, artists, Caltech and Art Center profs and students, Huntington docs... everyone who's anyone in Pasadena. 📷 ♻ ☼

[Kaldi] 1019 El Centro St., South Pasadena, 626.403.5951. Mon.-Fri. from 7 a.m., Sat.-Sun. from 7:30 a.m. AE, MC, V. **WHY** An authentic and appealing slice of European-style café life, right in the middle of Small Town, U.S.A. **WHAT** The sultry purple neon sign beckons passersby into this popular local hangout in a handsome old brick building across the street from the library. On the menu: well-made espresso drinks, a welcoming vibe and sunny sidewalk tables. **WHO** Students and game players who favor the outdoor tables; freshly coiffed patrons of the salon next door; errand-runners and library patrons. 📍 ☼

🏛 **ESSENTIALLY L.A.** ☺ **LATE** ♥ **ROMANTIC** 📷 **VALUE** 📍 **QUIET** ♻ **SUSTAINABLE**

[Langham Huntington Hotel] 1401 S. Oak Knoll Ave., Pasadena, 626.585.6218, pasadena.langhamhotels.com. Thurs.-Sun. from 1 p.m. AE, MC, V. **WHY** A proper silver tea service, heavenly scones and, for those who must, good Champagne. **WHAT** The swankiest afternoon tea east of Beverly Hills is served in the lobby lounge at this lovely Pasadena landmark. White linens, formal service, tiered trays of scones, sandwiches and pastries all reassure one that the barbarians are safely on the other side of the gate. The price will sober you up, but what a way to go! **WHO** Blue-blood grandmothers taking their granddaughters to tea. ♥ ◑ ☺

[Peet's Coffee & Tea] 605 S. Lake Ave., Pasadena, 626.795.7413, peets.com. Daily from 6 a.m. AE, MC, V. **WHY** Major Dickason's blend. **WHAT** If you must drink at a chain, this estimable Bay Area institution is the one to pick. The coffee drinks are robust and made by actual baristas, the take-home beans are addictive and thoughtfully ground, and all the Southern California locations seem to have been carefully chosen to showcase Peets' outdoor tables in lively, people-watching neighborhoods. Delectable baked goods, too. **WHO** Parents after drop-off at Pasadena's nearby Polytechnic School; Lake Avenue shoppers; Caltech profs; homesick Northern Californians. ◑ ☺ ✿

[Perry's Joint] 2051 Lincoln Ave., Pasadena, 626.798.4700, perrysjoint.com. Mon.-Fri. from 8 a.m., Sat. from 10 a.m. MC, V. **WHY** Can't beat the soundtrack — great jazz on the stereo. **WHAT** A sophisticated, spacious spot, Perry's is a terrific place to hold small business meetings or to work on your laptop (free WiFi). Good coffee, tasty sandwiches and a full range of Dreyer's ice cream. **WHO** The hipper sorts of northwest Pasadenans, after-school kids and employees of local nonprofits holding meetings. ▣ ◑ ☺

[Scarlet Tea Room] 18 W. Green St., Pasadena, 626.577.0051, scarlettearoom.com. Tues.-Sun. from 11 a.m. AE, MC, V. **WHY** A serene afternoon tea service with delectable scones and the best strawberry jam around. **WHAT** Tea-party groups meet here for the peaceful, gilt-trimmed setting and handy Old Pasadena location. If you can't make it for the finger sandwiches, check out the gourmet dinner on Friday and Saturday nights with live jazz. ♥ ◑

[Ten Ren & Tea Station] 154 & 158 W. Valley Blvd., San Gabriel, 626.288.1663, tenren.com. Daily from 11:30 a.m. Chinese. AE, MC, V. **WHY** A good range of teas, delicious fried tofu and tasty taro balls. **WHAT** This tea-dealing chain is part retail store, part Chinese tea room. You can buy bulk green, jasmine, black, Pouchong, flavored, organic and pretty much any other kind of tea, or sit down next door with a properly brewed cup or a refreshing boba. ▣ ✎ ☺

🍃 VEGETARIAN ◉ KID FRIENDLY ✿ PATIO DINING 🚍 DELIVERY 🏛 PRIVATE PARTY

[Ten Ren Tea] 111 W. Garvey Ave., Monterey Park, 626.288.2012, tenren.com. Daily from 9:30 a.m. Chinese. AE, MC, V. **WHY** Bulk teas, ginseng and hot teas, iced teas and iced milk teas to sip in the shop. **WHAT** A branch of the international tea company, this place has a loyal following for its bulk teas from around the world: green, jasmine, black, Pouchong, Ti Kuan, organic teas, flavored teas and more. Take a break and sit down with an iced bubble (*boba*) tea or a pot of King's Tea. 🍵 🎵 📞

[Zephyr Coffee House & Art Gallery] 2419 E. Colorado Blvd., East Pasadena, 626.793.7330, zephyrcoffeeandart.com. Mon.-Sat. from 8 a.m., Sun. from 9 a.m. MC, V. **WHY** A place to join the regulars and settle in for hours with newspaper or laptop. Often-worthwhile music on weekend nights. **WHAT** This hidden gem is a Craftsman cottage suffused with Zen-like beauty and calm. Comfy sofas, tree-shaded patio tables and a menu that includes tasty crêpes. **WHO** Art students, hookah smokers on the side patio, and the sort of Pasadenan who sends her child to a co-op nursery school and has her own vegetable garden. ♥📞☼

[Zona Rosa] 15 S. El Molino Ave., Pasadena, 626.793.2334, zonarosacaffe.com. Mon.-Sat. 7:30 a.m., Sun. from 9 a.m. Mexican. Cash only. **WHY** Heavenly Mexican hot chocolate to sip in the charming and romantic upstairs room. **WHAT** Tiny and vividly colorful, this coffeehouse has Mexican flair and a prime location next to the Pasadena Playhouse. **WHO** Shoppers, strollers, readers and theater-goers — in addition to the Playhouse next door, there's an art-house Laemmle multiplex and the great bookstore Vroman's just around the corner on Colorado. ♥ 🎵 ☼

EAST VALLEY

[Aroma Café] 🏠 4360 Tujunga Ave., Studio City, 818.508.0677, aromacoffeeandtea.com. Mon.-Sat. from 6 a.m., Sun. from 6:30 a.m. MC, V. **WHY** Well-made iced lattes, cappuccinos and chai drinks to drink on a patio of tremendous charm. **WHAT** Owned by the same folks behind Alcove in Los Feliz, this café/coffeehouse/bookstore is in a fetching old cottage with a lovely enclosed brick patio. The menu is extensive, but it's fine to just have coffee. Partial table service (order at the counter) can be spotty and a little full of attitude, and you'll have to wait at peak times, but the coffee, food and setting are usually worth it. **WHO** Studio City beautiful people, including lots of writers toiling away. ♥📞☼

[Coffee Roaster] 13567 Ventura Blvd., Sherman Oaks, 818.905.9719, thecoffeeroaster.net. Mon.-Sat. from 7 a.m. MC, V. **WHY** Roasted on-site beans sold by the pound, and robust coffee drinks to take away or drink in the tiny café. **WHAT** This longstanding Valley shop roasts beans to sell both retail and wholesale. That's it's main business, but it also makes lattes, mochas and brewed blends.

[M Street Coffee] 13251 Moorpark St., Sherman Oaks, 818.907.1400, mstreetcoffee.com. Mon.-Fri. from 7 a.m., Sat.-Sun. from 8 a.m. MC, V. **WHY** Nice people, good coffee and chai, copies of the *L.A. Weekly* and free WiFi. **WHAT** A bright yet soothing space done in earth tones makes for a comfortable spot to sit with a cappuccino or an iced chai latte. **WHO** Writers, artists, friends meeting to chat quietly and assorted Starbucks refugees. ☼

[Priscilla's Gourmet Coffee] 4150 W. Riverside Dr., Toluca Lake, 818.843.5707, priscillascoffee.com. Daily from 6 a.m. AE, MC, V. **WHY** A lovely, relaxed neighborhood hangout, and good cinnamon streusel, too. **WHAT** We wish the coffee was better, but we forgive Priscilla's any faults. It still has a lot more personality, not to mention better coffee, than Starbucks, and it's the best option in this neighborhood. Free WiFi, amusing industry eavesdropping and good coffeehouse snacks. **WHO** TV writers, production people, beautiful actress/moms — the usual Toluca Lake crowd. ☺ 📷🐾☺☼

WEST VALLEY

[Java Groove Coffee House] 14310 Victory Blvd., Van Nuys, 818.785.6593, javagroovecoffee.com. Mon.-Fri. from 7 a.m., Sat. from 9 a.m. MC, V. **WHY** Perfectly respectable Illy coffee drinks (lattes, americanos), teas and chai in a part of the Valley that is woefully short on indie coffeehouses. **WHAT** A fine, all-around coffeehouse with the usual offerings: coffee drinks, smoothies, bagels, panini, free WiFi and, for an extra treat, belgian waffles. ☺☼

[Peet's Coffee & Tea] 18973 Ventura Blvd., Tarzana, 818.401.0263, peets.com. Daily from 5 a.m. AE, MC, V. **WHY** True neighborhood coffeehouses are as rare as cool summer days in the West Valley, so Peet's is the next best thing — or the best thing, depending on how hooked you are on Major Dickason's Blend. **WHAT** If you must drink at a chain, this estimable Bay Area institution is the one to pick. The coffee drinks are robust and made by actual baristas, the take-home beans are addictive and thoughtfully ground, and all the Southern California locations seem to have been carefully chosen to showcase Peets' outdoor tables in lively, people-watching neighborhoods. Delectable baked goods, too. ☺☼

[Rocky Roaster] 7239 Canoga Ave., Canoga Park, 818.347.1378, rockyroaster.com. Mon.-Fri. from 6:30 a.m., Sat. from 8 a.m. MC, V. **WHY** For take-home organic and/or fair trade beans, roasted on-site, and an excellent cup of coffee while you're there. **WHAT** Rocky Rhodes (yes, that's his name) has a thriving roasting business here, and he

Coffee, Tea + Juices

🌿 **VEGETARIAN** ⊙ **KID FRIENDLY** ☼ **PATIO DINING** 🚚 **DELIVERY** 🎪 **PRIVATE PARTY**

also sells beans from fair-trade sources for the ambitious to roast at home. Next door is a no-frills coffeehouse that makes the best coffee for miles around. **WHO** Restaurateurs buying wholesale and everyday coffee junkies desperate for the real thing in the Valley. 🖼️ 🍃

WESTSIDE: CENTRAL

[The Conservatory] 🏠 10117 Washington Blvd., Culver City, 310.558.0436, conservatorycoffeeandtea.com. Mon.-Fri. from 7 a.m., Sat. from 8 a.m. AE, MC, V. **WHY** Subtle, artful roasting in a low-key yet cool environment where the bean is king. Seriously good cocoa, too. **WHAT** The on-site roasting makes this a coffeehouse for aficionados. Fans sing the praises of the nuanced brews and drive happily from the Valley or beyond just to buy a pound. The location, right across the street from Sony Studios, is a handy place to caffeinate before a pitch meeting. **WHO** Culver City locals, studio musicians, screenwriters and anyone with business at that big studio across the street. 🍃 ☺ ☼

[Espresso Profeta] 1129 Glendon Ave., Westwood, 310.208.3375. Mon.-Fri. from 6 a.m., Sat.-Sun. from 7 a.m. MC, V. **WHY** Just when you think Westwood is nothing but chains, you find this charming spot with rich, creamy espresso pulled by people who love it. **WHAT** In a 1927 brick building in the heart of the Village, Espresso Profeta has it all: beautiful coffee drinks made from custom-roasted beans, food from Breadbar and Buttercake Bakery, free WiFi and comfy spots to hang out. **WHO** Your more sophisticated UCLA student. ☼ 🍹

[Euro Caffé] 9559 S. Santa Monica Blvd., Beverly Hills, 310.274.9070. Mon.-Sat. from 7 a.m. Italian. MC, V. **WHY** For true Italian espresso drinks made from a giant brass R2-D2 machine, with good panini and baked goods, too. **WHAT** This small café is authentically Italian — which means no hanging around with your laptop for hours. Instead, drink your carefully pulled espresso or glass of Valpolicella (it's an enoteca, too) or eat your caprese salad at one of the three sidewalk tables or five indoor tables, and then move on. **WHO** The local Italian ex-pat community, all of whom seem to show up when Italian soccer is on TV, mixed with women who've had work done and men of a certain age who know their way around a tanning booth. 📷 ☼

[Graffeo Coffee] 🏠 315 N. Beverly Dr., Beverly Hills, 310.273.0817, graffeo.com. Mon.-Sat. from 9 a.m. AE, MC, V. **WHY** For rich, smooth, expertly roasted whole-bean coffee, ground to order. **WHAT** In this era of 427 kinds of coffee, it's a simple joy to shop at this no-frills retail store from San Francisco. You will have only four choices: dark, light, half-and-half or decaf (Swiss water process). They're all the same price, $13.75 a pound, except the decaf, which costs $1 more. And they're all delicious. **WHO** Restaurateurs, homesick San Franciscans and serious coffee people.

🏠 ESSENTIALLY L.A. ☺ LATE ♥ ROMANTIC 🖼️ VALUE 🍹 QUIET 🍃 SUSTAINABLE

[Le Palais des Thés] 401 N. Cañon Dr., Beverly Hills, 310.271.7922, lepalaisgourmet.com. Mon.-Sat. from 10 a.m. AE, MC, V. **WHY** The off-shoot of a Parisian emporium is said to source some of the world's finest teas. **WHAT** Beverly Hills is the obvious location for a tea boutique of this quality and price level. Indulge at the counter or take home a tin of a rare blend or varietal. **WHO** BevHills matrons, tourists from around the world and tea buffs with full wallets.

[Paddington's Tea Room] 355 S. Robertson Blvd., Beverly Hills, 310.652.0624, paddingtonstearoom.com. Daily from noon. English. AE, MC, V. **WHY** For either a proper British afternoon tea service or a more substantial high tea, both of which feature the Royal Blend from Fortnum & Mason and lovely finger sandwiches and scones with Devon cream. **WHAT** The stuffed-animal phobic may get itchy (Paddington Bears are everywhere), but everyone else will enjoy the charm of this English tea room. Kindly women serve afternoon tea, and in back is a shop stocked with such British must-haves as Cadbury chocolate and loose-leaf teas. **WHO** Ladies who take tea, grandmas taking granddaughters out and birthday celebrants. 🍴 ☺

[Royal/T Café] 🏠 8910 Washington Blvd., Culver City, 310.559.6300, royal-t.org/cafe. Tues.-Sun. from 10 a.m. Japanese. AE, MC, V. **WHY** For an L.A. take on a Japanese maid café, with very good, carefully presented matcha and milk teas and lovely tea-friendly sandwiches, Japanese dishes and pastries, served with performance-art flair. **WHAT** Royal/T provides the most singular tea experience you can possibly imagine, blending underground Japanese geek culture with English high-tea conventions, served by waitresses done up in French maids' costumes (a wee bit creepy in that Lolita way), set in the midst of a 10,000-square-foot collection of contemporary Japanese art. It's the strange and fascinating vision of collector/owner Susan Hancock, and you really must experience it. **WHO** Artists, collectors, tea ritualists and the curious. 🍴

[Urth Caffé] 267 S. Beverly Dr., Beverly Hills, 310.205.9311, urthcaffe. com. Daily from 6:30 a.m. MC, V. **WHY** Organic coffee, excellent teas and good food with a vegetarian/vegan emphasis. **WHAT** Except for the Lamborghinis parked out front and $200 T-shirts being worn by patrons inside, you could be at any of the other Urth locations. **WHO** Beautiful people, in a Beverly Hills way. ☼🍴☼

WEST OF THE 405

[18th Street Coffee House] 1725 Broadway, Santa Monica, 310.264.0662. Mon.-Fri. from 7 a.m., Sat. from 8:30 a.m. MC, V. **WHY** Homemade rugelach and 50-cent refills. **WHAT** This adorable historic brick building, complete with homey outdoor patio, has a folksy, East Bay/East Village vibe (but no, Bob Dylan does not own

🍴 **VEGETARIAN** ⊙ **KID FRIENDLY** ☼ **PATIO DINING** 🚚 **DELIVERY** 🏠 **PRIVATE PARTY** it, local rumor mill notwithstanding). **WHO** Young moms, students, writers and people without cell phone addictions (there's an outdoor-calling-only policy). ♻ ☺ ☼

[Abbot's Habit] **1401 Abbot Kinney Blvd., Venice, 310.399.1171, abbotshabit.com. Daily from 6 a.m. MC, V. WHY** Mellow vibe, good coffee, amusing people-watching. **WHAT** Try for a coveted sidewalk table at this funky (think Berkeley in the '70s) place in the heart of ultra-hip Abbot Kinney. Or check out the two inside rooms, where you can grab a quick sandwich or settle in for the afternoon with a laptop or sketchbook. **WHO** A happy mix of upwardly mobile Venice homeowners and hippie stoners. ♻ ☺ ☼

[Café Bolivar] **1741 Ocean Park Blvd., Santa Monica, 310.581.2344, cafebolivar.com. Mon.-Fri. from 7 a.m., Sat. from 9 a.m. Cash only. WHY** It's the perfect place to sit and finish your novel (the one you're reading or the one you're writing). **WHAT** This friendly, relaxed place is a real find in a sleeper Ocean Park neighborhood. It's got an open, modern look and warm Latin music on the stereo, along with excellent coffee and delicious lunches (grilled chicken sandwich with roasted pepper pesto, a true Spanish jamón serrano, a vegan torta.) Free WiFi, too. **WHO** Art lovers and poets drawn to the openings and readings that occasionally liven things up; friends looking for a relaxed spot to catch up. 📷 ☺

[Caffé Luxxe] **925 Montana Ave., Santa Monica, 310.394.2222, caffeluxxe.com. Mon.-Fri. from 6 a.m., Sat.-Sun. from 6:30 a.m. AE, MC, V. WHY** Each cup is a work of art. **WHAT** This place serves the best lattes and cappuccinos in Santa Monica (calm down — the new Intelligentsia is in Venice). The setting is serene and European, with high ceilings and framed mirrors. Only espresso drinks are served (no brewed coffee) along with a few high-quality baked goods including croissants, baguettes and cookies. But when the drinks are this good — the espresso creamy and almost sweet, the milk steamed with artistry and precision — who needs more? **WHO** Serious coffee lovers. ♻

[Dragon Herbs] **315 Wilshire Blvd., Santa Monica, 310.917.2288, dragonherbs.com. Daily from 11 a.m. Chinese. AE, MC, V. WHY** For adviser-designed herb tea drinks that just might cure what ails you. **WHAT** All sorts of Chinese herbs and teas are served at the tonic bar in this retail emporium. Tell the folks here what you're seeking (more energy, less weight, fewer hot flashes) and they'll fix you up with a drink that just might help. **WHO** The intensely health conscious. 🍃

[Funnel Mill] 📖 **930 Broadway, Santa Monica, 310.597.4395, funnelmill.com. Mon.-Fri. from 9 a.m., Sat. from 10 a.m. AE, MC, V. WHY** Siphon coffee and cold-water-infusion iced coffee, made with quality beans. **WHAT** Coffee is taken very seriously at this soothing,

Asian-themed spot, where a waterfall burbles and people work quietly on laptops (free WiFi). You can choose from a global menu of coffee beans to have ground and brewed in a glass siphon at your table, or explore the exceptional collection of teas, including an authentic Indian chai, fresh ginseng and many green and oolong varieties. **WHO** Studious sorts who love the quiet, but mostly people who are *really* into their coffee or their tea. 🍵

[Groundwork] **2908 Main St., Santa Monica, 310.392.9243, lacoffee. com. Mon.-Fri. from 6 a.m., Sat.-Sun. from 7 a.m. AE, MC, V. WHY** For house-roasted organic coffee, properly robust, to take home by the pound or order in a cup. **WHAT** Don't expect to hang out in this minia-ture storefront — it's a place to buy good whole beans to take home or a tasty brewed cup or latte to take with you. 🖥️♻️

[Infuzion Café] **1149 3rd St., Santa Monica, 310.393.9985, infuzi-oncafe.com. Mon.-Fri. from 6:30 a.m., Sat. from 7 a.m., Sun. from 8 a.m. MC, V. WHY** Delicious "infuzions," friendly people. **WHAT** This tiny coffeehouse just north of the Promenade draws a local, non-tourist crowd all day long. There's free WiFi, but the tables are too small to allow for hours of leisurely e-mailing. The coffee's fine and the café's signature "infuzions" — fruit-based iced-blended drinks — are deli-cious. **WHO** Local office workers and shoppers, who line up at peak hours. 🖥️☺️

[Intelligentsia Venice Coffeebar] 🔒 **1331 Abbot Kinney Blvd., Venice, 310.399.1233, intelligentsiacoffee.com. Mon.-Fri. from 6 a.m., Sat.-Sun. from 7 a.m. AE, MC, V. WHY** So you can be greeted by your own personal barista. **WHAT** When this offshoot of the Chicago-by-way-of-Silver Lake coffeehouse opened on Abbot Kinney in late spring 2009, you'd have thought the Obamas themselves were pulling espressos from the Synesso machines. Coffee geeks walk into this light-filled industrial space and begin hyperventilating at the sight of the Mazzer grinders and array of contraptions, from siphon to Chemex — but the gentle guidance of their personal barista soon calms the feverish excitement. Said baristas escort each guest through the space, guiding him or her to the station that best suits his or her desires (espresso, brewed, pressed). Yes, it's dreadfully precious, but the cof-fee is damn good. Seating is on uncomfortable stadium-style benches — this is a place for quietly worshipping your cup, not writing your screenplay. **WHO** The sort of people who can argue about whether the overtones in a particular brew suggest cherries or tamarind. ♻️

[Jin Patisserie] 🔒 **1202 Abbot Kinney Blvd., Venice, 310.399.8801, jinpatisserie.com. Tues.-Sun. from 10:30 a.m. AE, MC, V. WHY** Very good coffee and infused teas, sublime chocolates and scones, and a lovely garden patio on which to enjoy it all. **WHAT** This thoughtfully elegant patisserie showcases owner Kristy Choo's meticulously crafted works

🌿 VEGETARIAN ⊙ KID FRIENDLY ✿ PATIO DINING 🚗 DELIVERY 🎩 PRIVATE PARTY

of chocolate art, which go down well with a cup of coffee or tea.
WHO The most refined of Abbot Kinney's cool crowd take tea and
pastries on Jin's serene enclosed patio. ♥ 🌿 ♻ 🍵 ☼

[The Legal Grind] 2640 Lincoln Blvd., Santa Monica, 310.452.8160,
legalgrind.com. Mon.-Sat. from 10 a.m. MC, V. **WHY** Where else can $45
buy you "coffee & counsel" — a cuppa joe and 20 minutes of legal
consultation? **WHAT** Corporate law was a grind, so Jeff Hughes com-
bined his desire to become a "people's lawyer" with his love of a good
coffeehouse to create this unusual place. You can drop in or make an
appointment to get legal help with your latte. 🗫 🌿

[Newsroom the Espresso Café] 530 Wilshire Blvd., Santa Monica,
310.319.9100. Mon.-Fri. from 8 a.m., Sat.-Sun. from 9 a.m. AE, MC, V.
WHY Tasty oat bran muffins and other healthy treats. **WHAT** This
friendly café is well located in central Santa Monica, just a short walk
from the Promenade. The coffee drinks are carefully made and the
food is actually good for you: veggie burgers, quesadillas, organic
salads. Try to score a table on the outdoor patio. 🌿 ♻ 🍵 ☺ ☼

[The Novel Café & Bookstore] 212 Pier Ave., Santa Monica,
310.396.8566, novel.com. Mon.-Fri. from 7 a.m., Sat.-Sun. from 8 a.m.
Cash only. **WHY** A literary atmosphere and late hours — to 1 a.m. every
night but Sunday. **WHAT** Spend an afternoon — or a month — writing
your masterpiece in this book-lined haven. When you need sustenance,
head to the counter for coffee drinks, bagels, spinach Caesars or turkey quesadillas from the large-for-a-coffeehouse menu. **WHO** Night
owls and novelists. ☺ 🗫 🌿 🍵

[Peet's Coffee & Tea] 2439 Main St., Santa Monica, 310.399.8117;
1401 Montana Ave., Santa Monica, 310.394.8555, peets.com. Daily
from 5 a.m. AE, MC, V. **WHY** Major Dickason's blend. **WHAT** If you
must drink at a chain, this estimable Bay Area institution is the one
to pick. The coffee drinks are robust and made by actual baristas, the
take-home beans are addictive and thoughtfully ground, and all the
Southern California locations seem to have been carefully chosen to
showcase Peets' outdoor tables in lively, people-watching neighborhoods. Delectable baked goods, too. **WHO** Shoppers, after-beach
coffee seekers, scruffy-chic guys with laptops. ☺ ☼

[Tanner's Coffee Co.] 200 Culver Blvd., Playa del Rey,
310.574.2739. Mon.-Fri. from 6 a.m., Sat.-Sun. from 6:30 a.m. MC, V.
WHY The best coffee in the area, not to mention free WiFi, a few
choice sidewalk tables and a great location in a sort of secret beach
neigbhorhood in Playa del Rey. **WHAT** Tanner's is the community
hub for this great little beach village, which has resisted the glam
gentrification of neighboring towns. It is serious about its coffee but
is otherwise relaxed; it has baked goods, but if you get really hungry,

🏛 ESSENTIALLY L.A. ☺ LATE ♥ ROMANTIC 🗫 VALUE 🌿 QUIET ♻ SUSTAINABLE head to the charming little French-American café across the street. **WHO** Surfers, LMU students and Playa residents. 🌊 ☺ ☼

[Tudor House] 🔒 1403 2nd St., Santa Monica, 310.451.4107, thetudorhouse.com. Mon.-Tues. from 10:30 a.m., Wed.-Sun. from 9 a.m. English. AE, MC, V. **WHY** Steak and kidney pie, welsh rarebit, trifle and full afternoon tea with scones and tea sandwiches. There's also a shop full of British imports. **WHAT** Santa Monica used to have a thriving British community, and the Tudor House has been there for some 40 years. Inside, it resembles a British auntie — a bit dowdy but terribly cozy. **WHO** Tea-sipping ladies and British ex-pats longing for clotted cream. ☺

[UnUrban Coffee House] 3301 Pico Blvd., Santa Monica, 310.315.0056. Mon.-Fri. from 7 a.m., Sat.-Sun. from 8 a.m. MC, V. **WHY** Excellent double-shot cappuccino; highly entertaining evening performances. **WHAT** "Death Before Decaf" is the motto at this neighborhood café, and the baristas deliver the goods. As for the décor, think first apartment for theater majors — walls painted red and purple, thrift-store tables and chairs, old movie-theater seats and velvet drapes in bold colors. There's also free WiFi, plentiful tables and evening music and spoken-word performances. Note that the lease is tenuous, so it could disappear at any time. 📷🔌

[Urth Caffé] 🔒 2327 Main St., Santa Monica, 310.314.7040, urthcaffe. com. Daily from 6:30 a.m. MC, V. **WHY** Organic coffee, excellent teas and good food with a vegetarian/vegan emphasis. **WHAT** Robust coffee, loose-leaf teas and tasty café fare for health-conscious, environmentally aware, Prius-driving westsiders. On sunny days the outdoor tables are as prized as seats at the Oscars. A quintessential L.A. place. **WHO** Hip Match.com blind-daters, girlfriends catching up, and all sorts of beautiful Santa Monicans. 🌊🔌☼

SOUTH BAY TO SOUTH L.A.

[Aguas Tijuana's Juice Bar] 8530 Paramount Blvd., Downey, 562.928.0214, aguastijuanasjuicebar.com. Daily from 7 a.m. Mexican. MC, V. **WHY** For wonderful juice drinks — try the strawberries and cream made with fresh berries, the piña or the escamocha. **WHAT** This friendly juice and smoothie bar makes 11 drinks daily (papaya, watermelon, strawberry/banana, horchata), plus mixes smoothies and custom drinks to order. Ingredients are fresh, and the place is spotless. Tortas are offered, too. 📷🔌☺

[Aroma di Roma] 5327 E. 2nd St., Long Beach, 562.434.6353. Mon.-Fri. from 5:30 a.m., Sat.-Sun. from 6 a.m. AE, MC, V. **WHY** Good coffee, perfectly foamed lattes, a locals' vibe and Italian soccer on TV. **WHAT** Second Street's best coffeehouse is a real neighborhood hub,

🔌 VEGETARIAN ☺ KID FRIENDLY ☼ PATIO DINING 🚚 DELIVERY 🎉 PRIVATE PARTY where friends are always running into one another while ordering a latte or a gelato. Good Italian food (panini, salads), very good coffee and a great atmosphere both inside and on the sidewalk patio. **WHO** Neighbors who can walk here from their adorable Belmont Shore bungalows. ☺ ☼

[Catalina Coffee Company] **126 N. Catalina Ave., Redondo Beach, 310.318.2499, catalinacoffee.com. Daily from 7 a.m. MC, V. WHY** Roasted-on-site coffee, a decent selection of teas and an inviting, hang-out-for-a-while atmosphere. **WHAT** Outside is a sunny patio with thatched umbrellas, but inside it's more literary than beachy, with a fireplace, lots of books, comfy high-backed armchairs and a flea-market-chic look. Redondo's star indie coffeehouse doesn't have free WiFi, but everyone's busy reading, chatting or playing board games and doesn't seem to care. **WHO** Everyone who's anyone in Redondo. ☺ ☼

[Hot Java] **2101 E. Broadway, Long Beach, 562.433.0688. Daily from 6 a.m. MC, V. WHY** A relaxed vibe, very good brewed coffee (lattes and cappuccinos are unexceptional), pastries from Rossmoor Bakery and free WiFi. **WHAT** Two airy, modern rooms and some sidewalk tables provide lots of space for the regulars to hang out, but even then, it can get full, especially in the evening. The third Saturday of the month is a standup comedy showcase. **WHO** An interesting mix of beach people, gay neighbors and the laptop-obsessed. ☺ 🖫☺ ☼

[Library Coffeehouse] **3418 E. Broadway, Long Beach, 562.433.2393. Mon.-Fri. from 6 a.m., Sat.-Sun. from 7 a.m. MC, V. WHY** Perfectly fine coffee, respectable pastries and light meals, free WiFi and a very comfortable funky-chic setting in a great neighborhood. **WHAT** A longstanding Belmont Heights hangout, the Library is large and rambling, stuffed with pleasantly shabby Victorian furniture and bookcases stocked with used titles for sale. **WHO** The young 'n quirky, often with a goth-literary bent. ☺ 🖼🖫☼

[North End Café] **3421 Highland Ave., Manhattan Beach, 310.546.4782. Daily from 8:30 a.m. MC, V. WHY** The best takeout coffee in the area and, if you have time to sit down and eat, very good food, too. **WHAT** This is not really a place to sit with just a cup of coffee and linger — the people waiting for a table for breakfast or lunch will look daggers at you — but it's a great place to get a first-rate coffee drink to go. And what's your rush? You might as well sit down and have some beignets and fresh berries to go with your latte. **WHO** Locals who can walk here and El Porto surfers. 🖫☺ ☼

[Planet Earth – Eco Café] **509 Pier Ave., Hermosa Beach, 310.318.1888. Tues.-Fri. from 7 a.m., Sat.-Sun. from 8:30 a.m. MC, V. WHY** Well-made organic, fair-trade mochas, lattes, teas and chai drinks, tasty baked goods (including vegan options) and interesting music on the stereo. **WHAT** As you might guess from the name, this place has a sweet, beach-hippie vibe, a devotion to all things organic and sustainable, and friendly, hands-on owners who know how to make coffee properly. If only it stayed open in the evenings... **WHO** A beach crowd grateful for a green, indie alternative to the coffee chains. ✪✎☺✿

[Portfolio Coffeehouse] **2300 E. 4th St., Long Beach, 562.434.2486, portfoliocoffeehouse.com. Daily from 6 a.m. AE, MC, V. WHY** Excellent espresso, properly foamed cappuccinos, free WiFi and a stylishly studious vibe. **WHAT** The hub of life in the Broadway Corridor neighborhood, Portfolio wraps around the corner of 4th and Junipero near a collection of fun vintage shops. The back room is filled with silent, headphone-wearing people on laptops; the front room is chattier and has PCs to rent for a buck for ten minutes. Forgot your laptop? Pick up one of the smart magazines for sale. Superb coffee, good breakfast panini and baked goods, and lunch dishes that go beyond the coffeehouse basics. **WHO** Grad students, high-school girls with creative haircuts and black Converse sneakers, hip seniors... a diverse bunch. ☺🖭♪☺

[Tierra Mia Coffee] 🏠 **4914 Firestone Blvd., South Gate, 323.563.3948, tierramiacoffee.com. Mon.-Fri. from 6:30 a.m., Sat.-Sun. from 7 a.m. AE, MC, V. WHY** Authentic Cuban café con leche, heavenly mochas, lattes infused with horchata and all-around superb coffee. **WHAT** This suave and handsome spot, with leather comfy chairs and intoxicating aromas, takes its coffee — and its beans — very seriously, buying them from organic, artisanal roasters and handling them with care. But there's a sense of whimsy that cancels out any pretension, as witnessed by the Rice and Beans, a horchata-flavored blended espresso drink sprinkled with crushed coffee beans. **WHO** The coolest people in South Gate by a long shot. ☺🖭♪☺

🍃 VEGETARIAN ☺ KID FRIENDLY ✿ PATIO DINING 🚚 DELIVERY 🎩 PRIVATE PARTY

Food That's Fast

Hungry and in a hurry? You'll have no trouble resisting the Del Taco urge when you see the astonishing range of L.A.'s offerings, from ramen houses to taco trucks, burger joints to rib shacks, falafel stands to pizzerias.

ALSO CONSIDER THESE
SPEEDY GOURMET-TO-GO PLACES:
Artisan Cheese Gallery, Studio City (PAGE 265)
Auntie Em's, Eagle Rock (PAGE 183)
Bottega Louie, Downtown (PAGE 263)
Café Surfas, Culver City (PAGE 267)
Clementine, Century City (PAGE 268)
Food + Lab, West Hollywood (PAGE 260)
Gallego's Mexican Deli, Mar Vista (PAGE 269)
Joan's on Third, Beverly/Third (PAGE 260)
Julienne, San Marino (PAGE 264)
Larchmont Larder, Hancock Park (PAGE 261)
Ma 'n' Pa's Grocery, Long Beach (PAGE 316)
Marmalade, Santa Monica & Malibu (PAGES 266 & 269)
Mozza 2 Go, Melrose (PAGE 262)
Nicole's Gourmet Foods, South Pasadena (PAGE 265)
The Oaks Market, Hollywood (PAGE 262)
Porta Via, Pasadena (PAGE 265)
Tiara Café, South Park/Fashion District (PAGE 264)

🏛 ESSENTIALLY L.A. ☺ LATE ♥ ROMANTIC 💲 VALUE 🔇 QUIET ♻ SUSTAINABLE

[ESSENTIALLY L.A.]

🌿 VEGETARIAN ☺ KID FRIENDLY ☼ PATIO DINING 🚗 DELIVERY 🎩 PRIVATE PARTY

CITYWIDE

[Barbie's Q] 310.989.5110, @BarbiesQ (Twitter), barbiesq.com. **Barbecue. Cash only. $ - $$** **WHY** Sandwiches and ribs served out of a truck that's mostly in Venice but does private parties and hits various public events around town. **WHAT** This rider on the mobile-truck bandwagon makes respectable barbecue, notably the pulled-pork sandwich (better than the blah chicken), the faux-pork sandwich and the baby-back ribs. Most lunchtimes it's parked on Abbot Kinney at San Juan in Venice, and in the evenings it's often near one of the bars, but it might be in West Hollywood or El Segundo. Check the Twitter feed..

[Border Grill Truck] @BorderGrill (Twitter), bordergrill.com. **Mexican. Cash only. $** **WHY** Border Grill's excellent tacos (the Yucatan pork, potato and Baja-style fish are our faves) and quesadillas, served from a truck window all over town. **WHAT** At this writing, one of the city's newer food trucks was doing a lot of private events and showing up consistently at several spots, including in front of the Venice bar the Brig every Thursday night; at the Downtown Art Walk the second Thursday of the month; and at the Santa Monica Farmers' Market twice a month. By the time you read this, it'll probably be at more places; check the site or the Twitter feed for details.

[Dosa Truck] @dosatruck (Twitter), dosatruck.com. **Indian. Cash only. $** **WHY** A twist on the truck fad, serving Indian street-food snacks out a taco-truck window. **WHAT** While Dosa might seem like just another trendoid truck, it's true that Indian street food is well suited to serving out of a catering truck. This newish one specializes in *dosas* (sourdough rice-and-lentil cakes), cooked to order and topped with chutneys or things like eggs, curried potatoes and caramelized onions, mushrooms and cheese. We were disappointed in its early days with dosa that weren't crisp and flavors that needed work, but it has promise. At this writing, it was appearing regularly in Hollywood, Downtown, Venice and Santa Monica.

[Frysmith] 818.371.6814, @frysmith (Twitter), eatfrysmith.com. **Wed.-Sun. American. Cash only. $** **WHY** To paraphrase its own site... for stuff thrown on top of fries. **WHAT** We haven't yet tried this new truck, because it hadn't hit the streets at press time, but it will have by the time you read this, and it's a safe bet that it will be a hit. The custom-built truck will be fresh-frying Kennebec and sweet potatoes and topping them with beef chili and cheese, vegan chili, steak and caramelized onions, and kim chee. How could it not succeed?

[Green Truck] 310.204.0477, @Green_Truck (Twitter), greentruckonthego.com. **B, L & D Mon.-Fri. Vegetarian/modern American. Cash only. $ - $$** **WHY** Fresh, organic salads, soups, wraps and sandwiches, served out of two catering trucks at several locations. **WHAT** These sustainable twists on the roach coach, fueled by recycled vegetable oil, cruise Culver City, Santa Monica and the Wilshire/La Brea area on weekdays. Your ahi poke tacos, vegan sesame-tofu wraps and sweet potato fries are served in biodegradable packaging. To see where the trucks are parked, go to the web site's GPS tracker or follow it on Twitter. **WHO** Culver City studio folks, Miracle Mile office toilers and health-conscious Santa Monica office workers. ○○

[Kogi BBQ] 🏠 Locations vary, @kogibbq (Twitter), kogibbq.com. **Korean/Mexican. Cash only. $ WHY** Taco trucks hit the big time when this Korean/Mexican fusion coach arrived on the scene. **WHAT** Spicy pork and beef short-rib tacos along with kim chee quesadillas and other Kogi specialties are undoubtedly delicious Asian twists on Mexican favorites — but whether the wait time is worth it depends on the length of the line and your patience. The pioneer of the gourmet food truck movement, Kogi quickly gained fame from fans following the truck's Twitter feed, and at this writing its fleet had increased to three trucks, which stop all over L.A. (and will show up at your event with a $1,000 minimum order). Its food is more easily available at the Alibi Lounge in Culver City. **WHO** Trend-followers and addicts willing to wait for up to 90 minutes for a couple of short-rib tacos. 🗟

CENTRAL CITY

[Astro Burger] **7475 Santa Monica Blvd., West Hollywood, 323.874.8041. B, L & D daily until 4 a.m. American. Cash only. $ WHY** A good selection of veggie burgers, and respectable beef burgers, too. **WHAT** Better than its sibling on Melrose, this Astro is full day and night. It's the usual fast-food menu — burgers, dogs, fries, pastrami — with a few interesting additions, like the fiery chicken quesadilla. The crowd can get a little rowdy in the wee hours. **WHO** Lunch-break workers, vegetarians happy to find a burger joint that loves them and, late at night, drunk people. ○ ○ ○ ○

[Authentic Korean Dumplings] **698 S. Irolo St., Koreatown, 213.480.1289. L & D daily. Korean. Cash only. $ WHY** For the steamed King dumpling (a big daddy filled with beef or pork and either leeks, kim chee or rice noodles), the pan-fried dumplings and the kim chee dumplings. **WHAT** This Koreatown shack (really — it's an actual shack) lives up to its name and does serve authentic dumplings, but they're as much Chinese as they are Korean. They're cheap, tasty and served in an instant. 🗟 ○ ○

[Best Fish Taco in Ensenada] **1650 N. Hillhurst Ave., Los Feliz, No phone, bestfishtacoinensenada.com. L & D daily. Taqueria. No booze. Cash only. $ WHY** It's a place of tremendous simplicity: you got your fish tacos ($1.50) and your shrimp tacos ($2), and a choice of canned soda or fresh horchata ($1) to drink. That's it. The fish and shrimp are lightly breaded and served hot from the fryer (sometimes one at a

🗟 VEGETARIAN ○ KID FRIENDLY ○ PATIO DINING �DELIVERY 🏠 PRIVATE PARTY time); you dress them yourself with very good salsas, crisp cabbage and the traditional white sauce. **WHAT** This seriously funky taqueria, with a small outdoor patio and a few tall tables inside, is run by a guy named Joseph, who jokes and flirts and sometimes lays down the law with the steady stream of customers — the law mostly being that you can't take the tacos to go. Some have dubbed him the Taco Nazi, but he's doing it for a good reason — if you don't eat these little bits of heaven right away, they turn into a miserable, soggy mess. 🎨 ☺ ☼

[Cactus Taqueria] 950 Vine St., Hollywood, 323.464.5865. B, L & D daily until midnight. Taqueria. MC, V. $ **WHY** *Birria* (goat), chorizo, al pastor and delicious *camarón* (fried shrimp), all served as tacos and paired with a good salsa and marinated-veggie bar. **WHAT** Your basic taco joint, except the choices are better than the norm; you can eat at a picnic table outside or take your tacos back to work. **WHO** Cops, Hollywood eccentrics and workers from the many local studios, post houses and production-related small businesses. ☺ ☼

[Carney's] 8351 Sunset Blvd., West Hollywood, 323.654.8300, carneytrain.com. L & D daily until midnight or 1 a.m. (to 3 a.m. Fri.-Sat. American. Beer & wine. AE, MC, V. $ **WHY** A tasty turkey burger, good hot dogs and all-around decent fast food served until 3 a.m. on weekends at modest prices — in a high-priced neighborhood. Oh, and great free parking! **WHAT** An L.A. classic on the Sunset Strip, Carney's is a pretty standard fast-food joint in an atmospheric old train car plopped in a parking lot. The chili's on the bland side, and the fries are just okay, but the burgers and dogs are totally satisfying, and the people-watching is great. **WHO** Sunset Strip crawlers. ☺ 🎨 ☺ ☼ 🚙

[Cassell's] 3266 W. 6th St., Koreatown, 213.480.8668. L Mon.-Sat. American. MC, V. $ **WHY** For old-school burgers — large, flat, on big, plain white buns — that many people find delicious and comforting and others find too, well, old-school and bland. Everyone loves the potato salad, though. **WHAT** With roots going to 1948, Cassell's is one of L.A.'s culinary landmarks. The Cassell family no longer runs it, but it still boasts house-ground, high-quality meat, homemade mayo, excellent lemonade and an addictive, subtly spicy potato salad. Best of all: They'll actually cook your burger rare if that's how you want it. **WHO** Longtime customers from Wilshire Boulevard and Downtown's insurance and real estate offices. 🎨 ☺ ☼

[Deano's Gourmet Pizza] Farmers Market, 6333 W. 3rd St., Fairfax District, 323.935.6373, deanospizzala.com. L & D daily. Pizzeria. AE, MC, V. $$ - $$$ **WHY** Excellent upscale pizza by the slice, with a light, flavorful crust that holds up well. Good meatball sandwiches, too. **WHAT** Dean Schwartz's friendly pizzeria has a health focus — if you want your pizza gluten free or vegan, no problem (if you call ahead). Ingredients are fresh, and the crusts (cornmeal, herb-white or whole wheat) are tasty. We're partial to the pesto-spinach-garlic-shrimp combo. **WHO** The terrifically diverse Farmers Market crew. 🛍️☺️☼

[Dino's Burgers] **2575 W. Pico Blvd., Mid-City, 213.380.3554. B, L & D daily. American. Cash only. $ WHY** Orange-red chicken marinated in a chile-laced sauce and grilled, resting on a bed of fries deliciously imbued with the juices of the half chicken. **WHAT** Despite the name, it's not about the burgers at this very modest stand; the half-chicken plate has achieved near-legendary status among local connoisseurs of cheap eats. 📷☺️

[El Matador Taco Truck] **Western Ave. at Lexington Ave., Hollywood. D nightly. Taqueria. Cash only. $ WHY** Juicy, carefully prepared tacos al pastor and carne asada for just a buck, with a robust salsa roja that has a hint of habañero. **WHAT** This is the best taco truck in Hollywood, usually open from sunset until at least 2 a.m. and often bearing a line. **WHO** Neighborhood Latinos and after-club party people. ☺️📷☺️

[Falafel Arax] 🏛️ **5101 Santa Monica Blvd., Hollywood, 323.663.9687. B, L & early D daily. Middle Eastern/Armenian. Cash only. $ WHY** The best falafel in town, crisp on the outside and tender within. Succulent schwarma, too. **WHAT** This tiny diner has been attracting falafel addicts for 25 years, and the lines still haven't abated. **WHO** A long line of falafel junkies during the rush hours. 📷🍴

[I Panini di Ambra] **5633 Hollywood Blvd., Hollywood, 323.463.1200, thepaninilady.com. B, L & early D Mon.-Sat. Italian. MC, V. $ WHY** Focaccia with *cipolle* (onion) or rosemary and potato; panini with prosciutto and provolone. You can also get the house-made focaccia to go. **WHAT** The little storefront on the gentrifying stretch of Hollywood Boulevard that's home to Sabor y Cultura is run by a lovely Italian woman who's a longtime baker. Her focaccia is the key ingredient to the two main dishes served here: by-the-slice pizza and fresh-grilled panini. Opt for pizzas with the lighter toppings, so they won't overwhelm her delicious focaccia. You can eat here at a few tables or take it to go. 📷🍴

[JNJ Burger & Bar-B-Q] **5754 W. Adams Blvd., Mid-City, 323.933.7366. L & D Mon.-Sat. American. Cash only. $ WHY** Exceptionally tender and tasty pork and beef ribs and pulled pork, smoked by Jay Nelson with oak and almond woods. **WHAT** A shack in the best sense of the word, JNJ is indeed a burger joint, but that's not why you come here. You come for the honest-to-goodness barbecue: tender pork ribs, hefty beef ribs and juicy hot links (pass on the brisket); extras include great collard greens and sweet potato pie. **WHO** Culver City studio folks sneaking away from their vegetarian lunch meetings for some ribs. 📷☺️☼

🍴VEGETARIAN ☺️KID FRIENDLY ☼PATIO DINING �chDELIVERY 🏠PRIVATE PARTY

[Joe's Pizza] 8539 W. Sunset Blvd., West Hollywood, 310.358.0900, joespizza.com. L & D daily. Pizzeria. MC, V. $ **WHY** Really tasty thin crust, New York–style pizza (just enough sauce and cheese, no crazy toppings) for eating in or to go — and delivery is free. **WHAT** Joe Vitale of THE Joe's Pizza on Bleecker Street first tackled Santa Monica last year, and when he met with success, he opened this new pizzeria on the Sunset Strip. Besides the classic pies, you can get a few heroes and pastas. But it's really about the slices. **WHO** WeHo locals grateful for a place to get a great slice for just $2.75. ☺ 🍴☺�foodcar

[Loteria Grill] 🏛 Farmers Market, 6333 W. 3rd St., Fairfax District, 323.930.2211, loteriagrill.com. L & D daily. Taqueria. Beer at neighboring stall. MC, V. $ - $$ **WHY** Tacos stuffed with chicken mole, mushrooms, cactus or squash, huevos rancheros for brunch and stunning aguas frescas made from fresh fruits or jamaica flowers. **WHAT** This little Farmers Market stand turns out some of the best Mexican food for miles around with a creative Mexico City–style flair. For more of a sit-down meal with the same great food and a full bar, try the new Loteria Hollywood. 🗺☺☼

[Moishe's Fine Middle Eastern Cuisine] Farmers Market, 6333 W. 3rd St., Fairfax District, 323.936.4998. L & D daily. Middle Eastern. Cash only. $ - $$ **WHY** Quality falafel at a treasured spot in the old section of the Farmers Market. **WHAT** Don't worry about the impatient counter ladies — once you get past the ordering and into the eating, the falafel sandwiches at this gem of a spot are extraordinary, wrapped in super-thin pita, dolloped with great tahini dressing and served with ripe tomato and lettuce. There are some exceptional sides, too, such as the savory bulgur pilaf and the *muhammara* (walnut/pomegranate/pepper dip). 🗺🍴☺☼

[Phillips Bar-B-Que] 2619 Crenshaw Blvd., Mid-City, 323.731.4772; 4307 Leimert Blvd., Leimert Park, 323.292.7613. L & D Tues.-Sun. Barbecue. MC, V. $ - $$$ **WHY** Pork ribs and rib tips, a bit chewy, properly smoky and full of flavor; try the mixed sauce. **WHAT** This local chain of South L.A. takeout-only rib joints has its rabid followers and ornery detractors; we're somewhere in the middle, believing for one thing that even so-so ribs are still a gift from the gods. These are saucy and substantial, not as tender as some but quite tasty. Call ahead to place your order or you'll have a long wait. **WHO** A constant crowd of fans waiting for their ribs and jockeying for one of the few seats. 🗺

[Pink's] 709 N. La Brea Blvd., Hollywood, 323.931.4223, pinkshollywood.com. L & D daily until 2 a.m. (3 a.m. Fri.-Sat.). American. Cash only. $ **WHY** Old-school hot dogs of every conceivable topping combo, creatively named for celebrities and movies. **WHAT** These aren't the best wieners in town, but Pink's is still a must stop for visitors and L.A. newbies, for the atmosphere and to watch the tourists from all over the

world. There's always a line, but the people-watching is half the fun.
WHO Tourists, teenagers, Hollywood oddballs, you name it. ☺

[Pollos a la Brasa] 🏠 764 S. Western Ave., Koreatown,
213.382.4090. L & D Tues.-Sun. Peruvian. Cash only. $ **WHY** Where else
can you get a Peruvian-style chicken cooked over real wood in the
middle of a sea of Korean eateries? **WHAT** Come here for deeply flavored roast chicken that reflects the smoky flavor from cords of wood
piled outside the tiny restaurant. The addictive spicy *aji* (garlic) sauce
is the perfect foil to the crispy chicken skin. 🖼️☺

[Shinu Rang-Olke Rang] 🏠 1032 Crenshaw Blvd., Mid-City,
323.935.2724. L & D Tues.-Sun. Korean. AE, MC, V. $ **WHY** The truck-
stop rule: All those people in the line snaking out the door at lunchtime know that these are some of the best Korean dumplings around.
WHAT Plumply stuffed dumplings are gems at this modest café, whose
name means "All Family Restaurant." They're hand rolled and cut,
and the taste and texture are noticeably better than the machine-made
kinds. Order them deep-fried, boiled, steamed or in soup. 🖼️☺

[Singapore's Banana Leaf] Farmers Market, 6333 W. 3rd St.,
Fairfax District, 323.933.4627. L & D daily. Malaysian. No booze. MC, V.
$ **WHY** Satisfying Malaysian curries, salads and rendang chicken,
presented with more flair than you'd expect of a Farmers Market stall.
WHAT Melding the flavors of China, Thailand and even India, Malaysian cooking is richly spiced but not hot, sweet but not sugary, and
this order-at-the-counter spot in Farmers Market represents the cuisine
very well, especially given that everything is less than $10. 🍃☺☼

[Tomato Pie Pizza Joint] 7751 Melrose Ave., Melrose,
323.653.9993, tomatopiepizzajoint.com. L & D daily. Pizzeria. MC, V.
$ - $$$ **WHY** All the standard pies (plus an excellent white pie), along
with calzones, subs and pasta dishes. **WHAT** Flavorful New York–style
pies are sold at this modest shop with two locations, each of which has
friendly service and efficient delivery. 🖼️☺🚗

[Village Pizzeria] 131 N. Larchmont Blvd., Hancock Park,
323.465.5566, villagepizzeria.net. L & D daily. Pizzeria. Beer & wine. AE,
MC, V. $ - $$$ **WHY** Garlic rolls as addictive as cigarettes but not
quite as bad for you, as well as good salads and great pizza by the
slice or the pie. **WHAT** The lucky folks who live in Hancock Park can
get this pizza delivered whenever they like; the rest of us have to find
parking on Larchmont and a seat in this typically crowded little spot.
The reward is a first-class New York–style pizza, certainly one of the
better in L.A. All the varieties are good, but the simple cheese is pure
nirvana. The new branch on Ivar and Yucca in Hollywood has takeout,
a little seating and curbside delivery. **WHO** Marlborough girls and
Hancock Park regulars. 🖼️☺☼🚗

Food
That's Fast

🍃 VEGETARIAN ☺ KID FRIENDLY ☼ PATIO DINING 🚗 DELIVERY 🏠 PRIVATE PARTY

[Vito's Pizza] 🏠 846 N. La Cienega Blvd., West Hollywood, 310.652.6859. L & D daily (to midnight on weekends). Pizzeria. Beer & wine. AE, MC, V. $ **WHY** Carefully crafted, hand-tossed, New York–style pizzas with top-quality ingredients; try the signature white pie or the Terra Firma with the works. **WHAT** Fans waited years for Vito's to reopen after a break, and they weren't disappointed when it finally did. Vito's has L.A.'s best crust. ☺ 📝 ☺ ○ 🚗

[Woody's Bar-B-Que] 3446 W. Slauson Ave., Mid-City, 323.294.9443, woodysla.com. L & D daily. Barbecue. AE, MC, V. $ - $$ **WHY** Tasty, meaty pork ribs (they're better than the beef ribs), tender chicken, chicken links and greens; if you don't want your meat covered in sauce, ask for it on the side. **WHAT** Vying with Phillip's as L.A.'s kings of down-and-dirty takeout rib joints, Woody's smokes good-quality ribs and chicken and pairs them with a potent and spicy sauce; there's also a milder sauce option. 📝

[Yuca's] 🏠 2056 Hillhurst Ave., Los Feliz, 323.662.1214, yucasla.com. L & D daily. Taqueria. Cash only. $ **WHY** The carnitas burrito of your dreams, and great cochinita pibil, too. **WHAT** Not many 100-square-foot taco stands in a liquor store parking lot can boast a James Beard award, but Yuca's can. Since 1976, Socorro Herrera and her daughter, Dora, have been the queens of Hillhurst, turning out fantastic tortas, tacos, burritos and, on Saturdays, Yucatan-style tamales. It's an aggressively carnivorous place — they won't even make a cheese quesadilla for vegetarians. There's a new branch at 4666 Hollywood Blvd., the site of the old Casa Diaz. **WHO** Construction workers, grandmas, tattooed musicians — a wonderful L.A. mix. 📝 ○

[Zankou Chicken] 5065 W. Sunset Blvd., Hollywood, 323.665.7842. L & D daily. Lebanese. AE, MC, V. $ **WHY** Aromatic rotisserie chicken, the skin soaked just right with salt, seasonings and grease. **WHAT** Besides the legendary rotisserie chicken, the original Zankou location in a grim strip mall in an unglamorous part of Hollywood has a few more choices than its siblings, including tabbouleh, stuffed grape leaves and kebabs. It appears to be under different ownership than the others in the local chain, but the chicken tastes the same. 📝 ☺

EASTSIDE

[Al & Bea's] 2025 E. 1st St., Boyle Heights, 323.267.8810. B, L & D Mon.-Sat. Taqueria. Cash only. $ **WHY** A basic place for basic food: L.A. burritos that are cheap, juicy and delicious. **WHAT** For decades, this utilitarian stand has served as a hub of Boyle Heights life. Located near Mariachi Plaza and the spiffy new Hollenbeck police station, it's where everyone in the neighborhood goes for a burrito, to eat here or take over to Hollenbeck Park. Don't bother with anything but the specialty: a bean and cheese burrito, with either red or green chile; or the combo burrito, basically the same thing but with meat added. **WHO** Kids, cops, construction workers and old guys who've been coming here for decades. 📷😊☼

[Breed Street Food Fair] 🔒 **Breed St. and Cesar Chavez Ave., Boyle Heights. D Thurs.-Sun. Mexican/Latino. Cash only. $ WHY** The pozole lady, the pupusa lady, the churro guy and Anna, the queen of quesadillas. **WHAT** Four nights a week, about ten food carts set up in the parking lot at the corner of Breed and Cesar Chavez, and a food-lover's fiesta ensues. Bring cash (not much) and an appetite (a big one) and wander the stands, trying whatever strikes your fancy. We're partial to the Mexico City–style quesadillas with great fillings (including *huitlacoche*, sort of like a corn mushroom), *barbacoa* (barbecued lamb) tacos, and heavenly churros made from a homemade contraption. **WHO** Boyle Heights families and on-a-budget hungry people from all over the eastside. 📷😊

[Brownstone Pizza] **2108 Colorado Blvd., Eagle Rock, 323.257.4992. L & D daily. Pizzeria. MC, V. $ WHY** Huge, floppy New York-style pies and hearty traditional pasta dishes. Eat your pizza quickly — they get soggy if they sit around, and they don't take home well. **WHAT** Huge, ultra-thin-crust pizzas are served in a basic store-front setting. The pies and slices can be taken to Colorado Wine next door for a fun *vino con pizza* evening. 📷😊

[The Bucket] **4541 Eagle Rock Blvd., Eagle Rock, 323.257.5654. L & D Wed.-Sun. American. Beer & wine. MC, V. $ WHY** Hefty, juicy burgers with the secret Bucket sauce — live large (or not for long) and try the Cardiac burger (two half-pound patties, cheese, deep-fried bacon, ham and much more) or the more reasonable green-chile burger. **WHAT** A good selection of beers (some by the pitcher), football on TV and a large, funky outdoor patio add to the laid-back vibe at this historic neighborhood stand. **WHO** Hungry-boy Oxy students, sports fans and young, hip Eagle Rock families. 📷😊☼

[Cemitas Poblanas Elvirita #1] 🔒 **3012 E. 1st St., Boyle Heights, 323.881.0428. L & D daily. Mexican. Cash only. $ WHY** The cemitas carnitas and the cemitas with chicken in black mole are two of the best sandwiches in L.A.; the quesadillas filled with such things as squash flowers and mushrooms are also excellent. **WHAT** This hybrid restaurant-sandwich shop is a sit-down place, but we're putting it in Food That's Fast because it's really a place to get a quick sandwich — one of the best sandwiches you'll ever have in your life. The specialty is Mexican cemitas, made on soft, toasted buns that are filled to bursting with wonderful things: carnitas, milanesa beef, roasted chipotle, avocado, various cheese, salsas and more. Save room for just one *taco arabe*, a sort of a tortilla wrap filled with fantastic bits of pork, and bring quarters for the jukebox. **WHO** Ebullient Latino families. 📷😊

Food That's Fast

🌿VEGETARIAN ◎KID FRIENDLY ☼PATIO DINING 🚚DELIVERY 🏠PRIVATE PARTY

[Daikokuya] 327 E. 1st St., Little Tokyo/Arts District, 213.626.1680, daikoku-ten.com. L & D daily, brunch Sun. Japanese. Beer & wine. MC, V. $ **WHY** For 50 cents they'll add extra pork fat to your soup base. Need we say more? **WHAT** It's not as fast as we'd like, because of the lines of ramen addicts who slow things down at peak times. But the intensely flavorful pork broth served at this ramen-dive is worth the wait. And you won't stay long, because hungry people will be staring at you to hurry up and finish. Night owls note that it's open until midnight during the week and 1 a.m. on weekends. ☺ 🎬

[El Parian] 🏛 1528 Pico Blvd., Pico-Union, 213.386.7361. B, L & D daily. Mexican/taqueria. Beer. Cash only. $ **WHY** The best carne asada in the history of mankind, served on pressed-to-order tortillas. Remarkable *birria* (kid), too. **WHAT** Pay no mind to the graffiti and the bars on the windows, and step inside this friendly spot for gorgeous, grilled-to-order birria and carne asada, served in huge tacos, in burrito form or to go by the pound. Unlike at many taquerias, cold beer is served, and there's free parking in back. **WHO** Pico-Union locals and a few adventurous Downtown office workers. 🎬☺

[El Pique Taco Truck] 🏛 Parking lot at York Blvd. & Ave. 53, Highland Park. L & D daily. Taqueria. Cash only. $ **WHY** Meltingly tender al pastor and savory chorizo tacos and burritos, served late into the night. **WHAT** One of L.A.'s finest taco trucks lives in the parking lot of the car wash at the corner of York and Avenue 53, and it has a devoted following. The al pastor is smoky and richly spicy, the carne asada is lean and savory, and the chorizo is addictive. **WHO** Locals, workers from the car wash that shares this parking lot, and Mexican *futbol* fans (the truck bears its allegiance to Chivas). ☺ 🎬

[Hana-Ichimonme] 333 S. Alameda St., Little Tokyo/Arts District, 213.626.3514. L daily, D Mon.-Tues. & Thurs.-Sun. Japanese. Beer & wine. MC, V. $ **WHY** *Champon*, a robust, spicy broth with seafood and lots of noodles. **WHAT** This Little Tokyo warhorse has been turning out good, inexpensive ramen for years, and it's still going strong, despite the general decline of the little mall it's in. A handy spot for a quick bite Downtown. **WHO** Japanese-American regulars and Downtown partiers looking for a quick, cheap, tasty meal. 🎬☺

[India Sweets & Spices] 3126 Los Feliz Blvd., Atwater, 323.345.0360, indiasweetsandspices.net. L & D daily. Indian. AE, MC, V. $ **WHY** Cooked-to-order southern-style treats such as the pancake-like uthappam, spongy steamed idli dumplings and crispy crêpe-style dosa with *sambar*, a tart lentil stew. **WHAT** Vegetarian street food and the Indian snack fare chat are the main draws at this branch of the California mini-chain that offers takeout as well as a dining room with communal tables. Check out the vivid orange signs trumpeting the daily specials and be prepared for some intense chile-driven heat. At the market you can load up on spices and Indian groceries. **WHO** Indian families and eastside food adventurers and vegetarians. 🍴🌿🚲☺

[Juanita's] 20 E. Olvera St., Downtown, 213.628.1013. L & D daily. Mexican. MC, V. $ **WHY** For the best taquitos around, and a place to eat on Olvera Street that isn't a tourist trap. **WHAT** A plain-jane stall in the middle of Olvera Street, with a few tables and downright delicious fresh taquitos. You can also get pan dulce, enchiladas and a few other things, but most everyone gets the taquitos. **WHO** Your savvier tourists and longtime regulars, sometimes picking up a few dozen taquitos for a party (call ahead). 🍴☺☼

[King Taco] 🏛 1118 Cypress Ave., Mt. Washington, 323.223.2595, kingtaco.com. B, L & D daily. Taqueria. Cash only. $ **WHY** Famously savory, just-greasy-enough meats, especially carne asada and carnitas, served in very good tacos, burritos and sopes. **WHAT** The mothership of the King Taco empire, this is an L.A. classic, with great carne asada tacos and kickass salsa roja. Order at the counter, snag a patio table, and pick up lots of napkins. ☺🍴☺☼

[Mama's Hot Tamales] 🏛 2122 W. 7th St., Westlake, 213.487.7474, iurd.org/mamashottamales. L daily. Mexican. MC, V. $ **WHY** Indulge in these tamales not only because they're delicious, but because they're making L.A. a better place. Good coffee, too, and a gallery showcasing local artists. **WHAT** Sure, the tamales from every region of Mexico and Central America are wonderful, and yes, the café is a vividly colorful community center, but this nonprofit is really about doing good: providing job training and business skills for low-income local women. Have a quick lunch in the café or pick up a few to take back to the office. **WHO** West Downtown workers, artists, Koreatown residents. 🍴☺

[The Oinkster] 2005 Colorado Blvd., Eagle Rock, 323.255.OINK, oinkster.com. L & D daily. Barbecue. Beer & wine. AE, MC, V. $ **WHY** For "slow" fast food that's really tasty: pulled pork, rotisserie chicken, burgers, Belgian fries, fresh salads and monster cupcakes. **WHAT** A former drive-through got a near-complete makeover but still retained its '60s A-frame goofiness. The gimmick is fast food prepared the slow way, with quality ingredients — a burger joint for people who read *Cook's Illustrated*. **WHO** Oxy students and tastefully tattooed Eagle Rock parents with their adorably outfitted kids. 🍴☺☼

[Philippe the Original] 🏛 1001 N. Alameda St., Chinatown, 213.628.3781, philippes.com. B, L & D daily. American. Beer & wine. AE, MC, V. $ **WHY** Marvelously soggy dip sandwiches (beef, lamb, pork), which Philippe's claims to have invented. **WHAT** We've been coming to Philippe's since we were knee-high to a wooden stool, and there's nothing we love more than sitting on a wooden stool in this 1908

🌿 VEGETARIAN ☺ KID FRIENDLY ☼ PATIO DINING 🚐 DELIVERY 🏛 PRIVATE PARTY order-at-the-counter, sawdust-on-the-floor landmark. The French dips are delicious, the wine by the glass is surprisingly good, the candy counter is a vintage treasure, and the sandwich ladies wear fetching little hats. What's not to adore? **WHO** A marvelous array of Angelenos: miniature Chinese ladies, strapping cops, big-shot politicians, down-on-their-luckers who scraped together enough for a sandwich and a cup of the legendary ten-cent coffee. 🗺️ ☺

[Pitfire Pizza Company] 108 W. 2nd St., Downtown, 213.808.1200, pitfirepizza.com. L & D daily. Pizzeria. Beer & wine. AE, MC, V. $
WHY Neopolitan-style pizzas (try the burrata), well-filled panini and good salads, plus delivery in the Downtown zone bounded by Alameda, Figueroa, Temple and Olympic. **WHAT** Although it's a sit-down café, and a perfectly fine one, this is a handier place to know about for takeout and delivery, especially because it can get mobbed at lunchtime. (Note that lunchtime delivery orders need to be in by 11 a.m.) The individual pizzas are terrific, the crusts thin but with enough bite, and the grilled panini are just as tasty. **WHO** Students, gallery explorers and Caltrans and City Hall toilers. 🗺️ 🔦 ☺ 🚗

[Pollo Campero] 1605 W. Olympic Blvd., Pico-Union, 213.251.8594, campero.com. B, L & D daily. Guatemalan. AE, MC, V. $ **WHY** So legendary that food historian John T. Edge included it in his seminal *Fried Chicken*. **WHAT** Forget the Colonel and check out this branch of the Guatemalan chain famous for its achiote-pepper-crusted chicken. Biscuits, slaw, fried plantains and a nice salsa bar round out the accompaniments. **WHO** Guatemalan ex-pats happy to no longer have to lug this *pollo* back in their suitcases. 🗺️ ☺

[Pollos el Brasero] 2281 W. Pico Blvd., Pico-Union, 213.381.6060. L & D Tues.-Sun. Peruvian. No booze. MC, V. $ **WHY** Straightforward, tasty, very cheap Peruvian fire-roasted chicken served in a cheerful dive. **WHAT** We're not as gaga for this chicken as some — it's a wee bit bland, and it can get dry, depending on how long it's been sitting around — but it has a wonderful, mahogany skin and a nice smokiness, and it's a hell of a value, at about $5 for a quarter chicken meal. The fries and rice are good, and the green aji sauce (some call it Peruvian habañero) makes heat lovers ecstatic. Not worth a major drive, but a good spot for takeout or a cheap lunch for those who work or live not too far from Pico-Hoover. 🗺️ ☺

[Ricardo's Fish Tacos] Various locations, Silver Lake, @rickysfishtacos, L Sat.-Sun. Taqueria. Cash only. $ **WHY** Excellent Baja-style fish tacos. **WHAT** Ricardo (better known as Ricky) moves his *poquito* stand around Silver Lake, but you can reliably find him either in front of Le Bar (3922 Sunset Blvd.) or the laundromat on Saturdays during the Silver Lake Farmers' Market. He makes just one thing, fish tacos

($2.50), and they're terrific, the fish fresh from the fryer and the tortillas warmed to order. This is the real thing, made by an Ensenada native. **WHO** Farmers' market shoppers and surfers pining for Baja. 🖼

[Señor Fish] 🏠 4803 Eagle Rock Blvd., Eagle Rock, 323.257.7167. B, L & D daily. Taqueria. AE, MC, V. $ - $$ **WHY** Scallop enchiladas, seafood quesadillas, homemade salsas and heavenly beans, all of which you can eat in a setting of unusual (for a taqueria) charm. **WHAT** A fetching old bungalow with a stone fireplace and tree-shaded patio (it's very Berkeley) is home to L.A.'s most acclaimed seafood-focused taqueria. **WHO** Occidental students and their professors, with lots of new-era Eagle Rock yuppies mixed in. 🖼 ☺ ✿

[Señor Fish] 🏠 422 E. 1st St., Little Tokyo/Arts District, 213.625.0566, senorfishla.com. L & D daily. Mexican/seafood. Full bar. MC, V. $ - $$ **WHY** Grilled-scallop tacos (make sure to order the grilled, not fried), fish tacos and decadent seafood quesadillas. **WHAT** Now expanded with an adjacent full bar, this half-sibling to the Eagle Rock classic is home to equally good seafood tacos, burritos and quesadillas, which you can eat on a most pleasant walled patio. Be prepared for a line at lunchtime. Parking in the next-door 24-hour lot is just $3 with validation. **WHO** Workers from the local warehouses, residents of the local lofts and visitors to adjacent Little Tokyo. 🖼 ☺ ✿

[Spring Street Smoke House] 640 N. Spring St., Chinatown, 213.626.0535, sssmokehouse.com. L & D daily. American/Southern. Beer & wine. AE, MC, V. $ - $$ **WHY** An American barbecue joint is a fish out of water in Chinatown, but this place has proved to be a big success, with fine sauces and meat so good it (almost) doesn't need any sauce. **WHAT** The pitmaster in this simple rib joint mans a J & R Little Red smoker, and his meats benefit from the exquisite hickory smoking. Spice-rubbed brisket, tri-tip, ribs, baby backs, sandwich beef — all are standouts. House specialty: the bacon-wrapped Cajun-style smoked chicken breast, stuffed with onions and jalapeños. **WHO** Downtown business folks and Chinatown art-gallery types. 🖼 ☺

[Taco Zone] 🏠 Von's parking lot, 1342 N. Alvarado St., Echo Park. Nightly from 7 p.m. Taqueria. Cash only. $ **WHY** Simple, perfectly grilled pork, beef and chorizo tacos. **WHAT** Some love the carne asada, others prefer the *lengua* (tongue), but all agree this truck parked outside the Von's market on Alvarado grills up some of the best meats in the area. Come anytime after 7 p.m., but expect crowds later in the evening when hungry clubgoers start congregating. This truck is so beloved that when it was vandalized last year, neighborhood musicians mounted a fundraiser to help keep the tacos coming. **WHO** Echo Park families and fashionably attired young folks. ☺ 🖼 ☺

🍃 VEGETARIAN ☺ KID FRIENDLY ✿ PATIO DINING 🚗 DELIVERY 🎩 PRIVATE PARTY

[Tacos El Korita] **E. Olympic Blvd. at Herbert Ave., East L.A.. D nightly (until 2 a.m. weekends). Taqueria. Cash only. $ WHY** Tortillas *hechas a mano* (handmade) right on the truck are paired with good meats and either a smoky salsa verde or intense salsa roja. **WHAT** A taco truck's gotta be good to make it in this neighborhood, and El Korita is good, really good. Tortillas pressed to order, right on the truck — need we say more? **WHO** Pilgrims coming from as far away as the Valley, and families from just around the block. ☉ ▧ ☺

[Tacos Tumbras a Tomas] **Grand Central Market, 317 S. Broadway, Downtown, 213.620.1071, grandcentralsquare.com. B, L & early D daily. Taqueria. Cash only. $ WHY** Great Michoacan tacos that are so big you have to eat them with a knife and fork. **WHAT** This hugely popular stand in Grand Central Market serves the biggest tacos in town, so big that they come with an extra full-size tortilla so you can turn it into two tacos. All the meats are expertly seasoned; we're partial to the chicken. Very good tortas, too. **WHO** Latino immigrant shoppers, jury-duty lunch-breakers and, on weekends, day trippers. ▧ ☺

[Tomato Pie Pizza Joint] **2457 Hyperion Ave., Silver Lake, 323.661.6474, tomatopiepizzajoint.com. L & D daily. Pizzeria. MC, V. $ - $$$ WHY** All the standard pies (plus an excellent white pie), as well as calzones, subs and pasta dishes. **WHAT** Flavorful New York–style pies are turned out at this modest shop with a few locations, each of which has friendly service and efficient delivery. ▧ ☺ 🚗

[Tommy's] 🔒 **2575 Beverly Blvd., Westlake, 213.389.9060, original-tommys.com. B, L & D 24 hours daily. American. Cash only. $ WHY** For the chili burger and chili dog that have captivated three generations of Angelenos. **WHAT** It's a rite of passage that every self-respecting young Angeleno experiences — drink too much, stay out too late, and then go to Tommy's at 3 a.m. for a messy, greasy chili burger. We prefer the chili dog, but then again, we're getting too old for Tommy's anyway. **WHO** The drunk, the hungry and the possessors of cast-iron stomachs. ☉ ▧ ☺

[Two Boots] **1818 W. Sunset Blvd., Echo Park, 213.413.2668, twoboots.com. L Fri.-Sun., D nightly. Pizzeria. No booze. MC, V. $ WHY** Echo Park's first real pizza parlor comes with Cajun-via-New York flavor, and you can even get a slice to go. **WHAT** This acclaimed New York pizzeria came to Echo Park last year, making locals happy with hearty pies with slightly sweet crusts, bearing such whimsical names as the Big Maybelle and the Cleopatra Jones. Toppings are considerably broader than most pizzerias, including crayfish, shiitake mushrooms and tasso ham. Two Boots also delivers to the adjacent Echo music club. **WHO** Teens, families, clubgoers who like the late hours. ☉ 🚗

🔒 ESSENTIALLY L.A. ☉ LATE ♥ ROMANTIC ▧ VALUE 🔊 QUIET ♻ SUSTAINABLE

SAN GABRIEL VALLEY

[The Counter] 140 Shoppers Ln., Pasadena, 626.440.1008, thecounterburger.com. L & D daily. American. Beer & wine. AE, MC, V. $ - $$ **WHY** For a generous, messy, not-inexpensive burger (Angus beef, turkey, chicken, salmon or veggie), prepared in a nearly infinite number of ways. Also terrific are the sweet potato fries, crisp onion rings and thick shakes. **WHAT** Have a hankering for a burger with jalapeño jack cheese, carrot strings, a fried egg and apricot sauce? You can get just that in this brand-new outpost of the fast-growing, Santa Monica-born modern diner chain — in fact, you can get 312,120 possible combinations, including a simple cheeseburger. The beef is Angus, and they'll at least try to cook it on the rare side if you ask. **WHO** BMW-driving men and their iPod-wearing spawn. 🕮 ☺

[Doña Rosa] 577 S. Arroyo Pkwy., Pasadena, 626.449.2999, dona-rosa. com. B, L & D daily. Mexican. Full bar. AE, MC, V. $ - $$ **WHY** Although it's a taqueria swank enough that you could take Nancy Reagan there, Doña Rosa is not phony, as evidenced by its excellent huevos con chorizo, hearty pozole and, most of all, its acclaimed pan dulce of every type. **WHAT** How the food can be so good here and so, well, less than good at its parent, the El Cholo on Fair Oaks, is hard to fathom. So just ignore the family tree, step up to the counter, and order a sopes al pollo made with a freshly griddled masa cake. How they got a liquor license at an order-at-the-counter place we'll never know, but the superb $4 margaritas ($2.50 from Monday through Thursday) are the best deal in Pasadena. 🕮 ☺ ☼

[Dumpling House] 921 S. Baldwin Ave., Arcadia, 626.445.2755. L & D daily. Chinese/dumplings/noodles. MC, V. $ **WHY** Good, cheap dumplings and other Shanghai dishes that you can eat here or have made quickly to take out. The scallion pancakes are even more essential to order than the dumplings. **WHAT** A little more downmarket than nearby (and much more famous) Din Tai Fung, this friendly neighborhood café and takeout joint is also known for its *xiao long bao*, the juicy soup-filled dumplings that are the great addiction of Shanghainese cooking. These are good ones, richly flavorful and with skins that are satisfyingly doughy but not too heavy. Also try the cumin lamb and, most essentially, the scallion pancakes with sliced beef, the epitome of meaty, fried comfort food. 🕮 ☺

[El Taquito Mexicano] 467 N. Fair Oaks Ave., Pasadena, 626.577.3918, eltaquitomexicano.com. B, L & D daily. Taqueria. MC, V. $ **WHY** Sopes made with fat masa cakes, richly flavorful beans and tender chicken; all the meats (carne asada, lengua, carnitas) are good, too. By day you can eat in the bare-bones café, by night at the taco truck. **WHAT** The interior of this sunny yellow building isn't much to look at, but the women in the tiny kitchen turn out some of the best Mexican

🕮 VEGETARIAN ☺ KID FRIENDLY ☼ PATIO DINING 🚗 DELIVERY 🎪 PRIVATE PARTY food in the San Gabriel Valley, at rock-bottom prices. Night owls head for their taco truck, which is parked in the Nishikawa auto-repair shop lot at 510 S. Fair Oaks — it's open until at least midnight during the week and 3 a.m. on weekends. (Cash only at the truck.) **WHO** Day laborers, contractors, artists and in-the-know businesspeople fleeing Old Town. ☺ 🐖☺ ☼

[Gerlach's Grill] **1075 S. Fair Oaks Ave., Pasadena, 626.799.7575. L & D daily. Mexican/Middle Eastern. MC, V. $ WHY** For Mediterranean-Mexican kebabs and fresh seafood dishes to take home or back to the office (or eat in your car). Try the salmon tacos, mahi mahi burger, falafel or lamb kebabs. **WHAT** A tiny hut next to Gerlach's Liquor (which stocks a surprisingly impressive collection of wine) turns out delicious and inexpensive food that mixes Mexican influences (tacos, burritos) with Middle Eastern flavors (saffron-flavored rice, tangy salads, traditional kebabs). Simple but very good fresh grilled fish, too. **WHO** At lunch, workers from the Fair Oaks medical buildings; in the early evening, southwest Pasadenans driving up in their Mercedeses for a quick takeout dinner. 🐖🍖☺

[The Hat World Famous Pastrami] **491 N. Lake Ave., Pasadena, 626.449.1844, thehat.com. L & D daily. American. MC, V. $ WHY** Really good salty pastrami; long, thick fries, preferably doused with chili and cheese; and cold horchatas and Orange Bangs. **WHAT** Sparkling clean, featuring retro graphics and a constant background chant of "pastrami burger, pastrami burger," this cute little checkerboard place with a grandiose name has preserved the stripped-down ethos of fast food and the SoCal car culture that spawned it. 🐖☺

[La Estrella] **502 N. Fair Oaks Ave., Pasadena, 626.792.8559, la-estrellarestaurant.com. B, L & D daily (until 2 a.m. weekends). Taqueria. Cash only. $ WHY** Fried (Baja-style) fish tacos, ceviche and al pastor tacos and burritos. **WHAT** A vividly colorful stand that looks like it should be in a Mexican beach town, La Estrella has a crowd day and night. We prefer the meat dishes across the street at El Taquito Mexicano, but the fish tacos here are winners. **WHO** High school and college kids, day laborers and neighborhood families. ☺ 🐖☺ ☼

[Lola's Peruvian] **230 N. Brand Blvd., Glendale, 818.956.5888. L daily, D Tues.-Sun. Peruvian. Beer & wine. AE, MC, V. $ - $$ WHY** Profoundly addictive crisp-skinned chicken, one of the most delicious in all of Los Angeles, marinated in citrus juice, garlic and chiles and spit-roasted over a wood fire. **WHAT** A friendly little Peruvian café with amazing roast chicken and homemade french fries. Make sure to try the Peruvian chile sauce with your chicken. **WHO** Brand Boulevard shoppers and Glendale residents running in for a chicken to go. 🐖☺ ☼

[Los Tacos] 1 W. California Blvd., Pasadena, 626.795.9291. B, L & D daily. Taqueria. Cash only. $ **WHY** Savory carnitas and carne asada, Baja-style red-snapper tacos and good vegetarian tostadas and burritos. **WHAT** A cheerful, friendly taqueria with a nicer-than-the-norm setting (comfortable booths) and excellent tacos, burritos, menudo and horchata, all at low prices. They also do a fine job catering parties. **WHO** Huntington Hospital workers, Art Center students, moms 'n' kids. ☺ 🗊 🗲 ☺ ✿

[Lucky Boy] 640 S. Arroyo Pkwy, Pasadena, 626.793.0120. B, L & D daily. American/Mexican. Cash only. $ **WHY** Amazing breakfast burritos holding at least a pound of bacon, as well as all the burger-stand classics. **WHAT** A traditional burger joint, with concrete tables outside, Formica tables inside and an army of hard-working guys in the tiny short-order kitchen. **WHO** Young and hungry men, and everyone else in Pasadena. 🗊 ☺ ✿

[Mamma's Brick Oven Pizza] 710 S. Fair Oaks Ave., South Pasadena, 626.799.1344, mammasbrickoven.com. L & D daily. Pizzeria. MC, V. $ **WHY** Tasty, straightforward thin-crust pizzas served by the (large) slice or whole pie, to eat inside or on the patio or to get delivered. Make sure to get a couple of garlic knots, too. **WHAT** Lots of locals swear by Mamma's white pizza, but we find it too sweet and prefer the margherita, the shrimp or just plain cheese. Nice people man the busy counter. **WHO** South Pas High kids and local families. 🗊 ☺ ✿ 🚐

[Mario's Italian Deli & Market] 🏠 740 E. Broadway, Glendale, 818.242.4114, mariosdeli.com. L & early D Mon.-Sat. Italian. AE, MC, V. $ **WHY** Superb ten-inch Italian subs made before your eyes on fresh bread. While you're there, pick up some prosciutto, burrata and delicious, cheap homemade marinara to take home. **WHAT** Every day around 11:30 a.m., the crowds gather at this long glass deli case, waiting to order one of the famous subs. (It looks like total chaos, but there is a system, so make sure to take a number.) Pastas are so-so, pizzas aren't bad, but it's the sandwiches you come for, especially the prosciutto, the lemon turkey, the meatball and the chicken parmigiana. They're as good as the best in Brooklyn. Really. **WHO** Hungry working men, most of whom take the sandwiches out, because seating is limited. 🗊

[Mediterranean Delight] 126 S. Brand Blvd., Glendale, 818.543.3272. L & D daily. Mediterranean. MC, V. $ **WHY** For a quick bite, before or after a movie, that's homemade and delicious. Free delivery, too. **WHAT** Tasty Mediterranean food — kebabs, falafel, roast chicken, fresh mahi mahi, hummus — is served quickly and inexpensively by a husband-and-wife team. In a shopping-center spot where you'd expect a soulless chain, real people and real food thrive! **WHO** Glendale shoppers and moviegoers. 🗊 ☺ 🚐

Food That's Fast

🗲 VEGETARIAN ☺ KID FRIENDLY ✿ PATIO DINING 🚐 DELIVERY 🏠 PRIVATE PARTY

[Orean Health Express] 817 N. Lake Ave., Pasadena, 626.794.0861, oreanshealthexpress.com. B, L & D daily. Vegetarian/ vegan. MC, V. $ **WHY** Vegan and vegetarian fast food — there's even a drive-through window. **WHAT** All the fast-food staples are here — chili-cheese burgers, burritos, pastrami dips, soft-serve ice cream — except they're all vegetarian and/or vegan, made with tofu and soy, and they're pretty good, considering. The extensive menu includes air fries, miso-vegetable soup and ginseng slushies. 🗊❀🍴☺

[Señor Fish] 618 Mission St., South Pasadena, 626.403.0145. L & D daily, brunch Fri.-Sun. Taqueria. AE, MC, V. $ **WHY** Scallop enchiladas, seafood quesadillas, fish tacos, homemade salsas and heavenly beans. **WHAT** The generic strip-mall setting doesn't have a tenth of the charm of its Eagle Rock sibling, but the shrimp tacos and other Mexican taqueria dishes are every bit as good. **WHO** South Pasadena neighbors and shoppers fortifying themselves for a trip to the always-crowded Trader Joe's across the street. 🗊☺

[Teri & Yaki] 319 S. Arroyo Pkwy., Pasadena, 626.683.9865; 106 S. Myrtle Ave., Monrovia, 626.256.6705, teriandyaki.com. L & D Mon.-Sat. Asian. AE, MC, V. $ **WHY** Addictively sweet-savory teriyaki chicken, served over noodles and rice. **WHAT** A staple place for a hearty but not junky quick lunch and takeout meals after a long day at work. We're hooked on the teriyaki chicken, but others swear by the Korean-style beef and the noodle soup. Interesting spinach and bean-sprout side dishes. **WHO** Lunch-rushers and families after soccer practice. 🗊☺

[Tito's Market] 9814 E. Garvey Ave., El Monte, 626.579.1893. L & D daily. Argentinean. AE, MC, V. $ **WHY** Huge hoagie-style sandwiches with Argentinean flair (meaning lots of meat); try the steak milanese. **WHAT** You'd never think to stop in this ordinary-looking little market in a strip mall if you happened along Garvey, but inside is an Argentinean market and deli that turns out extraordinary sandwiches, both made to order and ready-made to take out. **WHO** A diverse mix that reflects the community. 🗊

[Tops] 🏛 3838 E. Colorado Blvd., East Pasadena, 626.449.4412, theoriginaltops.com. B, L & D daily. American/Mexican. MC, V. $ **WHY** The Kobe burger, made with American Kobe beef, smoked mozzarella, caramelized onion, tomato, mixed greens and herb mayo on a ciabatta bun, attracts burger buffs from as far away as Woodland Hills. **WHAT** This born-in-1952 fast-food institution has been spiffed up for a new era, with gleaming tile and shiny laminated tables. The food is generous and beautifully prepared; its Kobe burger, pastrami, turkey burgers, tuna melts, hand-cut fries, tortilla soup and bacon-and-egg sandwiches are as delicious as we hope they'll be in every American roadside diner but almost never are. **WHO** Middle-aged, middle-class working men, students and burger-joint foodies on a quest. 🗊☺✿

🏛 **ESSENTIALLY L.A.** ☺**LATE** ♥**ROMANTIC** 🗊 **VALUE** 🍴**QUIET** ✿**SUSTAINABLE**

[Zankou Chicken] 1415 E. Colorado Blvd., Glendale,
818.244.2237; 1296 E. Colorado Blvd., Pasadena, 626.405.1502,
zankouchicken.com. L & D daily. Lebanese. AE, MC, V. $ **WHY** Intensely
aromatic rotisserie chicken, the skin soaked just right with salt and
seasonings. **WHAT** The spits never stop spinning at Zankou, which
turns out hundreds of richly flavorful chickens a day, either to eat here
or take home. Once the chicken drops below the finger-melting tem-
perature (which takes a while), you tear it up and stuff it in a pita with
a schmear of the white garlic sauce, and enter poultry heaven. ☺

[Zeke's Smokehouse] 2209 Honolulu Ave., Montrose,
818.957.7045, zekessmokehouse.com. L & D daily. American/barbecue.
Beer & wine. AE, MC, V. $ - $$$ **WHY** Baby-back ribs to dream about:
smoky, succulent, with a nice char and light crust, and they take out
beautifully. Excellent brisket, too. **WHAT** Zeke's is a multi-denomina-
tional shrine to the art of the barbecue, with chefs channeling some of
the country's most renowned pit masters and turning out Kansas City,
Memphis, North Carolina and Texas styles. Their sauces are masterful
blends of hot, sweet, tangy and salty. Eat in or take out. **WHO** Locals,
families and 'cue fans from both valleys. ☺ ☼

[Zelo Cornmeal Crust Pizza] 328 E. Foothill Blvd., Arcadia,
626.358.8298, zelo.us. L Tues.-Sat., D Tues.-Sun. Pizzeria. Beer & wine.
AE, MC, V. $ - $$ **WHY** Unusual and very good pizza made with a corn-
meal crust that's almost like a good hush puppy, crunching with each
bite. Try the one with pancetta and red onions. **WHAT** A tiny, cheerful
café flagged with market umbrellas and small outdoor tables, serving
unusual and delicious pizza by the slice or whole, to eat here or to take
out. Worth a drive. ▣ ☺ ☼

EAST VALLEY

[Amir's Falafel] 11711 Ventura Blvd., Studio City, 818.509.8641.
L & D daily. Israeli. AE, MC, V. $ **WHY** For some of the city's finest
Israeli-style falafel, served in an accessible mini-mall spot near Universal City. **WHAT** A good, quick place serving freshly fried, pillowy
falafel sandwiches; chicken and beef schwarma and a good selection
of side dishes, including spicy carrot salad, tabbouleh, eggplant and
cabbage salads. Be prepared for a line at lunch. **WHO** Hurried workers
from production companies, post houses, Radford and even businesses
that have nothing to do with entertainment. ▣ ▨

[Carney's] 12601 Ventura Blvd., Studio City, 818.761.8300,
carneytrain.com. L & D daily. American. Beer & wine. AE, MC, V. $
WHY A tasty turkey burger, good hot dogs and all-around decent fast
food served until midnight on weekends at modest prices. Lunchtime
delivery, too! **WHAT** This Val offshoot of the Sunset Strip landmark is
a pretty standard fast-food joint in an atmospheric old train car. The

▨ VEGETARIAN ☺ KID FRIENDLY ☼ PATIO DINING ⊕ DELIVERY ▣ PRIVATE PARTY chili's on the bland side, and the fries are just okay, but the burgers and dogs are satisfying. **WHO** Valley families and gaggles of young people. 🎫😊☼🚗

[Jack's Classic Hamburgers] 🏛 **11375 Riverside Dr., North Hollywood, 818.761.4599, jacksclassichamburgers.com. L & D daily. American. Cash only. $ WHY** Great bacon-chili-cheeseburgers, classic burgers sparked with fresh jalapeños and slightly healthier turkey burgers (which we fatten up with bacon). **WHAT** In a parking lot next to the 170 Freeway is the best burger stand in the Valley, home to fresh, quality hamburgers, crispy skinny fries, good onion rings and tasty chili. 🎫😊☼

[Jody Maroni's] **CityWalk, 1000 Universal Center Dr., Universal City, 818.622.5639, jodymaroni.com. B, L & D daily. American. AE, MC, V. $ WHY** For the best fast food at CityWalk. Try the brat with grilled onions and peppers. **WHAT** Now found in markets across the country, Jody Maroni's sausages were first served at a little Venice stand in the late '70s and are now found at most of Southern California's upscale outdoor malls, like this one. **WHO** An endless river of teens and tourists cruising CityWalk. 🎫😊

[Ohana BBQ] **11269 Ventura Blvd., Studio City, 818.508.3192, ohanabbq.com. L & D Mon.-Sat. Hawaiian. AE, MC, V. $ WHY** The "Supah" salad is super, topped as it is with grilled chicken, and the dessert shave ices are the best. **WHAT** The Hawaiian word for delicious is *ono*, and that certainly applies to the Korean-influenced menu at this family-run spot. The Wiki Wiki noodle stir-fry (the Korean chap chae) is loaded with meat and vegetables, and the bibim bap features brown or white rice with veggies and a choice of barbecued pork, chicken, beef or tofu mixed with a sweet-hot chile sauce. Juicy beef short ribs and spicy pork ribs, too. 🎫😊

[Pitfire Pizza Company] **5211 Lankershim Blvd., North Hollywood, 818.980.2949, pitfirepizza.com. L & D daily. Pizzeria. Beer & wine. AE, MC, V. $ - $$ WHY** Neopolitan-style pizzas (try the burrata), well-filled panini and good salads (with farmers' market ingredients), plus delivery in NoHo, west Burbank and east Studio City (as far west as Laurel Canyon). **WHAT** Although it's a sit-down café, and a good one, this is a handy place to know about for takeout and delivery, especially because it can get mobbed at dinnertime. The modern individual pizzas are terrific, the crusts thin but with enough bite, and the grilled panini are just as tasty. **WHO** NoHo hipsters. 🎫😊☼🚗

[Poquito Mas] **3701 Cahuenga Blvd., Studio City, 818.760.8226, poquitomas.com. L & D daily. Taqueria. AE, MC, V. $ WHY** Shrimp tacos San Felipe, carne asada burrito and a particularly good salsa bar. **WHAT** The original Studio City location of this ten-store mini-chain long ago outgrew its parking lot, but patrons still throng to the tiny Baja-themed storefront with a minuscule outdoor eating area. Same menu and more spacious digs at the newer locations in Burbank, NoHo, West L.A., Sunset Strip, Torrance, Valencia, Chatsworth and Woodland Hills. **WHO** At the original location, hungry grips, best boys and Foley artists, along with the occasional celebrity. 🖅 ⊙ ☼

[Press Panini] **4389 Tujunga Ave., Studio City, 818.487.2564, press-panini.com. B, L & D Mon.-Fri. Italian. MC, V. $ WHY** High-quality pa-nini, including great vegetarian choices, served quickly. Extras include delivery and free parking in back. **WHAT** Warm, fresh, melting panini are the specialty here, from the classic (caprese or, for breakfast, prosciutto, egg, cheddar and Swiss) to the inventive (fajita chicken or teriyaki tofu). They're all good, as are the big salads. Eat here at a sidewalk table or take your sandwich back to work. 📞 ⊙ ☼ 🚗

[Tacos la Fonda] **NW corner of Vineland Ave. & Vanowen St., North Hollywood. D nightly. Taqueria. Cash only. $ WHY** Tortillas made fresh on the truck, juicy carne asada and excellent salsas, especially the smoky, spicy roja. **WHAT** Some of the best tacos in the Valley are handed through the window of this truck, which takes up residence in the car wash parking lot in the evenings. ⊙ 🖅 ⊙

[Tacos Texcoco] **Laurel Canyon Blvd. & Vanowen St., North Hollywood. D nightly. Taqueria. Cash only. $ WHY** Good, classic tacos and burritos at astonishingly low prices. **WHAT** An old-fashioned, tow-style taco wagon festooned with a vivid mural depicting the legend of the volcanoes turns out delicious carne asada and carnitas tacos. **WHO** Really frugal taco hounds — these cost just 80 cents! 🖅 ⊙

[Yaki's] **904 W. Alameda Ave., Burbank, 818.845.1016. L & D daily. Japanese/American. Cash only. $ WHY** Tasty sweet-savory teriyaki chicken or beef bowls. **WHAT** We can live without the Bulldog (a weird fried hot dog served with a teriyaki–Thousand Island dressing), but the small chicken and vegetable bowl makes for a very fine and affordable quick lunch. Eat at the counter or the little patio, or take it to go. 🖅 ⊙ ☼

WEST VALLEY

[Amer's Falafel] **17334 Ventura Blvd., Encino, 818.995.6332, amersfalafel.com. L & D daily. Middle Eastern. AE, MC, V. $ - $$ WHY** They do crispy right — even to the point of packaging takeout falafel in a separate paper bag to preserve that lightning-fast fry. **WHAT** The falafel doesn't hit the oil until you order, and the result is a revelation: thin, ultra-crisp exteriors with succulent steaming insides. Go with a sandwich, or, better yet, order as a plate so you can sample a couple of the Middle Eastern side dishes, including meaty roasted

🥬 **VEGETARIAN** ⊙ **KID FRIENDLY** ☼ **PATIO DINING** 🚗 **DELIVERY** 🏛 **PRIVATE PARTY**

mushrooms or eggplant in tomato sauce. 🗺️🍴☺

[Cemitas Poblanas Don Adrian] 🏠 14902 Victory Blvd., Van Nuys, 818.785.0328. L daily, D Mon.-Sat. Mexican. No booze. Cash only. **$**
WHY For the cemitas poblanas, like a hefty burger, only better.
WHAT This shop next to a laundromat draws big crowds for its *cemitas poblanas*, astonishingly large and delicious sandwiches that sell for just $4. The basic sandwich starts with a large, toasted round bun layered with avocado, creamy fresh panela cheese, the meaty filling of your choice, red onion, fresh herbs and either roasted red jalapeño or a scorching chipotle chile purée. Fillings include barbacoa of lamb, juicy pollo adobado, pickled beef tendon, pork loin *milanese* (pounded thin and pan fried) or the house special, *cecina*, marinated cured beef.
WHO Homesick families from the Puebla region, and newbies who've discovered this L.A. street-food-of-the-moment. 🗺️☺

[D'Amores Pizza] 7137 Winnetka Ave., Canoga Park, 818.348.5900, damorespizzawinnetka.com. L & D daily. Pizzeria. Beer & wine. AE, MC, V.
$ WHY For light, flavorful, even healthy thin-crust pizza — it's technically Boston style, but it's almost identical to the best by-the-slice pies in New York. Eat here, take it out or call for delivery. **WHAT** Delicious thin-crust pizza is sold by the slice or the pie at this casual café in the depths of the Valley. Owner Joe D'Amore, a Boston native, imports water from Massachusetts to make his dough, and he says the higher mineral content of the water makes the dough less wet and helps the crust hold up without becoming cracker-crisp. Purists stick with the plain cheese, but the pizza bianco is also a winner. ☺ 🗺️☺🚗

[Fab Hot Dogs] 6747 Tampa Ave., Reseda, 818.344.4336, fabhotdogs.com. L daily, D Mon.-Sat. American. MC, V. **$ WHY** For a ripper and tots. **WHAT** New Jersey native Joe Fabrocini missed the "rippers" (hot dogs deep-fried until the casings burst) of his youth, so he brought them to Reseda, and grateful Jersey boys and girls make the trek to this little storefront from all over. You can get your dog grilled or steamed — or turkey or veggie if you must — but rippers are the thing to get, possibly heaped with the house-made mustard relish or chili. The fries are fine, but trust us, you want the tater tots. 🗺️☺

[Italia Bakery & Deli] 11134 Balboa Blvd., Granada Hills, 818.360.2913, italiabakeryanddeli.com. L & early D Mon.-Sat. Italian. MC, V. **$ WHY** First-rate Italian sandwiches that would hold their own in New York. **WHAT** This well-stocked market and full-service deli gets slammed at lunchtime, so consider phoning in your order for a sandwich made on either a hard or soft roll, both fresh. Locals have been coming here for years and swear by their favorites — some say sausage is the best, others insist on the eggplant parmigiana, still others get the fresh turkey and provolone. We like 'em all. Make sure to take home some focaccia for later. 🗺️

🏠 ESSENTIALLY L.A. ☺ LATE ♥ ROMANTIC 🗺️ VALUE 🔊 QUIET ♻ SUSTAINABLE

[Panos Char Broiler] 16045 Victory Blvd., Van Nuys, 818.780.4041.
B, L & D daily to 8 p.m. Greek/Mediterranean. MC, V. $ **WHY** All-around
excellent fast food: tender, tasty gyros; crisp falafel; savory souvlaki;
pita or regular burgers; good fries. **WHAT** This long-established dive
serves great, cheap Greek-Medi-American comfort food, and it serves
it fast. Hours can be inconsistent, so don't be shocked if it's closed.
🖼️🔪☺️🚚

[Pita Pockets] 9127 Reseda Blvd., Northridge, 818.709.4444. L & D
daily. Israeli/Middle Eastern. MC, V. $ **WHY** Laffa wraps heaped with
lemony hummus and any number of savory, delicious fillings. One
of the best sandwiches in the West Valley. **WHAT** The heart of this
strip-mall spot is the round oven for baking *laffa*, the bubbly, doughy,
completely addictive naan-like bread that is made fresh for each order.
A cook spreads the warm laffa with hummus and then adds your
choice of good things — chicken or lamb schwarma, falafel, grilled
vegetables — as well as lettuce, onions, tomatoes and sauce. Try it
once, you'll be back for another soon. 🖼️🔪☺️☼

[The Stand] 17000 Ventura Blvd., Encino, 818.788.2700, thestandlink.
com. L & D daily. American. Beer & wine. AE, MC, V. $ **WHY** Chicago
dog, Downtown L.A. dog and a killer barbecue bacon cheeseburger.
Don't miss the $1 dog on Monday evenings. **WHAT** The hot dog stand
of your dreams, the Stand purveys an array of dogs, sausages and
burgers with every topping you've ever fantasized about. And neon
pickle relish, too! **WHO** Local families and others jonesing for a nitrite
fix. 🖼️☺️☼

[Tacos Don Chente] 9038 Sepulveda Blvd., North Hills,
818.892.7181, tacosdonchente.com. B, L & D daily. Taqueria. Beer. AE,
MC, V. $ **WHY** Homemade corn tortillas, sweet al pastor and salsa
roja with a kick. Also try the burritos, gorditas and sopes. **WHAT** A
fast-growing new taco chain that's out to give King Taco a run for its
money. It's not better than the King, but this is a good place to know
about in the depths of the Valley. **WHO** Large and exuberant families
and lively groups of friends. 🖼️☺️

WESTSIDE: CENTRAL

[The Apple Pan] 🏠 10801 W. Pico Blvd., Rancho Park,
310.475.3585. L & D Tues.-Sun. (to 1 a.m. Fri.-Sat.). American. Cash only.
$ **WHY** Flat, flavorful steak burgers and hickory burgers wrapped
in paper, fries and homemade pies are the mainstays of this classic
counter-only joint. **WHAT** More than six decades of cooking burgers
and pie in the same charming 1940s diner with servers of the same
vintage; always busy, but worth the wait. Don't dawdle — the waitresses aren't shy about wanting to turn their counter stations. ☺️

Food
That's Fast

🥬 VEGETARIAN ☺ KID FRIENDLY ☼ PATIO DINING 🚚 DELIVERY 🏠 PRIVATE PARTY

[Beverly Falafel] **8508 W. 3rd St., Beverly Hills, 310.652.1670. L & D daily. Middle Eastern. MC, V. $ WHY** The house falafel plate with smoky baba ganouj. **WHAT** Neon-lit and cosmopolitan, this Beverly Center–adjacent eatery features garlic-marinated chicken breast, lamb chop plates and perfectly balanced falafel — crispy on the outside, creamy within. **WHO** A polyglot clientele, judging from the overheard Korean, Russian and Tagalog accents at lunch. ☞ ☺

[Bibi's Warmstone Bakery & Café] **8928 W. Pico Blvd., Cheviot Hills, 310.246.1788. B, L & D Sun.-Fri. Middle Eastern/Israeli. AE, MC, V. $ WHY** Amazing savory treats baked in a stone oven: *sambusack* (Israeli calzone), pizzas and Jerusalem bagels, the thin, savory circles sold by vendors outside the ancient city's walls. **WHAT** Although it bills itself as a bakery first, Bibi's is a find for westsiders seeking something quick to eat that's both deeply delicious and not junky. Everything that comes out of the stone oven is wonderful, from the stuffed, sesame-encrusted pitas called toastees to the pizzas and individual quiches. **WHO** Kosher-keepers and devoted regulars who don't care about kosher but appreciate great food. ☺ ☞

[The Coop Pizza] 🏠 **10006 National Blvd., Cheviot Hills, 310.837.4462. L & D Tues.-Sun. Pizzeria. Cash only. $ WHY** Superb New York–style pizza, by the slice or the pie. **WHAT** Is this the best New York–style pizza in town? Many think so, and it's certainly on our very short list. There's no seating, just a stand-up counter with room for two to eat a slice or wait for a pie; Cheviot/Palms locals get delivery, and others happily drive a ways for takeout. Note that it's usually closed by 9:30 p.m., sometimes earlier if the kitchen runs out of dough. **WHO** True regulars who get this pizza far more often than is probably good for them. ☞🚗

[Falafel King] **1010 Broxton Ave., Westwood, 310.208.4444. L & D daily. Middle Eastern. MC, V. $ WHY** Decades of experience give this UCLA hangout (recently moved to a smaller spot down the street) the upper hand in fast yet healthy food. **WHAT** Great falafel, but also a wide selection of Middle Eastern salads to stuff in pita sandwiches, and schwarma, too. **WHO** A college and date-night crowd. ☞🍴☺

[Honey's Kettle Fried Chicken] **9537 Culver Blvd., Culver City, 310.202.5453, honeyskettle.com. L & D daily. American/Southern. AE, MC, V. $ WHY** The chicken, of course — whole bird, combo meal or even in an individual pot pie. **WHAT** The chicken is justly famous, lightly battered and spectacularly juicy. But there's more to Honey's than those golden birds. From the freshly squeezed lemonade to the small fruit pies and buttermilk biscuits, a meal in this cream-and-gold dining room is a treat. And don't forget to eat your vegetables; they're skewered, kettle-cooked and delicious. ☞☺

[Lamonica's NY Pizza] **1066 Gayley Ave., Westwood, 310.208.8671. L & D daily until midnight (to 1 a.m. Fri.-Sat.). Pizzeria. Cash only. $ WHY** For delicious New York pizza, best eaten by the slice and immediately. The plain cheese is best. **WHAT** Your basic pizza dive with thin-crust pies that boast the proper balance of cheese to sauce to crust. Pizza heads argue constantly about whether this is proper New York pizza or not, but we don't care. This is L.A., and Lamonica's tastes good. **WHO** UCLA students. ☺ 🖼🔖☺🚚

[Let's Be Frank] 🏠 **Helms Ave. between Washington Blvd. & Venice Blvd., Culver City, 888.2333.7265, letsbefrankdogs.com. L Wed.-Sun. American. Cash only. $ WHY** Because there's (almost) no guilt involved in enjoying the these all-natural, grass-fed beef hot dogs with organic accoutrements. It elevates the hot-dog cart to a haute new level. **WHAT** Even a Prius-driving liberal Democrat can feel good about this swank hot-dog cart parked near the old Helms Bakery building at lunchtime. Not only are the hot dogs, brats and Italian sausages artisanally produced, but they taste great and have just the right snap. Extras include organic sauerkraut and delicious freshly grilled onions. Thursday evenings they head over to Silverlake Wine (2395 Glendale Blvd.) to feed the tipsy masses after wine tastings. And with a $650 minimum order, they'll come to your next event. **WHO** Furniture shoppers and carefully rumpled families pushing $400 strollers. 🖼☺♻

[Paloma Selestial Taco Truck] **Overland Ave. at Pico Blvd., Century City. L daily. Taqueria. Cash only. $ WHY** *Cemita poblana de milanesa*, a Mexico City–style sandwich with thin-sliced, breaded beef, avocado and chipotle; good carnitas tacos, too. **WHAT** Also known as Tacos Wamu, this truck sets up lunch shop in the Chase (formerly Washington Mutual) parking lot every day, moving to the Pep Boys lot at Pico and Manning in the later afternoon. It's a reliable truck with respectable, consistent taco-truck fare. **WHO** Century City workers who don't want to spend $12 for a sandwich at the mall. 🖼

[Spoc's Sausage Stand] **972 Gayley Ave., Westwood, No phone. L & D daily. American. Cash only. $ WHY** Fast food that's two notches above the Westwood norm. **WHAT** A former sub-sandwich shack is now a first-rate sausage stand run by Samir Mohajer, owner/chef of Beverly Hills's Cabbage Patch. He's grilling Papa Cantela's sausages (smoked chicken-mango, honey smoked brats, linguiça), serving them on La Brea buns, and topping them with grilled onions and peppers. A combo meal with spicy fries and soda is a mere $5.50. **WHO** UCLA people and Westwood moviegoers and shoppers. 🖼☺

[The Stand] **2000 Avenue of the Stars, Century City, 310.785.0400, thestandlink.com. B & L Mon.-Fri. American. AE, MC, V. $ WHY** The "Loaded" dog, or any of the specialty hot dogs, such as the Chicago and the Downtown L.A. **WHAT** An alternative to Century City's

🥬 VEGETARIAN ☺ KID FRIENDLY ✿ PATIO DINING 🚚 DELIVERY 🎩 PRIVATE PARTY pricey restaurants, the Stand has become a lunchtime mainstay for local office workers who appreciate a good hot dog. 📺☺

[The Stand] 1116 Westwood Blvd., Westwood, 310.443.0400, thestandlink.com. L & D daily. American. Beer & wine. AE, MC, V. $ **WHY** Chicago dog, Downtown L.A. dog and a killer barbecue bacon cheeseburger. Don't miss the $1 dog on Monday evenings. **WHAT** The hot dog stand of your dreams, the Stand purveys an array of dogs, sausages and burgers with every topping you've ever fantasized about. And neon pickle relish, too! **WHO** UCLA students, moviegoers and date-nighters on a budget. 📺☺

[Zankou Chicken] 🏛 1716 S. Sepulveda Blvd., Westwood, 310.444.0550, zankouchicken.com. L & D daily. Lebanese. AE, MC, V. $ **WHY** Intensely aromatic rotisserie chicken, the skin soaked just right with salt and seasonings. **WHAT** The spits never stop spinning at Zankou, which turns out hundreds of richly flavorful chickens a day, either to eat here or take home. Once the chicken drops below the finger-melting temperature, you tear it up and stuff it in a pita with a schmear of the white garlic sauce, and enter poultry heaven. 📺☺

WEST OF THE 405

[Abbot's Pizza Company] 1407 Abbot Kinney Blvd., Venice, 310.396.7334. L & D daily. Pizzeria. AE, MC, V. $ **WHY** Huge slices of bagel-crust pizza to eat on the spot (the simple tomato-basil is best), or whole pizzas for takeout or delivery. **WHAT** The young folks just barely managing the $1,500 rent on their Venice dumps would starve if it weren't for the constantly replenished racks of by-the-slice pizza. Eat your slice at the narrow counter or at one of the highly prized outdoor tables. **WHO** Shaggy students and fake-shaggy (i.e., $100 haircuts) Abbot Kinney shoppers. 📺🍴☺🚗

[Baby Blues BBQ] 444 Lincoln Blvd., Venice, 310.396.7675, baby-bluesbarbq.com. L & D daily. Barbecue. Beer & wine. AE, MC, V. $ - $$$ **WHY** Memphis-style, slow-cooked, dry-rub ribs, both baby back and long bone. Also try the North Carolina-style pulled pork and the superb pork 'n' beans. **WHAT** A relaxed corner café with friendly people and a cheerful vibe. If you don't have time to eat here, you can take it out — and they deliver, too. **WHO** Venice carnivores — that's right, not everyone in Venice is vegetarian. 📺☺🚗

[Barney's Burgers] Brentwood Country Mart, 225 26th St., Santa Monica, 310.899.0133, barneyshamburgers.com. L & D daily. American. Beer & wine. MC, V. $$ **WHY** Flashback to the 1980s with spicy curly fries (great) and burgers topped with just about anything you want, all served al fresco at the Country Mart. **WHAT** Solid, if not brilliant, beef and turkey burgers. The fries, variety of burger toppings, and casual

🏛 ESSENTIALLY L.A. ☺LATE ♥ROMANTIC 📺 VALUE ᠀QUIET ❁SUSTAINABLE

outdoor picnic tables (perfect for messy tots) are the draw.
WHO After-school snackers, young families with picky eaters, and
too-cool-for-school teenagers. 🖼️☺️✿

[Bay Cities Italian Deli & Bakery] 🏛️ **1517 Lincoln Blvd., Santa
Monica, 310.395.8279, baycitiesitaliandeli.com. L Tues.-Sun. Italian. Beer
& wine. MC, V. $ WHY** The Godmother sub and the meatball sand-
wiches. **WHAT** This large Italian deli and grocery store is the westside
destination for huge sub sandwiches, especially the Godmother — a
massive heap of Genoa salami, mortadella, capicola, ham, prosciutto
and provolone on a house-baked roll. Get your sandwich to go or eat it
out front. **WHO** East Coasters hungry for a taste of home. ☺️

[Bravo Pizzeria] **2400 Main St., Santa Monica, 310.392.7466,
bravosantamonica.com. L & D daily until 1:30 a.m. Pizzeria. Beer & wine.
MC, V. $ - $$$ WHY** It nails the crust-sauce-cheese balance equation.
WHAT Bravo specializes in very good thin-crust pizza, with a richly
flavorful sauce and just the right amount of cheese. The service can be
spotty, but it delivers in the area. **WHO** Main Street revelers who buy
by the slice and locals who opt for a whole pie to take home. ☺️☺️🚗

[The Counter] **2901 Ocean Park Blvd., Santa Monica, 310.399.8383,
thecounterburger.com. L & D daily. American. Beer & wine. AE, MC, V.
$ - $$ WHY** For a generous, messy, not-inexpensive burger (Angus
beef, turkey, chicken, salmon or veggie), prepared in a nearly infinite
number of ways. Also terrific are the sweet potato fries, crisp onion
rings and thick shakes. **WHAT** Have a hankering for a burger with
jalapeño jack cheese, carrot strings, a fried egg and apricot sauce?
You can get just that in this concrete-and-glass modern diner — in
fact, you can get 312,120 possible combinations, including a simple
cheeseburger. The beef is Angus, and they'll at least try to cook it on
the rare side if you ask. **WHO** BMW-driving men and their iPod-
wearing spawn. 🍴☺️

[El Super Taco] **11923 Santa Monica Blvd., West L.A., 310.473.9692.
L & D daily until midnight. Taqueria. MC, V. $ WHY** Authentic Ensenada-
style fish tacos, juicy al pastor, an excellent salsa bar, pressed tortas
and an all-you-can-drink tamarindo fountain. **WHAT** What started as a
taco truck graduated to a strip-mall taqueria, in a westside neighborhood that's weak on taquerias — or rather, a westside neighborhood
that was weak on taquerias until now. **WHO** Westsiders who envy
their eastside taqueria-blessed friends. 🖼️

[Falafel King] **1315 3rd St. Promenade, Santa Monica, 310.587.2551.
L & D daily. Middle Eastern. MC, V. $ WHY** A rare reasonably priced yet
tasty place to eat on the Promenade. **WHAT** Great falafel, but also a
wide selection of Middle Eastern salads to stuff in pita sandwiches —
and schwarma, too. 🖼️🍴☺️✿

🍴 **VEGETARIAN** ☺️ **KID FRIENDLY** ✿ **PATIO DINING** 🚗 **DELIVERY** 🎩 **PRIVATE PARTY**

[Hole in the Wall Burger Joint] 11058 Santa Monica Blvd., West L.A., 310.312.7013, holeinthewallburgerjoint.com. L & D Mon.-Sat. American. MC, V. $ **WHY** For the cute knotted pretzel bun that tastes as good as it looks, house-made pickles and BBQ-style ketchup. **WHAT** This tiny burger joint may be nearly impossible to find (look for the Winchell's Donuts on Wilshire just east of the 405), but it's worth the effort. Longtime caterer Bill Dertouzos says he got tired of paying a fortune for quality burgers at fancy joints, so he opened this place. All the toppings on that $8 half-pound burger (beef, turkey or veggie) are house-made, and an order of fries (regular or sweet potato) will set you back just $2. Call ahead and your order will be ready in ten minutes, or grab one of the half-dozen counter stools or "patio" tables (really more of an outdoor garage). 🎫🍴☼

[Hot Dog on a Stick] 1633 Ocean Front Walk, Santa Monica, hotdogonastick.com. L & D daily. American. Cash only. $ **WHY** For one of the guiltiest pleasures of all: a low-class corn dog on a stick, washed down with super-sweet lemonade. **WHAT** Now found in malls across the nation, this simple, goofy chain started right here on Muscle Beach in 1946. A good amusement when you have out-of-town guests. **WHO** Tourists, bike-path cruisers and little kids. 🎫☺

[Howdy's Taqueria] 3835 Cross Creek Rd., Malibu, 310.317.4757. B, L & D daily. Mexican/Taqueria. MC, V. $ - $$ **WHY** For respectable, not-too-overpriced Mexican fast food that goes down well after a day at the beach. **WHAT** Howdy's is about as authentic as most of the breasts on the women around here, but hey, this is Malibu — and we're grateful for the mahi mahi tacos, Malibu chicken tostadas and salsa. **WHO** Local teens, surfers and Malibu beauty queens. ☺☼

[Hungry Pocket] 1715 Pico Blvd., Santa Monica, 310.450.5335. L & D daily. Middle Eastern. MC, V. $ **WHY** The best falafel on the westside, and good gyros and schwarmas, too. If you like it fiery, ask for the fresh hot sauce. **WHAT** This no-frills little counter joint boasts low prices, friendly owners and light, crunchy, delicious falafel. Juices are hand-squeezed (try the apple), and the lamb schwarma is dreamy. **WHO** Santa Monica College kids, local high school kids and Sunset Park neighbors. 🎫🍴☺☼

[Jody Maroni's] 🏛 2011 Ocean Front Walk, Venice, 310.822.5639, jodymaroni.com. L & D daily until sunset. American. AE, MC, V. $ **WHY** For the best fast food on the boardwalk. **WHAT** Now found in markets across the country, Jody Maroni's sausages were first served at this little boardwalk stand in the late '70s. There's nothing like a brat with grilled onions and peppers on a sunny summer day. **WHO** The circus of humanity that prowls the Venice boardwalk. 🎫☺

🏛 ESSENTIALLY L.A. ☺ LATE ♥ ROMANTIC 🎫 VALUE 🔇 QUIET ♻ SUSTAINABLE

[Jody Maroni's] The Promenade at Howard Hughes Center, 6081 Center Dr. Suite 218, Playa del Rey, 310.348.0007, jodymaroni.com. B, L & D daily. American. AE, MC, V. **$ WHY** Juicy brats with grilled onions and peppers. **WHAT** This Venice native may be a national chain, but it's your best bet if you're in a mall — like this one — and need something quick to eat. **WHO** Westside teens and mall-cruisers. 🖻 ☺

[Joe's Pizza] 111 Broadway, Santa Monica, 310.395.9222, joespizza. com. L & D daily. Pizzeria. M, V. **$ WHY** Very good thin crust, New York–style pizza (just enough sauce and cheese, no crazy toppings) for eating in or to go. **WHAT** After 35 years, Joe Vitale of THE Joe's Pizza on Bleecker Street decided to open a new joint … in Santa Monica. Not surprisingly, it's been a big hit, and he just opened another branch in WeHo. Sit down at one of the outdoor tables and enjoy a classic pie. **WHO** Pizza-crazed locals declaring an all-out war against Puck-inspired everything-goes pies. ☺ 🥢☺🚗

[La Playita] 3306 Lincoln Blvd., Santa Monica, 310.452.0090. B, L & D daily. Taqueria. Cash only. **$ WHY** Because this is one of the rare East L.A.–style taco stands on the westside, with delicious shrimp ceviche and carne asada burritos. **WHAT** A bare-bones taco stand with a couple of picnic tables and very good taqueria chow. **WHO** Latino working men and savvy locals from south Santa Monica. 🖻 ☼

[Mr. Cecil's California Ribs] 12244 W. Pico Blvd., West L.A., 310.442.1550, mrcecilscaliforniaribs.com. L & D daily. Barbecue. Beer & wine. MC, V. **$$ - $$$ WHY** Worth knowing about when you need a rib fix. **WHAT** "California" is the operative word in the name of this faux roadhouse; if you don't come expecting authentic smoked barbecue, you'll be happy with your tender baby-back ribs, dry-rub St. Louis ribs and tasty hush puppies. Parking can be an issue and the prices are high for what you get, but in these 'cue-challenged parts, we won't complain too loudly. ☺ ☼

[Reddi-Chick] Brentwood Country Mart, 225 26th St., Santa Monica, 310.393.5238. L & D daily to 8 p.m. American. Cash only. **$ WHY** A greasy-like-you-know-you-want-it half chicken covered in fries. **WHAT** North Santa Monica kids are practically raised on this simple, tasty rotisserie chicken, which you order from a window and either eat on the sunny brick courtyard in the posh Country Mart, or load into your Range Rover to take home. **WHO** Families delighting in a simple meal that costs less than they usually pay for valet parking. 🖻☺ ☼

[Santouka] 🏠 Mitsuwa Marketplace, 3760 S. Centinela Ave., Mar Vista, 310.391.1101, santouka.co.jp. L & dinner daily to 7:30 p.m. Japanese. Cash only. **$ WHY** The shio ramen with *chasu* (pork), which will have you ordering seconds. Come to think of it, all the ramens will.

🥢VEGETARIAN ☺KID FRIENDLY ☼PATIO DINING 🚗DELIVERY 🎩PRIVATE PARTY

WHAT This little place in the Mitsuwa food court with fake food on display doesn't look promising, but the broths are rich, filled with hearty noodles and topped with quality ingredients. Aromatic and satisfying, even if you have to eat it in an ugly food court. 🖼️😊

[Tacomiendo] **11462 Gateway Blvd., West L.A., 310.481.0804. L & D daily. Taqueria. MC, V. $ WHY** Fat, warm handmade tortillas, a good salsa bar and perfectly fine meats. **WHAT** You can eat in or take out from this friendly strip-mall taco joint, best known for its fresh tortillas. A good spot to know about in a taqueria-poor part of town. **WHO** Regulars stopping by for a satisfying, inexpensive lunch. 🖼️😊

[Taco Plus] **1525 S. Bundy Dr., West L.A. B, L & D daily. Taqueria. MC, V. $ WHY** Good soft tacos and burritos big enough to feed a small family. **WHAT** This tiny taqueria sells a to-go, too-good lunch for less than $2.50: fresh, doughy corn tortillas wrapped around grilled beef or chicken and sautéed onions, giant burritos, ceviche. **WHO** Dads picking up takeout, construction workers on break, teenagers hungry for a burrito *gigante*. 🖼️😊

[Tacos por Favor] **1406 Olympic Blvd., Santa Monica, 310.392.5768. B & L daily, D Mon.-Sat. Taqueria. Beer. AE, MC, V. $ WHY** Tender *birria* (baby goat), generous carne asada and carnitas tacos, acclaimed chorizo-cheese tacos and restorative menudo on weekends. Watch out for the fiery salsas. **WHAT** A friendly, capacious taqueria that manages to be both healthful (fresh tomatoes, lean meats, no lard) and authentic. **WHO** Lunchtime brings a long line of people from nearby low-key entertainment-industry and tech businesses. 🖼️🥄😊

[Wildflour Pizza] **2807 Main St., Santa Monica, 310.392.3300. L & D daily. Pizzeria. Beer & wine. AE, MC, V. $ WHY** Large, thin-crust pies, sold whole or by the slice, with every imaginable topping. **WHAT** Before Main Street got as hip as it is today, there was Wildflour. It's a classic pizza joint in a funky historic shack, with a wood-paneled, sawdust-floored room and a large patio in back. **WHO** Families, local AYSO teams and Ocean Park locals getting takeout. 🖼️🥄😊☼🚗

SOUTH BAY TO SOUTH L.A.

[Angelo's Italian Deli] 🏛️ **190 La Verne Ave., Long Beach, 562.434.1977. L Tues.-Sat. Italian. Beer & wine. AE, MC, V. $ WHY** For huge, exceptionally tasty sandwiches made from impeccable Italian cheeses, meats and seasonings. **WHAT** For a fast meal you won't forget, skip Belmont Shore's chain places and head to this tiny Italian market and deli for a sandwich (grilled or not) filled with things like fresh mozzarella, prosciutto, coppa, turkey, roasted peppers and fresh basil. There's nowhere to eat, so take it over to the nearby beach or back to work. One sandwich will feed two with gusto. Another branch just across the OC line in Seal Beach. **WHO** Beach picnickers, neighbors and loyal followers coming from as far as Downey.

[Bludso's BBQ] 🛗 811 S. Long Beach Blvd., Compton, 310.637.1342.
L & D Tues.-Sun. Barbecue. AE, MC, V. $ - $$ **WHY** Serious Texas-style
barbecue that doesn't disappoint. **WHAT** Bludso's proudly proclaims
itself to be "a li'l taste of Texas," but there's nothing small about these
flavors. There aren't any diminutive dishes, either: This storefront
joint is a purveyor of hearty, meat-heavy barbecue in the style of the
Lone Star State. And though it's is a relatively new place compared to
some of the Compton classics, it's already a powerhouse well known
for its expert brisket — but that doesn't mean you should discount the
ribs and links. Finish up with a giant slice of red velvet cake or some
cool banana pudding. **WHO** Well-traveled barbecue fiends and families
picking up extended-family-size meals. 📷 ☺

[Busy Bee Market] 2413 S. Walker St., San Pedro, 310.832.8660.
L & D Mon.-Sat. Italian/American. Cash only. $ **WHY** A sandwich institution of stomach-stretching proportions. **WHAT** Busy Bee earned its
reputation on both quality and quantity: The locally famous San Pedro
deli is home to a whole cast of hulking sandwiches. The market is a
no-frills place, a convenience store in a residential corner of town that
happens to house a great sandwich counter. The cold subs are plenty
filling (mortadella, tuna, prosciutto and the like), but the hot sandwiches (meatball, turkey pastrami, roast beef and others) are even better. **WHO** Hungry locals and belly busting fans from far and wide. 📷

[Dave's Burgers] 3396 Atlantic Ave., Long Beach, 562.424.3340.
L & early D Mon.-Sat. American. Cash only. $ **WHY** Excellent and
inexpensive turkey burgers, cheese dogs and hearty hamburgers. No
fries, but you can manage with the little bags of chips. **WHAT** A burger
shack in the parking lot of a gas station, with made-to-order fast food
that's better than most. 📷 ☺ ☼

[El Burrito Jr.] 919 Pacific Coast Hwy., Redondo Beach,
310.316.5058. B, L & D daily. Mexican/American. Cash only. $ **WHY** For
good, hearty breakfast burritos, burgers and chiles rellenos that go
down very well after a surf session or a run on Torrance Beach.
WHAT There's a constant crowd at this cheap, reliable fast-food stand.
Unless you're a 16-year-old who just surfed for four hours, get the
junior-size burrito — the regular size will hit you like a ton of bricks.
WHO Blond teens from South High, surfers, stoners and contractors
taking a break from remodeling fancy Palos Verdes houses. 📷 ☺

[El Taco Loco No. 3] 1465 Magnolia Ave., Long Beach,
562.437.6228. B, L & D 24 hours daily. Taqueria. MC, V. $ **WHY** An
honest taqueria that capably handles the classics. **WHAT** El Taco Loco
No. 3 earned its number as part of a South Bay chain, though many

Food
That's Fast

🥬 VEGETARIAN ⊙ KID FRIENDLY ✿ PATIO DINING 🚐 DELIVERY 🏛 PRIVATE PARTY of them share tenuous ties at best. This location is particularly true to the taqueria tradition: fresh-made tortillas and all the meat (offal and otherwise) that you could want. Tripe tacos are a specialty, but perhaps even better are the *buche* tacos stuffed with hunks of lightly fried pig stomach. There's a small but potent selection of salsas and a tub of blistered peppers for accompaniment. The menu also includes tortas and sopes and extends out to roasted chickens blanketed in mole. **WHO** Families and workers streaming in off the 710. ☺ 🗒 ☺

[Havana Sandwich Company] **229 Main St., El Segundo, 310.640.0014, havanasandwich.com. L & D daily. Cuban. AE, MC, V. $ WHY** Classic cubanos plus, for those who like to push the envelope, creative variations like spicy jerk chicken and corned beef. The Mediterranean — composed of roasted pork and feta cheese — is truly outstanding. **WHAT** Uncommonly well-crafted cubano sandwiches here transcend their ingredients (roasted pork, ham, Swiss cheese and a loaf that's crunchy on the outside and soft within) when skillfully grilled into hot, juicy masterpieces of the sandwich-maker's art. 🗒

[Honey's Kettle Fried Chicken] **2600 E. Alondra Blvd., Compton, 310.638.7871, honeyskettle.com. L & D daily. American/Southern. AE, MC, V. $ WHY** The chicken, of course — whole bird, combo meal or even in a pot pie. **WHAT** The chicken is justly famous, lightly battered and spectacularly juicy. But there's more to Honey's than those golden birds, which you can take away or eat here. From the freshly squeezed lemonade to the small fruit pies and buttermilk biscuits, a meal in this cream-and-gold dining room is a treat. And don't forget to eat your vegetables; they're skewered, kettle-cooked and delicious. 🗒 ☺

[Jay Bee's] 🏠 **15911 S. Avalon St., Gardena, 310.532.1064, jaybees-bbq.com. L Mon.-Sat., early D Mon., D Tues.-Sat. Barbecue. MC, V. $ - $$ WHY** Tender, just-fatty-enough pork ribs, pulled-pork sandwiches, rib tips, brisket and cornbread, to eat at the one picnic table or to take home — except most people can't wait until they get home and rip into the ribs in the car. **WHAT** Barbecue fans can (and do) argue for days, weeks, even years about whose ribs are best, and it often comes down to personal taste. Jay Bee's, however, has the consider-able distinction of winning a Chowhound blind taste test. Other than the generic cole slaw, the food at this takeout shack is really, really good — worth a detour. 🗒

[The Local Place] **18605 S. Western Ave., Torrance, 310.523.3233. L & D daily. Asian/Hawaiian. AE, MC, V. $ WHY** For island-style sweet-salty chicken and plantation-style bone-in chicken, both accompanied by potato-macaroni salad and rice. **WHAT** Local food, Hawaiian style, means Euro-Asian fusion fare, and this place does it well. It's ultra-modern in looks but owned by the family behind the old-school King's Hawaiian Bakery next door. 🗒 ☺

🏠 **ESSENTIALLY L.A.** ☺ **LATE** ♥ **ROMANTIC** 🗒 **VALUE** 🍷 **QUIET** ♻ **SUSTAINABLE**

[Los Muchachos] 118 Pier Ave., Hermosa Beach, 310.372.3633.
L & D daily. Taqueria. Cash only. $ **WHY** Tasty chicken or carnitas tacos,
vegetarian burritos and guac 'n chips, just a block from the beach.
WHAT A short stroll from the Hermosa Pier, this tiny stand makes the
best beach-friendly fast food around. You can eat your tacos at the
counter or at one of the teeny tables or, better yet, take it back on the
beach for a picnic. Good vegetarian choices. **WHO** Surfers, skaters and
every sort of hungry beach person. 🖼🦑☺

[Marukai Pacific Market] 🏠 1620 W. Redondo Beach Blvd.,
Gardena, 310.464.8888, marukai.com. L & D daily to 7:30 p.m. Asian.
MC, V. $ **WHY** For one of the best food courts in town; don't miss the
toasted honey butter bread from MamMoth Bakery, the udon from
Gen-Pei and the yakitori from Shin sen Gumi. **WHAT** The market's
fine, but the real reason to come to this Marukai is the food court,
which is resplendent with good, cheap, fast food: udon, gyoza, yakitori, bento boxes, sushi (the weakest thing here) and, to top it off,
cream puffs from Beard Papa's. 🖼☺

[Maui Chicken] 29217 S. Western Ave., Palos Verdes, 310.732.1886;
2100 Redondo Beach Blvd., Torrance, 310.715.6284. L & D Mon.-Sat.
Hawaiian. MC, V. $ **WHY** For a superior execution of the traditional
Hawaiian plate lunch ... oh, and for the bacon-fried rice. **WHAT** The
traditional Hawaiian plate lunch never had it so good. Muted tropical
colors add a nice note to an attractive setting in which to enjoy grilled
sesame-splashed salmon, shrimp or orange roughy with seared asparagus, as well as the customary rice and macaroni salad (this one comes
with potato chunks). Or go all out and order the poke with cubed raw
tuna and roasted sesame oil. 🖼☺

[Pavich's Brick Oven Pizzeria] 🏠 2311 S. Alma St., San Pedro,
310.519.1200, pavichspizza.com. L & D daily. Pizzeria/Croatian. MC, V.
$ - $$ **WHY** Distinctly unique Croatian pizzas that are among the best
in L.A. **WHAT** There's no room for interior dining at this San Pedro
pizza joint — Pavich's allots most of its square footage to a huge brick
oven. And it's with that enormous oven that owner Zdenko Pavic is
able to craft a whole menu's worth of truly excellent thin-crust pies.
The marquee pizza is the Croatian, a wonderfully flavorful creation
that's topped with smoked beef, roasted and fresh bell peppers, red
onions, olives, mushrooms and a sprinkling of feta. There are also
great brick-oven-baked calzones and Croatian specialties like stuffed
cabbage, *cevapcici* and *pljeskavica*, a Croatian sandwich that Pavich's
has turned into a burger of sorts by completing it with roasted bell
peppers, lettuce, tomatoes, onions, pickles and homemade garlic
sauce. **WHO** Neighbors strolling in for their weekly piece and pizza
seekers from as far away as Ventura. 🖼🦑☺✿

Food
That's Fast

🦑 VEGETARIAN ☺ KID FRIENDLY ✿ PATIO DINING �DELIVERY 🏠 PRIVATE PARTY

[Phillips BBQ] 1517 Centinela Ave., Inglewood, 310.412.7135. L & D Mon.-Sat. Barbecue. AE, MC, V. $ - $$$ W HY Pork ribs and rib tips, a bit chewy, properly smoky and full of flavor; try the mixed sauce. **WHAT** This local chain of takeout-only rib joints has its rabid followers and ornery detractors; we're somewhere in the middle, believing for one thing that even so-so ribs are still a gift from the gods. These are saucy and substantial, not as tender as some but quite tasty. Call ahead to place your order or you'll have a long wait. **WHO** A constant crowd of fans milling around the parking lot, waiting for their ribs.

[Porky's BBQ] 937 Redondo Ave., Long Beach, 562.434.9999, ribs123.com. L & D daily. Barbecue. MC, V. $ - $$ **WHY** Top-notch pulled pork plus other solid barbecue standards. **WHAT** Descended from the now-shuttered Porky's in Inglewood, this Long Beach rib joint stepped right into the region's relative barbecue void, offering hefty ribs, crisp fried chicken, worthy brisket and its signature dish, pulled pork. Unlike the wispy, flavorless strands of meat found at other spots, this pulled pork is as it should be: in tender, juicy hunks. It's available as a plate (with the usual sides) or in a sandwich so thoroughly stuffed with meat that it makes hand-held eating a mere fantasy. The Long Beach location doesn't have much in the way of seating, but for that, there's a newer, bigger branch just across the Vincent Thomas Bridge (362 W. 6th St., San Pedro).

[Rasraj] 18511 S. Pioneer Blvd., Artesia, 562.809.3141, rasraj.com. L & D Tues.-Sun. Indian. MC, V. $ **WHY** They keep the ovens fired up all day, so everything's fresh and hot. **WHAT** This Gujarati-style *chat* (snack) and *mithai* (sweets) shop in Little India packs 'em in with a menu featuring vegetarian *thalis* (combo plates), curried dishes and a marvelous array of fresh goodies — all made from ground grains and beans — that include crispy chips, noodles, pancake-style dosa and uttapam, steamed buns (*idli*), and dozens of varieties of sweets. **WHO** A discerning all-India clientele.

[Sergio's Tacos] 2216 S. Atlantic Blvd., Commerce, 323.261.3364. L & D daily. Taqueria. Cash only. $ **WHY** A perfect carne asada burrito. Good menudo, too. **WHAT** Neighborhoods — and taco stands — don't get any less glamorous than this one, but it's worth a quick detour off the 710 or the 5 for Sergio's carne asada. **WHO** Working folks and truck drivers.

[Shisen Ramen] 1730 W. Sepulveda Blvd., Torrance, 310.534.1698. L & D daily. Japanese. Beer & wine. AE, MC, V. $ **WHY** Fantastic *paiko* (fried pork in curry spices) and owners so fanatical about quality that they won't let you take the noodle soup to go (they don't want to ruin the ramen's characteristic bite by letting it sit too long in the hot broth.) **WHAT** Come here for imported Japanese ramen meticulously cooked and served in the style of China's Sichuan province. There's a generous array of noodle dishes and toppings that range from fried chicken chunks to fresh clams. Plus really great prices on the well-crafted, tapas-size offerings. 🍴

[Taqueria la Mexicana] **3270 E. 4th St., Long Beach, 562.433.6389. L & D daily. Taqueria. Cash only. $ WHY** Memorable carne asada burritos, a good vegetarian burrito, excellent tortas and vibrant watermelon agua fresca. **WHAT** Long Beach's best taco joint is this bare-bones stand with an order window, indoor and outdoor seating and damn fine carne asada. A local treasure. 🍴🛍️☺☼

[Valentino's Pizza] **975 Aviation Blvd., Manhattan Beach, 310.318.5959, valentinospizza.net. L & D daily. Pizzeria. AE, MC, V. $ WHY** Excellent Brooklyn-style pizza (thin-crust) sold by the slice here or delivered promptly by the whole pie. **WHAT** Former New Yorkers (yes, plenty of them live in MB) say this is the closest thing to home in L.A., and indeed the crust has that not-soggy-yet-floppy-enough-to-fold-in-half consistency so essential to a New York pie. You can get red-sauce Italian dishes, but most regulars get pizza, to go or delivered, because there are only a couple of tables. 🍴☺🚚

[Woody's Bar-B-Que] **475 S. Market St., Inglewood, 310.672.4200, woodysla.com. L & D Mon.-Sat. Barbecue. AE, MC, V. $ - $$ WHY** Tasty, meaty pork ribs (they're better than the beef ribs), tender chicken, chicken links and greens; if you don't want your meat covered in sauce, ask for it on the side. **WHAT** Vying with Phillip's as L.A.'s king of down-and-dirty rib joints, Woody's smokes good-quality ribs and chicken and pairs them with a potent and spicy sauce; there's also a milder sauce option. Unlike at the Slauson branch, there are a couple of places to sit outside, but most folks take their ribs to go. 🍴

[Ya-Ya's Burgers No. 2] **3202 E. Gage Ave., Huntington Park, 323.581.2383. B, L & D daily. Mexican. Cash only. $ WHY** They're all good, but we won't soon forget the Tepic-K, aka the chile relleno torta, filled with avocado, a smear of beans, a bit of crema, a slab of roast pork leg and a beautifully roasted chile stuffed with melted Oaxacan cheese. **WHAT** Forget the name — you don't come to this simple joint for burgers (though it makes them), you come for some 70 variations of the Mexico City (D.F.)–style torta, each as precisely constructed as the next. The menu just lists the names, not the descriptions, so newbies have to ask a lot of questions of the counter guy. 🍴☺

🍴 VEGETARIAN ☺ KID FRIENDLY ☼ PATIO DINING 🚚 DELIVERY 🏠 PRIVATE PARTY

Gourmet-to-Go

You don't feel like having pepperoni pizza or bad Chinese takeout — you want something really good to take home after work, bring to a party or turn into a Hollywood Bowl or beach picnic. From humble but meticulously made tamales to elegant salads and cheese platters, the food in the pages that follow will fulfill your take-away needs.

[ESSENTIALLY L.A.]

Antica Pizzeria, Marina del Rey (PAGE 268)

Artisan Cheese Gallery, Studio City (PAGE 265)

Bottega Louie, Downtown (PAGE 263)

Brent's Delicatessen, Northridge (PAGE 267)

Carrillo's Mexican Deli, Canoga Park (PAGE 267)

Claro's, San Gabriel & La Habra (PAGES 264 & 271)

Clementine, Century City (PAGE 268)

Greenblatt's Deli, West Hollywood (PAGE 260)

Joan's on Third, Beverly/Third (PAGE 260)

Julienne, San Marino (PAGE 264)

Mama's Hot Tamales, Westlake (PAGE 263)

Marmalade, Santa Monica (PAGE 269)

Mozza 2 Go, Melrose (PAGE 262)

Nicole's, South Pasadena (PAGE 265)

⌂ ESSENTIALLY L.A. ☽ LATE ♥ ROMANTIC ☞ VALUE ♪ QUIET ♻ SUSTAINABLE

MORE QUALITY TAKEOUT CAN BE FOUND
IN FOOD THAT'S FAST AND SHOPS.
HERE ARE SOME FAVORITES:

Angelo's Italian Deli, Long Beach (PAGE 253)
Bay Cities Italian Deli & Bakery, Santa Monica (PAGE 249)
Beverly Glen Marketplace, Bel-Air (PAGE 320)
CaCao Mexicatessen, Eagle Rock (PAGE 66)
Cheebo, Hollywood (PAGE 45)
Cube, Melrose (PAGE 313)
Cynthia's on the Corner, Santa Monica (PAGE 197)
Erewhon, Beverly/Third (PAGE 321)
Froma on Melrose, Melrose (PAGE 314)
India Sweets & Spices, Atwater & Canoga Park (PAGE 315)
Jons Marketplace, many locations (PAGE 322)
Koreatown Galleria Market, Koreatown (PAGE 322)
Koreatown Plaza Market, Koreatown (PAGE 315)
Larchmont Wine & Cheese, Hancock Park (PAGE 326)
Liborio Market, Koreatown & Downtown (PAGE 322)
Maui Chicken, Torrance & Rancho Palos Verdes (PAGE 255)
Mercado Buenos Aires, Van Nuys (PAGE 316)
Mitsuwa, West L.A. & Torrance (PAGES 322 & 323)
Naples Gourmet Grocer, Long Beach (PAGE 317)
Owen's Market, Century City (PAGE 318)
Pitfire Pizza, Downtown & North Hollywood (PAGES 234 & 242)
Pollos a la Brasa, Koreatown (PAGE 229)
Porky's BBQ, Long Beach (PAGE 256)
Samosa House, Culver City (PAGE 319)
Santa Monica Seafood, Santa Monica (PAGE 309)
Spring Street Smoke House, Chinatown/Downtown (PAGE 235)
Tito's Market, El Monte (PAGES 240 & 320)
Vallarta's Markets, various locations (PAGE 323)
Woody's Bar-B-Que, Mid-City (PAGE 257)

Gourmet
To Go

VEGETARIAN ⊙ KID FRIENDLY ✿ PATIO DINING 🚗 DELIVERY 🎩 PRIVATE PARTY

CENTRAL CITY

[The Deli at Little Dom's] 2128 Hillhurst Ave., Los Feliz, 323.661.0055, littledoms.com. Daily. Italian. AE, MC, V. $ - $$
WHY Fresh pasta, marinated white beans, farro with grilled vegetables, and panna cotta — everything you need to fake-cook an Italian dinner at home. **WHAT** The folks behind the neighboring (and currently hot) trattoria Little Dom's opened this tiny takeout deli, giving it a winning 1940s look and stocking its small glass case with a choice selection of good stuff: eggplant caponata, delicious roasted brusssels sprouts, cheeses, chocolate truffles… all the essentials (except wine) of Los Feliz life. Most people get their fresh pasta or warm panini to go, but there are a few places to sit, and espresso drinks, of course.

[Food + Lab] 7253 Santa Monica Blvd., West Hollywood, 323.851.7120, foodlabcatering.com. B, L & D daily. American/Austrian. AE, MC, V. $ - $$ **WHY** Fantastic sandwiches, excellent espresso, lovely patios both front and back, and good food to take home and pretend you made. **WHAT** Nino Linsmayer and his mom Esther built a successful business as caterers before opening this café and gourmet market, so they came into the business already knowing how to make crowd-pleasing food. They haven't been here long but already have a devout following for their sandwiches (Austrian meatloaf, prosciutto with ricotta and honey, veggie-pesto), salads, soups and breakfast dishes, made with organic ingredients. They're Austrian, which explains the Viennese coffee and flaky Austrian strudels. **WHO** Mostly neighborhood locals, including people who actually walk here. ☺️🔖☼

[Greenblatt's Deli] 🏛 8017 W. Sunset Blvd., West Hollywood, 323.656.0606, greenblattsdeli.com. L & D daily until 2 a.m. Deli. AE, MC, V. $ - $$ **WHY** Hefty deli sandwiches, potato knishes and famed matzo ball soup, to eat there or take out until 2 a.m. Free parking and $5 delivery in the area, too. **WHAT** Part wine store, part eat-in deli, part takeout destination, Greenblatt's has been a cherished Sunset Strip destination for decades. Have a restorative bowl of soup here and take some more substantial food home for later. **WHO** Sunset Strip partiers who need some good food to take home after a big night out. ☺️🚗

[Joan's on Third] 🏛 8350 W. 3rd St., Beverly/Third, 323.655.2285, joansonthird.com. B, L & early D daily. Modern American. AE, MC, V. $$ **WHY** Wonderful sandwiches (turkey meatloaf, pressed chicken, bacon and brie), lots of prepared salads (the lentil is particularly good), elegant cheese and charcuterie platters and famed cupcakes. **WHAT** Originally a caterer, Joan McNamara gradually expanded her business into a café, gourmet market and upscale takeout operation, and each facet has met with tremendous success. From the picnic baskets to the the office lunches to the daily takeout dinner entrees, Joan's food is uniformly excellent. Note that service on the café side can be erratic at busy times. **WHO** Chic women picking up a few things for a dinner

🏛 **ESSENTIALLY L.A.** ☺️ **LATE** ♥ **ROMANTIC** 🎥 **VALUE** 🔖 **QUIET** ♻️ **SUSTAINABLE**

party, personal assistants feeding their employers, and friends meeting for lunch, including a fair number of famous folks. 🦞

[Larchmont Larder] 626 N. Larchmont Blvd., Hancock Park, 323.962.9900, larchmontlarder.com. B, L & early D Mon.-Sat. American. AE, MC, V. $$ **WHY** "Humpday" dinners, a complete family meal for four for $37 to $44. **WHAT** Katie Trevino brings her business savvy, gregarious personality and network of Hancock Park friends to this new gourmet takeout place in a handsome restored bungalow, and partner Michael Beglinger brings his decade of cooking experience, including the demanding job as executive chef for Wolfgang Puck Catering. The result is a homey yet elegant place to sit down for a lunchtime sandwich, buy the kids a cherry chocolate chip muffin after school, or order a spread for a dinner party. **WHO** St. Brendan's and Marlborough families picking up meatloaf and braised swiss chard because the soccer games went late. 🦞👁️☼

[Little Next Door] 8142 W. 3rd St., Beverly/Third, 323.951.1010, thelittledoor.com. B, L & D daily. French/Mediterranean. AE, MC, V. $$ - $$$ **WHY** Rustic pastries and breads complement the pâtés and terrines, jewel-like salads, imaginative sandwiches and savory tarts. **WHAT** Gold-framed mirrors, cobalt-blue walls and a marble bar give this Parisian-style shop/café a glamorous atmosphere. Carefully chosen beers and wines, foodie gifts and house-made jams round out the collection of spiffy eat-in or takeout dishes. **WHO** French ex-pats lounging over pain au chocolat and cappuccino, fashionable young shoppers from the 3rd Street boutiques.

[Locali] 5825 Franklin Ave., Hollywood, 323.466.1360, localiyours.com. Daily. Modern American. AE, MC, V. $$ **WHY** Locali is like the opposite of Famima: Instead of convenience foods imported from Japan, the emphasis is on locally sourced edibles from some of our favorite producers. Don't miss the Ruby Jewel ice cream sandwiches — they may come all the way from Portland, but they rock. **WHAT** Locali packs a lot of interesting products into a tiny storefront, and they're all either sustainable, organic and/or local — wine, beer from Dales Bros. and the Bruery, sandwiches and salads from M Café, Carmela ice cream, La Guera Tamalera tamales, prepared food from several vegan suppliers, frozen foods, coffee and snacks. Books, shopping bags, water bottles and other tchotchkes for the green lifestyle are stocked as well — even a handy countertop compost bin. ☼🦞

[Luna Park] 672 S. La Brea Ave., Miracle Mile, 323.934.2110, lunaparkla.com. L Mon.-Fri., D nightly, brunch Sun. Modern American. AE, MC, V. $$ - $$$ **WHY** Free delivery, online ordering and easy takeout of things like Cobb salad, grilled artichokes, mac 'n cheese with broccoli, chic pizzas and grilled half chicken with a warm arugula salad.

Gourmet
To Go

🦞 **VEGETARIAN** 👁️ **KID FRIENDLY** ☼ **PATIO DINING** 🚙 **DELIVERY** 🏛️ **PRIVATE PARTY**

WHAT This shabby-chic San Francisco transplant delivers its reasonably priced, modern-American comfort food in the Miracle Mile area, and it also does a lot of takeout. The famed make-your-own s'mores don't travel well, but the blackberry-chocolate pie sure does. **WHO** Wilshire office workers picking up lunch-meeting food and Hancock Parkers getting dinner on their way home from work.

[Monsieur Marcel] Farmers Market, 6333 W. 3rd St., Fairfax District, 323.939.7792, mrmarcel.com. B, L & D daily. French. AE, MC, V. $ - $$
WHY Everything you need for a fabulous French picnic, plus a full menu of French classics that can be ordered to go. **WHAT** This large gourmet shop and café tucked into a corner of the Farmers Market has every kind of French cheese imaginable, along with charcuterie, an amazing olive selection, baguettes, chocolates, wine and more. Alas, there are no prepared foods in the glass cases, but the adjacent café will whip you up some takeout (quiches, salade de chèvre chaud, roast chicken, great garlic fries).

[Mozza 2 Go] 6610 Melrose Ave., Melrose, 323.297.1130, mozza2go.com. L & D Tues.-Sun. Italian. AE, MC, V. $$ - $$$ **WHY** All the things you most love about Pizzeria Mozza, without having to fight for a table. Great for Bowl picnics and office lunches. **WHAT** If you want to make your friends think you're a great cook, just call up this new takeout offshoot of the Mozza restaurants and order a tricolore salad, white-bean bruschetta, Mario's lasagne and butterscotch budino, and transfer everything to your own dishes. The small and swank shop has some pastries and Italian packaged goods on display, but everything else must be ordered at least an hour in advance. The pizzas are exactly as wonderful as in the pizzeria, but be warned that they won't hold up as well if they travel a long distance. You can pick up yourself or spring for the fee delivery.

[The Oaks Market] 1915 N. Bronson Ave., Hollywood, 323.871.8894, theoaksgourmet.com. B, L & D daily. Modern American. AE, MC, V. $ - $$ **WHY** All the yuppie-foodie essentials: pizzas cooked in a wood oven, beet salads, barista-pulled espresso made from beans roasted on-site, fresh-squeezed celery juice and rare sodas, all of which you can enjoy on the patio or take to your Hollywood Hills pad — or the Hollywood Bowl. **WHAT** The late, lamented Victor's is now the swankier Oaks Market, which is even more of a gourmet-to-go emporium and café than a market. You order at the counter, but this is no short-order sandwich shop: The menu runs to belgian waffles, smoked fish plates, baby arugula salads, sirloin burgers with Taleggio cheese, lobster club sandwiches and wood-fired pizzas.

[Real Food Daily] 414 N. La Cienega Blvd., West Hollywood, 310.289.9910, realfood.com. L Mon.-Sat., D nightly, brunch Sun. Vegan/American. AE, MC, V. $$ **WHY** Organic vegan food prepared in a kosher kitchen — and it actually tastes good. You can order takeout, order party platters or get lunch or dinner delivered. **WHAT** Real Food's meat- and dairy-free fare includes many dishes that take out well or work for small parties. Try the salad platters, the lentil-walnut pâté and the cold sesame-noodle salad. Your call on whether to try the tofu cheesecake (we passed). **WHO** Hollywood vegans and good-looking sorts who are just trying to eat more healthfully. 🌱🛍🚗

EASTSIDE

[Bottega Louie] 🏛 **700 S. Grand Ave., Downtown, 213.802.1470, bottegalouie.com. B, L & D daily. Italian. AE, MC, V. $$ - $$$**
WHY Pristine glass cases filled with so many good things to eat that you'll get woozy trying to decide. **WHAT** Downtown's shortage of quality takeout vanished overnight with the opening of this noisy, teeming trattoria. The entire west end of the massive space is devoted to takeout: good salads and sandwiches, even better sides (white beans, rosemary potatoes and peas and prosciutto are just the beginning), Italian classics (lasagne, chicken parm), roasted meats cut to order, delicious cookies and much more. The pizzas are worth waiting for. **WHO** Assistants picking up food for the office, and after-workers taking dinner home. 🛍

[Mama's Hot Tamales] 🏛 **2122 W. 7th St., Westlake, 213.487.7474, iurd.org/mamasHotTamales. L daily. Mexican. MC, V. $**
WHY Indulge in these tamales not only because they're delicious, but because they're making L.A. a better place. Good coffee, too, and a gallery showcasing local artists. **WHAT** Sure, the tamales from every region of Mexico and Central America are wonderful, and yes, the café is a vividly colorful community center, but this nonprofit is really about doing good: providing job training and business skills for low-income local women. Order a big bunch of tamales for your next party, or pick up a few to take back to the office. **WHO** West Downtown workers, artists, Koreatown residents. 🛍

[The Park] **1400 Sunset Blvd., Echo Park, 213.482.9209, thepark-1400sunset.com. L Tues.-Fri., D Tues.-Sun., brunch Sat.-Sun. Modern American. AE, MC, V. $ - $$ WHY** The excellent "game night" picnic boxes were designed for nearby Dodger Stadium, but they're available in all seasons and also work great for the Bowl, office meetings or even a take-home supper. **WHAT** One of the leaders of the Echo Park boom (it's not evil gentrification, it's a renaissance!), this starkly stylish café now offers great picnic boxes ($10 to $12), takeout dinners and party platters for a neighborhood that has almost no gourmet-to-go options. Young chef/owner Joshua Siegel makes tasty modern home cooking – composed salads, artful burgers, pot pies, roast chicken – that is just the thing for this era of modest consumption. 🛍

Gourmet
To Go

🛍 VEGETARIAN ⊙ KID FRIENDLY ☼ PATIO DINING 🚗 DELIVERY 🎩 PRIVATE PARTY

[Tiara Café] **127 E. 9th St., South Park/Fashion District, 213.623.3663, tiara-cafe-la.com. B & L daily, D Wed.-Sun., brunch Sat.-Sun. Modern American. AE, MC, V. $$ - $$$ WHY** The best pizza Downtown, which holds up well in a takeout box, plus other goodies to take away. **WHAT** This pink fashionista café has an adjacent mini-mart and gourmet-to-go counter, whose stock thins by the end of the day — but call ahead and they'll make you a fabulous pizza or salad to go. Worthy vegan and vegetarian options. **WHO** Fashion designers, their assistants and loft people picking up dinner to take home. 🜂🜲

SAN GABRIEL VALLEY

[Claro's] 🜂 **1003 E. Valley Blvd., San Gabriel, 626.288.2026, claros. com. B & L Mon.-Tues. & Thurs.-Sun. Italian. AE, MC, V. $ - $$ WHY** Prepared take-home dishes like lasagne and ravioli, huge and delicious sandwiches, savory sausages, take-and-bake pizzas and a bakery case lined with breads, cannoli and Italian cookies. **WHAT** This old-school Italian market and deli has been around since 1948, starting here in San Gabriel, and it now has five other locations. (This was once an Italian-immigrant neighborhood, which is hard to imagine in this Chinese era.) The deli offers sandwiches, sausages, antipasti and hot dishes. Good for a takeout dinner for one or a party for a dozen. **WHO** Third-generation loyalists and people proud of their Sicilian blood, even if it's only a little. 🜲

[Julienne] 🜂 **2649 Mission St., San Marino, 626.441.2299, juliennetogo.com. B, L & early D Mon.-Sat. Modern American. AE, MC, V. $ - $$$ WHY** Everything you need for a gracious picnic, dinner party or pantry-stocking, plus lots of irresistible extras, from Fleur de Sel finishing salt to an array of travel and food books that Francophiles, especially, will find delightful. **WHAT** This spectacular gourmet-to-go shop has a freezer full of dinner-for-two entrees and a deli case bountifully stocked with salads and main courses that might include Tuscan meatloaf, red-onion-crusted salmon, butterfly pasta with lemon and chives, and couscous salad with toasted pine nuts and cinnamon. The bakery case is justly famed, and the refrigerated dips, dressings and sauces are lifesavers for time-pressed party-givers. Nicely edited selection of wines, too, as well as gifts and books for food lovers. **WHO** People with Sub-Zeros to fill — and lots of zeroes on their bank balance. 🜲

[The Kitchen for Exploring Foods] **1434 W. Colorado Blvd., Pasadena, 626.793.7218, thekitchen.net. L & D Tues.-Sat. Modern American. AE, MC, V. $$ WHY** When you invited eight for dinner and forgot you had to be at a water-polo match and don't have time to cook. **WHAT** Pasadena's top caterer also has a great to-go section, where you can pick up something good just for you for dinner, or order a lasagne to feed a dozen for a last-minute gathering. **WHO** Everyone who's anyone in Pasadena.

[Nicole's Gourmet Foods] 🏛 **921 Meridian Ave., South Pasadena, 626.403.5751, nicolesgourmetfoods.com. B & L Mon.-Sat. French. AE, MC, V. $ - $$ WHY** Great selection of sandwiches, salads, charcuterie and, of course, cheese, along with an excellent array of frozen goods and pantry staples. Call a day ahead and Nicole will make you a gorgeous quiche or a proper potato gratin. **WHAT** It all started with the cheese, and that's still a prime take-home item here, but the deli case also beckons with pâtés, olives, French lentils and other delicacies. The freezer case is stocked with an impressive array of baking and hors d'oeuvre offerings, from croissants and quiches to miniature beef Wellingtons and pastas. The wines are well priced and interesting.

[Porta Via Italian Foods] **1 W. California Blvd., Pasadena, 626.793.9000, portaviafoods.com. B, L & early D daily. Italian. AE, MC, V. $$ WHY** Salumi platters, lasagnes, grilled salmon, amazing eggplant caponata and good design-your-own salads. **WHAT** Glass cases hold grilled baby lamb chops, quality prosciutti and salami, eggplant involontini, roasted vegetables and many more Italian lovelies to take home for dinner or parties. At lunchtime, west Pasadenans meet over salads and generous grilled panini. High-quality food at not-outrageous prices. **WHO** Lacrosse moms taking a break from Julienne. 🔖

[Recess] **1102 N. Brand Blvd., Glendale, 818.507.0592, recesseatery. com. B, L & D daily. Mediterranean/modern American. BYOB ($8 corkage). AE, MC, V. $ WHY** Beautiful salads, sandwiches, pizzas and other goodies to take out or eat here. **WHAT** A former Patina cook decided he wanted to do his own thing in his own neighborhood, and the result is an immediately popular new café and gourmet-to-go spot. Breakfast brings to-go croissants or eat-in eggs; lunch means prosciutto and mozzarella sandwiches, ahi tuna salads and lovely cheese pizzas; and dinner was just about to launch as we went to press. **WHO** North Glendale folks who can't believe their good luck with the opening of this appealing, modestly priced new spot. ♻🔖

EAST VALLEY

[Artisan Cheese Gallery] 🏛 **12023 Ventura Blvd., Studio City, 818.505.0207, artisancheesegallery.com. L daily. Modern American. AE, MC, V. $ - $$ WHY** For the duck confit sandwich, made with Breadbar's ciabatta, Le Merechal cheese and a fig spread. People drive across town for this sandwich. **WHAT** Call ahead or stop by to order cheese platters for a party or one of the superb sandwiches — the duck confit is most famous, but we're also terribly fond of the grilled cheese, the portobello with goat cheese, and the bacon, cheddar and apple. Order an assortment for your next casual party. 🔖�"

Gourmet To Go

🔖 VEGETARIAN ⊙ KID FRIENDLY ☼ PATIO DINING 🚗 DELIVERY 🏛 PRIVATE PARTY

[Caioti Pizza Café] 4346 Tujunga Ave., Studio City, 818.761.3588, caiotipizzacafe.com. L & D daily. Pizzeria. AE, MC, V. $ - $$ WHY Superb salads (try the Humble Salad, a romaine wedge with bacon, goat cheese and roma tomatoes), Caioti's rightly famed individual pizzas and delicious pastas and sandwiches; call ahead and your takeout order will be ready. WHAT Ed LaDou may have shuffled off this mortal coil, but the California pizza he invented (that's right, it was LaDou, not Puck) lives on in this casual, noisy café, which does a good job with to-go orders.

[Chenar Russian Deli] 4818 Laurel Canyon Blvd., Valley Village, 818.762.8980. Daily. Russian. MC, V. $$ WHY All manner of prepared Russian dishes, including such classics as Georgian-style chicken in creamy walnut sauce, cheese-stuffed khachapuri bread and traditional khinkali dumplings. WHAT Russian cuisine often summons visions of stodgy stroganoffs and leaden meats — until you visit Chenar, one of L.A.'s best Russian delis. Its cases hold a stunning array of buffet-worthy salads, soups, hot entrees and desserts, along with smoked fish, cured meats, international cheeses and, of course, caviar. Almost every dish from this tiny, decade-old strip-mall spot — including borscht that's light enough to suit the calorie conscious — is filled with wondrous flavors. WHO Eastern European ex-pats and Valleyites with a thing for cabbage and odd-looking cold cuts and smoked fish.

[Marmalade] 14910 Ventura Blvd., Sherman Oaks, 818.905.8872, marmaladecafe.com. B, L & D daily. Modern American/French. AE, MC, V. $$ WHY A vibrant range of prepared dishes, salads and baked goods to take out. WHAT This Valley branch of the Marmalade mini-empire is an eat-in café but also has loads of tempting choices for takeout. Salads range from herb chicken ravioli in pesto to roasted beets with oranges and candied walnuts in rosemary vinaigrette; panini and bakery treats are numerous; and take-home entrees run to such things as chicken enchiladas, vegetable lasagne and poached salmon with sour cream dill.

[Village Gourmet Cheese & Wine] 4357 Tujunga Ave., Studio City, 818.487.3807, villagegourmetcheeseandwine.com. L daily, early D Mon.-Sat. Modern American. AE, MC, V. $$ WHY Good last-minute party food from the freezer case — spinach-pesto puffs, gorgonzola-fig phyllo rolls — as well as lovely order-in-advance party platters (cheeses, crudités, caprese, caviar). Intelligently filled gift baskets, too. WHAT A convenient spot for all your high-end culinary essentials, from roasted-pepper-and-pesto sandwiches to chicken-apricot salad. Good lunch salads and sandwiches, party foods and prepared foods, both fresh and frozen. The wine and cheese selections are smart, though not cheap. WHO Regulars picking up some lasagne or frozen pasta for dinner, and special-occasion folks putting together Hollywood Bowl picnics.

⌂ESSENTIALLY L.A. ☺LATE ♥ROMANTIC ☞VALUE ♪QUIET ✿SUSTAINABLE

WEST VALLEY

[Bauducco's Italian Market] **2839 Agoura Rd., Westlake Village, 805.495.4623. Daily. Italian. AE, MC, V. WHY** Housemade Sicilian bread, either to take home or to have the deli make into a chicken-parmesan or sausage sandwich, as well as good pizzas, lasagnes and Italian prepared dishes to take home. **WHAT** Fabulous Sicilian bread and rolls are baked on the premises at this 40-year-old family business, where the deli cases are amply stocked with house-made sausages and salumi, both imported and domestic. The voluptuous sandwiches, pizzas and prepared foods to take home are very good — and if you don't want to take it home, there's a restaurant, too. 🚗

[Brent's Delicatessen] 🏠 **19565 Parthenia St., Northridge, 818.886.5679, brentsdeli.com. B, L & D daily. Deli. AE, MC, V. $$ - $$$ WHY** Very good deli, delivered anywhere in the greater L.A. area for a large group, or to pick up for a small one. **WHAT** Brent's fleet of vans scurry around the Valley and the L.A. side of the Santa Monicas every day, delivering trays of deli sandwiches, smoked fish, raw veggies and lemon bars to offices, schools and home gatherings. Lean meats, fresh breads, pretty fruit plates and a memorable whitefish salad, all at fair prices. For smaller orders, call ahead and it'll be ready for you to pick up. **WHO** Deli fans who need to feed a group for a meeting, a bridge party or a memorial.

[Carrillo's Mexican Deli] 🏠 **19744 Sherman Way, Canoga Park, 818.887.6118. B, L & D daily. Mexican. MC, V. $ WHY** Great tamales, which you can either order online to be shipped or can pick up at the deli or the factory (1242 Pico St., San Fernando, 818.365.1636). All the Mexican classics are first-rate. **WHAT** The atmosphere isn't much to speak of, so many regulars get this delicious food to take home — or, in larger quantities, to feed a party. The homemade tamales are righteous — get a few no matter what else you order — and you can feed a family on the $15.55 takeout special, which includes a pound of tender carnitas and sides of rice, beans, fresh salsa and homemade tortillas. 🖼

[Follow Your Heart Market & Café] **21825 Sherman Way, Canoga Park, 818.348.3240, followyourheart.com. B, L & D daily. Vegetarian/Vegan. AE, MC, V. $ - $$ WHY** Colorful, flavorful vegetarian and vegan cooking; many of the soup and main dishes (enchiladas corazón, spinach lasagne, spanakopita) take out very well. **WHAT** The '70s live on at this good-hearted natural-foods café and market, which was founded in 1970. But the food has kept up with the times, and it's all fresh and appealing. You can pick up staples from the market and takeout food from the café in back. **WHO** Vegetarians, vegans and seekers of healthful, organic foods. 🖼🌀🍃

Gourmet To Go

🍃 VEGETARIAN ⊙ KID FRIENDLY ✿ PATIO DINING 🚗 DELIVERY 🎩 PRIVATE PARTY

WESTSIDE: CENTRAL

[Café Surfas] 8777 W. Washington Blvd., Culver City, 310.558.1458, cafesurfas.com. B & L daily. Modern American. AE, MC, V. $ - $$
WHY Lovely pressed panini, Kobe beef burgers and creative salads, to take away or eat here. Try the smoked venison hot dog with Maytag blue cheese cream. **WHAT** The café next to famed restaurant-supply store Surfas serves predictably chic breakfast and lunch fare, and it's also a fine place to get food to take away, from daily soup specials to platters of artisanal cheeses. **WHO** Kitchen-supply junkies shopping at the adjacent Surfas. 🌀👜

[Clementine] 🏠 1751 Ensley Ave., Century City, 310.552.1080, clementineonline.com. B, L & early D Mon.-Sat. American. AE, MC, V. $$ - $$$ **WHY** Delicious updated feel-good food, like sloppy joes, saucy barbecue pork and vegetable lasagne, to feed two people or a crowd. **WHAT** In addition to being one of L.A.'s more popular caterers, Annie Miler also runs this café, bakery and takeout place. Some dishes, like sandwiches and breakfast items, are served on an individual basis; others are sold by the pound (brisket) or the tray (lasagne). Call ahead for curbside pickup and your food will be placed in your car for you. 👜

[Food] 10571 W. Pico Blvd., Rancho Park, 310.441.7770, food-la.com. B & L daily. Modern American. AE, MC, V. $ - $$ **WHY** The neighborhood is grateful for this relatively new gourmet market, café, takeout spot and caterer, specializing in healthy sandwiches, soups and salads that are rich in flavor. Call ahead for excellent picnic baskets or party platters. **WHAT** Not just the neon-red paint makes this West Pico storefront stand out — the quality of its takeout and café fare has won it the devotion of many locals. You'll pay more than $10 for a sandwich — slow-roasted grass-fed beef tenderloin on a baguette, for instance, or cilantro tofu with grilled corn relish, avocado and tomato on five-grain bread — but the ingredients are top drawer. 👜

[Rosti] 233 S. Beverly Dr., Beverly Hills, 310.275.3285, rostituscankitchen.com. L & D daily. Italian. AE, MC, V. $$ **WHY** Grilled Tuscan-style brick-pressed chicken with roasted potatoes, delivered to your door or to take out from the café. **WHAT** It's not the most amazing Italian food around, but it's just fine, and Rosti delivers in Beverly Hills. It also does a good job with takeout, including for larger orders. 👜🌀🚗

WEST OF THE 405

[Antica Pizzeria] 🏠 Villa Marina Marketplace, 13455 Maxella Ave., 2nd Fl., Marina del Rey, 310.577.8182, anticapizzeria.net. L & D daily. Pizzeria/Italian. AE, MC, V. $$ **WHY** Brilliantly balanced pizza with that elusive char on the underside of the crust, as well as many other worthy Italian dishes, all of which are delivered in the Marina/Venice

🏠 ESSENTIALLY L.A. ☺ LATE ♥ ROMANTIC 💲 VALUE 🤫 QUIET 🌀 SUSTAINABLE area. **WHAT** Real Naples-style pizza is crafted here by the first (and one of the only) U.S. members of the Associazione Verace Pizza Napoletana. They make the dough from just flour, natural yeast and water, and bake it in a wood-burning oven — a deceptively simple formula that produces a *fantastico* result. Also very good are the antipasti, salads and such takeout-friendly dishes as octopus with lemon, olive oil and garlic and arancini filled with mozzarella and peas. 🚐

[Cha Cha Chicken] 1906 Ocean Ave., Santa Monica, 310.581.1684, chachachicken.com. L & D daily. Caribbean. MC, V. $ **WHY** Chicken roasted and coated with an addictive, sweet-fiery jerk sauce and served with all the trimmings, for less than it costs to park at the neighboring Casa del Mar hotel. **WHAT** This cheap, lively, riotously colorful outdoor joint does a brisk phone-ahead takeout business and is also popular for its party packages for 15 people or more. Its signature Jamaican jerk chicken is the centerpiece; accompaniments include black beans, rice, fried plantains and salad. 🍴

[Gallegos Mexican Deli] 12470 Venice Blvd., Mar Vista, 310.391.2587, gallegosmexicandeli.com. B & L Mon.-Sat., D Mon.-Fri. to 7 p.m. Mexican. AE, MC, V. $ **WHY** Fresh tortillas (this place started as a tortilleria some 60 years ago), lovely homemade tamales (try the chicken chile verde tamale), substantial burritos and very good to-go trays of enchiladas, chile verde and such meats as carnitas and barbacoa. **WHAT** The Gallegos family has been making tamales and other good Mexican dishes in L.A. since 1945, and they're still going strong. You can eat here, but many get takeout or take advantage of the local delivery. **WHO** Generations of loyal fans, many of whom drive across town for a big order of tamales to go. 🍴🚐

[Javan] 11500 Santa Monica Blvd., West L.A., 310.207.5555, javanrestaurant.com. L & D daily. Persian. AE, MC, V. $$ **WHY** Tasty kebabs, delectable little grilled lamb chops, saffron rice and other Iranian dishes, delivered to your door. **WHAT** Javan's classic Iranian food takes out well and is good for a small dinner or a buffet party. Pass on the salads in favor of the kebabs, lamb chops and delicious lentil-based ashjoe soup. **WHO** Well-heeled Brentwood and West L.A. people getting food delivered for the family or a casual dinner party. 🚐

[Lemon Moon] Westside Media Center, 12200 W. Olympic Blvd., West L.A., 310.442.9191, lemonmoon.com. B & L daily. Modern American. AE, MC, V. $$ **WHY** Gorgeous but unpretentious takeout food from star chefs Josiah Citrin (Melisse) and Raphael Lunetta (JiRaffe); prices aren't low, but there's free validated parking in the underground structure. **WHAT** If we had one of those high-paying studio jobs that so many in this neighborhood have, we'd pick up takeout from here every day. Lots of the regulars take the rock shrimp ceviche, spicy Korean noodle salad or roasted mushroom salad with polenta back to the

---

🚐 VEGETARIAN ⊙ KID FRIENDLY ✿ PATIO DINING 🚐 DELIVERY 🏠 PRIVATE PARTY

office for lunch, but many of these dishes keep well for dinnertime, too. **WHO** Entertainment-industry folks who work in this building or nearby. 🦐

[Marmalade] 🏠 **710 Montana Ave., Santa Monica, 310.395.9196, marmaladecafe.com. B, L & early D daily. Modern American/French. AE, MC, V. $$ WHY** A vibrant range of prepared dishes, salads and baked goods to take out. **WHAT** This flagship of the Marmalade mini-empire doesn't have the seating of its siblings but has loads of tempting choices for takeout. Salads range from herb chicken ravioli in pesto to roasted beets with oranges and candied walnuts in rosemary vinaigrette; panini and bakery treats are numerous; and take-home entrees include chicken enchiladas, vegetable lasagne and poached salmon with sour cream dill. **WHO** Locals who have been coming here for years.

[Monsieur Marcel] **1260 3rd St. Promenade, Santa Monica, 310.587.1166, mrmarcel.com. L & D daily. French. AE, MC, V. $$ WHY** Straightforward bistro food, some of which (escargots, quiches, salads, cheeses) takes out well. If you have time, sit for a spell with a glass of wine and have fun watching the Promenade parade. **WHAT** Occupying the former newsstand smack in the middle of the Promenade, this Gallic market, wine bar and café is a good, if pricey, place to get food to take home or to the office. Check the chalkboard for the daily offerings. ☼

[Real Food Daily] **514 Santa Monica Blvd., Santa Monica, 310.451.7544, realfood.com. L & D daily. Vegan/American. AE, MC, V. $$ WHY** Organic vegan food that actually tastes good. You can order takeout, order party platters or get lunch or dinner delivered. **WHAT** Real Food's meat- and dairy-free fare includes many dishes that take out well or work for small parties. Try the salad platters, the lentil-walnut pâté and the cold sesame-noodle salad. Your call on whether to try the tofu cheesecake. (We passed.) **WHO** Santa Monica's many vegans and flexitarians. ☼🦐🚗

[SugarFISH] **4722 Admiralty Way, Marina del Rey, 310.306.6300; 11640 San Vicente Blvd., Brentwood, 310.820.4477, sugarfishsushi.com. L & D daily. Sushi. AE, MC, V. $$ - $$$ WHY** Takeout or eat-in sushi from the "sushi nazi" Kazunori Nozawa of Sushi Nozawa in Studio City — without the high-price tag or quite the same creative combinations. The Marina location has curbside service for people hustling to catch a plane. **WHAT** Nozawa has traded his omakase at the flagship restaurant for pre-set "Trust Me" combinations (hamachi nigiri, tuna sashimi with scallions) that are less expensive but just as fresh at this more laid-back strip-mall joint. The takeout is cleverly packaged and includes his famed "firm" nibbling instructions, so it almost feels like Nozawa is glaring over your shoulder at home. Note the new branch

🏠 ESSENTIALLY L.A. ☼ LATE ♥ ROMANTIC 🍽 VALUE 🦐 QUIET ☼ SUSTAINABLE

in Brentwood. **WHO** Just-landed Angelenos grabbing takeout on their way home from LAX or Marina locals popping in for a quick bite.

SOUTH BAY TO SOUTH L.A.

[Claro's] 🏠 **101 W. Whittier Blvd., La Habra, 562.690.2844, claros.com. B & L Mon.-Tues. & Thurs.-Sun. Italian. AE, MC, V. $ - $$ WHY** Prepared take-home dishes like lasagne and ravioli, huge and delicious sandwiches, savory sausages, take-and-bake pizzas and a bakery case lined with breads, cannoli and Italian cookies. **WHAT** This old-school Italian market and deli is a branch of the mothership in San Gabriel, which has been around since 1948. The deli offers sandwiches, sausages, antipasti and hot dishes. Good for a takeout dinner for one or a party for a dozen. **WHO** Third-generation loyalists and people proud of their Sicilian blood, even if it's only a little.

[Olives Gourmet Grocer] **3510 E. Broadway, Long Beach, 562.439.7758, olivesgourmetgrocer.com. B, L & early D daily. Modern American. AE, MC, V. $ - $$ WHY** For a food-lover's home away from home, not to mention a good place to pick up a rotisserie chicken for dinner or a platter for that potluck. **WHAT** This clean-lined store is as much a deli as a grocery store, with a terrific sandwich counter, a salad bar, an olive bar and a different dinner-to-go every night: perhaps chicken and dumplings on a Sunday, or pan-seared salmon with rice and roasted broccoli on a Wednesday.

[Olives Gourmet Grocer] **5000 E. 2nd St., Long Beach, 562.343.5580, olivesgourmetgrocer.com. B, L & early D daily. Modern American. AE, MC, V. $ - $$ WHY** Food for every need, from breakfast panini to party platters. **WHAT** Twice the size of its Broadway parent, this Belmont Shore Olives is as much a deli and gourmet-to-go place as a grocery store, with a pizza oven, grilled panini, traditional sandwiches, a salad bar, an olive bar and a different dinner-to-go every night: perhaps chicken Milanese or Southwest flatiron steak with roasted red potatoes and asparagus. There's a seating area if you want to eat in. **WHO** Passionate foodies from all over Long Beach and Seal Beach.

Gourmet To Go

🌱 VEGETARIAN ⊙ KID FRIENDLY ⊘ PATIO DINING 🚘 DELIVERY 🏠 PRIVATE PARTY

Bakeries + Sweets

Look here for bread bakers, cupcake makers and cake decorators, as well as chocolates, ice cream and more.

[ESSENTIALLY L.A.]

21 Choices, Pasadena (PAGE 280)

Big Sugar Bakeshop, Studio City (PAGE 285)

Breadbar, Beverly/Third & Century City (PAGES 275 & 287)

Brooklyn Bagel Bakery, Downtown (PAGE 278)

Bulgarini Gelato, Altadena (PAGE 281)

Diamond Bakery, Fairfax (PAGE 275)

Dr. Bob's Ice Cream, Pomona (PAGE 281)

El Gallo Bakery, East L.A. (PAGE 279)

Euro Pane, Pasadena (PAGE 282)

Fosselman's, Alhambra (PAGE 282)

Huckleberry, Santa Monica (PAGE 291)

Jin Patisserie, Venice (PAGE 292)

La Brea Bakery, Miracle Mile (PAGE 275)

L'Artisan du Chocolat, Silver Lake (PAGE 279)

La Mascota, Boyle Heights (PAGE 279)

Little Flower Candy Co., Pasadena (PAGE 283)

Littlejohn's English Toffee, Fairfax District (PAGE 276)

Partamian Armenian Bakery, Mid-City (PAGE 277)

Patisserie Chantilly, Torrance (PAGE 294)

Porto's, Glendale & Burbank (PAGES 284 & 286)

Scoops, Mid-City (PAGE 277)

Sprinkles Cupcakes, Beverly Hills (PAGE 289)

Susina Bakery, Beverly/Third (PAGE 277)

ESSENTIALLY L.A. LATE ROMANTIC VALUE QUIET SUSTAINABLE

QUALITY BAKED GOODS ARE
ALSO FOUND INSIDE THESE CAFÉS OR SHOPS:
Bauducco's Italian Market, Westlake Village (PAGE 267)
Bay Cities Italian Deli & Bakery, Santa Monica (PAGE 249)
Café Tropical, Silver Lake (PAGE 184)
Claro's, San Gabriel & La Habra (PAGES 264 & 271)
The Conservatory, Culver City (PAGE 214)
Cynthia's on the Corner, Santa Monica (PAGE 197)
Doña Rosa, Pasadena (PAGE 237)
Froma on Melrose, Melrose (PAGE 314)
Homegirl Café, Chinatown (PAGE 184)
Howie's Ranch Market, San Gabriel (PAGE 321)
I Panini di Ambra, Hollywood (PAGE 227)
Jongewaard's Bake N Broil, Long Beach (PAGE 200)
Julienne, San Marino (PAGE 188)
Koreatown Galleria Market, Koreatown (PAGE 322)
Le Pain Quotidien, various locations (PAGES 188 & 198)
Liborio Market, Downtown & Koreatown (PAGE 322)
Little Next Door, Beverly/Third (PAGE 261)
Lovebirds, Pasadena (PAGE 188)
Ma 'n' Pa's Grocery, Long Beach (PAGE 316)
Marmalade, various locations (PAGES 198, 266 & 269)
Marukai Pacific Market, Torrance (PAGE 255)
Nickel Diner, Downtown (PAGE 186)
Olives Gourmet Grocer, Long Beach (PAGE 317)
Owen's Market, Century City (PAGE 318)
Real Food Daily, W. Hollywood & Santa Monica (PAGES 140 & 262)
Recess, Glendale (PAGE 265)
Ugo's Italian Deli, Sierra Madre (PAGE 189)
Urth Caffé, various locations (PAGES 205, 209 & 219)

Bakeries
+ Sweets

VEGETARIAN ◎KID FRIENDLY ☼PATIO DINING 🚗DELIVERY 🏛PRIVATE PARTY

CITYWIDE

[Coolhaus Ice Cream Truck] @coolhaus (Twitter feed), eatcoolhaus.com. Ice cream. Cash only. **WHY** Handmade ice cream sandwiches that sport names based on architecture puns. **WHAT** All-natural, homemade ice cream sandwiches shaped vaguely like modern houses come in varieties including Frank Behry (sugar cookie and strawberry ice cream) and Mintimalism (chocolate cookie and mint chip ice cream). The truck roves around town to artsy events and shopping areas — check its website or follow its Twitter feed (@coolhaus) to see where it's parked. ☺

CENTRAL CITY

[Alcove Café & Bakery] 1929 Hillhurst Ave., Los Feliz, 323.644.0100, alcovecafe.com. Daily. American. AE, MC, V. **WHY** Sweet central: strawberry whip cake, banana cream cake and truly superb chocolate chip cookies. **WHAT** For every two people who are ordering a meal to enjoy on the oh-so-charming patio or in the old Craftsman house there's another person just getting something sweet to take away. The cupcakes are nothing special, but the chocolatechip cookies are well worth the calories, as is the See's Candy bundt cake, which is every bit as wonderful as it sounds. **WHO** Writers, musicians, costume designers, blind-daters and Los Feliz women sporting subtle tattoos and Kingsley-clad preschoolers. ☺ ♥🖅♻🐾☺☼

[The Bagel Broker] 7825 Beverly Blvd., Beverly/Third, 323.931.1258, bagelbroker.com. Daily. Deli. AE, MC, V. **WHY** All the traditional bagel varieties and variations, like blueberry or cheese jalapeño, are baked daily. Order them by the bag, or have a bagel sandwich or bagels and lox on the premises. **WHAT** Bagel connoisseurs and New York transplants say this basic mini-mall deli in the heart of the Fairfax Jewish district is one of the few places in L.A. to get something approaching an authentic bagel.

[Beard Papa's] Hollywood & Highland, 6801 Hollywood Blvd., Hollywood, 323.462.6100, beardpapa.com. Daily. Japanese/French. MC, V. **WHY** Two words: cream puffs. **WHAT** The craze that has swept Japan has arrived in L.A., with this Hollywood & Highland branch and more popping up like Pinkberries. In this case the obsession is over a cream puff. Fat balls of choux are baked all day long, and when you order yours, an employee fills it with sweetened cream (vanilla, chocolate, green tea, pumpkin), dusts it with powdered sugar, and off you go. More locations in San Gabriel, Gardena and beyond. **WHO** Food faddists who've just gotta try it. ☺

[Bennett's Ice Cream] Farmers Market, 6333 W. 3rd St., Fairfax District, 323.939.6786. Daily. Ice cream. Cash only. **WHY** For seasonal flavors like rose, for Rose Parade season, and pumpkin in the fall, and original creations like Fancy Nancy (coffee with bananas), along with shakes and sundaes. Bennett's also owns the Refresher soda-pop stand in the market and bottles its own sodas, including Spicy Hot Cola. **WHAT** Old-fashioned ice cream in dozens of flavors — no gelato here — made on the premises behind viewing windows at this folksy Farmers Market stand. **WHO** The marvelous cross-section of humanity that fills Farmers Market each day. ☺ ☼

[Breadbar] 🗋 8718 W. 3rd St., Beverly/Third, 310.205.0124, breadbar. net. Daily. American. AE, MC, V. **WHY** Hand-crafted whole grain and country breads, excellent croissants and tarts, as well as breakfast, sandwiches and salads. Don't miss the Alpine cheese bread. **WHAT** Baker Eric Kayser first won the hearts of Parisians (no easy thing) and is now out to conquer L.A., and he's off to a very fine start with this branch and the one in Century City. The patio fronts bustling 3rd Street, with more tables inside the chic industrial space. A display case runs the length of the café, showcasing pastries and colorful tarts. **WHO** Serious bread eaters and the 3rd Street café crowd. ☼

[Breadworks] Farmers Market, 6333 W. 3rd St., Fairfax District, 323.936.0785, breadworksbakery.com. Daily. American. MC, V. **WHY** Hearty, well-made breads in the La Brea vein, including baguettes, sourdoughs, seven grain, ciabatta and rosemary, supplied wholesale to many restaurants and markets and sold retail at this small shop. **WHAT** The folks here once worked at La Brea Bakery, and you'll note the similarity in the substantial, subtly sour breads. Good focaccia, too. Because it occupies the former Bread Bin space at Farmers Market, it's carrying on the Bread Bin's tradition of making wonderful Hungarian cinnamon bread.

[Diamond Bakery] 🗋 335 N. Fairfax Ave., Fairfax District, 323.655.0534. Daily. Deli/kosher. Cash only. **WHY** Kosher challah, delicious rye and heavenly cheesecakes. **WHAT** So maybe you have to wait a while, and maybe the fellow behind the counter could be a little less brusque. But these are the things one must endure to get a rye bread this good. Since you had to wait so long for your rye, you might as well get some chocolate chip rugelach. And maybe a cheesecake. **WHO** Longtime regulars and refugees from the trendy cupcakeries. 🗟

[La Brea Bakery] 🗋 624 S. La Brea Ave., Miracle Mile, 323.939.6813, labreabakery.com. Daily. American. AE, MC, V. **WHY** For its famous crusty baguettes and hearty artisanal loaves speckled with nuts, herbs and olives. **WHAT** The original bakery home of former Campanile pastry chef Nancy Silverton still has some of the best bread in town — and it's wholly different in quality from the grocery store brand bearing the same name. **WHO** Tourists checking it off their list and locals grabbing a baguette for dinner.

Bakeries + Sweets

🍃 VEGETARIAN ☺ KID FRIENDLY ☼ PATIO DINING 🚚 DELIVERY 🎩 PRIVATE PARTY

[La Maison du Pain] 5373 W. Pico Blvd., Mid-City, 323.934.5858, lamaisondupain.net. Closed Sun. French/American. AE, MC, V. **WHY** Kalamata olive bread, plain and chocolate croissants, macaroons and traditional Parisian baguettes wtih a crisp crust that shatters to reveal light, soft bread. **WHAT** No, it's not the House of Pain, it's the House of Bread, as well as the House of Tarts, Quiches and Cakes. It's both a sweet little café with very good breakfast and lunch goodies and a take-away bakery with good breads and sweets. ☺

[Littlejohn's English Toffee] 🛈 Farmers Market, 6333 W. 3rd St., Fairfax District, 323.936.5379, littlejohnscandies.com. Daily. Confections. AE, MC, V. **WHY** Buttery, crunchy, chocolatey English toffee that is impossible to stop eating. **WHAT** Good God, how we love this English toffee, the highlight of our childhood visits to Farmers Market. It's made fresh throughout the day and sold in hunks or in tidier sticks. Good almond bark and honeycomb, but that's not why you come here. **WHO** Wide-eyed children and chocolate-addicted women who stash their purchases in their purses and then nibble on the toffee furtively, so the calories don't stick. ☺ ○

[Mani's Bakery & Café] 519 S. Fairfax Ave., Fairfax District, 323.938.8800, manisbakery.com. Daily. French/American. AE, MC, V. **WHY** Mani's has been baking healthier baked goods for 20 years, with a full bakery as well as a café serving virtuous meals. **WHAT** Mani's baked goods are naturally sweetened with things like fruit juices or agave syrup, with many vegan items. Black-bottom banana tart, wheat-free pumpkin pie and whole-wheat éclairs are just a few of the choices, with many varieties of cakes available on special order. You won't mistake these for desserts with real butter and sugar, but you'll feel good about yourself. **WHO** Good-looking people intensely focused on their health. ○🍃

[Mashti Malone's Ice Cream] 1525 N. La Brea Ave., Hollywood, 323.874.0144, mashti.com. Daily. Ice cream. AE, MC, V. **WHY** The Mashti ice cream sandwich: your choice of ice cream stuffed between crisp wafers. **WHAT** Come here for Persian-style ice creams in inspired flavors that are as poetic sounding as they are delicious: orange blossom with pistachios, creamy rosewater, herbal snow, lavender, rose sorbet with sour cherry.... ☺

[Milk] 7290 Beverly Blvd., Beverly/Third, 323.939.6455, themilkshop. com. Daily. Ice cream/American. MC, V. **WHY** Ice cream creations like the grasshopper ice cream sandwich or banana-peanut malt, creative cakes like Blue Velvet, delicate cookies and handmade shaved ice (try the dulce de leche). Oh, and the vanilla-bean ice cream bar dipped in superb dark chocolate. **WHAT** When Milk opened on Beverly Boulevard, the charming, airy sweets spot filled a huge gap — there were few places to get good ice cream and dessert that stay open as late as 11 p.m. on weekends. The counter is piled with an array of tempting baked goods, and there are treats to take home in the cooler case. **WHO** Hancock Park moms picking up expensive but fantastic ice cream cakes and Beverly Boulevard date-nighters sharing shakes and sundaes. ☺

[Panos Pastry] 5150 Hollywood Blvd., Hollywood, 323.661.0335, panospastry.com. Daily. Armenian/French. AE, MC, V. **WHY** Superb baklava of every variety, as well as the full range of French and Armenian pastries. **WHAT** An elegant temple of French and Armenian delicacies, done up in marble and mirrors. There's another branch in Glendale. **WHO** Baklava junkies and brides-to-be looking for a beautiful cake.

[Partamian Armenian Bakery] 🏠 5410 W. Adams Blvd., Mid-City, 323.937.2870. Closed Sun. Armenian. AE, MC, V. **WHY** Devotees drive an hour for their *lahmajune*, aka Armenian pizza. **WHAT** This longstanding center of Armenian food culture in L.A. is now owned by two Mexican bakers — the devoted employees to whom Abraham Partanian left the business in his will. The lahmajune is as good as ever, and it does the heart good to see this place carry on so well. **WHO** Armenian-American famlies who've been coming here (often from great distances) for three generations, as well as lots of local lahmajune junkies. 📖☺

[Scoops] 🏠 712 N. Heliotrope Dr., East Hollywood, 323.906.2649. Daily. Ice cream/vegan. Cash only. **WHY** For ice cream and sorbet flavors you won't believe: chocolate-jasmine, cashew-ricotta, peanut-butter-celery-and-raisin, strawberry-lychee and many more; the roster changes daily. We adore the less-adventurous brown bread, a vanilla ice cream with caramel and Grape-Nuts. **WHAT** Tai Kim isn't a vegan who wishes he could eat ice cream — he's a passionate lover of gelato-style ice cream (a little lighter than true gelato) who wants everyone to enjoy it, including dairy-free vegans. He's come up with dozens of recipes for fantastic regular and vegan ice creams and sorbets, and in the process made his little East Hollywood joint a major foodie destination. **WHO** Adventurous ice cream lovers. 📖🍴☺

[Susina Bakery] 🏠 7122 Beverly Blvd., Beverly/Third, 323.934.7900, susinabakery.com. Daily. American. AE, MC, V. **WHY** Croissants for breakfast, quiches and such salads as dried cherry and brie for lunch, picnic boxes and lavish cakes — try the chocolate peanut butter mousse or berry blossom. **WHAT** Exquisite tarts and pastries are laid out in glass cases in this European-style bakery, with tables for enjoying sweets up to 11 p.m.

[Sweet Lady Jane] 8360 Melrose Ave., Melrose, 323.653.7145, sweetladyjane.com. Daily. American. AE, MC, V. **WHY** Gorgeous cakes, breakfast pastries and cookies that taste as good as they look. **WHAT** This is L.A.'s high-end birthday-cake central, turning out su-

Bakeries + Sweets

🍃 VEGETARIAN ☺ KID FRIENDLY ☼ PATIO DINING 🚗 DELIVERY 🎩 PRIVATE PARTY

perb almond roca, chocolate mocha praline, passion fruit with apricot, triple berry, even red velvet cakes. They're no bargain, though, and the service can be less than warm. But the cakes are so good that no one really minds. **WHO** Fred Segal-clad moms on birthday-cake patrol and neighborhood lunchgoers.

EASTSIDE

[Auntie Em's Marketplace] **4616 Eagle Rock Blvd., Eagle Rock, 323.255.0800, auntieemskitchen.com. Daily. American. AE, MC, V.**
WHY Dreamy scones, over-the-top coconut cupcakes, a great selection of domestic cheeses and a freezer full of take-home dishes.
WHAT Julienne for the pierced-nose set, Auntie Em's has evolved into a one-stop food-lovers' haven — part café, part gourmet-to-go, part caterer and part bakery. From the bakery operation in the restaurant, you can special-order a red velvet cake or take home some amazing chocolate cupcakes and muffins. **WHO** An Eagle Rock mix, from Oxy professors to tattooed Highland Park performance artists. 🐾 ☺ ☼

[Beard Papa's] **333 W. Alameda St., Little Tokyo/Arts District, 213.620.0710, beardpapa.com. Daily. Japanese/French. MC, V. WHY** Two words: cream puffs. **WHAT** The craze that has swept Japan has arrived in L.A., with this Little Tokyo branch and more popping up like Pinkberries. In this case the obsession is over a cream puff. Fat balls of choux are baked all day long, and when you order yours, an employee fills it with sweetened cream (vanilla, chocolate, green tea, pumpkin), dusts it with powdered sugar, and off you go. **WHO** Food faddists who've just gotta try it. ☺

[Brooklyn Bagel Bakery] 🏛 **2217 W. Beverly Blvd., Westlake, 213.413.4114. Daily. Deli. Cash only. WHY** Properly boiled and hearthbaked bagels, more compact and pleasingly dense than most in town, made fresh all day. **WHAT** Between Downtown and Koreatown lies one of L.A.'s most New York of businesses, a busy bakery with an equally busy retail outlet. Try the blueberry or the poppyseed, and don't miss Bagel Happy Hour (3 to 6 p.m.), when they're all half priced. **WHO** Wholesale customers (coffeehouse and café owners), homesick New Yorkers and bagel devotees from across L.A. 🗨

[Butter Tart] **4126 Verdugo Rd., Glassell Park, 323.258.8278, mybuttertart.com. Daily. American. Cash only. WHY** The bacon butter tart. **WHAT** Tossing its hat into the expanding eastside bakery-café ring, Butter Tart has opened in the far reaches of Glassell Park. Its namesake is a flaky pastry tart with a custardy butter-sugar filling familiar to Canadians, who seem to have endless opinions as to what consistency a true butter tart filling should have. Owner Karena Higgins has contributed to the debate with her own bacon butter tart, in keeping with this era's All Things Bacon theme. **WHO** People picking up a dozen butter tarts for the office, and indie youngsters who like the music on the stereo as much as the pastries. ☺ ☺

[El Gallo Bakery] 🔒 4546 Cesar E. Chavez Ave., East L.A., 323.263.5528, elgallobakery.com. Daily. Mexican. Cash only. **WHY** Bolillos, breads and all sorts of warm, fragrant, cinnamon-infused pan dulces. **WHAT** Perhaps the most cherished panaderia in East L.A., this no-frills place has been baking everyday breads and special-occasion sweets for six decades. Fans line up during the holidays to stock up on the rolls. **WHO** Grandparents bringing in their grandkids for pan dulce — and telling them about how they came here as a kid. 🖼☺

[Frances Bakery & Coffee] 404 E. 2nd St., Little Tokyo/Arts District, 213.680.4899. Closed Sun. French. AE, MC, V. **WHY** Cakes that are remarkably moist and delicious without being overly sugary; the chocolate hazelnut, green tea–chocolate and cheesecake are all stars. Sit and stay for a cup of very good coffee or a cup of afternoon tea. **WHAT** The Japanese-American baker who runs this longtime cake heaven is French in spirit and in baking technique, as evidenced by his lovely croissants, quiches and, especially, his superb cakes and handmade chocolates. The good stuff vanishes fast, so come early. **WHO** Longtime regulars in on the secret. ☺

[L'Artisan du Chocolat] 🔒 3364 W. 1st St., Silver Lake, 213.252.8721. Closed Sun.-Mon. Chocolatier. AE, MC, V. **WHY** Chocolates and truffles made here in Silver Lake with skill and taste; if you're adventurous, try the Aztec (with apricot and three chiles, including habañero) or Kalamata olive; if you're a classicist, have the straightforward truffle or the dark chocolate ganache with coffee bits. **WHAT** Master chocolatier Whajung Park and her husband Christian Alexandre turn out some of L.A.'s most sophisticated chocolates at this hidden spot near Beverly and Virgil. Some of the best creations are the most exotic, subtly flavored with herbs, spices, chiles and fruit, but the traditional chocolates are suave and delicious, too. **WHO** Regular customers buying lovely gift boxes.

[La Adelita] 1287 S. Union Ave., Pico/Union, 213.487.0176. Daily. Latino. MC, V. **WHY** Fluffy, ethereal tres leches cakes. **WHAT** An excellent Mexican and pan-Latin operation that bakes soft bolillos, pretty fruit tarts, tortillas and delicious cakes, most notably the tres leches cakes. Next door is a worthwhile café offering dishes from all the Central American countries. It also has a small shop in the Grand Central Market Downtown. **WHO** Pico-Union locals. 🖼☺

[La Mascota Bakery] 🔒 2715 Whittier Blvd., Boyle Heights, 323.263.5513, lamascotabakery.com. Daily. Mexican. MC, V. **WHY** The signature *bolillos* (white rolls) are a must-have for sandwiches, but the *quesadilla salvadoreña* (sour cream-parmesan coffee cake sprinkled

Bakeries + Sweets

🌱 VEGETARIAN ☺ KID FRIENDLY ☼ PATIO DINING 🚐 DELIVERY 🎩 PRIVATE PARTY

with toasted sesame seeds) and the house-made tamales are the secret gems here. **WHAT** The recently expanded bakery has been family run for more than 50 years, and it's still turning out some of the best classic Mexican pastries in town. Most pan dulce fans take their goodies to go, but there are a handful of patio tables for a quick bite and a bench out front where you can watch the tamale cooks in action. **WHO** The local postman, kids stopping by after school, and old-timers who have been coming for decades. ☺

[Lark Silver Lake Cake Shop] **3337 W. Sunset Blvd., Silver Lake, 323.667.2968, larkcakeshop.com. Daily. American. MC, V. WHY** Caramel cake, coconut cake, chocolate chip oatmeal cookies, a very fine sea-salt caramel cupcake and a homey apple pie. **WHAT** A welcome addition to the Silver Lake food scene, Lark makes good, reasonably priced cupcakes, special-occasion cakes, cookies (including Mexican wedding cookies), vegan cupcakes and pies. ☞☜☺

[Pazzo Gelato] **3827 Sunset Blvd., Silver Lake, 323.662.1410, pazzogelato.net. Daily. Ice cream/Italian. AE, MC, V. WHY** The always-rotating gelato flavors include a deep, concentrated pistachio that's sometimes paired with espresso, a mango-cayenne sorbet, mascarpone, and European yogurt. Intelligentsia coffee is also served. **WHAT** Silver Lake residents and gelato fans from a distance fill this popular dessert shop, which does a big after-dinner business (it's open until 11 p.m. during the week and midnight on weekends). **WHO** Little kids who already have their favorites to young couples on dates looking for something new to try. ☺ ☺

SAN GABRIEL VALLEY

[21 Choices] 🏛 **85 W. Colorado Blvd., Old Pasadena, 626.304.9521, 21choices.com. Daily. Yogurt. AE, MC, V. WHY** Delicious in-house yogurt creations (especially the fruit ones in summer, like peach crumble) and a dazzling array of mix-in options to pair with the French vanilla or Valrhona chocolate. **WHAT** Known for its exuberantly friendly staff and a line that typically stretches outside the door, 21 Choices actually offers untold thousands of possible combinations for its custom-made, mix-in frozen yogurts. Give 'em snaps for their efforts to be more sustainable with packaging and products. **WHO** Packs of Pasadena teens, families, date-nighters and, at least once a week, a gaggle of great-looking firefighters (they get to park the hook-and-ladder in the red outside!). ☺ ♻☜☺

[Ap-petite] **140 N. Lake Ave., Pasadena, 626.744.0337, ap-petite.com. Daily. Hungarian/French. MC, V. $ WHY** Tiny and delicious Hungarian and French pastries, priced so you can try a few. **WHAT** Okay, so the name Ap-petite™ is completely silly — almost all the pastries and open-faced sandwiches are petite (get it?) — but everything in this simple shop/café is delicious. The owners are Hungarian, as are many of the items, most notably the *pogi*: buttery, yeasty little pastry balls topped with bacon, cheese or poppy seeds. Also worth trying are the mini cinnamon twists; the small quiches, whose crusts don't hold up well but whose flavor is good; and the pretty $2 open-faced sandwiches, like the meatloaf, the mozzarella, and the roasted veggies. A big platter of these small tastes makes great party food. ☺

[Berolina Bakery] **3421 Ocean View Blvd., Glendale, 818.249.6506, berolinabakery.com. Closed Sun.-Mon. American/French. MC, V.**
WHY Limpa bread as it's meant to be baked, along with a daily lineup of artisanal loaves and daily specials ranging from sunflower to potato dill. **WHAT** A toe over the Montrose line, this shop has baked tasty Northern European and Scandinavian goods for two decades. The owners (he's Swedish, she's Belgian) specialize in breads, including limpa, Black Forest and Swiss Farmer loaves, along with rye-currant and 28 other varieties. Other treats include croissants, Danishes and buttery tortes. **WHO** Sensible folks from La Cañada, Glendale and Montrose, who pick up something to go or have a nosh on the sidewalk patio. ⌂

[Bulgarini Gelato] ⌂ **749 E. Altadena Dr., Altadena, 626.791.6174, bulgarinigelato.com. Closed Mon. Ice cream/Italian. MC, V.**
WHY Amazing gelati and sorbetti, with such flavors as Sicilian pistachio (the addiction of many), cherimoya, peach-moscato and zabaglione. **WHAT** Leo Bulgarini and Elizabeth Foldi were so obsessed with gelato that they apprenticed in Sicily before coming up with their flavors, which they originally served from a cart in the courtyard at the Pacific Asia Museum in Pasadena. After developing a rabid following, they opened this store way up in Altadena, which attracts fans from all over L.A. Make your next party a hit by hiring their mobile gelato cart. **WHO** Road-trippin' gelato aficionados and local moms 'n kids, many of whom come here several times a week. ☺

[Dr. Bob's Ice Cream] ⌂ **P.O. Box 2250, Pomona, 909.865.1956, drbobsicecream.com. By appt. Ice cream. Cash only. WHY** Small-batch ice creams with a 16% butterfat content and incredibly good flavors, especially Really Dark Chocolate, Lemon Custard and, at Christmastime, peppermint. **WHAT** Robert Small, aka Dr. Bob, is a professor at Cal Poly Pomona who turned his love of ice cream into a booming business. You can stop by the plant on the Pomona Fairgrounds property, but there's no real retail operation — instead, look for his ice creams at Gelson's, Vicente Foods, Surfas, Bristol Farms, Olives, Bay Cities, Market Gourmet, Julienne or Howie's Ranch Market. **WHO** Only the most diehard fans call the factory and stop by with a cooler and dry ice when in the Pomona area, and count us among those diehard fans.

Bakeries + Sweets

🍃 **VEGETARIAN** ☺ **KID FRIENDLY** ⌂ **PATIO DINING** 🚗 **DELIVERY** 🏠 **PRIVATE PARTY**

[Euro Pane] 950 E. Colorado Blvd., Pasadena, 626.577.1828. Daily. American/French. MC, V. **WHY** The croissants of your dreams, not to mention the best chocolate cake around, and substantial breads, too. **WHAT** Sumi Chang learned her craft in France and with La Brea's Nancy Silverton, and her bakery is now the most acclaimed in the San Gabriel Valley. Get there early if you hope to score a croissant. (And note that Jones Coffee on Raymond gets a stash of Euro Pane croissants most mornings.) **WHO** Pasadena's intelligentsia read their New Yorkers at small café tables over pains aux chocolats or lunchtime pressed sandwiches. ☺❧☼

[Fosselman's] 1824 W. Main St., Alhambra, 626.282.6533, fosselmans.com. Daily. Ice cream. Cash only. **WHY** The retro charm of old-fashioned banana splits, chocolate malts and grab-it-while-you-can seasonal flavors, especially the fresh peach. **WHAT** Its ice cream is on just about every "best of" list around, but Fosselman's remains at heart an old-fashioned, family-run parlor that draws diverse crowds to its modest brick storefront. Although seasonal flavors like eggnog, licorice and fresh peach beckon, the regular ice cream and sherbet menu also is dazzlingly varied, from real vanilla and white chocolate chip to green tea and dulce de leche. And the shakes, malts and hot fudge sundaes are just like you remember them — maybe better. **WHO** Whole families — from infants to grandparents — along with much of the San Gabriel Valley on hot summer nights. ☺

[Goldstein's Bagel Bakery] 1939 N. Verdugo Rd., Montrose, 818.952.2457; 412 N. Santa Anita Ave., Arcadia, 626.447.2457. Daily. Deli. AE, MC, V. **WHY** Large, chewy bagels that are boiled and baked, and good bagel wraps, too. **WHAT** A pioneer in Old Pasadena, Goldstein's became a victim of its neighborhood's success and was replaced by a Kenneth Cole store. Fortunately, by that point it had expanded to these two branches. The bagels are just as good, and there's even a drive-through window for people who need a dozen assorted bagels — stat! **WHO** During the week, folks hurrying to work or taking a turkey-wrap lunch break; on weekends, dads picking up bagels and cream cheese for the family. ☺☼

[Heirloom Bakery & Cafe] 807 Meridian Ave., South Pasadena, 626.441.0042. Closed Mon. American. AE, MC, V. **WHY** A dessert case packed with dreamy retro desserts, including Hostess-never-had-it-so-good chocolate cupcakes. **WHAT** Heirloom's first-rate breads and baked goods, fine sandwiches (try the Cuban) and excellent salads (especially the Cobb) have made it one of the most popular breakfast and lunch spots in South Pasadena. The setting is stylish, hip and friendly, and the appealing patio is a magnet for just about everybody in town on weekend mornings. **WHO** Outside: parents and their colorfully clad toddlers sharing space with dogs and their well-behaved owners. Inside: local business and creative types. ☺ ☼

[Little Flower Candy Co.] 🔒 **1424 W. Colorado Blvd., Pasadena, 626.304.4800, littleflowercandyco.com. Closed Sun. Confections/bakery. AE, MC, V. WHY** Divine salt caramels and other gift-worthy candies, as well as delicious bran muffins, berry scones and cookies. **WHAT** After finding success selling her candies online and to gourmet stores nationwide, Christine Moore has livened up this stretch of Colorado Boulevard with a friendly, relaxed bakery, confectionary and café. Great for to-go sweets, or for a relaxed latte and scone or lunchtime pressed sandwich, gorgeous salad or the best quiche in Pasadena. **WHO** West Pasadena moms and the Euro Pane crowd. ☺🛒☺

[Mignon Chocolate] **6 E. Holly St., Old Pasadena, 626.796.7100; 315 N. Verdugo Blvd., Glendale; mignonchocolate.com. Closed Mon. Chocolatier. AE, MC, V. WHY** Espresso-caramel chocolates with the subtlest hint of sea salt, and dozens of other superb chocolates, from the traditional to the inventive. **WHAT** The meticulously crafted, classic French-style chocolates, made in the Terpoghossian family's Van Nuys kitchen and displayed in this swank little shop, are deeply delicious; we're already addicted to the ones with the liquid caramel centers, and the dark chocolate with ginger and lime sea salt is remarkable. Beautiful gift boxes, too. The Glendale location is larger and serves coffee to go with your truffles.

[Mr. Baguette] **8702 Valley Blvd., Rosemead, 626.288.9166, mrbaguettesandwiches.com. Daily. Vietnamese/French. MC, V. WHY** As close to an authentic Parisian baguette as you can get in California. **WHAT** As the name suggests, baguettes are the focal point, either to take home or as part of the tasty *bahn mi* (Vietnamese-French sandwiches) made here. These are not robust like the ones at La Brea — they're airy on the inside and intensely crusty on the outside, so they'll make a mess all over your table, just like in Paris. **WHO** Locals grabbing a sandwich for lunch and home cooks picking up baguettes for dinner.

[Panos Pastry] **418 S. Central Ave., Glendale, 818.502.0549, panospastry.com. Daily. Armenian/French. AE, MC, V. WHY** Superb baklava of every variety, as well as the full range of French and Armenian pastries. **WHAT** An elegant temple of French and Armenian delicacies, done up in marble and mirrors. This is an offshoot of the original Hollywood location, and the pastries are just as good. **WHO** Baklava junkies and brides-to-be looking for a beautiful cake.

Bakeries + Sweets

🍃 VEGETARIAN ☺ KID FRIENDLY ☼ PATIO DINING �
 DELIVERY 🎩 PRIVATE PARTY

[Pie 'n' Burger] **913 E. California Blvd., Pasadena, 626.795.1123, pienburger.com. Daily. American. Cash only. WHY** The best pecan pie anywhere, and a host of dreamy meringue pies, including banana. **WHAT** For some reason most Pasadenans think of Pie 'n' Burger as a great place for breakfast or a lunchtime burger. But the name starts with "Pie" for a reason: These are pies that would make Mrs. Callender rend her garments in jealousy. If you have your heart set on a particular one, order in advance, but the kismet of seeing what's there is part of the joy. **WHO** Clever entertainers who don't bake, and during the holiday season a rush of desperate pie-seekers. 🖼️ ☺

[Polkatots] **720 N. Lake Ave., Pasadena, 626.798.3932, polkatots-cupcakes.com. Closed Sun. American. MC, V. WHY** Dulce de leche cupcakes, either regular size or mini. **WHAT** This relatively new spot hidden in a low-end strip mall on an unfashionable stretch of Lake Avenue rocketed to fame when its dulce de leche cupcake won the 2009 L.A. Cupcake Challenge. It deserved the win; we aren't riders on the cupcake fad-wagon and yet we cannot resist these caramel-y treasures. All the cupcakes are good, and the cupcake cakes are birthday-party faves, but all we care about are the mini dulce de leches. ☺

[Porto's] 🏛️ **315 N. Brand Blvd., Glendale, 818.956.5996, portosbakery. com. Daily. Cuban/American. AE, MC, V. WHY** The ornate tiered wedding cakes are award winners, and the Cuban sandwiches are worth driving across town for, as many do. **WHAT** This huge, gleaming café and bakery, founded by Cuban immigrants in the '60s, displays a gorgeous and staggeringly diverse array of goods. Where else can you find Cuban bread, all-American cheesecake and the guava-cheese strudel called *refugiado* all under one roof? ☺

[Sarkis Pastry] **1111 S. Glendale Ave., Glendale, 818.956.6636; 1776 E. Washington Blvd., Pasadena, 626.398.3999, sarkispastry.com. Daily. Armenian/Middle Eastern. AE, MC, V. WHY** For a terrific range of Middle Eastern sweets, notably the brioche-looking tahini cookies, the hand-rolled baklava, the layered bread pudding and the macaroons. **WHAT** The first Armenian/Middle Eastern bakery in Glendale, Sarkis is one of the focal points of Glendale's Armenian-American community. Glass cases are packed with all sorts of beautiful and delicious things. **WHO** A devoted and longstanding eastside clientele. 🖼️ ☺

[Sasoun Bakery] **625 E. Colorado Blvd., Glendale, 818.502.5059. Closed Mon. Armenian. MC, V. WHY** For excellent *lahmajune* (Armenian pizza), cheese boreks and tahini cookies. **WHAT** This meticulous bakery turns out excellent savory Armenian goodies, from cheese breads to the famed pizza-like addiction called lahmajune. Everything is very fresh. Another branch on Santa Monica in Hollywood. **WHO** Armenian-Americans and lahmajune buffs. 🖼️

🏛️ ESSENTIALLY L.A.   ☺ LATE   ♥ ROMANTIC   🖼️ VALUE   🔇 QUIET   ♻️ SUSTAINABLE

[Vrej Pastry] 1074 N. Allen Ave., Pasadena, 626.797.2331. Daily. Middle Eastern/Armenian. AE, MC, V. **WHY** For excellent *barazek* (sesame-pistacho cookies), cheese pastries and *burma* (rolls filled with kadayif nuts). **WHAT** A solid bakery with all the Middle Eastern classics, from baklavas to mamouls, with European petits fours, too. **WHO** Although smaller than in the neighboring town of Glendale, Pasadena has a thriving Armenian-American community, as well as those who hail from all over the Middle East, and they come here for a sweet taste of home. 🗺️ ☺

EAST VALLEY

[Big Sugar Bakeshop] 🏠 12182 Ventura Blvd., Studio City, 818.508.5855, bigsugarbakeshop.com. Daily. American. MC, V. **WHY** Heavenly American desserts, from the ubiquitous cupcake (they're good) to more interesting things, like an astonishing cinnamon cake studded with Red Hots, the Reverse Chocolate Chip Cookie and the rich seven-layer bars topped with coconut. **WHAT** Lisa Ritter has become a demi-goddess in Studio City for her wonderful desserts, from apple-pie bars to cheesecakes. The brownies and seven-layer bars are great to take to a party, and the friendly, family-oriented shop has good foodie gifts, too. **WHO** Studio foodies and after-school moms and kids. ☺

[Gelato Bar] 4342 Tujunga Ave., Studio City, 818.487.1717, gelatobar-la.com. Daily. Ice cream/Italian. AE, MC, V. **WHY** Classic and seasonal flavors, ranging from vanilla and chocolate chip to pink grapefruit, cinnamon-basil and fig mascarpone, served with excellent coffee and espresso. **WHAT** Homemade gelati in fun flavors from Gail Silverton, sister of L.A.'s culinary queen, Nancy Silverton, in a handsome Italian-country café setting. A real find on the most picturesque block in the Valley (also home to Caioti, Aroma Café and other culinary destinations). **WHO** Tujunga strollers and shoppers. ☺

[Leda's Bake Shop] 13722 Ventura Blvd., Sherman Oaks, 818.386.9644, ledasbakeshop.com. Hours irregular; for pickup only. American. MC, V. **WHY** For now, to special-order very good cupcakes (with surprise fillings) and cakes, including many choices for vegans. **WHAT** This place was doing mini-cupcakes before the craze began, and owner Ledette's little beauties are indeed among the best in town. She uses A-list ingredients (like organic eggs and Scharffen Berger chocolate) and makes each one look beautiful. But the real specialty is order-in-advance cakes, regular or vegan, all of which are carefully crafted and delicious. Leda's is currently baking only by special order, but Ledette promises an "exciting new concept" for this space in the future; it's been slow in coming, however. **WHO** Party planners and caterers picking up large orders, and small-scale customers getting two dozen mini-cupcakes for a birthday party.

Bakeries + Sweets

🍴VEGETARIAN ☺ KID FRIENDLY ☼PATIO DINING 🚙DELIVERY 🏠PRIVATE PARTY

[Martino's Bakery] 335 N. Victory Blvd., Burbank, 818.842.0715, martinosbakery.com. Closed Sun. American. AE, MC, V. **WHY** The historic and utterly addictive tea cakes, glazed square mini-cakes (blueberry, buttermilk or cranberry) that are wonderful for breakfast or a midnight snack. **WHAT** Founded as a pie bakery by Victor and Eva Martino in 1926, Martino's switched to making wholesale doughnuts during WWII until it came up with the "tea cake," a cupcake predecessor, in 1945. It's still making them, now in this new bakery/café, and they're as good as ever. Buy a lot — the first few will be gone by the time you get to your car. **WHO** Generations of Angelenos who grew up on Martino's tea cakes. ☺

[Natas Pastries] 13317 Ventura Blvd., Sherman Oaks, 818.788.8050, nataspastries.com. Daily. Portuguese. MC, V. **WHY** For the *nata*, Portugal's famous pastry — a custardy filling in puff pastry that's particularly cherished at Christmastime. Good espresso, too. **WHAT** This little Valley shop specializes in the very good sweets from Portugal, including the namesake nata, Portuguese sweet bread, and wonderful mini-coconut-lemon cupcakes and mini cheesecakes. And now the offerings are expanded — it took over a neighboring space and created a little dining room in which to serve breakfast and lunch. **WHO** Portuguese ex-pats and regulars who have become addicted to the *malassadas*, delicious little sugar-ball doughnuts. ☺

[Porto's] 🏛 3614 W. Magnolia Blvd., Burbank, 818.846.9100, portosbakery.com. Daily. Cuban/American. AE, MC, V. **WHY** The ornate tiered wedding cakes are award-winners, and the Cuban sandwiches are worth driving across town for, as many do. **WHAT** This offshoot of the Glendale original founded by Cuban immigrants in the '60s displays a gorgeous and staggeringly diverse array of goods. Where else can you find Cuban bread, all-American cheesecake and the guava-cheese strudel called *refugiado* all under one roof? ☺

[Rocket Fizz] 2112 Magnolia Blvd., Burbank, 818.846.7632. Daily. Confections. AE, MC, V. **WHY** It's hard to imagine a confection or soda this place doesn't have, and the cheerful surroundings will make you want to linger awhile. **WHAT** A retro candy and soda lover's paradise in the heart of Burbank, Rocket Fizz stocks more than 500 varieties of soda and even more kinds of classic and rare candy in a space decorated with vintage rock concert posters and even older tin signs. There's a patio out back, with plans afoot for summer B-movie nights, giving you plenty of time to enjoy your Sky Bar and cold bottle of Grape Crush. **WHO** Kids, candy geeks and a pre-movie crowd. ☺

[Studio Yogurt] 12050 Ventura Blvd., Studio City, 818.508.7811. Daily. Yogurt. Cash only. **WHY** For a side-by-side of chocolate and peanut butter yogurt. **WHAT** A good frozen yogurt shop; the toppings are limited (i.e., fruit is frozen, not fresh), but the house-developed flavors are often tasty. Huge portions, modest prices. **WHO** A constant line out the door of starlets, teens, seniors and families. 🖼🍷☺☼

WEST VALLEY

[Bea's Bakery] 18450 Clark St., Tarzana, 818.344.0100, beasbakery. com. Daily. Deli/kosher. Cash only. **WHY** For *hamantaschen* (three-sided filled cookies), black-and-white cookies, rugelach and cakes that would make your bubbe happy. **WHAT** A longstanding West Valley destination, this traditional Jewish bakery does a booming business in cookies, cakes, rye breads and challahs. Be prepared for a wait, but it's worth it. **WHO** Good Jewish sons and daughters picking up something to take to their mother's house for dinner. 🖼☺

WESTSIDE: CENTRAL

[Bluebird Cafe] 8572 National Blvd., Culver City, 310.841.0939, blue-birdcafela.com. Closed Sun. American. AE, MC, V. **WHY** For cupcakes that are just as good or better than Sprinkles, for considerably less money. **WHAT** House-baked goodies are served at this little breakfast-and-lunch café or can be ordered at the counter to take home — but don't think you can eat one of these moist, rich red velvet or chocolate cupcakes in your car without making a huge mess. Delicious scones, too. **WHO** Culver City studio workers and neighbors.

[Breadbar] 🏛 Westfield Century City, 10250 Santa Monica Blvd., Century City, 310.277.3770, breadbar.net. Daily. American. AE, MC, V. **WHY** Hand-crafted whole grain and country breads, excellent croissants and tarts, as well as breakfast, sandwiches and salads. Don't miss the Alpine cheese bread. **WHAT** This Parisian import now has a Century City mall branch, which is also a terrific place to have breakfast or lunch. Baker Eric Kayser first won the hearts of Parisians (no easy thing for a bread baker) and is now out to conquer L.A., and he's off to a very fine start with this branch and the one on 3rd. These superb breads are showing up in some of L.A.'s finest restaurants. **WHO** Chic Century City folks. ☼

[Buttercake Bakery] 10595 W. Pico Blvd., Rancho Park, 310.470.6770; 8616 Sunset Blvd., West Hollywood, 310.855.0770, but-tercakebakery.com. Daily. American. AE, MC, V. **WHY** For tender layer cakes and cookies that are the stuff of childhood dreams. **WHAT** Home-style cakes, cupcakes and mini-cupcakes done to perfection: German chocolate, coconut, red velvet, and of course, vanilla but-tercake. You'll also be tempted by criss-cross peanut butter cookies, bundt cakes and creamy cheesecakes that taste like they were baked in your mom's kitchen. Inscriptions on cookies and cakes at no extra charge. **WHO** People who believe there is a Betty Crocker, and cup-cake connoisseurs seeking true butter flavor and tender crumb. ☺

Bakeries + Sweets

🍃 VEGETARIAN ☺ KID FRIENDLY ☼ PATIO DINING 🚗 DELIVERY 🎪 PRIVATE PARTY

[Clementine] **1751 Ensley Ave., Century City, 310.552.1080, clementineonline.com. Closed Sun. American. AE, MC, V.** **WHY** Grown-up homemade granola, cookies and seasonal pies. **WHAT** This all-American bakery and caterer makes simple sweets the way you always hoped yours would turn out: flaky berry pie, tender buttermilk strawberry shortcake and delicious thumbprint cookies. **WHO** Business types on lunch break and locals lingering over coffee and cookies. ☺ ☼

[Dolce Forno Bakery] **3828 Willat Ave., Culver City, 310.280.6004, dolcefornobakery.com. Closed Sat.-Sun. Italian. AE, MC, V.** **WHY** Wonderful fresh filled pastas (in five-pound bags), Italian country breads (ciabatta, focaccia, noci, panini rolls), tiramisu and special-occasion cakes. **WHAT** Celestino Drago, one of L.A.'s star Italian chef/restaurateurs, runs this bakery to supply his own places and other Italian eateries; retail customers can shop here during the week. It's best to call a day in advance for your order, because not much is kept in stock for walk-ins. **WHO** Chefs, shop owners and some retail customers.

[Edelweiss Chocolate Factory] **444 N. Cañon Dr., Beverly Hills, 310.275.6003, edelweisschocolates.com. Daily. Chocolatier. MC, V.** **WHY** The dark chocolate Caramellow (with marshmallow and caramel) and the milk chocolate–coconut Snocap will have you bursting into songs from *The Sound of Music*. **WHAT** Beverly Hills's premier chocolatier since the 1940s is as good as ever, especially the chocolate-covered marshmallows, which the original owner invented and which remain big sellers today. The truffles aren't so hot, but the carefully made retro Swiss chocolates in the See's vein are good. ☺

[Jin Patisserie] **Intercontinental Hotel, 2151 Ave. of the Stars, Century City, 310.789.6485, jinpatisserie.com. Closed Sun. Chocolatier/French. AE, MC, V.** **WHY** For delicate, sculpturally gorgeous chocolates and pastries that taste as good as they look. **WHAT** After conquering Abbot Kinney with what may be L.A.'s most refined and serene chocolate shop and tea garden, Kristy Choo has branched out with this white-and-Lucite gallery-style shop in the Intercontinental. Same incredible chocolates and quality tea and coffee in a more modern setting.

[K Chocolatier] **9606 Little Santa Monica Blvd., Beverly Hills, 310.248.2626, dianekronchocolates.com. Daily. Chocolatier. AE, MC, V.** **WHY** For jewel-like (and jewel-priced) Swiss-style chocolates of good flavor and great beauty. **WHAT** Owner Diane Krön takes credit for inventing the chocolate-dipped strawberry back when she ran Krön Chocolatier in New York in the '70s; now she's returned from retirement to run this swank little Beverly Hills shop. If you take out a second mortgage, you can go wild with the milk mousse au chocolate, the crispy Teddy Bear chocolates and the dark-chocolate mints. **WHO** People pulling up in their Bentleys to pick up a hostess gift.

🏛 ESSENTIALLY L.A. ☺ LATE ♥ ROMANTIC 👓 VALUE 🔇 QUIET ♻ SUSTAINABLE

[Paulette Macaron] **9466 Charleville Blvd., Beverly Hills, 310.275.0023, paulettemacarons.com. Closed Sun. French. AE, MC, V.**
WHY Parisian-style macarons, displayed like objets d'art.
WHAT Parisian-style macarons are not the dumpling-style macaroons (normally made of coconut) that we see in the U.S. These are light, tender-crisp sandwich-style cookies that look rather like colorful, miniature hamburgers, except the fillings are luscious ganache. Try the Sicilian pistachio, salt caramel and Madagascar vanilla.

[Platine Sweet & Savories] **10850 Washington Blvd., Culver City, 310.559.9933, platinecookies.com. Closed Sun.-Mon. American/French. AE, MC, V. WHY** Customized, "couture" cookies, brownies and teeny pots de crème for parties and gifts, and impulse treats to take home. **WHAT** This boutique occupies a bare-bones commercial kitchen in still-untrendy west Culver City, with a tiny counter and no seating. But though the surroundings are spare, the product has all the preciousness of a Sprinkles — a daily assortment of such sweets as house-made Platinos (like Oreos); Camees (vanilla crème sandwiches); Short Stacks (weird, über-precious mini "pancakes" with caramelized bacon and maple-orange glaze); chocolate gingersnaps; and made-to-order ice cream sandwiches ($3.50 each; not large) made with Milk ice cream. Trendy bona fides also include coffee from LA Mill, caramels and marshmallows from Little Flower Candy Co., and jams from Mark & Stephen's. **WHO** People who like their cookies sweet and who think nothing of paying $1 to $2.50 for a two-inch cookie. ☺

[The Sensitive Baker] **10836 1/2 Washington Blvd., Culver City, 310.815.1800, thesensitivebaker.com. Closed Sat. American/vegan. MC, V. WHY** Just because you're gluten and dairy intolerant doesn't mean you have to tolerate bad baked goods. **WHAT** Located a couple of doors from butter- and flour-abundant Platine, this bare-bones kosher and vegan shop has figured out how to avoid those ingredients and still produce moist cupcakes with fluffy frosting, soft quinoa-cranberry cookies and fudgy brownies that will appeal to even the gluten-tolerant members of your family. The bakery's most popular bread — made with brown rice flour and hemp nuts — has a nice, bready pull, and the bagels (with almond meal) are satisfyingly chewy. In the freezer case are eggy brioche rolls, good scones, hamburger buns, pizza dough and vegan mac 'n "cheese." Come early if you want muffins or brownies, because they often sell out, and note that the bakery sells its mix by the bag, ships locally and makes birthday cakes. **WHO** People with good taste who need to avoid troublesome ingredients. 🔖

[Sprinkles Cupcakes] 🏛 **9635 Little Santa Monica Blvd., Beverly Hills, 310.274.8765, sprinklescupcakes.com. Daily. American. MC, V. WHY** For rich and beautiful (if sometimes too sweet) cupcakes; try the dark chocolate, lemon and cinnamon. If you call your order in ahead, you won't have to wait in line. **WHAT** We don't get the cupcake

Bakeries + Sweets

🔖 VEGETARIAN ⦿ KID FRIENDLY ☼ PATIO DINING 🚗 DELIVERY 🏛 PRIVATE PARTY

frenzy, but if you're among the obsessed, you will make a pilgrimage here, if you haven't already. Sprinkles is riding the cupcake wave and going national, and it's jumped on the truck fad-wagon — yes, you can follow the SprinklesMobile on Twitter. **WHO** Glamour moms and personal assistants who don't mind waiting in line a half hour for a dozen cupcakes. ☺

[Zen Bakery] 10988 W. Pico Blvd., Rancho Park, 310.475.6727, zenbakery.com. Closed Sun. American. Cash only. **WHY** Really good, and good for you, bran muffins — try the blueberry-raspberry oat-bran one. **WHAT** Zen's muffins are big sellers at Trader Joe's and Whole Foods, but you can come here to the source to buy them fresh from the ovens. The specialty is bran muffins of many types, as well as fiber cakes and vegan muffins. None of them taste like hay, which is too often the case with health-food baked goods. **WHO** Health-conscious and/or vegan westsiders. 📝 ✧ ☙ ☺

WEST OF THE 405

[3 Square Café & Bakery] 1121 Abbot Kinney Blvd., Venice, 310.399.6504, rockenwagner.com. Daily. German/American. AE, MC, V. **WHY** Can you say pretzel bread? **WHAT** Hans Röckenwagner's sunny, modern café is also a fine takeaway bakery, known for its meaty, delicious pretzel bread, as well as its pretzels, cinnamon rolls, ginger scones, cookies and rye bread. It's not cheap, but the goods are very good. **WHO** Venice hipster foodies who'll stop by Jin to pick up chocolates after getting their pretzel bread and scones here. ☙ ✧

[Amandine Patisserie] 12225 Wilshire Blvd., West L.A., 310.979.3211, amandinecafe.com. Closed Mon. French. AE, MC, V. **WHY** Absolutely perfect croissants, lovely birthday cakes and a small but free parking lot in back. **WHAT** As much a café as a patisserie, Amandine is a fine spot for breakfast (french toast) and lunch (croque madame). Or just pop in to pick up some croissants, quiches or tartlets or to order a special-occasion cake. Desserts are lush without being overly sugary. ✧

[Angel Maid] 4542 S. Centinela Ave., West L.A., 310.915.2078. Closed Mon. American/Japanese. MC, V. **WHY** Birthday cakes, tres leches cake, chocolate mousse cake and heavenly cinnamon rolls. **WHAT** An old-fashioned, family-run bakery in the heart of West L.A.'s Japanese-American community, with absolutely lovely desserts. **WHO** Longtime members of the local Japanese-American community, and everyone else in the know. 📝 ☺

[Angelato Cafe] 301 Arizona Ave., Santa Monica, 310.656.9999, angelatocafe.com. Daily. Ice cream/Italian. Cash only. **WHY** Enough flavors and colors of gelato and sorbetto to cause you to change your mind for hours. **WHAT** This bright, cheery storefront displays Italian gelato lined up like keys on a never-ending piano in both Italian flavors (hazelnut, tiramisu) and only-on-the-Promenade variations (blue bubble gum, apple pie). **WHO** Tourists and locals with kids in tow taking a break from Promenade shopping. ☺

[Belwood Bakery] 11625 Barrington Ct., Brentwood, 310.471.6855. Daily. American/French. MC, V. **WHY** Very good brioche, proper French croissants, mini baguettes and, for lunch, baguette sandwiches made to order. Excellent lattes, too. **WHAT** This relaxed, family-friendly bakery is a community center in this upscale community, a place to meet for coffee, grab a sandwich for lunch, order a birthday cake or take the kids after school for a macaroon treat. (And the macaroons are a treat.) The French-style breads and sweets are equally good. **WHO** Teens from the Brentwood School and Archer School, their parents and neighbors, including famous faces. ☺ ✿

[Compartes] 912 S. Barrington Ave., Brentwood, 310.826.3380, compartes.com. Closed Sun. Confections. AE, MC, V. **WHY** Superb contemporary bon bons, caramels, English toffee, truffles and single-origin chocolates with such exotic flavorings as smoked sea salt, pink peppercorns and even a summer Harry's Berries strawberry truffle. **WHAT** The 1950s-era fixture famous for its chocolate-dipped dried fruits is now run by 25-year-old Jonathan Grahm of the Bonny Doon Vineyard family. He's created a little chocolate salon: robin's-egg-blue banquettes, bougainvillea-covered walls and aromatic kaffir lime and pink lemonade trees on the patio. You'll also find proprietary gelati: chocolate, of course, but also fig balsamic and vanilla black pepper. If you really need a hit of chocolate's antioxidant powers, go for the European-style drinking chocolate, often prepared with cinnamon and cayenne, but no milk or cream. **WHO** People who linger over chocolates the way the rest of us sit down to coffee and pie. ♥ ☺ ✿

[Emil's Swiss Pastry] 11551 Santa Monica Blvd., West L.A., 310.473.6999, emilsswisspastry.com. Closed Mon. French. AE, MC, V. **WHY** Pastries in the classic, buttery, French/Swiss style: éclairs, napoleons, chocolate croissants, strudels and gorgeous fruit tarts. **WHAT** This venerable business is now run by a younger European couple (she's French, he's Austrian), and they're doing a wonderful job making classic European pastries and some worthy American ones, too, like the not-bad-at-all fat-free bran muffin. A new location brought room for café tables where you can sip good coffee and try the breakfast pastries, quiches, bread pudding and incredible apple strudel.

[Huckleberry Bakery and Cafe] 🏠 1014 Wilshire Blvd., Santa Monica, 310.451.2311, huckleberrycafe.com. Closed Mon. American. AE, MC, V. **WHY** Fabulous (and normal-size) chocolate chip, ginger and oatmeal-raisin cookies, as well as flaky tarts and perfect pastries.

Bakeries + Sweets

🌿 VEGETARIAN ☺ KID FRIENDLY ✿ PATIO DINING 🚗 DELIVERY 🏠 PRIVATE PARTY

WHAT This cacaphonous, always-packed café is also a superb bakery, featuring the work of Zoe Nathan, who's also the pastry chef at Rustic Canyon. We're all so over cupcakes, but the mini chocolate ones are divine, and for once this is a bakery that doesn't make one-pound cookies that no one can eat. **WHO** Impeccably groomed westside women who look like they've never eaten a cookie in their lives. 🥄

[Jin Patisserie] 🏠 1202 Abbot Kinney Blvd., Venice, 310.399.8801, jinpatisserie.com. Closed Mon. Chocolatier/French. AE, MC, V. **WHY** For delicate, sculpturally gorgeous chocolates and pastries that taste as good as they look. **WHAT** Former flight attendant turned pastry chef Kristy Choo's artful, investment-grade creations are as decadent as they are beautiful. Create a small box as a perfect hostess gift, or linger on the patio with a piece of chocolate cake or a couple of jasmine-scented truffles. **WHO** The most refined of Abbot Kinney's cool crowd take tea and pastries on Jin's serene enclosed patio. ♥ 🌙 🥄 ☼

[N'Ice Cream] 1410 Abbot Kinney Blvd., Venice, 310.396.7161, nielsens-ice.com. Daily. Ice cream. AE, MC, V. **WHY** Excellent gelati and sorbets, made fresh daily by a Danish couple. **WHAT** The Nielsens use organic milk and fresh fruit in their cool creations, which are creative without being twee and richly flavorful without being too sugary. Try the sour cherry or mint chocolate chip gelato or the lemon sorbet. Good lattes and gelato shakes, too. **WHO** Damned adorable Venice youngsters and their tattooed hardbody moms. 🙂

[Pioneer Boulangerie] 804 Montana Ave., Santa Monica, 310.451.4998, thecakecollection.com. Daily. American/French. MC, V. **WHY** Classic white sourdough in the San Francisco style — as good an example of the type as you can find in L.A. **WHAT** The remaining vestige of what used to be a large and thriving bakery in Venice, Pioneer is now a smaller Montana bakeshop that still makes the best San Francisco–style sourdough bread in town. The cakes and pastries are fine but unremarkable; come here for the bread, or a good sandwich made on the bread. 🙂

[SusieCakes] 11708 San Vicente Blvd., Brentwood, 310.442.2253, susiecakesla.com. Closed Sun. American. AE, MC, V. **WHY** For excellent homestyle sweets: German chocolate cake, banana pudding with vanilla wafers, layer cakes, cupcakes and lemon squares. **WHAT** This nostalgia-driven bake shop dressed in retro colors turns out sweets that owner Susan Sarich found on her grandmother's recipe cards. New locations in Calabasas (23653 Calabasas Rd., 818.591.2223) and Manhattan Beach (3500 N. Sepulveda Blvd., 310.303.3780). **WHO** Locals stopping by to pick up birthday-party treats and sneak a cupcake on the side. 🙂

[Vanilla Bake Shop] 512 Wilshire Blvd., Santa Monica, 310.458.6644, vanillabakeshop.com. Daily. American. MC, V. **WHY** The usual faddish cupcakes (red velvet, dark chocolate, vanilla bean) and beautiful whole cakes to order in advance — for true comfort, get the Mom's Birthday Cake, a yellow cake with milk-chocolate frosting that will leapfrog you back to the '50s. **WHAT** A small and stylish bake shop specializing in cupcakes to go (large or mini), tiny one-serving icebox desserts (key lime pie, Dirt Cake) and impeccably frosted whole cakes. **WHO** Chic Montana moms ordering party cakes and cupcake junkies. ☺

[The Yogurt Factory] 11870 Santa Monica Blvd., West L.A., 310.820.1992. Daily. Yogurt. MC, V. **WHY** Large portions (get a small) of delicious frozen yogurt, with non-dairy options for vegans and the lactose intolerant. **WHAT** A fine, mom 'n pop frozen-yogurt shop with quality products and nice people. Its YoBerry line is a competitor to Pinkberry, only better and cheaper. **WHO** Kids from Uni High, UCLA students and Westwood families. ☺ 🖼🥄☺

SOUTH BAY TO SOUTH L.A.

[Alpine Village Market] 833 W. Torrance Blvd., Torrance, 310.327.2483, alpinevillage.net. Daily. German. AE, MC, V. **WHY** Fresh pretzels that will have you yodeling on the way home. **WHAT** Sausages may be the claim to fame at this kitschy Bavarian market, but the bakery is not to be neglected. It turns out a variety of sturdy, delicious German rye breads along with strudel, kuchen, tortes and wonderful fresh pretzels sprinkled with rock salt. **WHO** Tourists and Angelenos who have been making the trek here for 40 years.

[Alsace Lorraine Pastries] 4334 Atlantic Ave., Long Beach, 562.427.5992, alsacelorrainepastries.com. Closed Sun.-Mon. French. MC, V. **WHY** Superb petits fours, which hardly anyone makes anymore, as well as remarkable cakes, including the St. Honoré and the wedding cakes. **WHAT** Classically trained Austrian bakers make gorgeous special-occasion cakes here, but the little things are lovely, too, like the macaroons and double-chocolate cookies.

[Babette Bakery] 1404 Atlantic Ave., Long Beach, 562.218.8877, babettebakery.com. Daily. French/American. MC, V. **WHY** Properly Parisian baguettes (crisp outside, airy inside), more substantial sandwich breads, croissants and addictive oatmeal cookies. **WHAT** Known for its breads and for fruit tarts that are far lovelier than the neighborhood outside, Babette is a great and affordable find for breads, breakfast pastries and desserts (but skip the cupcakes in favor of the cookies and tarts). Good panini and breakfast sandwiches, too. **WHO** Chefs, insiders and local high school kids with really good taste. 🖼☺

Bakeries + Sweets

🥬 VEGETARIAN ☺ KID FRIENDLY ☼ PATIO DINING 🚙 DELIVERY 🏠 PRIVATE PARTY

[Buona Forchetta] 1150 Gardena Blvd., Gardena, 310.532.8140, buonaforchetta.com. Closed Sat.-Sun. except for will call. American. MC, V. **WHY** For some of our very favorite breads in town — yes, some of them are better than La Brea's. They manage to be light and yet somehow substantial, crusty enough but not dry. The rosemary focaccia and sea-salt rolls are fabulous. **WHAT** Suzanne Dunaway went big-time when she sold her bread bakery to Mrs. Beasley's, but she's still very much the hands-on baker, and her products are as good as ever. You'll find her moist, substantial rusticos, baguettes, filoncinos and focaccias at the better markets throughout California, but it's fun to come to the mothership, where you get it super-fresh — plus they often have fun breads that you won't find in stores. Most products freeze beautifully. **WHO** Buyers from upscale markets, caterers, restaurateurs and fans who want to go straight to the source.

[Delicieuse] 2503 Artesia Blvd., Redondo Beach, 310.793.7979, icedreamonline.com. Open Fri.-Sun. Ice cream. AE, MC, V. **WHY** French-style sorbets, strawberry goats' milk ice cream and creamy, rich cinnamon or white peach ice cream — not to mention the profound romance of lavender ice cream made with crushed lavender petals. **WHAT** Now that this sophisticated ice cream is sold at Surfas, Whole Foods and Beverly Glen Marketplace, Angelenos don't have to trek to Redondo Beach, but the devout still do, at least on weekends, which is the only time it's open to the public. There's a sweet little café, too. **WHO** Chefs who don't want to make their own ice cream, locals in the know and aficionados from far and wide. ☺

[Grounds Bakery & Café] 6277 E. Spring St., Long Beach, 562.429.5661, groundscafe.com. Daily. American. AE, MC, V. **WHY** For the best bagels in Long Beach; good breads and muffins, too. **WHAT** Just-chewy-enough California-style bagels (that is, large and relatively light instead of small and dense) are the main draw at this large, open bakery and café; try the onion, the poppyseed and the pumpkin. Also worthwhile are the muffins, the sourdough breads and the various coffee brews. The brownies taste great but are ridiculously oversized. ☺

[Patisserie Chantilly] 🏛 2383 Lomita Blvd., Lomita, 310.257.9454, patisseriechantilly.com. Closed Tues. French/Jamaican. AE, MC, V. **WHY** Flawless French pastries with Japanese flair. **WHAT** Keiko Nojima's creations are as cross-cultural as they are classic: delicate and refined pastries that seamlessly balance tradition and intercontinental innovation. Take the matcha roll, for example, alternating layers of green tea chiffon cake and chestnut cream topped with sweet azuki beans. Or the fabulous cream puffs stuffed with either chantilly, chocolate, chestnut or black sesame cream. There are plenty of chocolate and seasonal treats for those with sweeter teeth, most of which are prepared in single-serving sizes — but it also makes party-sized desserts and special orders, too. **WHO** Dessert lovers of all ages and any language. 😊

[Portugal Imports] **11655 Artesia Blvd., Artesia, 562.809.7021, portugalimports.net. Closed Sun.-Mon. Portuguese. AE, MC, V. WHY** A rare chance to savor the sweet side of Portugal. **WHAT** This Artesia store serves what amounts to lunch — sausage sandwiches and a weekend-only selection of classic salt cod dishes — but the main reason to make the trip here is the selection of Portuguese breads and pastries. Try the *queijadas*, little tartlets flavored with almond, pineapple, caramel, coconut, sweet beans, orange or a creamy custard. There's a whole array of confections perfect for a cup of coffee, but above all else, make sure to grab a loaf of *massa sovada*, a sweet bread blessed with just a hint of cinnamon. **WHO** Expatriates hungry for a reminder of home and those curious about the tastes of the Iberian Peninsula.

[Powell's Sweet Shoppe] **5282 E. 2nd St., Long Beach, 562.434.6105. Daily. Confections. AE, MC, V. WHY** An astonishing selection of Jelly Bellies, Pez dispensers, gummies, candy and gum from sentimental Boomers' childhoods and, best of all, chocolate bars imported from the U.K. and Canada, where milk chocolate is much better than in the U.S. **WHAT** Willy Wonka is the patron saint of this place; there's a shrine to him, and the movie seems to run in a continuous loop in the back. Candy of every imaginable kind is sold here, from the retro (Squirrel Nut Zippers, Gold Nugget bubble gum) to the modern (green-tea chocolates) to the mainstream (gummy everything). The chocolate-truffle selection is just okay, but the gelati choices are good. **WHO** Kids, and lots of 'em. 😊

[Tropicana Bakery] **10218 Paramount Blvd., Downey, 562.806.8343. Daily. Cuban. AE, MC, V. WHY** Sweet Cuban classics and worthy sandwiches and entrees. **WHAT** Like Porto's, Tropicana blurs the line between bakery and restaurant. There are lots of great pastries — rum-soaked raspberry tarts, éclairs sweetened with dulce de leche, empanada-like *pastelitos* stuffed with the likes of cheese and guava — all of which go down even easier with a sip of Cuban coffee. But there are also equally good entrees, including pork-heavy sandwiches that make great use of the bakery's fresh bread. 😊

Bakeries + Sweets

Shops

Everyone knows about Trader Joe's, Whole Foods and
Sur la Table; the challenge is to find the great individual
cheesemonger, produce market, tofu maker, ethnic market,
kitchen store and soda-pop shop. Here's where you'll find the
things a food lover seeks.

MORE SHOPS IN EAT: LOS ANGELES

FOR BREAD, BAKED GOODS, ICE CREAM,
CHOCOLATE, CANDIES OR FROZEN YOGURT

[see Bakeries + Sweets]

FOR WHOLE-BEAN COFFEE OR LOOSE-LEAF TEA

[see Coffee, Tea + Juices]

FOR TAKEOUT AND PREPARED FOODS,
INCLUDING MORE OPTIONS FOR CHEESE AND CHARCUTERIE

[see Gourmet-to-Go]

ESSENTIALLY L.A. ☺ LATE ♥ ROMANTIC 🖼 VALUE 🔊 QUIET ♻ SUSTAINABLE

[ESSENTIALLY L.A.]

99 Ranch Market, San Gabriel (PAGE 320)

Andrew's Cheese, Santa Monica (PAGE 298)

Cheese Store of Beverly Hills (PAGE 298)

Cheese Store of Silverlake (PAGE 298)

Claro's, San Gabriel (PAGE 313)

E. Waldo Ward, Sierra Madre (PAGE 313)

Erewhon Natural Foods, Beverly/Third (PAGE 321)

Fish King, Glendale (PAGE 307)

Galco's Soda Pop Shop, Highland Park (PAGE 314)

Grand Central Market, Downtown (PAGE 315)

Harvey's Guss Meat Co., Miracle Mile (PAGE 307)

Heath Ceramics, Beverly/Third (PAGE 303)

Hollywood Farmers' Market (PAGE 300)

India Sweets & Spices, Atwater & Canoga Park (PAGE 315)

Koreatown Galleria Market, Koreatown (PAGE 322)

La Española Meats, Harbor City (PAGE 308)

Liborio Market, Downtown & Koreatown (PAGE 322)

Luna Garcia, Santa Monica (PAGE 304)

Marconda's Meat, Farmers Market (PAGE 308)

Mitsuwa, Torrance (PAGE 322)

Nicole's Gourmet Foods, South Pasadena (PAGE 299)

Santa Monica Farmers' Market (PAGE 301)

Schreiner's Fine Sausages, Glendale (PAGE 309)

Silverlake Wine, Silver Lake (PAGE 328)

Star Restaurant Equipment, Van Nuys (PAGE 305)

Super King Market, Altadena & Eagle Rock (PAGE 323)

Super Home Mart, Chinatown (PAGE 305)

Surfas, Culver City (PAGE 305)

Torrance Farmers' Market (PAGE 302)

Vinh Loi Tofu, Reseda (PAGE 320)

Wally's, Westwood (PAGE 328)

Wine Expo, Santa Monica (PAGE 329)

Wine House, West L.A. (PAGE 329)

Woodland Hills Wine Co. (PAGE 329)

Shops

🦑 VEGETARIAN ☺ KID FRIENDLY ☼ PATIO DINING 🚗 DELIVERY 🎩 PRIVATE PARTY

CHEESE & CHARCUTERIE

[Andrew's Cheese Shop] 728 Montana Ave., Santa Monica, 310.393.3308, andrewscheese.com. Daily. AE, MC, V. **WHY** Individual cheeses and party platters from one of L.A.'s most passionate cheeseheads. **WHAT** This handsome cheese shop is the work of Andrew Steiner, ex of Patina. "This Place Stinks" is the store's tagline, a clue to its lighthearted approach to what is, in fact, a very serious resource for high-quality cheese. Wine, beer and accoutrements also stocked.

[Artisan Cheese Gallery] 12023 Ventura Blvd., Studio City, 818.505.0207, artisancheesegallery.com. Daily. AE, MC, V. **WHY** Exotic cheeses from around the world, Fra' Mani salumi and great sandwiches. **WHAT** This small family-owned shop sells an array of artisanal cheeses and charcuterie, along with some gourmet products. Staffers encourage buyers to taste before buying, which means service can be v-e-r-y slow if it's crowded. Artisan Cheese also makes delicious panini daily from 11 a.m. until 4 p.m. **WHO** Val cheesehounds who don't want to trek over the hill to the Cheese Store of Beverly Hills.

[Barney Greengrass] Barney's, 9570 Wilshire Blvd., Beverly Hills, 310.777.5877. Daily. AE, MC, V. **WHY** For one thing: smoked fish. **WHAT** As a deli, we've found better. But the quality of the smoked fish (sturgeon, salmon, sable) is A-number-one. Get a platter for your next party and be prepared for happy guests. **WHO** The rich, the beautiful and the smoked-fish-obsessed rich and beautiful.

[Cheese Store of Beverly Hills] 419 N. Beverly Dr., Beverly Hills, 310.278.2855, cheesestorebh.com. Daily. AE, MC, V. **WHY** A selection of cheeses that is unmatched in Southern California. **WHAT** Since 1967 this tiny shop has purveyed the world's finest cheeses to the world's finickiest customers. An oasis of funky, cheesy aromas in the rarefied air of Beverly Hills, the Cheese Store is staffed with people who know their products and can discuss the finer points of fromage with all comers. There's also a good selection of wines. **WHO** Foodies, tourists and homesick Europeans.

[Cheese Store of Silverlake] 3926 W. Sunset Blvd., Silver Lake, 323.644.7511, cheesestoresl.com. Daily. AE, MC, V. **WHY** The widest selection of cheeses east of Beverly Hills, as well as a well-edited wine department, quality charcuterie, olives and choice gourmet items. **WHAT** Owner Chris Pollan may seem gruff at first, but his passion for Europe and America's finest cheeses shines through once he starts talking cheese. Ask him about the shelf of foods from his native Rhode Island. **WHO** Trendy young moms giving junior a taste of Taleggio, all stripes of Silver Lake residents stocking up for dinner parties.

[Gioia Cheese] 1605 Potrero Ave., El Monte, 949.922.8902, gioiacheeseinc.com. Closed Sat.-Sun. Italian. AE, MC, V. **WHY** Fresh burrata,

ESSENTIALLY L.A. LATE ROMANTIC VALUE QUIET SUSTAINABLE

made every single weekday, and other lovely soft Italian cheeses, too. **WHAT** Vito Girardi is a third-generation cheesemaker and the man responsible for most of the burrata you see in L.A.'s best restaurants. It is our good fortune that he also sells to the public — not just daily-fresh burrata, but also mozzarella, ricotta, mascarpone, affumicata, scamorza and other suave Italian beauties. Note that each cheese is made to order, so you must call in advance. **WHO** Chefs from many of California's best Italian restaurants, and home cooks willing to drive for fresh cheese.

[Nicole's Gourmet Foods] 🔒 **921 Meridian Ave., South Pasadena, 626.403.5751, nicolesgourmetfoods.com. Daily. French. AE, MC, V. WHY** A one-stop shop for French ingredients. Plus an amiable café and legendary cheese selection. **WHAT** If it's French, Nicole carries it: pâtés, cheeses, duck confit, truffles, chocolates, wines, pastry-making ingredients, pastry shells, puff pastry, French butter, olives, foie gras, sauce bases, frozen quiches, sea salts, lavender ... whether you want to cook a French meal or get a to-go French picnic, you'll find it here. **WHO** Serious French cooks and bakers, and eastsiders who don't want to trek to Surfas for their fix of Noel 72%.

[Wally's] **2107 Westwood Blvd., Westwood, 310.475.0606, wallywine. com. Daily. AE, MC, V. WHY** Cave-aged Swiss Gruyère, Gioia's bocconcini, Paul Bertoli's charcuterie, Catalonian sausages and, should the urge strike, Petrossian caviars. **WHAT** It has a big reputation for its wines, especially rare and high-end ones, but Wally's is also worth a trip for its high-quality international cheeses, its charcuterie and its terrific gift baskets, a Hollywood-agent staple during the holiday season. **WHO** Studio bigwigs, UCLA professors, Brentwood matrons.

COOKBOOKS

[Cook Books by Janet Jarvits] **1388 E. Washington Blvd., Pasadena, 626.296.1638, cookbkjj.com. Closed Sun.-Mon.; hours irregular. MC, V. WHY** More than 30,000 used cookbooks, cooking magazines, booklets and books on wine, the restaurant business and anything remotely having to do with food. **WHAT** Cookbooks upon cookbooks, all used and sometimes rare, are piled all the way up to the 15-foot ceiling and on every available surface. The bulk of the business is online, so don't expect a comfy hangout. **WHO** Collectors and aficionados.

FARMERS' MARKETS

[Beverly Hills Farmers' Market] **9300 Block of Civic Center Dr., Beverly Hills, 310.285.6830, beverlyhills.org. Sun. 9 a.m.-1 p.m. WHY** Beverly Hills's is the first SoCal market to sell wine — so with chickens and eggs available from Healthy Family Farms and grass-fed beef from J & J, you really can get everything you need for dinner.

Shops

🔖VEGETARIAN ☉KID FRIENDLY ⚘PATIO DINING � DELIVERY 🏛PRIVATE PARTY

WHAT This mid-size market has easy-breezy street parking, great variety and a Persian New Year celebration. The many A-list growers here include Harry's Berries, McGrath Family Farm, Weiser Family Farms, Finley Farms and Honey Crisp, which has exquisitely ripe summer fruit — their peaches brought Jeffrey Steingarten to his knees in his nationwide search for the best. Don't miss Westfield Farms' avocados — they have more varieties than you ever knew existed — and the organic wine from Gold Country grower/producer Brian Fitzpatrick. **WHO** Affluent seniors, young families, a large Persian community and a sprinkling of chefs.

[Culver City Farmers' Market] Culver at Main, Culver City, 310.253.5775, culvercity.org. Tues. 3-7 p.m. **WHY** A very good fish vendor (the same guy who's in Hollywood on Sunday), excellent cheeses and delicious fresh-ground peanut butter. And note that Culver City's parking structures provide free parking during the market. **WHAT** This afternoon/evening market draws both shoppers looking for organic produce and people looking to meet friends and graze from the many prepared-food vendors (check out the fresh coconuts at the Korean-food stand).

[Glendale Farmers' Market] Brand Blvd. between Wilson & Broadway, Glendale, 818.548.3155. Thurs. 9:30 a.m.-1:30 p.m. **WHY** An excellent selection of citrus, including some varieties you don't see elsewhere, and a good potato guy, too. **WHAT** A friendly, mellow market with more food than crafts, and a good selection of organic produce. It's a certified market, so all the vendors in the central produce area are from California and are selling directly.

[Hollywood Farmers' Market] 🏠 Ivar St. at Selma Ave., Hollywood, 323.463.3171, hollywoodfarmersmarket.net. Sun. 8 a.m.-1 p.m. **WHY** Excellent produce from McGrath's and Kenter Canyon Farms, among many others, as well as eggs and free-range chickens from Healthy Family Farms, a good fish vendor, a few bakers and Lindner's naturally raised bison. Switch from beef burgers to bison burgers — you won't be sorry. **WHAT** One of the finest markets in the state, with a superb selection and lots always going on: cooking demonstrations, cookbook signings, tastings, kids' amusements and live music. Parking is a challenge; you'll probably have to pay. Better yet, take the Metro — the Hollywood and Vine stop is a block away. Well worth a detour. **WHO** Chefs, caterers, families pushing tank-size strollers and European ex-pats with baskets on their arms.

[La Cienega Farmers' Market] S. La Cienega Blvd. at W. 18th St., Mid-City, 562.495.1764. Thurs. 3-7 p.m. **WHY** A great on-the-way-home-from-work stop for roast chicken, fresh berries in summer and particularly good apples, avocados and stone fruit. **WHAT** A small, neighborhoody market that's friendly, inexpensive and easy to maneuver. It doesn't start until 3 p.m., but some intrepid buyers show up as early as 2 for the best stuff. From among the dozen or so farmers, look for Polito for citrus, Tenerelli for stone fruit and Scarborough Farms for salad greens and micro-greens.

[Larchmont Village Farmers' Market] N. Larchmont Blvd. south of Beverly, Hancock Park, 818.591.8161. Sun. 10 a.m.-2 p.m. **WHY** Particularly good fruit vendors and bakers, with a respectable mix of seasonal produce, too. **WHAT** If you oversleep and miss the Hollywood market, head to this sweet little one on Larchmont. But if you want some of the fabulous unpasteurized fresh orange juice, don't get there too late — it always sells out.

[Long Beach Southeast Farmers' Market] Alamitos Bay Marina, Marina Dr. south of E. 2nd St., Long Beach, 866.466.3834. Sun. 9 a.m.-2 p.m. **WHY** An amazing scone baker, the fish guy (who gets the longest lines), the hummus guy, Lindner grass-fed bison and Garcia Farms grapes. **WHAT** A crowded market with challenging parking, but it's well worth the effort. While not huge, its selection of vendors is good, and there's also fun live music and some worthwhile prepared-food stands, especially for tamales.

[Pasadena Farmers' Market] N. Sierra Madre Blvd. & Paloma St., East Pasadena, 626.449.0179, pasadenafarmersmarket.org. Sat. 8:30 a.m.-1 p.m. **WHY** The best market east of Hollywood. **WHAT** This popular market on the edge of Victory Park is full of excellent farmers, including Ha's apples, ABC Rhubarb's herbs, Gless Ranch's citrus and Weiser Family Farms's eggplants, melons and sweet onions. Good flowers, too. The same group runs a good smaller market on Tuesday mornings at Villa Park, 363 E. Villa in Pasadena. **WHO** Parents stocking up while their kids play AYSO soccer on the neighboring fields.

[Santa Monica Farmers' Market: Arizona] 🔒 Arizona Ave. & 3rd St., Santa Monica, 310.458.8712, santa-monica.org/farmers_market. Wed. 8:30 a.m.-1:30 p.m. & Sat. 8:30 a.m.-1 p.m. **WHY** Harry's berries, Lily's eggs, Weiser melons, Coastal Farms tomatoes, Cirone apples, Maggie's Farm herbs, Redwood Hill cheeses, Tenerelli peaches, McGrath beets ... you won't believe your eyes, or your taste buds. **WHAT** The Wednesday market is pounced upon by the city's best chefs, as well as buyers who snatch up hot items and whisk them to LAX to fly to chefs around the country. But there's enough for everyone, including fruits and vegetables you've never seen before, which you can learn how to prepare — if you ask questions. The Saturday market is a little mellower and has a somewhat different mix of farmers. Also in town is a smaller market at Virginia Park (Cloverfield at Pico) on Saturday mornings, and the hugely popular Sunday market on Main Street (see next listing). **WHO** Chefs so famous they wear hats and sunglasses, and mobs of passionate food lovers. Lots of strollers.

Shops

🌿 VEGETARIAN ⊙ KID FRIENDLY ✿ PATIO DINING 🚐 DELIVERY 🎩 PRIVATE PARTY

[Santa Monica Farmers' Market: Main Street] 2640 Main St. at Ocean Park Ave., Santa Monica, 310.458.8712, santa-monica.org/farmers_market. Sun. 9:30 a.m.-1 p.m. **WHY** Kids' amusements, live music, great people-watching and very good produce. **WHAT** This sibling of the famous Arizona Avenue farmers' market is the social event of the week on Main Street, where neighbors meet and families shop. It may seem to be more about the face-painting and music, but there's also some terrific food from the likes of Spring Hill Cheese, Munak Ranch (heirloom tomatoes), Olson Farms (stone fruit) and Röckenwagner (pretzel bread). **WHO** Tons of families and Ocean Park/Venice locals.

[South Pasadena Farmers' Market] Meridian Ave. at Mission St., South Pasadena, 818.786.6612. Thurs. 4-8 p.m. **WHY** This is one of the greenest markets in town, because you don't have to drive to get here — it's right off the Gold Line Mission stop. **WHAT** A good-enough selection of produce and flowers, plus rotisserie chicken, tamales and addictive grilled corn on the cob. This is a social market for many people, who either get dinner from the stands or shop for produce and then go to one of the nearby restaurants. **WHO** Teens meeting to eat roast corn and tamales, families pushing strollers.

[Studio City Farmers' Market] Ventura Pl. at Ventura Blvd., Studio City, 818.655.7744, studiocityfarmersmarket.com. Sun. 8 a.m.-1 p.m. **WHY** Pretty good produce, most of which is local and organic, as well as Lily's Eggs, Corn Maiden tamales, fresh bread and a fishmonger. **WHAT** A family-friendly operation with a choo-choo train and pony rides, this is a small certified market that works just fine if you don't have the energy to drive over the hill to Hollywood's.

[Torrance Farmers' Market] 🔒 2400 Jefferson St., Torrance, 310.618.2930. Tues. & Sat. 8 a.m.-1 p.m. **WHY** Because the city of Torrance loves its farmers, and you can feel the vibe. **WHAT** The jewel of the South Bay, this market runs on two days — the Tuesday market celebrates 25 years in 2010; the bigger Saturday market is 17 years strong. Both have a tasty mix of seasonal produce, plus a strong Asian selection — Hmong grower Vang Thao's stand, for instance, is super popular for such items as fresh peanuts, bird chiles and bitter melon, as well as beautiful eggplants, basil and garlic. The community-focused offerings — breakfast, lunch (including Big Mista's great barbecue), entertainment, balloon sculpture — are plentiful. **WHO** A diverse crowd, ethnically, culturally and age-wise. On Tuesdays it's mostly seniors, mommies with strollers and summer-camp groups doing farmers' market scavenger hunts (that is, food education in the form of a game); Saturdays it's a grand mix.

[Venice Farmers' Market] Venice Way & Venice Blvd., Venice, 310.399.6690, venicefarmersmarket.com. Fri. 7 a.m.-11 a.m. **WHY** A full range of organic and/or local produce, as well as good eggs, a great berry guy and breads and sweets from a couple of skilled local bakers. **WHAT** Get up early to get the good stuff at this bustling, intimate Friday market, which packs a lot of good food into a compact park space.

KITCHEN & TABLE SUPPLY

[Bargain Fair] 7901 Beverly Blvd., Beverly/Third, 323.655.2227. Daily. AE, MC, V. **WHY** Total bargains on both quirky and basic kitchen and tableware. **WHAT** This cluttered discount store is always worth a stop. For one thing, you can pick up such essentials as chafing dishes and 99-cent tongs. And you might just find a Russian tea set that you can't live without and certainly can afford. Best of all, there's a great selection of glassware at almost-wholesale prices. **WHO** Savvy caterers.

[Bar Keeper] 3910 W. Sunset Blvd., Silver Lake, 323.669.1675, barkeepersilverlake.com. Closed Mon. AE, MC, V. **WHY** When you need not just one kind of absinthe spoon, but several. **WHAT** Given his name, it was probably destiny that Joe Keeper would someday open a store called Bar Keeper. In the Sunset Junction 'hood that is Silver Lake's foodie bulls-eye, he's put together a wonderful collection of gifts and essentials for drinkers, from glassware and shakers to books and vintage bar gear. **WHO** The sort of people who know that there is such a thing as an absinthe spoon.

[Charlie's Fixtures] 2251 Venice Blvd., Mid-City, 323.731.9023, charliesfixtures.com. Closed Sun. MC, V. **WHY** Great prices on high-quality restaurant- and home-kitchen-supply goods, from huge walk-ins to tabletop broilers. **WHAT** This cluttered, open-to-the-public wholesaler and retailer has most of the best names in professional-grade kitchen appliances and tableware at some of the lowest prices in town.

[Dish Factory] 310 S. Los Angeles St., Downtown, 213.687.9500, dishfactory.com. Closed Sun. AE, MC, V. **WHY** 60,000 square feet of china, glassware and new and refurbished heavy-duty cooking gear, all at unbeatable prices. **WHAT** This restaurant-supply warehouse is open to the public, and it's developed a loyal following for its dishware and flatware — firsts and seconds, all at great prices. Also notable is the very good glassware at 35 to 50% discounts by case quantity, and the refurbished mixers, refrigerators and ovens. **WHO** Restaurant managers, chefs, caterers and intrepid home entertainers looking for that extra case of wine glasses or a refurbished professional mixer.

[Heath Ceramics] 7525 Beverly Blvd., Beverly/Third, 323.965.0800, heathceramics.com. Daily AE, MC, V. **WHY** We know Angelenos who used to plan weekends in San Francisco around a trip to Heath Ceramics in Sausalito. Now the shrine has come to us. **WHAT** A partnership between Heath and longtime L.A. architect and

🍃 VEGETARIAN ☺ KID FRIENDLY ✿ PATIO DINING 🚗 DELIVERY 🎩 PRIVATE PARTY potter Adam Silverman, the airy space on the northeast corner of Beverly and Sierra Bonita includes gallery space for ceramic artists as well as plenty of display space for tableware, some kitchenware, a tightly edited book selection and an even smaller selection of food-stuffs and a couple of lines of artisanal preserves. **WHO** Appreciative Angelenos who now need a new excuse to travel up north.

[Intelligentsia Coffee] **3922 W. Sunset Blvd., Silver Lake, 323.663.6173, intelligentsiacoffee.com. Daily. AE, MC, V. WHY** Gleaming home espresso machines to drool over, and maybe even buy. **WHAT** Pasquini's got some competition in town, now that Intelligentsia is selling gear for the home barista. The range isn't large, but it's smart and thoughtful, from the $7,500 hard-plumbed La Marzocco espresso machine, good enough for a small café, to simple little machines that go for as little as $500. It also has good burr grinders, knock boxes and other accessories.

[Kelly Green] **4008 Santa Monica Blvd., Silver Lake, 323.660.1099, kellygreendesign.net. Closed Mon. AE, MC, V. WHY** Sustainably produced tableware, small composters and bowls made from reclaimed wood. **WHAT** Housewares that have a low impact on the environment are the focus here, and many of the products are for the table and kitchen. ♻

[La Tavola] **9859 Santa Monica Blvd. , Beverly Hills, 310.286.1333, latavolalinen.com. Closed Sat.-Sun. AE, MC, V. WHY** The most diverse and interesting array of rental table linens in town. **WHAT** The acclaimed Bay Area linen-rental firm has opened a Beverly Hills branch and immediately became the go-to place in L.A. for table linens. Fabulous fabrics, unusual designs, fun accessories and good service. **WHO** The best party planners and caterers in town.

[Luna Garcia] ⌂ **201 San Juan Ave., Venice, 800.905.9975, lunagarcia.com. Daily. AE, MC, V. WHY** You can change the mood of your tablescape by mixing and matching shapes and colors the same way you put together outfits from your closet. **WHAT** This venerable Venice pottery studio produces and sells its own collectible, durable dinnerware, bowls and serving pieces, which come in really interesting satin matte colors, shapes and sizes. Luna Garcia isn't an actual person — or rather, it's two: artist/owners Cindy and Curtis Ripley, who've been creating handmade forms, colors and patterns since 1979. Look for fabulous finds in the "seconds" room, party-like semi-annual sales and Cindy's unerring eye for intriguing accessories, many produced by the couple's talented friends. This place is sort of like the Slow Food of tableware. **WHO** Longtime regulars and couples who want a hip, arty alternative to bridal registries.

[Pasquini Espresso Co.] 1501 W. Olympic Blvd., Pico-Union, 213.739.0480, pasquini.com. Closed Sun. AE, MC, V. **WHY** For the hands-down best home-kitchen espresso machines — but you need to have a resale license to buy here. **WHAT** If you have a resale license or are working with a contractor or designer who does, come here to get a good deal on an ultra-high-quality home espresso machine/steamer/grinder setup that will have you making espresso as good as Intelligentsia's. If you don't have a resale license, call them up to find a retailer. **WHO** Hardcore coffeeheads.

[Rafu Bussan] 326 E. 2nd St., Little Tokyo/Arts District, 213.614.1181. Closed Wed. AE, MC, V. **WHY** For Mac knives, gorgeous Japanese tableware and clever kitchen gear sold by incredibly nice people. Watch for the twice-yearly sales. **WHAT** For a gift to please your food-loving friend, head to this wonderful store, where you'll find tableware, bento boxes, tea set, cookbooks, sushi knives, bowls, cooking gear and more. A fun place to browse, and nice gift-wrapping, too. **WHO** Chefs, restaurateurs and hip couples registering for their weddings.

[Star Restaurant Equipment] 🔒 6178 Sepulveda Blvd., Van Nuys, 818.782.4460, starkitchen.com. Closed Sun. MC, V. **WHY** A huge array of home and professional gear and accessories, at middle-of-the-road prices but with high-end service. **WHAT** Need a proofing cabinet or a panini grill? Make the trek to Van Nuys to Star, and plan on spending at least a couple of hours browsing the mouthwatering array of appliances, gadgets, tools, tableware, furniture and fixtures. It's open to the public, and if they don't have it, they can order it.

[Super Home Mart] 🔒 988 N. Hill St., Chinatown, 213.628.8898. Daily. AE, MC, V. **WHY** Fun, often bargain-priced Asian and American tableware and kitchen goods in a central Chinatown location. **WHAT** Attractive, festive and practical housewares are the draw here, and the prices can't be beat. You'll find Chinese stuff, of course, from woks to steamers, but also Japanese sake sets, Italian coffeemakers and much more. Particularly good tableware and glassware. **WHO** Chinatown tourists and savvy shoppers from Downtown, Silver Lake and Echo Park looking for a cool gift. 🖼

[Surfas] 🔒 8777 W. Washington Blvd., Culver City, 310.559.4770, surfasonline.com. Daily. AE, MC, V. **WHY** The ingredients and equipment for virtually every style of cooking in the world. **WHAT** This former restaurant supply store has morphed into a food-shopper's paradise complete with a little café. In addition to thousands of fresh, frozen and packaged gourmet food items, Surfas has equipment aisles devoted to a fascinating array of large-scale appliances and arcane cookware that you never knew existed, but now think you need. The goods aren't cheap, but the quality and service are high. **WHO** Professional chefs and semipro foodies.

🌿VEGETARIAN ◎KID FRIENDLY ☼PATIO DINING 🚗DELIVERY 🏠PRIVATE PARTY

MEAT & SEAFOOD

[Alexander's Prime Meats] Howie's Ranch Market, 6580 N. San Gabriel Blvd., San Gabriel, 626.286.8871. Closed Sun. AE, MC, V. **WHY** For some of the best prime beef in L.A. Consider going in with friends on a side of dry-aged beef. **WHAT** Inside the fetchingly old-school Howie's Ranch Market is this superb purveyor of beef — it's mostly from Harris Ranch, and it's mostly prime. The butchers know what they're doing. The marinated meats, notably the chicken and carne asada, are good, too. **WHO** Seekers of the perfect steak.

[Bel Air Prime Meats] 2964 N. Beverly Glen Blvd., Bel-Air, 310.475.5915. Daily. AE, MC, V. **WHY** The on-site smoker, the Harris Ranch beef dry-aged on the premises and the homemade sausages. **WHAT** Part of the elite Beverly Glen Marketplace is this high-end butcher, known for its prime beef, its veal chops and its kebabs and other prepared meats. Good movie-star-spotting, too. **WHO** Bel-Air locals, for whom the price of prime, dry-aged beef is of no more significance than change for the parking meter.

[Carniceria Sanchez] 4525 Inglewood Blvd., Mar Vista, 310.391.3640. Daily. Mexican. MC, V. **WHY** Pork shoulder, carne asada, marinated chicken and fresh salsas, too. **WHAT** The go-to carniceria for westsiders, Sanchez is in a little food-centric Latino neighborhood at Culver and Inglewood. The meats and marinades are very good. 🈂

[Crusty Crab] Ports O' Call, 1146 Nagoya Way, San Pedro, 310.519.9058. Daily. AE, MC, V. **WHY** Fresh, live crab — especially the unique-to-California coastal species. **WHAT** For more than 25 years, this has been crab central in San Pedro. Boiled, steamed or packed up live to cook at home, these succulent crustaceans are the stars at this family-run seafood market/restaurant. Longtime customers check the tanks to pick out their favorites, and they know how to pick 'em: The reds are the sweetest, while the browns have the largest claws.

[El Gaucho Meat Market] 2715 Manhattan Beach Blvd., Redondo Beach, 310.297.2617. Daily. Argentinean. MC, V. **WHY** Argentines know their meat, as do these butchers. Great for Argentine cuts (like beef for a parrillada), as well as empanadas and all kinds of good prepared foods. **WHAT** This butcher, market and café will handle all your Argentinean needs, from dulce de leche, to Ricci mayonnaise, to *aji molido* (crushed red pepper), to soccer matches on TV. There's also a bakery (decent medias lunas), good sandwiches and delicious empanadas. **WHO** Argentineans and meat lovers traveling from all over the westside.

[European Deluxe Sausage Kitchen] 9109 W. Olympic Blvd., Beverly Hills, 310.276.1331. Closed Sun. French. AE, MC, V. **WHY** Cold-smoked beef that's hung over hickory coals for 72 hours, and the house-smoked, very lean salumi (this is Beverly Hills, after all). **WHAT** This shop smokes its own meats and sausages over hickory chips in a brick pit in the back, and the German-trained owners stock their cases with impeccably spiced veal wieners, chubby bratwurst, smoked beef tongue and more. For the home sausage maker, this is a great place to order hard-to-get casings and caul fat.

[Fish King] 722 N. Glendale Ave., Glendale, 818.244.2161, fishkingseafood.com. Daily. AE, MC, V. **WHY** Hawaiian opah, sashimi-grade ahi, lobster bisque and everything seafood. **WHAT** The premier seafood market on the eastside (or perhaps in all of L.A.), Fish King also carries a few non-seafood essentials (pasta, bread, marinades, some fresh vegetables and citrus) and a few prepared dishes, notably excellent soups. The guys behind the counter know their stuff, and the fish and shellfish are outstanding.

[Fisherman's Outlet] 529 S. Central Ave., Downtown, 213.627.7231, fishermansoutlet.net. Closed Sun. Cash only. **WHY** Come for the adjacent seafood café and stay to pick out more fresh fish to cook yourself for dinner. But bring cash. **WHAT** A good all-around seafood market with a large section devoted to cooked crab and shrimp of every size. Low prices, a respectable selection and counter guys who move fast and know their stuff.

[Harmony Farms] 2824 Foothill Blvd., La Crescenta, 818.248.3068, harmonyfarmsonline.com. Daily. AE, MC, V. **WHY** Hey, they've got game — try the buffalo burgers. The turkey meatballs are great, too. **WHAT** Run by a goofy bunch of guys in butcher's whites, Harmony specializes in game and organic, free-range lamb, turkey, beef and chicken. Great for superb lamb chops and first-rate Thanksgiving turkeys.

[Harvey's Guss Meat Co.] 949 S. Ogden Dr., Miracle Mile, 323.937.4622. Daily. Cash only. **WHY** Lamb from Colorado and the Napa Valley; Kurobuta pork; and prime t-bones and porterhouse steaks from the Midwest, dry-aged on site for 30 days. **WHAT** Considered L.A.'s finest butcher, Harvey Gussman runs a wholesale operation that also sells to the public. It's not a place to browse — call the day before to see if they have what you want and then place your order. **WHO** Chefs, caterers and savvy home cooks.

[Huntington Meats & Sausage] Los Angeles Farmers Market, 6333 W. 3rd St., Fairfax District, 323.938.5383, huntingtonmeats.com. Daily. AE, MC, V. **WHY** A vast array of homemade sausages, Nancy Silverton's hamburger blend and Wagyu (Kobe-style) beef. **WHAT** The Huntington sells Harris Ranch beef, American lamb and an impressive selection of pork cuts, hams, bacon, house-made sausages and such specialties as Moffett's pot pies. The butchers give good advice on cooking and grilling techniques, too.

Shops

VEGETARIAN KID FRIENDLY PATIO DINING DELIVERY PRIVATE PARTY

[J & T European Gourmet] 1128 Wilshire Blvd., Santa Monica, 310.394.7227. Daily. Polish/Hungarian. AE, MC, V. **WHY** Incredible Polish and Middle European charcuterie made on the premises. **WHAT** Polish-trained meat masters John Pikula and Ted Maslo turn out several types of hams, smoked and cured meats and a grand supply of garlicky kielbasa, wiejska, kabanos and other sausages. The freezer holds homemade dumplings and soups, and in the cold case you'll find smoked fish and European butters to go with the German and Polish rye breads on the shelves. **WHO** Grateful Middle European ex-pats.

[Jim's Fallbrook Market] 5947 Fallbrook Ave., Woodland Hills, 818.347.5525. Daily. MC, V. **WHY** Ground-in-house meats, Harris Ranch prime cuts, very good tri-tip and some wild game. They corn their own beef — try it. **WHAT** It looks like your basic corner mom-and-pop market, which is what it was when it started back in the '40s. But today Jim's is the West Valley's best source for quality meats and full butcher service. Fresh fish, too.

[La Española Meats] 🏠 25020 Doble Ave., Harbor City, 310.539.0455, laespanolameats.com. Closed Sun. Spanish. AE, MC, V. **WHY** L.A.'s only outpost for house-made Spanish charcuterie. **WHAT** Inconspicuously lodged in an industrial side street, La Española makes the most of its Harbor City location by using its warehouse space to produce excellent sausages — including five types of chorizo and two types of morcilla — as well as cured Spanish meats. In the market are olive oils, canned fish, cheeses, even dry goods and desserts. On the small patio you can enjoy a *bocadillo*, a sandwich stuffed with the market's own jamón serrano, chorizo, roasted peppers and Manchego cheese — and a helping of some Saturday-only paella, which rightly requires a call ahead. 🗐 ○

[Marconda's Meat] 🏠 Los Angeles Farmers Market, 6333 W. 3rd St., Fairfax District, 323.938.5131, farmersmarketla.com. Daily. AE, MC, V. **WHY** Andouille, chorizo, Marconda's ready-to-bake meatloaf mixture and butterflied legs of lamb. **WHAT** Want to grill bistecca alla Fiorentina? Here's the place to get a custom-cut porterhouse for that, along with anything you might want in the way of pork, lamb (aged three weeks) or sausage; consider the Montana-grown Piedmontese beef from a breed of cattle naturally low in fat. Friendly, patient butchers who have seen it all make buying here a pleasure. **WHO** Everyone from famous chefs to little old ladies dragging their wooden Farmers Market carts and micromanaging their meat orders.

[Pacific Fresh Fish] 700 E. 6th St., Downtown, 213.623.6220, pacificfreshfish.com. Closed Sun. Cash only. **WHY** Very fresh fish at wholesale prices. **WHAT** A no-nonsense wholesale fish market with slippery floors, no prices posted and no filleting — just whole fish on ice. But the quality is acclaimed. Get there early (between 6 and

🏠 ESSENTIALLY L.A. ○ LATE ♥ ROMANTIC 🗐 VALUE ♪ QUIET ✿ SUSTAINABLE

9 a.m. on weekdays and 7 and 9 a.m. on Saturdays), know what you want, and bring cash. **WHO** Chefs, restaurant managers, shop owners and a few intrepid home cooks.

[Peking Poultry] **717 N. Broadway, Chinatown, 213.680.2588. Daily. MC, V. WHY** For live ducks and chickens, slaughtered to order if you want — or the more conventional (very) fresh poultry. Also a fine selection of cuts of pork, whole fish on ice and live tilapia and crab. **WHAT** Poultry is the claim to fame, both live and butchered, but fresh fish and pork are also in abundance, all at astonishingly low prices. The smell is on the intense side of intense (live and not-live chickens, ducks, fish, shellfish and meat will do that), but the place is scrupulously clean. And there's a free parking lot right in front!

[Santa Monica Seafood] **1000 Wilshire Blvd., Santa Monica, 310.393.5244, smseafood.com. Daily. AE, MC, V. WHY** The same great retail fish market Santa Monica has long depended upon, as well as a much-needed casual oyster bar, which was curiously lacking in this oceanside city. **WHAT** The new location of the seafood outpost has an expanded retail shop with beer, wine and everything you might want to rub beneath gills and between tentacles in its gorgeous seafood display case. Skip the café in favor of the attractive to-go sushi and salads but the oyster bar is worth a stop for an inexpensive glass of Prosecco and a changing selection of Fanny Bay, Kumamoto and other varietals. **WHO** Locals stocking up on paella party ingredients.

[Schreiner's Fine Sausages] 🏠 **3417 Ocean View Blvd., Glendale, 818.244.4735, schreinersfinesausages.com. Closed Sun. German. MC, V. WHY** Sausage-making as fine art, and especially worth a visit Thursday through Saturday, when the butchers prepare fresh brats, bangers, Swedish sausage and apple sausage. **WHAT** Schreiner's house-made sausages and cured meats are shipped all over the country, and with good reason. In addition to wondrous sausages, the smokehouse also makes marvelous Canadian bacon and Black Forest ham infused with sweet hickory. All sorts of European groceries, too, including Hungarian noodles and a good selection of German beer and wines.

[Seafood Paradise] **8955 Garvey Ave., Rosemead, 626.288.2088. Daily. MC, V. WHY** The most jaw-dropping array of live seafood swim in spotless tanks: striped bass, spot prawns, eel, catfish, conch, oysters, cultured abalone, even Taiwanese frogs. **WHAT** A large, clean space is lined with tanks holding everything from the sea or rivers you could possibly want to eat — and if you can't find it live, you'll likely find it on ice. Prices are excellent on popular items ($8.99 for live Maine lobster), but you'll pay dearly for the rarities, like live Australian coral trout for $45 a pound. **WHO** Chinese-American home cooks planning a special feast, and some local chefs.

Shops

🌿 VEGETARIAN ☺ KID FRIENDLY ✿ PATIO DINING 🚗 DELIVERY 🎩 PRIVATE PARTY

[Taylor's Ol' Fashioned Meat Market] Howie's Ranch Market, 14 E. Sierra Madre Blvd., Sierra Madre, 626.355.8267. Closed Sun. AE, MC, V. **WHY** High-quality marinated meats. **WHAT** Carnivores, rejoice: This is the place to go for prime and choice Midwestern beef, along with an array of marinated meats: tri-tips, carne asada, pollo asada, butterflied legs of lamb. Beautiful produce, too.

PRODUCE

[Figueroa Produce] 6312 N. Figueroa St., Highland Park, 323.255.3663, figueroaproduce.com. Daily. Cash only. **WHY** Fresh produce and some quality grocery items for a Highland Park neighborhood that needed them. **WHAT** Don't be put off by the location in between a 99 Cent store and a place selling discount clothing — this is local entrepreneurial spirit at its best. There's a good-size produce department; some international groceries; and a number of gourmet guilty pleasures, such as Dr. Bob's Scharffen Berger chocolate ice cream and Pasadena roaster Jones's coffee. The owners are keen to know what the locals want stocked, so pipe up!

[Grow: The Produce Shop] 1830 N. Sepulveda Blvd., Manhattan Beach, 310.545.2904, growtps.com. Daily. MC, V. **WHY** For produce as good as at the better farmers' markets, and not just produce: quality meats and poultry and great local-producer items like baby food, coffee and cookies. **WHAT** Grow carries local produce, as organic as possible, with varieties you don't see at Vons: blood oranges, unusual varieties of plums, sunchokes, frisée and so on. Prices are fair, the people are nice and they deliver (for free!) twice weekly. 🚐

[L.A. Wholesale Produce Market] 1601 E. Olympic Blvd., South Park/Fashion District, 213.896.4070. Midnight-8 a.m.; closed Sun. Cash only. **WHY** For fresh, often very high quality fruits, vegetables and flowers at wholesale prices. **WHAT** Get up really early (or stay up really late) and bring cash to shop at ground zero for L.A. produce — everything from mass-grown romaine to organic, small-producer blenheim peaches. Make sure to check out Davalan, which has some of the best fruit here. You have to buy in case quantity, so unless you have a big family, go in with friends. **WHO** Mostly professional buyers for markets and restaurants, but regular citizens show up, too. ☺ 🗺

[Marina Farms] 5454 S. Centinela Ave., Culver City, 310.827.3049. Daily. AE, MC, V. **WHY** If you can't hit a farmers' market, stop here for very good produce. **WHAT** It's a little hit-or-miss, but if you're lucky you'll find things like super-sweet pluots, ripe figs, baby carrots, Japanese eggplant and other less-commonly seen produce. It carries other grocery items, too, but they're pricey.

[Stan's Produce] 9307 W. Pico Blvd., Pico-Robertson, 310.274.1865.
Closed Sat. Cash only. **WHY** Farmers' market–quality produce at low
supermarket prices. **WHAT** Good produce shops like this are all over
cities like New York, but here in the land of three-acre supermarkets
and plentiful farmers' markets, they're as rare as blizzards. This makes
Stan's all the more special. Very good produce, rich seasonal variation,
and personal service from Stan. Note that it's closed on the Sabbath.

[Valley Produce] 18345 Vanowen St., Reseda, 818.609.1955. Daily.
Middle Eastern/Indian. AE, MC, V. **WHY** Any herb, green or fruit you
could ever imagine wanting, at great prices. **WHAT** With a focus on
Persian, Middle Eastern and Indian foods, this market has bargain
prices on avocados, stone fruits and lettuces, along with a vast selection of Mediterranean spices, Indian teas, Middle Eastern breads and
discounted olive oils. On weekends, hordes of shoppers mean cart
traffic moves as slowly as the 405 on Friday afternoon. 🖘

SPECIALTY & SMALL MARKETS

[Alpine Village Market] 833 W. Torrance Blvd., Torrance,
310.327.2483, alpinevillage.net. Daily. German. AE, MC, V. **WHY** Some
of the city's best sausages, plus a chance to pick up some freshly
baked German rye bread with your bierschinken. **WHAT** Sure, it looks
like a kitschy Bavarian tourist trap from the Harbor Freeway, but this
market inside the Alpine Plaza is an outpost of fine, authentic sausage
making. The market, which has its own smoking facilities, turns out
sausage several times a week — a freshness factor that means less
salt is needed as a preservative. There's also an immense selection
of salumi, as well as country pâté, European-style hams and lowfat
and low-sodium sausages. The bakery turns out German rye breads,
strudel, kuchen and tortes.

[Angelo's Italian Deli] 190 La Verne Ave., Belmont Shore,
562.434.1977. Closed Mon. Italian. MC, V. **WHY** To wallow in the
flavors of Italy. **WHAT** The size of this Long Beach market, hidden
just off busy 2nd Street, belies the amount of wonderful things found
inside: fresh pizza dough, fresh burrata from Gioia, a dazzling array
of olive oils and balsamic vinegars, dried and frozen pasta, cheeses,
tinned anchovies and tuna, every sort of cured meat, fresh cannoli,
all sorts of olives, even an Italian antacid, which you'll need. Great
sandwiches are made to take out. There's a second, larger branch just
across the OC line in Seal Beach. **WHO** Home chefs and party-throw-
ers who'll make a detour for good ingredients.

[Bangkok Market] 4757 Melrose Ave., East Hollywood,
323.662.9705. Daily. Thai. AE, MC, V. **WHY** Everything needed to con-
coct a Thai feast, from fresh lemongrass, kaffir lime leaves and Thai

🍃 VEGETARIAN ⊙ KID FRIENDLY ✿ PATIO DINING 🚗 DELIVERY 🎩 PRIVATE PARTY

basil to galangal and great deals on canned coconut milk and other essential ingredients. **WHAT** The first place in L.A. to find exotic Thai ingredients is still owned by the family of popular local chef and culinary teacher Jet Tila. 🍸

[Bangluck Market] **5170 Hollywood Blvd., East Hollywood, 323.660.8000; 12980 Sherman Way, North Hollywood, 818.765.1088. Daily. Thai. MC, V. WHY** All your Thai and Southeast Asian cooking needs packed into a small Hollywood market that shares a parking lot with the great Sanamluang Café — so allow time to stop for some pad see ew before or after you shop. **WHAT** Besides the expected range of produce and groceries needed to make Thai food, this packed little market has a great selection of inexpensive cookware and utensils, as well as products from Singapore and the Philippines. Look for the fresh kaffir lime leaves, palm sugar, tiny eggplants, curries, fish sauces and frozen banana leaves.

[Bauducco's Italian Market] **2839 Agoura Rd., Westlake Village, 805.495.4623. Daily. Italian. AE, MC, V. WHY** House-made Sicilian bread, to take home or to have the deli make into a chicken-parmesan or sausage sandwich. **WHAT** Fabulous Sicilian bread and rolls are baked on the premises at this 40-year-old family business, where the cases are stocked with house-made sausages and salumi, both imported and domestic. The voluptuous sandwiches, pizzas and prepared foods to take home are good, and the shop's shelves hold everything you need to cook *la bella cucina* — but if you don't want to cook, there's a restaurant, too. **WHO** Lunch-breakers stopping for a sandwich and shoppers staring at the deli case. 🚐

[Bay Cities Italian Deli & Bakery] **1517 Lincoln Blvd., Santa Monica, 310.395.8279, baycitiesitaliandeli.com. Closed Mon. Italian. MC, V. WHY** The Godmother sub and the meatball sandwiches, olives from the deli case and that red-checked-tablecloth Italian vibe. **WHAT** A classic Italian deli and grocery store, Bay Cities deserves the longevity award for making it in Santa Monica since the '20s. The deli packs 'em in for olives, salads and specialty sandwiches, including the famous Godmother, a massive heap of Genoa salami, mortadella, capicola, ham, prosciutto and provolone. The aisles are lined with imported pastas, olive oils, vinegars, anchovies, cookies and wine. The bread's baked on site, and if it isn't as good as eating a crusty loaf in Florence, it's a lot cheaper than a plane ticket. **WHO** East Coasters hungry for a taste of home.

[Bombay Spiceland] **8650 Reseda Blvd., Northridge, 818.701.9383. Daily. Indian. AE, MC, V. WHY** Think of it as the Dal House — the variety of beans and lentils is extraordinary. **WHAT** For a no-frills, warehouse-style Indian grocery store, Bombay Spiceland is amazingly well stocked. Whether you're looking for turmeric root, medicinal

---

🏠 **ESSENTIALLY L.A.** ☺ **LATE** ♥ **ROMANTIC** Ⓢ **VALUE** 🔉 **QUIET** ♻ **SUSTAINABLE** neem leaves, Bollywood's latest video rental or a phenomenal selection of *dals*, the beans and lentils central to Indian cooking, chances are you'll find it here. And don't miss the *chevdas*, those Indian snacks in the glass case near the front door — they're junk-food tasty but actually nutritious. 🖅

[Claro's] 🏠 1003 E. Valley Blvd., San Gabriel, 626.288.2026, claros. com. Closed Wed. Italian. AE, MC, V. **WHY** Prepared take-home dishes like lasagne and ravioli, a vast selection of imported pasta, cookies, breads and hard-to-find items from Italy, like pasta machines and espresso pots. Huge and delicious sandwiches, too. **WHAT** This well-stocked, old-school Italian market and deli has been around since 1948, starting in San Gabriel, and it now has five other locations. (This was once an Italian-immigrant neighborhood, which is hard to imagine in this Chinese era.) The deli offers sandwiches, meats, antipasti and hot dishes, and it's a great place to stock up for a party. **WHO** Third-generation loyalists and people proud of their Sicilian blood, even if it's only a little. 🖅

[Continental Shop] 1619 Wilshire Blvd., Santa Monica, 310.453.8655, thecontinentalshop.com. Daily. English. AE, MC, V. **WHY** This is L.A.'s supply depot for all things British, from taped TV shows to airline tickets and, yes, food. **WHAT** Let's say you've got a craving for bangers, a Cornish pasty or imported frozen Yorkshire pudding. The freezer of this tightly packed, slightly dowdy emporium is where to look. The cooler holds clotted Devon cream and packaged Stilton and Colby cheeses, and the shelves are filled with single-estate teas, all manner of shortbreads, jams, jellies, tinned biscuits and candy bars. **WHO** Homesick ex-pats and persnickety Anglophiles.

[Cube Marketplace] 615 N. La Brea Ave., Melrose, 323.939.1148, cubemarketplace.com. Closed Sun. Italian. AE, MC, V. **WHY** For its fresh and dried house-made pastas, along with an array of high-end olives, cheeses, salumi, sauces, olive oils and vinegars. **WHAT** Originally called the Divine Pasta Company, this business ramped it up and is now a high-end café and marketplace. Come here for more than 85 varieties of cheese; salumi from Salumi Salame, the Fatted Calf and Pio Tosini; an excellent selection of oils, vinegars, salts and syrups; and such foodie essentials as capers, fresh pesto and Laguiole knives. **WHO** The Eaters, the Shoppers, the Wine Bar Hoppers (and Sale Shoppers can usually snag an artisan honey or two).

[E. Waldo Ward] 🏠 273 E. Highland Ave., Sierra Madre, 626.355.1218, waldoward.com. Closed Sun. AE, MC, V. **WHY** Fantastic blood-orange marmalade, thin-sliced bread-and-butter pickles, pickled peaches, boysenberry jam and such modern creations as raspberry-chipotle sauce. **WHAT** This fourth-generation preserves maker still occupies the original family factory and citrus farm hidden in plain sight

Shops

🌿 VEGETARIAN ☺ KID FRIENDLY ✿ PATIO DINING 🚚 DELIVERY 🎩 PRIVATE PARTY in impossibly atmospheric Sierra Madre. It does the soul good to see places like this not just surviving, but thriving (thanks to the internet and savvy management by the founder's grandson, Richard Ward, and his son, Jeff Ward). Worth a trek.

[Epicure Imports] 6900 Beck Ave., North Hollywood, 818.985.9800. Open to the public only for occasional sales. AE, MC, V. **WHY** Vacuum-packed fresh foie gras, French nut oils, whole French cheeses and some wine buys. **WHAT** Several times a year (get on the e-mail list) this restaurant-industry wholesaler of gourmet imported products opens its doors to the public, permitting a sometimes chaotic supermarket sweep through aisles of plus-size food items (three kilograms of Valrhona dark chocolate, anyone?). The real gold mine is the refrigerated storage room, where the imported cheeses, hams and smoked salmon live. Bring a jacket. **WHO** Hardcore L.A. foodies. 🐭

[Follow Your Heart Market & Café] 21825 Sherman Way, Canoga Park, 818.348.3240, followyourheart.com. Daily. AE, MC, V. **WHY** An all-around well-stocked natural-foods market with good quality products at somewhat lower prices than at Whole Paycheck. **WHAT** The '70s live at this good-hearted natural-foods café and market, which was, in fact, founded in 1970. Besides organic produce, whole grains and all the expected natural foods, you'll find homeopathic remedies, green cleaning products and some home-décor items. The café in back is good for a fresh, healthy meal or takeout food. **WHO** Vegetarians, vegans and seekers of health. 🐭♻🥢

[Froma on Melrose] 7960 Melrose Ave., Melrose, 323.653.3700, fromaonmelrose.com. Daily. AE, MC, V. **WHY** It's one of the very few places in town to get the extraordinary (and expensive) jamón ibérico de bellota. **WHAT** A small, quality shop with top-tier products to assemble a luxe Hollywood Bowl picnic or pick up delicious sandwiches. The high-end charcuterie selection includes the famous La Quercia domestic prosciutto, chorizo, bresaola and soppressata. Also stocked are raw-milk cheeses and caviar, and you can special-order just about anything, including Kobe beef.

[Galco's Soda Pop Shop] 🏠 5702 York Blvd., Highland Park, 323.255.7115, sodapopstop.com. Daily. MC, V. **WHY** A vast wonderland of fizzy drinks. Not to mention the seriously old-school candy counter. **WHAT** For underage drinking, no place in the world beats Galco's, which stocks more than 250 kinds of soda (as well as a good selection of global beer). Looking for coffee soda, authentic Kickapoo Joy Juice or Guayaba from Brazil? Boy, have you come to the right place. You'll also find a strange and wonderful array of near-forgotten regional candy, including Owyhee Idaho Spuds, Mallo Cups and Chick-O-Sticks. And it ships. **WHO** Hipster kids, nostalgic boomers, immigrants seeking a fix of homeland carbonation. ☺

🏠 ESSENTIALLY L.A. � LATE ♥ROMANTIC 🐭 VALUE 🍃QUIET ♻SUSTAINABLE

[Grand Central Market] 🏛 **317 S. Broadway, Downtown, 213.624.2378, grandcentralsquare.com. Daily. Cash only. WHY** Stands specializing in very cheap produce of reasonable quality, rows of dried peppers and tubs of prepared mole, candies and staples, as well as lots of lunch counters. Make sure to get a taco at Tacos Tumbras a Tomas. **WHAT** A throwback to when Downtown really was the center of L.A., Grand Central Market is both a trip back in time and a daily shopping and eating destination for locals. The vast indoor market is filled with stands selling produce, meat, snacks, juices and such lunchtime staples as tacos and teriyaki. **WHO** Immigrant Latinos from the neighborhood, a few Downtown-dwelling yuppies and, at lunchtime, hordes descending from surrounding offices and jury duty. 🗺

[Holland American Market] **10343 E. Artesia Blvd., Bellflower, 562.925.6914, 1dutchmall.com. Daily. Dutch/Indonesian. MC, V. WHY** Come for the wooden shoes, stay for the sambal oelek. **WHAT** You could come here for the Dutch groceries (cheeses, herrings, pastries) that the name promises, but the bigger draw for many is the enormous stock of Indonesian foods. *Bumbus* (spice bases for curries) and chile-based sambals are on display, the essential sauce ketjap, fermented shrimp and Indonesian laurel leaves.

[India Sweets & Spices] 🏛 **3126 Los Feliz Blvd., Atwater, 323.345.0360; 22011 Sherman Way, Canoga Park, 818.887.0868, indiasweetsandspices.net. Daily. Indian. AE, MC, V. WHY** Large selection of rice, teas, frozen items and all the ingredients to make a world-class curry from scratch. **WHAT** Take a trip to India by way of Los Feliz or Canoga Park, exploring the rows of chutneys and well-priced spices, then noshing at the popular vegetarian cafeteria — it's known for its sweets, including several flavors of kulfi ice cream. **WHO** Indian families from miles around, and local hipsters who appreciate the reasonably priced steam-table curries and freshly made dosas. 🗺

[Koreatown Plaza Market] **928 S. Western Ave., Koreatown, 213.382.1234. Daily. Korean/Asian. AE, MC, V. WHY** An extraordinary variety of mild and spicy *panchan* — those small, flavorful side dishes at the heart of a Korean meal — plus validated parking. **WHAT** This contemporary market in a Euro-chic shopping mall features an impressive array of Korean prepared foods, notably highly flavored panchan, including marinated crab, pickled baby cucumbers, spicy squid strips and garlic-stem salad. Other standouts involve *mandu* (gyoza-type dumplings), fresh-frozen sea vegetables, and kim chee in its many forms — from the fiery hot stuff involving cabbage or "leek" (actually Chinese chive) to a cooling, salty variety made with white radish. The enormous meat department offers many precut meats suitable for all kinds of Asian cookery.

Shops

🥬 VEGETARIAN ⊙ KID FRIENDLY ❁ PATIO DINING 🚗 DELIVERY 🎩 PRIVATE PARTY

[LAX-C] **1000 N. Main St., Chinatown, 323.343.9000, lax-c.com. Daily. AE, MC, V. WHY** A remarkable selection of Thai ingredients, packaged foods, cookware, even furniture. **WHAT** Part supermarket, part Costco-style warehouse, this huge and shabby place is the go-to destination in town for everything you could possibly need to cook Thai food, all at very low prices (including produce). As at Costco, you may have to buy in huge quantities, so consider sharing with a friend or two. On weekends the parking lot fills with street-food vendors. **WHO** Thai restaurateurs and home cooks exploring Asian cuisines. 📝

[Locali] **5825 Franklin Ave., Hollywood, 323.466.1360, localiyours.com. Daily. AE, MC, V. WHY** Locally sourced edibles from some of our favorite producers. Don't miss the Ruby Jewel ice cream sandwiches — they may come all the way from Portland, but they rock. **WHAT** Locali packs a lot of interesting products into a tiny storefront, and they're all either sustainable, organic and/or local — wine, beer from Dales Bros. and the Bruery, sandwiches and salads from M Café, Carmela Ice Cream, La Guera Tamalera tamales, prepared food from several vegan suppliers, frozen foods, coffee and snacks. Books, shopping bags, water bottles and other tchotchkes for the green lifestyle are stocked as well — even a handy countertop compost bin. ♻🛍

[Ma 'n' Pa's Grocery] **346 Roycroft Ave., Long Beach, 562.438.4084. Daily. AE, MC, V. WHY** One of the finest small markets around, tiny and personal and packed with good things to eat. **WHAT** Oh how we love this wee little market in an old house. There's the quality produce, of course, and the good meat and fish. And there are those amazing scones made by the French guy who sells them at the farmers' markets, and the baguettes made by Babette. Oh, and the stupendous homemade beef and turkey jerky, and the burgers to eat on the picnic table outside, not to mention the daily entrees to take home for dinner. You'll pay for all this, of course, but it's worth it. **WHO** A devoted cadre of neighbors.

[Market Gourmet] **1800 Abbot Kinney Blvd., Venice, 310.305.9800. Daily. MC, V. WHY** A great place to find gourmet pantry items from around the world, from Australian marmite to Israeli olive oil. Ex-pats and returning travelers will delight at the nostalgic brands here. **WHAT** This quirky little market has an international focus and a great selection of imported goodies (check out the tapenades, ploufs, flours and Asian sauces), as well as fantastic homemade soup, a compact but diverse cheese area and good imported teas and coffees. A fabulous place to put together a food-lover's gift basket.

[Mercado Buenos Aires] **7540 Sepulveda Blvd., Van Nuys, 818.786.0522. Daily. Argentinean. AE, MC, V. WHY** Excellent meat dishes in the café, and quality Argentine and Italian goods in the market. **WHAT** Part deli, part butcher, part market and part restaurant, this place is all things to all Argentineans. The bakery cases hold wonderful pastries, both sweet and savory: spinach-cheese pie, ham torta and, of course, a variety of empanadas. In the cold-cut case look for imported Spanish and Italian prosciutto, delicate chicken-vegetable roll, matambre and tongue in vinaigrette. Upmarket groceries like Chilean sea salt and olive-oil mayonnaise belie the somewhat funky ambiance. **WHO** Who knew there were so many Argentineans in the Valley?

[Monsieur Marcel] Farmers Market, 6333 W. 3rd St., Fairfax District, 323.939.7792, mrmarcel.com. Daily. French. AE, MC, V. **WHY** Quality cheeses, olives, wine, duck confit and every preserve and oil made by man, as well as some everyday grocery-store essentials. **WHAT** This large gourmet market tucked into a corner of the Farmers Market offers one-stop shopping for Francophiles and, especially, cheese lovers — the cheese selection is dazzling. The selection of epicurean products is vast, including many private-label lines, and there's a good array of imported and domestic wines as well. Make sure to allow time for dejeuner at the adjacent outdoor café.

[Monte Carlo Deli] 3103 W. Magnolia Blvd., Burbank, 818.845.3516, montecarlodeli.com. Daily. Italian. AE, MC, V. **WHY** Prosciutto di Parma, fresh pizza dough, canned and marinated anchovies, excellent cold cuts. **WHAT** Despite adding a gelato bar and some tables at one end of the store, this venerable Italian grocery thankfully refuses to gentrify. Monte Carlo carries all the necessities of life, including Illy espresso beans, Italian sausage, Rustichella d'Abruzzo pasta, salt-packed capers, fresh basil, Grana Padano, mascarpone and biscotti. **WHO** Older native Italians, younger foodies and the rest of us.

[Naples Gourmet Grocer] 5650 E. 2nd St., Naples, 562.439.6518, naplesgourmetgrocer.com. Daily. AE, MC, V. **WHY** Cowgirl Creamery cheeses, Fra' Mani salumi, Breadbar breads, delicious boutique sodas and lots more gourmet goodies. **WHAT** The tiny Long Beach neighborhood of Naples has its own little Zabar's, stocked with the best food American food products out there — from such places as Niman Ranch, Paul Bertolli, Dr. Bob and Little Flower Candy Co. — and a few carefully chosen imports, too. The deli makes great sandwiches, and the cheese and salumi platters are showing up at the coolest Long Beach parties.

[The Oaks Market] 1915 N. Bronson Ave., Hollywood, 323.871.8894, theoaksgourmet.com. Daily. AE, MC, V. **WHY** A very good and surprisingly affordable selection of wine, beer and retro and rare sodas, as well as an extensive gourmet-to-go menu. **WHAT** The late lamented Victor's is now the swankier Oaks Market, which doesn't try to compete with Gelson's across the street for your upscale-grocery needs. Instead, it competes in just a few niches by offering a large and good-value collection of wine and beer, a coffee and juice bar, an on-

Shops

🌿 VEGETARIAN ⊙ KID FRIENDLY ☼ PATIO DINING 🚗 DELIVERY 🎩 PRIVATE PARTY

site coffee roaster, and a good selection of small-producer packaged foods, like Dewar's old-fashioned candy chews from Bakersfield and Casa de Fruta saltwater taffy from the Bay Area.

[Olives Gourmet Grocer] **3510 E. Broadway, Long Beach, 562.439.7758; 5000 E. 2nd St., Belmont Shore, 562.343.5580 olivesgourmetgrocer.com. Daily. AE, MC, V. WHY** For a food-lover's home away from home, not to mention a good place to pick up a rotisserie chicken for dinner or a platter for that potluck. **WHAT** The Broadway store is a compact, clean-lined gourmet market with particularly strong offerings in charcuterie and cheese, sophisticated sandwiches, sauces and oils, and prepared dishes to take home. You'll also find an olive bar (natch), a salad bar and just enough basic staples. Fun cooking classes, too. The newer Belmont Shore shop is twice the size of its parent, allowing room for a cheerful eat-in café.

[Owen's Market] **9769 W. Pico Blvd., Century City, 310.28.OWENS, owensla.com. Daily. AE, MC, V. WHY** For posh prepared foods and high-end groceries, delivered for westsiders. **WHAT** Mindy Weiss, a high-end event planner, has turned this little market into a sort of foodie boutique. Besides some basic grocery-store staples, you'll find naturally raised Angus beef from Montana Legend, prepared foods from Pasadena's Kitchen for Exploring Foods, desserts from the Cake Divas, eco-friendly cleaning products and a lovely (and organic) salad bar. If you have to ask the price of the cupcakes, you can't afford them.

[Petrossian] **321 N. Robertson Blvd., West Hollywood, 310.271.0576, petrossian.com. Daily. Russian/French. AE, MC, V. WHY** To pick up a great gift for a caviar lover — and it's not all $364-an-ounce Royal Sevruga stuff, either. There are some surprisingly affordable varieties. **WHAT** This newly expanded Euro-moderne West Hollywood outpost of the Parisian fancy-food emporium has a caviar-and-crème fraîche décor, 1950s Hollywood glam photos on the dining room walls and two big communal tall tables in the shop for tasting the goods. Shimmering cases hold Petrossian products: caviars, smoked fish, pâtés, Champagnes, chocolate truffles ... all the essentials of life, at least for some people. ♥

[Pondok Kaki Lima] **1200 Huntington Dr., Duarte, 626.357.0907. Sat. 10 a.m. - 2 p.m. Indonesian. Cash only. WHY** Indonesian street food in its natural habitat. **WHAT** Set up in a parking lot behind a Duarte motel, Pondok Kaki Lima is one of greater L.A.'s brightest beacons of Indonesian cooking. The weekly food fair is a collection of just under a dozen vendors, most of which specialize in a single dish, but often serve many. Some focus on skewers of sweet, charred pork, others on long-simmered curries and entire meals wrapped in banana leaves. Sip a durian shake and stop by the nearby brick-and-mortar Indonesian market on the way out. **WHO** All corners of the Indonesian diaspora, a few well-traveled surfers and curious eaters from all over.

[Roma Italian Deli & Grocery] **918 N. Lake Ave., Pasadena, 626.797.7748. Daily. Italian. AE, MC, V. WHY** Excellent Italian prosciutti, cheeses, sausages, salumi and gnocchi, sold with style and lots of sample tastes. **WHAT** Roma's fans are so passionate that they are almost a cult, and their leader is Rosario, who confidently proclaims his sandwiches, prosciutti and cheeses to be the best in the world. We're not sure about that, but they are damn good. Some swear by the inexpensive produce, but we don't.

[Samosa House] **11510 W. Washington Blvd., Culver City, 310.398.6766, samosahouse.net. Daily. Indian. AE, MC, V. WHY** One of the best-stocked Indian markets in town, with savvy owners who help customers hunt down elusive ingredients. **WHAT** The Punjabi owners stock ingredients for all kinds of Indian cooking, and they pride themselves on offering such exotic and hard-to-find foods as fresh curry leaves. And if you're looking for tandoori paste ready-made to smear on chicken or lamb before broiling, they've got it — part of Bharat's huge selection of "convenience" foods. The café, formally known as Bharat Bazaar, offers an all-vegetarian buffet, too.

[Savor the Flavor] **11 Kersting Ct., Sierra Madre, 626.355.5153, savortheflavor.net. Daily. AE, MC, V. WHY** A terrific selection of gifts for food lovers; good food samples, too. **WHAT** This storybook shop in the storybook town of Sierra Madre specializes in edibles, with some tableware and cookbooks thrown in for good measure. The kind staff love building custom gift baskets or helping you decide between the Chardonnay brittle, blueberry-acacia gummy pandas, and locally made dry rub for meats. You'll find sauces, marinades, soup mixes, vinegars, cookies and sweets galore, including many under their own label, as well as from such makers as Stonewall, Barefoot Contessa and Robert Rothschild. **WHO** Local ladies-who-shop and day-trippers exploring Sierra Madre.

[Selam Market] **5534 W. Pico Blvd., Mid-City, 323.935.5567. Daily. Ethiopian. MC, V. WHY** Neophytes can get a taste of the authentic Ethiopian culinary experience, and seasoned cooks can find exactly what they need (including three kinds of cardamon and green coffee). **WHAT** The meats here are cut for Ethiopian dishes, and the spice blends — including berberé, awazé and Nit'kr k'ibé spiced butter — are made in-house. Also on offer in this butcher shop/deli/grocery store are peppers, fenugreek, bulk cardamom and teff flour, if you'd like try your hand at making your own injera bread. (Those less adventurous in the kitchen can buy the quintessential Ethiopian bread ready-made.)

Shops

🌿 **VEGETARIAN** ☺ **KID FRIENDLY** ✿ **PATIO DINING** 🚐 **DELIVERY** 🎩 **PRIVATE PARTY**

[Teheran Market] 1417 Wilshire Blvd., Santa Monica, 310.393.6719. Daily. Persian/Middle Eastern. AE, MC, V. **WHY** Hard-to-find Persian and Middle Eastern ingredients at bargain prices. **WHAT** A great feta selection, unusual breads and baked goods, good spices and low prices on olives, fresh herbs and basmati rice draw cooks to this mid-size Middle Eastern market. Check out the Al Wadi hummus — it tastes like homemade.

[Tito's Market] 9814 E. Garvey Ave., El Monte, 626.579.1893. Closed Mon. Argentinean. AE, MC, V. **WHY** When you're running low on empanadas, dulce de leche and Malbec. **WHAT** You'd never think to stop in this ordinary-looking little market in a strip mall if you happened along Garvey, but inside is an extraordinary deli (steak milanese, empanadas, cured meats) and a fine grocery section stocked with Argentinean food products, fresh meat and wines. The huge sandwiches attract a lunch crowd. **WHO** A diverse mix that reflects the community.

[Village Gourmet Cheese & Wine] 4357 Tujunga Ave., Studio City, 818.487.3807, villagegourmetcheeseandwine.com. Daily. AE, MC, V. **WHY** Good last-minute party food from the freezer case — spinach-pesto puffs, gorgonzola-fig phyllo rolls — as well as lovely order-in-advance party platters (cheeses, crudités, caprese, caviar). Intelligently filled gift baskets, too. **WHAT** A convenient spot for all your high-end culinary essentials, from roasted-pepper-and-pesto sandwiches to chicken-apricot salad. Good lunch salads and sandwiches, party foods and prepared foods, both fresh and frozen. The wine and cheese selections are smart, though not cheap.

[Vinh Loi Tofu] 18625 Sherman Way, Reseda, 818.996.9779, vinhloitofu.com. Daily. Asian. MC, V. **WHY** Fresh tofu made on-site, as well as some vegan grocery essentials, including soy milk, tofu pudding and packaged vegan foods. **WHAT** Kevin Tran is L.A.'s king of fresh tofu. Come here to buy the good stuff, and allow time to eat in his amazing vegan Vietnamese café while you're there. **WHO** A steady stream of regulars, as diverse as they come: Asian chefs, vegan moms with toddlers in tow, bikers, women in hijabs.

SUPERMARKETS

[99 Ranch Market] 140 W. Valley Blvd., San Gabriel, 626.307.8899, 99ranch.com. Daily. Chinese. AE, MC, V. **WHY** Great prices and an amazingly varied selection of mainstream and esoteric Chinese grocery items. Worth a trip for the noodle case alone. **WHAT** The Gelson's of Chinese supermarkets, except instead of having 60 kinds of breakfast cereal, 99 Ranch has 60 kinds of fish sauce. An absolute must-visit, with a dazzling array of Chinese (not so much Korean or other Asian cultures) produce, sauces, noodles, kitchenware and ingredients, as well as terrific (and terrifically cheap) live seafood. More branches in Monterey Park, Rowland Heights and beyond. **WHO** A pan-Asian clientele, including tourists, locals, bargain-hunters, live-seafood shoppers and cooks. 📝

[Beverly Glen Marketplace] **2964 N. Beverly Glen Cir., Bel-Air, 310.475.0829. Daily. AE, MC, V. WHY** For small-town service with big-city products, from fine wines and prime meats to frozen organic baby food and boutique-label chocolates. **WHAT** This swank little market doesn't have 50 kinds of toilet paper, but it has everything a Bel-Air resident might need, including artisanal cheeses and sushi. There's an espresso bar, too. **WHO** Movie stars and captains of industry, as well as their personal assistants and nannies.

[Bob's Market] **1650 Ocean Park Blvd., Santa Monica, 310.452.2493, bobsmkt.com. Daily. AE, MC, V. WHY** Hand-cut steaks, house-made sausages, excellent prepared salads and sandwiches and neighborly service. The butcher will even custom make your favorite sausage, if you bring in the recipe and buy at least five pounds of it. **WHAT** A throwback in the best sense of the word, Bob's has personal service, a quality butcher counter, an excellent deli, carefully chosen produce and a well-edited wine collection — and the prices aren't as high as you'd expect for a little indie market. A community center in Ocean Park. **WHO** Ocean Park locals who know the employees by name. �

[Erewhon Natural Foods Market] 🔒 **7660 Beverly Blvd., Beverly/Third, 323.937.0777, erewhonmarket.com. Daily. Vegetarian. AE, MC, V. WHY** The salad bar, the sushi bar, the deli soups and the competitive prices on organic produce and healthy packaged food products. **WHAT** Before Whole Foods were popping up like so many organic chanterelles in a rain forest, Erewhon ("Nowhere" spelled backwards, sort of) was selling organic, natural foods. It stocks hormone-free chicken and organic eggs but sells no red meat; bulk grains, beans and dried fruits but no products made with white sugar; and lovely imported olive oils and cheeses but nothing made with hydrogenated vegetable fats. A spotless, well-organized new-age market with good prices. **WHO** Tie-dyed relics from the '70s meet glam vegan twentysomething development girls. 📝⚙🛍

[Grocery Warehouse] **1487 W. Sunset Blvd., Echo Park, 213.250.1446. Daily. Asian. AE, MC, V. WHY** For Chinese and Asian herbs and vegetables, from lemongrass to bok choy, as well as fresh noodles of many types, a remarkable selection of tofu and good, very cheap knives. **WHAT** Locals have been known to call it "the stinky-meat market" — not that there's anything wrong with the meat, mind you. It's just aromatic. Anyway, this is a very good market with a range of Asian foods at excellent prices. Great $5 knives, too. 📝

🥬 VEGETARIAN ◎ KID FRIENDLY ❀ PATIO DINING 🚐 DELIVERY 🎩 PRIVATE PARTY

[Howie's Ranch Market] **6580 N. San Gabriel Blvd., San Gabriel, 626.286.8871. Daily. AE, MC, V. WHY** Three reasons: Old-fashioned service with a smile. Famed meats from Alexander's. And classic goodies from Lisa's Bakery. **WHAT** This compact market is worth a detour. Look for the Harris Ranch beef, dry-aged prime cuts, excellent marinated poultry and carne asada, and locally made empanadas and tamales. The wine selection is very good, too. And it delivers! **WHO** Seniors who've been coming here for decades, and people who've ordered meat for a special occasion. 🚗

[Jons Marketplace] **3667 W. 3rd St., Koreatown, 213.382.5701, jonsmarketplace.com. Daily. AE, MC, V. WHY** The cheapest pita in town, a dizzying selection of Eastern European sausages and meats, fresh Middle Eastern cheeses and giant tubs of yogurt, as well as imported jams, candies and spices. The merchandise varies by the density of the ethnic groups in the area. **WHAT** This small chain specializes in ethnic groceries, primarily Middle Eastern and Latino items, depending on the neighborhood. They all have great delis and good produce (you might have to dig a little) at very low prices. Other locations in North Hollywood, Reseda, Hollywood and Glendale. 🖺

[Koreatown Galleria Market] 🖺 **3250 W. Olympic Blvd., Koreatown, 323.733.6000, koreatowngalleria.com. Daily. Korean/Asian. AE, MC, V. WHY** Paradise for Korean food-lovers and cooks, right in the middle of a glitzy shopping mall. While you're in the mall, check out Ho Won Dang, which sells special-occasion cookes. Try the tiny yellow cookies (their color comes from pine tree pollen) and the crisp, fried cookies coated with crushed pine nuts. **WHAT** It's worth a trip to Koreatown just to shop in this vast supermarket. It offers everything you need to prepare a Korean meal, and is often bustling with demonstrations and tastings of dumplings, meatballs or fried noodles. The produce section is lush with Korean greens, soy sprouts, a half-dozen types of Asian mushrooms, lipstick peppers and fat Korean zucchini. There's also a large section devoted to *panchan*, the side dishes served in Korean restaurants, as well as dinner-ready hot dishes, marinated meats, shelves of kim chee and gorgeous trays of sashimi. 🖺

[Liborio Market] 🖺 **864 S. Vermont Ave., Koreatown, 213.386.1458; 1831 W. 3rd St., Westlake, 213.483.1053; liborio.com. Daily. Latino/Cuban. AE, MC, V. WHY** The most wondrous array of Latin American foods: Brazilian manioc meal, dried Peruvian potatoes, Guatemalan mashed black beans, the Salvadoran coffee cake called *quesadilla*, squishy-sweet ripe plantains, the Mexican chorizos and marinated meat and, during the holidays, great tamales from many regions. **WHAT** This pan-Latin market draws cooks and enthusiastic eaters looking for a vast array of ingredients for the cuisines of Cuba, Brazil, El Salvador, Peru, Guatemala and the Yucatán and Campeche regions of southern Mexico, among others. The family-run Liborio — originally a Cuban market — has expanded substantially since it opened in the '60s and now features a bakery and a meat department that can sell you *lechón asado* (a whole roasted pig) or good, ready-to-use pupusa fillings. 🖼

[Mitsuwa] 🏠 **21515 Western Ave., Torrance, 310.782.0335, mitsuwa. com. Daily. Japanese. MC, V. WHY** The same great selection of Japanese foods as its siblings but with a huge 15-store food court/retail shop outlet next door. Pick up Japanese cosmetics, books or pottery and stay for dinner. There's even a fast-food Chinese restaurant (go figure). Did we mention the complimentary valet parking? **WHAT** Everything you need to stock your Japanese pantry, including 20-pound bags of rice and gummy-candies galore. Grab-and-go products like sushi and seaweed salad are good, too. But if you have a question, good luck — unless you speak Japanese or find the one employee who speaks English. Look for a kind customer instead.

[Mitsuwa] **3760 Centinela Ave., West L.A., 310.398.2113, mitsuwa. com. Daily. Japanese. MC, V. WHY** A Japanese food lovers' paradise: soft red-bean-paste buns from the bakery, some of the freshest (and hardest to find) seafood in town and a huge variety of tofu and soy sauce. There's an old-school snack-laden mini-mall across from the checkout stand to keep the kids busy while you shop – and there's even a dry cleaner. **WHAT** The full range of Japanese grocery items, prepared foods, produce, seafood and beyond.

[Super King Market] 🏠 **2260 N. Lincoln Ave., Altadena, 626.296.9311; 2716 N. San Fernando Rd., Eagle Rock, 323.225.0044 superkingmarkets.com. Daily. AE, MC, V. WHY** Low prices, good service, impeccable housekeeping and an unusual combination of mainstream American supermarket goods and a dazzling array of international foods. **WHAT** In 1993, the Fermanian family opened an unusual supermarket in Anaheim and over time found great success, and at last they've expanded to L.A. with these markets in Eagle Rock and Altadena. You'll find all your supermarket needs along with an incredible (and cheap) selection of Armenian, Greek, Middle Eastern and Latin American foods: fresh and aged cheeses, sauces, yogurts, grains, sauces, prepared meats and exotic produce that's sometimes a little over-ripe. Impressive bakery, extensive deli with fresh cheeses, and a beautiful nut bar. **WHO** The most wonderful L.A. mix: An Indian woman in a gorgeous sari, a Central American family with kids in soccer uniforms, young indie couples, little old Lebanese women walking so slow you want to scream.... 🖼

[Vallarta Supermarket] **13051 Victory Blvd., North Hollywood, 818.760.7021, vallartasupermarket.com. Daily. Mexican/Latino. AE, MC, V. WHY** Unending selection of Mexican and Latin American ingredients, plus great takeout. **WHAT** The 19 L.A. County branches of this regional chain have butchers that prepare your meat *corte al gusto* (cut

🥬 **VEGETARIAN** ◎ **KID FRIENDLY** ☼ **PATIO DINING** 🚚 **DELIVERY** 🏠 **PRIVATE PARTY**

with flair), as well as the largest selection of Mexican and Salvadoran cheeses (Oaxacan, requesón, asadero, enchilada) in town, a great bakery department, quirky Mexican products, candies and loads of bargain produce. This is the flagship store; other locations include Burbank, Canoga Park, East L.A., Northridge, Van Nuys, Baldwin Park and Sylmar.

[Vicente Foods] **12027 San Vicente Blvd., Brentwood, 310.472.5215, vicentefoods.com. Daily. AE, MC, V. WHY** Lots of good prepared and deli foods, pretty produce and a butcher that carries four kinds of beef: Kobe, Midwestern prime, certified Black Angus and hormone-free Angus. **WHAT** A family-owned market that's kind of like a small Whole Foods (and Whole Foods is just down the street). It's not cheap, but this ain't a cheap neighborhood, and surely you've earned that sushi and French chocolate! **WHO** Moneyed locals who are happy to pay for the convenience, quality and service.

WINE & SPIRITS

[55 Degrees] **3111 Glendale Blvd., Atwater, 323.662.5556, 55degreewine.com. Daily; tastings Tues.-Sun. AE, MC, V. WHY** A terrific array of Italians and a brick-walled, candlelit basement tasting room that's become the hippest spot in Atwater every night from 5 to 10 p.m. **WHAT** Ali Bignar, owner of Santa Monica's Wine Expo, has a new eastern outpost in gentrifying Atwater, and it immediately became an oenophile hot spot. As in Santa Monica, the specialty is small-producer Italian wines at very low prices; Champagnes are also a focus, and you'll also find some good choices from Spain. **WHO** Young wine buffs from Atwater, Highland Park and Silver Lake.

[Briggs Wine & Spirits] **13038 San Vicente Blvd., Brentwood, 310.395.9997, briggswine.com. Daily. AE, MC, V. WHY** A savvy staff that can lead you to that elusive vintage; alphabetically arranged bottles for those who prefer to snoop around on their own. **WHAT** Briggs is the place to go for that hard-to-find bottle of 2000 Château Haut-Brion — at $750 a pop. Big spenders will feel right at home in this 1940s institution, but there are also some affordable vintages amid the pricey French and California boutique wines. **WHO** Those for whom caviar is an impulse purchase.

[Brixwine] **1601 Pacific Coast Hwy., Hermosa Beach, 310.698.0745, brix1601.com. Closed Sun. AE, MC, V. WHY** A good place to get advice and to find a special bottle for a gift. **WHAT** An offshoot of the high-style Hermosa Beach restaurant brix@1601, this wine shop hosts Monday-night tastings and collaborates with the restaurant on winemaker dinners. It carries a mix of big-name and small-producer choices, with a focus on the mid-range. **WHO** Stylish, beachy young wine lovers.

[Chronicle Wine Shop] **919 E. California Blvd., Pasadena, 626.577.2549, cwcellar.com. Daily. AE, MC, V. WHY** The proximity to Pie 'n Burger adds to the eccentric charm of this wine emporium located in an old motel room. Sommelier Elizabeth Schweitzer knows her stuff but is unpretentious about it. **WHAT** The Chronicle Wine Shop is in a (quirky) world of its own. No high-end tasting room here, but the atmosphere, reminiscent of a plain-jane French cave, makes it worth a trip. When the flag is up on California Boulevard, the staff is in. **WHO** Caterers, party planners and low-key aficionados. 🖼

[Colorado Wine Company] **2114 Colorado Blvd., Eagle Rock, 323.478.1985, cowineco.com. Closed Mon. AE, MC, V. WHY** Fun and surprising wine bargains in an appealing, un-snooty atmosphere, with a great wine bar to boot. **WHAT** The slogan here is "Wine for everyone," and that's refreshingly evident in the large selection of bottles for less than $25 and the tastings, which feature generous pours of four wines for $12. (Bonus: The wine is served with artisanal cheeses from Auntie Em's.) **WHO** Attractive, friendly people in an attractive, friendly space in the newly hip heart of Eagle Rock. 🖼

[Du Vin Wine & Spirits] **540 N. San Vicente Blvd., West Hollywood, 310.855.1161, du-vin.net. Closed Sun. AE, MC, V. WHY** For its selection of French and Italian wines as well as a surprisingly large number of half-bottles. **WHAT** Tucked away behind an office bungalow is a tiny cottage housing Du Vin, a Mecca for lovers of European wines. This is the spot to find a big-ticket gift for a wine aficionado, as well as to snag esoteric varietals and regions that will spark cocktail-party chatter. Picpoul, anyone? There's a nice selection of upscale spirits, too, as well as a handful of gourmet foods. **WHO** Design professionals (it's around the corner from the Blue Whale) and wine lovers from WeHo and nearby Beverly Hills.

[The Duck Blind Fine Wine & Spirits] **1102 Montana Ave., Santa Monica, 310.394.6705, ducksblindwineandspirits.com. Daily. AE, MC, V. WHY** The specials. Sometimes you can luck into a $15 wine for $5. **WHAT** Don't let the outside fool you; what looks like a grungy liquor store is actually a perfectly fine wine shop. Lots of $10 and $15 bottles, plus some good local and international brews. **WHO** Neighborhood loyalists — this place has been around for half a century. 🖼🚚

[Fireside Cellars] **1421 Montana Ave., Santa Monica, 310.393.2888. Daily. AE, MC, V. WHY** Irresistible wine selections for those who know their Alexander Valley from their Languedoc. **WHAT** This tiny shop resembles a cozy home cellar filled with boutique wines, especially those from California and France. Visions of Cakebread and Stag's Leap will have you reaching for the stemware — and your checkbook. It's not that there aren't bargains here — there are some good $12 selections — but the pricier bottles from great wineries are just too

🍃 **VEGETARIAN** 👁 **KID FRIENDLY** ✿ **PATIO DINING** 🚚 **DELIVERY** 🏠 **PRIVATE PARTY** tempting. **WHO** Hybrid-driving, Viognier-drinking, Obama-voting Montana Avenue people.

[Flask Fine Wines] 12194 Ventura Blvd., Studio City, 818.761.5373, flaskfinewines.com. Daily. AE, MC, V. **WHY** A chic tasting bar (Friday nights and Saturday afternoons) and a smart choice of small-producer Californians. **WHAT** Excellent displays and little-seen Californian and French wines make this a fun place to browse. The monthly specials can be very good values. **WHO** Local tasters and producers' assistants who were dispatched to fetch an emergency $250 bottle for a gift.

[Gerlach's Liquor] 1075 S. Fair Oaks Ave., Pasadena, 626.799.1166. Daily. AE, MC, V. **WHY** Great buys on special wines (we've found swell Malbecs for $9), a small but thoughtful selection of French, Calfornian and Oregonian wines, and a terrific choice of port, sherry and dessert wine. **WHAT** It looks like your basic drive-up liquor store, but there's a lot more to Gerlach's than meets the eye. Brothers Lewy and Fred Fedail know their stuff, and they pack a lot of good wines into a small, climate-controlled room. A devoted clientele asks for their advice and takes it. **WHO** Blue-blood Pasadenans, artsy South Pasadenans and working guys picking up a six-pack. 🖙

[K & L Wine Merchants] 1400 Vine St., Hollywood, 323.464.WINE, klwines.com. Daily. AE, MC, V. **WHY** Great location, competitive prices and a parking lot. **WHAT** This terrific wine shop, a branch of the San Francisco Bay Area–based retailer, sits in the shadow of the ArcLight. Offering a superb selection of imported and domestic wines, K & L also boasts a well-edited shelf of single malts, small-batch bourbons, artisanal vodkas and digestifs. **WHO** Collectors who trickle in from the Hollywood Hills and Hancock Park.

[Larchmont Wine & Cheese] 223 N. Larchmont Blvd., Hancock Park, 323.856.8699. Closed Sun. AE, MC, V. **WHY** Savvy wine picks, delicious sandwiches and Michel Cordon Bleu smoked salmon. **WHAT** This almost oppressively tiny shop on Larchmont Boulevard stocks a well-chosen array of bottlings at a fair markup. Wine guy Simon Cocks offers trustworthy advice and doesn't hesitate to steer customers toward the best values (the "wine of the month" is always a good buy). The deli's succulent sandwiches are justifiably renowned. **WHO** Hancock Parkers catching up with each other about kids, vacations and remodelings.

[Los Angeles Wine Co.] 4935 McConnell Ave., West L.A., 310.306.9463, lawineco.com. Daily. AE, MC, V. **WHY** Drink globally, save locally. **WHAT** This warehouse-style merchant has spent years scouring the world for great deals, and it lives up to its motto: "Every wine in stock, always sale priced." Whether seeking a $95 Burgundy for $80 or a $40 Italian Sangiovese for $30, value hunters will appreciate the variety of steals and deals. **WHO** Penny-pinchers come for the Under $12 Club — more than 100 selections, some under $5.

[Mission Liquor] 1785 E. Washington Blvd., Pasadena, 626.797.0500, missionliquors.com. Closed Sun. AE, MC, V. **WHY** For neighborhood-wine-shop service with bigger-store selection; very good roster of spirits and liqueurs, too. **WHAT** Improbably anchoring Pasadena's Armenian Row with an imposing stone front, this 60-year-old liquor store has a bright, welcoming layout, expert advice and a surprisingly deep selection of wines, spirits and mixers. Look for the occasional tastings. **WHO** Wine-savvy Altadenans.

[Mission Wines] 1114 Mission St., South Pasadena, 626.403.9463, missionwines.com. Daily. AE, MC, V. **WHY** It's a nice spot to just hang out around wine. **WHAT** Former Patina sommelier Chris Meeske runs a charming, artisan-style shop that showcases handmade, distinctive bottlings at every price point. Wine education and pairing wine with food are specialties here, and the shop's frequent tastings have become a linchpin of South Pasadena's lively food-and-wine scene. The $10 and under bargains are always good. **WHO** People who wouldn't be caught dead buying wine at TJs.

[Moe's Fine Wines] 11740 San Vicente Blvd., Brentwood, 310.826.4444, moesfinewines.com. Closed Sun. AE, MC, V. **WHY** Wine is more fun than software, so thank you, Moe, for quitting your day job to open this place. **WHAT** Scott "Moe" Levy's high-end neighborhood shop looks like a dream home cellar, with stained-wood wine racks, Riedel stemware and a carefully chosen array of $8 to $800 wines, many from small California producers. Some international heavy-hitters are featured as well, along with delightful house chocolates and nuts. **WHO** Well-heeled Brentwood regulars, many of whom stop by for the Saturday-afternoon tastings.

[Off the Vine] 491 6th St., San Pedro, 310.831.1551, offthevinewines. com. Closed Mon. AE, MC, V. **WHY** Tasty, good-value bottles from the Santa Ynez Valley and the northern and southern Rhône. **WHAT** The selection is small at this tidy little shop, but it's creative and includes some very good monthly specials for less than $13. The focus is on just three regions: California's Central Coast, the Rhône and Spain. Regulars stop by for the Friday- and Saturday-night tastings.

[Palate Food & Wine] 933 S. Brand Blvd., Glendale, 818.662.9463, palatefoodwine.com. Daily. AE, MC, V. **WHY** For an international (and local) selection of superb wines, chosen and sold by people who are brimming with enthusiasm. **WHAT** Behind the happening restaurant Palate is a retail wine shop run by sommelier Steve Goldun, who has amassed a reasonably priced collection of carefully made wines from California and around the world. For your next party, consider a wine

VEGETARIAN ○ KID FRIENDLY ○ PATIO DINING ⊜ DELIVERY ⚑ PRIVATE PARTY and cheese tasting held at the cocktail tables between the wine shop and the restaurant's cheese cellar. **WHO** Eastside oenophiles who like to try new things and hang out for a while to talk about wine. 🍷

[Red Carpet] **400 E. Glenoaks Blvd., Glendale, 818.247.5544, redcarpetwine.com. Daily. AE, MC, V. WHY** For an impressive array of hard-to-find California bottlings. **WHAT** If Red Carpet doesn't carry it, you'll probably have to trek to the westside to find it. Staffed by enthusiasts, this venerable shop offers a vast selection of wine, beer and premium spirits, as well as cigars and stemware. The tasting bar is a popular hangout on weekends and Tuesday evenings. **WHO** Collectors who don't mind paying a few bucks more for good service.

[Rosso Wine Shop] **3459 N. Verdugo Rd., Glendale, 818.330.9130, rossowineshop.com. Closed Mon. AE, MC, V. WHY** To discover obscure vintners your tasting buddies haven't heard of. **WHAT** Tiny Rosso doesn't try to compete with the big guys; instead, owner Jeff Zimmitti focuses on France, Spain, Italy and California, selecting the best-value wines that go well with food. The result is a user-friendly shop that's a great addition to north Glendale's burgeoning "gourmet gulch" on Verdugo Road. Pick up a bottle here to enjoy with a very good dinner at Bashan next door. **WHO** A younger breed of collector and enthusiast.

[Silverlake Wine] 🔒 **2395 Glendale Blvd., Silver Lake, 323.662.9024, silverlakewine.com. Daily. AE, MC, V. WHY** Well-chosen selection at every price point. **WHAT** This female-friendly, no-attitude wine shop showcases small-production, artisanal wines from all over the world. And sometimes the best wine for your occasion might be a Pacific Northwest microbrew, or even a handmade sake. Tastings are happening events; Monday brings wines paired with cheeses from the Cheese Store of Silverlake, and on Thursday nights, the Let's Be Frank truck parks out front. If when you read this they're still organizing the Friday-night wine-tasting-and-tour of the Hollyhock House in Los Feliz, by all means join the fun. **WHO** Silver Lake hipsters, but the unhip are welcome, too.

[Topline Wine Company] **4718 San Fernando Rd., Glendale, 818.500.9670. Daily. AE, MC, V. WHY** Premium wine and spirits at not-so-premium prices. **WHAT** This no-frills shop in an industrial section of Glendale has a decent wine selection at very competitive prices. It's arranged warehouse-style, with stacks of cases, and it's worth poking through the boxes to find the buried treasures. Also check out the spirits room and the particularly good selection of aperitifs. **WHO** Price-conscious wine aficionados from all over.

[Wally's] 🔒 **2107 Westwood Blvd., Westwood, 310.475.0606, wallywine.com. Daily. AE, MC, V. WHY** For the phenomenal selection of hard-to-find trophy wines. **WHAT** Steve Wallace founded his West Los Angeles wine shop in 1968 and despite cramped quarters has built it into one of California's leading wine retailers. This is the spot to find rare and small-production bottlings from Napa, Burgundy, Bordeaux and other fine wine regions. Partner Christian Navarro handles the care and feeding of the shop's stable of heavy-hitting collectors. **WHO** Studio bigwigs, UCLA professors, Brentwood matrons.

[The Wine Country] **2301 Redondo Ave., Signal Hill, 562.597.8303, thewinecountry.com. Daily. AE, MC, V. WHY** Stuff you won't easily find anywhere else. **WHAT** Owner Randy Kemner has long championed offbeat varietals, off-the-beaten-track wine regions and underappreciated importers. The result is a shop with an eclectic array of wines selected for their ability to complement food, with particular strength in aromatic whites, including German, Austrian and Alsatian bottlings. **WHO** South Bay enthusiasts of ABC — "anything but Chardonnay."

[Wine Expo] 🍾 **2933 Santa Monica Blvd., Santa Monica, 310.828.4428, wineexpo.com. Daily. AE, MC, V. WHY** Educated and refreshingly honest staff members, who also know their way around tequila and beer. **WHAT** Wine Expo started life as a champagne specialty shop and has evolved into the westside's go-to source for Italian wines. Owners Ali Biglar and Robert Rogness cultivate great relationships with Italian winemakers and ship back via their own import business to keep prices low. Almost as entertaining as the vast selection of wines are the clever descriptions posted by the cases. Ditto the newsletter, which is a hoot. **WHO** Fans of *vino italiano*. 📧

[Wine House] 🍾 **2311 Cotner Ave., West L.A., 310.479.3731 or 800.626.9463, wineaccess.com/store/winehouse. Daily. AE, MC, V. WHY** For 18,000 square feet devoted to wine, beer and spirits. **WHAT** Arguably the best wine shop in Los Angeles, the Wine House has it all: great selection, good prices, informed staff and even a little gourmet food section, so you can get a tin of caviar to go with that magnum of Cristal. A year-round program of classes offers an easy way to improve your tasting skills and expertise. Also check out the cool automated tasting bar at the center of the store. **WHO** Wine buffs from all over Southern California.

[Woodland Hills Wine Company] 🍾 **22622 Ventura Blvd., Woodland Hills, 818.222.1111 or 800.678.WINE, whwc.com. Daily. AE, MC, V. WHY** It's all about the Burgs. **WHAT** A connoisseur's mecca, Woodland Hills Wine specializes in (sigh) Burgundies, but the selection of top wines from California, Bordeaux, the Rhône, Italy, Austria and Spain is worth the drive to the West Valley. Woodland Hills also direct-imports many hard-to-find bottlings, including some bargains. Staffers are highly knowledgeable and give good counsel. **WHO** Serious collectors as well as wine newbies.

🍃 VEGETARIAN ☺ KID FRIENDLY ✧ PATIO DINING 🚗 DELIVERY 🎪 PRIVATE PARTY

Services + Events

Need a caterer? Want to get lunch delivered or find an organic-produce service? Keen to bone up on your baking skills? Looking for a fun food festival? We're here to help.

[ESSENTIALLY L.A.]

[CATERERS]
Along Came Mary (PAGE 332)
Angeli Caffé Catering (PAGE 332)
Auntie Em's Kitchen (PAGE 333)
Border Grill & Ciudad Catering (PAGE 333)
Brent's Delicatessen (PAGE 334)
Clementine (PAGE 334)
Jennie Cook's (PAGE 336)
Lety's Catering Service (PAGE 337)
Lucques Catering (PAGE 337)
Pie 'n' Burger (PAGE 338)
Wolfgang Puck Catering (PAGE 339)

[COOKING SCHOOLS]
Epicurean School of Culinary Arts (PAGE 340)
New School of Cooking (PAGE 341)

[DELIVERY SERVICES]
Tierra Miguel Foundation (PAGE 343)

[FESTIVALS]
American Wine & Food Festival (PAGE 343)
California Avocado Festival (PAGE 344)
Indio International Tamale Festival (PAGE 345)
L.A. County Fair (PAGE 345)
Taste of the Nation L.A. (PAGE 347)

[KNIFE SHARPENERS]
Ross Cutlery (PAGE 348)

🏛 ESSENTIALLY L.A. ☺ LATE ♥ ROMANTIC 💲 VALUE 🔇 QUIET ♻ SUSTAINABLE

**A GREAT MANY RESTAURANTS CATER.
HERE ARE JUST A FEW TO CONSIDER:**

Bottega Louie, Downtown (PAGE 66)

Carnival, Sherman Oaks (PAGE 105)

Chichen Itza, Downtown (PAGE 67)

George's Greek Café, Long Beach (PAGE 151)

Gingergrass, Silver Lake (PAGE 72)

Koutoubia, Westwood (PAGE 120)

La Huasteca, Lynwood (PAGE 154)

La Serenata de Garibaldi, East L.A. (PAGE 74)

Loteria Grill, Hollywood (PAGE 52)

M Café de Chaya, Melrose & Culver City (PAGES 53 & 121)

Minestraio Trattoria, Beverly/Third (PAGE 54)

Typhoon, Santa Monica (PAGE 143)

Woodlands, Artesia & Chatsworth (PAGES 116 & 159)

Yxta Cocina Mexicana, Downtown (PAGE 81)

Zeke's Smokehouse, Montrose (PAGE 104)

NOT MANY RESTAURANTS DELIVER, BUT THESE DO!

Antica Pizzeria, Marina del Rey (PAGE 126)

Baby Blues BBQ, Venice (PAGE 248)

Bulan Thai Vegetarian, Melrose & Silver Lake (PAGES 44 & 66)

Café Flore, Beverly Hills (PAGE 193)

Chaba Thai Bay Grill, Redondo Beach (PAGE 148)

Cheebo, Hollywood (PAGE 45)

Green Street Restaurant, Pasadena (PAGE 187)

Holy Cow Indian Express, Beverly/Third (PAGE 49)

Javan, West L.A. (PAGE 134)

Luna Park, Mirale Mile (PAGE 53)

Mae Ploy, Echo Park (PAGE 75)

Mediterranean Delight, Glendale (PAGE 239)

Pitfire Pizza Co., Downtown & North Hollywood (PAGES 234 & 242)

Porky's BBQ, Long Beach (PAGE 256)

Press Panini, Studio City (PAGE 243)

Rambutan Thai, Silver Lake (PAGE 78)

Real Food Daily, W. Hollywood & Santa Monica (PAGES 140 & 270)

Shekarchi, South Park/Fashion District (PAGE 187)

Swan Restaurant, North Hollywood (PAGE 110)

🌿 VEGETARIAN ◎ KID FRIENDLY ☼ PATIO DINING 🚐 DELIVERY 🏠 PRIVATE PARTY

CATERERS

[Alligator Pear Catering] **818.347.7860, alligatorpearcatering.
com. WHY** Careful service and very good food. **WHAT** Abi Chilton's
serene, easygoing personality comes through in the events, large and
small, that her company caters. Everything is taken care of, and the
modern American/Mediterranean food is delicious. Lots of good vegetarian recipes in the repertoire, too. **WHO** Academy of Motion Picture
Arts & Sciences, USC, AFI, UCLA Anderson School, the Family
Channel and other media companies.

[Along Came Mary] **323.931.9082, alongcamemary.com.
WHY** When it's not just a party you're throwing, but a production
— and a lavish, meticulously staged, high-budget production at that.
WHAT L.A.'s most famous caterer is known for extravaganzas that
give new meaning to the word "extravaganza." If you're having 500
for your daughter's Super Sweet 16 or 1,000 for your film premiere,
Mary's the one to call. **WHO** The Oscars, the Grammys, MTV, all the
studios and a bunch of really rich people.

[Alyson Cook Gourmet Foods & Catered Events]
626.791.9757, alysoncookgourmet.com. WHY Very good food, ranging
from modern American classics to Indian and Thai dishes.
WHAT Cook is a longtime L.A. caterer who was classically trained in
Europe and worked as a private chef for such folks as Carol Burnett
and the Queen Mum. Now based in Pasadena, she's on the faculty at
the California School of Culinary Arts and runs a solidly professional
catering business that does weddings, dinner parties and the usual
shindigs.

[Angeli Caffé Catering] **7274 Melrose Ave., Melrose,
323.936.9086, angelicaffe.com. WHY** Deeply satisfying rustic cooking at prices that might inspire you to entertain more. **WHAT** Evan
Kleiman and her trattoria, Angeli, are known for irresistible Italian
fare — small pizzas, bruschetta, frittura mista, roast chicken — but
the catering operation can go beyond Italian to do Provençal, Indian,
American, even Irish food. The universal theme is a homey rusticity
and robust flavors. **WHO** A longstanding and loyal clientele of production companies, studios and hip L.A. businesses.

[Atmosphere] **818.914.4179, atmospherecatering.com. WHY** From
high-profile corporate dining to candlelight dinners for two — atmosphere's repeat client list pretty much tells the tale: You provide
the cause, atmosphere will provide the célébrée. **WHAT** French-born
and French-trained chef Nicolas Rolland partners in the kitchen with
German-born chef Erik Fischer, trained in classic French and German
cuisine. Their exquisite food will have you poking around the kitchen
well before your guests arrive. Dana Rolland, with a background in PR

and restaurant management, maintains a robust client list and oversees the atmosphere for which the company is famed (to say nothing of named).

[Auntie Em's Kitchen Catering] 🔒 **4616 Eagle Rock Blvd., Eagle Rock, 323.663.8688, auntieemscatering.com. WHY** Outstanding modern American party food, as organic as possible, with particularly memorable desserts. **WHAT** Before she opened her oh-so-hip bakery, café and store, Terri Wahl was a caterer specializing in production shoots. Nowadays she also feeds the cognoscenti at commitment ceremonies, 50th-birthday celebrations and publication parties all over the L.A. area. **WHO** Party-throwing Occidental professors, Silver Lake graphic designers, Highland Park gentrifiers and even Malibu wedding planners. 🔹🔍

[Baked It Myself] **14543 Erwin St., Van Nuys, 818.787.0601, bakeditmyself.com. WHY** For delicious, reasonably priced catered lunches for business meetings, script readings or production shoots; they do good dinner parties and showers, too. **WHAT** Cheryl Canter-Valesella first found success with cakes and desserts at her wholesale and retail bakery operation. But she doesn't just bake, and eventually she found herself in demand at studios and production companies for catered meals. Now her catering kitchen doubles as a cheerful lunch café during week, and she does private dinners in her kitchen at night. **WHO** Showtime, Variety, Warner Brothers, DreamWorks and many other Hollywood companies.

[Boneyard Bistro] **13539 Ventura Blvd., Sherman Oaks, 818.906.7427, boneyardbistro.com. Barbecue/American. WHY** These guys make damn good barbecue and damn fine party food. **WHAT** This Sherman Oaks restaurant has a thriving catering business as well. Chef Aaron Robins combines traditional, people-pleasing barbecue with a more modern approach to service and sides — so instead of generic cole slaw, with your ribs you can have such things as fire-roasted artichokes with ceviche, a vegetarian falafel salad and Thai-spiced crispy calamari.

[Border Grill & Cuidad Catering] 🔒 **445 S. Figueroa St., Downtown, 213.542.1102, marysueandsusan.com. WHY** For vividly flavorful food that's full of L.A. style, with good party management to boot — and if you want something funkier, they'll send their new taco truck. **WHAT** Mary Sue Milliken and Susan Feniger have been L.A.'s culinary divas since they founded City in the '80s; their Border Grill and Ciudad restaurants are both showcases of modern California-Latin cooking. From the margaritas to the ceviche tostaditas and legendary guacamole, this is great party fare. **WHO** Downtown offices, Santa Monica production studios and north of Montana homeowners. 🔹🔍

Services + Events

🔹 **VEGETARIAN** ⊙ **KID FRIENDLY** ☼ **PATIO DINING** 🚐 **DELIVERY** 🏠 **PRIVATE PARTY**

[Brent's Delicatessen] 🔒 **19565 Parthenia St., Northridge, 818.886.5679, brentsdeli.com. WHY** Very good deli, delivered anywhere in the greater L.A. area. **WHAT** Brent's fleet of vans scurry around the Valley and the L.A. side of the Santa Monicas every day, delivering trays of deli sandwiches, smoked fish, raw veggies and lemon bars to offices, schools and home gatherings. Lean meats, fresh breads, pretty fruit plates and a memorable whitefish salad, all at fair prices. **WHO** Deli fans who need to feed a group for a meeting, a bridge party or a memorial.

[Buckboard Catering Co.] **1386 E. Foothill Blvd., Upland, 909.608.7393, buckboardcatering.com. WHY** For authentic, crowd-pleasing Santa Maria barbecue, cooked at your site. **WHAT** Some parties demand the social consciousness of vegan cooking. Others cry out for the aroma of slow-grilled hunks o' meat. Buckboard puts on a very good traditional Central Coast barbecue, with tri-tip, beef ribs, chicken and the trimmings (cole slaw, pinquito beans, white bread rolls). Very nice people bring the wagon-wheel grill to your site and take care of everything for a modest price. **WHO** Mostly businesses and families from the San Bernandino area, but Buckboard will travel west into Pasadena and L.A. 📷

[Caramelized Productions] **954.599.6990. WHY** Fabulous food (especially for carnivores) and personal attention for a memorable wedding — if you are lucky enough to get on these boys' busy calendar. **WHAT** Vinny Dotolo and Jon Shook had their first 15 minutes as stars of 2 Dudes Catering on the Food Network, and now they're enjoying their second bout of fame as the proprietors of the happening restaurant Animal. In their spare time, they're also the hottest wedding caterers in town. They have neither a web site nor a marketing operation; it's all word of mouth, and they're booked a year in advance. **WHO** Actors, artists and people cool enough to book these dudes.

[Clementine] 🔒 **1751 Ensley Ave., West L.A., 310.552.1080, clementineonline.com. WHY** For Annie Miler's deeply comforting comfort food and her fabulous desserts. In fact, consider making your next event a Clementine dessert party. **WHAT** Workplace breakfasts and lunches are the specialty of this café/gourmet-to-go/catering operation run by chef Annie Miler, who worked at Campanile and Spago before finding success on her own. Her team can also cater a swell dinner party, but they'll contract out the serving staff. Particularly good for smaller parties that don't require full party management.

[Dickenson West Fine Catering] **181 E. Glenarm, Pasadena, 626.799.5252, dickensonwest.com. WHY** It's Pasadena's leading high-end caterer. **WHAT** Derek Dickenson and his team put on the finest weddings, benefits and 50th-birthday dinners in Pasadena, in addition to running a romantic restaurant. The French-California food is as delicious as it is elegant (and expensive), and Dickenson is particularly adept at managing the details and making sure everything looks beautiful. **WHO** San Marino couples throwing swank anniversary parties and old-line Pasadena businesses entertaining clients.

[Elements Kitchen] 107 S. Fair Oaks Ave., Pasadena, 626.440.0100, elementskitchen.com. **WHY** For inventive (but not too risky) food and good party management. **WHAT** Pasadena's got a hip new caterer (and café) in town, whose food combines the comfort of American classics with lots of Asian and Latin influences. So passed dishes might include Vietnamese-style beef skewers with chile and lemongrass as well as Italian-style caprese skewers with fresh mozzarella. Good for dinner parties and mid-size shindigs. **WHO** The kind of eastsiders who'd throw a wedding at the Pacific Asia Museum or a bar mitzvah at the Pasadena Museum of California Art.

[Food Art Events] 310.482.6986, foodartgroup.com. AE, MC, V. **WHY** A-list food for A-list events, prepared and served in a sustainable manner. **WHAT** A partnership between chef David Myers (Sona, Comme Ça), chef Jerry Baker (City Cuisine Catering) and events planner Chris Baker, Food Art takes party food beyond sliders and bruschetta. They're doing some of L.A.'s best weddings and premieres these days, and they're doing it green: vehicles run on biodiesel, disposable goods are compostable, and foods are local and organic as much as possible.

[Food Inc.] 310.457.2444, boldmultimedia.com/portfolio/foodinc/home. htm. **WHY** When you're ready to party like a rock star. **WHAT** Claudia Taylor specializes in big bashes — not just chic party food, but also art direction, live and DJ music, entertainers, parking, the whole shebang. **WHO** Record labels, movie studios, Cirque du Soleil, big companies and Malibu brides.

[Gallegos Mexican Deli] 12470 Venice Blvd., Mar Vista, 310.391.2587, gallegosmexicandeli.com. Mexican. **WHY** Delicious and affordable tamales, enchiladas, chile verde and other Mexican classics. **WHAT** The Gallegos family has been feeding Angelenos well for generations. If you're really on a budget, you can pick up trays of tamales, carnitas, beans and salsa from the deli, or if you can spend a little more, they'll bring everything to you and handle the service and clean up. Make sure to get some of their peach empanadas for dessert.

[Good Gracious Events] 323.954.2277, goodgraciousevents.com. **WHY** One of L.A.'s most prestigious caterers, known for staging mega events. **WHAT** High-end parties put on by Good Gracious routinely end up in swank magazines, and it counts many celebrities and corporations on its returning-customer list. Lavish weddings, fashion events, awards ceremonies and launch parties are specialties.

Services + Events

VEGETARIAN ◎ KID FRIENDLY ✿ PATIO DINING ➡ DELIVERY 🍴 PRIVATE PARTY

WHO The kind of big-time players who want to see artist renderings of their events before they happen.

[Green Truck] **310.204.0477, greentruckonthego.com. Vegetarian/ modern American. AE, MC, V. WHY** Fresh, organic salads, soups, wraps and sandwiches, served on-site for parties, shoots and meetings. **WHAT** This sustainable twist on the roach coach not only parks at different spots in L.A. each weekday, but it also caters. Not to worry about greenhouse gases — your ahi poke tacos, vegan sesame-tofu wraps and sweet potato fries will arrive via a truck running on re-cycled vegetable oil. Great for casual outdoor functions, especially if your guests will be hemp-wearing vegetarians. ☻☙

[Happy Trails Catering] **207 S. Fair Oaks Ave., Pasadena, 626.796.9526, happytrailscatering.com. WHY** For a lovely and rea-sonably priced in-their-garden wedding or garden party, as well as carry-out platters of comforting modern American food (grilled tri-tip, white-bean chicken chili, Southern fried chicken salad) for all sorts of events. **WHAT** Many a wedding has been held in this secret garden behind a brick storefront on the south end of Old Pasadena. Groups of up to 200 can celebrate under the massive old camphor tree; during the week, the garden is a lovely spot for lunch. **WHO** Brides from all over L.A., as well as Pasadena folks who need good food for a graduation party, anniversary or memorial. ▦

[Jennie Cook's] ⌂ **323.982.0052, jenniecooks.com. WHY** For richly flavorful and sustainably produced modern comfort food — for vegans and carnivores alike — at moderate prices. Ask about dinner parties in her kitchen. **WHAT** Jennie Cook's homey style of cooking suits her Pennsylvania Dutch roots — but the surprise is the commitment to sustainability and health. Her kitchen turns out great briskets and bacon-wrapped dates as well as sophisticated vegan and vegetarian dishes, and she's made a serious commitment to use local and organic goods, to recycle and to run an environmentally responsible busi-ness. Moderate prices, reliably good service. **WHO** Brides, bar and bat mitzvah celebrants, film-shoot producers and opening-night party throwers. ▦☻☙

[Joan's on Third] **8350 W. 3rd St., Beverly/Third, 323.655.2285, joansonthird.com. WHY** For a pick-up or delivery dinner for 12 or a full-service catered affair for 120, with equally good modern American cooking. **WHAT** Joan McNamara started as a caterer and opened a companion café some years ago; the café and gourmet-to-go operation is now hugely popular. Her team's food and style work well for sit-down dinner parties and mid-size weddings; they also do a lot of delivered-food catering for business meetings, office lunches and photo and commercial shoots. Good order-in-advance box lunches.

[Junior's] **2379 Westwood Blvd., Westwood, 310.475.5771, jrsdeli. com. WHY** Deli platters for a meeting or a full-service spread for a party or, God forbid, a memorial. **WHAT** A 50-year-old Westwood landmark, Junior's is the best westside deli and a reliable source for deli catering, from pick-up orders to full-service events. **WHO** Westside Jewish families preparing to feed a crowd after a bris or a funeral.

[The Kitchen for Exploring Foods] **1434 W. Colorado Blvd., Pasadena, 626.793.7218, thekitchen.net. WHY** Excellent food stations for large parties, as well as the full range of party services — and great gourmet-to-go goodies for that last-minute dinner party. **WHAT** If you've ever attended a big wedding, fundraiser or celebratory shindig in Pasadena and environs, you're likely to have enjoyed Peggy Dark's food. Her long-established firm, which has also catered many a Hancock Park and Los Feliz event, does a consistently good job, and the gourmet-to-go section is ideal for smaller parties. The menu is particularly strong in Mediterranean cooking. **WHO** Everyone who's anyone in Pasadena and the eastside. 🌿

[Lety's Catering Service] 🔒 **323.240.4719. Mexican. WHY** For made-to-order tacos, the hit of any party. **WHAT** L.A. has dozens of "taco ladies," but most are under-the-table businesses. Lety's is bigger than most, but not so big as to be inauthentic or overpriced. They'll send a taco lady (or taco guy) who will set up a great salsa bar and all the fixings (rice, beans, cilantro, onions) and will grill chicken, carne asade and al pastor on site, for a mere $6 a head. **WHO** Savvy entertainers on a budget. 🚚😊

[Lucky Leaf Food] **818.448.4810, luckyleaffood.com. WHY** Hand-crafted party food — Wolff even makes the ice cream himself — culled mostly from farmers' markets and organic purveyors. **WHAT** Brian Wolff is chef de cuisine at Lucques, so he's a busy and talented guy, but he still finds time to work with his wife Natalie to cater everything from backyard barbecues to boat christenings. Their style is intensely personal — as an architect would do before building you a house, they'll interview you before planning a party to get a handle on your style, personality and preferences. ✿

[Lucques Catering] 🔒 **323.246.0978, lucques.com. AE, MC, V. WHY** If you've always yearned to recreate Lucques's Sunday suppers in your own home, down to the little table setups of olives, bread, butter and fleur de sel. **WHAT** Run by Suzanne Goin's sister, Jessica, the catering arm of the Lucques empire handles everything from intimate birthday dinners to large events, including flower arrangements and wine if you like. Professional and thorough, the staff (including a Lucques chef) leaves your house as they found it. **WHO** Cal-Med seasonal aficionados with extra cash in their pockets. Not cheap, but not the end of the world either — you get what you pay for.

🌿 VEGETARIAN ⊙ KID FRIENDLY ✿ PATIO DINING 🚚 DELIVERY 🎩 PRIVATE PARTY

[Marmalade] 710 Montana Ave., Santa Monica, 310.828.3808, marmaladecafe.com. Modern American. **WHY** For a highly experienced, professional catering operation that isn't over-the-top expensive. **WHAT** Marmalade was once a friendly little gourmet-to-go and catering operation in Santa Monica, and now it's a rapidly growing corporate enterprise. So you won't get the personal service of years past, but you will get a well-tuned operation and crowd-pleasing Italian-French-California food. You can also order smaller-party platters to pick up from this branch or any of the others, which include Malibu, the Grove, Sherman Oaks, Rolling Hills Estates and Westlake Village.

[Papa Cristo's] 2771 W. Pico Blvd., Mid-City, 323.737.2970, papacristo.com. Greek. **WHY** Fun Greek party food at low prices: spanakopita, baba ganouj, kebabs, gyros, roast lamb and lots more. It ranges from pick-up platters to full-service catering. **WHAT** This landmark Greek market and restaurant is also a fine and affordable caterer; you can pick up smaller orders or get larger ones delivered. It puts together platters of mini-kebabs, spanakopita, hummus, lamb chops, baklava and all the standards, and will also set up a fun gyros bar ($200 for 20 people) or do a whole roasted lamb for a party. **WHO** Party-throwers on a budget who are tired of tacos and barbecue. 🗊🍖

[Patina Catering] 213.239.2508, patinagroup.com/catering. **WHY** For an A-list event at Disney Hall, Descanso Gardens, LACMA or one of the other prime locations for which Patina is the exclusive caterer. **WHAT** High-end corporate, society and Hollywood events, held at in-demand venues like MOCA or at your Hancock Park mini-mansion, are Patina's specialties. Crackerjack service, elegant French-California fare and not-insignificant prices. **WHO** USC, Center Theatre Group, L.A. Opera, Buena Vista Pictures and other luminaries in the arts, education and business.

[Pie 'n' Burger] 🏠 913 E. California Blvd., Pasadena, 626.795.1123, pienburger.com. American. **WHY** Cheeseburgers and peach pie with vanilla ice cream. **WHAT** Want to make your guests happy without spending a fortune? Serve them burgers and pie from Pie 'n' Burger, Pasadena's revered diner. It caters for parties of 50 or more, either burgers and pie or barbecue chicken and tri-tip and pie, with the usual trimmings (including ice cream for the pie). **WHO** Pasadenans with means who want to keep it casual. 🗊☺

[Versailles] 10319 Venice Blvd., Culver City, 310.558.3168, versailles-cuban.com. **WHY** Garlic roast chicken, Cuban roast pork and all the fixings, all of which makes for festive and inexpensive party food. **WHAT** Although it doesn't have a catering operation, this mini-chain is popular with on-a-budget party throwers for quantity takeout. A few orders of the famous marinated roast chicken, a few orders of the salty roast pork, some plantains, and a couple of quarts of black beans and white rice, and you're making your friends very happy. Branches on South La Cienega and in Encino and Manhattan Beach.

[Wolfgang Puck Catering] 🔒 **866.491.1270, wolfgangpuckcatering.com. WHY** For the celebrity caché, of course, but also because Puck remains the standard-bearer in modern American cooking. **WHAT** L.A.'s original celebrity chef is now a national superstar, with restaurants, airport cafés and catering operations from coast to coast. His food is universally appealing, and the entire operation is completely professional. It's no bargain, but no one expects it to be. **WHO** A-list wedding planners, A-list corporations and, of course, the Governor's Ball after the Oscars.

COOKING SCHOOLS

[A & J Cake & Candy Supplies] **2254 Rte. 66, Glendora, 626.335.7747, ajcake.com. Closed Sun. AE, MC, V. WHY** Who wouldn't want to learn how to make cluster candies, chocolate pizzas or marshmallow buddies? **WHAT** From the front this strip-mall place on a lost stretch of Route 66 looks like nothing more than a place to buy candy molds, and in fact it is an excellent supply house for bakers and candy makers. But a lot more goes on behind those doors: classes in candy and cake making, for the novice to the moderately experienced. Free candy-making demonstrations happen twice a month, and if you like what you see, you can sign up to learn how to make your own bonbons. The cake-decorating and fondant-making classes are also very popular. **WHO** Gaggles of middle-aged women friends, and moms with their teenage daughters. ☺

[Art Institute of California] **2900 31st St., Santa Monica, 310.752.4700, artinstitutes.edu/losangeles. WHY** A career-oriented program for aspiring professional cooks. **WHAT** This national chain of schools that provides professional training in the glamour careers — design, media arts, fashion and food — has a culinary school in Santa Monica. It offers associate and bachelor's degrees in culinary arts, culinary management and baking and pastry. These are full-time, expensive programs intended to launch a career.

[California School of Culinary Arts] **521 E. Green St., Pasadena, 626.229.1300, csca.edu. WHY** To get a professional culinary education without having to move to Hyde Park or Paris. **WHAT** First taking root in a small South Pasadena space, this school has grown faster than it can keep up with — it's sprawled over Pasadena (you see its uniformed student chefs everywhere) and most recently took over the former Kitchen Academy space next to the Arclight in Hollywood. This is a demanding school that's affiliated with Le Cordon Bleu and is geared toward the full-time student seeking degrees in culinary arts, patisserie and management. The only part-time program is for patis-

Services + Events

🍃 VEGETARIAN ☺ KID FRIENDLY ✿ PATIO DINING 🚙 DELIVERY 🎩 PRIVATE PARTY

serie and baking. **WHO** A mix of right-out-of-high-school kids and midlife career-changers.

[Chefmakers] **865 Swarthmore Ave., Pacific Palisades, 310.459.9444, chefmakersonline.com.** **WHY** Particularly good classes in baking, as well as a well-rounded learn-how-to-cook series and lots of programs for kids and teens. **WHAT** With a large crew of professional instructors, including occasional celebrity-chef visiting teachers like Neal Fraser of Grace, this is a good resource for far-westside food lovers. And there's a well-stocked kitchen store, so you can take home one of those knives you just learned how to use. ☺

[Chefs, Inc.] **10955 W. Pico Blvd., Cheviot Hills, 310.470.2277, chefsinc.net.** **WHY** A good, all-around cooking school with particularly worthwhile classes for teens, workshops with some of L.A.'s top restaurant chefs and summer camps for kids. **WHAT** Leslie McKenna cooked at Valentino, was a private chef for celebrities and now runs an all-around cooking school on the westside. Her kitchens are roomy and well equipped but have a homey warmth that will make non-pros feel at ease. It's a great place to hold a party, team-building event or teen party, and the classes range from the very basics for home cooks to serious training for future pastry chefs. **WHO** Kids, teens, groups of friends and more serious chefs in the professional programs. ☺

[Chez Cherie] **1401 Foothill Blvd., La Cañada, 818.952.7217, chezcherie.com.** **WHY** Trader Joe's cooking classes. **WHAT** This small school has a number of good classes, from knife skills to cooking basics, but what owner Cherie Twohy is best known for are her single-session classes in making the most of Trader Joe's products. These $55 classes are fun and full of great pointers and ideas. **WHO** La Cañada and Pasadena moms.

[Epicurean School of Culinary Arts] 🏛 **8500 Melrose Ave., West Hollywood, 310.659.5990, epicureanschool.com.** **WHY** Excellent facilities, 25 years of experience and some really fun workshops. **WHAT** The focus here is split between serious professional training and terrific, and terrifically fun, workshops: Beer Blast, Planet Organics, Ole Mole and more. The workshops reflect current trends and styles (including sustainability) but aren't faddishly trendy. **WHO** A mix of aspiring professionals and people who just love to cook — or want to learn to love to cook. 🍃

[Glendale Community College] **1500 N. Verdugo Rd., Glendale, 818.240.1000, glendale.edu/technology/culinaryarts.** **WHY** An extensive and affordable program offering certificates in culinary arts and restaurant management. **WHAT** Go ahead and spend $45K for a year at a fancy cooking school — or consider the professional program at Glendale College. It has wicked awesome kitchens, an accomplished faculty, a student-run white-tablecloth dining room and a practical, get-a-job focus.

[Hipcooks] **642 Moulton Ave., Lincoln Heights, 323.222.3663, hip-cooks.com. WHY** Casual, convivial, downright fun classes that end in a meal and are designed to help regular people learn to throw something delicious together without freaking out. **WHAT** Monika Reti is as much a therapist as a cooking teacher, giving planning advice and getting people to shed their inhibitions (and terror) about cooking for a date, throwing a dinner party or even following a recipe. Now that her newish, home-style classes/parties have become wildly popular, she's hired more teachers, expanded to a westside location on Robertson, and opened a branch in Portland. Classes end with a sit-down dinner with wine, making them a bargain at $55 a person ($65 on Robertson). Topics include a Romantic Dinner for Two, Tapas, Sushi and My Big Fat Greek Cooking Class. Great for a party of friends. **WHO** Couples, singles and birthday-party groups.

[Michael's Table] **1121 Hill St., Santa Monica, 310.450.5667, michaelstable.com. WHY** An advocate for sustainable living, are you? Then pull your chair up to Michael's table and begin by sustaining yourself. **WHAT** Michael Sieverts has consulted with Alice Waters and worked at Moosewood Restaurant, known for its best-selling vegetarian cookbooks. For Sieverts, it's all about the joy of cooking spectacular meals with local ingredients — whether it swam the seas, trod the pasture or grew in the field, he knows where it came from, and he'll teach you where to find it. Take all the notes you like, but he is the only one wielding a knife. This is demonstration cooking at its most blissful: With skill, joy, and sly humor, Sieverts cooks, and everyone eats together. **WHO** Anyone interested in cooking and local food foraging techniques that support eating for pleasure and immune-system-enhancing health.

[New School of Cooking] **8690 Washington Blvd., Culver City, 310.842.9702, newschoolofcooking.com. WHY** One of the best consum-er-oriented cooking-school programs in Southern California, with an underlying love of food and a general joie de vivre. Good summer kid and teen programs, too. **WHAT** Well established and very well run, the New School has a mouthwatering roster of classes for both the ama-teur and professional: Izakaya: Japanese Small Plates; Essential Knife Skills; Summer in Provence; Yeast Breads and the all-important class in Cupcakes. Acclaimed Thai-cuisine teacher Jet Tila is on the faculty, as are several other accomplished cooks and bakers.

VEGETARIAN ◎ KID FRIENDLY ✿ PATIO DINING 🚐 DELIVERY 🎩 PRIVATE PARTY

[Sushi Chef Institute] **222 S. Hewitt St., Little Tokyo/Arts District, 213.617.6825, sushischool.net. WHY** For a rigorous and rewarding approach to making sushi run by master chef Andy Matsuda. **WHAT** Chef Andy Matsuda is a highly regarded sushi master and teacher, and he and his team of chef/teachers run an excellent program. The core of the school is a professional program for aspiring full-time sushi chefs; it also offers short-term intensive workshops in things like being a sake sommelier. Private sushi-making lessons are also available. **WHO** A multicultural mix, mostly of in-training or skills-updating professionals but also of avid amateurs.

DELIVERY SERVICES

[Auntie Em's Organic Produce and Dinner Delivery] **4616 Eagle Rock Blvd., Eagle Rock, 323.255.0800, auntieemsdelivery.com. AE, MC, V. WHY** A great option for organic produce delivery for those who aren't lucky enough to score a farm share. **WHAT** Terri Wahl and her food-obsessed team at Auntie Em's cruise several weekly farmers' markets on behalf of their customers, then assemble boxes of produce (and such extras as cheeses and, on request, prepared foods). These boxes are delivered weekly, biweekly or monthly, and the basic price is $42 for a small (good for two people for a week or so) or $62 (for a family of four). ♻🛒🚚

[LAbite.com] **626.405.1101, 310.441.2483, 818.205.0500, 213.405.1500, labite.com. L Mon.-Fri., D nightly. AE, MC, V. WHY** Home and office delivery across L.A. from an extensive range of restaurants. **WHAT** This fast-growing operation has become the dominant restaurant-delivery business in town, with centers in Downtown, in Pasadena, in the Valley, the South Bay and on the westside. It's heavy on chain restaurants (Daily Grill, CPK, Louise's) but also represents some good individual places, from Bread and Porridge in Santa Monica to Figaro Bistro in Los Feliz. There's a $6 to $7 delivery fee and a 4% "convenience" fee (for whose convenience is that fee?), and you need to tip the driver. 🚚

[LOVE Delivery] **310.821.5683, lovedelivery.com. AE, MC, V. WHY** Quality, often-organic produce, delivered weekly to your house by very nice people. **WHAT** For a weekly fee, the LOVE folks will deliver a box of assorted seasonal fruits, vegetables and herbs; you can request certain produce and say which ones you don't want. The quality's about as good as at Gelson's or Whole Foods, and about as pricey, but the service is more convenient — and it can inspire you to try new things. 🛒🚚

[ParadiseO] **562.229.2096, paradiseo.com. AE, MC, V. WHY** For $25 to $35 boxes of seasonal, organic, locally grown fruits and vegetables, delivered weekly or biweekly to almost anywhere in L.A. County.

🏠 ESSENTIALLY L.A. 🌙 LATE ♥ ROMANTIC 💲 VALUE 🔕 QUIET ♻ SUSTAINABLE

WHAT Pick your own selection of organic, hand-selected fruits and vegetables, or go with the weekly selection available on the web site. We've heard some complaints about the timeliness of the service, but the business has many loyal customers. **WHO** Produce lovers who don't have time to hit the farmers' market. ○◡◠

[Tierra Miguel Foundation] 🔒 760.742.4213, tierramiguelfarm. org. MC, V. **WHY** You're supporting an organic, sustainable farming operation and getting first-rate produce, too. **WHAT** Part of the CSA (Community Supported Agriculture) movement, this nonprofit farm sells "farm shares" — you commit to an annual fee to support the farm, and in return you get a case of exceptionally delicious fruits and vegetables every week or two. The produce is delivered to several drop-off spots around town, so you'll have to do some driving to get it, but it's worth the trouble. ○◡

[Why Cook L.A.] 310.278.3955, whycookla.com. L Mon.-Fri., D nightly. AE, MC, V. **WHY** When you can afford to have food from Sushi Roku or Josie delivered instead of pizza. **WHAT** This westside delivery service works with a pretty high caliber of restaurant, including M Café de Chaya, Josie, Boa Hollywood and Xi'an. There's a $25 minimum, a delivery charge ranging from $8 to $20 (studios are a flat $10) and a 6% handling charge, and you need to tip, so this is not for the frugal. But the service is good, and you can eat very well indeed. **WHO** Studio folks and the westside work-through-lunch crowd. ◡◠

FESTIVALS

[American Wine & Food Festival] 🔒 Universal Studios Backlot, Universal City, 310.574.3663, awff.org. Early fall. **WHY** To support Meals on Wheels. Oh, and to network. Oh yeah, and to wallow in great food and wine. **WHAT** L.A.'s foodie event of the year takes over the backlot at Universal Studios on a Saturday in the fall and is typically a sellout, despite the high price of admission. Thanks to the clout of event founders (and former spouses) Wolfgang Puck and Barbara Lazaroff, it draws a glittering roster of chefs and winemakers from across the country. **WHO** Showbiz and foodbiz worlds collide, with an A-list crowd of chefs, winemakers, food journalists, studio execs, agents, entertainment lawyers and well-heeled gourmands.

[Armenian Festival] Holy Cross Cathedral, 900 W. Lincoln Ave., Montebello, 323.727.1113, armenianfoodfair.com. Early June. Armenian. **WHY** You can learn how to stuff grape leaves, and then go eat some made by a seasoned home cook. **WHAT** Not to diminish the music, dancing, backgammon or kids' games, but this festival is really about the food. An army of home cooks takes great pride in their kebabs, hummus, cheese boreg, piroshki, *lahmajoun* (Armenian pizza), baklava and more. Don't miss the cooking demonstrations. ▤☺

Services + Events

🍴VEGETARIAN ⊙KID FRIENDLY ☼PATIO DINING ◠DELIVERY ⌂PRIVATE PARTY

[California Avocado Festival] 🏛 **Downtown, Carpinteria, 805.684.0038, avofest.com. Early October. WHY** To see the world's largest vat of guacamole, of course. **WHAT** Now one of the state's largest food-focused events, the Avocado Festival is free and fun. Contests include largest avocado, best guacamole recipe and best-dressed avocado; music comes from lots of good local bands; and the kids' area includes an avocado rock-climbing wall. Early October also happens to be a superb time to visit this fetching little beach town — the sun is usually out, and the water is still warm. **WHO** Families with strollers but no dogs (they're not allowed, perhaps because dogs go crazy for avocados), seniors and backyard-avocado growers. 📷🍷☺

[California Strawberry Festival] **Strawberry Meadows, 3250 S. Rose Ave., Oxnard, 888.288.9242, strawberry-fest.org. Mid-May. WHY** To celebrate the Central Coast's most cherished fruit. **WHAT** Going strong for more than a quarter of a century, this celebration is a fine way to celebrate one of California's greatest products. Music ranges from the Oxnard High Marching Band to Big Bad Voodoo Daddy, and there's a strawberry-focused recipe contest, a strawberry tart toss, a strawberry-themed play area for kids and lots of good food, from fresh local berries to strawberry lemonade, strawberry pizza and even tri-tip sandwiches with strawberry sauce. **WHO** Families, farmers, bakers, retirees and food-festival junkies. 📷🍷☺

[Grilled Cheese Invitational] **Location varies, grilledcheeseinvitational.com. Late April. WHY** To wallow in the glory of bread, butter and cheese. **WHAT** Bread - Butter - Cheese - Victory! is the slogan of this fast-growing underground cheese-off that's typically held in April. The location changes and is kept secret until you're signed up to either enter or judge — and both categories fill up early. So if grilled cheese is your thing, check out the web site early and get on the e-mail list. And be warned that this is a rather loosely organized event — the 2009 one was chaotic and overcrowded. **WHO** Cheeseheads of all ages and culinary abilities. 📷☺

[Holland Festival] **Police Officers Association Park, 7390 Carson St., Long Beach, nassocal.org. Mid- to late May. WHY** A multicultural mix of excellent Dutch and Indonesian dishes. **WHAT** Despite two decades of history, the Holland Festival is a relatively secret celebration. That's partly because of its location (housed at a hidden park stashed behind Long Beach Towne Center), but also because the festival is something of a misnomer — though there is plenty of herring and Heineken, it is more directly dedicated to Indonesian street food. In fact, many of the vendors at the festival are regulars of Duarte's weekly Pondok Kaki Lima food fair. And that's a sure sign of great food, including everything from sweetly charred pork skewers and plastic-fork-tender beef rendang to airy potato croquettes and durian shakes. Between bites, expect bounce houses, bands and more. 📷🍷☺

🏛 **ESSENTIALLY L.A.** ☺ **LATE** ❤ **ROMANTIC** 📷 **VALUE** 🎵 **QUIET** ♻ **SUSTAINABLE**

[Indio International Tamale Festival] Downtown, Indio, 760.391.4175. Early December. **WHY** Really good, really homemade tamales from church groups, home-based tamale businesses and larger regional tamale makers. **WHAT** This free 18-year-old festival is devoted to the humble but heavenly tamale, held during the traditional tamale month, December, which also happens to be the most pleasant time of year in the desert. Tamale booths galore, a tamale-eating contest and tamale judging are balanced out with a parade, carnival rides, Folklorico dancing and other festival amusements. **WHO** A big crowd, 150,000 or more — mostly families, and mostly Latino families at that.

[L.A. County Fair] Los Angeles County Fairgrounds, 1101 W. McKinley Ave., Pomona, 909.623.3111, lacountyfair.com. 18 days in September. **WHY** For deep-fried Snickers, of course. Oh, and the good wine tastings (really). **WHAT** More than a million people attend the County Fair every year, and while some may be coming to go on the rides, hear War in concert or see the pigs, plenty come for the chance to see what new foodstuff is being deep-fried. The food's not all good, but there are some fun things to taste, including smoked turkey legs, churros, giant artichokes, fried sweet potatoes and some good Mexican dishes like pozole. Just don't try the deep-fried avocados, whatever you do. The beer and wine tastings can be rewarding.

[Los Angeles BBQ Festival] Santa Monica Beach, north of the Pier, Santa Monica, 310.709.3969, labbqfest.com. Early May. **WHY** Ribs, pulled pork and brisket from a dozen barbecuers from around the country. **WHAT** High-end cover bands meet ribs 'n slaw at this weekend-long festival, which pairs local barbecue operations (like Robin's and Baby Blues) with challengers from Illinois and Texas. Admission is $10, and you'll pay another $10 for a plate of 'cue.

[Los Angeles International Tamale Festival] Locations vary, Downtown area, eastlosangeles.net/tamalefestival. 1st weekend in November. **WHY** A fun, free street festival with local bands, kids' amusements and lots of tamale making, tasting and gorging (during the tamale-eating contest). **WHAT** An upstart competitor to the big Indio tamale fest, this is a smaller, more personal one that started near Mama's Hot Tamales but is moving to a larger venue near Olvera Street. Money raised goes to Mama's, a wonderful nonprofit that helps local immigrant women get business skills. Because the festival coincides with Dia de los Muertos, there's an altar-making contest, too, and some Halloween fun. **WHO** Families and young activists.

[National Date Festival] Riverside County Fairgrounds, Indio, 760.863.8247, datefest.org. Mid-February. **WHY** For date shakes, fresh dates and a big-ticket county fair to boot. **WHAT** Now folded into the large-scale Riverside County Fair, this 64-year-old week-long event has become more about the parades, concerts (with headliners like LeAnn Rimes), camel races and amusement-park fun than about food. But you can still learn a lot about dates, take part in the Blessing of the Dates, and wallow in the decadent joy of a date shake. **WHO** A robust crowd of Riverside County locals and families from as far away as San Diego and Santa Monica. ☺

[Ojai Wine Festival] Lake Casitas Recreational Area, Ojai, 805.646.3794, ojaiwinefestival.com. Early June. **WHY** To support the good works of the local Rotary Club while tasting wine in a beautiful place. **WHAT** The words "unpretentiousness" and "wine" don't often go together, but they do just that, and beautifully so, at this neighborly afternoon festival that supports Ojai's Rotary-West. Tickets range from $25 to $35, depending on when you buy them, and that entitles you to taste all sorts of terrific California wines, as well as meet the people who make them. Local restaurants offer small dishes for modest prices, and there's usually a lively local band playing. **WHO** Everyone who's anyone in Ojai, along with low-key wine lovers from L.A. and Santa Barbara. ♥

[Oxnard Salsa Festival] Downtown area, Oxnard, 800.269.6273, oxnardsalsafestival.com. Last weekend in July. **WHY** Tastings of some 50 salsas, amateur and professional recipe contests, great Latin music and salsa dancing — and all the chips you could ever hope to eat. **WHAT** You can dance the salsa and eat the salsas and this fun, free and friendly summertime fest in ocean-cooled Oxnard. The heart of the event is the huge salsa-tasting tent (little bags of chips are served as accompaniments). If you need something more than salsa, other booths sell beer, margaritas (made with wine) and such food as fish tacos. A fun day trip. 🥢☺

[Port of Los Angeles Lobster Festival] Ports o' Call Village, San Pedro, 310.831.6245, lobsterfest.com. Mid-September. **WHY** A Maine lobster meal for less than $10 (many people eat two), with all the attendant summertime-festival stands and bands. **WHAT** The lobsters don't come from this port, which is a good thing — 13 tons of them are flown in from Maine and served on paper plates with a "buttery topping" to hordes of festival goers. This won't be the best lobster meal you've ever had, but the price is right and the air is salty.

[Santa Barbara County Vintners' Festival] Location varies, Lompoc, 805.688.0881, sbcountywines.com. Mid-April. **WHY** Wine tastings from the 100-plus members of the SB County Vintners' Association and some really good food by local chefs to go with it. **WHAT** Sometimes held at an estate winery and sometimes at River Park, this is a lovely Saturday-afternoon festival that celebrates the thriving Santa Barbara wine community. The festival itself takes place

🏛 ESSENTIALLY L.A. ☺ LATE ♥ ROMANTIC 💲 VALUE 🔇 QUIET ♻ SUSTAINABLE

only for a few hours in the afternoon, but many of the area's best wineries host open houses, tastings and events from Friday through Monday. **WHO** Lots of locals, as well as L.A. wine buffs making a weekend of it. ♥

[Taste of the Nation L.A.] 🔒 **Media Park, Venice Blvd. & Culver Blvd., Culver City, taste.strength.org. Mid-June. WHY** To help the hungry in Los Angeles while eating some amazing food. **WHAT** L.A.'s best chefs show up at this family-friendly, shorts-and-flip-flops afternoon event in the park, and they outdo each other making beautiful little tastes for attendees, who pay $125 to gorge themselves silly and hobnob with an L.A. foodie A-list. Last year's chefs included Mary Sue Milliken (chair of the event), Jimmy Shaw, Octavio Becerra, Evan Kleiman, Suzanne Goin, Walter Manzke, Jon Shook and many more. Good California wines, too. The proceeds go to local organizations that combat hunger, especially for children. ☺

[Valley Greek Festival] **St. Nicholas Greek Orthodox Church, 9501 Balboa Blvd., Northridge, 818.886.4040, valleygreekfestival.com. Memorial Day weekend. Greek. WHY** The good ladies of the church make 48,000 pastries for the weekend, and the least you could do is try a couple of them. **WHAT** If you, like us, can never get your fill of moussaka, spanakopita, Kalamata olives, gyros and baklava, and if seeing *My Big Fat Greek Wedding* 47 times hasn't tired you of saying, "Opa!" over and over, then you'll want to spend a Memorial weekend afternoon at the annual Valley Greek Festival, an impressive shindig sponsored by St. Nicholas Church that draws some 50,000 visitors each year. There's lots more besides food, of course: dancing, music, church tours, and rides and games for kids. But really it's the food, which is robust, aromatic, inexpensive and plentiful. Fun cooking demonstrations, too. 🎦☺

KNIFE SHARPENERS

[Gary's Knife Sharpening Service] **310.560.3258, garysknife-sharpening.com. WHY** A sharp knife is a thing of beauty. **WHAT** Few things frustrate a cook more than a dull knife. Gary understands. Westsiders will find him and his sharpening tools at several farmers' markets, including Torrance, Culver City, Mar Vista and Beverly Hills; check his web site for the schedule. If you don't live on the westside, not to worry — with a $40 minimum order, Gary and his team make house calls; we let our neighbors know one of Gary's people was coming, and everyone brought their knives, scissors and gardening tools, so meeting the minimum was a snap. Make sure to go to Gary's web site and check out the YouTube video starring his wife — it's hilarious.

[Kitchen Outfitters] 5666 E. 2nd St., Long Beach, 562.434.2728, kitchenoutfitters.net. Mon. AE, MC, V. **WHY** For professional knife sharpening in Long Beach. **WHAT** Drop off your knives (standard, serrated, ceramic, Japanese) and shears by 2 p.m. on Monday, and you'll get them back professionally sharpened and/or repaired by 5 p.m., thanks to the Perfect Edge mobile truck. While you wait, you'll have a great time shopping for kitchen gear in this Naples store, and you can wander over to Naples Gourmet Grocer for something good to take home for dinner.

[Perfect Edge Knife Sharpening] 562.895.6567, perfectsharpening.com. MC, V. **WHY** This isn't the cheapest sharpening service around ($4.80 to $25 per knife), but it's worth it just to get a look in the mobile workshop, a handy guy's dream come true. And the work is excellent. **WHAT** This mobile sharpening truck appears at a half-dozen places in Southern California, incluidng Koontz Hardware (8914 Santa Monica Blvd., West Hollywood) on the second and fourth Friday of the month; Chefmakers (865 Swarthmore Ave., Pacific Palisades) on the fourth Wednesday of the month; and Kitchen Outfitters (5666 E. 2nd St., Long Beach) every Monday morning. The truck will also come to your house with a decent minimum order. Besides sharpening, it can repair broken knives, scissors and garden tools.

[Ross Cutlery] 🔒 310 S. Broadway, Downtown, 213.626.1897, rosscutlery.com. Daily. AE, MC, V. **WHY** For knife shopping, knife sharpening and to get to go inside the Bradbury Building. **WHAT** Made famous for its courtroom role in the O.J. murder trial, Ross is nowadays more known for its knife-sharpening services — and yes, it sharpens cuticle clippers and pocket knives. Plan on leaving your knives for a couple of days. And good luck resisting the temptation to buy a new blade from its fantastic collection, including ceramic knives. **WHO** Chefs with their beloved knives.

SPECIALTY SERVICES

[Hillside Produce Cooperative] Glassell Park, hillsideproducecooperative.org. **WHY** Free backyard fruit, vegetables and herbs from thoughtful urban farmers. **WHAT** Actress Hynden Walch has started a nonprofit co-op that just may go viral. Residents from Glassell Park and environs (including Silver Lake, Los Feliz and Eagle Rock) drop off their excess backyard crops at a pre-set time and place, and Walch and volunteers bag up assortments that are then delivered to all the participants. It's all free, it's all intended to make the world a better place, and Walch hopes her work will inspire other good folks across L.A. to organize their own backyard-produce co-ops (one has already formed in Merced). Check out the web site for details. 🗺️♻️

[Kirk's Urban Bees] **323.646.9651, kirksurbanbees.com. MC, V.**
WHY Doesn't everyone want to be a beekeeper? **WHAT** Like dog walking and closet organizing, beekeeping turns out to be a task that can be outsourced — thanks to Kirk Anderson, the Urban Beekeeper. Typically he removes unwanted swarms and moves them to a new home that wants them — your future hive may be rescued from someone's attic in Silver Lake! Once moved, the bees stay put in their adopted yards, and he maintains the hive, which consists of monthly visits and a honey harvest in June. Anderson doesn't feed them corn syrup, artificial pollen, chemicals or medicines. You can also buy jars of his locally produced honey online, and take a beekeeping class if you'd like to learn how to do it yourself. ☘

[Melting Pot Food Tours] **424.247.9666, meltingpotours.com.
MC, V. WHY** Warm-hearted tours for people who like to wander, explore and nosh. **WHAT** Sisters Lisa and Diane Scalia are friendly, energetic and hungry, so it's no surprise that they've gone in to the walking-tour business. Their repertoire recently doubled to two three-hour tours: the original, which explores the Original Farmers Market and ventures out onto 3rd Street, and the new one, of Old Pasadena. They make the effort to find the worthwhile places (in Old Pas, you'll be sampling at little mom 'n pop places, not the Cheesecake Factory), and they add history, architecture and culture into the mix.

Services
+ Events

Indexes

BY NEIGHBORHOOD

Index A to Z